For the Record

A DOCUMENTARY HISTORY

OF AMERICA

For the Record

A DOCUMENTARY HISTORY OF AMERICA

SEVENTH EDITION

VOLUME 2

From Reconstruction through Contemporary Times

DAVID EMORY SHI AND HOLLY A. MAYER

W · W · NORTON & COMPANY   NEW YORK · LONDON

W. W. Norton & Company has been independent since its founding in 1923, when William Warder Norton and Mary D. Herter Norton first published lectures delivered at the People's Institute, the adult education division of New York City's Cooper Union. The firm soon expanded its program beyond the Institute, publishing books by celebrated academics from America and abroad. By midcentury, the two major pillars of Norton's publishing program—trade books and college texts—were firmly established. In the 1950s, the Norton family transferred control of the company to its employees, and today—with a staff of four hundred and a comparable number of trade, college, and professional titles published each year—W. W. Norton & Company stands as the largest and oldest publishing house owned wholly by its employees.

Editor: Jon Durbin
Project Editor: Taylere Peterson
Editorial Assistant: Lily Gellman
Managing Editor, College: Marian Johnson
Managing Editor, College Digital Media: Kim Yi
Production Manager: Benjamin Reynolds
Marketing Manager, History: Sarah England Bartley
Photo Editor: Stacey Stambaugh
Director of College Permissions: Megan Schindel
Permissions Associate: Elizabeth Trammell
Composition: Westchester Publishing Services
Manufacturing: Maple Press—York, PA

Permission to use copyrighted material is included as a footnote on the first page of each reading.

Library of Congress Cataloging-in-Publication Data

Names: Shi, David Emory, author. | Mayer, Holly A. (Holly Ann), 1956– author.
Title: For the record : a documentary history of America / David Emory Shi and Holly A. Mayer.
Description: Seventh edition. | New York : W. W. Norton & Company, [2019]
Identifiers: LCCN 2018046023| ISBN 9780393673791 (pbk. : v.1) | ISBN 9780393673807 (pbk. : v.2)
Subjects: LCSH: United States—History—Sources.
Classification: LCC E173 .S487 2019 | DDC 973—dc23 LC record available at https://lccn.loc.gov/2018046023

ISBN: 978-0-393-67380-7 (vol. 2, pbk.)

W. W. Norton & Company, Inc., 500 Fifth Avenue, New York, NY 10110

wwnorton.com

W. W. Norton & Company Ltd., 15 Carlisle Street, London W1D 3BS

1 2 3 4 5 6 7 8 9 0

DAVID EMORY SHI is a professor of history and president emeritus of Furman University. He is the author of several books on American cultural history, including *America: A Narrative History, The Simple Life: Plain Living and High Thinking in American Culture* and *Facing Facts: Realism in American Thought and Culture (1850–1920)*.

HOLLY A. MAYER is a historian at Duquesne University in Pittsburgh, Pennsylvania. She has published multiple works about women and war in late eighteenth-century America. Dr. Mayer's continuing research on civil and military issues during the American Revolution has resulted in "Canada, Congress, and the Continental Army: Strategic Accommodations, 1774–1776" in the *Journal of Military History* (2014) and supports an ongoing book project about a regiment in the Continental Army.

For our students

CONTENTS

CHAPTER **18** ⌒ THE NEW SOUTH AND THE NEW WEST, 1865–1900   34

CHAPTER **19** ⌒ POLITICAL STALEMATE AND RURAL REVOLT, 1865–1900   58

CHAPTER 20 ∽ SEIZING AN AMERICAN EMPIRE, 1865–1913   88

CHAPTER 21 ∽ THE PROGRESSIVE ERA, 1890–1920   99

INTERPRETING VISUAL SOURCES: PHOTOGRAPHY AND PROGRESSIVE REFORM   125

CHAPTER 25 ◦◦ THE GREAT DEPRESSION, 1929–1939   197

CHAPTER 26 ◦◦ THE SECOND WORLD WAR, 1939–1945   215

CHAPTER 27 ❦ THE COLD WAR AND THE FAIR DEAL, 1945–1952   238

CHAPTER 28 ❦ COLD WAR AMERICA, 1950–1959   255

CHAPTER 29 ❦ A NEW FRONTIER AND A GREAT SOCIETY, 1960–1968   285

INTERPRETING VISUAL SOURCES: THE CIVIL RIGHTS MOVEMENT   313

CHAPTER 30 ⮑ REBELLION AND REACTION: THE 1960s AND 1970s   322

PREFACE FOR INSTRUCTORS

We know from our experiences in history classrooms that students can benefit greatly from studying the original sources that historians have used to craft their interpretations of the past. And, equally important, students can use such sources to develop their own historical perspectives. The exchange that occurs between students and instructors when working with primary sources is an exciting and invaluable part of the learning process. This passion has motivated our work and helped guide our selection process across all seven editions of *For The Record*.

This new edition of the reader features 268 primary source documents, both textual and visual, drawn from a vast range of media, including government documents, newspapers, speeches, letters, novels, and images. Thirty-eight new selections offer strengthened coverage of immigration, and the table of contents has been revised to align with *America: A Narrative History*, Eleventh Edition.

In selecting these documents, we have sought to represent the wide spectrum of historical developments by striking a balance among political, diplomatic, economic, social, and cultural perspectives. In general, we have tried to provide entire documents or substantial portions rather than brief snippets, which so often are pedagogically unsound and intellectually unsatisfying. We have edited several of these documents to eliminate extraneous material and to make them more accessible to students. Ellipses and asterisks indicate where passages or portions have been omitted. In a few cases, we have also modernized spelling and punctuation, taking care not to change the meaning of the original selection.

Chapter introductions set the stage for the accompanying selections by describing each historical period and highlighting key issues and actors. Each document in turn is introduced by a headnote that places it in the context of the period and suggests its historical significance. And each document is followed by a list of review questions to stimulate reflections about the material.

One of the unique features of *For the Record* is its recognition that visual artifacts are also important primary sources for the historian. Each volume contains two special sections to help students learn how to analyze and interpret visual sources. The four visual features include the following:

- *Picturing Development* presents examples of the relationship between words and images that, in turn, describe the relationship between the human-made and natural America.
- *Picturing the Civil War* explores the Civil War as the first "total war" represented through the camera lens of Mathew Brady and his associates.
- *Photography and Progressive Reform* explores the Progressive Era through the famous and controversial photos of the immigrant urban reformer Jacob Riis.
- *The Civil Rights Movement* explores the courageous and controversial efforts to gain racial equality and justice during the twentieth century.

For the Record: A Documentary History of America is primarily a companion reader for *America: A Narrative History*. With a rich collection of 268 primary-source documents, it can also be readily used on its own or in conjunction with other textbooks.

New Selections in the Seventh Edition

- Juan de Oñate, FROM *Letter From New Mexico* (1599)
- William Penn, Articles of Agreement with the Susquehanna Indians (1701)
- Board of Trade, Report on Charter & Proprietary Colonies (1701)
- Jonathan Edwards, *Sinners in the Hands of an Angry God* (1741)
- Peter Fontaine, *Slavery in Virginia* (1757)
- Atiwaneto, *Conditions for Peace* (1752)
- Elizabeth Drinker, Life in Occupied Philadelphia (1777-78)
- Benedict Arnold, FROM A Proclamation (1780)
- FROM Northwest Ordinance (1787)
- The *Supporter, Anecdotes of the Battle on Lake Erie* (1814)
- Hezekiah Niles, FROM Great National Interests (1826)
- Thomas Jefferson, Letter to John Holmes (April 1820)
- Alexis de Tocqueville, Parties in the United States (1835; trans. 1838)
- Gustavus Sohon, Fort Benton (1826/1863)
- Frances Flora Bond Palmer, *Across the Continent* (1868)
- The *Boston Investigator,* The Bible in the Common Schools (1854)
- The *Boston Daily Atlas*, FROM The El Dorado Discovered, &c. (1848)
- Julius Robert Voigt, FROM Letters of a German Confederate (1862–63)
- Jourdon Anderson, Letter to My Old Master (1865)
- The *Daily Cleveland Herald*, Women, War, And Negroes (1869)
- Mary Paik Lee, FROM *Quiet Odyssey* (1990)
- Alain Locke, FROM Enter the New Negro (1925)

Taken as a whole, *For the Record* reveals the diversity of sources that contribute to American history. In the process, it introduces students to important public documents and powerful personal accounts of events and experiences. The result is a more textured and comprehensive understanding of the ways in which we recreate and understand the past.

In compiling *For the Record*, we have benefited from the insights and talents of the editorial and marketing staff at W. W. Norton & Company. Jon Durbin has been our guide and our goad for this edition. He has provided wonderful advice in the first role and has been properly, thankfully amicably, persistent in the second. Kudos also go to Lily Gellman, Taylere Peterson, Stacey Stambaugh, and Elizabeth Trammell, who did truly fine work in shaping the final product.

WHERE TO BEGIN

This checklist contains a series of questions that can be used to analyze most of the documents in this reader.

✔ What type of document is it?

✔ Why does the document exist? What motives prompted the author to write the material in this form?

✔ Who wrote this document?

✔ Who or what is left out of the document—women, children, other minorities, members of the majority?

✔ In addition to the main subject, what other kinds of information can be obtained from the document?

✔ How do the subjects of the document relate to what we know about broader society?

✔ What was the meaning of the document in its own time? What is its meaning for the reader today?

✔ What does the document tell us about change in society?

---

16 ❧ THE ERA OF RECONSTRUCTION, 1865–1877

The assassination of Abraham Lincoln in April 1865 brought Vice President Andrew Johnson into the White House. A Tennessee Democrat who had served two terms as governor before being elected to the Senate in 1857, he was an ardent Unionist who blamed the slaveholding planter elite for secession and the Civil War. Johnson was the only southern senator who refused to embrace the Confederacy in 1861. Such credentials help explain why Lincoln invited him to be his running mate in 1864 on the union ticket.

The Radical Republicans hoped that President Johnson would embrace their comprehensive effort to reconstruct the defeated South. Johnson shared their disdain for the former Confederate leaders and for the planter class, but he also cherished states' rights and feared any effort to expand federal authority. He also retained many of the racial prejudices of his native region. "White men alone must manage the South," Johnson told a journalist. Unlike the Radical Republicans, he balked at putting freed blacks in control of southern politics.

Like Lincoln, Andrew Johnson hoped that middle-class white southern Unionists, along with repentant ex-Confederates, would take control of restoring the South to the Union. He required that the new state constitutional conventions formally abolish slavery, renounce secession, and void all war debts that the state had incurred. The states then could hold elections and officially return to the Union. By April 1866, all the southern states had fulfilled these requirements, albeit grudgingly, and had formed new governments. At the same time, they steadfastly refused to allow African Americans to vote. Johnson, however, was dismayed that the new political leaders were more often former Confederates than southern Unionists.

The Union victory in the Civil War and the official end of slavery created excited expectations among the freed slaves. Some adopted new names to express their new identity and to make a new beginning. Others discarded the clothes provided by their masters and took up new modes of dress. Many freedpeople left the plantations and migrated to neighboring towns and cities, where federal troops offered protection.

But freedom itself did not provide security or the resources necessary for meaningful lives. In March 1865 Congress created the Freedmen's Bureau, an agency administered by the War Department, to provide the former slaves with emergency supplies and to help them find employment, procure land, and pursue educational opportunities. By 1870 the bureau was supervising more than four thousand schools.

Yet for all of its heroic efforts, the Freedmen's Bureau could help only a small percentage of former slaves. Few freedpeople were able to acquire land of their own. Most of them were forced to become wage laborers, or sharecroppers or tenant farmers contracting with white landowners to work their land in exchange for food, tools, clothing, and a place to live. This agrarian system, however necessary in the face of the social and economic realities confronting the region, soon placed the freed slaves in a dependent relationship reminiscent of slavery itself.

As the new "lily white" state governments coalesced in 1865 and 1866, most of them drafted "Black Codes" limiting the rights and freedoms of African Americans. These laws varied from state to state, but all of them restricted the independence of blacks and channeled them into the service of the white-dominated social and economic order.

Some whites decided that such restrictive laws did not sufficiently impress upon blacks their subordinate status. In an effort to promote white supremacy, they founded secret organizations such as the Ku Klux Klan. The Klan, organized by former Confederate soldiers, used violence and terror to intimidate blacks and to disrupt the efforts of Radical Republicans to "reconstruct" the South. During one campaign season in Louisiana, over two hundred African Americans were killed in one parish alone. Congress passed laws intended to suppress the Klan, but to little avail.

Reconstruction officially ended in 1877 with the withdrawal of the last federal troops from the South. African Americans in the region retained certain constitutional rights, but in practice white supremacy had been reestablished through force and terror. With the loss of federal protection, blacks found themselves not only at the mercy of the southern political elite but locked into a dependent economic relationship through the sharecrop system as well.

JOURDON ANDERSON

Letter to My Old Master (1865)

The Civil War gave some four million slaves their freedom, but freedom wasn't quite so simple. Where would the former slaves live? How would they put food on the table? If those issues weren't challenging enough, freed slaves also had to contend with former owners who were not happy about what the war had done. Some ex-Confederates refused to acknowledge that defeat meant emancipation. They tried to force their slaves to stay under their control because they still needed help planting and harvesting their crops. Having become accustomed to the benefits of enslaved workers, most of them balked at paying their former slaves a living wage. Consider the example of Jourdon Anderson, who, like many slaves, had adopted the surname of his owner, Colonel P. H. Anderson of Big Spring, Tennessee. In 1864, as Union troops took control of Tennessee, Jourdon Anderson and his wife and children had seized their freedom and eventually relocated to Dayton, Ohio. Four months after the war ended, Colonel Anderson learned of Jourdon's whereabouts and sent him a letter urging him to return to work on the farm, promising to treat him well. Jourdon's tongue-in-cheek reply reveals both the complexities of emancipation and the resilience and courage that many freed slaves displayed.

"Letter from a Freedman to His Old Master," *New York Daily Tribune,* August 22, 1865. [Editorial insertions appear in square brackets—*Ed.*]

The following [is] a genuine document. It was dictated by the old servant, and contains his ideas and forms of expression. [*Cincinnati Commercial.*]

DAYTON, Ohio, August 7, 1865.

To my Old Master, Col. P. H. ANDERSON, *Big Spring, Tennessee.*

SIR: I got your letter and was glad to find that you had not forgotten Jourdon, and that you wanted me to come back and live with you again, promising to do better for me than anybody else can. I have often felt uneasy about you. I thought the Yankees would have hung you long before this for harboring Rebs, they found at your house. I suppose they never heard about your going to Col. Martin's to kill the Union soldier that was left by his company in their stable. Although you shot at me twice before I left you, I did not want to hear at your being hurt, and am glad you are still living. It would do me good to go back to the dear old home again and see Miss Mary and Miss Martin and Alion, Esther, Green and Leo. Give my love to them all, and tell them I hope we will meet in the better world, if not in this. I would have gone back to see you all when I was working in the Nashville Hospital, but one of the neighbors told me Henry intended to shoot me if he ever got a chance.

I want to know particularly what the good chance is you propose to give me. I am doing tolerably well here; I get $25 a month, with victuals [food] and clothing; have a comfortable home for Mandy (the folks here call her Mrs. Anderson), and the children; Milly, Jane and Grandy, go to school and are learning well; the teacher says Grandy has a head for a preacher. They go to Sunday School, and Mandy and me attend church regularly. We are kindly treated; sometimes we overhear others saying, "Them colored people were slaves" down in Tennessee. The children feel hurt when they hear such remarks, but I tell them it was no disgrace in Tennessee to belong to Col. Anderson. Many darkies would have been proud, as I used to was, to call you master. Now, if you will write and say what wages you will give me, I will be better able to decide whether it would be to my advantage to move back again.

As to my freedom, which you say I can have, there is nothing to be gained on that score, as I got my free-papers in 1861 from the Provost-Marshal-General of the Department at Nashville. Mandy says she would be afraid to go back without some proof that you are sincerely disposed to treat us justly and kindly—and we have concluded to test your sincerity by asking you to send us our wages for the time we served you. This will make us forget and forgive old scores, and rely on your justice and friendship in the future. I served you faithfully for thirty-two years, and Mandy twenty years, as $25 a month for me, and $2 a week for Mandy. Our earnings would amount to $11,680. Add to this the interest for the time our wages been kept back and deduct what you paid for our clothing and three doctor's visits to me, and pulling a tooth for Mandy, and the balance will show what we are in justice entitled to. Please send the money by Adams Express, in care of V. Winters, esq., Dayton, Ohio! If you fail to pay us for faithful labors in the past we can have little faith in your promises in the future. We trust the good Maker has opened your eyes to the wrongs which you and your fathers have done to me and my fathers, in making us toil for you for generations without recompense. Here I draw my wages every Saturday night, but in Tennessee there was never any pay day for the negroes any more than for the horses and cows. Surely there will be a day of reckoning for those who defraud the laborer of his hire.

In answering this letter please state if there would be any safety for my Milly and Jane, who are now grown up and both good looking girls. You know how it was with poor Matilda and Catherine. I would rather stay here and starve and die if it come to that than have my girls brought to shame by the violence and wickedness of their young masters. You will also please state if there has been any schools opened for the colored children in your neighborhood, the great desire of my life now is to give my children an education, and have them form virtuous habits.

From your old servant,   JOURDON ANDERSON.

P. S.—Say howdy to George Carter, and thank him for taking the pistol from you when you were shooting at me.

REVIEW QUESTIONS

1. What do you learn from this letter about the experience of enslaved African Americans in transitioning from being the property of others to being free?

2. Based on the information in the letter, how would you describe the conditions of being a slave in the former Confederacy?

THE *NEW YORK TIMES*

FROM The Late Convention of Colored Men (1865)

Freedom did not bring independence to many former slaves after the Civil War. They were no longer slaves, but they had no property, no money, and little education. In each state, groups of former slaves met to share their concerns and to request assistance from the federal government. The following message was sent from a convention of freedmen in Alexandria, Virginia, in 1865.

From "The Late Convention of Colored Men," *New York Times*, August 13, 1865.

We, the undersigned members of a convention of colored citizens of the State of Virginia, would respectfully represent that, although we have been held as slaves, and denied all recognition as a constituent of your nationality for almost the entire period of the duration of your government, and that by your permission we have been denied either home or country, and deprived of the dearest rights of human nature; yet when you and our immediate oppressors met in deadly conflict upon the field of battle, the one to destroy and the other to save your government and nationality, we, with scarce an exception, in our inmost souls espoused your cause, and watched, and prayed, and waited, and labored for your success.

When the contest waxed long, and the result hung doubtfully, you appealed to us for help, and how well we answered is written in the rosters of the two hundred thousand colored troops now enrolled in your service; and as to our undying devotion to your cause, let the uniform acclamation of escaped prisoners, "Whenever we saw a black face we felt sure of a friend," answer.

Well, the war is over, the rebellion is "put down," and we are declared free! Four-fifths of our enemies are paroled or amnestied, and the other fifth are being pardoned, and the President has, in his efforts at the reconstruction of the civil government of the States, late in rebellion, left us entirely at the mercy of these subjugated but unconverted rebels, in everything save the privilege of bringing us, our wives and little ones, to the auction block. He has, so far as we can understand the tendency and bearing of his action in the case, remitted us for all our civil rights, to men, a majority of whom regard our devotions to your cause and flag as that which decided the contest against them! This we regard as destructive of all we hold dear, and in the name of God, of justice, of humanity, of good faith, of truth and righteousness, we do most solemnly and earnestly protest. Men and brethren, in the hour of your peril you called upon us, and despite all time-honored interpretation of constitutional obligations, we came at your call and you are saved—and now we beg, we pray, we entreat you not to desert us in this the hour of our peril!

We know these men—know them well—and we assure you that, with the majority of them, loyalty is only "lip deep," and that their professions of loyalty are used as a cover to the cherished design of getting restored to their former relation with the Federal Government, and then, by all sorts of "unfriendly legislation," to render the freedom you have given us more intolerable than the slavery they intended for us.

We warn you in time that our only safety is in keeping them under Governors of the military persuasion until you have so amended the Federal Constitution that it will prohibit the States from making any distinction between citizens on account of race or color. In one word, the only salvation for us besides the power of the Government, is in the possession of the ballot. Give us this, and we will protect ourselves. No class of men relatively as numerous as we were ever oppressed when armed with the ballot. But, 'tis said we are ignorant. Admit it. Yet who denies we know a traitor from a loyal man, a gentleman from a rowdy, a friend from an enemy?

. . . All we ask is an equal chance with the white traitors varnished and japanned with the oath of amnesty. Can you deny us this and still keep faith with us? "But," say some, "the blacks will be overreached by the superior knowledge and cunning of the whites." Trust us for that. We will never be deceived a second time. "But," they continue, "the planters and landowners will have them in their power, and dictate the way their votes shall be cast." We did not know before that we were to be left to the tender mercies of these landed rebels for employment. Verily, we thought the Freedmen's Bureau was organized and clothed with power to protect us from this very thing, by compelling those for whom we labored to pay us, whether they liked our political opinions or not! . . .

We are "sheep in the midst of wolves," and nothing but the military arm of the Government prevents us and all the truly loyal white men from being driven from the land of our birth. Do not then, we beseech you, give to one of these "wayward sisters" the rights they abandoned and forfeited when they rebelled until you have secured our rights by the aforementioned amendment to the Constitution.

Let your action in our behalf be thus clear and emphatic, and our respected President, who, we feel confident, desires only to know your will, to act in harmony therewith, will give you his most earnest and cordial cooperation; and the Southern States, through your enlightened and just legislation, will speedily award us our rights. Thus not only will the arms of the rebellion be surrendered, but the ideas also.

REVIEW QUESTIONS

1. What services had former slaves performed that they believed entitled them to the protection of the federal government?
2. What did the petitioners mean when they said that the white Southerner was "subjugated but unconverted"?
3. What two steps did the freed blacks claim would ensure that their own rights would be guaranteed?

FROM Black Codes of Mississippi (1865)

The so-called Black Codes were enacted by the newly reconstituted southern state legislatures to address the legal status of the freed slaves after the Civil War. Some of the codes, such as Georgia's, were relatively lenient; others, such as those of Louisiana and Mississippi, sought to restore slavery in all but name. Most of the Black Codes were suspended by the federal military governors of the reconstructed states, and both the Civil Rights Act of 1866 and the Fourteenth Amendment were in part a response to these efforts to suppress the rights of blacks. The following sections from the Mississippi code deal with civil rights, apprenticeship, vagrancy, and penal crimes.

From *Laws of the State of Mississippi*, 1865 (Jackson, MS, 1866), pp. 82–90, 165.

1. Civil Rights of Freedmen in Mississippi

Sec. 1. *Be it enacted.* . . . That all freedmen, free negroes, and mulattoes may sue and be sued, implead and be impleaded, in all the courts of law and equity of this State, and may acquire personal property . . . by descent or purchase, and may dispose of the same in the same manner and to the same extent that white persons may: *Provided,* That the provisions of this section shall not be so construed as to allow any freedman, free negro, or mulatto to rent or lease any lands or tenements except in incorporated cities or towns, in which places the corporate authorities shall control the same. . . .

Sec. 3. . . . All freedmen, free negroes, or mulattoes who do now and have herebefore lived and cohabited together as husband and wife shall be taken and held in law as legally married, and the issue shall be taken and held as legitimate for all purposes: that it shall not be lawful for any freedman, free negro, or mulatto to intermarry with any white person; nor for any white person to intermarry with any freedman, free negro, or mulatto: and any person who shall so intermarry, shall be deemed guilty of felony, and on conviction thereof shall be confined in the State penitentiary for life; and those shall be deemed freedmen, free negroes, and mulattoes who are of pure negro blood, and those descended from a negro to the third generation, inclusive, though one ancestor in each generation may have been a white person.

Sec. 4. . . . In addition to cases in which freedmen, free negroes, and mulattoes are now by law competent witnesses, freedmen, free negroes, or mulattoes shall be competent in civil cases, when a party or parties to the suit, either plaintiff or plaintiffs, defendant or defendants, and a white person or white persons, is or are the opposing party or parties, plaintiff or plaintiffs, defendant or defendants. They shall also be competent witnesses in all criminal prosecutions where the crime charged is alleged to have been committed by a white person upon or against the person or property of a freedman, free negro, or mulatto: *Provided,* that in all cases said witnesses shall be examined in open court, on the stand; except, however, they may be examined before the grand jury, and shall in all cases be subject to the rules and tests of the common law as to competency and credibility. . . .

Sec. 6. . . . All contracts for labor made with freedmen, free negroes, and mulattoes for a longer period than one month shall be in writing, and in duplicate, attested and read to said freedman, free negro, or mulatto by a beat, city or county officer, or two disinterested white persons of the county in which the labor is to be performed, of which each party shall have one; and said contracts shall be taken and held as entire contracts, and if the laborer shall quit the service of the employer before the expiration of his term of service, without good cause, he shall forfeit his wages for that year up to the time of quitting.

Sec. 7. . . . Every civil officer shall, and every person may, arrest and carry back to his or her legal employer any freedman, free negro, or mulatto who shall have quit the service of his or her employer before the expiration of his or her term of service without good cause; and said officer and person shall be entitled to receive for arresting and carrying back every deserting employee aforesaid the sum of five dollars, and ten cents per mile from the place of arrest to the place of delivery; and the same shall be paid by the employer, and held as a set-off for so much against the wages of said deserting employee: *Provided,* that said arrested party, after being so returned, may appeal to the justice of the peace or member of the board of police of the county, who, on notice to the alleged employer, shall try summarily whether said appellant is legally employed by the alleged employer, and has good cause to quit said employer; either party shall have the right of appeal to the county court, pending which the alleged deserter shall be remanded to the alleged employer or otherwise disposed of, as shall be right and just; and the decision of the county court shall be final. . . .

Sec. 9. . . . If any person shall persuade or attempt to persuade, entice, or cause any freedman, free negro, or mulatto to desert from the legal employment of any person before the expiration of his or her term of service, or shall knowingly employ any such deserting freedman, free negro, or mulatto, or shall knowingly give or sell to any such deserting freedman, free negro, or mulatto, any food, raiment, or other thing, he or she shall be guilty of a misdemeanor, and, upon conviction, shall be fined not less than twenty-five dollars and not more than two hundred dollars and the costs; and if said fine and costs shall not be immediately paid, the court shall sentence said convict to not exceeding two months' imprisonment in the county jail, and he or she shall moreover be liable to the party injured in damages: *Provided,* if any person shall, or shall attempt to, persuade, entice, or cause any freedman, free negro, or mulatto to desert from any legal employment of any person, with the view to employ said freedman, free negro, or mulatto without the limits of this State, such person, on conviction, shall be fined not less than fifty dollars, and not more than five hundred dollars and costs; and if said fine and costs shall not be immediately paid, the court shall sentence said convict to not exceeding six months imprisonment in the county jail.

*   *   *

Mississippi Vagrant Law

Sec. 1. *Be it enacted, etc.* . . . That all rogues and vagabonds, idle and dissipated persons, beggars, jugglers, or persons practicing unlawful games or plays, runaways, common drunkards, common night-walkers, pilferers, lewd, wanton, or lascivious persons, in speech or behavior, common railers and brawlers, persons who neglect their calling or employment, misspend what they earn, or do not provide for the support of themselves or their families, or dependents, and all other idle and disorderly persons, including all who neglect all lawful business, habitually misspend their time by frequenting houses of ill-fame, gaming-houses, or tippling shops, shall be deemed and considered vagrants, under the provisions of this act, and upon conviction thereof shall be fined not exceeding one hundred dollars, with all accruing costs, and be imprisoned at the discretion of the court, not exceeding ten days.

Sec. 2. . . . All freedmen, free negroes and mulattoes in this State, over the age of eighteen years, found on the second Monday in January, 1866, or thereafter, with no lawful employment or business, or found unlawfully assembling themselves together, either in the day or night time, and all white persons so assembling themselves with freedmen, free negroes or mulattoes, or usually associating with freedmen, free negroes or mulattoes, on terms of equality, or living in adultery or fornication with a freed woman, free negro or mulatto, shall be deemed vagrants, and on conviction thereof shall be fined in a sum not exceeding, in the case of a freedman, free negro or mulatto, fifty dollars, and a white man two hundred dollars, and imprisoned at the discretion of the court, the free negro not exceeding ten days, and the white man not exceeding six months. . . .

Sec. 7. . . . If any freedman, free negro, or mulatto shall fail or refuse to pay any tax levied according to the provisions of the sixth section of this act, it shall be *prima facie* evidence of vagrancy, and it shall be the duty of the sheriff to arrest such freedman, free negro, or mulatto or such person refusing or neglecting to pay such tax, and proceed at once to hire for the shortest time such delinquent tax-payer to any one who will pay the said tax, with accruing costs, giving preference to the employer, if there be one.

*   *   *

4. Penal Laws of Mississippi

Sec. 1. *Be it enacted.* . . . That no freedman, free negro or mulatto, not in the military service of the United States government, and not licensed so to do by the board of police of his or her county, shall keep or carry fire-arms of any kind, or any ammunition, dirk or bowie knife, and on conviction thereof in the county court shall be punished by fine, not exceeding ten dollars, and pay the costs of such proceedings, and all such arms or ammunition shall be forfeited to the informer; and it shall be the duty of every civil and military officer to arrest any freedman, free negro, or mulatto found with any such arms or ammunition, and cause him or her to be committed to trial in default of bail.

Sec. 2. . . . Any freedman, free negro, or mulatto committing riots, routs, affrays, trespasses, malicious mischief, cruel treatment to animals, seditious speeches, insulting gestures, language, or acts, or assaults on any person, disturbance of the peace, exercising the function of a minister of the Gospel without a license from some regularly organized church, vending spirituous or intoxicating liquors, or committing any other misdemeanor, the punishment of which is not specifically provided for by law, shall, upon conviction thereof in the county court, be fined not less than ten dollars, and not more than one hundred dollars, and may be imprisoned at the discretion of the court, not exceeding thirty days.

Sec. 3. . . . If any white person shall sell, lend, or give to any freedman, free negro, or mulatto any fire-arms, dirk or bowie knife, or ammunition, or any spirituous or intoxicating liquors, such person or persons so offending, upon conviction thereof in the county court of his or her county, shall be fined not exceeding fifty dollars, and may be imprisoned, at the discretion of the court, not exceeding thirty days. . . .

Sec. 5. . . . If any freedman, free negro, or mulatto, convicted of any of the misdemeanors provided against in this act, shall fail or refuse for the space of five days, after conviction, to pay the fine and costs imposed, such person shall be hired out by the sheriff or other officer, at public outcry, to any white person who will pay said fine and all costs, and take said convict for the shortest time.

REVIEW QUESTIONS

1. Which crime carried the harshest penalty? Why?
2. Summarize the regulations related to employment of freed slaves. How did they represent a form of slavery?
3. The Black Codes were criticized for their vagueness. Cite an example of such vagueness, and note ways in which the codes could be interpreted or manipulated.

FROM Organization and Principles of the Ku Klux Klan (1868)

The Ku Klux Klan was the largest of several white supremacist societies that emerged in the post–Civil War era. Founded in Pulaski, Tennessee, in 1865, it gained support among many Confederate veterans across the South. Former Confederate general Nathan Bedford Forrest was the first grand wizard. The Klan used terror and violence to defy the efforts of Radical Republicans to reconstruct southern society. The following is an early statement of the Klan's principles.

From W. L. Fleming, J. C. Lester, and D. L. Wilson, *The Ku Klux Klan: Its Origin, Growth and Disbandment* (New York: Neale, 1905), pp. 154ff.

Creed

We . . . reverentially acknowledge the majesty and supremacy of the Divine Being, and recognize the goodness and providence of the same. And we recognize our relation to the United States Government, the supremacy of the Constitution, the Constitutional Laws thereof, and the Union of States thereunder.

Character and Objects of the Order

This is an institution of Chivalry, Humanity, Mercy, and Patriotism; embodying in its genius and its principles all that is chivalric in conduct, noble in sentiment, generous in manhood, and patriotic in purpose; its peculiar objects being

First: To protect the weak, the innocent, and the defenseless, from the indignities, wrongs, and outrages of the lawless, the violent, and the brutal; to relieve the injured and oppressed; to succor the suffering and unfortunate, and especially the widows and orphans of Confederate soldiers.

Second: To protect and defend the Constitution of the United States, and all laws passed in confor-mity thereto, and to protect the States and the people thereof from all invasion from any source whatever.

Third: To aid and assist in the execution of all constitutional laws, and to protect the people from unlawful seizure, and from trial except by their peers in conformity to the laws of the land.

Titles

Sec. 1. The officers of this Order shall consist of a Grand Wizard of the Empire, and his ten Genii; a Grand Dragon of the Realm, and his eight Hydras; a Grand Titan of the Dominion, and his six Furies; a Grand Giant of the Province, and his four Goblins; a Grand Cyclops of the Den, and his two Night Hawks; a Grand Magi, a Grand Monk, a Grand Scribe, a Grand Exchequer, a Grand Turk, and a Grand Sentinel.

Sec. 2. The body politic of this Order shall be known and designated as "Ghouls."

Territory and Its Divisions

Sec. 1. The territory embraced within the jurisdiction of this Order shall be coterminous with the States of Maryland, Virginia, North Carolina, South Carolina, Georgia, Florida, Alabama, Mississippi, Louisiana, Texas, Arkansas, Missouri, Kentucky, and Tennessee; all combined constituting the Empire.

Sec. 2. The Empire shall be divided into four departments, the first to be styled the Realm, and coterminous with the boundaries of the several States; the second to be styled the Dominion, and to be coterminous with such counties as the Grand Dragons of the several Realms may assign to the charge of the Grand Titan. The third to be styled the Province, and to be coterminous with the several counties; *Provided* the Grand Titan may, when he deems it necessary, assign two Grand Giants to one Province, prescribing, at the same time, the jurisdiction of each. The fourth department to be styled the Den, and shall embrace such part of a Province as the Grand Giant shall assign to the charge of a Grand Cyclops. . . .

Interrogations to be asked

1st. Have you ever been rejected, upon application for membership in the . . . or have you ever been expelled from the same?

2d. Are you now, or have you ever been, a member of the Radical Republican party, or either of the organizations known as the "Loyal League" and the "Grand Army of the Republic?"

3d. Are you opposed to the principles and policy of the Radical party, and to the Loyal League, and the Grand Army of the Republic, so far as you are informed of the character and purposes of those organizations?

4th. Did you belong to the Federal army during the late war, and fight against the South during the existence of the same?

5th. Are you opposed to negro equality, both social and political?

6th. Are you in favor of a white man's government in this country?

7th. Are you in favor of Constitutional liberty, and a Government of equitable laws instead of a Government of violence and oppression?

8th. Are you in favor of maintaining the Constitutional rights of the South?

9th. Are you in favor of the re-enfranchisement and emancipation of the white men of the South, and the restitution of the Southern people to all their rights, alike proprietary, civil, and political?

10th. Do you believe in the inalienable right of self-preservation of the people against the exercise of arbitrary and unlicensed power? . . .

REVIEW QUESTIONS

1. How could the Klan express such reverence for the Constitution while castigating Union Army veterans?
2. Why would poor whites have been attracted to the Klan?
3. How would freed slaves have reacted to the Klan's principles?

Klan Terrorism in South Carolina (1872)

During the early 1870s the Congress held hearings to investigate reports that the Ku Klux Klan was engaging in widespread intimidation and violence against blacks in the South. The following three documents relate to a series of racial incidents in York County, South Carolina, in 1871. Throughout the South, where Radical Reconstruction was being implemented, blacks were joining Union Leagues, Republican organizations that also had secret rituals. The first document from the Congressional hearings includes an article from the Yorkville Enquirer (South Carolina) *describing the rash of violence in the community. The second document is the courtroom testimony of an African American woman, Harriet Postle, whose family was assaulted by Klansmen. The third document is the testimony of Lawson B. Davis, a white Klansman accused of such terrorism.*

From U.S. Congress, *Report of the Joint Select Committee to Inquire into the Condition of Affairs in the Late Insurrectionary States* (Washington, DC, 1872), 3:1540–41, 1951–52, 1943–44.

Whipping and House-Burning.

The state of things which exists in many sections of our country is alarming. Scarcely a night passes but some outrage is perpetrated against the welfare of some community. Houses are burned, persons are whipped, and in some instances killed, by parties unknown, and for causes which no one can decipher. These things are not right; they are not prudent. They are grave crimes against God and the best interest of the country.

By common consent, the house-burning is charged upon the colored race, and the whipping and killing upon the so-called Ku-Klux. This is not certainly known to be the case, but the probability is that the supposition with regard to the perpetrators of these deeds is correct. One thing must be evident to every observing man: there is concert of action both in the house-burning and in the whipping and killing.

For some years there has been, and still is, we are informed by one who claims to know, an organization known as the Union League. Of this we know nothing, save what we have learned by observing its workings. From what we have been able to learn, we are convinced that the Union League is a secret political organization, and on this ground alone, if we knew nothing about its operations and results, we would condemn it. We take the broad ground that all secret political organizations are nothing but conspiracies against the established government of a country, and as such are ruinous to the peace and quiet and prosperity of the people.

Of the Ku-Klux we know even less than we do of the Union League. Sometimes we are disposed to believe that there is no such organization; at other times we think differently. Recent developments rather indicate that there is such an organization, and it is made of no mean material. This is mere conjecture on our part. We do not know one single individual who holds connection with the Ku-Klux. It is evident, however, that there is some sort of complicity of action in the whipping and killing that has recently been perpetrated in this country, and which is going on at present all over the State, and, in fact, all over the South.

We do not believe, from what we know of the political party which is opposed to the Union League and the political tenets of the dominant party in South Carolina, that the Ku-Klux is a political organization, in the strict sense of that term. Whatever may be its object, we are convinced that the Ku-Klux is doing much harm. To be honest and frank, we charge the Union League with the shameful state of things which now exists. It has placed its members in a predicament which is anything but enviable. The ostensible purpose for which the thing was organized was, we suppose, to protect the freedman; the real purpose, however, was, as is acknowledged by some of its members, to consolidate the votes of the freedman, that designing men might be elevated to positions of honor and profit. There is no doubt but the Union League has done the colored people a great injury. It has been the means of arraying them in hostility against the white man, and the result always has been that in every conflict between the white man and the colored man, the condition of the latter has been materially injured. We do not blame the colored people for joining the League; but we do blame those designing white men who enticed them into this snare of destruction.

However much we may reprobate the Union League, this does not cause us to love or approve of the Ku-Klux. Two wrongs never can make one right. Both the Union League and the Ku-Klux are founded upon dangerous principles, and are working the ruin of this county. We have no disposition to make prediction, especially while so unsettled a state of things continues as exists in this county at present; but we will venture to say that if this house-burning and whipping does not stop soon, it will culminate in a conflict which will be fatal to some party.

What is the duty of every good citizen, under existing circumstances? It is the duty, we believe, of the leading colored people to influence their race to abandon the League and to refrain from acts of violence. On the other hand, it is the duty of the white people, especially the old men, to advise the young men not to engage in whipping and murdering the colored people. So long as the present state of things exists, no one is safe. The minds of the white people are filled with anxiety lest their houses may be burned down at any time, and no doubt the minds of the colored people are filled with dread lest they be dragged from their beds and taken to the forest and whipped, or, perchance, shot. We have no party purposes to subserve by what we say. All we desire is to assist in restoring peace and quiet to our county. These outrages must stop now, or worse will come. If a few more houses are burned, the public mind will be so exasperated that, in all probability, something will be done that will be very injurious to the public good. It is the imperative duty of every good citizen to discourage house-burning and whipping. We must be permitted to say that it is our impression that, so long as the Union League exists, some kind of an opposing party will also exist. The sooner all such organizations cease to exist, the better it will be for all parties.

Testimony of Harriet Postle.

Examination by Mr. CORBIN:

I live in the eastern part of York County, about four miles from Rock Hill, on Mr. James Smith's plantation; I am about thirty years old; my husband is a preacher; I have a family of six children; the oldest is about fourteen; the Ku-Klux visited me last spring; it was some time in March; I was asleep when they came; they made a great noise and waked me up, and called out for Postle; my husband heard them and jumped up, and I thought he was putting on his clothes, but when I got up I found he was gone; they kept on hallooing for Postle and knocking at the door; I was trying to get on my clothes, but I was so frightened I did not get on my clothes at all; it looked like they were going to knock the door down; then the rest of them began to come into the house, and my oldest child got out and ran under the bed; one of them saw him and said, "There he is; I see him;" and with that three of them pointed their pistols under the bed; I then cried out, "It is my child;" they told him to come out; when my child came out from under the bed, one of them said, "Put it on his neck;" and the child commenced hallooing and crying, and I begged them not to hurt my child; the man did not hurt it, but one of them ran the child back against the wall, and ground a piece of skin off as big as my hand; I then took a chair and sat it back upon a loose plank, and sat down upon it; one of the men stepped up; seeing the plank loose, he just jerked the chair and threw me over, while my babe was in my arms, and I fell with my babe to the floor, when one of them clapped his foot upon the child, and another had his foot on me; I begged him, for the Lord's sake, to save my child; I went and picked up my babe, and when I opened the door and looked I saw they had formed a line; they asked me if Postle was there; I said no; they told me to make up a light, but I was so frightened I could not do it well, and I asked my child to make it up for me; then they asked me where my husband was; I told them he was gone; they said, "He is here somewhere;" I told them he was gone for some meal; they said he was there somewhere, and they called me a damned liar; one of them said: "He is under the house;" then one of them comes to me and says: "I am going to have the truth tonight; you are a damned, lying bitch, and you are telling a lie;" and he had a line, and commenced putting it over my neck; said he: "You are telling a lie; I know it; he is here;" I told them again he was gone; when he had the rope round my head he said, "I want you to tell where your husband is;" and, said he, "The truth I've got to have;" I commenced hallooing, and says he: "We are men of peace, but you are telling me a damned lie, and you are not to tell me any lies to-night;" and the one who had his foot on my body mashed me badly, but not so badly as he might have done, for I was seven or eight months gone in travail; then I got outside of the house and sat down, with my back against the house, and I called the little ones to me, for they were all dreadfully frightened; they said my husband was there, and they would shoot into every crack; and they did shoot all over the place, and there are bullet-holes there and bullet-marks on the hearth yet; at this time there were some in the house and some outside, and says they to me: "We're going to have the truth out of you, you damned, lying bitch; he is somewhere about here;" said I: "He is gone;" with that he clapped his hands on my neck, and with one hand put the line over my neck; and he says again: "We're going to have the truth out of you, you damned bitch;" and with that he beat my head against the side of the house till I had no sense hardly left; but I still had hold of my babe.

Mr. Corbin:

Question. Did you recognize anybody?

Answer. Yes, sir; I did; I recognized the first man that came into the house; it was Dr. Avery, [pointing to the accused.] I recognized him by his performance, and when he was entangling the line round my neck; as I lifted my hand to keep the rope off my neck, I caught his lame hand; it was his left hand that I caught, his crippled hand; I felt it in my hand, and I said to myself right then, "I knows you;" and I knew Joe Castle and James Matthews—the old man's son; I didn't know any one else; I suppose there was about a dozen altogether there; Dr. Avery had on a red gown with a blue face, with red about his mouth, and he had two horns on his cap about a foot long; the line that he tried to put over my neck was a buggy-line, not quite so wide as three fingers, but wider than two; they said to me that they rode thirty-eight miles that night to see

old Abe Broomfield and preacher Postle; they said that they had heard that preacher Postle had been preaching up fire and corruption; they afterward found my husband under the house, but I had gone to the big house with my children to take them out of the cold, and I did not see them pull him out from the house.

*   *   *

Testimony of Lawson B. Davis.

Witness for the prosecution:

I reside in York County, and have lived there two years. I was initiated as a member of the Ku-Klux Klan. I took the oath at my own house. Three persons were initiated at the same time. I attended one meeting and heard the constitution and by-laws. That was in last January. The contents of the oath, as near as I can remember, were that female friends, widows, and orphans were to be objects of our protection, and that we were to support the Constitution as it was bequeathed to us by our forefathers; and there was to be opposition to the thirteenth, fourteenth, and fifteenth amendments.[1] The fourteenth was particularly specified in the oath I took. The oath was repeated, and I repeated it after them. There was no written document present. The penalty for divulging its secrets was death.

The constitution and by-laws were here handed to the witness by Mr. Corbin.

The witness continued: That is the same oath that I took except the second section, which, as repeated to me, was "opposition to the thirteenth, fourteenth, and fifteenth amendments." The organization, when I joined it, was called the Invisible Empire of the South. After I joined I found it was the same as the Ku-Klux organization. When I found that I determined to leave them. The first

---

[1]Amendments to the U.S. Constitution associated with the Civil War. The Thirteenth, ratified in 1865, abolished slavery; the Fourteenth (1866) provided people "equal protection under the law"; and the Fifteenth (1870) granted the right to vote to black males. [Lee Guidon, 1872]

meeting I attended there were eight or ten persons sworn in, and a proposition was brought forward to make a raid upon such and such persons. I inquired the reason, and they said they were prominently connected with the Union League. Their object was to discountenance people from joining the League. I heard this from the members. They said that those who belonged to the League were to be visited and warned; that they must discontinue their connection with the League. If they did not, on the second visit they were to leave the country, and if they didn't leave they were to be whipped; and if after this they did not leave, they were to be killed. I know this was how the purposes of the order were to be carried out. I have known of instances of raiding for guns.

They made one raid upon Jerry Adams; Charley Byers told me they had whipped him; he was to be chief of the Klan; he said they had scared the boy very badly—they had fired several guns at him, but didn't mean to hit him. The only charge I ever heard against Jerry Adams was that he was a radical. He was a republican and a colored man. Charley Good, who was whipped very badly by the Klan, came to my house two or three days afterwards. He was a blacksmith, and a very good workman—the best in that part. Charley Good was whipped so badly that he could not follow his trade for several days. Two or three weeks after that he was killed.

Wesley Smith, and William Smith, and William White were among those who killed Charley Good. Smith said he was a member of Smarr's Klan, and some members of that Klan assisted in putting Charley Good's body out of the way. The two Smiths, I know, were members of the Klan. Charley Good was killed because he was a republican. He told me, in the presence of some other persons, that he knew who had whipped him. I told him it would be better for him to keep that to himself. Wesley Smith gave, as the reason for killing him, that Charley Good knew some of the party who had whipped him. I was ordered to assist in disposing of the body of Charley Good. I did not, till then, know that he was missing. They

came and summoned me and Mr. Howard to go and secrete the body, which was lying near to where he was murdered.

Wesley Smith said that all who were members of the organization were required to assist, so that they might be connected with it, and that the matter might not get out. I told him that I did not want to go, but he said that all the members had to go. We were ordered to meet at the gate about a quarter of a mile from his house. I left about 9 o'clock and went up to Mr. Howard's, and Wesley Smith had given him the same instructions. He did not feel willing to go, and I said those were my feelings exactly. We waited until the hour had passed, and then when we left we met some ten or fifteen of the party. It was a dark night, and I only recognized Thomas L. Berry, Pinckney Caldwell, Wesley Smith, and Madison Smarr. He is said to be the chief of the Klan. Madison Smarr said I had escaped a scouring. He said the body was very heavy to carry. And Pinckney Caldwell told me that "Charley Good is now at the bottom of the river. The body would not sink, and I jumped in upon him," he said, "and fastened him there, as well as I could, with a stake."

Charley Good was at one time a member of a militia company, and, being told it was not to his interest, he left it and returned his gun. He was regarded as a man of republican principles, and was considered a person of some influence in that neighborhood. I never heard him charged with being a member of the Union League.

*   *   *

REVIEW QUESTIONS

1. Based on these testimonies, characterize the methods used by the Klan to intimidate African Americans.
2. According to these excerpts, why did the KKK harass certain blacks?
3. How did blacks react to this kind of continuous treatment? What choices did they have?

SOJOURNER TRUTH

FROM Address to the First Annual Meeting of the American Equal Rights Association (1867)

In the aftermath of the Civil War, many Americans sought to help the almost four million former southern slaves, most of whom found themselves free but without jobs or homes or food—or civil rights. Most advocates for civil rights (voting privileges, social equality, equitable treatment, etc.) focused on black men and ignored the distinctive needs of black women. Sojourner Truth was one of the few advocates of equal rights for black women. Born a slave in 1797 in upstate New York and named Isabella Baumfree, she was sold several times to different owners before escaping with her infant daughter in 1826 (she later won custody of her son). As an adult she experienced an intense conversion to Christianity, renamed herself Sojourner Truth, and published her autobiography, The Narrative of Sojourner Truth: A Northern Slave. *Thereafter she became the most celebrated female black abolitionist. During the Civil War, she helped recruit black men to serve in the Union Army. Afterward, she earnestly promoted equal rights for black women until her death in Michigan in 1883. In the following speech delivered two years after the end of the Civil War, Sojourner Truth explains why women deserved equal treatment.*

From "Address to the First Annual Meeting of the American Equal Rights Association," in *Proceedings of the First Anniversary of the American Equal Rights Association* (New York: Robert J. Johnson, 1867), pp. 20–21. [Editorial insertion appears in square brackets—*Ed.*]

. . . My friends, I am rejoiced that you are glad, but I don't know how you will feel when I get through. I come from another field—the country of the slave. They have got their liberty—so much good luck to have slavery partly destroyed; not entirely. I want it root and branch destroyed. Then we will all be free indeed. I feel that if I have to answer for the deeds done in my body just as much as a man, I have a right to have just as much as a man. There is a great stir about colored men getting their rights, but not a word about the colored women; and if colored men get their rights, and not colored women theirs, you see the colored men will be masters over the women, and it will be just as bad as it was before. So I am for keeping the thing going while things are stirring; because if we wait till it is still, it will take a great while to get it going again. White women are a great deal smarter, and know more than colored women, while colored women do not know scarcely anything. They go out washing, which is about as high as a colored woman gets, and their men go about idle, strutting up and down; and when the women come home, they ask for their money and take it all, and then scold because there is no food. I want you to consider on that, chil'n. I call you chil'n; you are somebody's chil'n, and I am old enough to be mother of all that is here. I want women to have their rights. In the courts women have no right, no voice; nobody speaks for them. I wish woman to have her voice there among the pettifoggers [lawyers]. If it is not a fit place for women, it is unfit for men to be there.

I am above eighty years old; it is about time for me to be going. I have been forty years a slave and forty years free, and would be here forty years more to have equal rights for all. I suppose I am kept here because something remains for me to do; I suppose I am yet to help to break the chain. I have done a great deal of work; as much as a man, but did not get so much pay. I used to work in the field and bind grain, keeping up with the cradler; but men doing no more, got twice as much pay; so with the German women. They work in the field and do as much work, but do not get the pay. We do as much, we eat as much, we want as much. I suppose I am about the only colored woman that goes about to speak for the rights of the colored women. I want to keep the thing stirring, now that the ice is cracked. What we want is a little money. You men know that you get as much again as women when you write, or for what you do. When we get our rights we shall not have to come to you for money, for then we shall have money enough in our own pockets; and may be you will ask us for money. But help us now until we get it. It is a good consolation to know that when we have got this battle once fought we shall not be coming to you any more. You have been having our rights so long, that you think, like a slave-holder, that you own us. I know that it is hard for one who has held the reins for so long to give up; it cuts like a knife. It will feel all the better when it closes up again. I

have been in Washington about three years, seeing about these colored people. Now colored men have the right to vote. There ought to be equal rights now more than ever, since colored people have got their freedom. I am going to talk several times while I am here; so now I will do a little singing. I have not heard any singing since I came here.

Accordingly, suiting the action to the word, Sojourner sang, "We are going home." "There children," said she, "in heaven we shall rest from all our labors, first do all we have to do here. There I am determined to go, not to stop short of that beautiful place, and I do not mean to stop till I get there, and meet you there, too."

*   *   *

REVIEW QUESTIONS

1. Truth claimed that "white women are a great deal smarter, and know more than colored women, while colored women do not know scarcely anything." What was her point? Did she mean to be taken literally?
2. How does Truth try to get black men to realize that they treat black women in ways comparable to the way that whites treated slaves?

THE *DAILY CLEVELAND HERALD*

Women, War, and Negroes (1869)

Before and during the Civil War, many activists put abolition of slavery above suf-frage for women. Then the Constitution's Thirteenth Amendment ended slavery and the Fourteenth confirmed that the freedpersons, among others born and naturalized in the United States, were citizens with rights. But many men in the federal and state governments saw voting as a privilege rather than a right and thus restricted suffrage. A person had to meet certain qualifications—such as being a free, white, male citi-zen—in order to vote. When the proposal for the Fifteenth Amendment addressed the racial qualification but not the sexual or gendered one, women suffragists cried shame but were divided over what to do next. The result, in 1869, was that the activ-ists created two national organizations: the National Woman Suffrage Association (NWSA) argued against ratification until it was revised to include women or tied to another for woman's rights; the American Woman Suffrage Association (AWSA) sup-ported the Fifteenth Amendment and embarked on a strategy to win the vote for women state by state. In both cases, the activists faced questions about how women would serve states and nation in return for the right to vote.

"Women, War, and Negroes," The *Daily Cleveland Herald*, Cleveland, Ohio, June 10, 1869, issue 138, in 19th Century U.S. Newspapers, Gale Document GT305251117. [Editorial insertion appears in square brackets—*Ed.*]

The National Woman's Suffrage Association had a sederunt in New York on Tuesday, and among other matters discussed the subject of the belligerent duties and immunities of women in case of war. The question was started by a doubting sister who wanted to know if the right to vote carried with it the obliga-tion to fight if called upon; in other words if the bal-lot box had in all cases a draft wheel attached to it. Another lady flippantly replied that "men who vote are not obliged to serve in the kitchen," which was clearly irrelevant, the only point that could be made in that way being that disfranchised men are not obliged to serve in the kitchen.

Then arose Mrs. CADY STANTON. The subject was one not to be trifled away, but answered. She narrated how the sage [Horace Greeley] of the [New York] *Tribune* had once propounded to her in con-vention the conundrum "If women were permitted to vote would they go to war?" and how she cor-nered the drab coated philosopher by asking how many gentlemen present bore the mark of a bullet. As the class of men who usually attended Mrs. STANTON's gatherings were not of the fighting kind there was no answer, from H.G. himself fail-ing to uncover any honorable scars save those received from trenchant pens. Mrs. STANTON fol-lowed up her triumph by expressing her belief that many women actually served in the late war in men's garb, and that when their sex was discovered they were dismissed in disgrace without pay. But Mrs. STANTON added that when women obtained their rights there would be no occasion for fighting, as all State questions would be settled by peaceful, earnest discussions in council. It is scarcely neces-sary to remark that the women have set a good example in this respect in their political gatherings, their discussions, being eminently peaceful and their conclusions when arrived at thoroughly practical—barring a violent squabble every now and then and a difficulty in arriving at any satisfactory conclusion on anything.

One claim set up by Mrs. STANTON, and urged by other speakers, in connection with woman's place in war, is just. It was urged that in case of war there would be a division of labor, and that woman's work would mainly be found in the hospitals, where she did such good service during the recent war. One woman, who has had practical experience in the army, said that the late war would have been a failure without the noble women who emptied their wardrobes, linen closets, and cellars, for the sake of our wounded. They ran the hospitals, and saved two-thirds of the army. True, every word of it, and yet a large proportion of those who did this noble work are not in sympathy with the STANTON-ANTHONY movement. They were inspired with love and not with ambition. They carried with them to the bedside of the dying soldier the atmosphere of the home fireside and not of the caucus room or the political convention.

Towards the close of the Convention it became evident that all the women were not of one mind on any subject and that the woman's movement is not progressing as harmoniously as it could be wished by its friends. Mrs. STANTON called on Mrs. SAFFORD to say something concerning her recent experience in the South. Mrs. SAFFORD proceeded to say it, speaking favorably of the progress, of the negroes and discouragingly of the intellectual and moral condition of the "poor whites," the women of whom smoked, chewed, spit, and swore with as much freedom as the men. That brought Mrs. STANTON to her feet in wrath. She snappishly advised Mrs. SAFFORD to qualify her remarks. The South was highly intellectual. She knew it, for were not some of the best articles in the *Revolution* [woman's rights newspaper] written by Southern women? Then, as for smoking, chewing, et cetera, many of the noble and cultivated women of France did the same thing. Mrs. SAFFORD sat down extinguished.

The Southern topic brought up the Fifteenth Amendment, and this was the signal for a general squabble. Miss ANTHONY thought the denunciation of the Amendment too sweeping and illiberal. She could go a great way, but thought that was going too far. Mrs. STANTON turned in wrath upon the recalcitrant sister, and denounced the attempt to advance the negro and leave the woman sitting in the cold shade of political non-recognition. The Amendment was an insult to the women of America. Dr. HAEBER, who we infer to be a man, thought so too, and said he should cut the Republican party because of the Amendment, and he immediately performed that surgical operation without the aid of chloroform. The Republican party, at last accounts, was still alive. The conclusion of the meeting was significant.

Mrs. Stanton then proposed to discuss the "Coming Campaign."

Miss Anthony said she didn't like to talk about plans when there was no money with which to carry them out. We should sweep every State as thoroughly as we did Kansas. Here Miss Anthony became rather severe upon Massachusetts. Kansas gave us so many votes that the question was lost by a majority of only three. [In 1867 Kansas had first state referendum on woman's suffrage.] Massachusetts defeats us by 22 votes against 9. [Hisses.] There is much of the Boston Puritanical feeling, "I am holier than thou," throughout Massachusetts. The Bostonian thought and said that *The Revolution*-ists had no business to come to Boston. They carried on the work in a silver-slippered, kid-gloved sort of way, and looked askance upon real workers. Miss Anthony closed her somewhat long speech with an appeal for money with which to further their plans.

REVIEW QUESTIONS

1. Why and how did Elizabeth Cady Stanton take seriously the question whether the right to vote carried with it the duty to fight?
2. Were there sectional divisions and social biases in this national organization?
3. Did Susan Anthony's speech provide evidence as to why the NWSA doubted a bottom-up states approach to suffrage?

17 ❧ BIG BUSINESS AND LABOR IN THE INDUSTRIAL ERA

During the half century after the Civil War, the United States experienced an economic transformation that catapulted it into the front rank of industrial nations. The reconstruction of the South and the settlement of the West created an unceasing demand for goods and services. At the same time, the growing national economy created job opportunities that served as a powerful magnet luring millions of immigrants from foreign lands. The need to feed, clothe, and shelter such a rapidly growing population added more fuel to industrial expansion, and, in turn, fostered a dramatic increase in the number and size of cities, especially in the East and Midwest. By the end of the nineteenth century, the United States was no longer a decentralized agrarian republic. It was increasingly a nation of cities and factories.

A key development facilitating the urban-industrial revolution was the maturation of a national market. What had been local or regional economies before the Civil War assumed national proportions with the advent of the transcontinental railroad network, the telegraph system, and other innovations that enabled entrepreneurs to manufacture products for distribution across the country. Such a national market helped give rise to larger corporations and huge individual fortunes.

During this turbulent period of industrial expansion and consolidation, many business leaders engaged in unethical and even illegal practices in an effort to gain advantages in the marketplace. Critics charged that some of the most domineering corporate buccaneers, men such as railroad tycoons Jay Gould and Daniel Drew, oil baron John D. Rockefeller, banking magnate J. P. Morgan, and steel giant Andrew Carnegie, were robber barons who ruthlessly eliminated their competitors, gouged consumers, and rode roughshod over employees. In their defense, the business leaders pointed out that the new jobs that they were creating, the growing volume of goods and services they were making available to the public, the rising standard of living for the country as a whole, and the philanthropic contributions they were making helped improve the general welfare of their communities.

The rise of big business and its attendant excesses helped spawn a new era in the development of an organized labor movement. The first major national union, the Knights of Labor, was founded in 1869. It included all types of laborers, skilled and unskilled, and embraced a wide array of reform initiatives, ranging from the eight-hour workday to the increased use of paper money. Terence Powderly and other leaders of the Knights of Labor sought to gain their objectives through negotiation rather than strikes.

In the 1880s, however, such broad objectives and conciliatory tactics created fissures within the Knights that led to its demise by the end of the century. In its place emerged a new organization, the American Federation of Labor (AFL). Unlike the Knights of Labor, the AFL was a federation of many separate unions, each organized by special craft or skill. Unskilled workers were not allowed in the AFL, nor were women workers. The founder of the AFL, Samuel Gompers, disdained the comprehensive reform agenda of the Knights of Labor in favor of sharply focused bread-and-butter issues—higher wages, shorter working hours, and better working conditions. And unlike Powderly, he embraced the strike as the union's most effective weapon in wrenching concessions from recalcitrant corporate leaders. By the turn of the century, the AFL was the largest union in the United States, claiming over 500,000 members.

The AFL did not challenge the basic premises of capitalism. Its aim was simply to gain for its members a larger slice of the economic pie. A few labor leaders, however, grew enamored of the socialist ideas of Karl Marx. In the 1890s a West Indian immigrant, Daniel DeLeon, and a railway union organizer, Eugene Debs, organized separate labor movements grounded in socialist philosophy. Of the two, Debs proved to be the more successful. In 1901 he organized the Socialist Party of America, and three years later he garnered over 400,000 votes as a candidate in the presidential election. Eight years later he ran again and gained over 900,000 votes.

At the same time that Eugene Debs was mobilizing a socialist-based working-class movement, militant labor leaders in the western states were forming a parallel organization, the Industrial Workers of the World (IWW). Like the defunct Knights of Labor, the IWW sought to organize all types of workers into "One Big Union." But the "Wobblies," as IWW members were called, sought the complete destruction of the capitalist system and its replacement by autonomous workers' unions (syndicates). The IWW used confrontational strikes and tactics to assault the capitalist system. Its efforts, in turn, led to a violent counterattack by the police. During World War I, government officials used emergency powers to crack down on the IWW and arrest its leaders.

ANDREW CARNEGIE

FROM Wealth (1889)

Andrew Carnegie (1835–1919) was a Scottish immigrant who created the world's largest and most efficient steel company; in the process he became one of the wealthiest men in the world. In the following essay, published in the North American Review *in 1889, he articulated what came to be known as the "gospel of wealth." Carnegie steadfastly defended the principles of the free enterprise system and the right of individuals to amass huge fortunes, but he stressed that the rich should donate their money for the public good before they died. Carnegie himself gave away $350,000,000. He built thousands of free public libraries, supported scientific research and higher education, and promoted the cause of world peace.*

From the *North American Review* 148 (June 1889): 653–64. [Editorial insertion appears in square brackets—*Ed.*]

The problem of our age is the proper administration of wealth, so that the ties of brotherhood may still bind together the rich and poor in harmonious relationship. The conditions of human life have not only been changed, but revolutionized, within the past few hundred years. In former days there was little difference between the dwelling, dress, food, and environment of the chief and those of his retainers. . . . The contrast between the palace of the millionaire and the cottage of the laborer with us today measures the change which has come with civilization.

This change, however, is not to be deplored, but welcomed as highly beneficial. It is well, nay, essential for the progress of the race, that the houses of some should be homes for all that is highest and best in literature and the arts, and for all the refinements of civilization, rather than that none should be so. . . . The "good old times" were not good old times. Neither master nor servant was as well situated then as today. A relapse to old conditions would be disastrous to both—not the least so to him who serves—and would sweep away civilization with it. But whether the change be for good or ill, it is upon us, beyond our power to alter, and therefore to be accepted and made the best of. It is a waste of time to criticize the inevitable. . . .

The price we pay for this salutary change, is, no doubt, great. We assemble thousands of operatives in the factory, in the mine, and in the counting-house, of whom the employer can know little or nothing, and to whom the employer is little better than a myth. All intercourse between them is at an end. Rigid castes are formed, and, as usual, mutual ignorance breeds mutual distrust. Each caste is without sympathy for the other, and ready to credit anything disparaging in regard to it. Under the law of competition, the employer of thousands is forced into the strictest economies, among which the rates paid to labor figure prominently, and often there is friction between the employer and the employed, between capital and labor, between rich and poor. Human society loses homogeneity.

The price which society pays for the law of competition, like the price it pays for cheap comforts and luxuries, is also great; but the advantages of this law are also greater still, for it is to this law that we owe our wonderful material development, which brings improved conditions in its train. But, whether the law be benign or not, we . . . cannot evade it; no substitutes for it have been found; and while the law may be sometimes hard for the individual, it is best for the race, because it insures the survival of the fittest in every department. We accept and welcome, therefore, as conditions to which we must accommodate ourselves, great inequality of environment, the concentration of business . . . in the hands of a few, and the law of competition between these, as being not only beneficial, but essential for the future progress of the race. . . .

Objections to the foundations upon which society is based are not in order, because the condition of the race is better with these than it has been with any others which have been tried. Of the effect of any new substitutes proposed we cannot be sure. The Socialist or Anarchist who seeks to overturn present conditions is to be regarded as attacking the foundation upon which civilization itself rests, for civilization took its start from the day that the capable, industrious workman said to his incompetent and lazy fellow, "If thou dost not sow, thou shalt not reap," and thus ended primitive Communism by separating the drones from the bees. One who studies this subject will soon be brought face to face with the conclusion that upon the sacredness of property civilization itself depends—the right of the laborer to his hundred dollars in the savings bank, and equally the legal right of the millionaire to his million. To those who propose to substitute Communism for this intense Individualism the answer, therefore, is: The race has tried that. All progress from that barbarous day to the present time has resulted from its displacement. Not evil, but good, has come to the race from the accumulation of wealth by those who have the ability and energy that produce it.

*   *   *

We start, then, with a condition of affairs under which the best interests of the race are promoted, but which inevitably gives wealth to the few. Thus far, accepting conditions as they exist, the situation can be surveyed and pronounced good. The question then arises—and, if the foregoing be correct, it is the only question with which we have to deal—

What is the proper mode of administering wealth after the laws upon which civilization is founded have thrown it into the hands of the few? And it is of this great question that I believe I offer the true solution. . . .

There are but three modes in which surplus wealth can be disposed of. It can be left to the families of the decedents; or it can be bequeathed for public purposes; or, finally, it can be administered during their lives by its possessors. Under the first and second modes most of the wealth of the world that has reached the few has hitherto been applied. Let us in turn consider each of these modes. The first is the most injudicious. In monarchical countries, the estates and the greatest portion of the wealth are left to the first son, that the vanity of the parent may be gratified by the thought that his name and title are descend to succeeding generations, unimpaired. The condition of this class in Europe today teaches the futility of such hopes or ambitions. . . . Why should men leave great fortunes to their children? If this is done from affection, is it not misguided affection? Observation teaches that, generally speaking, it is not well for the children that they should be so burdened. Neither is it well for the state. . . . It is no longer questionable that great sums bequeathed oftener work more for injury than for the good of the recipients. . . .

As to the second mode, that of leaving wealth at death for public uses, it may be said that this is only a means for the disposal of wealth, provided a man is content to wait until he is dead before it becomes of much good in the world. Knowledge of the results of legacies bequeathed is not calculated to inspire the brightest hopes of much posthumous good being accomplished. . . . Besides this, it may fairly be said that no man is to be extolled for doing what he cannot help doing, nor is he to be thanked by the community to which he only leaves wealth at death. Men who leave vast sums in this way may fairly be thought men who would not have left it at all, had they been able to take it with them. . . .

The growing disposition to tax more and more heavily large estates left at death is a cheering indication of the growth of a salutary change in public opinion. The State of Pennsylvania now takes . . .

one-tenth of the property left by its citizens. . . . By taxing estates heavily at death, the state marks its condemnation of the selfish millionaire's unworthy life. . . .

There remains, then, only one mode of using great fortunes; but in this we have the true antidote for the temporary unequal distribution of wealth, the reconciliation of the rich and the poor—a reign of harmony—another ideal, differing indeed, from that of the Communist in requiring only the further evolution of existing conditions, not the total overthrow of our civilization. . . . Under its sway we shall have an ideal state, in which the surplus wealth of the few will become, in the best sense, the property of the many, because it is administered for the common good, and this wealth, passing through the hands of the few, can be made a much more potent force for the elevation of our race than it if had been distributed in small sums to the people themselves. Even the poorest can be made to see this, and to agree that great sums gathered by some of their fellow-citizens and spent for public purposes, from which the masses reap the principal benefit, are more valuable to them than if scattered among them through the course of many years in trifling amounts.

*   *   *

This, then, is held to be the duty of the Man of Wealth: First, to set an example of modest, unostentatious living, shunning display of extravagance; to provide moderately for the legitimate wants of those dependent upon him; and after doing so to consider all surplus revenues which come to him simply as trust funds, which he is called upon to administer . . . in the manner which, in his judgment, is best calculated to produce the most beneficial results for the community—the man of wealth thus becoming the mere agent and trustee for his poorer brethren, bringing to their service his superior wisdom, experience, and ability to administer, doing for them better than they would or could do for themselves. . . .

In bestowing charity, the main consideration should be to help those who will help themselves; to

provide part of the means by which those who desire to improve may do to; to give those who desire to rise the aids by which they may rise. . . . Neither the individual nor the race is improved by almsgiving. . . . The amount which can be wisely given. . . . [to] individuals is necessarily limited, . . . for in alms-giving more injury is probably done by rewarding vice than by relieving virtue. . . .

Thus is the problem of the Rich and Poor to be solved. The laws of accumulation will be left free; the laws of distribution free. Individualism will continue, but the millionaire will be but a trustee for the poor; entrusted for a season with a great part of the increased wealth of the community, but administering it for the community far better than it could or would have done for itself. The best minds will thus have reached a stage in the development of the race in which it is clearly seen that there is no mode of disposing of surplus wealth . . . save by using it year by year for the general good. The day already dawns. But a little while, and . . . the man who dies leaving behind him millions, . . . which was his to administer in life, will pass away "unwept, unhonored, and unsung," no matter to what uses he leave the dross which he cannot take with him. Of such as these the public verdict will then be: "The man who dies thus rich dies disgraced."

Such, in my opinion, is the true Gospel concerning Wealth, obedience to which is destined some day to solve the problem of the Rich and the Poor, and to bring "Peace on earth, among men Good-Will."

REVIEW QUESTIONS

1. How did Carnegie justify the accumulation of wealth?
2. What three ways did Carnegie suggest to dispose of personal wealth?
3. What criteria did Carnegie establish for administering charitable resources? Are his reasons consistent?

Preamble to the Constitution
of the Knights of Labor (1878)

Many disagreed with Andrew Carnegie's defense of unchecked free enterprise. One dissenting group was the Noble Order of the Knights of Labor, the first national union in the United States. Founded in 1869 as a secret fraternal order, it included workers of all types, skilled and unskilled, as well as women and African Americans. The Knights grew slowly until 1879 when Terence V. Powderly assumed leadership of the organization. He brought the Knights into the public arena, advocated an eight-hour working day for all workers, promoted an array of political reforms, and preferred boycotts over strikes. In 1886 the Knights boasted some 800,000 members. Yet their far-flung objectives and their utopian efforts to replace the wage-labor system of competitive free enterprise with a "cooperative" philosophy brought their demise. By 1900 the organization had disappeared. It was displaced by the American Federation of Labor, founded in 1886, which organized only skilled workers and used strikes to gain its objectives. Powderly helped draft the Preamble to the Constitution of the Knights of Labor, excerpted below.

From Terence V. Powderly, *Thirty Years of Labor* (Columbus, OH: Excelsior Publishing House, 1890), pp. 243–46.

The recent alarming development and aggression of aggregated wealth, which, unless checked, will invariably lead to the pauperization and hopeless degradation of the toiling masses, render it imperative, if we desire to enjoy the blessings of life, that a check should be placed upon its power and upon unjust accumulation, and a system adopted which will secure to the laborer the fruits of his toil; and as this much-desired object can only be accomplished by the thorough unification of labor, and the united efforts of those who obey the divine injunction that "In the sweat of thy brow shalt thou eat bread," we have formed the Knights of Labor with a view of securing the organization and direction, by co-operative effort, of the power of the industrial classes; and we submit to the world the object sought to be accomplished by our organization, calling upon all who believe in securing "the greatest good to the greatest number" to aid and assist us:

I. To bring within the folds of organization every department of productive industry, making knowledge a standpoint for action, and industrial and moral worth, not wealth, the true standard of individual and national greatness.

II. To secure to the toilers a proper share of the wealth that they create; more of the leisure that rightfully belongs to them; more societary advantages; more of the benefits, privileges, and emoluments of the world; in a word, all those rights and privileges necessary to make them capable of enjoying, appreciating, defending, and perpetuating the blessing of good government.

III. To arrive at the true condition of the producing masses in their educational, moral, and financial condition, by demanding from the various governments the establishment of bureaus of Labor Statistics.

IV. The establishment of co-operative institutions, productive and distributive.

V. The reserving of the public lands—the heritage of the people—for the actual settler;—not another acre for railroads or speculators.

VI. The abrogation of all laws that do not bear equally upon capital and labor, the removal of unjust technicalities, delays, and discriminations in the administration of justice, and the adopting of measures providing for the health and safety of those engaged in mining, manufacturing, or building pursuits.

VII. The enactment of laws to compel chartered corporations to pay their employees weekly, in full, for labor performed during the preceding week, in the lawful money of the country.

VIII. The enactment of laws giving mechanics and laborers a first lien on their work for their full wages.

IX. The abolishment of the contract system on national, state, and municipal work.

X. The substitution of arbitration for strikes, whenever and wherever employers and employees are willing to meet on equitable grounds.

XI. The prohibition of the employment of children in workshops, mines, and factories before attaining their fourteenth year.

XII. To abolish the system of letting out by contract the labor of convicts in our prisons and reformatory institutions.

XIII. To secure for both sexes equal pay for equal work.

XIV. The reduction of the hours of labor to eight per day, so that the laborers may have more time for social enjoyment and intellectual improvement, and be enabled to reap the advantages conferred by the labor-saving machinery which their brains have created.

XV. To prevail upon governments to establish a purely national circulating medium,[1] based upon the faith and resources of the nation, and issued directly to the people, without the intervention of any system of banking corporations, which money shall be a legal tender in payment of all debts, public or private.

REVIEW QUESTIONS

1. Whom did the preamble identify as enemies of social and economic equality? Explain.
2. How did the preamble characterize the impact of labor-saving machines?
3. How do you think Carnegie might have reacted to this document?

---

[1]Currency—*Ed.*

LEONORA M. BARRY

FROM Organizing Women Workers (1887)

Women workers during the nineteenth century suffered discrimination in hiring and pay. The Knights of Labor sought to organize women workers into unions on a national scale. The organization accepted women both in mixed assemblies and gender-segregated locals. The Knights hired Leonora M. Barry, a former mill worker herself, to work as an organizer. During her first year she visited numerous factories and mills across the country, documenting the conditions and prejudice she encountered. The following excerpt from her report reveals the special difficulties that women workers faced and helps explain why the Knights were generally unsuccessful in organizing them.

From Pamphlet. Sophia Smith Collection, Smith College, Northampton, MA. [Editorial insertions appear in square brackets—*Ed.*]

General Master Workman and Members of the General Assembly:

One year ago the Knights of Labor, in convention assembled at Richmond, Va., elected me to a position of honor and trust—the servant and representative of thousands of toiling women. . . .

Having no legal authority I have been unable to make as thorough an investigation in many places as I would like . . . consequently the facts stated in my report are not all from actual observation but from authority which I have every reason to believe truthful and reliable.

Upon the strength of my observation and experience I would ask of officers and members of this Order that more consideration be given, and more thorough educational measures be adopted on behalf of the working-women of our land, the majority of whom are entirely ignorant of the economic and industrial question which is to them of such vital importance; and they must ever remain so while the selfishness of their brothers in toil is carried to such an extent as I find it to be among those who have sworn to demand equal pay for equal work. Thus far in the history of our Order that part of our platform has been but a mockery of the principles intended. . . .

Men! ye whose earnings count from nine to fifteen dollars a week and upward, cease, in the name of God and humanity, cease your demands and grievances and give us your assistance for a time to bring some relief to the poor unfortunate, whose week's work of eighty-four hours brings her but $2.50 or $3 per week.

*   *   *

December 10 went to Newark to investigate the matter concerning the sewing-women of that city, which was referred to our committee at the General Assembly at Richmond. Found, after a careful study of the matter, that . . . in general the working-women of Newark were very poorly paid, and the system of fines in many industries were severe and unjust. Instance: a corset factory where a fine is imposed for eating, laughing, singing or talking of 10 cents each. If not inside the gate in the morning when the whistle stops blowing, an employee is locked out until half past seven; then she can go to work, but is docked two hours for waste power; and many other rules equally slavish and unjust. Other industries closely follow these rules, while the sewing-women receive wages which are only one remove from actual starvation. In answer to all my inquiries of employer and employed why this state of affairs exists, the reply was, monopoly and competition. . . .

Went to Auburn, N.Y., Feb. 20. I found the working-women of this city in a deplorable state, there being none of them organized. There were long hours, poor wages, and the usual results consequent upon such a condition. Not among male employers alone in this city, but women in whose heart we would expect to find a little pity and compassion for the suffering of her own sex. To the contrary, on this occasion, however, I found one who, for cruelty and injustice toward employees, has not an equal on the pages of labor's history—one who owns and conducts an establishment in which is manufactured women's and children's wear. Upon accepting a position in her factory an employee is compelled to purchase a sewing machine from the proprietress, who is agent for the S. M. Co. This must be paid for in weekly payments of 50 cents, provided the operative makes $3. Should she make $4 the weekly payment is 75 cents. At any time before the machine is paid for, through a reduction of the already meagre wages, or the enforcement of some petty tyrannical rule—sickness, anger, or any cause, the operative leaves her employ, she forfeits the machine and all the money paid upon it, and to the next applicant the machine is resold. She must also purchase the thread for doing the work, as she is an agent for a thread company. It takes four spools of thread at 50 cents a spool to do $5 worth of work, and when $2 is paid for thread, and 50 cents for the machine, the unfortunate victim has $2.50 wherewith to board, clothe and care for herself generally; and it is only experts who can make even this. . . .

I succeeded in organizing two Local Assemblies in this city, one of woodworkers, and one women's Local Assembly, numbering at organization 107 members, which has grown rapidly and is now one of the most flourishing Local Assemblies in the State. Here it was that Sister Annie Conboy was discharged from the silk mill for having taken me through the mill, although she had received permission from her foreman to take a friend through, yet, when the proprietor found out I was a Knight of Labor she was discharged without a moment's warning.

March 14 was sent to Paterson [New Jersey] to look into the condition of the women and children employed in the Linen-thread Works of that city. There are some fourteen or fifteen hundred persons employed in this industry, who were at that time out of employment for this reason: Children who work at what is called doffing[1] were receiving $2.70 per week, and asked for an increase of 5 cents per day. They were refused, and they struck, whereupon all the other employees were locked out. . . .

---

[1]Removing a bobbin from a spinning frame.

The abuse, injustice and suffering which the women of this industry endure from the tyranny, cruelty and slave-driving propensities of the employers is [sic] something terrible to be allowed existence in free America. In one branch of this industry women are compelled to stand on a stone floor in water the year round, most of the time barefoot, with a spray of water from a revolving cylinder flying constantly against the breast; and the coldest night in winter as well as the warmest in summer those poor creatures must go to their homes with water dripping from their underclothing along their path, because there could not be space or a few moments allowed them wherein to change their clothing. A constant supply of recruits is always on hand to take the places of any who dare rebel against the ironclad authority of those in charge.

*   *   *

In submitting my report to the members of the Order and the public at large, I ask only one favor, namely, a careful perusal and just criticism. . . . I can only hope that my labor will yet bear good fruit, and that in the near future fair consideration and justice will be meted out to the oppressed women of our nation. . . .

REVIEW QUESTIONS

1. Compare the data given for men's wages and women's wages. Were women receiving equal pay for equal work? What kinds of costs were often deducted from women's wages?
2. Describe the kinds of conditions that women faced at work.
3. Why was it easy to fire women workers? What does this suggest about the dynamics of nineteenth-century supply and demand for labor?

SAMUEL GOMPERS

FROM The American Federation of Labor (1883)

The American Federation of Labor supplanted the Knights of Labor, and it developed a quite different philosophy. Rather than trying to abolish the wage-labor system, it sought to use strikes to gain higher wages, reduced working hours, and better working conditions for its members. Unlike the Knights of Labor, the AFL organized only skilled workers into unions defined by particular trades. The AFL also required relatively high dues to create a treasury large enough to sustain the members during a prolonged strike. Under the leadership of Samuel Gompers (1850–1924), a London-born cigar maker, the AFL became not only a powerful force serving the interests of its members but also a conservative defender of capitalism against the appeal of socialism and communism. In 1883 Gompers testified before a Congressional committee about his organization.

From U.S. Senate, Testimony of Samuel Gompers, August 1883, *Report of the Committee of the Senate upon the Relations between Labor and Capital* (Washington, DC, 1885), 1:365–70.

. . . There is nothing in the labor movement that employers who have had unorganized workers dread so much as organization; but organization alone will not do much unless the organization provides itself with a good fund, so that the operatives may be in a good position, in the event of a struggle with their employers, to hold out. . . .

Modern industry evolves these organizations out of the existing conditions where there are two classes in society, one incessantly striving to obtain the labor of the other class for as little as possible, and to obtain the largest amount or number of hours of labor; and the members of the other class, being as individuals utterly helpless in a contest with their employers, naturally resort to combinations to improve their condition, and, in fact, they are forced by the conditions which surround them to organize for self-protection. Hence trades unions. Trade unions are not barbarous, nor are they the outgrowth of barbarism. On the contrary they are only possible where civilization exists. Trade unions cannot exist in China; they cannot exist in Russia; and in all those semi-barbarous countries they can hardly exist, if they can exist at all. But they have been formed successfully in this country, in Germany, in England, and they are gradually gaining strength in France. . . .

Wherever trades unions have organized and are most firmly organized, there are the rights of the people most respected. A people may be educated, but to me it appears that the greatest amount of intelligence exists in that country or that state where the people are best able to defend their rights, and their liberties as against those who are desirous of undermining them. Trades unions are organizations that instill into men a higher motive-power and give them a higher goal to look to. . . .

The trades unions are by no means an outgrowth of socialistic or communistic ideas or principles, but the socialistic and communistic notions are evolved from the trades unions' movements. As to the question of the principles of communism or socialism prevailing in trades unions, there are a number of men who connect themselves as workingmen with the trades unions who may have socialistic convictions, yet who never gave them currency. . . . On the other hand, there are men—not so numerous now as they have been in the past—who are endeavoring to conquer the trades-union movement and subordinate it to those doctrines, and in a measure, in a few such organizations that condition of things exists, but by no means does it exist in the largest, most powerful, and best organized trades unions. There the view of which I spoke just now, the desire to improve the condition of the workingmen by and through the efforts of the trades union, is fully lived up to. . . . I believe that the existence of the trades-union movement, more especially where the unionists are better organized, has evoked a spirit and a demand for reform, but has held in check the more radical elements in society.

REVIEW QUESTIONS

1. Why did Gompers believe that unions were necessary?
2. Why did Gompers claim that trade unions did not exist in China or Russia?
3. What were the advantages of Gompers's explicit rejection of socialism and communism?

EDWARD O'DONNELL

FROM Women as Bread Winners— The Error of the Age (1887)

The AFL excluded not only unskilled workers but also blacks, women, and recent immigrants. In 1900 only 3 percent of working women were represented by unions. At times the arguments against admitting women into unions grew hysterical, as illustrated by this AFL pamphlet.

From "Women as Bread Winners—The Error of the Age," *American Federationist* 48 (October 1887): 167–68.

The invasion of the crafts by women has been developing for years amid irritation and injury to the workman. The right of the woman to win honest bread is accorded on all sides, but with craftsmen it is an open question whether this manifestation is of a healthy social growth or not.

The rapid displacement of men by women in the factory and workshop has to be met sooner or later, and the question is forcing itself upon the leaders and thinkers among the labor organizations of the land.

Is it a pleasing indication of progress to see the father, the brother and the son displaced as the bread winner by the mother, sister and daughter?

Is not this evolutionary backslide, which certainly modernizes the present wage system in vogue, a menace to prosperity—a foe to our civilized pretensions? . . .

The growing demand for female labor is not founded upon philanthropy, as those who encourage it would have sentimentalists believe; it does not spring from the milk of human kindness. It is an insidious assault upon the home; it is the knife of the assassin, aimed at the family circle—the divine injunction. It debars the man through financial embarrassment from family responsibility, and physically, mentally and socially excludes the woman equally from nature's dearest impulse. Is this the demand of civilized progress; is it the desire of Christian dogma? . . .

Capital thrives not upon the peaceful, united, contented family circle; rather are its palaces, pleasures and vices fostered and increased upon the disruption, ruin or abolition of the home, because with its decay and ever glaring privation, manhood loses its dignity, its backbone, its aspirations. . . .

To combat these impertinent inclinations, dangerous to the few, the old and well-tried policy of divide and conquer is invoked, and to our own shame, it must be said, one too often renders blind aid to capital in its warfare upon us. The employer in the magnanimity of his generosity will give employment to the daughter, while her two brothers are weary because of their daily tramp in quest of work. The father, who has a fair, steady job, sees not the infamous policy back of the flattering propositions. Somebody else's daughter is called in the same manner, by and by, and very soon the shop or factory are full of women, while their fathers have the option of working for the same wages or a few cents more, or take their places in the large army of unemployed. . . .

College professors and graduates tell us that this is the natural sequence of industrial development, an integral part of economic claim.

Never was a greater fallacy uttered of more poisonous import. It is false and wholly illogical. The great demand for women and their preference over men does not spring from a desire to elevate humanity; at any rate that is not its trend.

The wholesale employment of women in the various handicrafts must gradually unsex them, as it most assuredly is demoralizing them, or stripping them of that mode's demeanor that lends a charm to their kind, while it numerically strengthens the multitudinous army of loafers, paupers, tramps and policemen, for no man who desires honest employment, and can secure it, cares to throw his life away upon such a wretched occupation as the latter.

The employment of women in the mechanical departments is encouraged because of its cheapness and easy manipulation, regardless of the consequent perils; and for no other reason. The generous sentiment enveloping this inducement is criminal design, since it comes from a thirst to build riches upon the dismemberment of the family or the hearthstone cruelly dishonored. . . .

But somebody will say, would you have women pursue lives of shame rather than work? Certainly not; it is to the alarming introduction of women into the mechanical industries, hitherto enjoyed by the sterner sex, at a wage uncommandable by them, that leads so many into that deplorable pursuit. . . .

REVIEW QUESTIONS

1. What did O'Donnell mean by female employment constituting an "insidious assault upon the home"?
2. According to the pamphlet, how did employment "unsex" women?

EUGENE V. DEBS

FROM Outlook for Socialism in the United States (1900)

By the end of the nineteenth century, some labor activists insisted that capitalism itself must give way to a socialist system. Eugene Debs (1855–1926) was a railroad union organizer who converted to socialism during a stint in jail. He later would run as the Socialist Party candidate for president in several elections.

From "Outlook for Socialism in the United States," *International Socialist Review* 1 (September 1900): 129–35. [Editorial insertion appears in square brackets—*Ed.*]

The sun of the passing century is setting upon scenes of extraordinary activity in almost every part of our capitalistic, old planet. Wars and rumors of wars are of universal prevalence . . . and through all the flame and furor of the fray can be heard the savage snarlings of the Christian "dogs of war" as they fiercely glare about them, and with jealous fury threaten to fly at one another's throats to settle the question of supremacy and the spoil and plunder of conquest. . . .

Cheerless indeed would be the contemplation of such sanguinary [violent] scenes were the light of Socialism not breaking upon mankind. . . . From out of the midnight of superstition, ignorance and slavery the disenthralling, emancipating sun is rising. I am not gifted with prophetic vision, and yet I see the shadows vanishing. I behold near and far prostrate men lifting their bowed forms from the dust. I see thrones in the grasp of decay; despots relaxing their hold upon scepters, and shackles falling, not only from the limbs, but also from the souls of men. . . .

Socialists generally will agree that the past year has been marked with a propaganda of unprecedented activity and that the sentiment of the American people in respect to Socialism has undergone a most remarkable change. It would be difficult to imagine a more ignorant, bitter and unreasoning prejudice than that of the American people against Socialism during the early years of its introduction. . . .

Socialism was cunningly associated with "anarchy and bloodshed," and denounced as a "foul foreign importation" to pollute the fair, free soil of America, and every outrage to which the early agitators were subjected won the plaudits of the people. But they persevered in their task; they could not be silenced or suppressed. Slowly they increased in number and gradually the movement began to take root and spread over the country. . . .

The subject has passed entirely beyond the domain of sneer and ridicule and now commands serious treatment. Of course, Socialism is violently denounced by the capitalist press and by all the brood of subsidized contributors to magazine literature, but this only confirms the view that the advance of Socialism is very properly recognized by the capitalist class as the one cloud upon the horizon which portends an end to the system in which they have waxed fat, insolent and despotic through the exploitation of their countless wage-working slaves.

In school and college and church, in clubs and public halls everywhere, Socialism is the central theme of discussion, and its advocates, inspired by its noble principles, are to be found here, there and in all places ready to give or accept challenge to battle. In the cities the corner meetings are popular and effective. But rarely is such a gathering now molested by the "authorities," and then only where they have just been inaugurated. They are too numerously attended by serious, intelligent and self-reliant men and women to invite interference. . . .

Needless is it for me to say to the thinking workingman that he has no choice between these two capitalist parties,[1] that they are both pledged to the same system and that whether the one or the other succeeds, he will still remain the wage-working slave he is today.

What but meaningless phrases are "imperialism," "expansion," "free silver," "gold standard," etc., to the wage-worker? The large capitalists represented by Mr. McKinley and the small capitalists represented by Mr. Bryan[2] are interested in these "issues," but they do not concern the working class.

What the workingmen of the country are profoundly interested in is the private ownership of the means of production and distribution, the enslaving and degrading wage-system in which they toil for a pittance at the pleasure of their masters and are bludgeoned, jailed or shot when they protest—this is the central, controlling, vital issue of the hour, and neither of the old party platforms has a word or even a hint about it. . . .

Whether the means of production—that is to say, the land, mines, factories, machinery, etc.—are owned by a few large Republican capitalists, who organize a trust, or whether they be owned by a lot of small Democratic capitalists, who are opposed to the trust, is all the same to the working class. Let the capitalists, large and small, fight this out among themselves.

The working class must get rid of the whole brook of masters and exploiters, and put themselves in possession and control the means of production, that they may have steady employment without consulting a capitalist employer, large or small, and that they may get the wealth their labor produces, all of it, and enjoy with their families the fruits of their industry in comfortable and happy homes, abundant and wholesome food, proper clothing and all other things necessary to "life, liberty and the pursuit of happiness." It is therefore a question not of "reform," the mask of fraud, but of evolution. The capitalist system must be overthrown, class-rule abolished and wage-slavery supplanted by cooperative industry.

We hear it frequently urged that the Democratic Party is the "poor man's party," "the friend of labor." There is but one way to relieve poverty and to free labor, and that is by making common property of the tools of labor. . . .

The differences between the Republican and Democratic parties involve no issue, no principle in which the working class has any interest. . . . For a time the Populist Party had a mission, but it is practically ended. The Democratic Party has "fused" it out of existence. The "middle-of-the-road" element will be sorely disappointed when the votes are counted, and they will probably never figure in another national campaign. Not many of them will go back to the old parties. Many of them have already come to Socialism, and the rest are sure to follow.

There is no longer any room for a Populist Party, and progressive Populists realize it, and hence the "strongholds of Populism" are becoming the "hotbeds" of Socialism.

It is simply a question of capitalism or Socialism, of despotism or democracy, and they who are not wholly with us are wholly against us. . . . Oh, that all the working class could and would use their eyes and see; their ears and hear; their brains and think. How soon this earth could be transformed and by the alchemy of social order made to blossom with beauty and joy.

REVIEW QUESTIONS

1. Why did Debs say that Socialists should shun both Republicans and Democrats?
2. By what means did Socialists gain power?
3. Critics then and since dismissed Socialists as utopians. Do you agree?

---

[1]Republican and Democratic.
[2]The 1896 presidential candidates, William Jennings Bryan (1860–1925) and William McKinley (1843–1901).

18 ❧ THE NEW SOUTH AND THE NEW WEST, 1865–1900

The end of the Civil War found Americans confronting two frontiers of opportunity: the devastated South and the untamed West. The sprawling regions were—and are—the most distinctive sections of the country, and both regions exerted a magnetic attraction for adventurers and entrepreneurs. In the postwar South, people set about rebuilding railroads, mills, stores, barns, and homes. In the process of such renewal, a strenuous debate arose over the nature of the "New South." Should it try to re-create the agrarian culture of the antebellum period? Or should it adopt the northern model of a more diversified economy and urban-industrial society? The debate was never settled completely, and as a result both viewpoints competed for attention throughout the last quarter of the nineteenth century. By 1900, the South remained primarily an agricultural region, but it also had developed a far-flung network of textile mills, railroad lines, and manufacturing plants.

African Americans in the former Confederacy often found themselves at the center of the economic and political debate in the New South. By the end of the century, black leaders themselves were divided over the best course to follow. For his part, Booker T. Washington counseled southern blacks to focus on economic and educational opportunities at the expense of asserting their political and legal rights. Not so, declared W. E. B. Du Bois. He attacked Washington's "accommodationist" strategy and urged blacks to undertake a program of "ceaseless agitation" for political and social equality.

Controversy also swirled around the frenzied renewal of western settlement after the Civil War. During the century after 1865, fourteen new states were carved out of the western territories. To encourage new settlers, the federal government helped finance the construction of four transcontinental railroads, conquered and displaced the Indians, and sold public land at low prices to farmers and developers. Propelled by a lust for land and profits, millions of Americans headed west across the Mississippi River to establish homesteads, stake out mining claims, and set up shop in the many boom towns cropping up across the Great Plains and in the Far West.

This postwar surge of western migration had many of the romantic qualities so often depicted in novels, films, and television. The varied landscape of prairies, rivers, deserts, and mountains was stunning. And the people who braved incredibly harsh conditions to begin new lives in the West were indeed courageous and tenacious. Cowboys and Indians, outlaws and vigilantes, farmers and herders populated the plains, while miners and trappers led nomadic lives in hills and backwoods.

But these familiar images of western life tell only part of the story. Drudgery and tragedy were as commonplace as adventure and success. Droughts, locusts, disease, tornadoes, and the erratic fluctuations of commodity markets made life relentlessly precarious. The people who settled the trans-Mississippi frontier were in fact a diverse lot: they included women as well as men, African Americans, Hispanics, Asians, and European immigrants.

Many of the settlers were also blinded by short-sighted greed and prone to irresponsible behavior. In the process of "removing" the Indians, soldiers sometimes exterminated them. By the 1890s there were only 250,000 Native Americans left in the United States. The feverish quest for quick profits also helped fuel a boom–bust economic cycle that injected a chronic instability into the society and politics of the region.

The history of the Old West is thus a much more complicated story than that conveyed through popular culture—or through the accounts of some historians. In 1893 the historian Frederick Jackson Turner announced his so-called frontier thesis. The process of taming and settling an ever-receding frontier, Turner declared, gave American culture its distinctive institutions, values, and energy. The rigors and demands of westward settlement, for example, helped implant in Americans their rugged individualism and hardihood, and such qualities helped reinforce the democratic spirit that set them apart from other peoples. "Up to our day," Turner said, "American history has been in large degree the history of the colonization of the Great West. The existence of an area of free land, its continuous recession, and the advance of American settlement westward, explain American development." He was both right and wrong. The frontier experience explains much about the development of American society, but not all. And while the settling of the West planted seeds of democracy, it also involved the brutal exploitation of the land and its native peoples.

HENRY W. GRADY

FROM The New South (1886)

Atlanta newspaper editor Henry W. Grady was one of the most ardent promoters of a New South after the Civil War. In numerous speeches during the 1880s, he praised efforts to encourage industrial development and gave a glowing—and exaggerated—description of improved race relations in his native region. The excerpt below comes from a speech to the New England Society in New York City.

From Samuel Harding, ed., *Select Orations Illustrating American Political History* (Indianapolis: Hollenbeck Press, 1908), pp. 490–500.

We[1] have established a thrift in city and country. We have fallen in love with work. We have restored comfort to homes from which culture and elegance never departed. We have let economy take root and spread among us as rank as the crabgrass which sprung from Sherman's[2] cavalry camps, until we are ready to lay odds on the Georgia Yankee as he manufactures relics of the battlefield in a one-story shanty and squeezes pure olive oil out of his cotton seed, against any down-easter that ever swapped wooden nutmegs for flannel sausage in the valleys of Vermont. Above all, we know that we have achieved in these "piping times of peace" a fuller independence for the South than that which our fathers sought to win in the forum by their eloquence or compel in the field by their swords.

It is a rare privilege, sir, to have had part, however humble, in this work. Never was nobler duty confided to human hands than the uplifting and upbuilding of the prostrate and bleeding South— misguided, perhaps, but beautiful in her suffering, and honest, brave and generous always. In the record of her social, industrial and political illustration we await with confidence the verdict of the world.

But what of the negro? Have we solved the problem he presents or progressed in honor and equity toward solution? Let the record speak to the point. No section shows a more prosperous laboring population than the negroes of the South, none in fuller sympathy with the employing and landowning class. He shares our school fund, has the fullest protection of our laws and the friendship of our people.

Self-interest, as well as honor, demand that he should have this. Our future, our very existence depend upon our working out this problem in full and exact justice. We understand that when Lincoln signed the emancipation proclamation, your victory was assured, for he then committed you to the cause of human liberty, against which the arms of man cannot prevail—while those of our statesmen who trusted to make slavery the corner-stone of the Confederacy doomed us to defeat as far as they could, committing us to a cause that reason could not defend or the sword maintain in sight of advancing civilization. . . .

The relations of the southern people with the negro are close and cordial. We remember with what fidelity for four years he guarded our defenseless women and children, whose husbands and fathers were fighting against his freedom. To his eternal credit be it said that whenever he struck a blow for his own liberty he fought in open battle, and when at last he raised his black and humble hands that the shackles might be struck off, those hands were innocent of wrong against his helpless

[1] I.e., Southerners.
[2] Union general William T. Sherman (1820–1891).

charges, and worthy to be taken in loving grasp by every man who honors loyalty and devotion.

Ruffians have maltreated him, rascals have misled him, philanthropists established a bank for him, but the South, with the North, protests against injustice to this simple and sincere people. To liberty and enfranchisement is as far as law can carry the negro. The rest must be left to conscience and common sense. It must be left to those among whom his lot is cast, with whom he is indissolubly connected, and whose prosperity depends upon their possessing his intelligent sympathy and confidence. Faith has been kept with him, in spite of calumnious assertions to the contrary by those who assume to speak for us or by frank opponents. Faith will be kept with him in the future, if the South holds her reason and integrity.

But have we kept faith with you? In the fullest sense, yes. When Lee[3] surrendered . . . the South became, and has since been, loyal to this Union. We fought hard enough to know that we were whipped, and in perfect frankness accept as final the arbitrament[4] of the sword to which we had appealed. The South found her jewel in the toad's head of defeat. The shackles that had held her in narrow limitations fell forever when the shackles of the negro slave were broken. Under the old regime the negroes were slaves to the South; the South was a slave to the system. The old plantation, with its simple police regulations and feudal habit, was the only type possible under slavery. Thus was gathered in the hands of a splendid and chivalric oligarchy the substance that should have been diffused among the people, as the rich blood, under certain artificial conditions, is gathered at the heart, filling that with affluent rapture but leaving the body chill and colorless.

The old South rested everything on slavery and agriculture, unconscious that these could neither give nor maintain healthy growth. The new South presents a perfect democracy, the oligarchs leading in the popular movement—a social system compact and closely knitted, less splendid on the surface, but stronger at the core—a hundred farms for every plantation, fifty homes for every palace—and a diversified industry that meets the complex need of this complex age.

The new South is enamored of her new work. Her soul is stirred with the breath of a new life. The light of a grander day is falling fair on her face. She is thrilling with the consciousness of growing power and prosperity. As she stands upright, full-statured and equal among the people of the earth, breathing the keen air and looking out upon the expanded horizon, she understands that her emancipation came because through the inscrutable wisdom of God her honest purpose was crossed, and her brave armies were beaten.

---

[3]Confederate general Robert E. Lee (1807–1870).
[4]To settle a dispute by force.

REVIEW QUESTIONS

1. How does Grady characterize the "Negro"?
2. According to Grady, what were the negative effects of slavery on the South?
3. In what respects might Grady have tailored his remarks to his New York audience?

FROM **A Sharecrop Contract (1882)**

After the Civil War, farm folk of both races who could not afford to buy their own land were forced to work for others, either as rent-paying tenants or, more often, as sharecroppers. The farm owner would provide the "cropper" with a plot of land, seed, fertilizer, tools, and a line of credit at the general store for other necessities. In exchange, the cropper would give the owner a "share" of the crop. The following contract with the Grimes family of North Carolina illustrates the arrangement.

From The Grimes Family Papers (3357), 1882. Southern Historical Collection, University of North Carolina, Chapel Hill.

To every one applying to rent land upon shares, the following conditions must be read, and *agreed to.*

To every 30 or 35 acres, I agree to furnish the team,[1] plow, and farming implements, except cotton planters, and I *do not* agree to furnish a cart to every cropper. The croppers are to have half of the cotton, corn and fodder (and peas and pumpkins and potatoes if any are planted) if the following conditions are complied with, but—if not—they are to have only two fifths. Croppers are to have no part or interest in the cotton seed raised from the crop planted and worked by them. No vine crops of any description, that is, no watermelons, muskmelons, . . . squashes or anything of that kind, except peas and pumpkins, and potatoes are to be planted in the cotton or corn. All must work under my direction. All plantation work to be done by the croppers. My part of the crop to be *housed* by them, and the fodder and oats to be hauled and put in the house. All the cotton must be topped about 1st August. If any cropper fails from any cause to save all the fodder from his crop, I am to have enough fodder to make it equal to one half of the whole if the whole amount of fodder had been saved.

For every mule or horse furnished by me there must be 1000 good sized rails . . . hauled, and the fence repaired as far as they will go, the fence to be torn down and put up from the bottom if I so direct. All croppers to haul rails and work on fence whenever I may order. Rails to be split when I may say. Each cropper to clean out every ditch in his crop, and where a ditch runs between two croppers, the cleaning out of that ditch is to be divided equally between them. Every ditch bank in the crop must be scrubbed down and cleaned off before the crop is planted and must be cut down every time the land is worked with his hoe and when the crop

is "laid by," the ditch banks must be left clean of bushes, weeds, and seeds. The cleaning out of all ditches must be done by the first of October. The rails must be split and the fence repaired before corn is planted.

Each cropper must keep in good repair all bridges in his crop or over ditches that he has to clean out and when a bridge needs repairing that is outside of all their crops, then any one that I call on must repair it.

Fence jams to be done as ditch banks. If any cotton is planted on the land outside of the plantation fence, I am to have *three fourths of* all the cotton made in those patches, that is to say, no cotton must be planted by croppers in their home patches.

All croppers must clean out stables and fill them with straw, and haul straw in front of stables whenever I direct. All the cotton must be manured, and enough fertilizer must be brought to manure each crop highly, the croppers to pay for one half of all run in the plantation after crops are gathered.

If the fence should be blown down, or if trees should fall on the fence outside of the land planted by any of the croppers, any one or all that I may call upon must put it up and repair it. Every cropper must feed, or have fed, the team he works, Saturday nights, Sundays, and every morning before going to work, beginning to feed his team (morning, noon, and night *every day* in the week) on the day he rents and feeding it to and including the 31st day of December. If any cropper shall from any cause fail to repair his fence as far as 1000 rails will go, or shall fail to clean out any part of his ditches, or shall fail to leave his ditch banks, any part of them, well scrubbed and clean when his crop is laid by, or shall fail to clean out stables, fill them up and haul straw in front of them whenever he is told, he shall have only two-fifths of the cotton, corn, fodder, peas and pumpkins made on the land he cultivates.

---

[1]Horses or mules.

If any cropper shall fail to feed his team Saturday nights, all day Sunday and all the rest of the week, morning/noon, and night, for every time he so fails he must pay me five cents.

No corn nor cotton stalks must be burned, but must be cut down, cut up and plowed in. Nothing must be burned off the land except when it is *impossible* to plow it in.

Every cropper must be responsible for all gear and farming implements placed in his hands, and if not returned must be paid for unless it is worn out by use.

Croppers must sow & plow in oats and haul them to the crib, but *must have no part of them*. Nothing to be sold from their crops, nor fodder nor corn to be carried out of the fields until my rent is all paid, and all amounts they owe me and for which I am responsible are paid in full.

I am to gin[2] & pack all the cotton and charge every cropper an eighteenth of his part, the cropper to furnish his part of the bagging, ties, & twine.

The sale of every cropper's part of the cotton to be made by me when and where I choose to sell, and after deducting all they owe me and all sums that I may be responsible for on their accounts, to pay them their half of the net proceeds. Work of every description, particularly the work on fences and ditches, to be done to my satisfaction, and must be done over until I am satisfied that it is done as it should be. . . .

---

[2]The process of removing seeds from cotton.

REVIEW QUESTIONS

1. Does the sharecrop arrangement seem fair to all parties? Explain.
2. What alternative did landless farmers have?
3. Why was the landowner so determined to prevent croppers from planting cotton and other staple crops in their "home" patches?

FROM *Plessy v. Ferguson* (1896)

The growing social separation of the races in the South during the 1880s varied from county to county and state to state, but by the 1890s the trend was clear: white southerners were determined to enforce a racially segregated society. A Louisiana ordinance of 1890 required that railroads "provide equal but separate accommodations for the white and colored races." A group of New Orleans blacks resolved to test the constitutionality of the law. One of them, Homer Plessy, sat in a whites only section of a railcar in 1892 and was arrested. Four years later the U.S. Supreme Court heard his case when Plessy appealed a ruling by District Judge John H. Ferguson. Seven judges upheld Plessy's conviction and only one, John Marshall Harlan, son of a slaveholder from Kentucky, dissented. Harlan put forth a powerful defense of equal rights.

From *Plessy v. Ferguson*, 163 U.S. 537 (1896).

Justice Henry Brown for the majority: This case turns upon the constitutionality of an act of the general assembly of the state of Louisiana, passed in 1890, providing for separate railway carriages for the white and colored races. . . .

The constitutionality of this act is attacked upon the ground that it conflicts both with the 13th Amendment of the Constitution, abolishing slavery, and the 14th Amendment, which prohibits certain restrictive legislation on the part of the states.

1. That it does not conflict with the 13th Amendment, which abolished slavery and involuntary servitude, except as a punishment for crime, is too clear for argument. . . . Indeed, we do not understand that the 13th Amendment is strenuously relied upon by the plaintiff. . . .

The object of the (14th) amendment was undoubtedly to enforce the absolute equality of the two races before the law, but in the nature of things it could not have been intended to abolish distinctions based upon color, or to enforce social, as distinguished from political, equality or a commingling of the two races upon terms unsatisfactory to either. Laws permitting, and even requiring their separation in places where they are liable to be brought into contact do not necessarily imply the inferiority of either race to the other, and have been generally, if not universally, recognized as within the competency of the state legislatures in the exercise of their police power. . . .

We consider the underlying fallacy of the plaintiff's argument to consist in the assumption that the enforced separation of the two races stamps the colored race with a badge of inferiority. If this be so, it is not by reason of anything found in the act, but solely because the colored race chooses to put that construction upon it. . . .

The argument also assumes that social prejudice may be overcome by legislation, and that equal rights cannot be secured to the Negro except by an enforced commingling of the two races. We cannot accept this proposition. If the two races are to meet on terms of social equality, it must be the result of natural affinities, a mutual appreciation of each other's merits and a voluntary consent of individuals. . . . Legislation is powerless to eradicate racial instincts or to abolish distinctions based upon physical differences, and the attempt to do so can only result in accentuating the difficulties of the present situation. If the civil and political right of both races be equal, one cannot be inferior to the other civilly or politically. If one race be inferior to the other socially, the Constitution of the United States cannot put them upon the same plane.

———

Justice John Harlan, dissenting: . . . In respect of civil rights, common to all citizens, the Constitution of the United States does not, I think, permit any public authority to know the race of those entitled to be protected in the enjoyment of such rights. . . . I deny that any legislative body or judicial tribunal may have regard to the race of citizens when the civil rights of those citizens are involved. Indeed such legislation as that here in question is inconsistent not only with that equality of rights which pertains to citizenship, national and state, but with the personal liberty enjoyed by everyone within the United States. . . .

The white race deems itself to be the dominant race in this country. And so it is, in prestige, in achievements, in education, in wealth and power. So, I doubt not, it will continue to be for all time, if it remains true to its great heritage and holds fast to the principles of constitutional liberty. Our Constitution is color-blind, and neither knows nor tolerates classes among citizens. In respect to civil rights, all citizens are equal before the law. . . .

The destinies of the two races in this country are indissolubly linked together, and the interests of both require that the common government of all shall not permit the seeds of race hate to be planted under the sanction of law. What can more certainly arouse race hate, what more certainly create and perpetuate a feeling of distrust between these races, than state enactments which in fact proceed on the ground that colored citizens are so inferior and degraded that they cannot be allowed to sit in public coaches occupied by white citizens? That, as all will admit, is the real meaning of such legislation as was enacted in Louisiana. . . .

State enactments regulating the enjoyment of civil rights, upon the basis of race, and cunningly devised to defeat legitimate results of the war,[1] under the pretense of recognizing equality of rights, can have no other result than to render permanent peace impossible, and keep alive a conflict of races, the continuance of which must do harm to all concerned.

We boast of the freedom enjoyed by our people above all other peoples. But it is difficult to reconcile that boast with a state of the law which, practically,

———

[1] The Civil War.

puts the brand of servitude and degradation upon a large class of our fellow citizens, our equals before the law. The thin disguise of "equal" accommodations for passengers in railroad coaches will not mislead anyone, or atone for the wrong this day done. . . .

I am of opinion that the state of Louisiana is inconsistent with the personal liberty of citizens, white and black, in that state, and hostile to both the spirit and letter of the Constitution of the United States. If laws of like character should be enacted in the several states of the Union, the effect would be in the highest degree mischievous. . . .

I am constrained to withhold my assent from the opinion and judgment of the majority.

REVIEW QUESTIONS

1. The majority opinion drew a sharp distinction between political and social equality. How could the justices maintain such a distinction?
2. The majority opinion also insisted that segregation was a symbol of racial inferiority/superiority only if African Americans chose to view it as such. Assess the logic of this argument.
3. Which of Harlan's arguments would be used by later jurists to dismantle segregation? Explain.

BOOKER T. WASHINGTON

The Atlanta Compromise (1895)

How best to improve the plight of blacks in the so-called New South generated intense debate among African American leaders. Booker T. Washington (1856–1915) emerged as the most eloquent advocate of what his critics labeled the "accommodationist" perspective. Born a slave in Virginia, Washington was educated at Hampton Institute, which provided blacks with vocational training. In 1881 Washington created a similar school in Alabama, the Tuskegee Institute. Its success catapulted Washington into the national spotlight. In 1895 he was invited to deliver a speech at the Cotton States Exposition in Atlanta. His remarks seemed to condone social segregation. Journalists later labeled Washington's proposal the "Atlanta Compromise."

From Booker T. Washington, *The Story of My Life and Work* (Cincinnati, OH: W. H. Ferguson Company, 1900), pp. 165–71. Reprinted in *Up from Slavery: The Autobiography of Booker T. Washington* (Garden City, NY: Doubleday, 1959), pp. 153–58.

One-third of the population of the South is of the Negro race. No enterprise seeking the material, civil, or moral welfare of this section can convey to you, Mr. President and Directors, the sentiment of the masses of my race when I say that in no way have the value and manhood of the American Negro been more fittingly and generously recognized than by the managers of this magnificent Exposition at every stage of its progress. It is a recognition that will do more to cement the friendship of the two races than any occurrence since the dawn of our freedom.

Not only this, but the opportunity here afforded will awaken among us a new era of industrial progress. Ignorant and inexperienced, it is not strange that in the first years of our new life we began at the top instead of at the bottom; that a seat in Congress or the State Legislature was more sought than real estate or industrial skill; that the political convention or stump speaking had more attractions than starting a dairy farm or truck garden.

A ship lost at sea for many days suddenly sighted a friendly vessel. From the mast of the unfortunate vessel was seen a signal: "Water, water, we die of thirst." The answer from the friendly vessel at once came back, "Cast down your bucket where you are." A second time the signal, "Water, water, send us water," ran up from the distressed vessel and was answered, "Cast down your bucket where you are." The captain of the distressed vessel, at last heeding the injunction, cast down his bucket and it came up full of fresh, sparkling water from the mouth of the Amazon River. To those of my race who depend on bettering their condition in a foreign land, or who underestimate the importance of cultivating friendly relations with the Southern white man who is their next-door neighbor, I would say: Cast down your bucket where you are; cast it down in making friends, in every manly way, of the people of all races by whom we are surrounded.

Cast it down in agriculture, mechanics, in commerce, in domestic service, and in the professions. And in this connection it is well to bear in mind that whatever other sins the South may be called upon to bear, when it comes to business pure and simple, it is in the South that the Negro is given a man's chance in the commercial world, and in nothing is this Exposition more eloquent than in emphasizing this chance. Our greatest danger is that, in the great leap from slavery to freedom, we may overlook the fact that the masses of us are to live by the productions of our hands and fail to keep in mind that we shall prosper in the proportion as we learn to dignify and glorify common labor, and put brains and skill into the common occupations of life; shall prosper in proportion as we learn to draw the line between the superficial and the substantial, the ornamental gewgaws[1] of life and the useful. No race can pros-

per until it learns that there is as much dignity in tilling a field as in writing a poem. It is at the bottom of life we must begin, and not at the top. Nor should we permit our grievances to overshadow our opportunities.

To those of the white race who look to the incoming of those of foreign birth and strange tongue and habits for the prosperity of the South, were I permitted I would repeat what I say to my own race, "Cast down your bucket where you are." Cast it down among the 8,000,000 Negroes whose habits you know, whose fidelity and love you have tested in days when to have proved treacherous meant the ruin of your firesides. Cast down your bucket among these people who have, without strikes and labor wars, tilled your fields, cleared your forests, built your railroads and cities, and brought forth treasures from the bowels of the earth and helped make possible this magnificent representation of the progress of the South. Casting down your bucket among my people, helping and encouraging them as you are doing on these grounds, and, with education of head, hand and heart, you will find that they will buy your surplus land, make blossom the waste places in your fields, and run your factories. While doing this, you can be sure in the future, as in the past, that you and your families will be surrounded by the most patient, faithful, law-abiding and unresentful people that the world has seen. As we have proved our loyalty to you in the past, in nursing your children, watching by the sick-bed of your mothers and fathers, and often following them with tear-dimmed eyes to their graves, so in the future, in our humble way, we shall stand by you with a devotion that no foreigner can approach, ready to lay down our lives, if need be, in defense of yours; interlacing our industrial, commercial, civil, and religious life with yours in a way that shall make the interest of both races one. In all things that are purely social we can be as separate as the fingers, yet one as the hand in all things essential to mutual progress.

There is no defense or security for any of us except in the highest intelligence and development of all. If anywhere there are efforts tending to curtail the fullest growth of the Negro, let these efforts

---

[1]Trinkets.

be turned into stimulating, encouraging, and making him the most useful and intelligent citizen. Effort or means so invested will pay a thousand per cent interest. These efforts will be twice blessed—"blessing him that gives and him that takes."

There is no escape, through law of man or God, from the inevitable:

The laws of changeless justice bind
Oppressor with oppressed,
And close as sin and suffering joined
We march to fate abreast.

Nearly sixteen million hands will aid you in pulling the load upward, or they will pull against you the load downward. We shall constitute one-third and more of the ignorance and crime of the South, or one-third its intelligence and progress; we shall contribute one-third to the business and industrial prosperity of the South, or we shall prove a veritable body of death, stagnating, depressing, retarding every effort to advance the body politic.

Gentlemen of the Exposition: As we present to you our humble effort at an exhibition of our progress, you must not expect over much. Starting thirty years ago with ownership here and there in a few quilts and pumpkins and chickens (gathered from miscellaneous sources), remember: the path that has led us from these to the invention and production of agricultural implements, buggies, steam engines, newspapers, books, statuary carving, paintings, the management of drugstores and banks, has not been trodden without contact with thorns and thistles. While we take pride in what we exhibit as a result of our independent efforts, we do not for a moment forget that our part in this exhibition would fall far short of your expectations but for the constant help that has come to our educational life, not only from the Southern states, but especially from Northern philanthropists who have made their gifts a constant stream of blessing and encouragement.

The wisest among my race understand that the agitation of questions of social equality is the extremist folly, and that progress in the enjoyment of all the privileges that will come to us must be the result of severe and constant struggle rather than of artificial forcing. No race that has

anything to contribute to the markets of the world is long in any degree ostracized. It is important and right that all privileges of the law be ours, but it is vastly more important that we be prepared for the exercise of those privileges. The opportunity to earn a dollar in a factory just now is worth infinitely more than the opportunity to spend a dollar in an opera house.

In conclusion, may I repeat that nothing in thirty years has given us more hope and encouragement, and drawn us so near to you of the white race, as this opportunity offered by the Exposition; and here bending, as it were, over the altar that represents the results of the struggles of your race and mine, both starting practically empty-handed three decades ago, I pledge that, in your effort to work out the great and intricate problem which God has laid at the door of the South, you shall have at all times the patient, sympathetic help of my race; only let this be constantly in mind that, while from representations in these buildings of the product of field, of forest, or mine, of factory, letters and art, much good will come—yet far above and beyond material benefits, will be that higher good, that let us pray God will come, in a blotting out of sectional difference and racial animosities and suspicions, in a determination to administer absolute justice, in a willing obedience among all classes to the mandates of law. This, coupled with material prosperity, will bring into our beloved South a new heaven and a new earth.

REVIEW QUESTIONS

1. In the previous selection (page 39), Justice Harlan insisted that the destinies of whites and blacks were "indissolubly linked together." How would Washington have responded to this assertion?
2. Why did many African Americans agree with Washington's statement that it was more important to *earn* a dollar than to *spend* one?
3. Does Washington suggest how long it would take for social equality to develop?

JOHN HOPE

A Critique of the Atlanta Compromise (1896)

Many younger African American activists criticized Washington's accommodation-ist strategy and advocated a more comprehensive effort to gain civil rights and social equality for all blacks. In a speech to the Colored Debating Society, John Hope (1868–1936), a young professor at Roger Williams University in Nashville, Tennessee, rejected Washington's emphasis on vocational education and called for more militant efforts to improve the political status and economic opportunities of African Americans. Hope was the son of a white father and black mother. He graduated from Brown University in Rhode Island and later would become president of Morehouse College and Atlanta University, the first graduate university for blacks.

Reprinted with the permission of Scribner, a division of Simon & Schuster, Inc., from *The Story of John Hope* by Ridgeley Torrence. Copyright © 1948 by Ridgeley Torrence. Copyright renewed © 1976 by Ellen W. Dunbar. All rights reserved.

If we are not striving for equality, in heaven's name for what are we living? I regard it as cowardly and dishonest for any of our colored men to tell white people or colored people that we are not struggling for equality. If money, education, and honesty will not bring to me as much privilege, as much equality as they bring to any American citizens, then they are to me a curse, and not a blessing. God forbid that we should get the implements with which to fashion our freedom, and then be too lazy or pusillanimous to fashion it. Let us not fool ourselves nor be fooled by others. If we cannot do what other freemen do, then we are not free. Yes, my friends, I want equality. Nothing less. I want all that my God-given powers will enable me to get, then why not equality? Now, catch your breath, for I am going to use an adjective: I am going to say we demand *social* equality. In this republic we shall be less than freemen, if we have a whit less than that which thrift, education, and honor afford other freemen. If equality, political, economic, and social, is the boon of other men in this great country of *ours*, then equality, political, economic, and social, is what we demand. Why build a wall to keep me out? I am no wild beast, nor am I an unclean thing.

Rise, Brothers! Come let us possess this land. Never say: "Let well enough alone." Cease to console yourselves with adages that numb the moral sense. Be discontented. Be dissatisfied. "Sweat and grunt" under present conditions. Be as restless as the tempestuous billows on the boundless sea. Let your discontent break mountain-high against the wall of prejudice, and swamp it to the very foundation. Then we shall not have to plead for justice nor on bended knee crave for mercy; for we shall be men. Then and not until then will liberty in its highest sense be the boast of our Republic.

REVIEW QUESTIONS

1. How would Booker T. Washington have responded to Hope's arguments?
2. In what ways does Hope suggest that the lack of social equality would impede the progress of African Americans?
3. If you were a black person living at the turn of the twentieth century, whose arguments, Hope's or Washington's, would you find more appealing? Why?

The Life of an Illinois Farmer's Wife (1905)

In 1905 the editors of The Independent *asked an Illinois farmer's wife to write a candid account of her life on the prairie. They granted her request for anonymity.*

From "One Farmer's Wife," *The Independent* 58 (February 9, 1905): 294–98. [Editorial insertions appear in square brackets—*Ed.*]

I have been a farmer's wife in one of the States of the Middle West for thirteen years, and everybody knows that the farmer's wife must of necessity be a very practical woman, if she would be a successful one.

I am not a practical woman and consequently have been accounted a failure by practical friends and especially by my husband, who is wholly practical. . . .

I was reared on a farm, was healthy and strong, was ambitious, and the work was not disagreeable, and having no children for the first six years of married life, the habit of going whenever asked to became firmly fixed, and he had no thought of hiring a man to help him, since I could do anything for which he needed help.

I was always religiously inclined; brought up to attend Sunday school . . . every Sunday all the year round. . . .

I was an apt student at school and before I was eighteen I had earned a teacher's certificate of the second grade and would gladly have remained in school a few more years, but I had, unwittingly, agreed to marry the man who is now my husband, and tho I begged to be released, his will was so much the stronger that I was unable to free my self without wounding a loving heart, and could not find it in my heart to do so. . . .

I always had a passion for reading; during girlhood it was along educational lines; in young womanhood it was for love stories, which remained ungratified because my father thought it sinful to read stories of any kind, and especially love stories.

Later, when I was married, I borrowed everything I could find in the line of novels and stories, and read them by stealth still, for my husband thought it a willful waste of time to read anything and that it showed a lack of love for him if I would rather read than to talk to him when I had a few moments of leisure, and, in order to avoid giving offense and still gratify my desire, I would only read when he was not at the house, thereby greatly curtailing my already too limited reading hours. . . .

It is only during the last three years that I have had the news to read, for my husband is so very penurious that he would never consent to subscribing for [news]papers of any kind and that old habit of avoiding that which would give offense was so fixed that I did not dare to break it.

The addition of two children to our family never altered or interfered with the established order of things to any appreciable extent. My strenuous outdoor life agreed with me, and even when my children were born I was splendidly prepared for the ordeal and made rapid recovery. I still hoed and tended the truck [garden] patches and garden, still watered the stock and put out feed for them, still went to the hay field and helped harvest and house the bounteous crops; still helped harvest the golden grain later on when the cereals ripened; often took one team [of horses] and dragged ground to prepare the seed-bed for wheat for weeks at the time, while my husband was using the other team on another farm which he owns several miles away.

While the children were babies they were left at the house, and when they were larger they would go with me to my work; now they are large enough to help a little during the summer and to go to school in winter; they help a great deal during the fruit canning season—in fact, [they] can and do work at almost everything, pretty much as I do. . . .

Any bright morning in the latter part of May I am out of bed at four o'clock [A.M.]; next, after I have dressed and combed my hair, I start a fire in the kitchen stove . . . sweep the floors and then cook breakfast.

While the other members of the family are eating breakfast I strain away the morning's milk (for my husband milks the cows while I get breakfast), and fill my husband's dinner-pail, for he will go to work on our other farm for the day.

By this time it is half-past five o'clock, my husband is gone to his work, and the stock loudly pleading to be turned into the pastures. The younger cattle, a half-dozen steers, are left in the pasture at night, and I now drive the two cows a half-quarter mile and then turn them in with the others, come back, and then there's a horse in the barn that belongs in a field where there is no water, which I take to a spring quite a distance from the barn; bring it back and turn it into a field with the sheep, a dozen in number, which are housed at night.

The young calves are then turned out into the warm sunshine, and the stock hogs, which are kept in a pen, are clamoring for feed, and I carry a pailful of swill to them, and hasten to the house and turn out the chickens and put out feed and water for them, and it is, perhaps, 6:30 A.M.

I have not eaten breakfast yet, but that can wait; I make the beds next and straighten things up in the living room, for I dislike to have the early morning caller find my house topsy-turvy. When this is done I go to the kitchen, which also serves as a dining room, and uncover the table, and take a mouthful of food occasionally as I pass to and fro at my work until my appetite is appeased.

By the time the work is done in the kitchen it is about 7:15 A.M., and the cool morning hours have flown, and no hoeing done in the garden yet, and the children's toilet has to be attended to and churning has to be done.

Finally the children are washed and churning done, and it is eight o'clock, and the sun getting hot, but no matter, weeds die quickly when cut down in the heat of day, and I use the hoe to a good advantage until the dinner hour, which is 11:30 A.M. We come in, and I comb my hair, and put fresh flowers

in it, and eat a cold dinner, put out feed and water for the chickens; set a hen, perhaps, sweep the floors again; sit down and rest and read a few moments, and it is nearly one o'clock, and I sweep the door yard while I am waiting for the clock to strike the hour.

I make and sow a flower bed, dig around some shrubbery, and go back to the garden to hoe until time to do the chores at night. . . .

. . . I hoe in the garden till four o'clock; then I go into the house and get supper . . . when supper is all ready it is set aside, and I pull a few hundred plants of tomato, sweet potato or cabbage for transplanting . . . I then go after the horse, water him, and put him in the barn; call the sheep and house them, and go after the cows and milk them, feed the hogs, put down hay for three horses, and put oats and corn in their troughs, and set those plants and come in and fasten up the chickens. . . . By this time it is 8 o'clock P.M.; my husband has come home, and we are eating supper; when we are through eating I make the beds ready, and the children and their father go to bed, and I wash the dishes and get things in shape to get breakfast quickly next morning. . . .

All the time that I have been going about this work I have been thinking of things I have read . . . and of other things which I have a desire to read, but cannot hope to while the present condition exists.

As a natural consequence, there are, daily, numerous instances of absentmindedness on my part; many things left undone that I really could have done, by leaving off something else of less importance, if I had not forgotten the thing of more importance. My husband never fails to remind me that it is caused by my reading so much; that I would get along much better if I should never see a book or paper, while really I would be distracted if all reading matter was taken from me.

I use an old fashioned [dairy] churn, and the process of churning occupies from thirty minutes to three hours, according to the condition of the cream, and I always read something while churning, and tho that may look like a poor way to attain self-culture, yet if your reading is of the nature to bring about the desirable result, one will surely be greatly benefited by these daily exercises. . . .

I suppose it is impossible for a woman to do her best at everything which she would like to do, but I really would like to. I almost cut sleep out of my routine in trying to keep up all the rows which I have started in on . . . when the work for the day is over, or at least the most pressing part of it, and the family are all asleep and no one to forbid it, I spend a few hours writing or reading. . . .

I might add that the neighbors among whom I live are illiterate and unmusical, and that my redeeming qualities, in their eyes, are my superior education and musical abilities; they are kind enough to give me more than justice on these qualities because they are poor judges of such matters.

But money is king, and if I might turn my literary bent to account, and surround myself with the evidences of prosperity, I may yet hope fully to redeem myself in their eyes, and I know that I will have attained my ambition in that line.

REVIEW QUESTIONS

1. Do you think this woman's outlook was representative of most farm women? Why or why not?
2. What activities did this woman find most fulfilling? Why?

BENJAMIN SINGLETON

FROM Negro Exodus from the Southern States (1880)

With the return of white supremacy in the post-Reconstruction South, thousands of African Americans migrated to the West in search of economic opportunities and social equality. Most of them flocked to Kansas. Their quest for a new "promised land" on the Great Plains led people to call them "Exodusters." Benjamin Singleton was the foremost promoter of black migration to the West. Born a slave in Tennessee, he escaped and settled in Detroit, Michigan, where he operated a boardinghouse that became a refuge for other runaway slaves. After the Civil War he returned to Tennessee. To help African Americans free themselves from the surge of racism that accompanied the withdrawal of federal troops from the South in the 1870s, he bought land in Kansas and began recruiting settlers. So many heeded his call that Southerners grew worried about the loss of laborers in their region, and Congress agreed to investigate the matter.

From U.S. Senate, Select Committee Investigating the "Negro Exodus from the Southern States," April 17, 1880 (Washington, DC).

Benjamin Singleton (colored) sworn and examined by Mr. Windom:
Question. Where were you born, Mr. Singleton?
Answer. I was born in the State of Tennessee, sir.
Q. Where do you now live?

A. In Kansas.
Q. What part of Kansas?
A. I have a colony sixty miles from Topeka, sir. . . .
Q. When did you commence the formation of that colony?

A. It was in 1875, perhaps. . . .

Q. *When did you change your home from Tennessee to Kansas?*

A. I have been going there for the last six or seven years, sir.

Q. *Going between Tennessee and Kansas, at different times?*

A. Yes, sir; several times.

Q. *Well, tell us about it.*

A. I have been fetching out people; I believe I fetched out 7,432 people.

Q. *You have brought out 7,432 people from the South to Kansas?*

A. Yes, sir; brought and sent.

Q. *That is, they came out to Kansas under your influence?*

A. Yes, sir; I was the cause of it.

Q. *How long have you been doing that—ever since 1869?*

A. Yes, sir; ever since 1869. . . .

Q. *What was the cause of your going out, and in the first place how did you happen to go there, or to send these people there?*

A. Well, my people, for the want of land—we needed land for our children—and their disadvantages— that caused my heart to grieve and sorrow; pity for my race, sir, that was coming down, instead of going up—that caused me to go to work for them. I sent out there perhaps in '66—perhaps so; or in '65, any way—my memory don't recollect which; and they brought back tolerable favorable reports; then I jacked up three or four hundred, and went into Southern Kansas, and found it was a good country, and I thought Southern Kansas was congenial to our nature, sir; and I formed a colony there, and bought about a thousand acres of ground—the colony did—my people.

Q. *And they went upon it and settled there?*

A. Yes, sir; they went and settled there. . . .

Q. *Tell us how these people are getting on in Kansas.*

A. I am glad to tell you, sir.

Q. *Have they any property now?*

A. Yes; I have carried some people in there that when they got there they didn't have fifty cents left, and now they have got in my colony—Singleton colony—a house, nice cabins, their milk cows, and pigs, and sheep, perhaps a span of horses, and trees before their yards, and some three or four or ten acres broken up, and all of them has got little houses that I carried there. They didn't go under no relief assistance; they went on their own resources; and when they went in there first the country was not overrun with them; you see they could get good wages; the country was not overstocked with people; they went to work, and I never helped them as soon as I put them on the land.

Q. *Well, they have been coming continually, and adding from time to time to your colony these few years past, have they?*

A. Yes, sir; I have spent, perhaps, nearly six hundred dollars flooding the country with circulars.

Q. *You have sent the circulars yourself, have you?*

A. Yes, sir; all over these United States.

Q. *Did you send them into other southern states besides Tennessee?*

A. O, yes, sir. . . . I then went out to Kansas, and advised them all to go to Kansas; and, sir they are going to leave the Southern country. The Southern country is out of joint. The blood of a white man runs through my veins. That is congenial, you know, to my nature. That is my choice. Right emphatically, I tell you today, I woke up the millions right through me! The great God of glory has worked in me. I have had open air interviews with the living spirit of God for my people; and we are going to leave the South. We are going to leave it if there ain't an alteration and signs of change. I am going to advise the people who left that country (Kansas) to go back. . . .

Q. *And you attribute this movement to the information you gave in your circulars?*

A. Yes, sir; I am the whole cause of the Kansas immigration!

Q. *You take all that responsibility on yourself?*

A. I do, and I can prove it; and I think I have done a good deal of good, and I feel relieved!

Q. *You are proud of your work?*

A. Yes, sir; I am! (Uttered emphatically.)

REVIEW QUESTIONS

1. According to Singleton, what was the primary motive for African American migration to Kansas?

2. How did Singleton entice blacks to leave their homes?

3. Why do you think Congress felt the need to investigate the Exoduster movement?

CHIEF JOSEPH

An Indian's Perspective (1879)

Chief Joseph was the heroic leader of a large band of Nez Percé (a misnomer, meaning "pierced noses") who had been converted to Christianity in the early nineteenth century. He was born in 1840 in the Wallowa Valley of Oregon. Like many other tribes, the Nez Percé negotiated treaties with the American government only to see the treaties violated, tensions erupt, and conflict ensue. In 1877, after months of ferocious fighting and a spectacular retreat across Idaho and Montana, Chief Joseph's band of some four hundred Indians surrendered with the understanding that they would be allowed to return home. Instead, they were taken first to Kansas and then to what is now Oklahoma. Joseph thereafter made repeated appeals to the federal government to let his people return to their native region; he visited Washington, D.C., in 1879 to present his grievances against the federal government to President Rutherford B. Hayes. But it was not until 1885 that he and several others were relocated to Washington State, where he died in 1904.

From Chester Anders Fee, *Chief Joseph: The Biography of a Great Indian* (New York: Wilson-Erickson, 1936), pp. 78–79, 262–63, 281–83.

White men found gold in the mountains around the land of the Winding Water. They stole a great many horses from us and we could not get them back because we were Indians. The white men told lies for each other. They drove off a great many of our cattle. Some white men branded our young cattle so they could claim them. We had no friends who would plead our cause before the law councils. It seemed to me that some of the white men in Wallowa were doing these things on purpose to get up a war. They knew we were not strong enough to fight them. I labored hard to avoid trouble and bloodshed.

We gave up some of our country to the white men, thinking that then we could have peace. We were mistaken. The white men would not let us alone. We could have avenged our wrongs many times, but we did not. Whenever the Government has asked for help against other Indians we have never refused. When the white men were few and we were strong we could have killed them off, but the Nez Percé wishes to live at peace. . . .

We have had a few good friends among the white men, and they have always advised my people to bear these taunts without fighting. Our young men are quick tempered and I have had great trouble in keeping them from doing rash things. I have carried a heavy load on my back ever since I was a boy. I learned then that we were but few while the white men were many, and that we could not hold our own with them. We were like deer. They were like grizzly bears. We had a small country. Their country was large. We were contented to let things remain as the Great Spirit Chief made them. They were not; and would change the mountains and rivers if they did not suit them.

* * *

Tell General Howard that I know his heart.[1] What he told me before I have in my heart. I am tired of fighting. Our chiefs are killed. . . . The old men are all dead. . . . It is cold and we have no blankets. The little children are freezing to death. My people—some of them have run away to the hills and have no blankets and no food. No one knows where they are—perhaps freezing to death. I want to have time to look for my children and see how many of them I can find. Maybe I shall find them among the dead. Hear me, my chiefs, my heart is sick and sad. From where the sun now stands I will fight no more against the white man.

* * *

At last I was granted permission to come to Washington and bring my friend Yellow Bull and our interpreter with me.[2] I am glad I came. I have shaken hands with a good many friends, but there are some things I want to know which no one seems able to explain. I cannot understand how the Government sends a man out to fight us, as it did General Miles, and then breaks his word. Such a government has something wrong about it. . . .

I have heard talk and talk but nothing is done. Good words do not last long unless they amount to something. Words do not pay for my dead people. They do not pay for my country now overrun by white men. They do not protect my father's grave. They do not pay for my horses and cattle. Good words do not give me back my children. Good words will not make good the promise of your war chief,

General Miles. Good words will not give my people a home where they can live in peace and take care of themselves. I am tired of talk that comes to nothing. It makes my heart sick when I remember all the good words and all the broken promises. There has been too much talking by men who had no right to talk. Too many misinterpretations have been made; too many misunderstandings have come up between the white men and the Indians. . . .

I know that my race must change. We cannot hold our own with the white men as we are. We only ask an even chance to live as other men live. We ask to be recognized as men. We ask that the same law shall work alike on all men. If an Indian breaks the law, punish him by the law. If a white man breaks the law, punish him also.

Let me be a free man, free to travel, free to stop, free to work, free to trade where I choose, free to choose my own teachers, free to follow the religion of my fathers, free to talk, think and act for myself— and I will obey every law or submit to the penalty.

Whenever the white man treats the Indian as they treat each other then we shall have no more wars. We shall be all alike—brothers of one father and mother, with one sky above us and one country around us and one government for all. Then the Great Spirit Chief who rules above will smile upon this land and send rain to wash out the bloody spots made by brothers' hands upon the face of the earth. For this time the Indian race is waiting and praying. I hope no more groans of wounded men and women will ever go to the ear of the Great Spirit Chief above, and that all people may be one people.

REVIEW QUESTIONS

1. What initially provoked hostilities between whites and the Nez Percé?
2. What were Chief Joseph's basic demands? Why would whites have balked at meeting them?
3. Analyze Chief Joseph's comments about the historic relationship between whites and Native Americans.

---

[1]This section refers to events after Chief Joseph's surrender in 1877.

[2]This section refers to Chief Joseph's visit to Washington, D.C., in 1879.

HELEN HUNT JACKSON

FROM *A Century of Dishonor* (1881)

The surge of settlers streaming westward across the Mississippi River after the Civil War brought increasing conflict with Native Americans. Federal troops engaged in a series of frontier wars with the Comanche, the Apache, the Kiowa, the Cheyenne, and the Sioux. At the same time, white hunters devastated the buffalo herds that were essential to the survival of Indian culture. One of the few whites who sympathized with the plight of the Indians was Helen Hunt Jackson. Born in Amherst, Massachusetts, in 1830, she was a childhood friend of the poet Emily Dickinson. After the death in 1863 of Jackson's first husband, a Union Army officer, she earned her living by writing poems, stories, and travel accounts. In 1872 she moved to Colorado where she married a financier, grew indignant at the mistreatment of the Indians, and wrote A Century of Dishonor, *published in 1881. Jackson sent the book to every member of Congress with a graphic message printed in red on the cover: "Look upon your hands: they are stained with the blood of your relations." The book had little impact initially, but Jackson's unrelenting crusade for a more enlightened federal Indian policy eventually helped convince Congress to pass the Dawes Act of 1887. She died two years before it was enacted.*

From *A Century of Dishonor* (1881; New York: Indian Head Books, 1994), pp. 335–42.

There are within the limits of the United States between two hundred and fifty and three hundred thousand Indians, exclusive of those in Alaska. The names of the different tribes and bands . . . number nearly three hundred. . . . There is not among these three hundred bands of Indians one which has not suffered cruelly at the hands either of the Government or of white settlers. The poorer, the more insignificant, the more helpless the band, the more certain the cruelty and outrage to which they have been subjected. This is especially true of the bands on the Pacific slope. These Indians found themselves of a sudden surrounded by and caught up in the great influx of gold-seeking settlers, as helpless creatures on a shore are caught up in a tidal wave. There was not time for the Government to make treaties; not even time for communities to make laws. The tale of the wrongs, the oppressions, the murders of the Pacific-slope Indians in the last thirty years would be a volume by itself, and is too monstrous to be believed.

It makes little difference, however, where one opens the record of the history of the Indians; every page and every year has its dark stain. The story of one tribe is the story of all, varied only by differences of time and place; but neither time nor place makes any difference in the main facts. Colorado is as greedy and unjust in 1880 as was Georgia in 1830, and Ohio in 1795; and the United States Government breaks promises now as deftly as then, and with an added ingenuity from long practice.

One of its strongest supports in so doing is the widespread sentiment among the people of dislike to the Indian, of impatience with his presence as a "barrier to civilization" and distrust of it as a possible danger. The old tales of the frontier life, with its horrors of Indian warfare, have gradually, by two or three generations' telling, produced in the average mind something like an hereditary instinct of questioning and unreasoning aversion which it is almost impossible to dislodge or soften. . . .

President after president has appointed commission after commission to inquire into and report upon Indian affairs, and to make suggestions as to the best methods of managing them. The reports are filled with eloquent statements of wrongs done to the Indians, of perfidies on the part of the Government; they counsel, as earnestly as words can, a trial of the simple and unperplexing expedients of telling truth, keeping promises, making fair bargains, dealing justly in all ways and all things. These reports are bound up with the Government's Annual Reports, and that is the end of them. . . .

The history of the Government connections with the Indians is a shameful record of broken treaties and unfulfilled promises. The history of the border white man's connection with the Indians is a sickening record of murder, outrage, robbery, and wrongs committed by the former, as the rule, and occasional savage outbreaks and unspeakably barbarous deeds of retaliation by the latter, as the exception.

Taught by the Government that they had rights entitled to respect, when those rights have been assailed by the rapacity of the white man, the arm which should have been raised to protect them has ever been ready to sustain the aggressor.

The testimony of some of the highest military officers of the United States is on record to the effect that, in our Indian wars, almost without exception, the first aggressions have been made by the white man. . . . Every crime committed by a white man against an Indian is concealed and palliated. Every offense committed by an Indian against a white man is borne on the wings of the post or the telegraph to the remotest corner of the land, clothed with all the horrors which the reality or imagination can throw around it. Against such influences as these are the people of the United States need to be warned.

To assume that it would be easy, or by any one sudden stroke of legislative policy possible, to undo the mischief and hurt of the long past, set the Indian policy of the country right for the future, and make the Indians at once safe and happy, is the blunder of a hasty and uninformed judgment. The notion which seems to be growing more prevalent, that simply to make all Indians at once citizens of the United States would be a sovereign and instantaneous panacea for all their ills and all the Government's perplexities, is a very inconsiderate one. To administer complete citizenship of a sudden, all round, to all Indians, barbarous and civilized alike, would be as grotesque a blunder as to dose them all round with any one medicine, irrespective of the symptoms and needs of their diseases. It would kill more than it would cure. Nevertheless, it is true, as was well stated by one of the superintendents of Indian Affairs in 1857, that, "so long as they are not citizens of the United States, their rights of property must remain insecure against invasion. The doors of the federal tribunals being barred against them while wards and dependents, they can only partially exercise the rights of free government, or give to those who make, execute, and construe the few laws they are allowed to enact, dignity sufficient to make them respectable. While they continue individually to gather the crumbs that fall from the table of the United States, idleness, improvidence, and indebtedness will be the rule, and industry, thrift, and freedom from debt the exception. The utter absence of individual title to particular lands deprives every one among them of the chief incentive to labor and exertion— the very mainspring on which the prosperity of a people depends."

All judicious plans and measures for their safety and salvation must embody provisions for their becoming citizens as fast as they are fit, and must protect them till then in every right and particular in which our laws protect other "persons" who are not citizens. . . .

However great perplexity and difficulty there may be in the details of any and every plan possible for doing at this late day anything like justice to the Indian, however, hard it may be for good statesmen and good men to agree upon the things that ought to be done, there certainly is, or ought to be, no perplexity whatever, or difficulty whatever, in agreeing upon certain things that ought not to be done, and which must cease to be done before the first steps can be taken toward righting the wrongs, curing the ills, and wiping out the disgrace to us of the present conditions of our Indians.

Cheating, robbing, breaking promises—these three are clearly things which must cease to be done. One more thing, also, and that is the refusal of the protection of the law to the Indian's rights of property, "of life, liberty, and the pursuit of happiness."

When these four things have ceased to be done, time, statesmanship, philanthropy, and Christianity can slowly and surely do the rest. Till these four things have ceased to be done, statesmanship and philanthropy alike must work in vain, and even Christianity can reap but small harvest.

Review Questions

1. Why did the federal government repeatedly violate its treaties with the various Indian tribes, according to Jackson?
2. Why did Jackson oppose the granting of immediate citizenship to all Indians?

The Dawes Act (1887)

The relentless advance of settlers into the West created constant tensions with Native Americans and sparked numerous wars during the post–Civil War era. President Rutherford B. Hayes acknowledged in 1877 that most "of our Indian wars have had their origin in broken promises and acts of injustice on our part." As a result of such growing concern, federal policy toward the Indians seemingly grew more benevolent. The Dawes Act of 1887, named after its sponsor, Senator Henry L. Dawes of Massachusetts, was intended to improve the lot of the Indians by providing them with private property and opportunities for citizenship. But most of the land grants were inadequate, and the emphasis on individual land ownership eroded tribal unity.

From *United States Statutes at Large*, 24:388–91.

An act to provide for the allotment of lands in severalty to Indians on the various reservations, and to extend the protection of the laws of the United States and Territories over the Indians, and for other purposes.

Be it enacted, that in all cases where any tribe or band of Indians has been, or shall hereafter be, located upon any reservation created for their use, either by treaty stipulation or by virtue of an act of Congress or executive order setting apart the same for their use, the President of the United States be, and he hereby is, authorized . . . to allot the lands in said reservation in severalty to any Indian located thereon in quantities as follows:

To each head of a family, one-quarter of a section;

To each single person over eighteen years of age, one-eighth of a section;

To each orphan child under eighteen years of age, one-eighth of a section; and,

To each other single person under eighteen years now living, or who may be born prior to the date of the order of the President directing an allotment of the lands embraced in any reservation, one-sixteenth of a section. . . .

Sec. 5. That upon the approval of the allotments provided for in the act by the Secretary of the Interior, he shall . . . declare that the United States does and will hold the land thus allotted, for the period of twenty-five years, in trust for the sole use and benefit of the Indian to whom such allotment shall have been made, . . . and that at the expiration of said period the United States will convey the same by patent to said Indian, or his heirs as aforesaid, in fee, discharged of such trust and free of all charge or incumbrance whatsoever. . . .

Sec. 6. That upon the completion of said allotments and the patenting of the lands to said allottees, each and every member of the respective bands or tribes of Indians to whom allotments have been made shall have the benefit of and be subject to the laws, both civil and criminal, of the State or Territory in which they may reside; . . . And every Indian born within the territorial limits of the United States to whom allotments shall have been made under the provisions of this act, or under any law or treaty, and every Indian born within the territorial limits of the United States who has voluntarily taken up, within said limits, his residence separate and apart from any tribe of Indians therein, and has adopted the habits of civilized life, is hereby declared to be a citizen of the United States, and is entitled to all the rights, privileges, and immunities of such citizens, whether said Indian has been or not, by birth or otherwise, a member of any tribe of Indians within the territorial limits of the United States without in any manner impairing or otherwise affecting the right of any such Indian to tribal or other property. . . .

Sec. 10. That nothing in this act contained shall be so construed as to affect the right and power of Congress to grant the right of way through any lands granted to an Indian, or a tribe of Indians, for railroads, or other highways, or telegraph lines, for the public use, or to condemn such lands to public uses, upon making just compensation. . . .

REVIEW QUESTIONS

1. How might the emphasis on private property in the Dawes Act have conflicted with Native American customs?
2. Why did Congress feel the need to retain title to the land allotments for twenty-five years?
3. To qualify for citizenship under the Dawes Act, Native Americans had to adopt "the habits of civilized life." Assess the meaning and implications of such a standard.

FREDERICK JACKSON TURNER

FROM *The Frontier in American History* (1893)

More than any other scholar, historian Frederick Jackson Turner influenced attitudes toward the role of the West in shaping American values and institutions. Born in Portage, Wisconsin, in 1861, he taught at the University of Wisconsin from 1889 until 1910, when he joined Harvard's faculty. In 1893 he presented his "frontier thesis" to the American Historical Society. Turner claimed that the process of western settlement was the defining characteristic of American society. Yet he concluded that at the end of the nineteenth century the frontier era had ended, and he worried that its beneficial effects would be lost to future generations of Americans. His frontier thesis was widely accepted. Today, however, historians criticize him for ignoring the role of women, evading the moral issues associated with the exploitation of the Native Americans, and asserting a simplistic connection between geography and political ideology.

From *The Frontier in American History* (New York: Holt, Rinehart & Winston, 1920), pp. 1–4, 22–23, 29–31, 32, 37–38.

In a recent bulletin of the Superintendent of the Census for 1890 appear these significant words: "Up to and including 1880 the country had a frontier of settlement, but at present the unsettled area has been so broken into by isolated bodies of settlement that there can hardly be said to be a frontier line. In the discussion of its extent, its westward movement, etc., it can not, therefore, any longer have a place in census reports." This brief official statement marks the closing of a great historic movement. Up to our own day American history has been in a large degree the history of the colonization of the Great West. The existence of an area of free land, its continuous recession, and the advance of American settlement westward explain American development.

Behind institutions, behind constitutional forms and modifications, lie the vital forces that call these organs into life and shape them to meet changing conditions. The peculiarity of American institutions is the fact that they have been compelled to adapt themselves to the changes of an expanding people—to the changes involved in crossing a continent, in winning a wilderness, and in developing at each area of this progress out of the primitive economic and political conditions of the frontier into the complexity of city life. Said Calhoun[1] in 1817, "we are great, and rapidly—I was about to say fearfully—growing!" So saying, he touched the distinguishing feature of American life.

*   *   *

In the case of most nations, however, the development has occurred in a limited area; and if the nation has expanded, it has met other growing peoples whom it has conquered. But in the case of the United States we have a different phenomenon. Limiting our attention to the Atlantic coast, we have the familiar phenomenon of the evolution of institutions in a limited area, such as the rise of representative government; the differentiation of simple colonial governments into complex organs; the progress from primitive industrial society, without division of labor, up to manufacturing civilization. But we have in addition to this a recurrence of the process of evolution in each western area reached in the process of expansion. Thus American development has exhibited not merely advance along a single line, but a return to primitive conditions on a continually advancing frontier line, and a new development for that area.

American social development has been continually beginning over again on the frontier. This perennial rebirth, this fluidity of American life, this expansion westward with its new opportunities, its continuous touch with the simplicity of primitive society, furnish the forces dominating American character. The true point of view in the history of this nation is not the Atlantic coast, it is the Great West. . . .

In this advance, the frontier is the outer edge of the wave—the meeting point between savagery and civilization. . . . The most significant thing about

---

[1] South Carolina statesman John C. Calhoun (1782–1850).

the American frontier is, that it lies at the hither edge of free land.

*   *   *

In the settlement of America we have to observe how European life entered the continent, and how America modified and developed that life and reacted on Europe. Our early history is the study of European germs developing in an American environment.... The frontier is the line of most rapid and effective Americanization. The wilderness masters the colonist. It finds him a European in dress, industries, tools, modes of travel, and thought. It takes him from the railroad car and puts him in the birch canoe. It strips off the garments of civilization and arrays him in the hunting shirt and the moccasin. It puts him in the log cabin of the Cherokee and Iroquois and runs an Indian palisade around him. Before long he has gone to planting Indian corn and plowing with a sharp stick; he shouts the war cry and takes the scalp in orthodox Indian fashion. In short, at the frontier the environment is at first too strong for the man. He must accept the conditions which it furnishes, or perish, and so he fits himself into the Indian clearings and follows the Indian trails. Little by little he transforms the wilderness, but the outcome is not the old Europe....

The fact is, that here is a new product that is American. At first, the frontier was the Atlantic coast. It was the frontier of Europe in a very real sense. Moving westward the frontier becomes more and more American.... Thus the advance of the frontier has meant a steady movement away from the influence of Europe, a steady growth of independence on American lines. And to study this advance, the men who grew up under these conditions, and the political, economic, and social results of it, is to study the really American part of our history.

*   *   *

First, we note that the frontier promoted the formation of a composite nationality for the American people. The coast was preponderantly English, but the later tides of continental immigration flowed across to the free lands.... In the crucible of the frontier the immigrants were Americanized, liberated, and fused into a mixed race, English in neither nationality nor characteristics. The process has gone on from the early days to our own....

But the most important effect of the frontier has been in the promotion of democracy here and in Europe. As has been indicated, the frontier is productive of individualism. Complex society is precipitated by the wilderness into a kind of primitive organization based on the family. The tendency is anti-social. It produces antipathy to control, and particularly to any direct control.

The frontier States that came into the Union in the first quarter of a century of its existence came in with democratic suffrage provisions, and had reactive effects of the highest importance upon the older States whose peoples were being attracted there. An extension of the franchise became essential....

But the democracy born of free land, strong in selfishness and individualism, intolerant of administrative experience and education, and pressing individual liberty beyond its proper bounds, has its dangers as well as its benefits. Individualism in America has allowed a laxity in regard to governmental affairs which has rendered possible the spoils system and all the manifest evils that follow from the lack of a highly developed civil spirit....

The works of travelers along each frontier from colonial days onward describe certain common traits, and these traits have, while softening down, still persisted as survivals in the place of their origin, even when a higher social organization succeeded. The result is that to the frontier the American intellect owes its striking characteristics. The coarseness and strength combined with acuteness and inquisitiveness; that practical, inventive turn of mind, quick to find expedients; that masterful grasp of material things, lacking in the artistic but powerful to effect great ends; that restless nervous energy; that dominant individualism, working for good and for evil, and withal that buoyancy and exuberance which comes with freedom—these are traits of the frontier, or traits called out elsewhere because of the existence of the frontier.

Since the days when the fleet of Columbus sailed into the waters of the New World, America has been another name for opportunity, and the people of the United States have taken their tone from the incessant expansion which has not only been open but has even been forced upon them. He would be a rash prophet who should assert that the expansive character of American life has now entirely ceased. Movement has been its dominant fact, and, unless this training has no effect upon a people, the American energy will continually demand a wider field for its exercise. . . . yet, in spite of environment, and in spite of custom, each frontier did indeed furnish a new field of opportunity. . . . And now, four centuries from the discovery of America, at the end of a hundred years of life under the Constitution, the frontier has gone, and with its going has closed the first period of American history.

REVIEW QUESTIONS

1. What do you think Turner meant by the term *Americanization*?
2. According to Turner, in what crucial respect did western states differ from those on the Atlantic coast?
3. Turner equated the frontier with the American character. Does his set of national characteristics accurately describe Americans today? Explain.
4. In suggesting that the frontier was ultimately synonymous with a "new field of opportunity," what did Turner imply about other living environments in nineteenth-century American life?

19 ∽ POLITICAL STALEMATE AND RURAL REVOLT, 1865–1900

American political life during the last quarter of the nineteenth century has long been viewed in negative terms. Novelist Mark Twain labeled the era "The Gilded Age" because of the corrupt connections between business tycoons and political leaders. Political life during the period was preoccupied with patronage, the long-established pattern of rewarding loyal supporters with government jobs. Prominent senators such as Roscoe Conkling of New York and Benjamin Butler of Massachusetts, as well as urban bosses like New York City's William Marcy Tweed and George Washington Plunkitt, were masters of the so-called spoils system, a term derived from the saying, "To the victor belongs the spoils." They and other political "bosses" used the patronage system to reward supporters and to maintain powerful political "machines."

Eventually, however, the abuses of the spoils system sparked protests and legislation. In 1881 concerned citizens founded the National Civil Service Reform League, and in 1883 they helped push through Congress the Pendleton Civil Service Act. It created a federal civil service commission to establish job qualifications and competitive exams for a variety of government positions, thereby removing them from the patronage system.

While Republicans controlled the White House, the two major political parties were evenly balanced in the Congress. Tariff and monetary policies dominated public debate. Republicans generally supported high tariffs (taxes on imported goods) as a means of protecting American farmers and manufacturers from foreign competition. Republicans also tended to promote a conservative monetary policy based on the gold standard so as to limit the money supply and avoid inflation. To maintain its base of support among northern voters, the Grand Old Party (GOP) also consistently supported generous government pensions for Union war veterans. For their part, Democrats were more divided on such issues, with factions on opposite sides. This reflected the geographic diversity of the party. The Democrats found their reliable base of support in two contrasting regions: *the rural South and the northern cities with large immigrant populations.*

Unlike today, voter participation during the Gilded Age was remarkably high. Elections aroused enormous interest. Of course, women could not yet vote in national elections, and most African American males were prevented from voting in the former Confederacy as the century came to a close. Indians and Asians were also the subjects of racial prejudice and legal discrimination. Both Native Americans and Chinese Americans were denied citizenship. The white men who did vote across the country were most keenly interested in local concerns rooted in ethnic and cultural issues such as Sunday closing laws, liquor prohibition, and immigration restriction.

The phenomenal economic development after the Civil War fostered a massive wave of foreign immigration to the United States. Europeans and Asians flocked to America in search of jobs and freedom. The massive influx eventually provoked a rising nativist sentiment to limit immigration. During the mid–nineteenth century, for instance, thousands of Chinese began streaming into the United States, most of them settling in California. Although initially encouraged to migrate to the United States, they soon found themselves the victims of violent harassment. A new California constitution drafted in 1879 included numerous anti-Chinese provisions, prohibiting them from owning land or engaging in particular professions. Courts also refused to accept testimony from Chinese. Anti-Chinese riots killed dozens of the newcomers.

By 1880 there were over a hundred thousand Chinese on the West Coast, and the rising numbers prompted efforts to prohibit further immigration. This culminated in the Chinese Exclusion Act of 1882, the first significant law restricting immigration into the United States. Although President Chester A. Arthur vetoed the bill, Congress passed it to protect "American" jobs and to maintain white "racial purity." The new restrictions provided a precedent for a series of laws thereafter limiting foreign access.

Perhaps the most salient political issue during the last quarter of the nineteenth century was a tension between city and country, industry and agriculture. Millions of distressed farmers during the late nineteenth century felt ignored or betrayed by the city-dominated political process. While the industrial economy and urban culture witnessed unprecedented expansion, farmers confronted a chronic boom–bust cycle characterized by falling prices, growing indebtedness and dependence on local merchants and middlemen, and the high cost of credit. In the rural South and in the Midwest, discontented farmers first formed grassroots Granges or Alliances that provided opportunities for both social recreation and political action. By the 1890s these regional efforts had combined to form a third national political party, the People's Party, whose members were called Populists. The new party promoted a variety of reforms and policies, but it soon fastened on a seeming panacea: the free and unlimited coinage of silver. A massive coinage of silver, they argued, would inflate the money supply and thereby increase the prices for farm commodities, make credit cheaper, and relieve debtors of their paralyzing burdens.

In 1892 Populists participated in their first presidential elections, with candidate James B. Weaver garnering 9 percent of the popular vote. A year later a sharp financial panic triggered the onset of the worst depression in American history up to that time. This prolonged crisis gave sudden credibility to many Populist ideas, and the free-silver crusade made inroads into the Democratic Party, especially in the West and South. In 1896 the Democrats and the Populists nominated Congressman William Jennings Bryan of Nebraska to run against Republican William McKinley, thus setting the stage for one of the most important presidential elections in American history. The Republicans and McKinley emerged triumphant, but Populists succeeded in creating momentum for a more activist government in the early twentieth century.

JOSIAH STRONG

FROM *Our Country* (1885)

During the so-called Gilded Age, many social commentators worried about the effects of unchecked urban development. Josiah Strong, a prominent Congregationalist minister from Ohio, was among the most concerned. In 1885 he published Our Country, *a comprehensive critique of modern developments. Strong viewed large cities as a menace to morals and to the social order. He also feared that the vices of urban culture warred against the teachings of Christianity.*

From *Our Country: Its Possible Future and Its Present Crisis* (New York: The American Home Missionary Society, 1885), pp. 128–43. [Editorial insertion appears in square brackets—*Ed.*]

The city is the nerve center of our civilization. It is also the storm center. The fact, there-fore, that it is growing much more rapidly than the whole population is full of significance. In 1790, one-thirtieth of the population of the United States lived in cities of 8,000 inhabitants and over; in 1800, one twenty-fifth; in 1810, and also in 1820, one-twentieth; in 1830, one-sixteenth; in 1840, one-twelfth; in 1850, one-eighth; in 1860, one-sixth; in 1870, a little over one-fifth; and in 1880, 22.5 per cent, or nearly one-fourth. From 1790 to 1880 the whole population increased a little less than four fold, the urban population thirteen fold. . . . In 1790 there were only six cities in the United States which had a population of 8,000 or more. In 1880 there were 286.

The city has become a serious menace to our civilization. . . . It has a peculiar attraction for the immigrant. Our fifty principal cities contain 39.3 per cent of our entire German population, and 45.8 per cent of the Irish. Our ten larger cities [host] only nine per cent of the entire population, but 23 per cent of the foreign. While a little less than one-third of the population of the United States is foreign by birth or parentage, sixty-two per cent of the population of Cincinnati are foreign, eighty-three per cent of Cleveland, sixty-three per cent of Boston, eighty-eight per cent of New York, and ninety-one per cent of Chicago.

Because our cities are so largely foreign, Romanism[1] finds in them its chief strength. For the same reason the saloon, together with the intemperance and the liquor power which it represents, is multiplied in the city. East of the Mississippi there was, in 1880, one saloon to every 438 of the population; in Boston, one to every 329; in Cleveland, one to every 192; in Chicago, one to every 179; in New York, one to every 171; in Cincinnati, one to every 124. Of course the demoralizing and pauperizing power of the saloons and their debauching influence in politics increase with their numerical strength.

It is the city where wealth is massed; and here are the tangible evidences of it piled many stories high. Here the sway of Mammon[2] is widest, and his worship the most constant and eager. Here are luxuries gathered—everything that dazzles the eye, or tempts the appetite; here is the most extravagant expenditure. Here, also, is the *congestion* of wealth severest. Dives and Lazarus[3] are brought face to face; here, in sharp contrast, are the *ennui* of surfeit and the desperation of starvation. The rich are richer, and the poor are poorer, in the city than

[1] Roman Catholicism.
[2] The false god of riches in the New Testament.
[3] Dives was the rich man in the biblical parable of Lazarus, the diseased beggar.

elsewhere; and, as a rule, the greater are the riches of the rich and the poverty of the poor. Not only does the proportion of the poor increase with the growth of the city, but their condition becomes more wretched. The poor of a city with 8,000 inhabitants are well off compared with many in New York; and there are no such depths of woe, such utter and heart-wringing wretchedness in New York as in London. . . .

Socialism not only centers in the city, but is almost confined to it; and the materials of its growth are multiplied with the growth of the city. Here is heaped the social dynamite; here roughs, gamblers, thieves, robbers, lawless and desperate men of all sorts, congregate; men who are ready on any pretext to raise riots for the purpose of destruction and plunder; here gather foreigners and wage-workers; here skepticism and irreligion abound; here inequality is the greatest and most obvious, and the contrast between opulence and penury the most striking; here is suffering the sorest. As the greatest wickedness in the world is to be found not among the cannibals of some far off coast, but in Christian lands where the light of truth is diffused and rejected, so the utmost depth of wretchedness exists not among savages, who have few wants, but in great cities, where, in the presence of plenty and of every luxury men starve. . . .

"During the past three years, 220,976 persons in New York have asked for outside aid in one form or another." Said a New York Supreme judge, not long since: "There is a large class—I was about to say a majority—of the population of New York area Brooklyn, who just live, and to whom the rearing of two or more children means inevitably a boy for the penitentiary, and a girl for the brothel." Under such conditions smolder the volcanic fires of a deep discontent.

As a rule, our largest cities are the worst governed. It is natural, therefore, to infer that, as our cities grow larger and more dangerous, the government will become more corrupt, and control will pass more completely into the hands of those who themselves most need to be controlled. If we would

appreciate the significance of these facts and tendencies, we must bear in mind that the disproportionate growth of the city is undoubtedly to continue, and the number of great cities to be largely increased. . . .

But the supreme peril, which will certainly come, eventually, and must probably be faced by multitudes now living, will arise, when, the conditions having been fully prepared, some great industrial or other crisis precipitates an open struggle between the destructive and the conservative elements of society. As civilization advances, and society becomes more highly organized, commercial transactions will be more complex and immense. As a result, all business relations and industries will be more sensitive. Commercial distress in any great business center will the more surely create widespread disaster. Under such conditions, industrial paralysis is likely to occur from time to time, more general and more prostrating than any heretofore known. When such a commercial crisis has closed factories by the ten thousand, and wageworkers have been thrown out of employment by the million; when the public lands, which hitherto at such times have afforded relief, are all exhausted; when our urban population has been multiplied several fold; and our Cincinnatis have become Chicagos, our Chicagos and our New Yorks, Londons; when class antipathies are deepened; when socialistic organizations, armed and drilled, are in every city, and the ignorant and vicious power of crowded populations has fully found itself; when the corruption of city governments is grown apace; when crops fail, or some gigantic "corner" doubles the price of bread; with starvation in home; with idle workingmen gathered, sullen and desperate, in the saloons with unprotected wealth at hand; with the tremendous forces of chemistry within easy reach; then with *the opportunity, the means, the fit agents; the motive, the temptation to destroy, all brought into evil conjunction,* THEN will come the real test of our institutions, then will appear whether we are capable of self-government.

REVIEW QUESTIONS

1. Why was Strong concerned that immigrants made up such a high percentage of urban dwellers?

2. What kinds of problems did the disparity of wealth create in cities?

3. What forces did Strong overlook as possible causes for urban woes?

GEORGE W. PLUNKITT

A Defense of Political Graft (1905)

The most powerful political machine during the Gilded Age was Tammany Hall, an Irish-based organization that dominated New York City politics throughout the nineteenth century. It involved a network of Democratic politicians and party workers in alliance with various contractors who provided kickbacks in exchange for government favors. George Washington Plunkitt was district leader of Tammany Hall who took for granted the patronage system. In 1905 he participated in a series of interviews with a local reporter in which he defended the political machine against the criticisms of reformers.

From William Riordan, ed., *Plunkitt of Tammany Hall* (1905; New York: E. P. Dutton, 1963), pp. 3–4, 11, 12–13. [Editorial insertions appear in square brackets—*Ed.*]

Everybody is talkin' these days about Tammany men growin' rich on graft, but nobody thinks of drawin' the distinction between honest graft and dishonest graft. There's all the difference in the world between the two. Yes, many of our men have grown rich in politics. I have myself. I've made a big fortune out of the game, and I'm gettin' richer every day, but I've not gone in for dishonest graft—blackmailin' gamblers, saloon-keepers, disorderly people, etc.—and neither has any of the men who have made big fortunes in politics.

There's an honest graft, and I'm an example of how it works. I might sum up the whole thing by sayin': "I seen my opportunities and I took 'em."

Just let me explain by examples. My party's in power in the city, and it's goin' to undertake a lot of public improvements. Well, I'm tipped off, say, that they're going to lay out a park at a certain place.

I see my opportunity and I take it. I go to that place and I buy up all the land I can in the neighborhood. Then the board of this or that makes its plan public, and there is a rush to get my land, which nobody cared particular for before.

Ain't it perfectly honest to charge a good price and make a profit on my investment and foresight? Of course, it is. Well, that's honest graft.

*   *   *

. . . This civil service law is the biggest fraud of the age. It is the curse of the nation. There can't be no real patriotism while it lasts. How are you goin' to interest our young men in their country if you have no offices to give them when they work for their party? Just look at things in this city today. There are ten thousand good offices, but we can't get at more than a few hundred of them. How are we goin' to provide for the thousands of men who worked for the Tammany ticket? It can't be done. These men were full of patriotism a short time ago. They expected to be servin' their city, but when we tell them that we can't place them [in government jobs], do you think their patriotism is goin' to last? Not much. They say: "What's the use workin' for your country anyhow? There's nothin' in the game [for us]." And what can they do? I don't know, but I'll tell you what I do know. I know more than one young man in past years who worked for the ticket and was overflowin' with patriotism, but when he was knocked out by the civil service humbug he got to hate his country and became an Anarchist.

*   *   *

When the people elected Tammany, they knew just what they were doin'. We didn't put up any false pretenses. We didn't go in for humbug civil service and all that rot. We stood as we always have stood, for rewardin' the men that won the victory. They call that the spoils system. All right: Tammany is for the spoils system, and when we go in we fire every anti-Tammany man from office that can be fired under the law. It's an elastic sort of law and you can bet it will be stretched to the limit. . . .

The civil service humbug is underminin' our institutions and if a halt ain't called soon this great republic will tumble down like a Park Avenue house when they were buildin' the subway, and on its ruins will rise another Russian government.

REVIEW QUESTIONS

1. How does Plunkitt distinguish between "honest" and "dishonest" graft? Is his distinction persuasive?
2. According to Plunkitt, what is the primary motivation behind political involvement?

FROM The Chinese Exclusion Act (1882)

The Chinese Exclusion Act of 1882 suspended all Chinese immigration for ten years and declared the Chinese ineligible for citizenship. Chinese workers already in the country challenged the constitutionality of the law, but their efforts failed. The act was renewed in 1892 for another ten years, and in 1902 Chinese immigration was permanently prohibited. Not until 1943 did Congress grant Chinese Americans eligibility for citizenship.

From *United States Statutes at Large*, 22:58ff.

An act to execute certain treaty stipulations relating to Chinese:

WHEREAS, in the opinion of the Government of the United States the coming of Chinese laborers to this country endangers the good order of certain localities within the territory thereof: Therefore, Be it enacted, That from and after the expiration of ninety days next after the passage of this act, and until the expiration of ten years next after the passage of this act, the coming of Chinese laborers to the United States be . . . suspended; and during such suspension it shall not be lawful for any Chinese laborer to come, or, having so come after the expiration of said ninety days, to remain within the United States.

*   *   *

SEC. 2. That the master of any vessel who shall knowingly bring within the United States on such vessel, and land or permit to be landed, any Chinese laborer, from any foreign port or place, shall be deemed guilty of a misdemeanor, and on conviction thereof shall be punished by a fine of not more than five hundred dollars for each and every such Chinese laborer so brought, and may be also imprisoned for a term not exceeding one year.

SEC. 3. That the two foregoing sections shall not apply to Chinese laborers who were in the United States on the seventeenth day of November, eighteen hundred and eighty, or who shall have come into the same before the expiration of ninety days next after the passage of this act. . . .

*   *   *

SEC. 6. That in order to the faithful execution of articles one and two of the treaty in this act before mentioned, every Chinese person other than a laborer who may be entitled by said treaty and this act to come within the United States, and who shall be about to come to the United States, shall be identified as so entitled by the Chinese Government in each case, such identity to be evidenced by a certificate issued under the authority of said government, which certificate shall be in the English language or (if not in the English language) accompanied by a translation into English, stating such right to come, and which certificate shall state the name, title, or official rank, if any, the age, height, and all physical peculiarities former and present occupation or profession and place of residence in China of the person to whom the certificate is issued and that such person is entitled conformably to the treaty in this act mentioned to come within the United States. . . .

*   *   *

SEC. 12. That no Chinese person shall be permitted to enter the United States by land without pro-ducing to the proper office of customs the certificate in this act required of Chinese persons seeking to land from a vessel. Any Chinese person found unlawfully within the United States shall be caused to be removed therefrom to the country from whence he came, by direction of the President of the United States, and at the cost of the United States, after being brought before some justice, judge, or commissioner of a court of the United States and found to be one not lawfully entitled to be or remain in the United States.

SEC. 13. That this act shall not apply to diplomatic and other officers of the Chinese Government traveling upon the business of that government, whose credentials shall be taken as equivalent to the certificate in this act mentioned, and shall exempt them and their body and household servants from the provisions of this act as to other Chinese persons.

SEC. 14. That hereafter no State court or court of the United States shall admit Chinese to citizenship; and all laws in conflict with this act are hereby repealed.

SEC. 15. That the words "Chinese laborers," whenever used in this act, shall be construed to mean both skilled and unskilled laborers and Chinese employed in mining.

REVIEW QUESTIONS

1. What do you think the phrase "endangers the good order of certain localities" meant? Do you think its vagueness was intentional?
2. What types of penalties did the act prescribe?
3. Who would have supported this legislation? Who would have opposed it?

ROBERT G. INGERSOLL

FROM Should the Chinese Be Excluded? (1893)

Among the critics of the anti-Chinese legislation, the most articulate was Illinois attorney Robert G. Ingersoll (1833–1899). The era's most eloquent orator and an outspoken agnostic, he addressed more people than any other public figure in the nineteenth century. Ingersoll was a Civil War veteran who after 1865 promoted civil rights for the freed slaves and equal rights for women. He once declared that there was "but one use for law, but one excuse for government—the preservation of liberty." In the following speech he condemned the racist attitudes that lay behind the legislation renewing the Exclusion Act in 1892, known as the Geary Act.

From *North American Review* 157 (July 1893): 52–58.

The average American, like the average man of any country, has but little imagination. People who speak a different language, or worship some other god, or wear clothing unlike his own, are beyond the horizon of his sympathy. He cares but little or nothing for the sufferings or misfortunes of those who are of a different complexion or of another race. His imagination is not powerful enough to recognize the human being, in spite of peculiarities.

Instead of this he looks upon every difference as an evidence of inferiority, and for the inferior he has but little if any feeling. If these "inferior people" claim equal rights he feels insulted, and for the purpose of establishing his own superiority tramples on the rights of the so-called inferior.

In our own country the native has always considered himself as much better than the immigrant, and as far superior to all people of a different complexion. At one time our people hated the Irish, then the Germans, then the Italians, and now the Chinese. The Irish and Germans, however, became numerous. They became citizens, and, most important of all, they had votes. They combined, became powerful, and the political parties sought their aid. They had something to give in exchange for protection—in exchange for political rights. In consequence of this, they were flattered by candidates, praised by

the political press, and became powerful enough not only to protect themselves, but at last to govern the principal cities in the United States. As a matter of fact the Irish and the Germans drove the native Americans out of the trades and from the lower forms of labor. They built the railways and canals. They became servants. Afterward the Irish and the Germans were driven from the canals and railways by the Italians.

The Irish and Germans improved their condition. They went into other businesses, into the higher and more lucrative trades. They entered the professions, turned their attention to politics, became merchants, brokers, and professors in colleges. They are not now building railroads or digging on public works. They are contractors, legislators, holders of office, and the Italians and Chinese are doing the old work.

If matters had been allowed to work in a natural way, without the interference of mobs or legislators, the Chinese would have driven the Italians to better employments, and all menial labor would, in time, be done by the Mongolians. . . .

In our country, as a matter of fact, there is but little prejudice against emigrants coming from Europe, except among naturalized citizens; but nearly all foreign-born citizens are united in their prejudice against the Chinese. The truth is that the Chinese came to this country by invitation. . . .

These Chinese laborers are inoffensive, peaceable and law-abiding. They are honest, keeping their contracts, doing as they agree. They are exceedingly industrious, always ready to work and always giving satisfaction to their employers. They do not interfere with other people. They cannot become citizens. They have no voice in the making or the execution of the laws. They attend to their own business. They have their own ideas, customs, religion and ceremonies—about as foolish as our own; but they do not try to make converts or to force their dogmas on others. They are patient, uncomplaining, stoical and philosophical. They earn what they can, giving reasonable value for the money they receive, and as a rule, when they have amassed a few thousand dollars, they go back to their own country. They do not interfere with our ideas, our ways or customs. They are silent workers, toiling without any object, except to do their work and get their pay. They do not establish saloons and run for Congress. Neither do they combine for the purpose of governing others. Of all the people on our soil they are the least meddlesome. Some of them smoke opium, but the opium-smoker does not beat his wife. Some of them play games of chance, but they are not members of the Stock Exchange. They eat the bread that they earn; they neither beg nor steal, but they are of no use to parties or politicians except as they become fuel to supply the flame of prejudice. They are not citizens and they cannot vote.

Their employers are about the only friends they have. In the Pacific States the lowest became their enemies and asked for their expulsion. They denounced the Chinese and those who gave them work. The patient followers of Confucius were treated as outcasts—stoned by boys in the streets and mobbed by the fathers. Few seemed to have any respect for their rights or their feelings. They were unlike us. They wore different clothes. They dressed their hair in a peculiar way, and therefore they were beyond our sympathies. These ideas, these practices, demoralized many communities; the laboring people became cruel and the small politicians infamous.

When the rights of even one human being are held in contempt the rights of all are in danger. We cannot destroy the liberties of others without losing our own. By exciting the prejudices of the ignorant we at last produce a contempt for law and justice, and sow the seeds of violence and crime. . . .

Both of the great parties ratified the outrages committed by the mobs, and proceeded with alacrity to violate the treaties and solemn obligations of the Government. These treaties were violated, these obligations were denied, and thousands of Chinamen were deprived of their rights, of their property, and hundreds were maimed or murdered. They were driven from their homes. They were hunted like wild beasts. All this was done in a country that sends missionaries to China to tell the benighted savages of the blessed religion of the United States. . . .

The idea of imprisoning a man at hard labor for a year, and this man a citizen of a friendly nation, for the crime of being found in this country without a certificate of residence, must be abhorrent to the mind of every enlightened man. Such punishment for such an "offense" is barbarous and belongs to the earliest times of which we know. This law makes industry a crime and puts one who works for his bread on a level with thieves and the lowest criminals, treats him as a felon, and clothes him in the stripes of a convict,—and all this is done at the demand of the ignorant, of the prejudiced, of the heartless, and because the Chinese are not voters and have no political power.

The Chinese are not driven away because there is no room for them. Our country is not crowded. There are many millions of acres waiting for the plow. There is plenty of room here under our flag for five hundred millions of people. These Chinese that we wish to oppress and imprison are people who understand the art of irrigation. They can redeem the deserts. They are the best of gardeners. They are modest and willing to occupy the lowest seats.

They only ask to be day-laborers, washers and ironers. They are willing to sweep and scrub. They are good cooks. They can clear lands and build railroads. They do not ask to be masters—they wish only to serve. In every capacity they are faithful;

but in this country their virtues have made enemies, and they are hated because of their patience, their honesty and their industry. . . .

*   *   *

This law is contrary to the laws and customs of nations. The punishment is unusual, severe, and contrary to our Constitution, and under its provisions aliens—citizens of a friendly nation—can be imprisoned without due process of law. The law is barbarous, contrary to the spirit and genius of American institutions, and was passed in violation of solemn treaty stipulations.

The Congress that passed it is the same that closed the gates of the World's Fair on the "blessed Sabbath," thinking it wicked to look at statues and pictures on that day. These representatives of the people seem to have had more piety than principle.

After the passage of such a law by the United States is it not indecent for us to send missionaries to China? Is there not work enough for them at home? We send ministers to China to convert the heathen; but when we find a Chinaman on our soil, where he can be saved by our example, we treat him as a criminal. It is to the interest of this country to maintain friendly relations with China. We want the trade of nearly one-fourth of the human race. . . .

After all, it pays to do right. This is a hard truth to learn—especially for a nation. A great nation should be bound by the highest conception of jus-

tice and honor. Above all things it should be true to its treaties, its contracts, its obligations. It should remember that its responsibilities are in accordance with its power and intelligence.

Our Government is founded on the equality of human rights—on the idea, the sacred truth, that all are entitled to life, liberty and the pursuit of happiness. Our country is an asylum for the oppressed of all nations—of all races. Here, the Government gets its power from the consent of the governed. After the abolition of slavery these great truths were not only admitted, but they found expression in our Constitution and laws. Shall we now go back to barbarism? . . .

Let us retrace our steps, repeal the law and accomplish what we justly desire by civilized means. Let us treat China as we would England; and, above all, let us respect the rights of Men.

REVIEW QUESTIONS

1. Why did Ingersoll believe that the differences among people led to charges of racial inferiority?
2. What were some of the positive characteristics that Ingersoll attributed to the Chinese?
3. Why did Ingersoll think that the exclusion law contradicted American principles?

MARY PAIK LEE

FROM *Quiet Odyssey* (1990)

During the early twentieth century, the United States experienced a surge of immigrants from around the world. Among them was Mary Paik Lee, born Paik Kuang Sun in 1900, a Korean girl who left her native country in 1905. She and her parents traveled as political refugees after Japan seized control over Korea at the close of the Russo-Japanese War. Lee's father worked on Hawaii sugar plantations before taking his family to California in 1906. There the parents earned their living as farm labor-

ers, tenant farmers, cooks, and janitors, and the family always took in laundry to supplement their meager earnings. Mary Paik Lee's autobiography, Quiet Odyssey, *tells their story of persistence and resilience in the face of hardship and discrimination, a story that represents the experiences of most poor immigrants who came to America between 1900 and 1920.*

From Mary Paik Lee, *Quiet Odyssey: A Pioneer Korean Woman in America*, pp. 12–16; 21–23. (Seattle: University of Washington Press, 1990). © 1990. Reprinted with permission of the University of Washington Press. [Editorial insertion appears in square brackets—*Ed.*]

Mother told me there had been a lot of discussion for several days before the final decision was made for my parents, my brother, and me to leave Korea to find a better life elsewhere. Father was reluctant to leave, but his parents insisted, saying that his presence would not help them. They knew what would happen to them in the near future. They were prepared to face hardship or worse, but they wanted at least one member of their family to survive and live a better life somewhere else. Such strong, quiet courage in ordinary people in the face of danger is really something to admire and remember always.

My second brother, Paik Daw Sun, was born on October 6, 1905, in Hawaii. Father was desperate, always writing to friends in other places, trying to find a better place to live. Finally, he heard from friends in Riverside, California, who urged him to join them: they said the prospects for the future were better in America; that a man's wages were ten to fifteen cents an hour for ten hours of work a day. After his year in Hawaii was up, Father borrowed enough money from friends to pay for our passage to America on board the *S. S. China*.

We landed in San Francisco on December 3, 1906. As we walked down the gangplank, a group of young white men were standing around, waiting to see what kind of creatures were disembarking. We must have been a very queer-looking group. They laughed at us and spit in our faces; one man kicked up Mother's skirt and called us names we couldn't understand. Of course, their actions and attitudes left no doubt about their feelings toward us.

I was so upset. I asked Father why we had come to a place where we were not wanted. He replied that we deserved what we got because that was the same kind of treatment that Koreans had given to the first American missionaries in Korea: the children had thrown rocks at them, calling them "white devils" because of their blue eyes and yellow or red hair. He explained that anything new and strange causes some fear at first, so ridicule and violence often result. He said the missionaries just lowered their heads and paid no attention to their tormentors. They showed by their action and good works that they were just as good or even better than those who laughed at them. He said that is exactly what we must try to do here in America—study hard and learn to show Americans that we are just as good as they are. That was my first lesson in living, and I have never forgotten it.

Many old friends came with us from Hawaii. Some stayed in San Francisco, others went to Dinuba, near Fresno, but most headed for Los Angeles. We ourselves went straight to the railroad depot nearby and boarded a train for Riverside, where friends would be waiting for us. It was our first experience on a train. We were very excited, but we felt lost in such a huge country. When we reached Riverside, we found friends from our village in Korea waiting to greet us.

In those days, Orientals and others were not allowed to live in town with the white people. The Japanese, Chinese, and Mexicans each had their own little settlement outside of town. My first glimpse of what was to be our camp was rows of one-room shacks, with a few water pumps here and there and little sheds for outhouses. We learned later that the shacks had been constructed for the Chinese men who had built Southern Pacific Railroad in the 1880s.

We had reached Riverside [California] without any plans and with very little money, not knowing what we could do for a living. After much discussion with friends, it was decided that Mother should cook for about thirty single men who worked in the citrus groves. Father did not like her to work, but it seemed to be the only way we could make a living for ourselves. She would make their breakfast at 5 A.M., pack their lunches, and cook them supper at 7 P.M. But my parents did not have the cooking utensils we needed, so Father went to the Chinese settlement and told them of our situation. . . . He asked for credit, promising to make regular payments from time to time. They trusted him and agreed to give us everything we needed to get started: big iron pots and pans, dishes, tin lunch pails, chopsticks, and so forth. They also gave us rice and groceries.

The Korean men went to the dumpyard nearby and found the materials to build a shack large enough for our dining area. They made one long table and two long benches to seat thirty men. Father made a large stove and oven with mud and straw, and he found several large wine barrels to hold the water for drinking and cooking. That was the start of our business. Mother had long, thick black hair that touched the ground. It became a nuisance in her work, so Father cut it short, leaving just enough to coil in a bun on the back of her head. It must have caused her much grief to lose her beautiful hair, but she never complained. We had already lost everything else that meant anything to us.

We lived in a small one-room shack built in the 1880s. The passing of time had made the lumber shrink, so the wind blew through the cracks in the walls. There was no pretense of making it livable—just four walls, one window, and one door—nothing else. We put mud in the cracks to keep the wind out. The water pump served several shacks. We had to heat our bath water in a bucket over an open fire outside, then pour it into a tin tub inside. There was no gas or electricity. We used kerosene lamps, and one of my chores was to trim the wicks, clean the glass tops, and keep the bowls filled with kerosene.

The Chinese men who had lived there in the 1880s must have slept on the floor. Father solved the problem of where we were going to sleep by building shelves along the four walls of our shack. Then he found some hay to put on each shelf. He put a blanket over the hay, rolled up some old clothes for a pillow—and that was a bed for a child. I used a block of wood for my pillow. It became such a habit with me that even to this day I do not like a soft pillow. . . .

Every Saturday, Meung and I went to a slaughterhouse some distance away to get the animal organs that the butchers threw out—pork and beef livers, hearts, kidneys, entrails, tripe—all the things considered unfit for human consumption. We were not alone—Mexican children came there also. They needed those things to survive just as we did. The butchers stood around laughing at us as we scrambled for the choice pieces. When I told Father I didn't want to go there anymore because they were making fun of us, he said we should thank God that they did not know the value of what they threw out; otherwise, we would go hungry.

. . . My first day at school was a very frightening experience. As we entered the schoolyard, several girls formed a ring around us, singing a song and dancing in a circle. When they stopped, each one came over to me and hit me in the neck, hurting us and frightening me. They ran away when a tall woman came towards us. Her bright yellow hair and big blue eyes looking down at me were a fearful sight; it was my first close look at such a person. She was welcoming me to her school, but I was frightened. When she addressed me, I answered in Korean, "I don't understand you." I turned around, ran all the way home, and hid in our shack. Father laughed when he heard about my behavior. He told me there was nothing to be afraid of; now that we were living here in America, where everything is different from Korea, we would have to learn to get along with everyone.

*   *   *

We lived in Riverside for four or five years, but Father became concerned about Mother's health—the work of cooking for thirty men was too much for her. She was a small woman, only four feet eleven inches tall, and she was expecting another baby. So we paid off the Chinese merchants who had helped us get started, paid all our debts to friends, and moved to Claremont, not too far away. It was a quiet college town with many school buildings. We moved into a duplex building, where an old friend, Martha Kim, was living with her parents. It was across the street from the railroad station and a huge citrus-packing house. Those were the days before frozen fruit juices, so after the choice fruit was packed, the culls were piled up in boxes back of the buildings to be taken to the dump once a week. Because of this, we were fortunate that we could enjoy all the discarded fruit.

Our move to Claremont turned out to be our first experience with the American way of living. The new house seemed huge after our little shack. It had several rooms with beds, chairs, and other furniture. The kitchen had a gas stove, electric lights, and a sink with faucets for cold and hot water. But all that was as nothing compared to what we found in the bathroom. There was a big white tub with faucets at one end—I couldn't believe it was the place for taking our baths. And the biggest surprise of all was the toilet. Father flushed it to show us how it operated. He must have seen these wonders before somewhere, because he wasn't surprised at anything. For the first time, I felt glad that we had come to America.

Father found a job as a janitor in the nearby apartment buildings. He told Meung and me to ask the tenants if we could do their laundry, and also to ask our schoolteachers the same thing. On foot, Meung had to pick up the dirty laundry in a big basket and return it later. I helped with the laundry before and after school and with the ironing at night.

In Claremont we had our first experience with an electric iron. Before this we had heard the old "sad irons," as they were called in those days, on the wood stove. It was such a relief to use the electric iron. No more kerosene lamps, hunting for firewood, and outhouses.

Life was getting better. Every Saturday Father bought a beef roast, and every Sunday we had pot roast with mashed potatoes and bread. This was our introduction to American food, and it tasted wonderful. . . . Unfortunately, Father's wages were so low in Claremont that it was difficult to make a living. So, a year later, we moved to Colusa in northern California, hoping to find work there. It turned out we had made a disastrous move. Father could not find any kind of work. There was a depression in 1911, and the situation was so bad the Salvation Army offered a bowl of soup and a piece of bread to each hungry person in town. But when I asked if we could go and get some, Father said no. He didn't want us to be humiliated by asking for help.

The feeling towards Orientals in southern California had not been friendly, but we had been tolerated. In the northern part of the state, we found the situation to be much worse. Although we found a house on the outskirts of town, the townspeople's attitude towards us was chilling. Father told Meung and me to ask our schoolteachers for their laundry. Once again, Meung had to fetch and deliver, carrying a basket on foot. Since we lived on the outskirts of town, it was a hard job for him, but he never complained. But because of the negative feeling towards Orientals in Colusa, we never got enough clothes to launder, and we could not earn enough money to meet our needs.

After paying the rent, light, water, and other bills, we had very little left over for food. Mother would tell me to buy a five-pound sack of flour, a small can of baking powder, salt, and two cans of Carnation milk for the baby. The two cans of milk had to last for one week: it was diluted with so much water, it didn't look like anything nourishing. Mother made tiny biscuits each morning and served one biscuit and a tin cup of water to us three times a day. During the time we lived in Colusa, we had no rice, meat, or anything besides biscuits to eat.

Nonetheless, when we sat down to eat, Father would pray, thanking God for all our blessings. This used to irritate me. At the age of eleven years, I couldn't think of anything to be thankful for. Once he was sitting out on the porch smoking after dinner, and I asked him what we had to be so thankful for. He said, "Don't you remember why we came here?" I had forgotten that the fate of our family in Korea was much worse than ours. Nevertheless, my stomach ached of lack of food, and I had severe cramps.

One evening the pain was so bad I got up to fill myself with water, which helped somewhat. As I neared the kitchen, I saw Father and Mother sitting across from each other at the table holding hands, with tears flowing down their faces. I realized then how much agony they were suffering, and that my own feelings were as nothing compared with theirs. I had been so absorbed in myself that the thought of my parents' suffering had never entered my mind. Seeing them that way made me realize how ignorant I was. It awakened me to the realities of life. . . .

REVIEW QUESTIONS

1. What was Lee's "first lesson in living" upon arriving in California? Is it relevant today?
2. What qualities did Lee's parents display in helping their family adapt to life in the United States?

ROCCO CORRESCA

FROM The Biography of a Bootblack (1902)

At the end of the nineteenth century, a surge of immigrants from southern and eastern Europe generated concern among American "nativists" that such "alien" newcomers could not be easily assimilated. For their part, many of these "new immigrants" stressed that they were just like the "old immigrants" in their desire to participate in the American Dream. In 1902, Rocco Corresca, a recently arrived immigrant from Italy, wrote an account of his experience trying to make his way in America. He tried several jobs before fastening on bootblacking—shining shoes.

From *The Independent* 54 (Dec. 4, 1902): 2863–67. [Editorial insertions appear in square brackets—*Ed.*]

. . . Now and then I had heard things about America that it was a far off country where everybody was rich and that Italians went there and made plenty of money, so that they could return to Italy and live in pleasure ever after. One day I met a young man who pulled out a handful of gold and told me he had made that in America in a few days.

I said I should like to go there, and he told me that if I went he would take care of me and see that I was safe. I told Francisco and he wanted to go, too. So we said goodby to our good friends. Teresa cried and kissed us both and the priest came and shook our hands and told us to be good men, and that no matter where we went God and his saints were always near us and that if we lived well we should all meet again in heaven. We cried, too, for it was our home, that place. . . .

*   *   *

We were so long on the water that we began to think we should never get to America or that, perhaps, there was not any such place, but at last we saw land and came up to New York We were glad to get over [to America] without giving money, but I have heard since that we should have been paid for our work among the coal and that the young man who had sent us got money for it. We were all landed on an island [Ellis Island], and the bosses there said that Francisco and I must go back because we had not enough money, but a man named Bartolo came up and told them that we were brothers and he was our uncle and would take care of us. He brought two other men who swore that they knew us in Italy and that Bartolo was our uncle. I had never seen any of them before, but even then Bartolo might be my uncle, so I did not say anything. The bosses of the island let us go out with Bartolo after he had made the oath.

We came to Brooklyn to a wooden house in Adams Street that was full of Italians from Naples. Bartolo had a room on the third floor and there were fifteen men in the room, all boarding with Bartolo. He did the cooking on a stove in the middle of the room and there were beds all around the sides, one bed above another. It was very hot in the room, but we were soon asleep, for we were very tired.

*   *   *

Most of the men in our room worked at digging the sewer. Bartolo got them the work and they paid him about one quarter of their wages. Then he charged them for board and he bought the clothes for them, too. So they got little money after all.

Bartolo was always saying that the rent of the room was so high that he could not make anything, but he was really making plenty. He was what they call a *padrone* and is now a very rich man. The men that were living with him had just come to the country and could not speak English. They had all been sent by the young man we met in Italy. Bartolo told us all that we must work for him and that if we did not the police would come and put us in prison.

He gave us very little money, and our clothes were some of those that were found on the street. Still we had enough to eat and we had meat quite often, which we never had in Italy. Bartolo got it from the butcher the meat that he could not sell to other people but it was quite good meat Bartolo cooked it in the pan while we all sat on our beds in the evening. Then he cut it into small bits and passed the pan around, saying, "See what I do for you and yet you are not glad I am too kind a man, that is why I am so poor."

We were with Bartolo nearly a year, but some of our countrymen who had been in the place a long time said that Bartolo had no right to us and we could get work for a dollar and a half a day, which, when you make it *lire* [Italian currency] is very much. So we went away one day to Newark and got work on the street. Bartolo came after us and made a great noise, but the boss said that if he did not go away soon the police would have him. Then he went, saying that there was no justice in this country.

We paid a man five dollars each for getting us the work and we were with that boss for six months. He was Irish, but a good man and he gave us our money every Saturday night. We lived much better than with Bartolo, and when the work was done we each had nearly $200 saved. Plenty of the men spoke English and they taught us, and we taught them to read and write. That was at night, for we had a lamp in our room, and there were only five other men who lived in that room with us.

We got up at half past five o'clock every morning and made coffee on the stove and had a breakfast of bread and cheese, onions, garlic and red herrings. We went to work at seven o'clock and in the middle of the day we had soup and bread in a place where we got it for two cents a plate. In the evenings we had a good dinner with meat of some kind and potatoes. We got from the butcher the meat that other people would not buy because they said it was old, but they don't know what is good. We paid four or five cents a pound for it and it was the best, though I have heard of people paying sixteen cents a pound.

When the Newark boss told us that there was no more work, Francisco and I talked about what we would do and we went back to Brooklyn to a saloon near Hamilton Ferry, where we got a job cleaning it out and slept in a little room upstairs. There was a bootblack named Michael on the corner, and when I had time I helped him and learned the business. Francisco cooked the lunch in the saloon and he, too, worked for the bootblack and we were soon able to make the best polish.

Then we thought we would go into business and we got a basement on Hamilton Avenue, near the

Ferry, and put four chairs in it. We paid $75 for the chairs and all the other things. We had tables and looking glasses there and curtains. We took the papers that have the pictures in and made the place high toned. Outside we had a big sign that said:

THE BEST SHINE FOR TEN CENTS

Men that did not want to pay ten cents could get a good shine for five cents, but it was not an oil shine. We had two boys helping us and paid each of them fifty cents a day. The rent of the place was $20 a month, so the expenses were very great, but we made money from the beginning. We slept in the basement, but got our meals in the saloon till we could put a stove in our place, and then Francisco cooked for us all. That would not do, tho, because some of our customers said that they did not like to smell garlic and onions and red herrings. I thought that was strange, but we had to do what the customers said So we got the woman who lived upstairs to give us our meals and paid her $1.50 a week each She gave the boys soup in the middle of the day five cents for two plates.

*   *   *

We had said that when we saved $1,000 each we would go back to Italy and buy a farm, but now that the time is coming we are so busy and making so much money that we think we will stay. We have opened another parlor near South Ferry, in New York. We have to pay $30 a month rent, but the business is very good. The boys in the place charge sixty cents a day because there is so much work.

These people are without a king such as ours in Italy. It is what they call a Republic . . . and every year in the fall the people vote. They wanted us to vote last fall, but we did not. A man came and said that he would get us made Americans for fifty cents and then we could get two dollars for our votes. I talked to some of our people and they told me that we should have to put a paper in a box telling who we wanted to govern us.

*   *   *

There are two kinds of people that vote here, Republicans and Democrats. I went to a Republican meeting and the man said that the Republicans want a Republic and the Democrats are against it. He said that Democrats are for a king whose name is [William Jennings] Bryan and who is an Irishman. There are some good Irishmen, but many of them insult Italians. They call us Dagoes. So I will be a Republican.

I like this country now and I don't see why we should have a king. . . . I and Francisco are to be Americans in three years. The court gave us papers and said we must wait and we must be able to read some things and tell who the ruler of the country is.

There are plenty of rich Italians here, men who a few years ago had nothing and now have so much money that they could not count all their dollars in a week The richest ones go away from the other Italians and live with the Americans.

*   *   *

On Sundays we get a horse and carriage from the grocer and go down to Coney Island. We go to the theatres often and other evenings we go to the houses of our friends and play cards. I am nineteen years of age now and have $700 saved. Francisco is twenty one and has about $900. We shall open some more [shoeshine] parlors soon. I know an Italian who was a bootblack ten years ago and now bosses bootblacks all over the city, who has so much money that if it was turned into gold it would weigh more than himself. . . .

Brooklyn N. Y.

*   *   *

REVIEW QUESTIONS

1. How were immigrants enticed to vote in elections?
2. What was Corresca's notion of the American Dream?

A Black Woman

Racism in the South (1902)

The era of Progressive reform (1890–1920) was fraught with contradictions. At the same time that social idealists were assaulting political corruption and promoting laws protecting women and children in the workplace, racial prejudice was flourishing. During the 1890s, state after state in the South passed "Jim Crow" laws mandating racial segregation of public facilities and schools. Efforts to use fraud and intimidation to reduce black voting continued unabated. The following article, written by a black woman from Alabama who felt the need to withhold her name, describes the racial abuses suffered by blacks at the turn of the century.

From "The Negro Problem: How It Appears to a Southern Colored Woman," *The Independent* 54 (September 18, 1902): 2221–24. [Editorial insertions appear in square brackets—*Ed.*]

I am a colored woman, wife and mother. I have lived all my life in the South, and have often thought what a peculiar fact it is that the more ignorant the Southern whites are of us, the more vehement they are in their denunciation of us. They boast that they have little intercourse with us, never see us in our homes, churches or places of amusement, but still they know us thoroughly.

They also admit that they know us in no capacity except as servants, yet they say we are at our best in that single capacity. What philosophers they are! The Southerners say we negroes are a happy, laughing set of people, with no thought of tomorrow. How mistaken they are! The educated, thinking Negro is just the opposite. There is a feeling of unrest, insecurity, almost panic among the best class of negroes in the South. In our homes, in our churches, wherever two or three are gathered together, there is a discussion of what is best to do. Must we remain in the South or go elsewhere? Where can we go to feel that security which other people feel? Is it best to go in great numbers or only in several families? These and many other things are discussed over and over.

People who have security in their homes, whose children can go on the street unmolested, whose wives and daughters are treated as women, cannot,

perhaps, sympathize with the Southern negro's anxieties and complaints. I ask forebearance of such people.

It is asserted that we are dying more rapidly than other people in the South. It is not remarkable when the houses built for sale or rent to colored people are usually placed in the lowest and most unhealthy spots. I know of houses occupied by poor negroes in which a respectable farmer would not keep his cattle. It is impossible for them to rent elsewhere. All Southern real estate agents have "white property" and "colored property." In one of the largest Southern cities there is a colored minister, a graduate of Harvard, whose wife is an educated, Christian woman, who lived for weeks in a tumble-down rookery because he could neither rent nor buy in a respectable locality.

Many colored women who wash, iron, scrub, cook or sew all the week to help pay the rent for these miserable hovels and help fill the many small mouths, would deny themselves some of the necessaries of life if they could take their little children and teething babies on the cars to the parks of a Sunday afternoon and sit under trees, enjoy the cool breezes and breathe God's pure air for only two or three hours; but this is denied them. Some of the parks have signs, "No negroes allowed on these grounds except as servants." Pitiful, pitiful customs and laws that make war on women and babes! There is no wonder that we die; the wonder is that we persist in living.

Fourteen years ago I had just married. My husband had saved sufficient money to buy a small home. On account of our limited means we went to the suburbs, on unpaved streets, to look for a home, only asking for a high, healthy locality. Some real estate agents were "sorry, but had nothing to suit," some had "just the thing," but we discovered on investigation that they had "just the thing" for an unhealthy pigsty. Others had no "colored property." One agent said that he had what we wanted, but we should have to go to see the lot after dark, or walk by and give the place a casual look; for, he said, "all the white people in the neighborhood would be down on me." Finally, we bought this lot. When the house was being built we went to see it. Consternation reigned. We had ruined this [all-white] neighborhood of poor people; poor as we, poorer in manners at least. The people who lived next door received the sympathy of their friends. When we walked on the street (there were no sidewalks) we were embarrassed by the stare of many unfriendly eyes.

Two years passed before a single woman spoke to me, and only then because I helped one of them when a little sudden trouble came to her. Such was the reception, I a happy young woman, just married, received from people among whom I wanted to make a home. Fourteen years have now passed, four children have been born to us, and one has died in this same home, among these same neighbors. Although the neighbors speak to us, and occasionally one will send a child to borrow the morning's paper or ask the loan of a pattern, not one woman has ever been inside of my house, not even at the times when a woman would doubly appreciate the slightest attention of a neighbor. . . .

. . . A colored woman, however respectable, is lower [in status] than the white prostitute. The Southern white woman will declare that no Negro women are virtuous, yet she placed her innocent children in their care. . . .

White agents and other chance visitors who come into our homes ask questions that we must not dare ask their wives. They express surprise that our children have clean faces and that their hair is combed. . . .

. . . We were delighted to know that some of our Spanish-American [War] heroes were coming where we could get a glimpse of them. Had not black men helped in a small way to give them their honors? In the cities of the South, where these heroes went, the white school children were assembled, flags waved, flowers strewn, speeches made, and "My Country, 'Tis of Thee, Sweet Land of Liberty," was sung. Our children, who need to be taught so much, were not assembled, their hands waved no flags, they threw no flowers, heard no thrilling speech, sang no song of their country. And this is the South's idea of justice. Is it surprising that [racist] feeling grows more bitter, when the white mother teaches her boy to hate my boy, not because he is mean, but because his skin is dark? I have seen very small white children hang their black dolls. It is not the child's fault, he is simply an apt pupil. . . .

Why does not the mistreatment of thousands of the [black] citizens of our country call forth a strong, influential champion? It seems to me that the very weakness of the negro should cause at least a few of our great men to come to the rescue. Is it because an espousal of our cause would make any white man unpopular, or do most of our great men think that we are worthless? Are there greater things to do than to "champion the rights of human beings and to mitigate human suffering?"

The way seems dark, and the future almost hopeless, but let us not despair, "For right is right, since God is God, and right the day must win." Some one will at last arise who will champion our cause and compel the world to see that we deserve justice, as other heroes compelled it to see that we deserved freedom.

REVIEW QUESTIONS

1. To what extent are racist prejudices the result of ignorance and stereotypes?
2. Are patterns of racial segregation still visible in American society? Explain.

FROM The Populist Party Platform (1892)

The People's Party, more commonly known as the Populist Party, was organized in St. Louis in 1892 to represent the common folk—especially farmers—against the entrenched interests of railroads, bankers, processors, corporations, and the politicians in league with such interests. At its first national convention in Omaha in July 1892, the party nominated James K. Weaver for president and ratified the so-called Omaha Platform, drafted by Ignatius Donnelly of Minnesota.

From "People's Party Platform," *Omaha Morning World–Herald*, July 5, 1892. [Editorial insertions appear in square brackets—*Ed.*]

Assembled upon the 116th anniversary of the Declaration of Independence, the People's Party of America, in their first national convention, invoking upon their action the blessing of Almighty God, put forth in the name and on behalf of the people of this country, the following preamble and declaration of principles:

Preamble

The conditions which surround us best justify our cooperation; we meet in the midst of a nation brought to the verge of moral, political, and material ruin. Corruption dominates the ballot-box, the Legislatures, the Congress, and touches even the ermine of the bench.[1] The people are demoralized; most of the States have been compelled to isolate the voters at the polling places to prevent universal intimidation and bribery. The newspapers are largely subsidized or muzzled, public opinion silenced, business prostrated, homes covered with mortgages, labor impoverished, and the land concentrating in the hands of capitalists. The urban workmen are denied the right to organize for self-protection, imported pauperized labor beats down their wages, a hireling standing army, unrecognized by our laws, is established to shoot them down, and they are rapidly degenerating

into European conditions. The fruits of the toil of millions are badly stolen to build up colossal fortunes for a few, unprecedented in the history of mankind; and the possessors of these, in turn, despise the Republic and endanger liberty. From the same prolific womb of governmental injustice we breed the two great classes—tramps and millionaires. The national power to create money is appropriated to enrich bond-holders; a vast public debt payable in legal-tender currency has been funded into gold-bearing bonds, thereby adding millions to the burdens of the people.

Silver, which has been accepted as coin since the dawn of history, has been demonetized to add to the purchasing power of gold by decreasing the value of all forms of property as well as human labor, and the supply of currency is purposely abridged to fatten usurers, bankrupt enterprise, and enslave industry. A vast conspiracy against mankind has been organized on two continents, and it is rapidly taking possession of the world. If not met and overthrown at once it forebodes terrible social convulsions, the destruction of civilization, or the establishment of an absolute despotism.

We have witnessed for more than a quarter of a century the struggles of the two great political parties for power and plunder, while grievous wrongs have been inflicted upon the suffering people. We charge that the controlling influences dominating both these parties have permitted the existing

---

[1] A valuable white fur adorning the robes of some judges.

dreadful conditions to develop without serious effort to prevent or restrain them. Neither do they now promise us any substantial reform. They have agreed together to ignore, in the coming campaign, every issue but one. They propose to drown the outcries of a plundered people with the uproar of a sham battle over the tariff, so that capitalists, corporations, national banks, rings, trusts, watered stock, the demonetization of silver and the oppressions of the usurers may all be lost sight of. They propose to sacrifice our homes, lives, and children on the altar of mammon; to destroy the multitude in order to secure corruption funds from the millionaires.

Assembled on the anniversary of the birthday of the nation, and filled with the spirit of the grand general and chief who established our independence, we seek to restore the government of the Republic to the hands of the "plain people," with which class it originated. We assert our purposes to be identical with the purposes of the National Constitution; to form a more perfect union and establish justice, insure domestic tranquillity, provide for the common defense, promote the general welfare, and secure the blessings of liberty for ourselves and our posterity. . . .

Our country finds itself confronted by conditions for which there is not precedent in the history of the world; our annual agricultural productions amount to billions of dollars in value, which must, within a few weeks or months, be exchanged for billions of dollars' worth of commodities consumed in their production; the existing currency supply is wholly inadequate to make this exchange; the results are falling prices, the formation of combines and rings, the impoverishment of the producing class. We pledge ourselves that if given power we will labor to correct these evils by wise and reasonable legislation, in accordance with the terms of our platform.

We believe that the power of government—in other words, of the people—should be expanded (as in the case of the postal service) as rapidly and as far as the good sense of an intelligent people and the teaching of experience shall justify, to the end that oppression, injustice, and poverty shall eventually cease in the land. . . .

Platform

We declare, therefore—

First.—That the union of the labor forces of the United States this day consummated shall be permanent and perpetual; may its spirit enter into all hearts for the salvation of the republic and the uplifting of mankind.

Second.—Wealth belongs to him who creates it, and every dollar taken from industry without an equivalent is robbery. "If any will not work, neither shall he eat." The interests of rural and civil labor are the same; their enemies are identical.

Third.—We believe that the time has come when the railroad corporations will either own the people or the people must own the railroads; and should the government enter upon the work of owning and managing all railroads, we should favor an amendment to the constitution by which all persons engaged in the government service shall be placed under a civil-service regulation of the most rigid character, so as to prevent the increase of the power of the national administration by the use of such additional government employees.

FINANCE.—We demand a national currency, safe, sound, and flexible issued by the general government only, a full legal tender for all debts, public and private, and that without the use of banking corporations; a just, equitable, and efficient means of distribution direct to the people, at a tax not to exceed 2 per cent, per annum, to be provided as set forth in the sub-treasury plan of the Farmers' Alliance, or a better system; also by payments in discharge of its obligations for public improvements.

1. We demand free and unlimited coinage of silver and gold at the present legal ratio of 16 to 1.
2. We demand that the amount of circulating medium[2] be speedily increased to not less than $50 per capita.
3. We demand a graduated income tax.
4. We believe that the money of the country should be kept as much as possible in the hands of the people, and hence we demand

---

[2]Currency or coin.

that all State and national revenues shall be limited to the necessary expenses of the government, economically and honestly administered.

We demand that postal savings banks be established by the government for the safe deposit of the earnings of the people and to facilitate exchange.

TRANSPORTATION.—Transportation being a means of exchange and a public necessity, the government should own and operate the railroads in the interest of the people. The telegraph and telephone, like the post-office system, being a necessity for the transmission of news, should be owned and operated by the government in the interest of the people.

LAND.—The land, including all the natural sources of wealth, is the heritage of the people, and should not be monopolized for speculative purposes, and alien ownership of land should be prohibited. All land now held by railroads and other corporations in excess of their actual needs, and all lands now owned by aliens should be reclaimed by the government and held for actual settlers only.

Expressions of Sentiments

Your Committee on Platform and Resolutions beg leave unanimously to report the following:

Whereas, Other questions have been presented for our consideration, we hereby submit the following, not as a part of the Platform of the People's Party, but as resolutions expressive of the sentiment of this Convention.

1. RESOLVED, That we demand a free ballot and a fair count in all elections and pledge ourselves to secure it to every legal voter without Federal Intervention, through the adoption by the States of the unperverted Australian or secret ballot system.

2. RESOLVED, That the revenue derived from a graduated income tax should be applied to the reduction of the burden of taxation now levied upon the domestic industries of this country.

3. RESOLVED, That we pledge our support to fair and liberal pensions to ex-Union soldiers and sailors.

4. RESOLVED, That we condemn the fallacy of protecting American labor under the present system, which opens our ports to the pauper and criminal classes of the world and crowds out our wage-earners; and we denounce the present ineffective laws against [foreign] contract labor, and demand the further restriction of undesirable emigration.

5. RESOLVED, That we cordially sympathize with the efforts of organized workingmen to shorten the hours of labor, and demand a rigid enforcement of the existing eight-hour law on Government work, and ask that a penalty clause be added to the said law.

6. RESOLVED, That we regard the maintenance of a large standing army of mercenaries, known as the Pinkerton system, as a menace to our liberties, and we demand its abolition. . . .

7. RESOLVED, That we commend to the favorable consideration of the people and the reform press the legislative system known as the initiative and referendum.

8. RESOLVED, That we favor a constitutional provision limiting the office of President and Vice-President to one term, and providing for the election of Senators of the United States by a direct vote of the people.

9. RESOLVED, That we oppose any subsidy or national aid to any private corporation for any purpose.

10. RESOLVED, That this convention sympathizes with the Knights of Labor and their righteous contest with the tyrannical combine of clothing manufacturers of Rochester, and declare it to be a duty of all who hate tyranny and oppression to refuse to purchase the goods made by the said manufacturers, or to patronize any merchants who sell such goods.

REVIEW QUESTIONS

1. In what ways did the Populists present a class-based interpretation of American politics? Who made up the social classes described by the Populists?

2. What were some of the Populists' specific demands? What groups would have opposed these demands?

3. Compare Populist proposals with those advocated by Democrats and Republicans. Were Populists truly radical?

MARY E. LEASE

The Money Question (1892)

The Populist movement provided unprecedented opportunities for women to participate in politics. Among the most active and impassioned was Mary Elizabeth Lease. Born in Pennsylvania in 1853, she moved to Kansas at the age of twenty. There she married, had four children, practiced law, and became a fiery orator on behalf of Populism. She urged farmers to "raise less corn and more hell!" The following excerpt from one of her speeches reveals her impassioned style.

From Elizabeth N. Barr, "The Populist Uprising," in *History of Kansas, State, and People,* ed. W. E. Connelly (Topeka: Lewis Publishing, 1928), 2:1167. [Editorial insertions appear in square brackets—*Ed.*]

This is a nation of inconsistencies. The Puritans fleeing from oppression [in England] became oppressors [in New England]. We fought England for our liberty and put chains on four million of blacks. We wiped out slavery and by our tariff laws and national banks began a system of white wage slavery worse than the first.

Wall Street owns the country. It is no longer a government of the people, by the people, and for the people, but a government of Wall Street, by Wall Street, and for Wall Street.

The great common people of this country are slaves, and monopoly is the master. The West and South are bound and prostrate before the manufacturing East.

Money rules. . . . The parties lie to us and the political speakers mislead us. We were told two years ago to go to work and raise a big crop, that was all we needed. We went to work and plowed and planted; the rains fell, the sun shone, nature smiled, and we raised the big crop that they told us to; and what came of it? Eight-cent corn, ten-cent oats, two-cent beef, and no price at all for butter and eggs—that's what came of it.

Then the politicians said we suffered from overproduction. Overproduction, when 10,000 little children, so statistics tell us, starve to death every year in the United States, and over 100,000 shopgirls in New York are forced to sell their virtue for the bread that niggardly wages deny them.

Tariff is not the paramount question. The main question is the money question. . . . Kansas suffers from two great robbers, the Santa Fe Railroad and the loan companies. The common people are robbed to enrich their masters. . . .

*   *   *

We want money, land, and transportation. We want the abolition of the national banks, and we want the power to make loans direct from the government. We want the accursed foreclosure system wiped out. . . .

We will stand by our homes and stay by our fireside by force if necessary, and we will not pay our debts to the loan-shark companies until the government pays its debt to us. The people are at bay; let the bloodhounds of money who have dogged us thus far beware.

REVIEW QUESTIONS

1. What did Lease mean when she wrote, "Wall Street owns the country"?
2. How did Lease interpret the conflict in geographic terms? How might such a regional outlook inhibit the effort to build political coalitions?
3. Characterize Lease's attitude toward the federal government. Explain your response.

J. STERLING MORTON

What Farm Problem? (1896)

The People's Party and its reform agenda aroused intense opposition. Democrat J. Sterling Morton of Nebraska served as secretary of agriculture under Grover Cleveland from 1893 to 1897. He vigorously denied that there was a serious "farm problem" and staunchly opposed the Populist movement's efforts to gain government benefits for farmers.

From *The Report of Secretary of Agriculture, 1896* (Washington, DC, 1896), pp. xlv–vi.

Out of each thousand farms in the United States only 282 are mortgaged, and three-fourths of the money represented by the mortgages upon the 282 farms was for the purchase of those farms or for money borrowed to improve those farms. And the prevalent idea that the West and the South are more heavily burdened with farm mortgages than the East and North-east sections of the United States is entirely erroneous. . . .

The constant complaint by the alleged friends of farmers, and by some farmers themselves, is that the Government does nothing for agriculture. In conventions and congresses it has been proclaimed that the farmers of the country are almost universally in debt, despondent, and suffering. Largely these decla-rations are without foundation. Their utterance is a belittlement of agriculture and an indignity to every intelligent and practical farmer of the United States. The free and independent farmers of this country are not impoverished; they are not mendicants; they are not wards of the Government to be treated to annuities, like Indians upon reservations. On the other hand, they are the representatives of the oldest, most honorable, and most essential occupation of the human race. Upon it all other vocations depend for subsistence and prosperity. The farmer is the copartner of the elements. His intelligently directed efforts are in unison with the light and heat of the sun, and the success of his labors represents the commingling of the raindrops and his own sweat.

Legislation can neither plow nor plant. The intelligent, practical, and successful farmer needs no aid from the Government. The ignorant, impractical, and indolent farmer deserves none. It is not the business of Government to legislate in behalf of any class of citizens because they are engaged in any specific calling, no matter how essential the calling may be to the needs and comforts of civilization. Lawmakers can not erase natural laws nor restrict or efface the operation of economic laws. It is a beneficent arrangement of the order of things and the conditions of human life that legislators are not permitted to repeal, amend, or revise the laws of production and distribution.

REVIEW QUESTIONS

1. What did Morton mean by "practical" farmers and "impractical" farmers?
2. In what ways was the farmer the "copartner of the elements"? What important factor did he omit in this context?
3. What relationship, if any, did the government have with natural or economic laws? How does this reflect late-nineteenth-century notions about governance?

FROM The Republican Party Platform of 1896

In 1896 the Republican Party National Convention convened in St. Louis. The delegates nominated former governor William McKinley of Ohio as their standard bearer, and they adopted a conservative platform reaffirming the sanctity of the gold standard and the benefits of high tariffs, thus setting the stage for a climactic election contest.

From Donald Bruce Johnson and Kirk H. Porter, eds., *National Party Platforms, 1840–1972* (Urbana: University of Illinois Press, 1973), pp. 107–08. [Editorial insertion appears in square brackets—*Ed.*]

. . . For the first time since the civil war the American people have witnessed the calamitous consequence of full and unrestricted Democratic control of the government. It has been a record of unparalleled incapacity, dishonor, and disaster. In administrative management it has ruthlessly sacrificed indispensable revenue, entailed an unceasing deficit, eked out ordinary current expenses with borrowed money, piled up the public debt by $262,000,000, in time of peace, forced an adverse balance of trade, kept a perpetual menace hanging over the redemption fund, pawned American credit to alien syndicates and reversed all the measures and results of successful Republican rule. In the broad effect of its policy it has precipitated panic, blighted industry and trade with prolonged depression, closed factories, reduced work and wages, halted enterprise and crippled American production, while stimulating foreign production for the American market. Every consideration of public safety and individual interest demands that the government shall be wrested from the hands of those who have shown themselves incapable of conducting it without disaster at home and dishonor abroad and shall be restored to the party which for thirty years administered it with unequaled success and prosperity. And in this connection, we heartily endorse the wisdom, patriotism and success of the administration of Benjamin Harrison.

We renew and emphasize our allegiance to the policy of [tariff] protection as the bulwark of American industrial independence and the foundation of American development and prosperity. This true American policy taxes foreign products and encourages home industry. It puts the burden of revenue on foreign goods; it secures the American market for the American producer. It upholds the American standard of wages for the American workingman; it puts the factory by the side of the farm, and makes the American farmer less dependent on foreign demand and price; it diffuses general thrift, and founds the strength of each. In its reasonable application it is just, fair and impartial, equally opposed to foreign control and domestic monopoly, to sectional discrimination and individual favoritism. . . .

We demand such an equitable tariff on foreign imports which come into competition with the American products as will not only furnish adequate revenue for the necessary expense of the Government, but will protect American labor from degradation and the wage level of other lands. We are not pledged to any particular schedules. The question of rates is a practical question, to be governed by the condition of time and of production.

The ruling and uncompromising principle is the protection and development of American labor and industries. . . .

The Republican party is unreservedly for sound money. It caused the enactment of a law providing for the resumption of specie payments in 1879. Since then every dollar has been as good as gold. We are unalterably opposed to every measure calculated to debase our currency or impair the credit of our country. We are therefore opposed to the free coinage of silver. . . . All of our silver and paper currency must be maintained at parity with gold, and we favor all measures designated to maintain inviolable the obligations of the United States, of all our money, whether coin or paper, at the present standard, the standard of most enlightened nations of the world. . . .

REVIEW QUESTIONS

1. What were some of the "calamitous consequences" linked to Democratic policies?
2. In discussing tariff protection for American industries, which aspect of the production process did the platform emphasize? Whose political support was being courted?
3. How might a Populist have responded to the Republican platform?

WILLIAM JENNINGS BRYAN

FROM The "Cross of Gold" Speech (1896)

The 1896 presidential election was one of the most significant in American history. Having suffered a humiliating defeat in the 1894 congressional elections, the Democratic Party faced a turning point: either embrace the "free silver" issue promoted by the Populists or echo the Republican platform by reaffirming the "gold standard" and "sound money" principles. At the party's national convention in Chicago in 1896, the silverites prevailed during the platform debate. What turned the tide was a rousing address to the 15,000 delegates by William Jennings Bryan of Nebraska. The thirty-six-year-old reformer was one of the greatest orators of his day, and his dramatic speech propelled the convention to nominate him as the Democratic presidential candidate. His references to "bimetallism" refer to proposals to allow for the coining of both gold and silver.

From William Jennings Bryan, *The First Battle: A Story of the Campaign of 1896* (Chicago: W. B. Conkey, 1896), pp. 199–206.

Mr. Chairman and Gentlemen of the Convention:

I would be presumptuous, indeed, to present myself against the distinguished gentlemen to whom you have listened if this were a mere measuring of abilities; but this is not a contest between persons. The humblest citizen in all the land, when clad in the armor of a righteous cause, is stronger than all the hosts of error. I come to speak to you in defense of a cause as holy as the cause of liberty—the cause of humanity. . . .

Never before in the history of this country has there been witnessed such a contest as that through which we have just passed. Never before in the history of American politics has a great issue been fought out as this issue has been, by the voters of a great party. On the fourth of March, 1895, a few Democrats, most of them members of Congress, issued an address to the Democrats of the nation, asserting that the money question was the paramount issue of the hour; declaring that a majority of the Democratic party had the right to control the action of the party on this paramount issue; and concluding with the request that the believers in the free coinage of silver in the Democratic party should organize, take charge of, and control the policy of the Democratic party.

Three months later, at Memphis, an organization was perfected, and the silver Democrats went forth openly and courageously proclaiming their belief, and declaring that, if successful, they would crystallize into a platform the declaration which they had made. Then began the conflict. With a zeal approaching the zeal which inspired the Crusaders who followed Peter the Hermit, our silver Democrats went forth from victory unto victory until they are now assembled, not to discuss, not to debate, but to enter up the judgment already rendered by the plain people of this country. In this contest brother has been arrayed against brother, father against son. The warmest ties of love, acquaintance, and association have been disregarded; old leaders have been cast aside when they have refused to give expression to the sentiments of those whom they would lead, and new leaders have sprung up to give direction to this cause of truth. Thus has the contest been waged, and we have assembled here under as binding and solemn instructions as were ever imposed upon representatives of the people. . . .

When you[1] come before us and tell us that we are about to disturb your business interests, we reply that you have disturbed our business interests by your course. We say to you that you have made the definition of a business man too limited in its application. The man who is employed for wages is as much a business man as his employer; the attorney in a country town is as much a business man as the corporation counsel in a great metropolis; the merchant at the cross-roads store is as much a business man as the merchant of New York; the farmer who goes forth in the morning and toils all day, who begins in spring and toils all summer, and who by the application of brain and muscle to the natural resources of the country creates wealth, is as much a business man as the man who goes upon the Board of Trade and bets upon the price of grain; the miners who go down a thousand feet into the earth, or climb two thousand feet upon the cliffs, and bring forth from their hiding places the precious metals to be poured into the channels of trade are as much businessmen as the few financial magnates who, in a back room, corner the money of the world. We come to speak of this broader class of business men.

Ah, my friends, we say not one word against those who live upon the Atlantic Coast, but the hardy pioneers who have braved all the dangers of the wilderness, who have made the desert to blossom as the rose—the pioneers away out there,[2] who rear their children near to Nature's heart, where they can mingle their voices with the voices of the birds—out there where they have erected schoolhouses for the education of their young, churches where they praise their creator, and cemeteries where rest the ashes of their dead—these people, we say, are as deserving of the consideration of our party as any people in this country. It is for these that we speak. We do not come as aggressors. Our

war is not a war of conquest; we are fighting in the defense of our homes, our families, and posterity. We have petitioned, and our petitions have been scorned; we have entreated, and our entreaties have been disregarded; we have begged, and they have mocked when our calamity came. We beg no longer; we entreat no more; we petition no more. We defy them!

The gentleman from Wisconsin has said that he fears a Robespierre.[3] My friends, in this land of the free you need not fear that a tyrant will spring up from among the people. What we need is an Andrew Jackson to stand, as Jackson stood, against the encroachments of organized wealth.

They tell us that this platform was made to catch votes. We reply to them that changing conditions make new issues; that the principles upon which Democracy rests are as everlasting as the hills, but that they must be applied to new conditions as they arise. Conditions have arisen, and we are here to meet those conditions. They tell us that the income tax ought not to be brought in here; that it is a new idea. They criticize us for our criticism of the Supreme Court of the United States. My friends, we have not criticized; we have simply called attention to what you already know. If you want criticisms, read the dissenting opinions of the court. There you will find criticisms. They say that we passed an unconstitutional law; we deny it. The income tax law was not unconstitutional when it was passed; it was not unconstitutional when it went before the Supreme Court for the first time; it did not become unconstitutional until one of the judges changed his mind, and we cannot be expected to know when a judge will change his mind. The income tax is just. It simply intends to put the burdens of government justly upon the backs of the people. I am in favor of an income tax. When I find a man who is not willing to bear his share of the burdens of the government which protects him, I find a man who is unworthy to enjoy the blessings of a government like ours.

They say that we are opposing national bank currency; it is true. . . . We say in our platform that

[1]Bryan is referring to the delegates committed to a gold-only currency.
[2]The West.

[3]The ruthless leader of the French Revolution who was himself guillotined in 1794.

we believe that the right to coin and issue money is a function of government. We believe it. We believe that it is a part of sovereignty, and can no more with safety be delegated to private individuals than we could afford to delegate to private individuals the power to make penal statutes or levy taxes. Mr. Jefferson, who was once regarded as good Democratic authority, seems to have differed in opinion from the gentleman who has addressed us on the part of the minority. Those who are opposed to this proposition tell us that the issue of paper money is a function of the bank, and that the government ought to go out of the banking business. I stand with Jefferson rather than with them, and tell them, as he did that the issue of money is a function of government, and that the banks ought to go out of the governing business. . . .

And now, my friends, let me come to the paramount issue. If they ask us why it is that we say more on the money question than we say upon the tariff question, I reply that, if protection has slain its thousands, the gold standard has slain its tens of thousands. If they ask us why we do not embody in our platform all the things that we believe in, we reply that when we have restored the money of the Constitution all other necessary reforms will be possible; but that until this is done there is no other reform that can be accomplished.

Why is it that within three months such a change has come over the country? Three months ago when it was confidently asserted that those who believe in the gold standard would frame our platform and nominate our candidates, even the advocates of the gold standard did not think that we could elect a President. And they had good reason for their doubt, because there is scarcely a state here today asking for the gold standard which is not in the absolute control of the Republican party.

But note the change. Mr. McKinley was nominated at St. Louis upon a platform which declared for the maintenance of the gold standard until it can be changed into bimetallism by international agreement. Mr. McKinley was the most popular man among the Republicans, and three months ago everybody in the Republican party prophesied his election. How is it to-day? Why, the man who

was once pleased to think that he looked like Napoleon—that man shudders today when he remembers that he was nominated on the anniversary of the battle of Waterloo. . . .

Why this change? Ah, my friends, is not the reason for the change evident to any one who will look at the matter? No private character, however pure, no personal popularity, however great, can protect from the avenging wrath of an indignant people a man who will declare that he is in favor of fastening the gold standard upon this country, or who is willing to surrender the right of self-government and place the legislative control of our affairs in the hands of foreign potentates and powers.

We go forth confident that we shall win. Why? Because upon the paramount issue of this campaign there is not a spot of ground upon which the enemy will dare to challenge battle. If they tell us that the gold standard is a good thing, we shall point to their platform and tell them that their platform pledges the party to get rid of the gold standard and substitute bimetallism.

If the gold standard is a good thing, why try to get rid of it? I call your attention to the fact that some of the very people who are in this Convention today and who tell us that we ought to declare in favor of international bimetallism—thereby declaring that the gold standard is wrong and that the principle of bimetallism is better—these very people four months ago were open and avowed advocates of the gold standard, and were then telling us that we could not legislate two metals together, even with the aid of all the world. If the gold standard is a good thing, we ought to declare in favor of its retention and not in favor of abandoning it; and if the gold standard is a bad thing why should we wait until other nations are willing to help us to let go?

Here is the line of battle, and we care not upon which issue they force the fight; we are prepared to meet them on either issue or on both. If they tell us that the gold standard is the standard of civilization, we reply to them that this, the most enlightened of all the nations of the earth, has never declared for a gold standard and that both the great parties this year are declaring against it. If the gold standard is the standard of civilization, why, my friends, should we not have it? If they come to meet us on that issue we can present the history of our nation. More than that; we can tell them that they will search the pages of history in vain to find a single instance where the common people of any land have ever declared themselves in favor of the gold standard. They can find where the holders of fixed investments have declared for a gold standard, but not where the masses have. . . .

My friends, the question we are to decide is: Upon which side will the Democratic party fight; upon the side of "the idle holders of idle capital" or upon the side of "the struggling masses"? That is the question which the party must answer first, and then it must be answered by each individual hereafter. The sympathies of the Democratic party, as shown by the platform, are on the side of the struggling masses who have ever been the foundation of the Democratic party.

There are two ideas of government. There are those who believe that, if you will only legislate to make the well-to-do prosperous, their prosperity will leak through on those below. The Democratic idea, however, has been that if you legislate to make the masses prosperous, their prosperity will find its way up through every class which rests upon them.

You come to us and tell us that the great cities are in favor of the gold standard; we reply that the great cities rest upon our broad and fertile prairies. Burn down your cities and leave our farms, and your cities will spring up again as if by magic; but destroy our farms and the grass will grow in the streets of every city in the country.

My friends, we declare that this nation is able to legislate for its own people on every question, without waiting for the aid or consent of any other nation on earth; and upon that issue we expect to carry every state in the Union. I shall not slander the inhabitants of the fair state of Massachusetts

nor the inhabitants of the state of New York by saying that, when they are confronted with the proposition, they will declare that this nation is not able to attend to its own business.

It is the issue of 1776 over again. Our ancestors, when but three millions in number, had the courage to declare their political independence of every other nation; shall we, their descendants, when we have grown to seventy millions, declare that we are less independent than our forefathers?

No, my friends, that will never be the verdict of our people. Therefore, we care not upon what lines the battle is fought. If they say bimetallism is good, but that we cannot have it until other nations help us, we reply that, instead of having a gold standard because England has, we will restore bimetallism, and then let England have bimetallism because the United States has it.

If they dare to come out in the open field and defend the gold standard as a good thing, we will fight them to the uttermost. Having behind us the producing masses of this nation and the world, supported by the commercial interests, the laboring interests and the toilers everywhere, we will answer their demand for a gold standard by saying to them: You shall not press down upon the brow of labor this crown of thorns, you shall not crucify mankind upon a cross of gold.

REVIEW QUESTIONS

1. Why did Bryan profess such a distaste for banks?
2. Why did Bryan support an income tax?
3. Bryan claimed that the cities' survival depended on the farms, and therefore the urban dwellers should support the silverite position. Do you find this argument convincing? Explain.

20 ∽ SEIZING AN AMERICAN EMPIRE, 1865–1913

In 1889 the prominent Massachusetts Congressman Henry Cabot Lodge observed that "our relations with foreign nations today fill but a slight place in American politics, and excite generally only a languid interest." Indeed, Americans after the Civil War gave scant attention to world affairs. They instead focused their energies on the domestic concerns associated with industrial development and the settling of the western frontier. At the same time, presidents and the Congress steadfastly refused to entangle the nation in foreign crises and controversies.

During the 1890s, however, this period of "splendid isolationism" abruptly ended as the United States rushed to join European nations in competing for overseas empires. By 1900 U.S. army and naval forces had won an easy victory over Spain, acquired far-flung possessions in the Pacific and Caribbean, and assumed a significant new role in world affairs.

How did this happen? How was it that a nation long committed to a non-interventionist foreign policy had become an expansionist imperial power and world leader? The reasons are many and complex, involving long-developing commercial and strategic interests, missionary impulses, and a quest for international prestige, but the catalytic event was the War of 1898, in which the United States forced Spain to grant independence to Cuba while America took control of the Philippines and Puerto Rico.

Elected president in 1896, William McKinley pursued a diplomatic solution to the protracted war in Cuba between Spanish forces and Cuban rebels seeking independence. But after the mysterious sinking of the American battleship Maine *in Havana harbor on February 15, 1898, Republican leaders such as Theodore Roosevelt and Henry Cabot Lodge urged immediate military action against Spain. Even the pacifist Democrat William Jennings Bryan argued that "the time for intervention has arrived. Humanity demands that we shall act." But President McKinley counseled caution and asked the nation to withhold judgment until an investigation of the tragic event could determine the cause of the explosion.*

On March 27, 1898, the investigating board reported that an external explosion caused the sinking of the Maine. Most people assumed the culprits were the Spanish, but skeptics asked why they would do something to provoke American intervention. McKinley used the report as an excuse to send the Spanish government an ultimatum: either accept American efforts to mediate the dispute and allow for Cuban independence or risk war. When the Spanish refused, McKinley succumbed to public pressure and asked for a declaration of war.

The "splendid little war" against Spain, as Republican John Hay called it, lasted only 113 days. During the summer of 1898, American forces defeated the Spanish army and navy, and on August 12, Spanish officials signed a preliminary peace treaty. Some 5,500 Americans had died in the War of 1898, but only 379 of them were killed in battle. The rest fell victim to a variety of accidents and diseases: yellow fever, malaria, and typhoid.

Although the United States officially declared war against Spain on behalf of the Cuban struggle for independence, America in the end took control of the Spanish colonies, Puerto Rico, the Philippine Islands, Guam, and Wake Island, completed the annexation of Hawaii, and established a protectorate over Cuba. Soon thereafter, the United States "acquired" the right to build an interoceanic canal in Panama, repeatedly used military force to intervene in the internal affairs of Central American nations, and undertook a major diplomatic initiative in Asia known as the Open Door policy.

By 1900 the United States had thus become a world power with global responsibilities. While advocates of American expansionism rejoiced in such developments, others lamented the abandonment of many principles and policies that had served the nation well since 1776. "Mr. Dooley," the popular cartoon character created by Finley Peter Dunne, looked back to "th' good old days befur we became . . . a wurrld power." He recalled that "our favrite sport was playin' solytare," but now that the nation had become a participant in the game of power politics, "be Hivens we have no peace iv mind."

Under President Theodore Roosevelt (1901–09), the United States asserted its right to intervene in the internal affairs of Latin American nations. In perhaps his most controversial action, Roosevelt helped Panama break away from Colombia to facilitate the building of an American canal across the isthmus. In 1904 a financial crisis in the debt-ridden Dominican Republic led Roosevelt to announce his "corollary" modifying the Monroe Doctrine: it allowed for American intervention in other countries in the Western Hemisphere to preempt such actions by European governments eager to collect debts. However well intentioned, such interventionist policies helped generate among Latin Americans an intense resentment of the United States and "Yankee imperialism." Roosevelt's swaggering rhetoric and bold actions led one Argentine writer to lament the bullying tactics of the "Colossus of the North."

WILLIAM McKINLEY

FROM Declaration of War (1898)

President William McKinley found it impossible to resist the mounting public and political pressure for war against Spain. In requesting a declaration of war from the Senate on April 11, 1898, he listed several concerns but stressed the nation's humanitarian sympathy for the Cuban independence movement. He said little about the long-range implications of war.

From James D. Richardson, ed., *Messages and Papers of the Presidents* (Washington, DC, 1899), 10:139–50. [Editorial insertions appear in square brackets—*Ed.*]

To the Congress of the United States:

... The present revolution is but the successor of other similar insurrections which have occurred in Cuba against the dominion of Spain, extending over a period of nearly half a century, each of which during its progress has subjected the United States to great effort and expense in enforcing its neutrality laws, caused enormous losses to American trade and commerce, caused irritation, annoyance, and disturbance among our citizens, and, by the exercise of cruel, barbarous, and uncivilized practices of warfare, shocked the sensibilities and offended the human sympathies of our people. ...

Our trade has suffered, the capital invested by our citizens in Cuba has been largely lost, and the temper and forbearance of our people have been so sorely tried as to beget a perilous unrest among our own citizens, which has inevitably found its expression from time to time in the National Legislature, so that issues wholly external to our own body politic engross attention and stand in the way of that close devotion to domestic advancement that becomes a self-contained commonwealth whose primal maxim has been the avoidance of all foreign entanglements.

All this must needs awaken, and has, indeed, aroused, the utmost concern on the part of this Government, as well during my predecessor's term as in my own. ... The overtures of this Government [to the Spanish government] ... were met by assurances that home rule in an advanced phase would be forthwith offered to Cuba, without waiting for the war to end, and that more humane methods should thenceforth prevail in the conduct of hostilities.

*   *   *

The war in Cuba is of such a nature that, short of subjugation or extermination, a final military victory for either side seems impracticable. The alternative lies in the physical exhaustion of the one or the other party, or perhaps of both. ... The prospect of such a protraction and conclusion of the present strife is a contingency hardly to be contemplated with equanimity by the civilized world, and least of all by the United States, affected and injured as we are, deeply and intimately, by its very existence. ...

The spirit of all our acts hitherto has been an earnest, unselfish desire for peace and prosperity in Cuba, untarnished by differences between us and Spain and unstained by the blood of American citizens. The forcible intervention of the United States as a neutral to stop the war ... is justifiable on rational grounds ... [which] may be briefly summarized as follows:

First. In the cause of humanity and to put an end to the barbarities, bloodshed, starvation, and horrible miseries now existing there, and which the parties to the conflict are either unable or unwilling to stop or mitigate. It is no answer to say this is all in another country, belonging to another nation, and is therefore none of our business. It is specially our duty, for it is right at our door.

Second. We owe it to our citizens in Cuba to afford them that protection and indemnity for life and property which no government there can or will afford, and to that end to terminate the conditions that deprive them of legal protection.

Third. The right to intervene may be justified by the very serious injury to the commerce, trade, and business of our people and by the wanton destruction of property and devastation of the island.

Fourth, and which is of the utmost importance. The present condition of affairs in Cuba is a constant menace to our peace and entails upon this Government an enormous expense. With such a conflict waged for years in an island so near us and with which our people have such trade and business relations; when the lives and liberty of our citizens are in constant danger and their property destroyed and themselves ruined; where our trading vessels are liable to seizure and are seized at our very door by war ships of a foreign nation; the expeditions of filibustering that we are powerless to prevent altogether, and the irritating questions and entanglements thus arising—all these and others that I need not mention, with the resulting strained relations, are a constant menace to our peace and compel us to keep on a semiwar footing with a nation with which we are at peace.

These elements of danger and disorder already pointed out have been strikingly illustrated by a tragic event which has deeply and justly moved the American people. I have already transmitted to Congress the report of the naval court of inquiry on the destruction of the battleship *Maine* in the harbor of Havana during the night of the 15th of February. The destruction of that noble vessel has filled the national heart with inexpressible horror.

*   *   *

The naval court of inquiry, which, it is needless to say, commands the unqualified confidence of the Government, was unanimous in its conclusion that the destruction of the *Maine* was caused by an exte-

rior explosion—that of a submarine mine. It did not assume to place the responsibility. That remains to be fixed. In any event, the destruction of the *Maine*, by whatever exterior cause, is a patent and impressive proof of a state of things in Cuba that is intolerable. That condition is thus shown to be such that the Spanish Government can not assure safety and security to a vessel of the American Navy in the harbor of Havana on a mission of peace, and rightfully there. . . .

The long trial has proved that the object for which Spain has waged the war can not be attained. The fire of insurrection may flame or may smolder with varying seasons, but it has not been and it is plain that it can not be extinguished by present methods. The only hope of relief and repose from a condition which can no longer be endured is the enforced pacification of Cuba. In the name of humanity, in the name of civilization, in behalf of endangered American interests which give us the right and the duty to speak and to act, the war in Cuba must stop.

In view of these facts and of these considerations I ask the Congress to authorize and empower the President to take measures to secure a full and final termination of hostilities between the Government of Spain and the people of Cuba, and to secure in the island the establishment of a stable government, capable of maintaining order and observing its international obligations, insuring peace and tranquility and the security of its citizens as well as our own, and to use the military and naval forces of the United States as may be necessary for these purposes. . . .

REVIEW QUESTIONS

1. What were the specific interests of the United States in Cuba? Were they legitimate and significant enough to warrant intervention?
2. How did President McKinley justify going to war against Spain over events in Cuba?
3. Had McKinley indeed "exhausted every effort" short of war, as he claimed in his statement to Congress?

ALBERT J. BEVERIDGE

FROM The March of the Flag (1900)

Although the ostensible reason for declaring war against Spain was to stop the oppression of Cubans, the McKinley administration decided to dispatch Commodore George Dewey's Pacific naval task force to Manila Bay, where on May 1, 1898, it destroyed the Spanish Pacific fleet and took control of the Philippines. Spain ceded the Philippines to the United States in the Treaty of Paris, which officially ended the war on December 10, 1898. This posed an unexpected dilemma. What was to be done with the Philippines now that they were in American hands? Those supporting annexation were led by a small but prominent group of imperialists that included Theodore Roosevelt, senators Henry Cabot Lodge and Albert Beveridge, and John Hay, soon to become secretary of state. In the following selection, Beveridge articulated why he supported annexation of the Philippines—and perhaps other areas in the future.

From the *Congressional Record*, 56th Cong., 1st sess., January 9, 1900, pp. 4–12.

Fellow citizens, It is a noble land that God has given us; a land that can feed and clothe the world; a land whose coast lines would enclose half the countries of Europe; a land set like a sentinel between the two imperial oceans of the globe, a greater England with a nobler destiny. It is a mighty people that He has planted on this soil; a people sprung from the most masterful blood of history; a people perpetually revitalized by the virile, man-producing working folk of all the earth; a people imperial by virtue of their power, by right of their institutions, by authority of their Heaven directed purposes—the propagandists and not the misers of liberty.

It is a glorious history our God has bestowed upon His chosen people; a history whose keynote was struck by Liberty Bell; a history heroic with faith in our mission and our future; a history of statesmen who flung the boundaries of the Republic out into unexplored lands and savage wildernesses; a history of soldiers who carried the flag across the blazing deserts and through the ranks of hostile mountains, even to the gates of sunset; a history of a multiplying people who overran a con-

tinent in half a century; a history of prophets who saw the consequences of evils inherited from the past and of martyrs who died to save us from them; a history divinely logical, in the process of whose tremendous reasoning we find ourselves today. . . .

Shall the American people continue their resistless march toward the commercial supremacy of the world? Shall free institutions broaden their blessed reign as the children of liberty wax in strength, until the empire of our principles is established over the hearts of all mankind?

Have we no mission to perform, no duty to discharge to our fellowman? Has the Almighty Father endowed us with gifts beyond our deserts and marked us as the people of His peculiar favor, merely to rot in our own selfishness, as men and nations must, who take cowardice for their companion and self for their deity—as China has, as India has, as Egypt has?

Shall we be as the man who had one talent and hid it, or as he who had ten talents and used them until they grew to riches? And shall we reap the reward that waits on our discharge of our high duty as the sovereign power of earth; shall we occupy new markets for what our farmers raise, new markets for what our factories make, new markets for what our merchants sell—aye, and, please God, new markets for what our ships shall carry?

*   *   *

Hawaii is ours; Porto Rico is to be ours; at the prayer of her people Cuba will finally be ours; in the islands of the East, even to the gates of Asia, coaling-stations are to be ours at the very least; the flag of a liberal government is to float over the Philippines, and I pray God it may be the banner that Taylor unfurled in Texas and Frémont[1] carried to the coast—the Stars and Stripes of glory. . . .

The Opposition tells us that we ought not to govern a people without their consent. I answer, The rule of liberty that all just government derives its authority from the consent of the governed, applies only to those who are capable of self-government. I answer, We govern the Indians without their consent, we govern our territories without their consent, we govern our children without their consent. I answer, How do you assume that our government would be without their consent? Would not the people of the Philippines prefer the just, humane, civilizing government of this Republic to the savage, bloody rule of pillage and extortion from which we have rescued them? . . .

Today, we are raising more than we can consume. Today, we are making more than we can use. Today, our industrial society is congested; there are more workers than there is work; there is more capital than there is investment. We do not need more money—we need more circulation, more employment. Therefore we must find new markets for our produce, new occupation for our capital, new work for our labor. And so, while we did not need the territory taken during the past century at the time it

was acquired, we do need what we have taken in 1898, and we need it now. . . .

Think of the tens of thousands of Americans who will invade mine and field and forest in the Philippines when a liberal government, protected and controlled by this republic, if not the government of the republic itself, shall establish order and equity there! Think of the hundreds of thousands of Americans who will build a soap-and-water, common-school civilization of energy and industry in Cuba, when a government of law replaces the double reign of anarchy and tyranny!—think of the prosperous millions that Empress of Islands will support when, obedient to the law of political gravitation, her people ask for the highest honor liberty can bestow, the sacred Order of the Stars and Stripes, the citizenship of the Great Republic!

What does all this mean for every one of us? It means opportunity for all the glorious young manhood of the republic—the most virile, ambitious, impatient, militant manhood the world has ever seen. It means that the resources and the commerce of these immensely rich dominions will be increased as much as American energy is greater than Spanish sloth; for Americans henceforth will monopolize those resources and that commerce. . . .

Fellow Americans, we are God's chosen people. . . . His power . . . delivered the Spanish fleet into our hands on the eve of Liberty's natal day, as he delivered the elder Armada[2] into the hands of our English sires two centuries ago. His great purposes are revealed in the progress of the flag, which surpasses the intentions of Congresses and Cabinets, and leads us like a holier pillar of cloud by day and pillar of fire by night into situations unforeseen by finite wisdom, and duties unexpected by the unprophetic heart of selfishness. The American people cannot use a dishonest medium of exchange; it is ours to set the world its example of right and honor. We cannot fly from our world duties; it is ours to execute the purpose of a fate that has driven us to be greater than our small intentions. We cannot

---

[1]John Charles Frémont was an American soldier and explorer who seized California for the United States during the Mexican War in the mid-nineteenth century. General Zachary Taylor led American troops in the Mexican War.

[2]The Spanish Armada was a naval fleet sent to attack England in 1588. It fell victim to powerful storms.

retreat from any soil where Providence has unfurled our banner; it is ours to save that soil for Liberty and Civilization. . . .

REVIEW QUESTIONS

1. How did Beveridge justify American acquisition of new territories? Does one country have the right to control another country, without "the consent of the governed"?

2. What did he mean by asserting that Americans were "God's chosen people"?

3. Do you share his belief that it was the "manifest destiny" of the United States to bring the blessings of its civilization to other peoples?

4. How did Beveridge imply that domestic economic concerns were dictating American foreign policy?

FROM Platform of the American Anti-Imperialist League (1899)

Those opposed to the new expansionism included Republicans and Democrats, business leaders such as Andrew Carnegie, the philosopher William James, prominent scholars such as William Graham Sumner, and literary figures such as Mark Twain and William Dean Howells. Many of them joined the Anti-Imperialist League, formed in Boston in 1898 for the purpose of galvanizing public opinion against the Philippine War and the evils of imperialism. Anti-imperialists almost prevented the annexation of the Philippines through their lobbying efforts against the Treaty of Paris, which the Senate ultimately ratified by only one vote on February 6, 1899. The following excerpt outlines the anti-imperialist critique of American foreign policy.

From "Platform of the American Anti-Imperialist League," in *Speeches, Correspondence, and Political Papers of Carl Schurz*, ed. Frederick Bancroft, vol. 6 (New York: G. P. Putnam's Sons, 1913), pp. 77–79.

We hold that the policy known as imperialism is hostile to liberty and tends toward militarism, an evil from which it has been our glory to be free. We regret that it has become necessary in the land of Washington and Lincoln to reaffirm that all men, of whatever race or color, are entitled to life, liberty, and the pursuit of happiness. We maintain that governments derive their just powers from the consent of the governed. We insist that the subjugation of any people is "criminal aggression" and open disloyalty to the distinctive principles of our Government.

We earnestly condemn the policy of the present National Administration in the Philippines. It seeks to extinguish the spirit of 1776 in those islands. We deplore the sacrifice of our soldiers and sailors, whose bravery deserves admiration even in an unjust war. We denounce the slaughter of the Filipinos as a needless horror. We protest against the extension of American sovereignty by Spanish methods.

We demand the immediate cessation of the war against liberty, begun by Spain and continued by us. We urge that Congress be promptly convened to announce to the Filipinos our purpose to concede to them the independence for which they have so long fought and which of right is theirs.

The United States have always protested against the doctrine of international law which permits the subjugation of the weak by the strong. A self-governing state cannot accept sovereignty over an unwilling people. The United States cannot act upon the ancient heresy that might makes right.

Imperialists assume that with the destruction of self-government in the Philippines by American hands, all opposition here will cease. This is a grievous error. Much as we abhor the war of "criminal aggression" in the Philippines, greatly as we regret that the blood of the Filipinos is on American hands, we more deeply resent the betrayal of American institutions at home. The real firing line is not in the suburbs of Manila. The foe is of our own household. The attempt of 1861 was to divide the country. That of 1899 is to destroy its fundamental principles and noblest ideals.

Whether the ruthless slaughter of the Filipinos shall end next month or next year is but an incident in a contest that must go on until the Declaration of Independence and the Constitution of the United States are rescued from the hands of their betrayers. Those who dispute about standards of value while the Republic is undermined will be listened to as little as those who would wrangle about the small economies of the household while the house is on fire. The training of a great people for a century, the aspiration for liberty of a vast immigration are forces that will hurl aside those who in the delirium of conquest seek to destroy the character of our institutions.

We deny that the obligation of all citizens to support their Government in times of grave national peril applies to the present situation. If an Administration may with impunity ignore the issues upon which it was chosen, deliberately create a condition of war anywhere on the face of the globe, debauch the civil service for spoils to promote the adventure, organize a truth-suppressing censorship and demand of all citizens a suspension of judgment and their unanimous support while it chooses to continue the fighting, representative government itself is imperiled.

We propose to contribute to the defeat of any person or party that stands for the forcible subjugation of any people. We shall oppose for reelection all who in the White House or in Congress betray American liberty in pursuit of un-American gains. We still hope that both of our great political parties will support and defend the Declaration of Independence in the closing campaign of the century. . . .

REVIEW QUESTIONS

1. What arguments did the Anti-Imperialist League offer against the annexation of any new territories?
2. What did they plan to do to oppose annexation efforts?
3. How would you have felt about these issues?

JOHN HAY

FROM The Open Door in China (1899–1900)

Having extended American control over the Philippines, the McKinley administration next turned its attention to the most coveted economic market in Asia—China. In 1899 Secretary of State John Hay issued the first "Open Door Note," a letter sent to each of the nations engaged in commercial activity in China—the United Kingdom,

France, Germany, Italy, Japan, and Russia. In an effort to thwart the efforts of Japan and Russia to carve out exclusive economic spheres of interest in China, the letter affirmed the commercial equality of all nations trading in China. Although most major powers ignored or evaded the Open Door Note, Hay announced their acceptance on March 20, 1900.

From U.S. Department of State, *Papers Relating to Foreign Relations of the United States, 1899* (Washington, DC, 1901), pp. 129–30.

At the time when the Government of the United States was informed by that of Germany that it had leased from His Majesty the Emperor of China the port of Kiaochao and the adjacent territory in the province of Shantung, assurances were given to the ambassador of the United States at Berlin by the Imperial German minister for foreign affairs that the rights and privileges insured by treaties with China to citizens of the United States would not thereby suffer or be in anywise impaired within the area over which Germany had thus obtained control.

More recently, however, the British Government recognized by a formal agreement with Germany the exclusive right of the latter country to enjoy in said leased area and the contiguous "sphere of influence or interest" certain privileges, more especially those relating to railroads and mining enterprises; but, as the exact nature and extent of the rights thus recognized have not been clearly defined, it is possible that serious conflicts of interest may at any time arise, not only between British and German subjects within said area, but that the interests of our citizens may also be jeopardized thereby.

Earnestly desirous to remove any cause of irritation and to insure at the same time to the commerce of all nations in China the undoubted benefits which should accrue from a formal recognition by the various powers claiming "spheres of interest" that they shall enjoy perfect equality of treatment for their commerce and navigation within such "spheres," the Government of the United States would be pleased to see His German Majesty's Government give formal assurances and lend its cooperation in securing like assurances

from the other interested powers that each within its respective sphere of whatever influence—

First. Will in no way interfere with any treaty port or any vested interest within any so-called "sphere of interest" or leased territory it may have in China.

Second. That the Chinese treaty tariff of the time being shall apply to all merchandise landed or shipped to all such ports as are within said "sphere of interest" (unless they be "free ports"), no matter to what nationality it may belong, and that duties so leviable shall be collected by the Chinese Government.

Third. That it will levy no higher harbor dues on vessels of another nationality frequenting any port in such "sphere" than shall be levied on vessels of its own nationality, and no higher railroad charges over lines built, controlled, or operated within its "sphere" on merchandise belonging to citizens or subjects of other nationalities transported through such "sphere" than shall be levied on similar merchandise belonging to its own nationals transported over equal distances. . . .

The commercial interests of Great Britain and Japan will be so clearly served by the desired declaration of intentions, and the views of the Governments of these countries as to the desirability of the adoption of measures insuring the benefits of equality of treatment of all foreign trade throughout China are so similar to those entertained by the United States, that their acceptance of the propositions herein outlined and their cooperation in advocating their adoption by the other powers can be confidently expected. . . .

REVIEW QUESTIONS

1. How did the United States justify an "open door policy"?

2. What did it ask the other foreign powers in China to do?

3. What do you think was the primary motive for such a policy?

FROM The Roosevelt Corollary to the Monroe Doctrine (1904)

When he became president in 1901, Theodore Roosevelt brought with him to the White House a candid assumption of American superiority in the affairs of the Western Hemisphere. Within a few years, he grew concerned about the chronic instability of Latin American governments and economies. He especially worried that European powers might intervene to collect overdue debts. In 1904 a financial crisis in the Dominican Republic provoked him to formulate a new policy that came to be known as the Roosevelt Corollary to the Monroe Doctrine. His reasoning rested on the assumption that nations are not equal in stature. Those governments unable to manage their affairs must submit to outside supervision by "first-class" powers.

From James D. Richardson, ed., *Messages and Papers of the Presidents* (Washington, DC, 1905), 14:6923ff.

... It is not true that the United States feels any land hunger or entertains any projects as regards the other nations of the Western Hemisphere save such as are for their welfare. All that this country desires is to see the neighboring countries stable, orderly, and prosperous. Any country whose people conduct themselves well can count upon our hearty friendship. If a nation shows that it knows how to act with reasonable efficiency and decency in social and political matters, if it keeps order and pays its obligations, it need fear no interference from the United States.

Chronic wrongdoing, or an impotence which results in a general loosening of the ties of civilized society, may in America, as elsewhere, ultimately require intervention by some civilized nation, and in the Western Hemisphere the adherence of the United States to the Monroe Doctrine may force the United States, however reluctantly, in flagrant cases of such wrongdoing or impotence, to the exercise of an international police power. If every country washed by the Caribbean Sea would show the progress in stable and just civilization which with the aid of the Platt amendment Cuba has shown since our troops left the island, and which so many of the republics in both Americas are constantly and brilliantly showing, all question of interference by this Nation with their affairs would be at an end.

Our interests and those of our southern neighbors are in reality identical. They have great natural riches, and if within their borders the reign of law and justice obtains, prosperity is sure to come to them. While they thus obey the primary laws of civilized society they may rest assured that they will be treated by us in a spirit of cordial and helpful sympathy. We would interfere with them only in the last resort, and then only if it became evident that their inability or unwillingness to do justice at home and abroad had violated the rights of the United States or had invited foreign aggression to the detriment of the entire body of American nations. It is a mere truism to say that every nation, whether in America or anywhere else, which desires to maintain its freedom, its independence, must ultimately realize that the right of such independence can not be separated from the responsibility of making good use of it.

In asserting the Monroe Doctrine, in taking such steps as we have taken in regard to Cuba, Venezuela, and Panama, and in endeavoring to circumscribe the theater of war in the Far East, and to secure the open door in China, we have acted in our own interest as well as in the interest of humanity at large. There are, however, cases in which, while our own interests are not greatly involved, strong appeal is made to our sympathies. . . . But in

extreme cases action may be justifiable and proper. What form the action shall take must depend upon the circumstances of the case; that is, upon the degree of the atrocity and upon our power to remedy it. The cases in which we could interfere by force of arms as we interfered to put a stop to intolerable conditions in Cuba are necessarily very few.

REVIEW QUESTIONS

1. Why did Roosevelt claim that the United States should interfere in the internal affairs of nations in Central and South America?
2. What factors contributed to the Roosevelt Corollary? Do you agree with his reasoning? Why?
3. In reflecting on the expansion of American power around the world at the turn of the century, do you think it was motivated more by moral idealism or by power politics? Why?

21 ❧ THE PROGRESSIVE ERA, 1890–1920

The capitalists and entrepreneurs who during the late nineteenth century built the United States into one of the world's leading economies took full advantage of America's free-enterprise culture to launch an industrial revolution of unprecedented scope. With few state or federal laws to hinder them, many business leaders used questionable tactics to drive out competitors and establish monopolies or near-monopolies in their respective industries. Along the way they cajoled, bribed, or blackmailed political leaders to facilitate their efforts.

To address such excesses, a diverse group of reformers set about trying to gain political power and public support at the end of the nineteenth century. Progressivism, as historians have come to label this reform movement, found its support primarily in urban areas among the middle and upper-middle classes—business executives, professionals, teachers, and government workers. They promoted greater efficiency in the workplace and greater honesty in government. Their fervent hope was to restore democratic control of the economic and political sectors.

There was no all-encompassing "progressive" organization, agenda, or motive. The movement cut across both political parties, appeared in every geographic region, and contained many conflicting elements. Some activists were spurred by strong religious convictions while others were animated by secular ideals. Some were earnest humanitarians and others were more concerned with issues of efficiency and productivity. Prominent men such as Robert La Follette, Theodore Roosevelt, and Woodrow Wilson are most often associated with the progressive movement, yet women were disproportionately involved in the array of "progressive" causes and issues.

While varied in motivation and mission, Progressives believed that government should take a more active role in promoting the public good. More specifically, this meant the passage of laws breaking up the huge corporate trusts, regulating child and female labor, promoting better working conditions, and conserving the environment. In addition, Progressives supported voluntary associations such as settlement houses and other charitable organizations intended to help immigrants, the poor, and the disabled.

Progressivism changed the social and political landscape of American life by enlarging the sphere of government action. New laws, regulations, and attitudes resulted from the efforts of self-styled progressives to deal with many persistent social ills. The glaring failure of the progressive movement was its unwillingness to address racial injustice. For the most part, progressivism was for whites only. African Americans in the South were increasingly victims of disfranchisement, Jim Crow laws, vigilante assaults, and poverty.

WASHINGTON GLADDEN

The Social Gospel (1902)

*During the last quarter of the nineteenth century, many Americans began to pro-
mote what came to be called the social gospel. They used Christian ethics to address
the many problems spawned by rapid urbanization and industrialization: poverty,
unsanitary living conditions, racial and ethnic tensions, and labor strife. Among the
early champions of the social gospel was Washington Gladden, a prominent Congre-
gational minister who pastored large churches in Springfield, Massachusetts, and
Columbus, Ohio. Gladden was the first minister to endorse the labor union movement. He also spoke out against anti-Catholicism and racial segregation. In the following selection from his book* Social Salvation, *he explains why Christians need to
become social reformers.*

From *Social Salvation* (Boston: Houghton Mifflin, 1902), pp. 14–15, 25–28, 206–08, 226.

Any treatment of social questions which failed to
bring the responsibility for right social actions
home to individuals would, indeed, be defective
treatment; on the other hand, any discussion of the
problems of the individual life which did not keep
the social environment steadily in view would be
utterly inadequate.

I am therefore unable to understand how Christianity, whether as a law or as a gospel, can be
intelligently or adequately preached or lived in
these days without a constant reference to social
questions. No individual is soundly converted until
he comprehends his social relations and strives to
fulfill them; and the work of growth and sanctifi-
cation largely consists in a clearer apprehension of
these relations and a more earnest effort to fill them
with the life of the divine Spirit. The kingdom of
heaven is *within* us and *among* us; the preposition,
in Christ's saying, seems to have the double meaning. It cannot be among us unless it is within us, and
it cannot be within us without being among us.

It would seem, therefore, that the minister's
work, in these days, must lie, very largely, along the
lines of social amelioration. He is bound to under-

stand the laws of social structure. It is just as needful
that he should understand the constitution of human
society as that he should understand the constitution
of the human soul; the one comes under his purview
no less directly than the other. He does not know
definitely what sin is, unless he understands the
nature of the social bond; he does not surely know
what salvation means until he has comprehended
the reciprocal action of society upon the individual
and of the individual upon society. The men who are
working out their own salvation are doing it largely
through the establishment of right relations between
themselves and their neighbors, and he cannot help
them in this unless he has some clear idea of what
these right relations are.

*   *   *

. . . The minister who has become merely or mainly
political, or sociological, or economical, or scientific,
has abandoned his vocation. The minister to whom
religion is not the central and culminating power in
all his teaching has no right in any Christian pulpit.
It is *the religion* of politics, of economics, of sociology
that we are to teach,—nothing else. We are to bring

the truths and the powers of the spiritual world, the eternal world, to bear upon all these themes. This is what we have to do with these social questions, and we have nothing else to do with them.

The first thing for us to understand is that God is in his world, and that we are workers together with him. In all this industrial struggle he is present in every part of it, working according to the counsel of his perfect will. In the gleams of light which sometimes break forth from the darkness of the conflict we discern his inspiration; in the stirrings of goodwill which temper the wasting strife we behold the evidence of his presence; in the sufferings and losses and degradations which wait upon every violation of his law of love we witness the retributions with which that law goes armed. In the weltering masses of poverty; in the giddy throngs that tread the paths of vice; in the multitudes distressed and scattered as sheep having no shepherd; in the brutalized ranks marching in lock-step through the prison yard; in the groups of politicians scheming for place and plunder,—in all the most forlorn and untoward and degrading human associations, the One who is never absent is that divine Spirit which brooded over the chaos at the beginning, nursing it to life and beauty, and which is

> nearer to every creature he hath made,
> Than anything unto itself can be.

Nay, there is not one of these hapless, sinning multitudes in whose spirit he is not present to will and to work according to his good pleasure; never overpowering the will, but gently pressing in, by every avenue open to him, his gifts of love and truth. As he has for every man's life a plan, so has he for the common life a perfect social order into which he seeks to lead his children, that he may give them plenty and blessedness and abundance of peace as long as the moon endureth. Surely he has a way for men to live in society; he has a way of organizing industry; he has a way of life for the family, and for the school, and for the shop, and for the city, and for the state; he has a way for preventing poverty, and a way for helping and saving the poor and the sick and the sinful; and it is his way that we are to seek and point out and follow. We cannot know it perfectly, but if we are humble

and faithful and obedient, we shall come to understand it better and better as the years go by. The one thing for us to be sure of is that God has a way for human beings to live and work together, just as truly as he has a way for the stars over our heads and the crystals under our feet; and that it is man's chief end to find this way and follow it.

*   *   *

No one who has lived and labored for many years in ill-governed cities, in the interests of virtue, can fail to be aware of the evil influence which bad government exerts upon the characters of those who live under it. The tone of public morality is affected; the convictions of the youth are blurred; the standards of honor and fidelity are lowered. That which in the family and in the Sunday-school and in the day-school and in the pulpit we are teaching our children to regard as sacred, the bad city government, by the whole tenor of its administration, openly despises; the things which we tell them are detestable and infamous, the bad city government, by its open connivance or inaction, proclaims to be honorable. The whole weight of the moral influence of a municipal government like that which has existed until recently in New York, like that which exists to-day in Philadelphia, and in many other cities, is hostile to honesty, honor, purity, and decency. The preacher of righteousness finds, therefore, in bad municipal government, one of the deadliest of the evil forces with which he is called to contend. The problem of the city is a problem in which he has a vital interest, a question on which he has an undoubted right to speak.

The American city of the nineteenth century has been notable for two things, the rapidity of its growth and the corruptness of its civic administration. The population of the whole land has been growing apace, but the cities have grown at the expense of the rural districts. . . .

*   *   *

Let us not underrate our problem. These people of the cities—many of them ignorant, depraved, superstitious, unsocial in their tempers and habits; many of them ignorant of the language in which our laws are written, and unable freely to communicate with those who wish to influence them for good; having no conception of government but that of an enemy to be eluded or an unkind providence from which dole may be extorted; and no idea of a vote higher than that of a commodity which can be sold for money—these are the "powers that be" who must give us good government in our cities, if we are ever to get it.

REVIEW QUESTIONS

1. How convincing is Gladden's argument for a social gospel? Explain.
2. Should ministers be social activists and political reformers? Why or why not?
3. How does Gladden characterize the foreign immigrants streaming into American cities in the late nineteenth century?

JANE ADDAMS

FROM The Subjective Necessity for Social Settlements (1892)

Women provided much of the energy, idealism, and leadership during the Progressive Era. Jane Addams (1860–1935) was one of the most prominent and tireless social reformers. After graduating from Rockford College in Illinois in 1881 and studying medicine in Philadelphia, she toured Europe and England several times, examining efforts to deal with spreading urban poverty. After her return she and Ellen Gates Starr formed Hull House in Chicago's West Side in 1889. Modeled after Toynbee Hall in London, it served as a "halfway" settlement house and social center for immigrants streaming into the city. It was staffed by middle- and upper-class men and women animated by a desire to do something about social problems.

From *Philanthropy and Social Progress* (New York: Thomas Y. Crowell, 1893), pp. 1–26. [Editorial insertions appear in square brackets—*Ed.*]

Hull House, which was Chicago's first Settlement, was established in September, 1889 . . . in the belief that the mere foothold of a house, easily accessible, ample in space, hospitable and tolerant in spirit, situated in the midst of the large foreign colonies which so easily isolate themselves in American cities, would be in itself a serviceable thing for Chicago. Hull House endeavors to make social intercourse express the growing sense of the economic unity of society. It is an effort to add the social function to democracy. It was opened on the theory that the dependence of classes on each other is reciprocal; and that as "the social relation is essentially a reciprocal relation, it gave a form of expression that has peculiar value."

This paper is an attempt to treat of the subjective necessity for Social Settlements, to analyze the motives which underlie a movement based not only upon [spiritual] conviction, but genuine emotion. Hull House of Chicago is used as an illustration, but so far as the analysis is faithful, it obtains wherever educated young people are seeking an outlet for that sentiment of universal brotherhood which the best spirit of our times is forcing from an emotion into a motive.

I have divided the motives which constitute the subjective pressure toward Social Settlements into three great lines: the first contains the desire to make the entire social organism democratic, to extend democracy beyond its political expression; the second is the impulse to share the race life, and to bring as much as possible of social energy and the accumulation of civilization to those portions of the race which have little; the third springs from a certain renaissance of Christianity, a movement toward its early humanitarian aspects.

It is not difficult to see that although America is pledged to the democratic ideal, the view of democracy has been partial, and that its best achievement thus far has been pushed along the line of the franchise [vote]. Democracy has made little attempt to assert itself in social affairs. We have refused to move beyond the position of its eighteenth-century leaders, who believed that political equality alone would secure all good to all men. We conscientiously followed the gift of the ballot hard upon the gift of freedom to the negro, but we are quite unmoved by the fact that he lives among us in a practical social ostracism. We hasten to give the franchise to the immigrant from a sense of justice, from a tradition that he ought to have it, while we dub him with epithets deriding his past life or present occupation, and feel no duty to invite him to our houses. We are forced to acknowledge that it is only in our local and national politics that we try very hard for the ideal so dear to those who were enthusiasts when the century was young. We have almost given it up as our ideal in social intercourse.

*   *   *

The social organism has broken down through large districts of our great cities. Many of the people living there are very poor, the majority of them without leisure or energy for anything but the gain of subsistence. They move often from one wretched lodging to another. They live for the moment side by side, many of them without knowledge of each other, without fellowship, without local tradition or

public spirit, without social organization of any kind.

Practically nothing is done to remedy this. The people who might do it, who have the social tact and training, the large houses, and the traditions and custom of hospitality, live in other parts of the city. The clubhouses, libraries, galleries, and semi-public conveniences for social life are also blocks away. We find working-men organized into armies of producers because men of executive ability and business sagacity have found it to their interests thus to organize them. But these working-men are not organized socially; although living in crowded tenement-houses, they are living without a corresponding social contact. The chaos is as great as it would be were they working in huge factories without foreman or superintendent. Their ideas and resources are cramped. The desire for higher social pleasure is extinct. They have no share in the traditions and social energy which make for progress.

Too often their only place of meeting is a saloon, their only host a bartender; a local demagogue forms their public opinion. Men of ability and refinement, of social power and university cultivation, stay away from them. Personally, I believe the men who lose most are those who thus stay away. But the paradox is here: when cultivated people do stay away from a certain portion of the population, when all social advantages are persistently withheld, it may be for years, the result itself is pointed at as a reason, is used as an argument, for the continued withholding.

It is constantly said that because the masses have never had social advantages they do not want them, that they are heavy and dull, and that it will take political or philanthropic machinery to change them. This divides a city into rich and poor; into the favored, who express their sense of the social obligation by gifts of money, and into the unfavored, who express it by clamoring for a "share"—both of them actuated by a vague sense of justice. This division of the city would be more justifiable, however, if the people who thus isolate themselves in certain streets and use their social ability for each other gained enough thereby and added sufficient to the sum total of social progress to justify the withholding of the pleasures and results of that progress from so many people who ought to have them. But they cannot accomplish this. "The social spirit discharges itself in many forms, and no one form is adequate to its total expression." We are all uncomfortable in regard to the sincerity of our best phrases, because we hesitate to translate our philosophy into the deed.

It is inevitable that those who feel most keenly this insincerity and partial living should be our young people, our so-called educated young people who accomplish little toward the solution of this social problem, and who bear the brunt of being cultivated into unnourished, oversensitive lives. They have been shut off from the common labor by which they live and which is a great source of moral and physical health. They feel a fatal want of harmony between their theory and their lives, a lack of coordination between thought and action. I think it is hard for us to realize how seriously many of them are taking to the notion of human brotherhood, how eagerly they long to give tangible expression to the democratic ideal. These young men and women, longing to socialize their democracy, are animated by certain hopes.

These hopes may be loosely formulated thus: that if in a democratic country nothing can he permanently achieved save through the masses of the people, it will be impossible to establish a higher political life than the people themselves crave; that it is difficult to see how the notion of a higher civic life can be fostered save through common intercourse; that the blessings which we associate with a life of refinement and cultivation can be made universal and must be made universal if they are to be permanent; that the good we secure for ourselves is precarious and uncertain, is floating in mid-air, until it is secured for all of us and incorporated into our common life.

These hopes are responsible for results in various directions, pre-eminently in the extension of educational advantages. We find that all educational matters are more democratic in their political than in their social aspects. The public schools in the poorest and most crowded wards of the city are inadequate to the number of children, and many of the teachers are ill-prepared and over-worked; but in each ward there is an effort to secure public education. The schoolhouse itself stands as a pledge that the city recognizes and endeavors to fulfill the duty of educating its children. But what becomes of these children when they are no longer in public schools? Many of them never come under the influence of a professional teacher nor a cultivated friend after they are twelve. Society at large does little for their intellectual development. The dream of transcendentalists that each New England village would be a university, that every child taken from the common school would be put into definite lines of study and mental development, had its unfulfilled beginning in the village lyceum and lecture courses, and has its feeble representative now in the multitude of clubs for study which are so sadly restricted to educators, to the leisure class, or only to the advanced and progressive wage-workers.

*   *   *

I find it somewhat difficult to formulate the second line of motives which I believe to constitute the trend of the subjective pressure toward the Settlement. There is something primordial about these motives, but I am perhaps over-bold in designating them as a great desire to share the race life. We all bear traces of the starvation struggle which for so long made up the life of the race. Our very organism holds memories and glimpses of that long life of our ancestors which still goes on among so many of our contemporaries. Nothing so deadens the sympathies and shrivels the power of enjoyment as the . . . continual ignoring of the starvation struggle which makes up the life of at least half the race. To shut one's self away from that half of the race life is to shut one's self away from the most vital part of it; it is to live out but half the humanity which we have been born heir to and to use but half our faculties. We have all had longings for a fuller life which should include the use of these faculties. . . .

You may remember the forlorn feeling which occasionally seizes you when you arrive early in the morning a stranger in a great city. The stream of laboring people goes past you as you gaze through the plate-glass window of your hotel. You see hard-working men lifting great burdens; You hear the driving and jostling of huge carts. Your heart sinks with a sudden sense of futility. The door opens behind you and you turn to the man who brings you in your breakfast with a quick sense of human fellowship. You find yourself praying that you may never lose your hold on it at all. A more poetic prayer would be that the great mother breasts of our common humanity, with its labor and suffering and its homely comforts, may never be withheld from you. You turn helplessly to the waiter. You feel that it would be almost grotesque to claim from him the sympathy you crave. Civilization has placed you far apart, but you resent your position with a sudden sense of snobbery.

*   *   *

We have in America a fast-growing number of cultivated young people who have no recognized outlet for their active faculties. They bear constantly of the great social maladjustment, but no way is provided for them to change it, and their uselessness bangs about them heavily. . . . These young people have had advantages of college, of European travel and economic study, but they are sustaining this shock of inaction. They have pet phrases, and they tell you that the things that make us all alike are stronger than the things that make us different. They say that all men are united by needs and sympathies far more permanent and radical than anything that temporarily divides them and sets them in opposition to each other. . . . Our young people feel nervously the need of putting theory into action, and respond quickly to the Settlement form of activity.

The third division of motives which I believe make toward the Settlement is the result of a certain renaissance going forward in Christianity. The impulse to share the lives of the poor, the desire to make social service, irrespective of propaganda, express the spirit of Christ, is as old as Christianity itself. . . .

I believe that there is a distinct turning among many young men and women toward this simple acceptance of Christ's message. They resent the assumption that Christianity is a set of ideas which belong to the religious consciousness, whatever that may be, that it is a thing to be proclaimed and instituted apart from the social life of the community. They insist that it shall seek a simple and natural expression in the social organism itself. The Settlement movement is only one manifestation of that wider humanitarian movement which throughout Christendom, but pre-eminently in England, is endeavoring to embody itself, not in a sect, but in society itself. . . .

Certain it is that spiritual force is found in the Settlement movement, and it is also true that this force must be evoked and must be called into play before the success of any Settlement is assured. There must be the overmastering belief that all that is noblest in life is common to men as men, in order to accentuate the likenesses and ignore the differences which are found among the people whom the Settlement constantly brings into juxtaposition. . . .

REVIEW QUESTIONS

1. What were the three motives that Addams identified with social settlements?
2. What were some of the serious social problems that Addams discussed?
3. Addams's emphasis on the role of the well educated as reform leaders suggested what about her view of social change?

UPTON SINCLAIR

FROM *The Jungle* (1906)

Muckraking (investigative) journalists and novelists were the shock troops of progressive efforts to promote government regulation of corporate America. One of the most powerful of these reform-minded writers was Upton Sinclair. In 1906 he published The Jungle, a novel set in Chicago's horrific meatpacking district. With graphic detail, it tells the story of Jurgis Rudkus, a Lithuanian immigrant, and his travails in Dunham's, a fictional meatpacking plant. Soon after the book appeared, Congress passed the Meat Inspection Act in an effort to address the abuses cited by Sinclair and others.

From *The Jungle* (1906; New York: Signet, 1960), pp. 100–102.

There was another interesting set of statistics that a person might have gathered in Packingtown—those of the various afflictions of the workers. When Jurgis had first inspected the packing plants . . . he had marveled while he listened to the tale of all the things that were made out of the carcasses of animals, and of all the lesser industries that were maintained there; now he found that each one of these lesser industries was a separate little inferno, in its way as horrible as the killing-beds, the source and fountain of them all. The workers in each of them had their own peculiar diseases. And the wandering visitor might be sceptical about all the swindles, but he could not be sceptical about these, for the worker bore the evidences of them about his own person—generally he had only to hold out his hand.

There were the men in the pickle rooms, for instance, where old Antanas had gotten his death; scarce a one of these that had not some spot of horror on his person. Let a man so much as scrape his finger pushing a truck in the pickle rooms, and he might have a sore that would put him out of the world; all the joints in his fingers would be eaten by the acid one by one. Of the butchers and floorsmen, the beef boners and trimmers, and all those who used knives, you could scarcely find a person who had the use of his thumb; time and time again the base of it had been slashed, till it was a mere lump of flesh against which the man pressed the knife to hold it. The hands of these men would be crisscrossed with cuts, until you could no longer pretend to count them or trace them. They would have no nails,—they had worn them off pulling hides; their knuckles were swollen so that their fingers spread out like a fan. There were men who had worked in the cooking rooms, in the midst of steam and sickening odors, by artificial light; in these rooms the germs of tuberculosis might live for two years, but the supply was renewed every hour. There were the beef luggers, who carried two-hundred-pound quarters into the refrigerator cars, a fearful kind of work, that began at four o'clock in the morning, and that wore out the most powerful men in two years. There were those who worked in the chilling rooms, and whose special disease was rheumatism, the time limit that a man could work in the chilling rooms was said to be five years. There were the wool pluckers, whose hands went to pieces even sooner than the hands of the pickle men; for the pelts of sheep had to be painted with acid to loosen the wool, and then the pluckers had to pull out this wool with their bare hands, till the acid had eaten their fingers off.

There were those who made tile tins for the canned meat, and their hands, too, were a maze of cuts, and each cut represented a chance for blood poisoning. Some worked at the stamping machines, and it was very seldom that one could work long there at the pace that was set, and not give out and forget himself, and have a part of his hand chopped off. There were the "hoisters," as they were called, whose task it was to press the level which lifted the dead cattle off the floor. They ran along upon a rafter, peering down through the damp and the steam, and as old Dunham's architects had not built the killing room for the convenience of the hoisters, at every few feet they would have to stop under a beam, say four feet above the one they ran on, which got them into the habit of stooping, so that in a few years they were walking like chimpanzees. Worst of any, however, were the fertilizer men, and those who served in the cooking rooms. These men could not be shown to the visitor—for the odor of a fertilizer man would scare any ordinary visitor at a hundred yards, and as for the other men, who worked in the tank rooms full of steam, and in some of which there were open vats near the level of the floor, their peculiar trouble was that they fell into the vats; and when they were fished out, there was never enough of them left to be worth exhibiting—sometimes they would be overlooked for days, till all but the bones of them had gone out to the world as Dunham's Pure Beef Lard!

REVIEW QUESTIONS

1. Why would such a description of working conditions prompt calls for regulation?
2. Why did workers have to endure such working conditions?

FROM *Muller v. Oregon* (1908)

Dangerous and unhealthy working conditions prevailed in American industry at the turn of the century, and regulating them became a major concern of progressive reformers. In 1903 the Oregon state legislature passed a law mandating that women employed in laundries could be required to work no more than ten hours a day. It was challenged by conservatives as a violation of the right of contract and an infringement of free enterprise. They cited the Court's ruling in Lochner v. New York *(1905) disallowing a law regulating the hours of bakers. Yet the Supreme Court ruled in favor of the Oregon statute. Evidence presented by attorney Louis Brandeis (who later would become a Supreme Court justice) that documented the sociological and medical effects of long working hours on women proved persuasive to the Court.*

From *Muller v. Oregon*, 208 U.S. 412 (1908).

BREWER, J. . . . The single question is the constitutionality of the statute under which the defendant was convicted so far as affects the work of a female in a laundry. . . .

It is the law of Oregon that women, whether married or single, have equal contractual and personal rights with men. . . .

It thus appears that, putting to one side the elective franchise, in the matter of personal and contractual rights they stand on the same plane as the other sex. Their rights in these respects can no more be infringed than the equal rights of their brothers. We held in *Lochner v. New York*, 198 U.S. 45, that a law providing that no laborer shall be required or permitted to work in a bakery more than sixty hours in a week or ten hours in a day was not as to men a legitimate exercise of the police power of the State, but an unreasonable, unnecessary and arbitrary interference with the right and liberty of the individual to contract in relation to his labor, and as such was in conflict with, and void under, the Federal Constitution. That decision is invoked by plaintiff in error as decisive of the question before us. But this assumes that the difference between the sexes does not justify a different rule respecting a restriction of the hours of labor.

It may not be amiss, in the present case, before examining the constitutional question, to notice the course of legislation as well as expressions of opinion from other than judicial sources. In the brief filed by Mr. Louis D. Brandeis, for the defendant in error is a very copious collection of all these matters. . . .

The legislation and opinions referred to[1] . . . may not be, technically speaking, authorities, and in them is little or no discussion of the constitutional question presented to us for determination, yet they are significant of a widespread belief that woman's physical structure, and the functions she performs in consequence thereof, justify special legislation restricting or qualifying the conditions under which she should be permitted to toil. Constitutional questions, it is true, are not settled by even a consensus of present public opinion, for it is the peculiar value of a written constitution that it places in unchanging form limitations upon legislative action, and thus gives a permanence and stability to popular government which other-wise would be lacking. At the same time, when a question of fact is debated and debatable, and the extent to which a special constitutional limitation goes is affected by the truth in respect to that fact, a widespread and long-continued belief concerning it is worthy of consideration. We take judicial cognizance of all matters of general knowledge . . .

That woman's physical structure and the performance of maternal functions place her at a disadvantage in the struggle for subsistence is obvious. This is especially true when the burdens of motherhood are

upon her. Even when they are not, by abundant testimony of the medical fraternity continuance for a long time on her feet at work, repeating this from day to day, tends to injurious effects upon the body, and as healthy mothers are essential to vigorous offspring, the physical well-being of woman becomes an object of public interest and care in order to preserve the strength and vigor of the race. . . .

Differentiated by these matters from the other sex, she is properly placed in a class by herself, and legislation designed for her protection may be sustained, even when like legislation is not necessary for men and could not be sustained. It is impossible to close one's eyes to the fact that she still looks to her brother and depends upon him. Even though all restrictions on political, personal and contractual rights were taken away, and she stood, so far as statutes are concerned, upon an absolutely equal plane with him, it would still be true that she is so constituted that she will rest upon and look to him for protection; that her physical structure and a proper discharge of her maternal functions—having in view not merely her own health, but the well-being of the race—justify legislation to protect her from the greed as well as the passion of man. The limitations which this statute places upon her contractual powers, upon her right to agree with her employer as to the time she shall labor, are not imposed solely for her benefit, but also largely for the benefit of all. Many words cannot make this plainer. The two sexes differ in structure of body, in the functions to be performed by each, in the amount of physical strength, in the capacity for long-continued labor, particularly when done standing, the influence of vigorous health upon the future well-being of the race, the self-reliance which enables one to assert full rights, and in the capacity to maintain the struggle for subsistence. This difference justifies a difference in legislation and upholds that which is designed to compensate for some of the burdens which rest upon her. . . .

For these reasons, and without questioning in any respect the decision in *Lochner v. New York*, we are of the opinion that it cannot be adjudged that the act in question is in conflict with the federal Constitution, so far as it respects the work of a female in a laundry. . . .

---

[1] I.e., in Brandeis's brief.

REVIEW QUESTIONS

1. According to Justice Brewer, why didn't the decision in *Lochner* invalidate the Oregon statute?
2. What role did women perform that was vital to maintaining the "vigor of the race"? How might harsh working conditions interfere with this role?
3. In the eyes of some feminists how might the Court's opinion that women required special legislation produce negative consequences?

IDA B. WELLS

FROM The Lynch Law in America (1900)

While progressives helped improve the lives of immigrants, convince Congress to provide the vote to women, and establish national parks, they did little to address the surge of racism that welled up at the turn of the century. Throughout the South during the 1890s, state after state passed laws effectively disenfranchising African Americans and instituting statutory segregation of public facilities. The most vicious manifestation of this new racism was the vigilante lynching of blacks accused of various crimes. On average, over one hundred African Americans were lynched each year, most of them in the South. An investigative journalist, Ida Wells, born a slave in 1862, organized in the early twentieth century a national crusade against lynching. Despite her efforts it would be another generation before Congress addressed the issue.

From *Arena* 23 (January 1900): 15–24.

Our country's national crime is *lynching*. It is not the creature of an hour, the sudden outburst of uncontrolled fury, or the unspeakable brutality of an insane mob. It represents the cool, calculating deliberation of an intelligent people who openly avow that there is an "unwritten law" that justifies them in putting to death without complaint under oath, without trial by jury, without opportunity to make defense, without right of appeal. . . .

The alleged menace of universal suffrage having been avoided by the absolute suppression of the negro vote, the spirit of mob murder should have been satisfied and the butchery of negroes should have ceased. But men, women, and children were the victims of murder by individuals and murder by mobs, just as they had been when killed at the demands of the "unwritten law" to prevent "negro domination." Negroes were killed for disputing over terms of contracts with their employers. If a few barns were burned some colored man was killed to stop it. If a colored man resented the imposition of a white man and the two come to blows, the colored man had to die, either at the hands of the white man then and there or later at the hands of the mob that speedily gathered. If he showed a spirit of courageous manhood he was hanged for his pains, and the killing was justified by the declaration that he was a "saucy nigger." Colored women have been murdered because they refused to tell the mobs where relatives could be found for "lynching bees." Boys of fourteen years have been lynched by white representatives of American civilization. In fact, for all kinds of offenses—and for no offenses—from murders to misdemeanors, men and women are put to death without judge or jury; so that, although the political excuse was no longer necessary, the wholesale murder of human beings went on just the same. A new name was given to the killings and a new excuse was invented for doing so.

Again the aid of the "unwritten law" is invoked, and again it comes to the rescue. During the last ten years a new statute has been added to the "unwritten law." This statute proclaims that for certain crimes or alleged crimes no negro shall be allowed a trial; that no white woman shall be compelled to charge an assault under oath or to submit any such charge to the investigation of a court of law. The result is that many men have been put to death whose innocence was afterward established; and today, under the reign of the "unwritten law," no colored man, no matter what his reputation, is safe from lynching if a white woman, no matter what her standing or motive, cares to charge him with insult or assault.

It is considered a sufficient excuse and reasonable justification to put a prisoner to death under this "unwritten law" for the frequently repeated charge that these lynching horrors are necessary to prevent crimes against women. The sentiment of the country has been appealed to, in describing the isolated condition of white families in thickly populated negro districts; and the charge is made that these homes are in as great danger as if they were surrounded by wild beasts. And the world has accepted this theory without let or hindrance. In many cases there has been open expression that the fate meted out to the victim was only what he deserved. In many other instances there has been a silence that says more forcibly than words can proclaim it that it is right and proper that a human being should be seized by a mob and burned to death upon the unsworn and the uncorroborated charge of his accuser. No matter that our laws presume every man innocent until he is proved guilty;

no matter that it encourages those criminally disposed to blacken their faces and commit any crime in the calendar so long as they can throw suspicion on some negro as is frequently done, and then lead a mob to take his life; no matter that mobs make a farce of the law and a mockery of justice; no matter that hundreds of boys are being hardened in crime and schooled in vice by the repetition of such scenes before their eyes—if a white woman declares herself insulted or assaulted, some life must pay the penalty, with all the horrors of the Spanish Inquisition and all the barbarism of the Middle Ages. The world looks on and says it is well.

*   *   *

Quite a number of the one-third alleged cases of assault that have been personally investigated by the writer have shown that there was no foundation in fact for the charges; yet the claim is not made that there were no real culprits among them. The negro has been too long associated with the white man not to have copied his vices as well as his virtues. But the negro resents and utterly repudiates the effort to blacken his good name by asserting that assaults suffered far more from the commission of this crime against the women of his race by white men than the white race has ever suffered through his crimes. Very scant notice is taken of the matter when this is the condition of affairs. What becomes a crime deserving capital punishment when the tables are turned is a matter of small moment when the negro woman is the accusing party. . . .

REVIEW QUESTIONS

1. According to Wells, what rights were denied to accused blacks?
2. What was one of the most common charges leveled against black men? In what way did this reveal a double standard?

BENJAMIN R. TILLMAN

The Use of Violence against Southern Blacks (1900)

During the last quarter of the nineteenth century, southern whites brazenly acceler-ated their efforts to restore all-white rule in the region's social, economic, and politi-cal life. Senator Benjamin R. Tillman, whose nickname was "Pitchfork Ben" (because he once threatened to stick a pitchfork in President Grover Cleveland because of his conservative financial policies) played a leading role in the efforts to disenfranchise blacks and enforce racial segregation. A vocal white supremacist from Edgefield County, South Carolina, Tillman recruited and inspired racist white militias and vigilantes. He served as governor of South Carolina from 1890 to 1894. Elected to the Senate in 1895, he promoted the interests of small farmers and greater regulation of railroads. He also continued to promote white supremacy—by any means necessary. In the following speech to the Senate, Tillman defended the use of violence to intimi-date African Americans.

From "Speech of Senator Benjamin R. Tillman, March 23, 1900," *Congressional Record,* 56th Cong., 1st sess., pp. 3223–24. [Editorial insertions appear in square brackets—*Ed.*]

[I]t can not be denied that the slaves of the South were a superior set of men and women to the freed-men of today, and that the poison in their minds—the race hatred of the whites—is the result of the teachings of Northern fanatics. Ravishing [sexually assaulting] a woman, white or black, was never known to occur in the South till after the Reconstruction era. So much for that phase of the subject. . . .

. . . And he [Senator John C. Spooner of Wis-consin] said we had taken their [blacks'] rights away from them. He asked me was it right to mur-der them in order to carry the elections. I never saw one murdered. I never saw one shot at an election. It was the riots before the elections, precipitated by their own hot-headedness in attempting to hold the government, that brought on conflicts between the races and caused the shotgun to be used. That is what I meant by saying we used the shotgun.

I want to call the Senator's attention to one fact. He said that the Republican Party [during Recon-struction] gave the negroes the ballot in order to pro-tect themselves against the indignities and wrongs that were attempted to be heaped upon them by the enactment of the black code. I say it was because the Republicans of that day, led by [Congressman] Thad Stevens, wanted to put white necks under black heels and to get revenge. There is a difference of opinion. You have your opinion about it, and I have mine, and we can never agree.

I want to ask the Senator this proposition in arithmetic: In my State there were 135,000 negro voters, or negroes of voting age, and some 90,000 or 95,000 white voters. General [Edward] Canby set up a carpetbag government there [after the Civil War] and turned our State over to this [black] major-ity. Now, I want to ask you, with a free vote and a fair count, how are you going to beat 135,000 by 95,000? How are you going to do it? You had set us an impos-sible task. You had handcuffed us and thrown away the key, and you propped your carpetbag negro government with [federal] bayonets. Whenever it was necessary to sustain the [Reconstruction] government you held it up by the Army.

Mr. President, I have not the facts and figures here, but I want the country to get the full view of the [white] Southern side of this question and the justification for anything we did. We were sorry we had the necessity forced upon us, but we could not help it, and as white men we are not sorry for it, and we do not propose to apologize for anything we have done in connection with it. We took the government away from them [blacks] in 1876. We did take it. If no other Senator has come here previous to this time who would acknowledge it, more is the pity. We have had no fraud in our elections in South Carolina since 1884. There has been no organized Republican party in the State.

We did not disfranchise the negroes until 1895. Then we had a constitutional convention convened which took the matter up calmly, deliberately, and avowedly with the purpose of disfranchising as many of them as we could under the fourteenth and fifteenth amendments. We adopted the educational qualification [for voting] as the only means

left to us, and the negro is as contented and as prosperous and as well protected in South Carolina today as in any State of the Union south of the Potomac. He is not meddling with politics, for he found that the more he meddled with them the worse off he got. As to his "rights"—I will not discuss them now. We of the South have never recognized the right of the negro to govern white men, and we never will. We have never believed him to be equal to the white man, and we will not submit to his gratifying his lust on our wives and daughters without lynching him. I would to God the last one of them was in Africa and that none of them had ever been brought to our shores. . . .

REVIEW QUESTIONS

1. What is Tillman's underlying premise for justifying the forceful restoration of all-white rule in South Carolina?
2. How does Tillman justify the benefits of slavery to slaves?

THE NIAGARA MOVEMENT

Declaration of Principles (1905)

The progressive reform impulse at the turn of the century fostered efforts by black activists to promote the interests of African Americans. Dr. W. E. B. Du Bois, the first African American to earn a doctoral degree from Harvard University, emerged as a powerful counter force to the accommodationist stance promoted by Booker T. Washington. Du Bois insisted that African Americans focus on obtaining full political rights and social equality, not simply vocational opportunities. In 1905 Du Bois and twenty-eight other black activists met at Niagara Falls (on the Canadian side because no American hotel would host them), where they drafted a list of political and social demands. The Niagara Movement provided the foundation for the formation of the National Association for the Advancement of Colored People (NAACP) in 1910.

From Joanne Grant, ed., *Black Protest: History, Documents, and Analyses, 1619 to the Present* (New York: Fawcett, 1968), pp. 206–09. [Editorial insertions appear in square brackets—*Ed.*]

Progress: The members of the conference, known as the Niagara Movement . . . congratulate the Negro-Americans on certain undoubted evidences of progress in the last decade, particularly the increase of intelligence, the buying of property, the checking of crime, the uplift in home life, the advance in literature and art, and the demonstration of constructive and executive ability in the conduct of great religious, economic and educational institutions.

Suffrage: At the same time, we believe that this class of American citizens should protest emphatically and continually against the curtailment of their political rights. We believe in manhood suffrage; we believe that no man is so good, intelligent or wealthy as to be entrusted wholly with the welfare of his neighbor.

Civil Liberty: We believe also in protest against the curtailment of our civil rights. All American citizens have the right to equal treatment in places of public entertainment according to their behavior and deserts.

Economic Opportunity: We especially complain against the denial of equal opportunities to us in economic life; in the rural districts of the South this amounts to peonage and virtual slavery; all over the South it tends to crush labor and small business enterprises; and everywhere American prejudice, helped often by iniquitous laws, is making it more difficult for Negro-Americans to earn a decent living.

Education: Common school education should be free to all American children and compulsory. High school training should be adequately provided for all, and college training should be the monopoly of no class or race in any section of our common country. We believe that, in defense of our own institutions, the United States should aid common school education, particularly in the South, and we especially recommend concerted agitation to this end. We urge an increase in public high school facilities in the South, where the Negro-Americans are almost wholly without such provisions. We favor well-equipped trade and technical schools for the training of artisans, and the need of adequate and liberal endowment for a few institutions of higher education must be patent to sincere well-wishers of the race.

Courts: We demand upright judges in courts, juries selected without discrimination on account of color and the same measure of punishment and the same efforts at reformation for black as for white offenders. We need orphanages and farm schools for dependent children, juvenile reformatories for delinquents, and the abolition of the dehumanizing convict-lease system.[1]

Public Opinion: We note with alarm the evident retrogression in this land of sound public opinion on the subject of manhood rights, republican government and human brotherhood, and we pray God that this nation will not degenerate into a mob of boasters and oppressors, but rather will return to the faith of the fathers, that all men were created free and equal, with certain unalienable rights.

Health: We plead for health—for an opportunity to live in decent houses and localities, for a chance to rear our children in physical and moral cleanliness.

Employers and Labor Unions: We hold up for public execration the conduct of two opposite classes of men: The practice among employers of importing ignorant Negro-American laborers in emergencies, and then affording them neither protection nor permanent employment; and the practice of labor unions in proscribing and boycotting and oppressing thousands of their fellow-toilers, simply because they are black. These methods have accentuated and will accentuate the war of labor and capital, and they are disgraceful to both sides.

Protest: We refuse to allow the impression to remain that the Negro-American assents to inferiority, is submissive under oppression and apologetic before insults. Through helplessness we may submit, but the voice of protest of ten million Americans must never cease to assail the ears of their fellows, so long as America is unjust.

Color-Line: Any discrimination based simply on race or color is barbarous, we care not how hallowed it be by custom, expediency or prejudice. Difference made on account of ignorance, immorality, or disease are legitimate methods of fighting evil, and

[1] After the Civil War, southern governments rented convicts, mostly African Americans, to landowners.

against them we have no word of protest; but discriminations based simply and solely on physical peculiarities, place of birth, color of skin, are relics of that unreasoning human savagery of which the world is and ought to be thoroughly ashamed.

"Jim Crow Cars": We protest against the "Jim Crow" [railroad] car, since its effect is and must be to make us pay first-class fare for third-class accommodations, render us open to insults and discomfort and to crucify wantonly our manhood, womanhood and self-respect.

Soldiers: We regret that this nation has never seen fit adequately to reward the black soldiers who, in its five wars, have defended their country with their blood, and yet have been systematically denied the promotions which their abilities deserve. And we regard as unjust, the exclusion of black boys from the military and naval training schools.

War Amendments: We urge upon Congress the enactment of appropriate legislation for securing the proper enforcement of those articles of freedom, the thirteenth, fourteenth and fifteenth amendments of the Constitution of the United States.

Oppression: We repudiate the monstrous doctrine that the oppressor should be the sole authority as to the rights of the oppressed. The Negro race in America stolen, ravished and degraded, struggling up through difficulties and oppression, needs sympathy and receives criticism; needs help and is given hindrance, needs protection and is given mob-violence, needs justice and is given charity; needs leadership and is given cowardice and apology, needs bread and is given a stone. This nation will never stand justified before God until these things are changed.

The Church: Especially are we surprised and astonished at the recent attitude of the church of Christ—of an increase of desire to bow to racial prejudice, to narrow the bounds of human brotherhood, and to segregate black men to some outer sanctuary. This is wrong, unchristian and disgraceful to the twentieth-century civilization.

Agitation: Of the above grievances we do not hesitate to complain, and to complain loudly and insistently. To ignore, overlook, or apologize for these wrongs is to prove ourselves unworthy of freedom. Persistent agitation is the way to liberty, and toward this goal the Niagara Movement has started and asks the cooperation of all men of all races.

Help: At the same time we want to acknowledge with deep thankfulness the help of our fellowmen from the Abolitionist down to those who today still stand for equal opportunity and who have given and still give of their wealth and of their poverty for our advancement.

Duties: And while we are demanding and ought to demand, and will continue to demand the rights enumerated above, God forbid that we should ever forget to urge corresponding duties upon our people:

The duty to vote.
The duty to respect the rights of others.
The duty to obey the laws.
The duty to be clean and orderly.
The duty to send our children to school.
The duty to respect ourselves, even as we respect others.

This statement, complaint and prayer we submit to the American people, and Almighty God.

REVIEW QUESTIONS

1. Summarize the rights that Du Bois demanded for African Americans.
2. Why do you think Du Bois included a list of "duties" for African Americans? What was the significance of each?
3. How might whites have claimed that Du Bois was demanding social as well as political equality?

THEODORE ROOSEVELT

FROM Message to Congress (1901)

Although the Sherman Anti-Trust Act of 1890 ostensibly dealt with the problem of corporate monopolies, in practice it left much to be desired, at least so far as progressives were concerned. Its phrasing was vague. It never defined what a "trust" or "monopoly" involved. And the Supreme Court threw out many of the government's efforts to prosecute trusts under the Sherman Act. When Theodore Roosevelt assumed the presidency in 1901, he recognized that the trust issue remained an acute economic and political problem. In his first message to Congress he distinguished between good and bad trusts, with the good ones led by executives of sterling character who promoted the public interest and the bad ones led by rascals pursuing selfish motives at the expense of consumers.

From First Annual Message to Congress, December 3, 1901, in *The Works of Theodore Roosevelt* (New York: Charles Scribner's Sons, 1926), 15:87–93.

. . . The tremendous and highly complex industrial development which went on with ever accelerated rapidity during the latter half of the nineteenth century brings us face to face, at the beginning of the twentieth, with very serious social problems. The old laws, and the old customs which had almost the binding force of law, were once quite sufficient to regulate the accumulation and distribution of wealth. Since the industrial changes which have so enormously increased the productive power of mankind, they are no longer sufficient.

The growth of cities has gone on beyond comparison faster than the growth of the country, and the upbuilding of the great industrial centers has meant a startling increase, not merely in the aggregate of wealth, but in the number of very large individual, and especially of very large corporate, fortunes. The creation of these great corporate fortunes has not been due to the tariff nor to any other governmental action, but to natural causes in the business world, operating in other countries as they operate in our own.

The process has aroused much antagonism, a great part of which is wholly without warrant. . . .

The captains of industry who have driven the railway systems across this continent, who have built up our commerce, who have developed our manufactures, have on the whole done great good to our people. Without them the material development of which we are so justly proud could never have taken place.

Moreover, we should recognize the immense importance of this material development by leaving as unhampered as is compatible with the public good the strong and forceful men upon whom the success of business operations inevitably rests. The slightest study of business conditions will satisfy any one capable of forming a judgment that the personal equation is the most important factor in a business operation; that the business ability of the man at the head of any business concern, big or little, is usually the factor which fixes the gulf between striking success and hopeless failure.

An additional reason for caution in dealing with corporations is to be found in the international commercial conditions of today. The same business conditions which have produced the great aggregations of corporate and individual wealth have made them very potent factors in international commercial competition. Business concerns which have the largest means at their disposal and are managed by the ablest men are naturally those which take the lead in the strife for commercial supremacy among the nations of the world. America has only just begun to assume that commanding position in the international business world which we believe will more and more be hers. It is of the utmost importance that this position be not jeopardized, especially at a time when the overflowing abundance of our own natural resources and the skill, business energy, and mechanical aptitude of our people make foreign markets essential. Under such conditions it would be most unwise to cramp or to fetter the youthful strength of our nation.

Moreover, it cannot too often be pointed out that to strike with ignorant violence at the interests of one set of men almost inevitably endangers the interests of all. The fundamental rule in our national life—the rule which underlies all others— is that, on the whole, and in the long run, we shall go up or down together.

*　　*　　*

The mechanism of modern business is so delicate that extreme care must be taken not to interfere with it in a spirit of rashness or ignorance. Many of those who have made it their vocation to denounce the great industrial combinations which are popularly, although with technical inaccuracy, known as "trusts," appeal especially to hatred and fear. These are precisely the two emotions, particularly when combined with ignorance, which unfit men for the exercise of cool and steady judgment. In facing new industrial conditions, the whole history of the world shows that legislation will generally be both unwise and ineffective unless undertaken after calm inquiry and with sober self-restraint. . . .

All this is true; and yet it is also true that there are real and grave evils, one of the chief being overcapitalization because of its many baleful consequences; and a resolute and practical effort must be made to correct these evils.

There is a widespread conviction in the minds of the American people that the great corporations known as trusts are in certain of their features and tendencies hurtful to the general welfare. This . . . is based upon sincere conviction that combination and concentration should be, not prohibited, but, supervised and within reasonable limits controlled; and in my judgment this conviction, is right.

It is no limitation upon property rights or freedom of contract to require that when men receive from government the privilege of doing business under corporate form, which frees them from individual responsibility, and enables them to call into their enterprises the capital of the public, they shall do so upon absolutely truthful representations as to the value of the property in which the capital is to be invested.

Corporations engaged in interstate commerce should be regulated if they are found to exercise a license working to the public injury. It should be as much the aim of those who seek for social betterment to rid the business world of crimes of cunning as to rid the entire body politic of crimes of violence. Great corporations exist only because they are created and safeguarded by our institutions; and it is therefore our right and our duty to see that they work in harmony with these institutions.

The first essential in determining how to deal with the great industrial combinations is knowledge of the facts—publicity. In the interest of the public, the government should have the right to inspect and examine the workings of the great corporations engaged in interstate business. Publicity is the only sure remedy which we can now invoke. What further remedies are needed in the way of governmental regulation, or taxation, can only be determined after publicity has been obtained, by process of law, and in the course of administration. The first requisite is knowledge, full and complete— knowledge which may be made public to the world.

*　　*　　*

The large corporations, commonly called trusts, though organized in one State, always do business in many States, often doing very little business in the State where they are incorporated. There is utter lack of uniformity in the State laws about them; and as no State has any exclusive interest in or power over their acts, it has in practice proved impossible to get adequate regulation through State action.

Therefore, in the interest of the whole people, the nation should, without interfering with the power of the States in the matter itself, also assume power of supervision and regulation over all corporations doing an interstate business. This is especially true where the corporation derives a portion of its wealth from the existence of some monopolistic element or tendency in its business. There would be no hardship in such supervision; banks are subject to it, and in their case it is now accepted as a simple matter of course. . . .

When the Constitution was adopted, at the end of the eighteenth century, no human wisdom could foretell the sweeping changes, alike in industrial and political conditions, which were to take place by the beginning of the twentieth century. At that time it was accepted as a matter of course that the several States were the proper authorities to regulate, so far as was then necessary, the comparatively insignificant and strictly localized corporate bodies of the day.

The conditions are now wholly different and wholly different action is called for. I believe that a law can be framed which will enable the National Government to exercise control along the lines above indicated; profiting by the experience gained through the passage and administration of the Interstate Commerce Act. If, however, the judgment of the Congress is that it lacks the constitutional power to pass such an act, then a constitutional amendment should be submitted to confer the power.

REVIEW QUESTIONS

1. According to Roosevelt, were the "captains of industry" contributing to the public good?
2. What specific recommendations did Roosevelt make with respect to corporations?
3. Did Roosevelt's views imply an expansion or reduction of government powers?

WOODROW WILSON

FROM *The New Freedom* (1913)

Unlike Theodore Roosevelt, who distinguished between "good" and "bad" trusts, Democrat Woodrow Wilson believed that all trusts were inherently bad. The federal government, he felt, had the responsibility to dismantle them to restore competition and to allow individual enterprise and small businesses to flourish again. The following selection includes extracts from Wilson's 1912 campaign speeches.

From *The New Freedom* (New York: Doubleday, Page, 1913), pp. 163–91.

I admit the popularity of the theory that the trusts have come about through the natural development of business conditions in the United States, and that it is a mistake to try to oppose the processes by which they have been built up, because those processes belong to the very nature of business in our time, and that therefore the only thing we can do, and the only thing we ought to attempt to do, is to accept them as inevitable arrangements and make the best out of it that we can by regulation.

I answer, nevertheless, that this attitude rests upon a confusion of thought. Big business is no doubt to a large extent necessary and natural. The development of business upon a great scale, upon a great scale of cooperation, is inevitable, and, let me add, is probably desirable. But that is a very different matter from the development of trusts, because the trusts have not grown. They have been artificially created; they have been put together, not by natural processes, but by the will, the deliberate planning will, of men who were more powerful than their neighbors in the business world, and who wished to make their power secure against competition.

*   *   *

Did you ever look into the way a trust was made? It is very natural, in one sense, in the same sense in which human greed is natural. If I haven't efficiency enough to beat my rivals, then the thing I am inclined to do is to get together with my rivals and say: "Don't let's cut each other's throats; let's combine and determine prices for ourselves; determine the output, and thereby determine the prices: and dominate and control the market."

That is very natural. That has been done ever since freebooting was established. That has been done ever since power was used to establish control. The reason that the masters of combination have sought to shut out competition is that the basis of control under competition is brains and efficiency. I admit that any large corporation built up by the legitimate processes of business, by economy, by efficiency, is natural; and I am not afraid of it, no matter how big it grows. It can stay big only by doing its work more thoroughly than anybody else. And there is a point of bigness, as every business man in this country knows, though some of them will not admit it, where you pass the limit of efficiency and get into the region of clumsiness and unwieldiness.

*   *   *

I take my stand absolutely, where every progressive ought to take his stand, on the proposition that private monopoly is indefensible and intolerable. And there I will fight my battle. And I know how to fight

it. . . . What these gentlemen do not want is this: they do not want to be compelled to meet all comers on equal terms. I am perfectly willing that they should beat any competitor by fair means; but I know the foul means they have adopted, and I know that they can be stopped by law. . . .

I have been told by a great many men that the idea I have, that by restoring competition you can restore industrial freedom, is based upon a failure to observe the actual happenings of the last decades in this country; because, they say, it is just free competition that has made it possible for the big to crush the little. I reply, it is not free competition that has done that; it is illicit competition. It is competition of the kind that the law ought to stop, and can stop,—this crushing of the little man.

You know, of course, how the little man is crushed by the trusts. He gets a local market. The big concerns come in and undersell him in his local market, and that is the only market he has; if he cannot make a profit there, he is killed. They can make a profit all through the rest of the Union, while they are underselling him in his locality, and recouping themselves by what they can earn elsewhere. Thus their competitors can be put out of business, one by one, wherever they dare to show a head. Inasmuch as they rise up only one by one, these big concerns can see to it that new competitors never come into the larger field. . . .

But unless you have unlimited capital (which of course you wouldn't have when you were beginning) or unlimited credit (which these gentlemen can see to it that you shan't get), they can kill you out in your local market any time they try. . . .

That is the difference between a big business and a trust. A trust is an arrangement to get rid of competition, and a big business is a business that survived competition by conquering in the field of intelligence and economy. A trust does not bring efficiency to the aid of business; it buys efficiency out of business. I am for big business, and I am against the trusts.

*   *   *

You know that Mr. Roosevelt long ago classified trusts for us as good and bad, and he said that he was afraid only of the bad ones. Now he does not desire that there be any more bad ones, but proposes that they should all be made good by discipline, directly applied by a commission of executive appointment. All he explicitly complains of is a lack of publicity and lack of fairness; not the exercise of power, for throughout that plank the power of the great corporations is accepted as the inevitable consequence of the modern organization of industry.

*   *   *

We are at a parting of the ways. We have, not one or two or three, but many established and formidable monopolies in the United States. We have, not one or two, but many fields of endeavor into which it is difficult, if not impossible, for the independent man to enter. We have restricted credit, we have restricted opportunity, we have controlled development, and we have come to be . . . no longer a government by free opinion . . . but a government by the opinion and duress of small groups of dominant men. . . .

America stands for opportunity. America stands for a free field and no favor. . . . Our purpose is restoration of freedom. We propose to prevent private monopoly by law, to see to it that the methods by which monopolies have been built up are legally made impossible. We design that the limitations on private enterprise shall be removed, so that the next generation of youngsters, as they come along, will not have to become proteges of benevolent trusts, but will be free to go about making their own lives what they will. . . .

REVIEW QUESTIONS

1. Why did Wilson consider "local markets" so important?
2. What did Wilson mean when he said that he was "for big business, and I am against the trusts"?
3. Which social groups would have been most supportive of Wilson's position?

KELLY MILLER

The Risk of Woman Suffrage (1915)

The heroic efforts of women (and men) to convince Congress to provide voting rights to women began to bear fruit in 1915 as a proposed constitutional amendment gained growing support across the United States. It is surprising that many progressive African American proponents of civil rights balked at the idea of allowing women to vote. In 1915 Kelly Miller, a celebrated African American professor and dean at Howard University in Washington, D.C., endorsed longstanding arguments opposing suffrage for women. A South Carolina native, born in 1863, Miller was the sixth of ten children born to Kelly Miller, a free black who served in the Confederate Army during the Civil War. A graduate of Howard University, Miller became the first African American student admitted to the Johns Hopkins University in Baltimore, the nation's first graduate school. Miller was appointed to the faculty of Howard University in 1890, where he taught mathematics and sociology. While a professor at Howard, he also earned a master's degree in mathematics and a law degree. In 1915 he presented his views on women's suffrage in The Crisis, *the journal of the National Association for the Advancement of Colored People (NAACP), which he helped edit.*

From *The Crisis* 11 (November 1915): 37.

The August number of THE CRISIS contained an interesting symposium on woman suffrage. The symposium was unusual, in that it involved only one side of a disputed issue. The contributors represent some of the ablest and most thoughtful names among us. They presented, presumably, the best possible putting of the cause espoused. The public, however, should not be misled to suppose that they represent the general attitude of the colored race on that question. Despite the ardent advocacy and plausible pleas of the propagandists, I am wholly unable to see wherein the experiment of woman suffrage promises any genuine advantage to social well-being.

The human race is divided horizontally by age, vertically by sex and diagonally by race. Each individual passes from the minor to the adult stage in course of a life time; the cleavage of race is subject to indefinite modification through environment and intermingling of blood; but sex is the one fixed and unalterable separatrix of mankind. The function of sex in human economy is clearly defined and well understood. The bearing and rearing of the young constitute the chief duty and responsibility of the female, and this task absorbs her highest energies during the most energetic period of her life. The family constitutes the fundamental social unit. Woman's sphere of activity falls mainly within while man's field of action lies largely without the domestic circle. This represents the traditional and, presumably, the ideal relation between the sexes. It has the sanction of divine authority and the test of human experience. Woman suffrage could not possibly enhance the harmoniousness of this relationship, but might seriously jeopardize it.

Woman is physically weaker than man and is incapable of competing with him in the stern and strenuous activities of public and practical life. In the final analysis, politics is a game of force, in which no weakling may expect to be assigned a conspicuous role.

As part of her equipment for motherhood, woman has been endowed with finer feelings and a more highly emotional nature than man. She shows tender devotion and self sacrifice for those close to her by ties of blood or bonds of endearment. But by the universal law of compensation, she loses in extension what is gained in intensity. She lacks the sharp sense of public justice and the common good, if they seem to run counter to her personal feeling and interest. She is far superior to man in purely personal and private virtue, but is his inferior in public qualities and character. Suffrage is not a natural right, like life and liberty. The common sense of mankind has always limited it by age, sex, possession, attainment and moral character. It is merely a convenient agency through which to secure the best result of government, and to make secure life, liberty and happiness to all. It cannot be maintained that woman is deprived of any of these objects under male suffrage. It is inconceivable that man would legislate against his wife and daughter, who are dearer to him than life itself, and who, he knows, must fall back upon his strong arm for protection, whether they be given the suffrage or not.

The historical hardships and legal disabilities against which women complain so bitterly were incidental imperfections of social development. Most of these have already been swept away, as all of them are bound to be, by man's growing sense of justice and fair play.

Female suffrage has been tried in twelve states of the Union, but so far no genuine public benefit has resulted therefrom, nor has the lot of woman been ameliorated more rapidly than in other states under exclusive male suffrage.

There may be some argument for suffrage for unfortunate females, such as widows and hopeless spinsters, but such status is not contemplated as a normal social relation.

Women as voters would undoubtedly stand against the purely masculine vices such as drunkenness and the social evil, but they can be equally or even more efficacious through non-political influence.

The logical sequence of suffrage is office-holding. Female suffrage will never reach its full fruition until fully one-half of all public offices, legislative, judicial and executive, local and national, are filled by women. Is the public mind ready for this risky innovation?

It is alleged that Negro suffrage and woman suffrage rest on the same basis. But on close analysis it is found that there is scarcely any common ground between them. The female sex does not form a class separate and distinct from the male sex in the sense that the Negro forms a class separate and distinct from the whites. Experience and reason both alike show that no race is good enough to govern another without that other's consent. On the other hand both experience and reason demonstrate that the male seeks the welfare and happiness of the female even above his own interest. The Negro can not get justice or fair treatment without the suffrage. Woman can make no such claim, for man accords her not only every privilege which he himself enjoys but the additional privilege of protection.

The fundamental defect in the propaganda of woman suffrage consists in the fact that instead of confining its effort to the improvement of woman's lot along the line of her obvious sphere and function in the social scheme, it insists upon her privilege and opportunities being artificially identical with those of man. It is amusing to note that women are to be allowed to vote at twenty-one merely because men are accorded the privilege at that age; whereas according to their physical and mental developments, the sexes have a different order of maturity. If the strictly physiological and psychological basis of male suffrage is placed at twenty-one, female suffrage should be placed at eighteen. If man should be allowed to vote on the first appearance of a mustache, some woman would doubtless demand the same privilege.

Male and female created He them; what God has made different man strives in vain to make identical.

REVIEW QUESTIONS

1. Why does Miller insist that allowing women to vote would be unnatural and injurious?
2. In what way could many of Miller's arguments against women voting also be used against providing African Americans with equal rights?

W. E. B. DU BOIS

Woman Suffrage (1915)

William Edward Burghardt "W. E. B." Du Bois was the most prominent African American activist in the first half of the twentieth century. Born in 1868 in western Massachusetts, he graduated from Harvard and became a professor at Atlanta University. A prolific author, he also served as the influential editor of the NAACP's The

Crisis, a quarterly journal focused on civil rights, history, politics, and culture. In 1915 he denounced an article in The Crisis *by Kelly Miller opposing the granting of the vote to women. During his long tenure as the editor of* The Crisis, *Du Bois wrote over twenty essays advocating women's suffrage.*

From *The Crisis,* November 1915.

This month 200,000 Negro voters will be called upon to vote on the question of giving the right of suffrage to women. THE CRISIS sincerely trusts that everyone of them will vote Yes. But THE CRISIS would not have them go to the polls without having considered every side of the question. Intelligence in voting is the only real support of democracy. For this reason we publish with pleasure Dean Kelly Miller's article against woman suffrage. We trust that our readers will give it careful attention and that they will compare it with that marvelous symposium which we had the pleasure to publish in our August number. Meantime, Dean Miller will pardon us for a word in answer to his argument.

Briefly put, Mr. Miller believes that the bearing and rearing of the young is a function which makes it practically impossible for women to take any large part in general, industrial and public affairs; that women are weaker than men; that women are adequately protected under man's suffrage; that no adequate results have appeared from woman suffrage and that office-holding by women is "risky."

All these arguments sound today ancient. If we turn to easily available statistics we find that instead of the women of this country or of any other country being confined chiefly to childbearing they are as a matter of fact engaged and engaged successfully in practically every pursuit in which men are engaged. The actual work of the world today depends more largely upon women than upon men. Consequently this man-ruled world faces an astonishing dilemma: either Woman the Worker is doing the world's work successfully or not. If she is not doing it well why do we not take from her the necessity of working? If she is doing it well why not treat her as a worker with a voice in the direction of work?

The statement that woman is weaker than man is sheer rot: It is the same sort of thing that we hear about "darker races" and "lower classes." Difference, either physical or spiritual, does not argue weakness or inferiority. That the average woman is spiritually different from the average man is undoubtedly just as true as the fact that the average white man differs from the average Negro; but this is no reason for disfranchising the Negro or lynching him. It is inconceivable that any person looking upon the accomplishments of women today in every field of endeavor, realizing their humiliating handicap and the astonishing prejudices which they face and yet seeing despite this that in government in the professions, in sciences, art and literature and the industries they are leading and dominating forces and growing in power as their emancipation grows,—it is inconceivable that any fair-minded person could for a moment talk about a "weaker sex." The sex of Judith, Candace, Queen Elizabeth, Sojourner Truth and Jane Addams was the merest incident of human function and not a mark of weakness and inferiority.

To say that men protect women with their votes is to overlook the flat testimony of the facts. In the first place there are millions of women who have no natural men protectors: the unmarried, the widowed, the deserted and those who have married failures. To put this whole army incontinently out of court and leave them unprotected and without voice in political life is more than unjust, it is a crime.

There was a day in the world when it was considered that by marriage a woman lost all her individuality as a human soul and simply became a machine for making men. We have outgrown that idea. A woman is just as much a thinking, feeling, acting person after marriage as before. She has opinions and she has a right to have them and she has a right to express them. It is conceivable, of course, for a country to decide that its unit of representation should be the family and that one person in that family should express its will. But by what possible process of rational thought can it be decided that the person to express that will should always be the male, whether he be genius or drunkard, imbecile or captain of industry? The meaning of the twentieth century is the freeing of the individual soul; the soul longest in slavery and still in the most disgusting and indefensible slavery is the soul of womanhood. God give her increased freedom this November!

Mr. Miller is right in saying that the results from woman suffrage have as yet been small but the answer is obvious: the experiment has been small. As for the risks of allowing women to hold office: Are they nearly as great as the risks of allowing working men to hold office loomed once in the eyes of the Intelligent Fearful?

REVIEW QUESTIONS

1. How convincing are Du Bois's arguments in favor of women's suffrage?
2. How did Du Bois compare the rationale for denying women the vote with similar arguments supporting racial prejudice?

INTERPRETING VISUAL SOURCES: PHOTOGRAPHY AND PROGRESSIVE REFORM

JACOB RIIS

Progressive reformers eager to improve the living and working conditions of the urban poor found a powerful weapon in the new medium of documentary photography. Like the muckraking writers who exposed political corruption and corporate excesses, talented journalists began to use cameras to shed light on the miseries of contemporary social life. Photographs not only served as witnesses to reality but also served as weapons of reform. Compelling visual evidence of the wretchedness of life in the city tenements and of the exploitation of children and adult poor in the workplace captured the attention of the public and helped provoke remedial legislation.

The pioneer of documentary journalism was Jacob Riis (pronounced Reese), a Danish immigrant turned reporter and reformer who used photojournalism to excite public concern for the hidden poor. His book, How the Other Half Lives, *remains a classic example of documentary photography, and his career epitomizes the fact-worshiping approach of progressive reform. "Ours is an age of facts," Riis once insisted. "It wants facts, not theories, and facts I have endeavored to put down on these pages."*

Soon after arriving in the United States from Denmark in 1870, Riis found himself jobless and homeless. He wandered the streets of Manhattan, sleeping in police station lodging houses and rummaging for scraps outside restaurants. Filthy and unkempt, he "was too shabby to get work, even if there had been any to get." Riis finally made his way to Philadelphia, where the Danish consul helped him find work as a lumberjack, hunter, and trapper in upstate New York. But his "desire to roam" kept him moving, and in 1877 he became a reporter for the New York Tribune.

As a journalist Riis developed a passion for human interest stories drawn from the back alleys and tenements of Manhattan's congested Lower East Side. There he saw throngs of poor Irish, Italians, Bohemians, African Americans, and Jews crammed into unsanitary hovels that bred disease, ignorance, and crime. His own encounters with the pinch of poverty and the sting of discrimination seasoned his observations and ignited his fervor for reform. Convinced that a bad environment was the primary cause of poverty, Riis began writing graphic exposés of the miserable conditions in the slums. "The power of fact," he decided, "is the mightiest lever of this or of any day."

Yet merely printing the "facts" about urban squalor failed to arouse much public outcry. "I wrote, but it seemed to make no impression," Riis recalled in his autobiography. To heighten the impact of his written testimony, he began to use photographs of crowded streets, decrepit tenements, and poorly clothed slum dwellers. The camera, he realized, had a special evidentiary power to lay bare hidden truths, and few facts were as visually compelling as poverty.

In 1887 Riis and his colleagues began taking photographs to accompany his articles, and their exhausting efforts provided the first graphic images of the seamy underside of New York life. They lugged around cumbersome cameras on tripods and used flash-lit photography—a dangerous new process requiring a pistol lamp that fired magnesium flash-powder cartridges with a flaming bang. "Twice I set fire to the house with my apparatus," Riis admitted, "and once to myself."

Through such explosive illumination, Riis literally brought light into some of the darkest corners of American society. His intriguing pictures of tenement life helped people see that poverty was not simply an evil to be condemned as it was a condition to be remedied. Eager to go beyond mere reportage and to promote concrete reforms, Riis began giving slide lectures to church and civic groups throughout the city and across the nation. "Neighbors," he would say at the end of his presentation, go out and "find your neighbors." Many found this a compelling challenge. A midwestern journalist reported that to those of "us who are unfamiliar with life in a large city," Riis's slide presentation "was a revelation." His photographs "were certainly more realistic than any words could be."

Riis's graphic account of bitter poverty so impressed the editor of Scribner's Monthly that he invited Riis to write an illustrated article for the popular middle-class magazine. "How the Other Half Lives" appeared in the Christmas 1889 issue accompanied by nineteen photographs transformed into line drawings. The article described sordid tenements "nurtured in the greed and avarice" of rapacious slumlords, disease-ridden ghettos where people were shoehorned into windowless warrens. In one thirteen-square-foot Bayard Street room, Riis found twelve male and female lodgers. Another two-room apartment on Essex Street hosted a family of fourteen plus six boarders.

Riis's shocking revelations excited so much interest that he agreed to expand his article into a book. Published in 1890, How the Other Half Lives: Studies among the Tenements of New York created an immediate sensation and went *through eleven editions in the next five years. "No book of the year," proclaimed the* Dial, *"has aroused a deeper interest or wider discussion than Mr. Riis's earnest study of the poor and outcast." In spirited prose, Riis detailed the crowded life of the "unventilated and fever-breeding" tenements, the ravages of disease and alcohol, the tragedy of homeless street urchins, the violence of "gangs," the sound of tubercular coughs, the oppressive atmosphere of sweatshops, and the "queer, conglomerate mass of heterogeneous elements" forming New York's diverse ethnic tapestry.*

Forty-three illustrations and fifteen halftone reproductions authenticated Riis's narrative. Riis, however, refused to let his pictures speak for themselves. He combined preaching prose with his photographs. "What then are the bald facts with which we have to deal in New York?" he asked. "That we have a tremendous, even swelling crowd of wage-earners which it is our business to house decently. . . . This is the fact from which we cannot get away, however we deplore it." Riis offered neither easy solutions nor the salve of consolation to bruised consciences. "We know now," he wrote, "that there is no way out; that the 'system' that was the awful offspring of public neglect and private greed has come to stay, a storm center forever of our civilization. Nothing is left but to make the best of a bad bargain." His own plan of action called for rigorous enforcement of building codes and the construction of new, sanitary, well-ventilated, and affordable housing, more city parks, and better playgrounds. Riis goaded the hesitant: "What are you going to do about it?" Some readers were moved to take action. Theodore Roosevelt, then serving as president of the board of New York City's police commissioners, visited Riis's office and left a note: "I have read your book, and I have come to help."

Riis rarely asked people for permission to enter their hovels and take their pictures. Many of the destitute and powerless resented the uninvited efforts of Riis's "raiding party," however noble their intentions. Some people pelted Riis and his associates with rocks, others fled their hovels or demanded to be paid for their cooperation. Such reactions reveal again the fine line separating well-intentioned reform from intrusive manipulation.

Despite the intrusive nature of his methods, the crusading Riis revealed to Americans how much of their contemporary social reality had been overlooked. From his pictures, he asserted, "there was no appeal." The poor of the inner city "compelled recognition." They were "dangerous less because of their own crimes than because of the criminal ignorance of those who are not of their kind." Riis's photographs revealed more than the degradations of slum life; they illuminated the dark side of the American Dream, and in the process they startled many into a keener sense of social responsibility. The muckraking journalist and novelist Ernest Poole remembered how "hungrily" he read How the Other Half Lives *because it revealed to him "a tremendous new field, scarcely touched by American writers."*

Five Cents a Spot

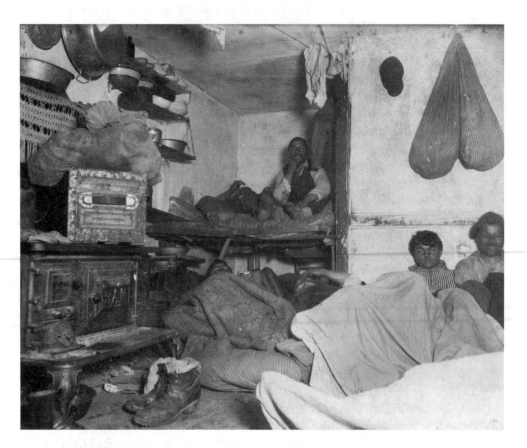

FIVE CENTS A SPOT
Paul Fearn/Alamy Stock Photo

A typical example of Riis's photographic technique is Lodgers in a Crowded Bayard Street Tenement: Five Cents a Spot. *It exposes a catacomb-like room, only thirteen square feet, clogged with twelve immigrant "lodgers" and their motley possessions. Awakened by Riis at midnight in their wretched roost, the bleary-eyed tenants stare at the camera in the midst of pots, pans, boots, caps, clothes, trunks, duffel bags, and firewood. The precise details of such a mundane scene heighten its emphatic immediacy, but its strength derives from its stark contrast with the norms of middle-class domesticity. The room's filth and claustrophobia pricked the consciences of well-to-do suburbanites preoccupied with clean homes and wholesome families.*

A Black-and-Tan Dive

A Black-and-Tan Dive
FAY 2018/Alamy Stock Photo

Riis revealed the ethical ambiguities embedded in his brand of documentary photography in A Black-and-Tan Dive, *a photograph of two white women and a black man in a darkened cellar saloon where a fastidious Riis witnessed the "commingling of the utterly depraved of both sexes." The sudden flash of illumination invades the secret sanctuary and catches the patrons off guard. Seated on a keg, the black man betrays both surprise and perhaps anger. The white woman on his left, face smudged with grime, looks down with a visage suggesting sullen resentment or embarrassment. The hand of another black man (off camera) rests on her shoulder, providing a controversial nuance in an age when racial mixing was deemed an abomination. Most striking is the third figure, a woman with her back turned to the camera and a shawl draped over her head in a spontaneous effort to shield her eyes from the glare and protect her privacy from the invasive lens. The photograph gave Riis's middle-class audience voyeuristic access into an alluring world of sensual gratification and forbidden behavior.*

Dens of Death

DENS OF DEATH
FAY 2018/Alamy Stock Photo

The relentless stream of immigrants arriving in New York City prompted landowners to erect ramshackle shanties. They were often built so hastily and carelessly that they soon collapsed. In this picture of immigrant housing on Baxter Street, Riis revealed how crowded and unsafe the living quarters were. He also learned that a chronic foul odor in the neighborhood prompted a visit from a sanitary inspector. Upon investigation he discovered that the sewage pipe from the buildings was not connected to the sewer drain. It simply poured its contents directly into the ground under the buildings.

Police Station Lodger

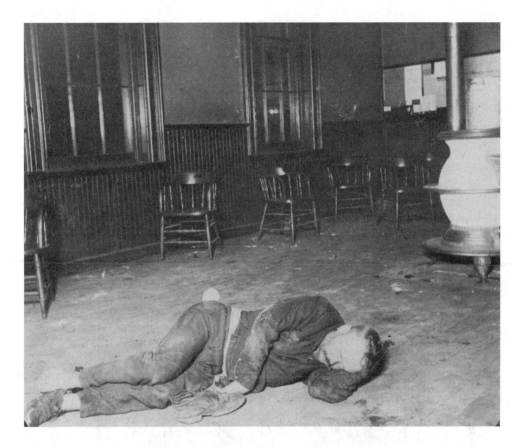

POLICE STATION LODGER
FAY 2018/Alamy Stock Photo

In the late nineteenth century the homeless had few options in dealing with difficult circumstances. During the winter months, police stations allowed people to come in at night and sleep on the floor. This photograph shows a vagrant suffering from typhus, lying on the bare floor near the stove for warmth. Sockless and sick, he offered poignant testimony to the plight of the downtrodden.

Tenement Yard

TENEMENT YARD
FAY 2018/Alamy Stock Photo

Riis was particularly concerned about the fate of children consigned to life in the congested tenements. Here he encountered a group of urchins forced to play in a confined space. "There was about as much light in this 'yard,'" he observed, "as in the average cellar." He counted 128 children living among the forty families in the building.

In a Sweatshop

Child labor was one of the chief targets of progressive reformers. Riis visited numerous sweatshops in New York, where he witnessed children as young as six years old working ten to twelve hours each day. They were given no time off for meals; they kept working while eating. In this photograph of an East Side sweatshop, he shows a boy at work pulling threads. The state law in New York said that children under sixteen could not be employed unless they could read and write English; and none could be employed under fourteen. Riis found that this boy had a certificate claiming he was sixteen, but he confessed to being only twelve.

SECTION REVIEW QUESTIONS

1. Why might photographs have been a more powerful medium for social documentary than sketches or drawings?

2. Was Riis practicing a form of "yellow journalism"? Why or why not?

3. Taken as a whole, what do these photographs suggest about urban growth during this period?

4. What is your reaction to the fact that Riis frequently "staged" his photographs, positioning people and their possessions for dramatic effect?

22   AMERICA AND THE GREAT WAR, 1914–1920

President Woodrow Wilson and Secretary of State William J. Bryan were diplomatic idealists who hoped that international tensions could always be settled peaceably. To this end they negotiated "cooling off" treaties with thirty nations, whereby disputes between two countries would be handed over to an international arbitration commission. However logical such agreements might have seemed in theory, they ignored the fact that international disputes often involved emotional issues and self-interests that were nonnegotiable.

Nowhere was this truer than in Europe. There the great powers during the late nineteenth century had divided themselves into two large interlocking military alliances. Germany, Austria-Hungary, and Italy formed the Triple Alliance, and Britain, France, and Russia formed the Triple Entente. Intended to maintain a rough balance of power, these alliances also ensured that when conflict erupted it would rapidly escalate into a major war. In 1914 the unthinkable occurred when a Serbian nationalist assassinated Archduke Franz Ferdinand, heir to the Austro-Hungarian Empire. The archduke and his wife were gunned down in Sarajevo, the capital of Bosnia in the Balkans. The Austrians resolved to punish the Serbs for the killings, triggering Russia to mobilize its army in defense of Serbia's large population of Slavs. Germany rushed to support Austria-Hungary, preemptively declaring war on Russia and France. When Germany invaded Belgium (thereby violating its neutrality) in order to attack France, the British declared war on Germany. The Great War had begun.

Americans were stunned by the sudden outbreak of European war, but were quickly reassured by the beliefs—mistaken, as it turned out—that the United States had no vital interests at stake in the conflict and that the Atlantic Ocean would insulate America from the conflagration. But it soon became obvious that Americans could not long remain neutral or uninvolved in an expanding world war. By virtue of their own ethnic background, political ideals, and economic interests, most Americans supported the Allies (as Britain, France, and Russia became known). Wilson, as it turns out, also sought to support the Allies behind the scenes while calling publicly for neutrality. By insisting on the American right to maintain trade with the belligerent nations, he was in effect aiding the Allies, for they received the vast majority of supplies.

Germany sought to cut off the pipeline of American shipments to Great Britain. In 1915 the German navy unleashed its submarines against transatlantic shipping and announced a blockade of the British Isles. Wilson warned the German government that he would hold them to "strict accountability" if any American lives were lost. The sinking of the huge British passenger liner Lusitania *in May 1915 killed nearly 1200 people, including over 100 Americans. The loss of the* Lusitania *horrified Americans. Some commentators called for a declaration of war. Wilson instead sent strident protests to the German government, demanding payment for the lost lives and a pledge not to sink passenger vessels. The Germans agreed and tensions eased. But Wilson predicted that the fragile peace would not last. As he confided to an aide in 1916, "I can't keep the country out of war. . . . Any little German lieutenant [submarine commander] can put us into war at any time by some calculated outrage."*

On January 31, 1917, the Germans announced the renewal of unrestricted submarine attacks on Atlantic shipping. A few days later the United States broke off diplomatic relations with Germany. Soon thereafter, on March 1, an intercepted telegram from the German foreign secretary, Arthur Zimmermann, to the German ambassador in Mexico inflamed public opinion in the United States. The Zimmermann telegram promised Mexico the restoration of Texas, New Mexico, and Arizona if Mexico supported Germany in a war against the United States.

More immediately, however, American officials in early 1917 were preoccupied with the escalating number of ships sunk by German submarines. Between March 12 and 21, five American ships were lost. This was the last straw. On April 2, Wilson asked Congress to declare war. The war resolution swept through the Senate by a vote of 82 to 6 and the House by 373 to 50.

No sooner had the United States officially entered the war than President Wilson began to turn the conflict into a crusade—not only to transform the nature of international relations but also to create a permanent peace. On January 8, 1918, in part to counter the Bolshevik claim that the Allies were fighting for imperialist aims, Wilson announced his Fourteen Point peace plan outlining allied intentions.

By the end of 1918 the war was winding down. American intervention proved decisive in turning the tide against the Germans and their allies. In December Wilson made the controversial decision to join the peace conference convening in Paris. This proved to be a political disaster because the Republican-controlled Senate felt that President Wilson was purposely ignoring its historic role in shaping foreign policy. When Wilson presented the peace plan—with its controversial provision for a League of Nations to police world affairs—to the American public, it aroused intense debate. Critics led by powerful Republican senator Henry Cabot Lodge balked at American participation in the League, arguing that it would transfer war-making authority to an outside body.

Wilson struggled to win passage of the Versailles Treaty. Worn down by a public speaking tour intended to arouse public support for the treaty, the crusading president suffered a stroke in the summer of 1919 that left him bedridden for months. Wilson's absence proved fatal to his hopes to gain Senate support. After much maneuvering and many votes, the Senate refused to ratify the Versailles Treaty in March 1920.

American involvement in the so-called Great War signaled the arrival of the United States on the center stage of world affairs. Yet in the immediate aftermath of the war, most Americans returned to their earlier stance of isolation from the turmoil of international events. Little did they know that the United States was more intertwined than ever in the fate of other nations.

The Zimmermann Telegram (1917)

One of the incidents inflaming American public opinion against Germany was the disclosure of the so-called Zimmermann telegram. It was in fact a secret message sent in January 1917 from the German foreign secretary, Arthur Zimmermann, to the German ambassador in Mexico. British intelligence officers intercepted the message and excitedly informed the United States of its provocative contents.

From James B. Scott, ed., *Diplomatic Correspondence between the United States and Germany, August 1, 1914–April 6, 1917* (New York: Oxford University Press, 1918), p. 338.

Berlin, January 19, 1917

On the first of February we intend to begin submarine warfare unrestricted. In spite of this it is our intention to keep neutral the United States of America.

If this attempt is not successful we propose an alliance on the following basis with Mexico: That we shall make war together and together make peace. We shall give general financial support, and it is understood that Mexico is to reconquer the lost territory in New Mexico, Texas, and Arizona. The details are left for your settlement.

You are instructed to inform the President of Mexico of the above in the greatest confidence as soon as it is certain there will be an outbreak of war with the United States, and we suggest that the President of Mexico on his own initiative should communicate with Japan suggesting adherence at once to this plan; at the same time offer to mediate between Germany and Japan.

Please call to the attention of the President of Mexico that the employment of ruthless submarine warfare now promises to compel England to make peace in a few months.

Zimmermann

REVIEW QUESTIONS

1. What in this message would have most angered Americans? Why?
2. What did the Germans believe that unrestricted submarine warfare would cause the British to do?
3. If you were a newspaper editor in 1917, what headline would you choose for the discovery of the Zimmermann telegram?

WOODROW WILSON

FROM Declaration of War against Germany (1917)

On April 2, 1917, President Wilson spoke to a joint session of Congress and summarized his two-year effort to maintain American neutrality in the face of the German submarine campaign. He called for a war not only to punish the Germans and reaffirm neutral rights but also to make the world "safe for democracy." In this sense he viewed the war as a "great crusade" to establish legal and moral principles for all nations to follow.

From "Address by the President of the United States," *Congressional Record*, 65th Cong., 1st sess., 1917, 55:102–04.

I have called the Congress into extraordinary session because there are serious, very serious, choices of policy to be made, and made immediately, which it was neither right nor constitutionally permissible that I should assume the responsibility of making.

On the third of February last I officially laid before you the extraordinary announcement of the Imperial German Government that on and after the first day of February it was its purpose to put aside all restraints of law or of humanity and use its submarines to sink every vessel that sought to approach either the ports of Great Britain and Ireland or the western coasts of Europe or any of the ports controlled by the enemies of Germany within the Mediterranean. . . .

I was for a little while unable to believe that such things would in fact be done by any government that had hitherto subscribed to the humane practices of civilized nations. International law had its origin in the attempt to set up some law which would be respected and observed upon the seas, where no nation had right of dominion and where lay the free highways of the world. . . .

This minimum of right the German Government has swept aside under the plea of retaliation and necessity and because it had no weapons which it could use at sea except these which it is impossible to employ as it is employing them without throwing to the winds all scruples of humanity or of respect for the understandings that were supposed to underlie the intercourse of the world.

I am not now thinking of the loss of property involved, immense and serious as that is, but only of the wanton and wholesale destruction of the lives of non-combatants, men, women, and children, engaged in pursuits which have always, even in the darkest periods of modern history, been deemed innocent and legitimate. Property can be paid for; the lives of peaceful and innocent people cannot be.

The present German submarine warfare against commerce is a warfare against mankind.

It is a war against all nations. American ships have been sunk, American lives taken, in ways which it has stirred us very deeply to learn of, but the ships and people of other neutral and friendly nations have been sunk and overwhelmed in the waters in the same way. There has been no discrimination. The challenge is to all mankind. Each nation must decide for itself how it will meet it. The choice we make for ourselves must be made with a moderation of counsel and a temperateness of judgment befitting our character and our motives as a nation. We must put excited feeling away. Our motive will not be revenge or the victorious assertion of the physical might of the nation, but only the vindication of right, of human right, of which we are only a single champion. . . .

With a profound sense of the solemn and even tragic character of the step I am taking and of the grave responsibilities which it involves, but in unhesitating obedience to what I deem my constitutional duty, I advise that the Congress declare the recent course of the Imperial German Government to be in fact nothing less than war against the government and people of the Unites States; that it formally accept the status of belligerent which has thus been thrust upon it; and that it take immediately steps not only to put the country in a more thorough state of defense but also to exert all its power and employ all its resources to bring the Government of the German Empire to terms and end the war. . . .

We have no quarrel with the German people. We have no feeling towards them but one of sympathy and friendship. It was not upon their impulse that their government acted in entering this war. It was not with their previous knowledge or approval. It was a war determined upon as wars used to be determined upon in the old, unhappy days when peoples were nowhere consulted by their rulers and wars were provoked and waged in the interest of dynasties or of little groups of ambitious men who were accustomed to use their fellow men as pawns and tools. . . .

The world must be made safe for democracy. Its peace must be planted upon the tested foundations of political liberty. We have no selfish ends to serve. We desire no conquest no dominion. We seek no indemnities for ourselves, no material compensation for the sacrifices we shall freely make. We are but one of the champions of the rights of mankind. We shall be satisfied when those rights have been made as secure as the faith and the freedom of nations can make them. . . .

Just because we fight without rancor and without selfish object, seeking nothing for ourselves but what we shall wish to share with all free peoples, we shall, I feel confident, conduct our operations as belligerents without passion and ourselves observe with proud punctilio[1] the principles of right and of fair play we profess to be fighting for.

We enter this war only where we are clearly forced into it because there are no other means of defending our rights. It will be all the easier for us to conduct ourselves as belligerents in a high spirit of right and fairness because we act without animus, not in enmity towards a people or with the desire to bring any injury or disadvantage upon them, but only in armed opposition to an irresponsible government which has thrown aside all considerations of humanity and of right and is running amuck.

We are, let me say again, the sincere friends of the German people, and shall desire nothing so much as the early reestablishment of intimate relations of mutual advantage between us,—however hard it may be for them, for the time being, to believe that this is spoken from our hearts. We have borne with their present Government through all these bitter months because of that friendship,—exercising a patience and forbearance which would otherwise have been impossible.

We shall, happily, still have an opportunity to prove that friendship in our daily attitude and actions towards the millions of men and women of German birth and native sympathy who live amongst us and share our life, and we shall be proud to prove it towards all who are in fact loyal to their neighbors and to the Government in the hour of test. They are, most of them, as true and loyal Americans as if they had never known any other fealty or allegiance. They will be prompt to stand with us in rebuking and restraining the few who may be of a different mind and purpose. If there should be disloyalty, it will be dealt with a firm hand of stern repression; but, if it lifts its head at all, it will lift it only here and there and without countenance except from a lawless and malignant few.

It is a distressing and oppressive duty, Gentlemen of the Congress, which I have performed in thus addressing you. There are, it may be, many months of fiery trial and sacrifice ahead of us. It is a fearful thing to lead this great peaceful people into war, into the most terrible and disastrous of all wars, civilization itself seeming to be in the balance.

But the right is more precious than peace, and we shall fight for the things which we have always carried nearest our hearts,—for democracy, for the right of those who submit to authority to have a voice in their own Governments, for the rights and liberties of small nations, for a universal dominion of right by such a concert of free peoples as shall bring peace and safety to all nations and make the world itself at last free.

To such a task we can dedicate our lives and our fortunes, everything that we are and everything that we have, with the pride of those who know that the day has come when America is privileged to spend her blood and her might for the principles that gave her birth and happiness and the peace which she has treasured. God helping her, she can do no other.

REVIEW QUESTIONS

1. What did Wilson mean when he claimed, "We have no quarrel with the German people"?
2. How did Wilson deal with the topic of German Americans?
3. Were Wilson's ultimate war goals realistic? Explain.

---

[1]A scrupulous adherence to laws or rules.

GEORGE WILLIAM NORRIS

Opposing U.S. Entry into World War I (1917)

Senator George William Norris (1861–1944), a progressive Republican from Nebraska, was one of the most outspoken critics of President Woodrow Wilson's call for a declaration of war against Germany in the spring of 1917. In the following speech to the Senate, he charged that self-interested financiers and industrialists were pushing for war.

From *Congressional Record*, 65th Cong., 1st Sess., Vol. LV, pt. I April 4, 1917, pp. 212–13. [Editorial insertion appears in square brackets—*Ed.*]

. . . The resolution now before the Senate is a declaration of war. Before taking this momentous step, and while standing on the brink of this terrible vortex, we ought to pause and calmly and judiciously consider the terrible consequences of the step we are about to take.

We ought to consider likewise the route we have recently traveled and ascertain whether we have reached our present position in a way that is compatible with the neutral position which we claimed to occupy at beginning and through the various stages of this unholy and unrighteous war. No close student of recent history will deny that both Great Britain and Germany have, on numerous occasions since the beginning of the war, flagrantly violated in the most serious manner the rights of neutral vessels and neutral nations under existing international law as recognized up to the beginning of this war by the civilized world.

The reason given by the President [Woodrow Wilson] in asking Congress to declare war against Germany is that the German government has declared certain war zones, within which, by the use of submarines, she sinks, without notice, American ships and destroys American lives. . . . The first war zone was declared by Great Britain. She gave us and the world notice of it on, the 4th day of November, 1914. The zone became effective Nov. 5, 1914. . . . This zone so declared by Great Britain covered the whole of the North Sea. . . .

The first German war zone was declared on the 4th day of February, 1915, just three months after the British war zone was declared. Germany gave fifteen days' notice of the establishment of her zone, which became effective on the 18th day of February, 1915. The German war zone covered the English Channel and the high seawaters around the British Isles. . . .

It is unnecessary to cite authority to show that both of these orders declaring military zones were illegal and contrary to international law. It is sufficient to say that our government has officially declared both of them to be illegal and has officially protested against both of them. The only difference is that in the case of Germany we have persisted in our protest, while in the case of England we have submitted.

What was our duty as a government and what were our rights when we were confronted with these extraordinary orders declaring these military zones? First, we could have defied both of them and could have gone to war against both of these nations for this violation of international law and interference with our neutral rights.

Second, we had the technical right to defy one and to acquiesce in the other.

Third, we could, while denouncing them both as illegal, have acquiesced in them both and thus remained neutral with both sides, although not agreeing with either as to the righteousness of their respective orders. We could have said to American shipowners that, while these orders are both contrary to international law and are both unjust, we do not believe that the provocation is sufficient to cause us to go to war for the defense of our rights as a neutral nation, and, therefore, American ships and American citizens will go into these zones at their own peril and risk.

Fourth, we might have declared an embargo against the shipping from American ports of any merchandise to either one of these governments that persisted in maintaining its military zone. We might have refused to permit the sailing of any ship from any American port to either of these military zones. . . .

There are a great many American citizens who feel that we owe it as a duty to humanity to take part in the war. Many instances of cruelty and inhumanity can be found on both sides. Men are often biased in their judgment on account of their sympathy and their interests. To my mind, what we ought to have maintained from the beginning was the strictest neutrality. If we had done this, I do not believe we would have been on the verge of war at the present time.

We had a right as a nation, if we desired, to cease at any time to be neutral. We had a technical right to respect the English war zone and to disregard the German war zone, but we could not do that and be neutral. I have no quarrel to find with the man who does not desire our country to remain neutral. While many such people are moved by selfish motives and hopes of gain, I have no doubt that in a great many instances, through what I believe to be a misunderstanding of the real condition, there are many honest, patriotic citizens who think we ought to engage in this war and who are behind the President in his demand that we should declare war against Germany.

I think such people err in judgment and to a great extent have been misled as to the real history and the true facts by the almost unanimous demand of the great combination of wealth that has a direct financial interest in our participation in the war. . . . The enormous profits of munition manufacturers, stockbrokers, and bond dealers must be still further increased by our entrance into the war.

*   *   *

This has brought us to the present moment, when Congress urged by the President and backed by the artificial sentiment, is about to declare war and engulf our country in the greatest holocaust that the world has ever known.

*   *   *

We have loaned many hundreds of millions of dollars to the Allies in this controversy. While such action was legal and countenanced by international law, there is no doubt in my mind but the enormous amount of money loaned to the Allies in this country has been instrumental in bringing about a public sentiment in favor of our country taking a course that would make every bond worth a hundred cents on the dollar and making the payment of every debt certain and sure.

Through this instrumentality and also through the instrumentality of others who have not only made millions out of the war in the manufacture of munitions, etc., and who would expect to make millions more if our country can be drawn into the catastrophe, a large number of the great newspapers and news agencies of the country have been controlled and enlisted in the greatest propaganda that the world has ever known to manufacture sentiment in favor of war.

*   *   *

War brings no prosperity to the great mass of common and patriotic citizens. It increases the cost of living of those who toil and those who already must strain every effort to keep soul and body together. War brings prosperity to the stock gambler on Wall Street—to those who are already in possession of more wealth than can be realized or enjoyed.

*   *   *

We are taking a step to-day that is fraught with untold danger. We are going into war upon the command of gold. We are going to run the risk of sacrificing millions of our countrymen's lives in order that other countrymen may coin their lifeblood into money. And even if we do not cross the Atlantic and go into the trenches, we are going to pile up a debt that the toiling masses that shall come many generations after us will have to pay. Unborn millions will bend their backs in toil in order to pay for the terrible step we are now about to take.

We are about to do the bidding of wealth's terrible mandate. By our act we will make millions of our countrymen suffer, and the consequences of it may well be that millions of our brethren must shed their lifeblood, millions of brokenhearted women must weep, millions of children must suffer with cold, and millions of babes must die from hunger, and all because we want to preserve the commercial right of American citizens to deliver munitions of war to belligerent nations.

*   *   *

REVIEW QUESTIONS

1. Why did Norris object to the United States entering the war in Europe?
2. What alternatives to war did Norris claim were available to the American government in 1917?

JULIA C. SIMPSON

We Have Begun Our Hard Work (1917)

No sooner did the United States enter the Great War in Europe than many women volunteered to serve as nurses at field hospitals. Perhaps the most dedicated and courageous of those volunteer nurses was Julia C. Simpson, a graduate of Vassar College who worked as a nurse in a St. Louis hospital before joining the Army Nurse Corps. In May 1917 she went to France with Base Hospital 21. Within a year, she was named chief nurse of the American Red Cross in France. She eventually headed up the nursing service of the American Expeditionary Forces. She was the first woman to be awarded the rank of major in the U.S. Army and received the Distinguished Service Medal at the end of the war. In these letters to her family, she described the wartime conditions faced by the nurses.

From *Finding Themselves: The Letters of an American Army Chief Nurse in a British Hospital in France* (New York: Macmillan, 1918). [Editorial insertions appear in square brackets—*Ed.*]

Liverpool, England
The Adelphi Hotel.

Monday, May 29, 1917.

Dearest Family:—
I do not know how I am ever going to manage to write down all the things I am learning and all the wonderful impressions that are beginning to crowd upon me. But I feel as though I could not bear to lose them; and so many new ones will come every day, I surely will lose them if I don't write them down at once.

We arrived last evening but did not dock until this a.m. at 7.30. We were met by a Colonel B., who . . . was an extremely affable old tall thin boy in a much-decorated uniform and a swagger stick. He told us we were to stay in Liverpool 24 hours . . . and that tomorrow at 11 we are to be conducted to London, to stay there at the Waldorf Hotel four or five days, and then to be sent to France. . . . We know where we are to go, but if I should tell you now the censor would cut it out. We can tell you later, not before. Anyway we are delighted, for we are to have lots of work, and mighty hard work too. We have been told considerable details about what we are to do, but I shall have to wait before I can tell you about it all.

*   *   *

And now I must hustle to bed, for tomorrow will be an exciting day. Good night and so much love to you all. If only you were all having this wonderful experience with me nothing more could be desired.

Julia

Wednesday, June 6, 1917.

Dearest Family:—

I have not written since that day in Liverpool, and now we have been ten days in London. If only I had the ability to write what we have seen and what we have felt. The contrasts have been so great some of us have almost lost our mental equilibrium. We are feted [honored] and cheered and taken from one entertainment to another and made much of by people of every class; and then between such social affairs we visit hospitals, military hospitals, because it is necessary for us to see how such hospitals are run.

First we see 1700 men, young men with faces or arms or legs blown off, and then we go to a tea at a fancy club; next we see 500 blinded men fighting their way back into normal life by learning various occupations, then we are taken in a body to the silliest musical comedy that was ever staged. Again we see thousands of crippled soldiers brought out to see the King give decorations to 350 heroes and heroines, soldiers and nurses, or "the next of kin" all in black, and we nearly choke when a blinded officer is led up to the King by his orderly who directs his every move, and lame men go hobbling up to receive their medals, and we watch the King use his left hand to shake hands with one man, because the man's right arm is gone, and then we go to St. Paul's [church] and see the Stars and Stripes carried up to the altar with the 64 British flags to be blessed at an "Empire day" service, while thousands and thousands of people sing "O God, our help in ages past."

Do you wonder that our emotions are wearing us to a frazzle? It is not only feminine emotions that are affected, because there are those of our directors who said they could not go to St. Dunstan's (the hospital school for blind soldiers) because they would not be able to sleep for nights afterwards. It is a mistake not to see such a wonderful place, however. There never was a more cheerful, hopeful place in the world.... There were men learning cobbling and carpentry, and chicken-farming and shorthand and typewriting and matmaking and weaving and basketry. The whole place was full of whistling, singing men who were going about their business as though they were like everybody else in the world instead of in total darkness forever. There were 500 of these men.

People tell me that English men and women have passed the emotional stage and have now settled down to work without the waste of riotous emotions and bursting feelings. It must be so or they would be dead, and they could not be doing the wonderful "war work" that each one of them is engaged in. From the highest to the lowest each woman has her work, her nursing, her preparing vegetables in hospitals (as Mrs. Waldorf Astor's sister was doing), her making of supplies, her managing a hospital in a private house, her organizing "hostels" for nurses, raising funds, everything that one can conceive of as a job for women is being done, as never before. Of course the street-sweeping by women is a kind of war work, and the bus conductoring, and delivering mail and telegrams, and driving cars and ambulances. The streets are full of women in uniforms of all sorts, all smart and business-like. Women in England are coming into their own. What is to happen after the war when the men come back can well fill the minds of those who are given to prophesy changes, for a change is taking place here that can never be undone. In addition to women taking a new place in the working world, class distinctions are being broken down in a way that is making itself felt to those who a few years ago could never have dreamt that such a change was possible....

Lovingly,

Julia.

France, Monday, June 11, 1917.

Dearest Daddy and Mother
and all of you:—

We have at last arrived [in France]! I wish I could tell you where, but I can't. This much I believe I can say, that it is on the outskirts of a large city, a beautiful old city. Our particular hospital is on a race course, which looks now like a vast circus establishment or a county fair, for it is covered with rows and rows of canvas tents, each of which holds about 14 beds. . . .

Rouen, France.

Sunday, June 17, 1917.
We have been told in our instructions about letter-writing that we may now state where we are. So now you can all know definitely just where we are. We got our first mail from home day before yesterday, and I can tell you there was great excitement. It is just a month to-day since we left St. Louis and it seems like a year.

* * *

We have very badly wounded men and their dressings are terrible.

Amputations are being done almost every day. Yesterday I went down to the "Theater Hut" to see how our nurses were going to handle a very bad case. . . . The poor boy whose leg had to be amputated was in such bad shape, he could have only the minimum of a general anaesthetic, but local anaesthesia was given. Besides having both legs badly hurt, his lower back is in terrible shape from injury; after the operation he was put on his face on his bed. Before eight o'clock one of the nurses held his head up so he could have a smoke! And this morning he says he is "in the pink," which means feeling fine. It is perfectly wonderful, their fortitude, and it is making us all so ashamed for all the complaining we have done. Their bravery is harder to bear than anything else. . . .

* * *

There are hundreds of stories like these. . . . One of the most pitiful groups are the "shell shocks." The other night the explosion of shells could be distinctly heard, and almost all these cases shook as though they were having convulsions all night. As one of them said, "Some poor devils are getting theirs now." One interesting case was brought in unable to speak several days ago. The other night he fell out of bed, and sat up and said "Sister, I can talk now." These

shell-shock cases are always falling out of bed, it seems.

* * *

It is my job of course to keep before my people the why of our coming and to keep their spirits up. As the director said this morning, we must never be discouraged or depressed, that our biggest job is to keep our people full of enthusiasm. Sometimes it is hard if one's own head aches, but it really is not hard for those of us who understand the meaning of our being here. . . .

* * *

July 25, 1917.
. . . Well, we have begun our hard work, and for our own sakes we are glad of it. In the past 24 hours we have admitted more patients than the total capacity of the Barnes and Children's Hospital, not the average number of patients, but the total capacity. And all these patients have been bathed, fed, and had their wounds dressed. Some of course were able to walk and could go to the bath house and the mess tents, but most of them to-day are stretcher cases, and oh, so dirty, hungry, and miserable. . . .

Many of the nurses have worked 14 straight hours to-day, and many of the doctors had only two or three hours' sleep last night, and were working all day. . . .

We have been receiving patients that have been gassed, and burned in a most mysterious way. Their clothing is not burned at all, but they have bad burns on their bodies, on parts that are covered by clothing. The doctors think it has been done by some chemical that gets its full action on the skin after it is moist, and when the men sweat, it is in these places that are the most moist that the burns are the worst. The Germans have been using a kind of oil in bombs, the men say it is oil of mustard. These bombs explode and the men's eyes, noses, and throats are so irritated they do not detect the poison gas fumes that come from the bombs that follow these oil ones, and so they either inhale it and die like flies, or have a delayed action and are affected by it terribly several hours later. We have had a lot of these delayed-action gassed men, who cough and cough continuously, like children with whooping cough. . . .

It is diabolical the things they [the Germans] do, simply fiendish, and like the things that would be expected from precocious degenerates. I cannot imagine what kind of change is going to take place in our minds before we get home. There are so many changes coming over our ideas every day. They are not new ideas, for many people have had them before, since the beginning of this war, but they are new to us. Human life seems so insignificant, and individuals are so unimportant. . . .

*   *   *

But what will we think when we get through with it all? How are we going to stand the mental strain?

Yet others do, and go on being normal, cheerful human beings, teaching bayoneting one hour, and playing tennis the next, or having tea with pretty nurses. "Oh, it's a queer world!" as the orderly said who came to tell me of a few more hundred wounded expected in soon. "Isn't it a cruel world?"

*   *   *

REVIEW QUESTIONS

1. Why were Simpson's letters censored by military officials?
2. What motivated Simpson and others to work so hard and lovingly during the war?

WOODROW WILSON

The League of Nations (1919)

When the Paris Peace Conference convened in 1919, Woodrow Wilson lobbied strenuously for inclusion of a League of Nations covenant in the final peace settlement. He was convinced that such a collective security organization was essential to the maintenance of peace. In June he returned to the United States from France, confident that the Senate would ratify the treaty and thereby commit the United States to membership in the new League of Nations. He greatly underestimated the issues at stake and the opposition they would arouse. Soon he found himself struggling to defend many of the treaty's provisions.

From *Senate Documents*, No. 76, 66th Cong., 1st Sess., 1919, 13:6–19.

To the Senate Committee on Foreign Relations

Mr. Chairman: I have taken the liberty of writing out a little statement in the hope that it might facilitate discussion by speaking directly on some points that I know have been points of controversy and upon which I thought an expression of opinion would not be unwelcome. . . .

Nothing, I am led to believe, stands in the way of ratification of the treaty except certain doubts with regard to the meaning and implication of certain articles of the Covenant of the League of Nations; and I must frankly say that I am unable to understand why such doubts should be entertained. . . . It was pointed out that . . . it was not expressly provided that the League should have no authority to act or to express a judgment of matters of domestic policy; that the right to withdraw from the League was not expressly recognized; and that the constitutional right of the Congress to determine all questions of peace and war was not sufficiently safeguarded.

On my return to Paris all these matters were taken up again by the Commission on the League of Nations and every suggestion of the United States was accepted.

The views of the United States with regard to the questions I have mentioned had, in fact, already been accepted by the commission and there was supposed to be nothing inconsistent with them in the draft of the Covenant first adopted—the draft which was the subject of our discussion in March—but no objection was made to saying explicitly in the text what all had supposed to be implicit in it. There was absolutely no doubt as to the meaning of any one of the resulting provisions of the Covenant in the minds of those who participated in drafting them, and I respectfully submit that there is nothing vague or doubtful in their wording.

The Monroe Doctrine is expressly mentioned as an understanding which is in no way to be impaired or interfered with by anything contained in the Covenant and the expression "regional understandings like the Monroe Doctrine" was used, not because any one of the conferees thought there was any comparable agreement anywhere else in existence or in contemplation, but only because it was thought best to avoid the appearance of dealing in such a document with the policy of a single nation. Absolutely nothing is concealed in the phrase.

With regard to domestic questions, Article 16 of the Covenant expressly provides that, if in case of any dispute arising between members of the League, the matter involved is claimed by one of the parties "and is found by the council to arise out of a matter which by international law is solely within the domestic jurisdiction of that party, the council shall so report, and shall make no recommendation as to its settlement." The United States was by no means the only Govern-

ment interested in the explicit adoption of this provision, and there is no doubt in the mind of any authoritative student of international law that such matters as immigration, tariffs, and naturalization are incontestably domestic questions with which no international body could deal without express authority to do so. No enumeration of domestic questions was undertaken because to undertake it, even by sample, would have involved the danger of seeming to exclude those not mentioned.

The right of any sovereign State to withdraw[1] had been taken for granted, but no objection was made to making it explicit. Indeed, so soon as the views expressed at the White House conference were laid before the commission it was at once conceded that it was best not to leave the answer to so important a question to inference. No proposal was made to set up any tribunal to pass judgment upon the question whether a withdrawing nation had in fact fulfilled "all its international obligations and all its obligations under the covenant." It was recognized that that question must be left to be resolved by the conscience of the Nation proposing to withdraw; and I must say that it did not seem to me worthwhile to propose that the article be made more explicit, because I knew that the United States would never itself propose to withdraw from the League if its conscience was not entirely clear as to the fulfillment of all its international obligations. It has never failed to fulfill them and never will. . . .

The United States will, indeed, undertake under Article 10 to "respect and preserve as against external aggression the territorial integrity and existing political independence of all members of the League," and that engagement constitutes a very grave and solemn moral obligation. But it is a moral, not a legal, obligation, and leaves our Congress absolutely free to put its own interpretation upon it in all cases that call for action. It is binding in conscience only, not in law.

Article 10 seems to me to constitute the very backbone of the whole Covenant. Without it the League would be hardly more than an influential debating society. . . .

---

[1] I.e., from the League.

If the United States were to qualify the document in any way, moreover, I am confident from what I know of the many conferences and debates which accompanied the formulation of the treaty that our example would immediately be followed in many quarters, in some instances with very serious reservations, and that the meaning and operative force of the treaty would presently be clouded from one end of its clauses to the other.

Pardon me, Mr. Chairman, if I have been entirely unreserved and plainspoken in speaking of the great matters we all have so much at heart. If excuse is needed, I trust that the critical situation of affairs may serve as my justification. The issues that manifestly hang upon the conclusions of the Senate with regard to peace and upon the time of its action are so grave and so clearly insusceptible of being thrust on one side or postponed that I have felt it necessary in the public interest to make this urgent plea, and to make it as simply and as unreservedly as possible.

REVIEW QUESTIONS

1. What specific objections did Wilson address in this speech?
2. Did Wilson expect the League to be a strong or weak organization? Explain.
3. Do you believe that American participation in the League would have represented a sharp break with American tradition? Why or why not?

HENRY CABOT LODGE

The League of Nations Must Be Revised (1919)

Republican senator Henry Cabot Lodge of Massachusetts led the opposition to Woodrow Wilson's promotion of America's membership in a League of Nations. As the powerful leader of the Senate Foreign Relations Committee, he emerged as the pivotal figure in the protracted debate over the League. Lodge offered to support it only if substantial revisions were made in its key provisions, especially Article X, which in his view transferred from the Senate to the League of Nations the authority to wage war. In an August 1919 speech Lodge summarized his objections.

From *Congressional Record*, 66th Cong., 1st Sess., 1919, 3779–84.

For ourselves we asked absolutely nothing. We have not asked any government or governments to guarantee our boundaries or our political independence. We have no fear in regard to either. We have sought no territory, no privileges, no advantages, for ourselves. That is the fact. It is apparent on the face of the treaty. I do not mean to reflect upon a single one of the powers with which we have been associated in the war against Germany, but there is not one of them which has not sought individual advantages for their own national benefit. I do not criticize their desires at all. The services and sacrifices of England and France and Belgium and Italy are beyond estimate and beyond praise. I am glad they should have what they desire for their own welfare and safety. But they all receive under the peace territorial and commercial benefits. We are asked to give, and we in no way seek to take. Surely it is not too much to insist that when we are offered nothing but the opportunity to give and to aid others we should have the right to say what sacrifices we shall make and what the magnitude of our gifts shall be. In the prosecution of the war we have unstintedly given American lives and American treasure. When the war closed we had 3,000,000 men under arms. We were turning the country into a vast workshop for war. We advanced ten billions to our allies. We refused no assistance that we could possibly render. All the great energy and power of the Republic were put at the service of the good cause. We have not been ungenerous. We have been devoted to the cause of freedom, humanity, and civilization everywhere. Now we are asked, in the making of peace, to sacrifice our sovereignty in important respects, to involve ourselves almost without limit in the affairs of other nations and to yield up policies and rights which we have maintained throughout our history. We are asked to incur liabilities to an unlimited extent and furnish assets at the same time which no man can measure. I think it is not only our right but our duty to determine how far we shall go. Not only must we look carefully to see where we are being led into endless disputes and entanglements, but we must not forget that we have in this country millions of people of foreign birth and parentage.

Our one great object is to make all these people Americans so that we may call on them to place America first and serve America as they have done in the war just closed. We can not Americanize them if we are continually thrusting them back into the quarrels and difficulties of the countries from which they came to us. We shall fill this land with political disputes about the troubles and quarrels of other countries. We shall have a large portion of our people voting not on American questions and not on what concerns the United States but dividing on issues which concern foreign countries alone. That is an unwholesome and perilous condition to force upon this country. We must avoid it. We ought to reduce to the lowest possible point the foreign questions in which we involve ourselves. Never forget that this league is primarily—I might say overwhelmingly—a political organiza-

tion, and I object strongly to having the policies of the United States turn upon disputes where deep feeling is aroused but in which we have no direct interest. It will all tend to delay the Americanization of our great population, and it is more important not only to the United States but to the peace of the world to make all these people good Americans than it is to determine that some piece of territory should belong to one European country rather than to another. For this reason I wish to limit strictly our interference in the affairs of Europe and of Africa. We have interests of our own in Asia and in the Pacific which we must guard upon our own account, but the less we undertake to play the part of umpire and thrust ourselves into European conflicts the better for the United States and for the world.

It has been reiterated here on this floor, and reiterated to the point of weariness, that in every treaty there is some sacrifice of sovereignty we are justified in sacrificing. In what I have already said about other nations putting us into war I have covered one point of sovereignty which ought never to be yielded—the power to send American soldiers and sailors everywhere, which ought never to be taken from the American people or impaired in the slightest degree. Let us beware how we palter with our independence. We have not reached the great position from which we were able to come down into the field of battle and help to save the world from tyranny by being guided by others. Our vast power has all been built up and gathered together by ourselves alone. We forced our way upward from the days of the Revolution, through a world often hostile and always indifferent. We owe no debt to anyone except to France in that Revolution, and those policies and those rights on which our power has been founded should never be lessened or weakened. It will be no service to the world to do so and it will be of intolerable injury to the United States. We will do our share. We are ready and anxious to help in all ways to preserve the world's peace. But we can do it best by not crippling ourselves. . . .

. . . I am thinking of what is best for the world, for if the United States fails the best hopes of mankind fail with it. I have never had but one allegiance—I can not divide it now. I have loved but one flag and I can not share that devotion and give affection to the mongrel banner invented by a league. Internationalism, illustrated by the Bolshevik and by the man to whom all countries are alike provided they can make money out of them, is to me repulsive. National I must remain, and in that way I like all other Americans can render the amplest service to the world. The United States is the world's best hope, but if you fetter her in the interests and quarrels of other nations, if you tangle her in the intrigues of Europe, you will destroy her power for good and endanger her very existence. . . .

We are told that we shall "break the heart of the world" if we do not take this league just as it stands. I fear that the hearts of the vast majority of mankind would beat on strongly and steadily and without any quickening if the league were to perish altogether. . . .

No doubt many excellent and patriotic people see a coming fulfillment of noble ideals in the word "League for Peace." We all respect and share these aspirations and desires, but some of us see no hope, but rather defeat, for them in this murky covenant. For we, too, have our ideals, even if we differ from those who have tried to establish a monopoly of idealism. Out first ideal is our country, and we see her in the future, as in the past, giving service to all her people and to the world. Our ideal of the future is that she should continue to render that service of her own free will. She has great problems of her own to solve, very grim and perilous problems, and a right solution, if we can attain to it, would largely benefit mankind. We would have our country strong to resist a peril from the West, as she has flung back the German menace from the East. We would not have our politics distracted and embittered by the dissensions of other lands. We would not have our country's vigor exhausted, or her moral force abated, by everlasting meddling and muddling in every quarrel, great and small, which afflicts the world. Our ideal is to make her ever stronger and better and finer because in that way alone, as we believe, can she be of the greatest service to the world's peace and to the welfare of mankind.

REVIEW QUESTIONS

1. Why did Lodge emphasize that America has "millions" of foreign-born residents?
2. Why did Lodge call the League primarily a "political organization"? Do you agree?
3. In what respects could Lodge's remarks have been interpreted as a partisan campaign speech aimed at undermining the Democratic presidential hopes for 1920?

W. E. B. Du Bois

Returning Soldiers (1919)

More than 350,000 African Americans served in racially segregated units during World War I, mostly as support troops well behind the front lines. But several black units—commanded by white officers—participated in combat alongside French and British soldiers. Some 171 African Americans were awarded the French Legion of Honor for valor under fire. Yet many people resented the discriminatory treatment black soldiers and sailors received while defending American values. In response to

such protests, several hundred African American men eventually received officers'
training. By October 1917, over 600 blacks were commissioned as officers, but they
were not allowed to supervise white troops. The racially discriminatory practices in
the military during World War I galvanized the black community in their continuing
efforts to ensure full citizenship for all Americans. Leading that effort was W. E. B.
Du Bois. In his role as editor of The Crisis, *the magazine published by the National*
Association for the Advancement of Colored People (NAACP), which he had helped
found, Du Bois relentlessly called for the United States to live up to its own ideals
and provide true civil rights for all Americans.

From *The Crisis*, May 1919.

We are returning from war! *The Crisis* and tens of thousands of black men were drafted into a great struggle. For bleeding France and what she means and has meant and will mean to us and humanity and against the threat of German race arrogance, we fought gladly and to the last drop of blood; for America and her highest ideals, we fought in far-off hope; for the dominant southern oligarchy entrenched in Washington, we fought in bitter resignation. For the America that represents and gloats in lynching, disfranchisement, caste, brutality and devilish insult—for this, in the hateful upturning and mixing of things, we were forced by vindictive fate to fight also.

But today we return! We return from the slavery of uniform which the world's madness demanded us to do to the freedom of civil garb. We stand again to look America squarely in the face and call a spade a spade. We sing: This country of ours, despite all its better souls have done and dreamed, is yet a shameful land.

It *lynches*.

And lynching is barbarism of a degree of contemptible nastiness unparalleled in human history. Yet for fifty years we have lynched two Negroes a week, and we have kept this up right through the war.

It *disfranchises* its own citizens.

Disfranchisement is the deliberate theft and robbery of the only protection of poor against rich and black against white. The land that disfranchises its citizens and calls itself a democracy lies and knows it lies.

It encourages *ignorance*.

It has never really tried to educate the Negro. A dominant minority does not want Negroes educated. It wants servants, dogs, whores and monkeys. And when this land allows a reactionary group by its stolen political power to force as many black folk into these categories as it possibly can, it cries in contemptible hypocrisy: "They threaten us with degeneracy; they cannot be educated."

It *steals* from us.

It organizes industry to cheat us. It cheats us out of our land; it cheats us out of our labor. It confiscates our savings. It reduces our wages. It raises our rent. It steals our profit. It taxes us without representation. It keeps us consistently and universally poor, and then feeds us on charity and derides our poverty.

It *insults* us.

It has organized a nation-wide and latterly a world-wide propaganda of deliberate and continuous insult and defamation of black blood wherever found. It decrees that it shall not be possible in travel nor residence, work nor play, education nor instruction for a black man to exist without tacit or open acknowledgment of his inferiority to the dirtiest white dog. And it looks upon any attempt to question or even discuss this dogma as arrogance, unwarranted assumption and treason.

This is the country to which we Soldiers of Democracy return. This is the fatherland for which we fought! But it is our fatherland. It was right for us to fight. The faults of our country are our faults.

Under similar circumstances, we would fight again. But by the God of Heaven, we are cowards and jackasses if now that that war is over, we do not marshal every ounce of our brain and brawn to fight a sterner, longer, more unbending battle against the forces of hell in our own land.

We *return*.

We *return from fighting*.

We *return fighting*.

Make way for Democracy! We saved it in France, and by the Great Jehovah, we will save it in the United States of America, or know the reason why.

REVIEW QUESTIONS

1. In what ways did Du Bois highlight the social hypocrisies in American life revealed by African American participation in World War I?
2. How would you have felt if you were a black veteran returning from military service in France in 1919?

A. MITCHELL PALMER

FROM The Case against the Reds (1920)

After the outbreak of strikes and riots in 1919, Democratic Attorney General A. Mitchell Palmer organized a carefully coordinated series of raids against communists and anarchists on January 3, 1920. He was a Quaker attorney from Pennsylvania who had served three terms in Congress. Driven by hatred of foreign radicals and a desire to gain the Democratic presidential nomination in 1920, he often acted on his own without informing or consulting President Wilson. In the article that follows, he sought to counter the many critics of the "Palmer raids."

From *The Forum* 63 (February 1920): 63–75. [Editorial insertions appear in square brackets—*Ed.*]

Like a prairie-fire, the blaze of revolution was sweeping over every American institution of law and order a year ago. It was eating its way into the homes of the American workman, its sharp tongues of revolutionary heat were licking into the altars of the churches, leaping into the belfry of the school bell, crawling into the sacred corners of American homes, seeking to replace marriage vows with libertine laws, burning up the foundations of society.

Robbery, not war, is the ideal of communism. This has been demonstrated in Russia, Germany, and in America. As a foe, the anarchist is fearless in his own life, for his creed is a fanaticism that admits no respect for any other creed. Obviously it is the creed of any criminal mind, which reasons always from motives impossible to clean thought. Crime is the degenerate factor in society.

Upon these two basic certainties, first that the "Reds" were criminal aliens, and secondly that the American Government must prevent crime, it was decided that there could be no nice distinctions drawn between the theoretical ideals of the radicals and their actual violations of our national laws. An assassin may have brilliant intellectuality, he may be able to excuse his murder or robbery with fine oratory, but any theory which excuses crime is not wanted in America. This is no place for the criminal to flourish, nor will he do so, so long as the rights of common citizenship can be exerted to prevent him. . . .

By stealing, murder and lies, Bolshevism has looted Russia not only of its material strength, but of its moral force. A small clique of outcasts from the East Side of New York has attempted this, with what success we all know. Because a disreputable alien—Leon Bronstein, the man who now calls himself Trotzky—can inaugurate a reign of terror from his throne room in the Kremlin: because this lowest of all types known to New York can sleep in the Czar's bed, while hundreds of thousands in Russia are without food or shelter, should Americans be swayed by such doctrines? . . .

My information showed that communism in this country was an organization of thousands of aliens, who were direct allies of [Leon] Trotzky. Aliens of the same misshapen cast of mind and indecencies of character, and it showed that they were making the same glittering promises of lawlessness, of criminal autocracy to Americans, that they had made to the Russian peasants. How the Department of Justice discovered upwards of 60,000 of these organized agitators of the Trotzky doctrine in the United States, is the confidential information upon which the Government is now sweeping the nation clean of such alien filth. . . .

One of the chief incentives for the present activity of the Department of Justice against the "Reds" has been the hope that American citizens will, themselves, become voluntary agents for us, in a vast organization for mutual defense against the sinister agitation of men and women aliens, who appear to be either in the pay or under the spell of Trotzky and Lenine [*sic*]. . . .

The whole purpose of communism appears to be a mass formation of the criminals of the world to overthrow the decencies of private life, to usurp property that they have not earned, to disrupt the present order of life regardless of health, sex, or religious rights. By a literature that promises the wildest dreams of such low aspirations, that can occur to only the criminal minds, communism distorts our social law. . . .

These are the revolutionary tenets of Trotzky and the Communist Internationale. Their manifesto further embraces the various organizations in this country of men and women obsessed with discontent, having disorganized relations to American society. These include the I.W.W.'s, the most radical socialists, the misguided anarchists, the agitators who oppose the limitations of unionism, the moral perverts and the hysterical neurasthenic women who abound in communism. The phraseology of their manifesto is practically the same wording as was used by the Bolsheviks for their International Communist Congress.

. . . The Department of Justice will pursue the attack of these "Reds" upon the Government of the United States with vigilance, and no alien, advocating the overthrow of existing law and order in this country, shall escape arrest and prompt deportation.

It is my belief that while they have stirred discontent in our midst, while they have caused irritating strikes, and while they have infected our social ideas with the disease of their own minds and their unclean morals, we can get rid of them! And not until we have done so shall we have removed the menace of Bolshevism for good.

REVIEW QUESTIONS

1. What crimes did Palmer accuse the Reds of committing?
2. How did Palmer address the legal rights of aliens?
3. What would be the public response to such a statement today? Explain.

WILLIAM ALLEN WHITE

The Red Scare Is Un-American (1920)

The majority of Americans supported the actions of Attorney General A. Mitchell Palmer and shared his fears of communist conspiracies. A few people, however, raised concerns about the arbitrary use of police powers to deal with aliens. William Allen White, the crusading editor of the Emporia Gazette *in Kansas and a prominent Republican progressive, criticized Palmer's crusade.*

From the *Emporia Gazette* (Kansas), January 8, 1920. [Editorial insertions appear in square brackets—*Ed.*]

The Attorney General [A. Mitchell Palmer] seems to be seeing red. He is rounding up every manner of radical in the country; every man who hopes for a better world is in danger of deportation by the Attorney General. The whole business is un-American. There are certain rules which should govern in the treason cases.

First, it should be agreed that a man may believe what he chooses.

Second, it should be agreed that when he preaches violence he is disturbing the peace and should be put in jail. Whether he preaches violence in politics, business, or religion, whether he advocates murder and arson and pillage for gain or for political ends, he is violating the common law and should be squelched—jailed until he is willing to quit advocating force in a democracy.

Third, he should be allowed to say what he pleases so long as he advocates legal constitutional methods of procedure. Just because a man does not believe this government is good is no reason why he should be deported.

Abraham Lincoln did not believe this government was all right seventy-five years ago. He advocated changes, but he advocated constitutional means, and he had a war with those who advocated force to maintain the government as it was.

Ten years ago Roosevelt[1] advocated great changes in our American life—in our Constitution, in our social and economic life. Most of the changes he advocated have been made, but they were made in the regular legal way. He preached no force. And if a man desires to preach any doctrine under the shining sun, and to advocate the realization of his vision by lawful, orderly, constitutional means—let him alone. If he is Socialist, anarchist, or Mormon, and merely preaches his creed and does not preach violence, he can do no harm. For the folly of his doctrine will be its answer.

The deportation business is going to make martyrs of a lot of idiots whose cause is not worth it.

REVIEW QUESTIONS

1. Was White concerned that the views of socialists might be true? Explain.
2. How did White suggest social change could be promoted?
3. What did White mean when he wrote that the "deportation business" would create martyrs?

[1]Theodore Roosevelt (1858–1919).

23 ❧ A CLASH OF CULTURES, 1920–1929

The Great War unleashed forces that caused severe social strains in the United States. The cultural conflicts during the 1920s resulted largely from explosive tensions between rural and urban ways of life. For the first time in the nation's history, more people lived in cities than in rural areas. While the urban middle class prospered during the twenties, farmers suffered from the end of the wartime boom in the exports of grains and livestock to Europe. Four million people moved from farms to cities in the twenties, in part because of the better quality of life and in part because of the prolonged agricultural recession. Amid this massive rural/urban population shift, bitter fights erupted between traditionalists and modernists, as old and new values fought a cultural civil war that continues today.

During the twenties, the new and unusual clashed openly with the conventional and the commonplace. Modernists and traditionalists waged cultural warfare with one another, one group looking to the future for inspiration and the other looking to the past for guidance. Clashes between traditional rural values and urban modernism were especially evident as young people in cities rebelled against the moral standards of their parents and grandparents. Many young adults—especially affluent college students—discarded old prohibitions. They engaged in sensual dancing, public kissing and swimming, cigarette smoking, and alcohol consumption that shocked and angered moral guardians. Many modernists joined Margaret Sanger in promoting the use of birth control to free mothers from the burden of supporting unwanted children. In the face of such cosmopolitan challenges, many rural traditionalists countered with an aggressive conservatism that coupled religious and cultural fundamentalism.

Nothing symbolized the emergence of controversial new social beliefs and practices more than the phenomenal popularity of the newly invented moving pictures. By 1924, there were 20,000 theaters showing 700 new "silent" films a year, and the movie business had become the nation's chief form of mass enter-

tainment. Hollywood, California, became the international center of movie pro-duction, grinding out cowboy Westerns, crime dramas, murder mysteries, and the timeless comedies of Mack Sennett's Keystone Studios, where a raft of slap-stick comedians—most notably London-born Charlie Chaplin, a comic genius—perfected their art, transforming it into a form of social criticism.

Movie attendance during the 1920s averaged 80 million people a week, more than half the national population, and attendance surged even more after 1927 with the appearance of "talkies," movies with sound. In 1930, 115 million people attended weekly movies out of a total population of 123 million (many people went more than once). Americans spent ten times as much on movies as they did on tickets to baseball and football games.

But movies did much more than entertain. They helped expand the con-sumer culture by feeding the desires of moviegoers, setting standards and tastes in fashion, music, dancing, and hairstyles. They also helped stimulate the sexual revolution. One boy admitted that it was the movies that taught him how "to kiss a girl on her ears, neck, and cheeks, as well as on the mouth." A social researcher concluded that movies made young Americans in the twenties more "sex-wise, sex-excited, and sex-absorbed" than previous generations.

What most shocked old-timers during the Jazz Age was a defiant sexual rev-olution among young people, especially those on college campuses. "None of the Victorian mothers—and most of the mothers were Victorian—had any idea how casually their daughters were accustomed to being kissed," wrote F. Scott Fitzger-ald in This Side of Paradise *(1920).*

During the twenties, Americans learned about the hidden world of "flaming youth" (the title of a popular novel): wild "petting parties," free love, speakeasies, "joyriding," and skinny-dipping. A promotional poster for the 1923 silent film Flaming Youth *asked: "How Far Can a Girl Go?" Other ads claimed the movie appealed especially to "neckers, petters, white kisses, red kisses, pleasure-mad daughters, [and] sensation-craving mothers."*

Some of the decade's most popular magazines were those that focused on romance and sex: True Confessions, Telling Tales, *and* True Story. *Their story titles revealed their themes: "The Primitive Lover" ("She wanted a cave-man husband"), "Indolent Kisses," and "Innocents Astray." Likewise, the most popular female movie stars—Madge Bellamy, Clara Bow, and Joan Crawford—projected an image of sensual freedom, energy, and independence. Advertisements for new movies reinforced the stereotypical self-indulgent images of the Jazz Age: "brilliant men, beautiful jazz babies, champagne baths, midnight revels, petting parties in the purple dawn, all ending in one terrific climax that makes you gasp." Traditionalists were shocked at the behavior of rebellious young women. "One hears it said," lamented a Baptist magazine, "that the girls are actually tempting the boys more than the boys do the girls, by their dress and conversation."*

The Great War also disrupted race relations during the twenties. The mass movement of blacks (and poor whites) to the North began at the start of the twentieth century but accelerated in 1915–1916, when rapidly expanding war industries in the northern states needed new workers. It continued throughout the twenties, as poor blacks boarded trains with one-way tickets, bound for the "promised land" up north.

Between 1920 and 1930, almost a million African Americans, mostly sharecroppers, joined the black exodus from the South. Many of them landed in New York City, Chicago, Detroit, Cleveland, Washington, D.C., Philadelphia, and other large cities in the northeast and midwest. The Great Migration continued in fits and starts throughout the twentieth century, producing dramatic social, economic, and political changes across the nation. In 1900, only 740 thousand African Americans lived outside the South, just 8 percent of the nation's total black population. By 1970, more than 10.6 million African Americans lived outside the South, 47 percent of the nation's total.

Blacks from the rural South who served in the military during the Great War were less willing to tolerate racial abuse and Jim Crow segregation laws once they returned home. Thousands of southern blacks also migrated north and west in search of higher wages and racial equality, only to discover that racism was not limited to the deep South. White mobs in communities across the nation assaulted blacks for various reasons or for no reason at all. In a Chicago riot, thirty-eight people were killed and hundreds injured; soldiers had to be called in to restore order. Some African Americans despaired of ever gaining true equality in the United States, and promoted black nationalism. Led by the charismatic Marcus Garvey, a large number of American blacks began to dream of returning to Africa and establishing their own ideal society.

In 1916, Garvey brought to Harlem the headquarters of the Universal Negro Improvement Association (UNIA), which he had started in his native Jamaica two years before. Garvey insisted that blacks had nothing in common with whites. To him, that was a good thing, for he preferred racial separation rather than integration. In passionate speeches and in editorials in the UNIA's popular newspaper, The Negro World, *Garvey urged African Americans to remove themselves from the surrounding white culture in order to cultivate black solidarity and "black power."*

The UNIA grew rapidly amid the racial tensions of the postwar years. By 1923, Garvey, who often wore gaudy military uniforms and feather-plumed hats, claimed to have as many as 4 million UNIA members served by 800 offices. The UNIA became the largest black political organization in the twentieth century. Garvey's goal was to build an all-black empire in Africa: "We will let white men have America and Europe, but we are going to have Africa." To that end, he began calling himself the "Provisional President of Africa," raising funds to send Americans to Africa, and expelling any UNIA member who married a white.

Garvey was both loved and hated. His message of black nationalism and racial solidarity appealed especially to the black working poor in northern cities, but also had supporters across the rural South. Garveyism, however, appalled other black leaders, especially those involved with the NAACP. W. E. B. Du Bois, for example, labeled Garvey "the most dangerous enemy of the Negro race. . . . He is either a lunatic or a traitor." An African American newspaper pledged to help "drive Garvey and Garveyism in all its sinister viciousness from the American soil."

Garvey's eccentric crusade collapsed in 1923 when he was convicted of fraud for overselling shares of stock in a steamship corporation (the Black Star Line) he founded to transport American blacks to Africa. Sentenced to a five-year prison term, he was pardoned in 1927 by President Calvin Coolidge on the condition that he be deported to Jamaica, where he received a hero's welcome. Garvey died in obscurity in 1940, but the memory of his movement kept alive an undercurrent that would reemerge in the 1960s under the slogan "black power."

MARGARET SANGER

The Need for Birth Control (1922)

During the 1920s New Yorker Margaret Sanger (1883–1966) became the crusading champion for a woman's right to birth control devices. Her mother was a devout Roman Catholic who went through eighteen pregnancies before dying of tuberculosis, and Sanger was determined to give women access to contraceptives to free them from such childbearing burdens. Her tireless efforts ignited fierce opposition from the Catholic Church and other religious organizations.

From *The Pivot of Civilization* (New York, 1922), pp. 196–219.

Religious propaganda against Birth Control is crammed with contradiction and fallacy. It refutes itself. Yet it brings the opposing views into vivid contrast. In stating these differences we should make clear that advocates of Birth Control are not seeking to attack the Catholic Church. We quarrel with that church, however, when it seeks to assume authority over non-Catholics and to dub their behavior immoral because they do not conform to the dictatorship of Rome. The question of bearing and rearing children we hold is the concern of the mother and the potential mother. If she delegates the responsibility, the ethical education, to an external authority, that is her affair. We object, however, to the State or the Church which appoints itself as arbiter and dictator in this sphere and attempts to force unwilling women into compulsory maternity. . . .

The sex instinct in the human race is too strong to be bound by the dictates of any church. The Church's failure, its century after century of failure, is now evident on every side: for, having convinced men and women that only in its baldly propagative phase is sexual expression legitimate, the teachings of the Church have driven sex underground, into secret channels, strengthened the conspiracy of silence, concentrated men's thoughts upon the "lusts of the body," have sown, cultivated and reaped a crop of bodily and mental diseases, and developed a society congenitally and almost hope-

lessly unbalanced. How is any progress to be made, how is any human expression or education possible when women and men are taught to combat and resist their natural impulses and to despise their bodily functions? . . .

Humanity, we are glad to realize, is rapidly freeing itself from this "morality" imposed upon it by its self-appointed and self-perpetuating masters. From a hundred different points the imposing edifice of this "morality" has been and is being attacked. Sincere and thoughtful defenders and exponents of the teachings of Christ now acknowledge the falsity of the traditional codes and their malignant influence upon the moral and physical well-being of humanity. . . .

Psychology and the outlook of modern life are stressing the growth of independent responsibility and discrimination as the true basis of ethics. The old traditional morality, with its train of vice, disease, promiscuity and prostitution, is in reality dying out, killing itself off because it is too irresponsible and too dangerous to individual and social well-being. The transition from the old to the new, like all fundamental changes, is fraught with many dangers. But it is a revolution that cannot be stopped.

The smaller family, with its lower infant mortality rate, is, in more definite and concrete manner than many actions outwardly deemed "moral," the expression of moral judgment and responsibility. It is the assertion of a standard of living, inspired by the wish to obtain a fuller and more expressive life for the children than the parents have enjoyed. If the morality or immorality of any course of conduct is to be determined by the motives which inspire it, there is evidently at the present day no higher morality than the intelligent practice of Birth Control.

The immorality of many who practice Birth Control lies in not daring to preach what they practice. What is the secret of the hypocrisy of the well-to-do, who are willing to contribute generously to charities and philanthropies, who spend thousands annually in the upkeep and sustenance of the delinquent, the defective and the dependent; and yet join the conspiracy of silence that prevents the poorer classes from learning how to improve their conditions, and elevate their standards of living? It is as though they were to cry: "We'll give you anything except the thing you ask for—the means whereby you may become responsible and self-reliant in your own lives."

The brunt of this injustice falls on women, because the old traditional morality is the invention of men. . . . In the moral code developed by the Church, women have been so degraded that they have been habituated to look upon themselves through the eyes of men. Very imperfectly have women developed their own self-consciousness, the realization of their tremendous and supreme position in civilization. Women can develop this power only in one way; by the exercise of responsibility, by the exercise of judgment, reason or discrimination. They need ask for no "rights." They need only assert power. Only by the exercise of self-guidance and intelligent self-direction can that inalienable, supreme, pivotal power be expressed. More than ever in history women need to realize that nothing can ever come to us from another. Everything we attain we must owe to ourselves. Our own spirit must vitalize it. Our own heart must feel it. For we are not passive machines. We are not to be lectured, guided and molded this way or that. We are alive and intelligent, we women, no less than men, and we must awaken to the essential realization that we are living beings, endowed with will, choice, comprehension, and that every step in life must be taken at our own initiative.

Moral and sexual balance in civilization will only be established by the assertion and expression of power on the part of women. This power will not be found in any futile seeking for economic independence or in the aping of men in industrial and business pursuits, nor by joining battle for the so-called "single standard." Woman's power can only be expressed and make itself felt when she refuses the task of bringing unwanted children into the world to be exploited in industry and slaughtered in wars. When we refuse to produce battalions of babies to be exploited; when we declare to the nation; "Show us that the best possible chance in life is given to every child now brought into the world, before you cry for more! At present our children are a glut on the market. You hold infant life cheap. Help us to make the world a fit place for children. When you have done this, we will bear you children,—then we shall be true women." . . .

Moreover, woman shall further assert her power by refusing to remain the passive instrument of sensual self-gratification on the part of men. Birth Control, in philosophy and practice, is the destroyer of that dualism of the old sexual code. It denies that the sole purpose of sexual activity is procreation; it also denies that sex should be reduced to the level of sensual lust, or that woman should permit herself to be the instrument of its satisfaction. In increasing and differentiating her love demands, woman must elevate sex into another sphere, whereby it may subserve and enhance the possibility of individual and human expression. Man will gain in this no less than woman; for in the age-old enslavement of woman he has enslaved himself; and in the liberation of womankind, all of humanity will experience the joys of a new and fuller freedom. . . .

To the foregoing contentions, it might be objected, you are encouraging passion. My reply would be, passion is a worthy possession—most men, who are any good, are capable of passion. You all enjoy ardent and passionate love in art and literature. Why not give it a place in real life? Why some people look askance at passion is because they are confusing it with sensuality. Sex love without passion is a poor, lifeless thing. Sensuality, on the other hand, is on a level with gluttony—a physical excess—detached from sentiment, chivalry, or tenderness. It is just as important to give sex love its place as to avoid its over-emphasis. Its real and effective restraints are those imposed by a loving and sympathetic companionship, by the privileges of parenthood, the exacting claims of career and that civic sense which prompts men to do social service.

*　　*　　*

Birth Control is an ethical necessity for humanity today because it places in our hands a new instrument of self-expression and self-realization. It gives us control over one of the primordial forces of nature, to which in the past the majority of mankind have been enslaved, and by which it has been cheapened and debased. It arouses us to the possibility of newer and greater freedom. It develops the power, the responsibility and intelligence to use this freedom in living a liberated and abundant life. It permits us to enjoy this liberty without danger of infringing upon the similar liberty of our fellow men, or of injuring and curtailing the freedom of

the next generation. It shows us that we need not seek in the amassing of worldly wealth, nor in the illusion of some extra-terrestrial Heaven or earthly Utopia of a remote future the road to human development. The Kingdom of Heaven is in a very definite sense within us. Not by leaving our body and our fundamental humanity behind us, not by aiming to be anything but what we are, shall we become ennobled or immortal. By knowing ourselves, by expressing ourselves, by realizing ourselves more completely than has ever before been possible, not only shall we attain the kingdom ourselves but we shall hand on the torch of life undimmed to our children and the children of our children.

REVIEW QUESTIONS

1. Why, according to Sanger, was the "traditional morality" related to sexual intercourse dying out?
2. What did Sanger say were the advantages of smaller families?
3. Why did she believe that birth control was an "ethical necessity"?

The Flappers of the 1920s:
Debating Bobbed Hair (1927)

The rebellious young women of the 1920s, called "flappers," rejected the styles and standards of the older generation. They smoked and drank in public, celebrated the sexual revolution, and embraced new fashions designed to set them apart. Popular magazines such as Ladies Home Journal *and* Pictorial Review *took time to debate the merits of "bobbing" hair, cutting it short and sculpting into the "bob." In these magazine excerpts, singer Mary Garden and film star Mary Pickford explained their views about bobbed hair.*

Originally published in *Pictorial Review* Vol. 28, April 1927, pp. 8, 9. Reprinted with permission. [Editorial insertions appear in square brackets—*Ed.*]

Why I Bobbed My Hair

Mary Garden

Why did I bob my hair? For several reasons. I did it because I wanted to, for one thing; because I found it easier to take care of; because I thought it more becoming; and because I felt freer without long, entangling tresses. But above and beyond these and several other reasons I had my hair cut short because, to me, it typified a progressive step, in keeping with the inner spirit that animates my whole existence.

In one way, whether I wear my hair short or not is of little importance. But viewed in another way, bobbed hair is not just a trivial, independent act of hair-dressing separate and apart from my life itself. It is part and parcel of life—one of the myriad things which by themselves may apparently mean nothing, but which in the aggregate help to form that particular complexity of expression which is myself.

This sounds a bit cryptic; but let me elucidate a little. Whether we know it or not, every single thing we do has a relationship to our lives as a whole, for the simple reason that what we do is the expression of what we think—consciously or unconsciously. You may say that it matters very little whether a woman wears her hair long or has it cut short, but that is really not true.

Bobbed hair is a state of mind and not merely a new manner of dressing my head. It typifies growth, alertness, up-to-dateness, and is part of the expression of the *élan vital* [spirit]! It is not just a fad of the moment, either like mah jong or cross-word puzzles. At least I don't think it is. I consider getting rid of our long hair one of the many little shackles that women have cast aside in their passage to freedom. Whatever helps their emancipation, however small it may seen, is well worth while.

Bobbing the hair is one of those things that show us whether or not we are abreast of the age in which we find ourselves. For instance, can you imagine any woman with a vivid consciousness of being alive, walking along the street in 1927 with skirts trailing on the ground, wearing elastic-side shoes, a shawl, and also a mid-Victorian bonnet? If you saw such a sight you would instantly put her down as one who had ceased to grow, as one who was *passé* [out of style] and very far from being an up-to-date woman.

Well, I carry that thought a little further in my whole scheme of things. I do my best to be constantly on the alert and up to the moment. On my toes, as the boys say. I could no more imagine myself wearing a long, trailing skirt in 1927 when all the world was wearing short skirts than I could wear long, trailing tresses when all the world (or nearly all of it) had wisely come to the conclusion that bobbed hair was more youthful, more *chic*, and, if I may say so, much more sanitary.

This attention to what is of the living present has a special application, I think, to those of us who are what the world designates as creative artists. We, of all people, must be very careful not to allow ourselves to stagnate in any manner whatsoever—mentally, artistically, or physically.

To be an artist means to grow. An artist can not afford to do anything else. To stand still means, paradoxically enough, to go backward, and for an artist that is fatal. To keep on growing means the constant necessity for getting a correct perspective of ourselves. We must stand off, so to speak, and look at ourselves through very critical glasses. If we once lose our perspective we lose all.

Life itself is growth, and the minute we allow ourselves to stop growing we really stop being vitally alive. And it is so fatally easy for people to get into a rut, to bask in the noonday sun of self-satisfaction, to cease to grow. Take my own profession, for instance. In the realm of grand opera, ignoring precedent and striking out into new paths is one of the hardest things to achieve. How easy it is for the producers of opera to be content with age old traditions, to go on going the easy thing. The antiquated thing that has become so much a matter of habit that thinking about it becomes unnecessary!

. . . When I consider the achievements of women in the past few years in the field of athletics I find it impossible to do so without taking into account the tremendous freedom-giving changes in fashion that have accompanied them. And enjoying the blessings of short hair is a necessary part of those fashion changes. To my way of thinking, long hair belongs to the age of general feminine helplessness. Bobbed hair belongs to the age of freedom, frankness, and progressiveness.

This is my view of the situation, but I should like to state most emphatically that I have no desire to lay down any fixed arbitrary rule for any one else to follow. Whether a woman wears her hair long or short, is her individual affair. I only know which *I* prefer. I can see nothing but what is progressive or beneficial in bobbed hair for women, altho I must admit there is one very tragic situation that is the direct result of women bobbing their hair, and that is, of course, the sorry plight of the hairpin manufacturers.

*   *   *

Why I Have Not Bobbed Mine

Mary Pickford

In the epidemic of hair-cutting which has swept the country, I am one of the few who have escaped. That does not mean that I have been inoculated by the germ, but that I have resisted valiantly. It has been a hard-fought battle, and the problem has occupied many of my waking and sleeping hours. I say "sleeping" because it often intrudes itself into my dreams.

Sometimes it comes in a pleasant guise, where I gaze enraptured at the mirrored reflection of my sleek bobbed head, and sometimes it is a dreadful nightmare, when I feel the cold shears at the back of my neck and see my curls fall one by one at my feet, useless, lifeless things to be packed away in tissue-paper with other outworn treasures.

I suppose almost every woman in the world has had a moment of trepidation before she made the final and momentous decision to part with her crowning glory; but in my case there are, perhaps, more reasons for hesitation than in the case of most people.

In the first place, my curls have become so identified with me that they have become almost a

trademark, and what old-established firm would change its trade-mark without giving considerable thought to the matter? Perhaps I am not quite fair to myself when I say "a trademark." I think they mean more than that—in some strange way they have become a symbol—and I think shorn of them I should become almost as Samson after his unfortunate meeting with Delilah.

It seems, no matter what my desires, that I am dedicated to little-girl roles for the rest of my screen life, and the curls here, of course, are invaluable to me. Curls are the one distinctive attribute left to little girls. Their older sisters, mothers, and grandmothers have robbed them of everything else. It is true that there are many small girls with short hair, but where could you find a mother or grandmother with long curls?

I could give a lengthy and, I think, convincing discourse about long hair making a woman more feminine, but there is some doubt in my mind as to whether it does or not. Of one thing I am sure: she looks smarter with a bob, and smartness rather than beauty seems to be the goal of every woman these days.

Whenever I go to the theater and see the rows of heads in front of me, I send up a little prayer of thanksgiving that we no longer have to view great masses of false hair, curls and puffs of varying shades, and that dreadful abomination once known as the "rat." But I cannot confess to any liking for shaved necks. They are dreadful and take away all charm and femininity from the most attractive woman.

Some gray-haired women look well with a bob. I think it depends upon the shape of the head and the size of the woman. If she is large, bobbed hair will make her head seem disproportionately small and will cause her neck to look too large for the face above it. After all, there is nothing more feminine than a beautiful head of well-cared-for hair simply coiled. Men admire it. They like the Greek line which some women are able to achieve with their smooth, shining coils of hair.

Then, too, in spite of the great variety of haircuts, one can achieve many more effects with long hair. This is, to me, of vital importance. A wind-blown bob or boyish bob has to remain just what it is until the next visit to the barber or until nature repairs the damage, but long hair can be dressed according to mood or circumstance. . . .

All the lovely ladies of history and romance have had long hair. Can you imagine a fairy princess with short, bobbed locks? It is unthinkable and almost shocking. Can you picture Elaine, the lily maid, floating down to Camelot on her barge without her golden curls over her shoulders? How could the prince have climbed to *Rapunzel,* "let down your hair"? And what a predicament *Lady Godiva* would have been in!

Then there is my family to consider. I think I should never be forgiven by my mother, my husband, or my maid if I should commit the indiscretion of cutting my hair. The last in particular seems to take a great personal pride in its length and texture, and her horror-stricken face whenever I mention the possibility of cutting it makes me pause and consider. Perhaps I have a little sentimental feeling for it myself. I have had my curls quite a while now and have become somewhat attached to them. Besides, there is no use denying the fact, no matter how much I should like to do so, that I am not a radical.

I am by nature conservative and even a bit old-fashioned, which is a dreadful thing to admit in this day and age. But the real reason why I do not bob my hair is undoubtedly on account of the requests received in my "fan" mail. Every day letters come in from the children saying, "Please do not bob your hair." "Please do not cut off your curls." I should feel that I was failing them if I ignored such an insistent plea. I haven't the courage to fly in the face of their disapproval nor have I the wish. If I am a slave, at least I am a willing slave. For their love and affection and loyalty I owe them everything, and if curls are the price I shall pay it.

Now, after giving all these arguments against the bob, I feel the old irresistible urge, and it is quite likely that some day in frenzied haste casting all caution to the winds, forgetting fans and family, I shall go to a coiffeur and come out a shorn lamb to join the great army of the bobbed.

* * *

REVIEW QUESTIONS

1. Which of the two women provides the more convincing argument and why?
2. In what ways are the terms *progressive* and *conservative* used to justify Garden's and Pickford's perspectives on bobbing hair?

HENRY L. MYERS

Motion Pictures a Source of Concern (1922)

As motion pictures grew in popularity, they also grew more controversial. Traditionalists viewed movies as a source of immoral and even criminal behavior. During the early 1920s, religious, social, and political leaders demanded that the government investigate the new industry and create regulations to enforce proper behavior. Among the leaders of the effort to regulate and "censor" movies was Senator Henry L. Myers of Montana. On June 29, 1922, he explained to the U.S. Senate his concerns.

Senator Henry L. Myers, U.S. Senate Speech, *Congressional Record*, June 29, 1922, pp. 9655–57. [Editorial insertions appear in square brackets—*Ed.*]

The motion picture is a great invention, and it has . . . great educational power for good or bad in our civilization. . . .

Through motion pictures the young and the old may see depicted every good motive, laudable ambition, commendable characteristic, ennobling trait of humanity. They may be taught that honesty is the best policy; that virtue and worth are rewarded; that industry leads to success. Those who live in the country or in small interior towns, and who never visit large cities, may see pictured the skyscrapers, the crowded streets, the rush and jam of metropolitan cities. . . .

However, from all accounts, the business has been conducted, generally speaking, upon a low plane and in a decidedly sordid manner. Those who own and control the industry seem to have been of the opinion that the sensual, the sordid, the prurient, the phases of fast life, the ways of extravagance, the risqué, the paths of shady life, drew the greatest attendance and coined for them the most money, and apparently they have been out to get the coin, no matter what the effect upon the public, young or old; and when thoughtful people have suggested or advocated official censorship, in the interest of good citizenship and wholesome morals, the owners of the industry have resented it and, in effect, declared that it was nobody's business other than theirs and concerned nobody other than them what kind of shows they produced; that if people did not like their shows they could stay away from them; that it was their business, and they would conduct it as they might please. At least they have vigorously fought all attempts at censorship and resented them. . . .

In that they are mistaken. The State [all levels of government] has an interest in citizenship and a concern in the education of the young. The State has an interest in good morals. It regulates in many ways all of those things. The motion-picture industry vitally concerns all of those things—citizenship, education, morals—and is therefore subject to regulation by the State. It has become a public utility, and is therefore the legitimate subject of State regulation. . . .

The industry has gone so far in defying public sentiment, and has been so flagrant in its abuse of its privileges that a public sentiment for censorship has been aroused which will not be brooked. It may be temporarily checked; it may be temporarily lulled by fair promises, but it is bound to grow, because censorship is needed and would be a good thing. . . .

I believe that a great deal of the extravagance of the day, a great deal of the disposition to live beyond one's means, yea, a great deal of the crime of the day comes from moving pictures. Through them young people gain ideas of fast life, shady ways, laxity of living, loose morals. Crime is freely depicted in alluring colors. Lax morals are held up lightly before them. The sensual is strongly appealed to. Many of the pictures are certainly not elevating; some, at least, are not fit to be seen.

About 18 months ago, in this city, there occurred a foul and most shocking murder. . . . Four youths of this city, in age from 15 to 20 years, as I recollect, stole an automobile, and in it followed an honest, peaceable, industrious barber as he was going to his loving family and quiet home after a day's work, and overtaking him, one of the youths jumped out of the automobile, in a residential section of the city, and murdered him by firing a pistol at him at close range. The victim dropped dead. The youths became panic-stricken on account of close-at-hand pedestrians and fled in the stolen machine. . . .

I have no doubt those young criminals got their ideas of the romance of crime from moving pictures. I believe moving pictures are doing as much harm to-day as saloons did in the days of the open saloon—especially to the young. They are running day and night, Sunday and every other day, the year round, and in most jurisdictions without any regulation by censorship. I would not abolish them. . . . I would close them on Sunday and regulate them week days by judicious censorship. . . .

When we look to the source of the moving pictures, the material for them, the personnel of those who pose for them, we need not wonder that many of the pictures are pernicious. . . .

At Hollywood, Calif., is a colony of these people, where debauchery, riotous living, drunkenness, ribaldry, dissipation, free love, seem to be conspicuous.... These are some of the characters from whom the young people of to-day are deriving a large part of their education, views of life, and character-forming habits. From these sources our young people gain much of their views of life, inspirations, and education. Rather a poor source, is it not? Looks like there is some need for censorship, does it not?

*   *   *

The Great Black Migration (1917)

One of the most important social developments triggered by World War I was a massive migration of African Americans from the rural South to other regions of the country. Over a half million men, women, and children relocated between 1915 and 1920, and thousands more followed during the 1920s. They left in search of better paying jobs and the hope of greater social equality and political participation. Black newspapers such as the Chicago Defender *actively encouraged the exodus. Most of the migrants settled in cities such as New York, Philadelphia, and Chicago, forming African American neighborhoods that became fertile centers of black culture. The following letters from southern blacks requesting information about life in the North poignantly reveal the challenges for those wishing to migrate.*

From Emmet J. Scott, ed., "Letters of Negro Migrants of 1916–1918," *Journal of Negro History* 4 (July 1, 1919): 290–340.

Palestine, Tex. 1/2/1917—Sir: I hereby enclose you a few lines to find out some things if you will be so kind to word them to me. I am a southerner lad and has never been in the north no further than Texas and I has heard much talk about the north and how much better the colard people are treated up there than down here and I has ben striving so hard in my coming up and now I see that I cannot get up there without the ade of some one and I wants to ask you Dear Sir to please direct me in your best manner the step that I shall take to get there and if there are any way that you can help me to get there I am kindly asking for your ade. And if you will ade me please notify me by return mail because I am sure ancious to make it in the north because these southern white people ar so mean and they seems to be getting worse and I wants to get away and they wont pay me in getting up there please give me information how I can get there I would like to get there in the early spring, if I can get there if possible. Our southern white people are so cruel we collard people are almost afraid to walke the streets after night. So please let me hear from you by return mail. I will not say very much in this letter I will tell you more about it when I hear from you please ans. soon.

REVIEW QUESTIONS

1. According to Senator Myers, what problems resulted from an unregulated movie industry?
2. How did Myers propose to regulate and censor the movie business?

Newbern, Ala. 4/17/1917—Sir: . . . Doubtless you have learned of the great exodus of our people to the north and west from this and other states. I wish to say that we are forced to go when one thinks of a grown man wages is only fifty to seventy cents per day for all grades of work. He is compelled to go where there is better wages and sociable conditions, believe me. When I say that [at] many places here in this state the only thing that the black man gets is a peck of meal and from three to four lbs. of bacon per week, and he is treated as a slave. As leaders we are powerless for we dare not resent such or to show even the slightest disapproval. Only a few days ago more than 1,000 people left here for the North and West. They cannot stay here. The white man is saying that you must not go, but they are not doing anything by way of assisting the black man to stay. As a minister of the Methodist Episcopal Church I am on the verge of starvation simply because of the above conditions. I shall be glad to know if there is any possible way by which I could be of real service to you as director of your society. Thanking you in advance for an early reply, and for any suggestions that you might be able to offer.

Dapne, Ala., 4/20/17—Sir: I am writing you to let you know that there is 15 or 20 familys wants to come up there at once but cant come on account of money to come with and we cant phone you here we will be killed they dont want us to leave here & say if we dont go to war and fight for our country they are going to kill us and wants to get away if we can if you send 20 passes there is no doubt that every one of us will com at once. we are not doing any thing here we cant get a living out of what we do now some of these people are farmers and som are cooks

barbers and black smiths but the greater part are farmers & good worker & honest people & up to date the trash pile dont want to go no where These are nice people and respectable find a place like that & send passes & we all will come at once we all wants to leave here out of this hard luck place if you cant use us find some place that does need this kind of people we are called Negroes here. I am a reader of the Defender and am delighted to know how times are there & was to glad to, know if we could get some one to pass us away from here to a better land. We work but cant get scarcely any thing for it & they dont want us to go away & there is not much of anything here to do & nothing for it. Please find some one that need this kind of a people & send at once for us. We dont want anything but our wareing and bed clothes & have not got no money to get away from here with & beging to get away before we are killed and hope to here from you at once. We cant talk to you over the phone here we are afraid to they dont want to hear one say that he or she wants to leave here if we do we are apt to be killed. They say if we dont go to war they are not going to let us stay here with their folks and it is not any thing that we have done to them.

REVIEW QUESTIONS

1. According to these accounts, what role did racial discrimination play in provoking southern blacks to migrate to the North?
2. Describe some of the economic hardships faced by blacks in the South.
3. Why might southern elites have wanted blacks to remain in the South?

ALAIN LOCKE

FROM Enter the New Negro (1925)

The economic boom triggered by the military needs of the First World War spawned the Great Migration of African Americans from the South to the Northeast and Midwest. One result of the Great Migration was the transformation of the Harlem neighborhood in New York City into a thriving center of black cultural life. Among the leaders of the Harlem Renaissance was Alain Leroy Locke, a professor of philosophy at historically black Howard University in Washington, D.C. Locke was born in Philadelphia in 1886. The child of well-educated professionals, he attended Harvard University and was the first African American to win a Rhodes Scholarship to England's Oxford University. He later earned a Ph.D. at Harvard and became the philosophy department chair at Howard University. During the twenties, Locke was an ardent champion of the emerging Harlem Renaissance and the New Negro movement, both of which sought to encourage African Americans to take pride in their heritage and to engage in artistic creativity while integrating themselves into mainstream American culture. He urged black poets, writers, artists, and sculptors to take pride in their black identity as expressed through the arts.

From "Enter the New Negro," *Survey Graphic*, March 1925. [Editorial insertions appear in square brackets—*Ed.*]

In the last decade something beyond the watch and guard of statistics has happened in the life of the American Negro and the three norns [mythological Norse rulers] who have traditionally presided over the Negro problem have a changeling in their laps. The Sociologist, the Philanthropist, the Race-leader are not unaware of the New Negro, but they are at a loss to account for him. He simply cannot be swathed in their formulae. For the younger generation is vibrant with a new psychology; the new spirit is awake in the masses, and under the very eyes of the professional observers is transforming what has been a perennial problem into the progressive phases of contemporary Negro life.

Could such a metamorphosis have taken place as suddenly as it has appeared to? The answer is no; not because the New Negro is not here, but because the Old Negro had long become more of a myth than a man. The Old Negro, we must remember, was a creature of moral debate and historical controversy. He has been a stock figure perpetuated as an historical fiction partly in innocent sentimentalism, partly in deliberate reactionism.

The Negro himself has contributed his share to this through a sort of protective social mimicry forced upon him by the adverse circumstances of dependence. So for generations in the mind of America, the Negro has been more of a formula than a human being—a something to be argued about, condemned or defended, to be "kept down," or "in his place," or "helped up," to be worried with or worried over, harassed or patronized, a social bogey or a social burden.

The thinking Negro even has been induced to share this same general attitude, to focus his attention on controversial issues, to see himself in the distorted perspective of a social problem. His shadow, so to speak, has been more real to him than his personality. Through having had to appeal from the unjust stereotypes of his oppressors and traducers to those of his liberators, friends and benefactors he has had to subscribe to the traditional positions from which his case has been viewed. Little true social or self-understanding has or could come from such a situation.

[T]he mind of the Negro seems suddenly to have slipped from under the tyranny of social intimidation and to be shaking off the psychology of imitation and implied inferiority. By shedding the old chrysalis [butterfly pupa] of the Negro problem we are achieving something like a spiritual emancipation. Until recently, lacking self-understanding, we have been almost as much of a problem to ourselves as we still are to others. But the decade that found us with a problem has left us with only a task. The multitude perhaps feels as yet only a strange relief and a new vague urge, but the thinking few know that in the reaction the vital inner grip of prejudice has been broken.

With this renewed self-respect and self-dependence, the life of the Negro community is bound to enter a new dynamic phase, the buoyancy from within compensating for whatever pressure there may be of conditions from without. The migrant masses, shifting from countryside to city, hurdle several generations of experience at a leap, but more important, the same thing happens spiritually in the life-attitudes and self-expression of the Young Negro, in his poetry, his art, his education and his new outlook, with the additional advantage, of course, of the poise and greater certainty of knowing what it is all about. From this comes the promise and warrant of a new leadership. As one of them has discerningly put it:

> We have tomorrow
> Bright before us
> Like a flame.
>
> Yesterday, a night-gone thing
> A sun-down name.
>
> And dawn today
> Broad arch above the road we came.
> We march!

This is what, even more than any "most creditable record of fifty years of freedom," requires that the Negro of to-day be seen through other than the dusty spectacles of past controversy. The day of "aunties," "uncles" and "mammies" is equally gone. Uncle Tom and Sambo have passed on, and even the "Colonel" and "George" play barnstorm roles from which they escape with relief when the public spotlight is off. The popular melodrama has about played itself out, and it is time to scrap the fictions, garret the bogeys and settle down to a realistic facing of facts.

First we must observe some of the changes which since the traditional lines of opinion were drawn have rendered these quite obsolete. A main change has been, of course, that shifting of the Negro population which has made the Negro problem no longer exclusively or even predominantly Southern. Why should our minds remain sectionalized, when the problem itself no longer is? Then the trend of migration has not only been toward the North and the Central Midwest, but city-ward and to the great centers of industry—the problems of adjustment are new, practical, local and not peculiarly racial. Rather they are an integral part of the large industrial and social problems of our present-day democracy. And finally, with the Negro rapidly in process of class differentiation, if it ever was warrantable to regard and treat the Negro *en masse* it is becoming with every day less possible, more unjust and more ridiculous.

In the very process of being transplanted, the Negro is becoming transformed. The tide of Negro migration, northward and city-ward, is not to be fully explained as a blind flood started by the demands of war industry coupled with the shutting off of foreign migration, or by the pressure of poor crops coupled with increased social terrorism in certain sections of the South and Southwest. Neither labor demand, the boll-weevil nor the Ku Klux Klan is a basic factor, however contributory any or all of them may have been. The wash and rush of this human tide on the beach line of the northern city centers is to be explained primarily in terms of a new vision of opportunity, of social and economic freedom, of a spirit to seize, even in the face of an extortionate and heavy toll, a chance for the improvement of conditions. With each successive wave of it, the movement of the Negro becomes more and more a mass movement toward the larger and the more democratic chance—in the Negro's case a deliberate flight not only from countryside to city, but from medieval America to modern.

Take Harlem as an instance of this. Here in Manhattan is not merely the largest Negro community in the world, but the first concentration in history of so many diverse elements of Negro life. It has attracted the African, the West Indian, the Negro American; has brought together the Negro of the North and the Negro of the South; the man from the city and the man from the town and village; the peasant, the student, the business man, the professional man, artist, poet, musician, adventurer and worker, preacher and criminal, exploiter and social outcast. Each group has come with its own separate motives and for its own special ends, but their greatest experience has been the finding of one another.

Proscription and prejudice have thrown these dissimilar elements into a common area of contact and interaction. Within this area, race sympathy and unity have determined a further fusing of sentiment and experience. So what began in terms of segregation becomes more and more, as its elements mix and react, the laboratory of a great race-welding. Hitherto, it must be admitted that American Negroes have been a race more in name than in fact, or to be exact, more in sentiment than in experience. The chief bond between them has been that of a common condition rather than a common consciousness; a problem in common rather than a life in common.

In Harlem, Negro life is seizing upon its first chances for group expression and self-determination. It is, or promises at least to be, a race capital. That is why our comparison is taken with those nascent centers of folk-expression and self-determination which are playing a creative part in the world to-day. Without pretense to their political significance, Harlem has the same role to play for the New Negro as Dublin has had for the New Ireland or Prague for the New Czechoslovakia.

Harlem, I grant you, isn't typical—but it is significant, it is prophetic. No sane observer, however sympathetic to the new trend, would contend that the great masses are articulate as yet, but they stir, they move, they are more physically restless. The challenge of the new intellectuals among them is clear enough—the "race radicals" and the realists who have broken with the old epoch of philanthropic guidance, sentimental appeal and protest. But are we after all only reading into the stirrings of a sleeping giant the dreams of an agitator? The answer is in the migrating peasant. It is the "man farthest down" who is most active in getting up. One of the most characteristic symptoms of this is the professional man himself migrating to recapture his constituency after a vain effort to maintain in some Southern corner what for years back seemed an established living and clientele. The clergyman following his errant flock, the physician or lawyer trailing his clients, supply the true clues. In a real sense it is the rank and file who are leading, and the leaders who are following. A transformed and transforming psychology permeates the masses.

When the racial leaders of twenty years ago spoke of developing race-pride and stimulating race-consciousness, and of the desirability of race solidarity, they could not in any accurate degree have anticipated the abrupt feeling that has surged up and now pervades the awakened centers. Some of the recognized Negro leaders and a powerful section of white opinion identified with "race work" of the older order have indeed attempted to discount this feeling as a "passing phase," an attack of "race nerves" so to speak, an "aftermath of the war," and the like. It has not abated, however, if we are to gauge by the present tone and temper of the Negro press, or by the shift in popular support from the officially recognized and orthodox spokesmen to those of the independent, popular, and often radical type who are unmistakable symptoms of a new order. It is a social disservice to blunt the fact that the Negro of the Northern centers has reached a stage where tutelage, even of the most interested and well-intentioned sort, must give place to new relationships, where positive self-direction must be reckoned with in ever-increasing measure. The American mind must reckon with a fundamentally changed Negro.

The Negro too, for his part, has idols of the tribe to smash. If on the one hand the white man has erred in making the Negro appear to be that which would excuse or extenuate his treatment of him, the Negro, in turn, has too often unnecessarily excused himself because of the way he has been treated. The intelligent Negro of to-day is resolved not to make discrimination an extenuation for his shortcomings in performance, individual or collective; he is trying to hold himself at par, neither inflated by sentimental allowances nor depreciated by current social discounts. For this he must know himself and be known for precisely what he is, and for that reason he welcomes the new scientific rather than the old sentimental interest. Sentimental interest in the Negro has ebbed. We used to lament this as the falling off of our friends; now we rejoice and pray to be delivered both from self-pity and condescension. The mind of each racial group has had a bitter weaning, apathy or hatred on one side matching disillusionment or resentment on the other; but they face each other to-day with the possibility at least of entirely new mutual attitudes.

*   *   *

It must be increasingly recognized that the Negro has already made very substantial contributions, not only in his folk-art, music especially, which has always found appreciation, but in larger, though humbler and less acknowledged ways. For generations the Negro has been the peasant matrix of that section of America which has most undervalued him, and here he has contributed not only materially in labor and in social patience, but spiritually as well. The South has unconsciously absorbed the gift of his folk-temperament. In less than half a generation it will be easier to recognize this, but the fact remains that a leaven of humor, sentiment, imagination and tropic nonchalance has gone into the making of the South from a humble, unacknowl-edged source. A second crop of the Negro's gifts promises still more largely. He now becomes a conscious contributor and lays aside the status of a beneficiary and ward for that of a collaborator and participant in American civilization.

The great social gain in this is the releasing of our talented group from the arid fields of controversy and debate to the productive fields of creative expression. The especially cultural recognition they win should in turn prove the key to that revaluation of the Negro which must precede or accompany any considerable further betterment of race relationships.

But whatever the general effect, the present generation will have added the motives of self-expression and spiritual development to the old and still unfinished task of making material headway and progress. No one who understandingly faces the situation with its substantial accomplishment or views the new scene with its still more abundant promise can be entirely without hope. And certainly, if in our lifetime the Negro should not be able to celebrate his full initiation into American democracy, he can at least, on the warrant of these things, celebrate the attainment of a significant and satisfying new phase of group development, and with it a spiritual Coming of Age.

REVIEW QUESTIONS

1. What did Locke mean by the "Old Negro" sensibility? How was the "New Negro" fashioning a different outlook?
2. In what ways did Locke see the flowering of African American culture as aiding the larger quest for civil liberties and social equality?

MARCUS GARVEY

FROM The Negro's Greatest Enemy (1923)

During the early twentieth century, Marcus Garvey, an energetic and ambitious Jamaican-born black journalist, organized an international movement to promote the civil rights of the "colored races" and encourage the migration of blacks to Africa so that they could govern themselves. In 1916, he moved to New York City, where he transformed the Universal Negro Improvement Association into a thriving organization boasting millions of worldwide members. In 1919 he created the Black Star Line, a transatlantic steamship company, to transport blacks from the United States and the West Indies to Africa. Convicted of mail fraud as a result of his fund-raising efforts, he was incarcerated at the Tombs Prison in New York City in 1923. While jailed, Garvey wrote the following autobiographical account to address the attacks on him by critics and the media.

From *Current History* 18 (September 1923), pp. 951–57. Reprinted with permission from *Current History* magazine. © 2018 Current History, Inc. [Editorial insertions appear in square brackets—*Ed.*]

I was born in the island of Jamaica, British West Indies, on Aug. 17, 1887. My parents were black negroes. . . . I grew up with other black and white boys. I was never whipped by any, but made them all respect the strength of my arms. I got my education from many sources—through private tutors, two public schools, two grammar or high schools and two colleges.

*   *   *

To me, at home in my early days, there was no difference between white and black. . . . All of us were playmates. We romped and were happy children playmates together. The little white girl whom I liked most knew no better than I did myself. We were two innocent fools who never dreamed of a race feeling and problem. As a child, I went to school with white boys and girls, like all other negroes. We were not called negroes then. I never heard the term negro used once until I was about fourteen.

At fourteen, my little white playmate and I parted. Her parents thought the time had come to separate us and draw the color line. They sent her and another sister to Edinburgh, Scotland, and told her that she was never to write or try to get in touch with me, for I was a "nigger." It was then that I found for the first time that there was some difference in humanity, and that there were different races, each having its own separate and distinct social life. . . .

*   *   *

At maturity, the black and white boys separated, and took different courses in life. I grew up then to see the difference between the races more and more. My schoolmates as young men did not know or remember me anymore. Then I realized that I had to make a fight for a place in the world, that it was not so easy to pass on to office and position. Personally, however, I had not much difficulty in finding and holding a place for myself, for I was aggressive.

At eighteen, I had an excellent position as manager of a large printing establishment having under my control several men old enough to be my grand-fathers. But I got mixed up with public life. I started to take an interest in the politics of my country, and then I saw the injustice done to my race because it was black, and I became dissatisfied on that account.

I went traveling to South and Central America and parts of the West Indies to find out if it was so elsewhere, and I found the same situation. I set sail for Europe to find out if it was different there, and again I found the same stumbling-block—"You are black." I read of the conditions in America. I read "Up From Slavery," by Booker T. Washington, and then my doom—if I may so call it—of being a race leader dawned upon me in London after I had traveled through almost half of Europe.

I asked, "Where is the black man's government?" "Where is his king and his kingdom?" "Where is his president, his country, and his ambassador, his army, his navy, his men of big affairs?" I could not find them, and then I declared, "I will help to make them."

Becoming naturally restless for the opportunity of doing something [for] the advancement of my race, I was determined that the black man would not continue to be kicked about by all the other races and nations of the world. . . . My young and ambitious mind led me into flights of great imagination. I saw before me then, even as I do now, a new world of black men, not peons, serfs, dogs and slaves, but a nation of sturdy men making their impress upon civilization and causing a new light to dawn upon the human race. I could not remain in London any more.

My brain was afire. There was a world of thought to conquer. I had to start ere it became too late and the work be not done. Immediately I boarded a ship at Southampton for Jamaica, where I arrived on July 15, 1914. The Universal Negro Improvement Association and African Communities (Imperial) League was founded and organized five days after my arrival, with the program of uniting all the negro peoples of the world into one great body to establish a country and Government absolutely their own.

*　　*　　*

I got in touch with Booker Washington [in the United States] and told him what I wanted to do. He invited me to America and promised to speak with me in the southern and other states to help my work. Although he died in the fall of 1915, I made my arrangements and arrived in the United States on March 23, 1916.

Here I found a new and different problem. I immediately visited some of the then so-called negro leaders, only to discover, after a close study of them, that they had no program, but were mere opportunists who were living off their so-called leadership while the poor people were groping in the dark. I traveled through thirty-eight states and everywhere found the same condition. I visited Tuskegee [Alabama] and paid my respects to the dead hero, Booker Washington, and then returned to New York, where I organized the New York division of the Universal Negro Improvement Association. . . .

*　　*　　*

The organization under my presidency grew by leaps and bounds. I started The Negro World. Being a journalist, I edited this paper free of cost for the association, and worked for them without pay until November, 1920. I traveled all over the country for the association at my own expense, and established branches until in 1919 we had about thirty branches in different cities. By my writings and speeches, we were able to build up a large organization of over 2,000,000 by June, 1919, at which time we launched the program of the Black Star Line.

*　　*　　*

The first year of our activities for the Black Star Line added prestige to the Universal Negro Improvement Association. . . . Our first ship, the steamship "Yarmouth," had made two voyages to the West Indies and Central America. The white press had flashed the news all over the world. I, a young negro, as President of the corporation, had become famous. My name was discussed on five continents. The Universal Negro Improvement Association gained millions of followers all over the world. By August, 1920, over 4,000,000 persons had joined the movement. A convention of all the negro peoples of the world was called to meet in New York that month. Delegates came from all parts of the known world. Over 25,000 persons packed the Madison Square Garden on Aug. 1 to hear me speak to the first International Convention of Negroes. It was a record-breaking meeting, the first and the biggest of its kind. The name of Garvey had become known as a leader of his race.

Such fame among negroes was too much for other race leaders and politicians to tolerate. My downfall was planned by my enemies. They laid all kinds of traps for me. They scattered their spies among the employees of the Black Star Line and the Universal Negro Improvement Association. Our office records were stolen. Employees started to be openly dishonest; we could get no convictions against them; even if on complaint they were held by a Magistrate, they were dismissed by the Grand Jury.

The ships' officers started to pile up thousands of dollars of debts against the company without the knowledge of the officers of the corporation. Our ships were damaged at sea, and there was a general riot of wreck and ruin. Officials of the Universal Negro Improvement Association also began to steal and be openly dishonest. I had to dismiss them. They joined my enemies, and thus I had an endless fight on my hands to save the ideals of the association and carry out our program for the race. My negro enemies, finding that they alone could not destroy me, resorted to misrepresenting me to the leaders of the white race, several of whom, without proper investigation, also opposed me. . . .

The temporary ruin of the Black Star Line in no way affected the larger work of the Universal Negro Improvement Association, which now has 900 branches with an approximate membership of 6,000,000. This organization has succeeded in organizing the negroes all over the world and we now look forward to a renaissance that will create a new people and bring about the restoration of Ethiopia's ancient glory.

Being black, I have committed an unpardonable offense against the very light colored negroes in America and the West Indies by making myself famous as a negro leader of millions. In their view, no black man must rise above them, but I still forge ahead determined to give to the world the truth about the new negro who is determined to make and hold for himself a place in the affairs of men. The Universal Negro Improvement Association has been misrepresented by my enemies. They have tried to make it appear that we are hostile to other races. This is absolutely false. We love all humanity. We are working for the peace of the world which we believe can only come about when all races are given their due.

We feel that there is absolutely no reason why there should be any differences between the black and white races, if each stop to adjust and steady itself. We believe in the purity of both races. We do not believe the black man should be encouraged in the idea that his highest purpose in life is to marry a white woman, but we do believe that the white man should be taught to respect the black woman in the same way as he wants the black man to respect the white woman. It is a vicious and dangerous doctrine of social equality to urge, as certain colored leaders do, that black and white should get together, for that would destroy the racial purity of both.

We believe that the black people should have a country of their own where they should be given the fullest opportunity to develop politically, socially and industrially. . . . We believe that with the rising ambition of the negro, if a country is not provided for him in another 50 or 100 years, there will be a terrible clash that will end disastrously to him and disgrace our civilization. We desire to prevent such a clash by pointing the negro to a home of his own. We feel that all well-disposed and broad-minded white men will aid in this direction. It is because of this belief no doubt that my negro enemies, so as to prejudice me further in the opinion of the public, wickedly state that I am a member of the Ku Klux Klan, even though I am a black man.

I have been deprived of the opportunity of properly explaining my work to the white people of America through the prejudice worked up against me by jealous and wicked members of my own race. My success as a[n] organizer was much more than rival negro leaders could tolerate. They, regardless of consequences, either to me or to the race, had to destroy me by fair means or foul. The thousands of anonymous and other hostile letters written to the editors and publishers of the white press by negro rivals to prejudice me in the eyes of public opinion are sufficient evidence of the wicked and vicious opposition I have had to meet from among my own people, especially among the very lightly colored. . . . No wonder, therefore, that several Judges, District Attorneys and other high officials have been against me without knowing me. No wonder, therefore, that the great white population of this country and of the world has a wrong impression of the aims and objects of the Universal Negro Improvement Association and of the work of Marcus Garvey.

Having had the wrong education as a start in his racial career, the negro has become his own greatest enemy. Most of the trouble I have had in advancing the cause of the race has come from negroes. Booker Washington aptly described the race in one of his lectures by stating that we were like crabs in a barrel, that none would allow the other to climb over, but on any such attempt all would continue to pull back into the barrel the one crab that would make the effort to climb out. Yet, those of us with vision cannot desert the race, leaving it to suffer and die.

Looking forward a century or two, we can see an economic and political death struggle for the survival of the different race groups. Many of our present-day national centers will have become overcrowded with vast surplus populations. The fight for bread and position will be keen and severe. The weaker and unprepared group is bound to go under. That is why, visionaries as we are in the Universal Negro Improvement Association, we are fighting for the founding of a negro nation in Africa, so that there will be no clash between black and white and that each race will have a separate existence and civilization all its own without courting suspicion and hatred or eyeing each other with jealousy and rivalry within the borders of the same country.

White men who have struggled for and built up their countries and their own civilizations are not disposed to hand them over to the negro or any other race without let or hindrance. It would be unreasonable to expect this. Hence any vain assumption on the part of the negro to imagine that he will one day become president of the nation, governor of the state, or mayor of the city in the countries of white men, is like waiting on the devil and his angels to take up their residence in the Realm on High and direct there the affairs of Paradise.

*   *   *

REVIEW QUESTIONS

1. Why did Garvey promote black nationalism?
2. According to Garvey, who were his greatest enemies in his effort to provide a homeland in Africa for blacks from across the world?

24 ❧ THE REACTIONARY TWENTIES

By the end of 1920, the race riots that swept across the country after the Great War had dissipated, but they left in their wake an atmosphere of venomous racism and ethnic prejudice that repeatedly erupted in violence. During the early 1920s, the Ku Klux Klan witnessed a dramatic revival, and anti-immigration sentiment culminated in new laws intended specifically to restrict the number of newcomers from southern and eastern Europe.

The clash between rural and urban values reached a theatrical climax in 1925, during the famous "monkey trial" in the small town of Dayton, Tennessee. A state law prohibiting the teaching of Charles Darwin's theory of evolution was challenged by a high school biology teacher named John Scopes, and the resulting trial pitted the forces of fundamentalism against liberalism. The state court ruled against Scopes, but the widely publicized trial helped generate a nationwide assault against fundamentalism that further eroded the foundations of biblical and social orthodoxy. Liberal Protestants and advocates of modern scientific methods heaped scorn on fundamentalists, initiating a cultural civil war over Christianity that persists today.

In the political arena, the twenties witnessed the resurgence of the Republican Party and the rapid decline of progressivism. In early 1921, the new Republican president, Warren G. Harding, promised the nation a "return to normalcy." This meant abandoning the progressive efforts of Wilson and Theodore Roosevelt to promote political reform and economic regulation. Instead, Harding and the Republicans revived the pro-business outlook that had served the party so well during the Gilded Age. Harding's successors, Calvin Coolidge and Herbert Hoover, shared this philosophy and presided over the greatest economic boom in the nation's history during the 1920s. Coolidge, who assumed office in 1923 upon Harding's death, proclaimed that the "business of America is business." To foster business growth, the Republicans emphasized reduced government spending, lower taxes, and higher tariffs. Coolidge once remarked that if the federal government disappeared, few would notice and even fewer would regret it.

The Republican success in restoring prosperity in the 1920s worked almost too well. In 1928, Herbert Hoover rode a wave of economic growth into the White House. Hoover was the best qualified of all the Republican presidents during the twenties, but he assumed office in March 1929, the year in which the nation's economy began to spiral downward into the worst depression in its history. To be sure, Hoover did not cause the Great Depression, but he failed to recognize the ominous warning signals, and he underestimated the downturn's scope and its human devastation.

WARREN G. HARDING

FROM The South and the Negro (1921)

For all his political conservatism, President Warren G. Harding was remarkably progressive in his stance toward race relations. Unlike his predecessor, Woodrow Wilson, who staunchly believed in white supremacy, Harding sought to convince the South to allow African Americans to participate fully in political and economic life. To that end, he used the occasion of a 1921 visit to Birmingham, Alabama, to deliver a speech to a largely white audience in which he expressed his candid views on the "race question, whether you like it or not." The race question, he stressed, was no longer simply a southern issue; it was a national issue. Large numbers of southern blacks had moved to the North and Midwest during the Great War and many others had served with distinction in the military. That blacks served with distinction in the military led many whites outside the South to change their thinking on racial issues. It was time for southern whites to do the same. While assuring his audience that he had no interest in promoting social equality for whites and African Americans, Harding encouraged whites and blacks to "lay aside old prejudices and old antagonisms."

From "The South and the Negro," *New York Times*, October 27, 1921.

HARDING SAYS NEGRO MUST HAVE EQUALITY IN POLITICAL LIFE

. . . Here, it has seemed to me, is suggestion of the true way out [of the racial dilemma]. Politically and economically there need be no occasion for great and permanent differentiation, for limitations of the individual's opportunity, provided that on both sides there shall be recognition of the absolute divergence in things social and racial. When I suggest the possibility of economic equality between the races I mean it in precisely the same way and to the same extent that I would mean if I spoke of equality of economic opportunity as between members of the same race. In each case I would mean equality proportioned to the honest capacities and deserts of the individual.

Men of both races may well stand uncompromisingly against every suggestion of social equality. Indeed, it would be helpful to have that word 'equality' eliminated from this consideration; to have it accepted on both sides that this is not a question of social equality, but a question of inescapable differences. We shall have made real progress when we develop an attitude in the public and community thought of both races which recognizes this difference.

Take the political aspect. I would say let the black man vote when he is fit to vote: prohibit the white man voting when he is unfit to vote. Especially would I appeal to the self-respect of the colored race. I would inculcate in it the wish to improve itself as a distinct race, with a heredity, a set of traditions, an array of aspirations all its own. Out of such racial ambitions and pride will come natural segregations, without narrowing and rights, such as are proceeding in both rural and urban communities now in Southern States, satisfying natural inclinations and adding notably to happiness and contentment.

On the other hand I would insist upon equal educational opportunity for both. This does not mean that both would become equally educated within a generation or two generations or ten generations. Even men of the same race do not accomplish such an equality as that. There must be such education among the colored people as will enable them to develop their own leaders, capable of understanding and sympathizing with such a differentiation between the races as I have suggested—leaders who will inspire the race with proper ideals of race pride, of national pride, of honorable destiny; and important participation in the universal effort of advancement of as a whole. Racial amalgamation [intermarriage between blacks and whites] there cannot be. Partnership of the races in developing the highest aims of all humanity there must be if humanity, not only here but everywhere, is to achieve the end which we have set for it.

I can say to you people of the South, both white and black, that the time has passed when you are entitled to assume that this problem of races is peculiarly and particularly your problem. More and more it is becoming a problem of the North, more and more it is the problem of Africa, of South America, of the Pacific, of the South Seas, of the world. It is the problem of democracy everywhere, if we mean the things we say about democracy as the ideal political state.

The one thing we must sedulously avoid is the development of group and class organizations in this country. There has been time when we heard too much about the labor vote, the business vote, the Irish vote, the Scandinavian vote, the Italian vote, and so on. But the demagogues who would array class against class and group against group have fortunately found little to reward their efforts. That is because, despite the demagogues, the idea of our oneness as Americans has risen superior to every appeal to mere class and group.

And so I would wish it might be in this matter of our national problem of races. I would accept

that a black man cannot be a white man, and that he does not need and should not aspire to be as much like a white man as possible in order to accomplish the best that is possible for him. He should seek to be, and he should be encouraged to be, the best possible black man, and not the best possible imitation of a white man.

It is a matter of the keenest national concern that the South shall not be encouraged to make its colored population a vast reservoir of ignorance, to be drained away by the processes of migration into all other sections. That is what has been going on in recent years at a rate so accentuated that it has caused this question of races to be, as I have already said, no longer one of a particular section. Just as I do not wish the South to be politically entirely one party; just as I believe that is bad for the South, and for the rest of the country as well, so I do not want the colored people to be entirely of one party. I wish that both the tradition of a solidly Democratic South and the tradition of a solidly Republican black race might be broken up. Neither political sectionalism nor any system of rigid groupings of the people will in the long run prosper our country.

With such convictions one must urge the people of the South to take advantage of their superior understanding of this problem and to assume an attitude toward it that will deserve the confidence of the colored people. Likewise, I plead with my own political party to lay aside every program that looks to lining up the black man as a mere political adjunct. Let there be an end of prejudice and of demagogy in this line. Let the South understand the menace which lies in forcing upon the black race an attitude of political solidarity.

Every consideration, it seems to me, brings us back at last to the question of education. When I speak of education as a part of this race question, I do not want the States or the nation to attempt to educate people, whether white or black, into something they are not fitted to be. I have no sympathy with the half-baked altruism that would overstock us with doctors and lawyers of whatever color, and leave us in need of people fit and willing to do the manual work of a workaday world. But I would like to see an education that would fit every man not only to do his particular work as well as possible but to rise to a higher plane if he would deserve it. For that sort of education I have no fears, whether it be given to a black man or a white man. From that sort of education, I believe, black men, white men, the whole nation, would draw immeasurable benefit.

It is probable that as a nation we have come to the end of the period of very rapid increase in our population. Restricted immigration will reduce the rate of increase, and force us back upon our older population to find people to do the simpler, physically harder manual tasks. This will require some difficult readjustments.

In anticipation of such a condition, the South may well recognize that the North and West are likely to continue their drafts upon its colored population, and that if the South wishes to keep its fields producing and its industry still expanding it will have to compete for the services of the colored man. If it will realize its need for him and deal quite fairly with him, the South will be able to keep him in such numbers as your activities make desirable.

Is it not possible, then, that in the long era of readjustment upon which we are entering, for the nation to lay aside old prejudices and old antagonisms, and in the broad, clear light of nationalism enter upon a constructive policy in dealing with these intricate issues? Just as we shall prove ourselves capable of doing this we shall insure the industrial progress, the agricultural security, the social and political safety of our whole country, regardless of race or sections, and along the lines of ideals superior to every consideration of groups or class, of race or color or section or prejudices.

REVIEW QUESTIONS

1. What kind of "equality" did Harding endorse for African Americans? Why did he insist that "social equality" would never work in the South?
2. According to Harding, why had race become a national problem in the United States after the First World War?

HIRAM W. EVANS

FROM The Klan's Fight for Americanism (1926)

The backlash against "alien" groups "infesting" American life after World War I assumed its most virulent form in a revival of the Ku Klux Klan. The organization had first emerged in the rural South after the Civil War, seeking to intimidate blacks from voting or holding office, and had pretty much died out by 1900. The zealous patriotism fostered by American intervention in World War I helped revive the Klan. In its new form it was more of an urban than a rural phenomenon. It adopted a broader agenda than the original organization, and its membership grew across the nation. By 1926 it boasted over 3 million members. Klan intolerance now went beyond blacks to include Jews, Catholics, communists, and labor unionists. Texas dentist Hiram Evans assumed leadership of the organization in 1926. In this speech he reveals that the Klan was fundamentally a protest against all of the ills associated with modern culture.

From *North American Review* 223 (March 1926): 38–39, 41, 44, 49, 52. Reprinted by permission of the North American Review.

... The Klan, therefore, has now come to speak for the great mass of Americans of the old pioneer stock. We believe that it does fairly and faithfully represent them, and our proof lies in their support. To understand the Klan, then, it is necessary to understand the character and present mind of the mass of old-stock Americans. The mass, it must be remembered, as distinguished from the intellectually mongrelized "Liberals."

These are, in the first place, a blend of various peoples of the so-called Nordic race, the race which, with all its faults, has given the world almost the whole of modern civilization. The Klan does not try to represent any people but these. ...

These Nordic Americans for the last generation have found themselves increasingly uncomfortable, and finally deeply distressed. There appeared first confusion in thought and opinion, a groping and hesitancy about national affairs and private life alike, in sharp contrast to the clear, straightforward purposes of our earlier years. There was futility in religion, too, which was in many ways even more distressing. Presently we began to find that we were dealing with strange ideas; policies that always sounded well but somehow always made us still more uncomfortable.

Finally came the moral breakdown that has been going on for two decades. One by one all our traditional moral standards went by the boards or were so disregarded that they ceased to be binding. The sacredness of our Sabbath, of our homes, of chastity, and finally even of our right to teach our own children in our own schools fundamental facts and truths were torn away from us. Those who maintained the old standards did so only in the face of constant ridicule. ...

The old-stock Americans are learning, however. They have begun to arm themselves for this new type of warfare. Most important, they have broken away from the fetters of the false ideals and philanthropy which put aliens ahead of their own children and their own race. ...

One more point about the present attitude of the old-stock American: he has revived and increased his long-standing distrust of the Roman Catholic Church. It is for this that the native Americans, and the Klan as their leader, are most often denounced as intolerant and prejudiced. ...

The Ku Klux Klan, in short, is an organization which gives expression, direction and purpose to the most vital instincts, hopes, and resentments of the old-stock Americans, provides them with leadership, and is enlisting and preparing them for militant, constructive action toward fulfilling their racial and national destiny. ... The Klan literally is once more the embattled American farmer and artisan, coordinated into a disciplined and growing army, and launched upon a definite crusade for Americanism! ...

Thus the Klan goes back to the American racial instincts, and to the common sense which is their first product, as the basis of its beliefs and methods. ...

There are three of these great racial instincts, vital elements in both the historic and the present attempts to build an America which shall fulfill the aspirations and justify the heroism of the men who made the nation. These are the instincts of loyalty to the white race, to the traditions of America, and to the spirit of Protestantism, which has been an essential part of Americanism ever since the days of Roanoke and Plymouth Rock. They are condensed into the Klan slogan: "Native, white, Protestant supremacy."

REVIEW QUESTIONS

1. What "evils" did Evans claim were infecting modern American society?
2. According to Evans, what were the implied objectives of the Klan?
3. To what extent do you think the Klan's philosophy was consistent with other American ideals and principles? Explain.

The Need for Immigration Restriction (1923)

The Red Scare after World War I helped generate pervasive fears of foreign radicals streaming into the United States. A postwar depression also fueled concerns that a wave of new immigrants would take jobs away from Americans. At the same time, people continued to worry that "alien" peoples from eastern Europe and Asia could not be assimilated into American culture. These concerns took legislative form in the passage of restrictive immigration laws in 1921 and 1924. The 1921 act limited the number of immigrants from any country to 3 percent of that nation's proportion of the American population as of 1910. The 1924 act was even more restrictive. In the following selection, the federal official in charge of immigration policy explains the context for these new laws.

From U.S. Department of Labor, *Annual Report of the Commissioner-General of Immigration to the Secretary of Labor* (Washington, DC, 1923), pp. 3–4.

Even a casual survey of congressional discussions of the immigration problem during the past quarter of a century demonstrates very clearly that while the law makers were deeply concerned with the mental, moral, and physical quality of immigrants, there developed as time went on an even greater concern as to the fundamental racial character of the constantly increasing numbers who came.

The record of alien arrivals year by year had shown a gradual falling off in the immigration of northwest European peoples, representing racial stocks which were common to America even in colonial days, and a rapid and remarkably large increase in the movement from southern and eastern European countries and Asiatic Turkey. Immigration from the last-named sources reached an annual average of about 750,000 and in some years nearly a million came, and there seems to have been a general belief in Congress that it would increase rather than diminish. At the same time no one seems to have anticipated a revival of the formerly large influx from the "old sources," as the countries of northwest Europe came to be known.

This remarkable change in the sources and racial character of our immigrants led to an almost continuous agitation of the immigration problem both in and out of Congress, and there was a steadily growing demand for restriction, particularly of the newer movement from the south and east of Europe. During the greater part of this period of agitation the so-called literacy test for aliens was the favorite weapon of the restrictionists, and its widespread popularity appears to have been based quite largely on a belief, or at least a hope, that it would reduce to some extent the stream of "new" immigration, about one-third of which was illiterate, without seriously interfering with the coming of the older type, among whom illiteracy was at a minimum.

Presidents Cleveland and Taft vetoed immigration bills because they contained a literacy test provision, and President Wilson vetoed two bills largely for the same reason. In 1917, however, Congress passed a general immigration bill which included the literacy provision over the President's veto, and, with certain exceptions, aliens who are unable to read are no longer admitted to the United States. At that time, however, the World War had already had the effect of reducing immigration from Europe to a low level, and our own entry into the conflict a few days before the law in question went into effect practically stopped it altogether.

Consequently, the value of the literacy provision as a means of restricting European immigration was never fairly tested under normal conditions.

The Congress, however, seemingly realized that even the comprehensive immigration law of 1917, including the literacy test, would afford only a frail barrier against the promised rush from the war-stricken countries of Europe, and in December, 1920, the House of Representatives, with little opposition, passed a bill to suspend practically all immigration for the time being. The per centum limit plan was substituted by the Senate, however, and the substitute prevailed in Congress, but it failed to become a law at the time because President Wilson withheld executive approval. Nevertheless, favorable action was not long delayed, for at the special session called at the beginning of the present administration the measure was quickly enacted, and, with President Harding's approval, became a law on May 19, 1921. This law expired by limitation June 30, 1922, but by the act of May 11, 1922, its life was extended to June 30, 1924, and some strengthening amendments were added.

The principal provisions of the per centum limit act, or the "quota," as it is popularly known, are as follows:

The number of aliens of any nationality who may be admitted to the United States in any fiscal year shall not exceed 3 per cent of the number of persons of such nationality who were resident in the United States according to the census of 1910. Monthly quotas are limited to 20 per cent of the annual quota. For the purposes of the act, "nationality" is determined by country of birth.

The law does not apply to the following classes of aliens: Government officials; aliens in transit; aliens visiting the United States as tourists or temporarily for business or pleasure; aliens from countries immigration from which is regulated in accordance with treaties or agreement relating solely to immigration, otherwise China and Japan; aliens from the so-called Asiatic barred zone; aliens who have resided continuously for at least five years in Canada, Newfoundland, Cuba, Mexico, Central or South America, or adjacent islands; aliens under the age of 18 who are children of citizens of the United States.

Certain other classes of aliens who are counted against quotas are admissible after a quota is exhausted. The following are included in this category: Aliens returning from a temporary visit abroad; aliens who are professional actors, artists, lecturers, singers, ministers of any religious denomination, professors for colleges or seminaries, members of any recognized learned profession, or aliens employed as domestic servants.

So far as possible preference is given to the wives and certain near relatives of citizens of the United States, applicants for citizenship and honorably discharged soldiers, eligible to citizenship, who served in the United States military or naval forces at any time between April 6, 1917, and November 11, 1918.

Transportation companies are liable to a fine of $200 for each alien brought to a United States port in excess of the quota and where such fine is imposed the amount paid for passage must be returned to the rejected alien.

The quota limit law is in addition to and not in substitution for the provisions of the immigration laws.

REVIEW QUESTIONS

1. What did the distinction between "new" and "old" immigrants suggest about the ethnic and religious tensions of the era?
2. Why did support for a literacy test skyrocket during this period?
3. How would members of the Klan have responded to these immigration restrictions?

Shut the Door to Immigrants (1924)

In the five years after the First World War, more than 600,000 people from southern and eastern Europe, mostly Italians, entered the United States, along with 150,000 Poles and 50,000 Russians. Some were socialists or anarchists, and a few endorsed violence to achieve their political goals.

Fears of foreign radicals led Congress to pass the Emergency Immigration Act of 1921, also called the Quota Act, which limited total immigration to 150,000 a year and restricted newcomers from each European country to 3 percent of the total number of that nationality represented in the 1910 census.

Three years later, Congress responded to complaints that too many eastern and southern Europeans were still being admitted by passing the Immigration Act of 1924 (the Johnson-Reed Act). The bill, set to take effect in 1929, reduced the number ("quota") of visas from 3 to 2 percent of the total number of people of each national-ity in the United States as of the 1890 rather than the 1910 national census, since there were far fewer eastern and southern Europeans in the nation in 1890. It also banned almost all immigrants from Asia. The Immigration Act of 1924 would govern the admission of foreigners until the 1960s.

During the Congressional debate over the proposed Immigration Act of 1924, Sen-ator Ellison DuRant Smith of South Carolina, a white supremacist who sought to "keep the Niggers down and the price of cotton up," drew upon the theories of Madi-son Grant, an American writer who claimed in The Passing of the Great Race *(1916) that the United States must shut the door to the "inferior" peoples of the world in order to preserve the superiority of the white, Anglo-Saxon ("Nordic") race. He wanted to confine America's future "to native Americans, who are anthropologically, socially, and politically sound, no Bolsheviki need apply." Although blatant racists like Smith were in the minority in the Senate, almost all senators supported the proposal to restrict immigration. The Johnson-Reed bill passed with only six dissenting votes.*

Speech by Ellison DuRant Smith, April 9, 1924, *Congressional Record*, 68th Cong., 1st Sess., 1924, 65: 5961–62. [Editorial insertions appear in square brackets—*Ed.*]

It seems to me the point as to this measure—and I have been so impressed for several years—is that the time has arrived when we should shut the door [to immigrants]. We have been called the melting pot of the world. We had an experience just a few years ago, during the great World War, when it looked as though we had allowed influences to enter our borders that were about to melt the pot in place of us being the melting pot.

I think that we have sufficient stock [of newcom-ers] in America now for us to shut the door, Ameri-canize what we have, and save the resources of America for the natural increase of our population. We all know that one of the most prolific causes of war is the desire for increased land ownership for the overflow of a congested population. We are increasing at such a rate that in the natural course of things in a comparatively few years the landed resources, the natural resources of the country, shall be taken up by the natural increase of our population. It seems to me the part of wisdom now that we have throughout the length and breadth of continental America a population which is beginning to encroach upon the reserve and virgin resources of the country to keep it in trust for the multiplying population of the country.

I do not believe that political reasons should enter into the discussion of this very vital question. It is of greater concern to us to maintain the institutions of America, to maintain the principles upon which this Government is founded, than to develop and exploit the underdeveloped resources of the country.

There are some things that are dearer to us, fraught with more benefit to us, than the immediate development of the undeveloped resources of the country. I believe that our particular ideas, social, moral, religious, and political, have demonstrated, by virtue of the progress we have made and the character of people that we are, that we have the highest ideals of any member of the human family or any nation. We have demonstrated the fact that the human family, certainly the predominant breed in America, can govern themselves by a direct government of the people.

If this Government shall fail, it shall fail by virtue of the terrible law of inherited tendency. Those who come from the nations which from time immemorial have been under the dictation of a master fall more easily by the law of inheritance and the inertia of habit into a condition of political servitude than the descendants of those who cleared the forests, conquered the savage, stood at arms and won their liberty from their mother country, England.

I think we now have sufficient population in our country for us to shut the door and to breed up a pure, unadulterated American citizenship. I recognize that there is a dangerous lack of distinction between people of a certain nationality and the breed of the dog. Who is an American? Is he an immigrant from Italy? Is he an immigrant from Germany? If you were to go abroad and someone were to meet you and say, "I met a typical American," what would flash into your mind as a typical American, the typical representative of that new Nation? Would it be the son of an Italian immigrant, the son of a German

immigrant, the son of any of the breeds from the Orient, the son of the denizens of Africa? We must not get our ethnological distinctions mixed up without anthropological distinctions. It is the breed of the dog in which I am interested.

I would like for the members of the Senate to read that book just recently published by Madison Grant, *The Passing of a Great Race*. Thank God we have in America perhaps the largest percentage of any country in the world of the pure, unadulterated Anglo-Saxon stock; certainly the greatest of any nation in the Nordic breed. It is for the preservation of that splendid stock that has characterized us that I would make this not an asylum for the oppressed of all countries, but a country to assimilate and perfect that splendid type of manhood that has made America the foremost nation in her progress and in her power, and yet the youngest of all the nations. I myself believe that the preservation of her institutions depends upon us now taking counsel with our condition and our experience during the last World War.

Without offense, but with regard to the salvation of our own, let us shut the door and assimilate what we have, and let us breed pure American citizens and develop our own American resources. I am more in favor of that than I am of our quota proposition. Of course, it may not meet the approbation of the Senate that we shall shut the door—which I unqualifiedly and unreservedly believe to be our duty—and develop what we have, assimilate and digest what we have into pure Americans, with American aspirations, and thoroughly familiar with the love of American institutions, rather than the importation of any number of men from other countries. If we may not have that, then I am in favor of putting the quota down to the lowest possible point, with every selective element in it that may be. . . .

REVIEW QUESTIONS

1. What reasons does Smith cite for "shutting the door" to further immigration?
2. How convincing is Smith's racial argument that the "Anglo-Saxon stock" in the American population was its source of salvation?

ROBERT H. CLANCY

FROM The Immigration Act of 1924

The new immigration quota law of 1921 substantially reduced immigration from southern and eastern Europe. Even more restrictive was the Immigration Act of 1924 (Johnson-Reed Act). Only six representatives in Congress voted against this act. One of the dissenters was Robert H. Clancy, a Republican congressman from Detroit, a city with a large immigrant population. In a speech to Congress on April 8, 1924, he criticized the quota provisions of the new Immigration Act for being racially discriminatory and "un-American."

From a speech, April 8, 1924, *Congressional Record*, 68th Cong., 1st Sess., 1924, 65:5929–32. [Editorial insertions appear in square brackets—*Ed.*]

Since the foundations of the American commonwealth were laid in colonial times over 300 years ago, vigorous complaint and more or less bitter persecution have been aimed at newcomers to our shores. . . . Old citizens in Detroit of Irish and German descent have told me of the fierce tirades and propaganda directed against the great waves of Irish and Germans who came over from 1840 on for a few decades to escape civil, racial, and religious persecution in their native lands.

The "Know-Nothings," lineal ancestors of the Ku-Klux Klan, bitterly denounced the Irish and Germans as mongrels, scum, foreigners, and a menace to our institutions, much as other great branches of the Caucasian race of glorious history and antecedents are berated to-day. All are riff-raff, unassimilables, "foreign devils," swine not fit to associate with the great chosen people—a form of national pride and hallucination as old as the division of races and nations.

But today it is the Italians, Spanish, Poles, Jews, Greeks, Russians, Balkanians, and so forth, who are [considered] the racial lepers. And it is eminently fitting and proper that so many Members of this House with names as Irish as Paddy's pig, are taking the floor these days to attack once more as their kind has attacked for seven bloody centuries the fearful fallacy of chosen peoples and inferior peoples. The fearful fallacy is that one is made to rule and the other to be abominated. . . .

In this bill we find racial discrimination at its worst—a deliberate attempt to go back 84 years in our census taken every 10 years so that a blow may be aimed at peoples of eastern and southern Europe, particularly at our recent allies in the Great War—Poland and Italy.

Jews in Detroit Are Good Citizens

Of course the Jews too are aimed at, not directly, because they have no country in Europe they can call their own, but they are set down among the inferior peoples. Much of the animus against Poland and Russia, old and new, with the countries that have arisen from the ruins of the dead Czar's European dominions, is directed against the Jew.

We have many American citizens of Jewish descent in Detroit, tens of thousands of them—active in every profession and every walk of life. They are particularly active in charities and merchandising. One of our greatest judges, if not the greatest, is a Jew. Surely no fair-minded person with a knowledge of the facts can say the Jews of Detroit are a menace to the city's or the country's well-being. . . .

Forty or fifty thousand Italian-Americans live in my district in Detroit. They are found in all walks and classes of life—common hard labor, the trades, business, law, medicine, dentistry, art, literature, banking, and so forth. They rapidly become Americanized, build homes, and make themselves into good citizens. They brought hardihood, physique, hope, and good humor with them from their outdoor life in Sunny Italy, and they bear up under the terrific strain of life and work in busy Detroit.

One finds them by the thousands digging streets, sewers, and building foundations, and in the automobile and iron and steel fabric factories of various sorts. They do the hard work that the native-born American dislikes. Rapidly they rise in life and join the so-called middle and upper classes. . . .

The Italian-Americans of Detroit played a glorious part in the Great War. They showed themselves as patriotic as the native born in offering the supreme sacrifice. In all, I am informed, over 300,000 Italian-speaking soldiers enlisted in the American Army, almost 10 percent of our total fighting force. Italians formed about 4 percent of the population of the United States and they formed 10 percent of the American military force. Their casualties were 12 percent. . . .

Detroit Satisfied with the Poles

I wish to take the liberty of informing the House that from my personal knowledge and observation of tens of thousands of Polish-Americans living in my district in Detroit that their Americanism and patriotism are unassailable from any fair or just standpoint.

The Polish-Americans are as industrious and as frugal and as loyal to our institutions as any class of people who have come to the shores of this country in the past 300 years. They are essentially home builders, and they have come to this country to stay. They learn the English language as quickly as possible, and take pride in the rapidity with which they become assimilated and adopt our institutions. Figures available to all show that in Detroit in the

World War the proportion of American volunteers of Polish blood was greater than the proportion of Americans of any other racial descent. . . . Polish-Americans do not merit slander nor defamation. If not granted charitable or sympathetic judgment, they are at least entitled to justice and to the high place they have won in American and European history and citizenship.

The force behind the Johnson bill and some of its champions in Congress charge that opposition to the racial discrimination feature of the 1800 quota basis arises from "foreign blocs." They would give the impression that 100 percent of Americans are for it and that the sympathies of its opponents are of the "foreign-bloc" variety, and bear stigma of being "hyphenates." I meet that challenge willingly. I feel my Americanism will stand any test.

Every American Has Foreign Ancestors

The foreign born of my district writhe under the charge of being called "hyphenates." The people of my own family were all hyphenates—English-Americans, German-Americans, Irish-Americans. They began to come in the first ship or so after the *Mayflower*. But they did not come too early to miss the charge of anti-Americanism. Roger Williams was driven out of the Puritan colony of Salem to die in the wilderness because he objected "violently" to blue laws and the burning or hanging of rheumatic old women on witchcraft charges. He would not "assimilate" and was "a grave menace to American Institutions and democratic government."

My family put 11 men and boys into the Revolutionary War, and I am sure they and their women and children did not suffer so bitterly and sacrifice until it hurt to establish the autocracy of bigotry and intolerance which exists in many quarters to-day in this country. Some of these men and boys shed their blood and left their bodies to rot on American battle fields. To me real Americanism and the American flag are the product of the blood of men and of the tears of women and children of a different type than the rampant "Americanizers" of to-day.

My mother's father fought in the Civil War, leaving his six small children in Detroit when he marched away to the southern battle fields to fight against racial distinctions and protect his country. My mother's little brother, about 14 years old, and the eldest child, fired by the traditions of his family, plodded off to the battle fields to do his bit. He aspired to be a drummer boy and inspire the men in battle, but he was found too small to carry a drum and was put at the ignominious task of driving army mules, hauling cannons and wagons. I learned more of the spirit of American history at my mother's knee than I ever learned in my four years of high school study of American history and in my five and a half years of study at the great University of Michigan. All that study convinces me that the racial discriminations of this bill are un-American. . . .

It must never be forgotten also that the Johnson bill, although it claims to favor the northern and western European peoples only, does so on a basis of comparison with the southern and western Euro-

pean peoples. The Johnson bill cuts down materially the number of immigrants allowed to come from northern and western Europe, the so-called Nordic peoples. . . .

Then I would be true to the principles for which my forefathers fought and true to the real spirit of the magnificent United States of today. I can not stultify myself by voting for the present bill and overwhelm my country with racial hatreds and racial lines and antagonisms drawn even tighter than they are to-day. [Applause.]

REVIEW QUESTIONS

1. Why did Congress seek to use the Immigration Act of 1924 to discriminate against immigrants from southern and western Europe?
2. Why did the United States restrict immigration at all?

HARRY EMERSON FOSDICK

FROM Shall the Fundamentalists Win? (1922)

The reactionary temper of the 1920s sparked a resurgence of Protestant fundamentalism. So-called liberal Protestants sought to reconcile religion and reason, faith and science, and to challenge the backward tendencies of fundamentalism. The Reverend Harry Emerson Fosdick exemplified such liberal Protestantism. His influential 1922 sermon, excerpted here, enraged fundamentalists and eventually forced his resignation from New York City's First Presbyterian Church. Fosdick went on to become one of the nation's most influential clergymen.

From *Christian Work* 102 (June 10, 1922): 716–22.

This morning we are to think of the fundamentalist controversy which threatens to divide the American churches as though already they were not sufficiently split and riven. . . . Already all of us

must have heard about the people who call themselves the Fundamentalists. Their apparent intention is to drive out of the evangelical churches men and women of liberal opinions. I speak of them the more freely because there are no two denominations more affected by them than the Baptist and the Presbyterian. We should not identify the Fundamentalists with the conservatives. All Fundamentalists are conservatives, but not all conservatives are Fundamentalists. The best conservatives can often give lessons to the liberals in true liberality of spirit, but the Fundamentalist program is essentially illiberal and intolerant.

The Fundamentalists see, and they see truly, that in this last generation there have been strange new movements in Christian thought. A great mass of new knowledge has come into man's possession—new knowledge about the physical universe, its origin, its forces, its laws; new knowledge about human history and in particular about the ways in which the ancient peoples used to think in matters of religion and the methods by which they phrased and explained their spiritual experiences; and new knowledge, also, about other religions and the strangely similar ways in which men's faiths and religious practices have developed everywhere. . . .

Now, there are multitudes of reverent Christians who have been unable to keep this new knowledge in one compartment of their minds and the Christian faith in another. They have been sure that all truth comes from the one God and is His revelation. Not, therefore, from irreverence or caprice or destructive zeal but for the sake of intellectual and spiritual integrity, that they might really love the Lord their God, not only with all their heart and soul and strength but with all their mind, they have been trying to see this new knowledge in terms of the Christian faith and to see the Christian faith in terms of this new knowledge.

Doubtless they have made many mistakes. Doubtless there have been among them reckless radicals gifted with intellectual ingenuity but lacking spiritual depth. Yet the enterprise itself seems to them indispensable to the Christian Church. The new knowledge and the old faith cannot be left antagonistic or even disparate, as though a man on Saturday could use one set of regulative ideas for his life and on Sunday could change gear to another altogether. We must be able to think our modern life clear through in Christian terms, and to do that we also must be able to think our Christian faith clear through in modern terms.

There is nothing new about the situation. It has happened again and again in history, as, for example, when the stationary earth suddenly began to move and the universe that had been centered in this planet was centered in the sun around which the planets whirled. Whenever such a situation has arisen, there has been only one way out—the new knowledge and the old faith had to be blended in a new combination. Now, the people in this generation who are trying to do this are the liberals, and the Fundamentalists are out on a campaign to shut against them the doors of the Christian fellowship. Shall they be allowed to succeed?

It is interesting to note where the Fundamentalists are driving in their stakes to mark out the deadline of doctrine around the church, across which no one is to pass except on terms of agreement. They insist that we must all believe in the historicity of certain special miracles, preeminently the virgin birth of our Lord; that we must believe in a special theory of inspiration—that the original documents of the Scripture, which of course we no longer possess, were inerrantly dictated to men a good deal as a man might dictate to a stenographer; that we must believe in a special theory of the Atonement—that the blood of our Lord, shed in a substitutionary death, placates an alienated Deity and makes possible welcome for the returning sinner; and that we must believe in the second coming of our Lord upon the clouds of heaven to set up a millennium here, as the only way in which God can bring history to a worthy denouement.

Such are some of the stakes which are being driven to mark a deadline of doctrine around the church. If a man is a genuine liberal, his primary protest is not against holding these opinions, although he may well protest against their being considered the fundamentals of Christianity. This is a free country and anybody has a right to hold these opinions or any others if he is sincerely convinced of them. The question is—Has anybody a right to deny the Christian name to those who differ with him on such points and to shut against them the doors of the Christian fellowship? The Fundamentalists say that this must be done. In this country and on the foreign field they are trying to do it. They have actually endeavored to put on the statute books of a whole state binding laws against teaching modern biology. If they had their way, within the church, they would set up in Protestantism a doctrinal tribunal more rigid than the pope's. In such an hour, delicate and dangerous, when feelings are bound to run high, I plead this morning the cause of magnanimity and liberality and tolerance of spirit. . . .

Here in the Christian churches are these two groups of people and the question which the Fundamentalists raise is this—Shall one of them throw the other out? Has intolerance any contribution to make to this situation? Will it persuade anybody of anything? Is not the Christian Church large enough to hold within her hospitable fellowship people who differ on points like this and agree to differ until the fuller truth be manifested? The Fundamentalists say not. They say the liberals must go. Well, if the Fundamentalists should succeed, then out of the Christian Church would go some of the best Christian life and consecration of this generation—multitudes of men and women, devout and reverent Christians, who need the church and whom the church needs. . . .

I do not believe for one moment that the Fundamentalists are going to succeed. Nobody's intolerance can contribute anything to the solution of the situation which we have described. If, then, the Fundamentalists have no solution of the problem, where may we expect to find it? In two concluding comments let us consider our reply to that inquiry.

The first element that is necessary is a spirit of tolerance and Christian liberty. When will the world learn that intolerance solves no problems? This is not a lesson which the Fundamentalists alone need to learn; the liberals also need to learn it. . . .

Nevertheless, it is true that just now the Fundamentalists are giving us one of the worst exhibitions of bitter intolerance that the churches of this country have ever seen. As one watches them and listens to them he remembers the remark of General Armstrong of Hampton Institute, "Cantankerousness is worse than heterodoxy." There are many opinions in the field of modern controversy concerning which I am not sure whether they are right or wrong, but

there is one thing I am sure of: courtesy and kindliness and tolerance and humility and fairness are right. Opinions may be mistaken; love never is.

As I plead thus for an intellectually hospitable, tolerant, liberty-loving church, I am, of course, thinking primarily about this new generation. We have boys and girls growing up in our homes and schools, and because we love them we may well wonder about the church which will be waiting to receive them. Now, the worst kind of church that can possibly be offered to the allegiance of the new generation is an intolerant church. . . .

My friends, nothing in all the world is so much worth thinking of as God, Christ, the Bible, sin and salvation, the divine purposes for humankind, life everlasting. But you cannot challenge the dedicated thinking of this generation to these sublime themes upon any such terms as are laid down by an intolerant church.

The second element which is needed if we are to reach a happy solution of this problem is a clear insight into the main issues of modern Christianity and a sense of penitent shame that the Christian Church should be quarreling over little matters when the world is dying of great needs. If, during the war, when the nations were wrestling upon the very brink of hell and at times all seemed lost, you chanced to hear two men in an altercation about some minor matter of sectarian denominationalism, could you restrain your indignation? You said, "What can you do with folks like this who, in the face of colossal issues, play with the tiddledywinks and peccadillos of religion?" . . .

The present world situation smells to heaven! And now, in the presence of colossal problems, which must be solved in Christ's name and for Christ's sake, the Fundamentalists propose to drive out from the Christian churches all the consecrated souls who do not agree with their theory of inspiration. What immeasurable folly!

Well, they are not going to do it; certainly not in this vicinity. I do not even know in this congregation whether anybody has been tempted to be a Fundamentalist. Never in this church have I caught one accent of intolerance. God keep us always so and ever increasing areas of the Christian fellow-ship; intellectually hospitable, open-minded, liberty-loving, fair, tolerant, not with the tolerance of indifference, as though we did not care about the faith, but because always our major emphasis is upon the weightier matters of the spirit.

1. Do you agree that religious fundamentalists are "illiberal and intolerant"? Why or why not?
2. Why did fundamentalists feel threatened by new scientific knowledge?

The Scopes Trial (1925)

In the 1920s the Tennessee legislature passed a law forbidding teachers in the state-supported (but not private) schools to teach the Darwinian theory of evolution. John T. Scopes, a young biology teacher, defied the law and was brought to trial in the backwoods hamlet of Dayton. The case drew the attention of the nation. Scopes's defense team was buttressed by the celebrated attorney and agnostic, Clarence G. Darrow; aiding the prosecution was the famed orator and fundamentalist William J. Bryan, who had long spearheaded the nationwide crusade against evolution. Bryan was induced to take the stand as an expert witness on the Bible, and Darrow proceeded to skewer him and his "fool religion."

From *The World's Most Famous Court Trial: Tennessee Evolution Case* (Cincinnati, OH: National Book Club, 1925), pp. 303–04.

DARROW: Do you believe the story of the temptation of Eve by the serpent?

BRYAN: I do.

DARROW: Do you believe that after Eve ate the apple, or gave it to Adam, whichever way it was, that God cursed Eve, and at that time decreed that all womankind thenceforth and forever should suffer the pains of childbirth in the reproduction of the earth?

BRYAN: I believe what it says, and I believe the fact as fully—

DARROW: That is what it says, doesn't it?

BRYAN: Yes.

DARROW: And for that reason, every woman born of woman, who has to carry on the race, the reason they have childbirth pains is because Eve tempted Adam in the Garden of Eden?

BRYAN: I will believe just what the Bible says. I ask to put that in the language of the Bible, for I pre-fer that to your language. Read the Bible and I will answer.

DARROW: All right, I will do that.

[*Darrow reads from Genesis 3:15–16.*]

BRYAN: I accept it as it is.

DARROW: And you believe that came about because Eve tempted Adam to eat the fruit?

BRYAN: Just as it says.

DARROW: And you believe that is the reason that God made the serpent to go on his belly after he tempted Eve?

BRYAN: I believe the Bible as it is, and I do not permit you to put your language in the place of the language of the Almighty. You read that Bible and ask me questions, and I will answer them. I will not answer your questions in your language.

DARROW: I will read it to you from the Bible: "And the Lord God said unto the serpent, because thou hast done this, thou art cursed above all cattle, and above every beast of the field; upon thy belly shalt thou go and dust shalt thou eat all the days of thy life." Do you think that is why the serpent is compelled to crawl upon its belly?

BRYAN: I believe that.

DARROW: Have you any idea how the snake went before that time?

BRYAN: No, sir.

DARROW: Do you know whether he walked on his tail or not?

BRYAN: No, sir. I have no way to know. (Laughter in audience.)

DARROW: Now, you refer to the cloud that was put in the heaven after the flood, the rainbow. Do you believe in that?

BRYAN: Read it.

DARROW: All right, I will read it for you.

BRYAN: Your Honor, I think I can shorten this testimony. The only purpose Mr. Darrow has is to slander the Bible, but I will answer his question.

I will answer it all at once, and I have no objection in the world, I want the world to know that this man, who does not believe in a God, is trying to use a court in Tennessee—

DARROW: I object to that.

BRYAN: (continuing)—to slur at it, and while it will require time, I am willing to take it.

DARROW: I object to your statement. I am examining you on your fool ideas that no intelligent Christian on earth believes.

REVIEW QUESTIONS

1. How did Bryan indicate his belief that the Bible is the literal word of God?
2. What do you think Darrow meant by an "intelligent Christian"?
3. Why do you think Bryan became the hero of biblical fundamentalists?

WARREN G. HARDING

A Return to Normalcy (1920)

During the 1920 presidential campaign, Republican candidate Warren G. Harding stressed in a speech in Boston that America needed to turn away from the government activism of Woodrow Wilson and other progressive idealists and revive the traditions of "normalcy." A prominent Ohio newspaper editor, Harding was elected a U.S. senator (1915–21). When the 1920 Republican Convention deadlocked over the selection of a presidential nominee, "Old Guard" party leaders tapped the handsome, fun-loving Harding as a compromise candidate. Harding's promise to return American life to normalcy after the disruptions of war and reformism pleased voters. Harding won by the largest landslide to date, capturing some 60 percent of the popular vote over the Democratic candidate, James Cox.

From "Back to Normal: Address before Home Market Club" [May 14, 1920], in *Rededicating America: Life and Recent Speeches of Warren G. Harding*, ed. Frederick E. Schortemeier (Indianapolis: Bobbs-Merrill, 1920), pp. 223–27.

There isn't anything the matter with the world's civilization except that humanity is viewing it through a vision impaired in a cataclysmal war. Poise has been disturbed and nerves have been racked, and fever has rendered men irrational; sometimes there have been draughts upon the dangerous cup of barbarity and men have wandered far from safe paths, but the human procession still marches in the right direction.

Here, in the United States, we feel the reflex, rather than the hurting wound, but we still think straight, and we mean to act straight, and mean to hold firmly to all that was ours when war involved us, and seek the higher attainments which are the only compensations that so supreme a tragedy may give mankind.

America's present need is not heroics, but healing; not nostrums, but normalcy; not revolution, but restoration; not agitation, but adjustment; not surgery, but serenity; not the dramatic, but the dispassionate; not experiment, but equipoise; not submergence in internationality, but sustainment in triumphant nationality.

It is one thing to battle successfully against world domination by military autocracy, because the infinite God never intended such a program, but it is quite another thing to revise human nature and suspend the fundamental laws of life and all of life's acquirements.

*   *   *

This republic has its ample tasks. If we put an end to false economics which lure humanity to utter chaos, ours will be the commanding example of world leadership today. If we can prove a representative popular government under which a citizenship seeks what it may do for the government rather than what the government may do for individuals, we shall do more to make democracy safe for the world than all armed conflict ever recorded. The world needs to be reminded that all human ills are not curable by legislation, and that quantity of statutory enactment and excess of government offer no substitute for quality of citizenship.

The problems of maintained civilization are not to be solved by a transfer of responsibility from citizenship to government, and no eminent page in history was ever drafted by the standards of mediocrity. More, no government is worthy of the name which is directed by influence on the one hand, or moved by intimidation on the other.

Nothing is more vital to this republic to-day than clear and intelligent understanding. Men must understand one another, and government and men must understand each other. For emergence from the wreckage of war, for the clarification of fevered minds, we must all give and take, we must both sympathize and inspire, but must learn griefs and aspirations, we must seek the common grounds of mutuality.

There can be no disguising everlasting truths. Speak it plainly, no people ever recovered from the distressing waste of war except through work and denial. There is no other way. We shall make no recovery in seeking how little men can do, our restoration lies in doing the most which is reasonably possible for individuals to do. Under production and hateful profiteering are both morally criminal, and must be combated. America can not be content with minimums of production to-day, the crying need is maximums. If we may have maximums of production we shall have minimums of cost, and profiteering will be speeded to its deserved punishment.

Money values are not destroyed, they are temporarily distorted. War wasted hundreds of billions, and depleted world store-houses, and cultivated new demands, and it hardened selfishness and gave awakening touch to elemental greed. Humanity needs renewed consecrations to what we call fellow citizenship.

Out of the supreme tragedy must come a new order and a higher order, and I gladly acclaim it. But war has not abolished work, has not established the processes of seizure or the rule of physical might. Nor has it provided a governmental panacea for human ills, or the magic touch that makes failure a success. Indeed, it has revealed no new reward for idleness, no substitute for the sweat of a man's face in the contest for subsistence and acquirement.

There is no new appraisal for the supremacy of law. That is a thing surpassing and eternal. A contempt for international law wrought the supreme tragedy, contempt for our national and state laws will rend the glory of the republic, and failure to abide the proven laws of to-day's civilization will lead to temporary chaos.

No one need doubt the ultimate result, because immutable laws have challenged the madness of all experiment. But we are living to-day, and it is ours to save ourselves from colossal blunder and its excessive penalty.

My best judgment of America's needs is to steady down, to get squarely on our feet, to make sure of the right path. Let's get out of the fevered delirium of war, with the hallucination that all the money in the world is to be made in the madness of war and the wildness of its aftermath. Let us stop to consider that tranquility at home is more precious than peace abroad, and that both our good fortune and our eminence are dependent on the normal forward stride of all the American people.

*　　*　　*

REVIEW QUESTIONS

1. How does Harding characterize America's greatest needs after the end of the Great War?
2. In what ways was his speech a direct attack on Woodrow Wilson's effort to involve the United States with a new League of Nations designed to ensure the peace?

CALVIN COOLIDGE

FROM Government and Business (1925)

President Calvin Coolidge was an outspoken champion of America's free enterprise system. He was convinced that America's postwar domination of the world economy and the growing size of American corporations were compatible with American ideals. In this 1925 speech to the New York State Chamber of Commerce, he outlined his faith in American economic values and international leadership.

From *Foundations of the Republic: Speeches and Addresses* (New York, 1926), pp. 317–32. [Editorial insertions appear in square brackets—*Ed.*]

This time and place naturally suggest some consideration of commerce in its relation to Government and society. We are finishing a year which can justly be said to surpass all others in the overwhelming success of general business. We are met not only in the greatest American metropolis [New York City], but in the greatest center of population and business that the world has ever known. If any one wishes to gauge the power which is represented by the genius of the American spirit, let him contemplate the wonders which have been wrought in this region in the short space of 200 years. Not only does it stand unequaled by any other place on earth, but it is impossible to conceive of any other place where it could be equaled. . . .

The foundation of this enormous development rests upon commerce. New York is an imperial city, but it is not a seat of government. The empire over which it rules is not political, but commercial. The great cities of the ancient world were the seats of both government and industrial power. The Middle Ages furnished a few exceptions. The great capitals of former times were not only seats of government but they actually governed. In the modern world government is inclined to be merely a tenant of the city. Political life and industrial life flow on side by side, but practically separated from each other. When we contemplate the enormous power, autocratic and uncontrolled, which would have been created by joining the authority of government with the influence of business, we can better appreciate the wisdom of the [founding] fathers in their wise dispensation which made Washington the political center of the country and left New York to develop into its business center. . . .

Everyone knows that it was our resources that saved Europe from a complete collapse immediately following the armistice [ending World War I]. Without the benefit of our credit, an appalling famine would have prevailed over great areas. In accordance with the light of all past history, disorder and revolution, with the utter breaking down of all legal restraints and the loosing of all the passions which had been aroused by four years of conflict, would have rapidly followed. Others did what they could, and no doubt made larger proportionate sacrifices, but it was the credits and food which we supplied that saved the situation.

When the work of restoring the fiscal condition of Europe began, it was accomplished again with our assistance. When Austria determined to put her financial house in order, we furnished a part of the capital. When Germany sought to establish a sound fiscal condition, we again contributed a large portion of the necessary gold loan. Without this, the reparations plan would have utterly failed. Germany could not otherwise have paid. The armies of occupation would have gone on increasing international irritation and ill will. It was our large guarantee of credit that assisted Great Britain to return to a gold basis. What we have done for France, Italy, Belgium, Czechoslovakia, Poland, and other countries, is all a piece of the same endeavor. These efforts and accomplishments, whether they be appreciated at home or received with gratitude abroad, which have been brought about by the business interests of our country, constitute an enormous world service. Others have made plans and adopted agreements for future action which hold a rank of great importance. But when we come to the consideration of what has been done, when we turn aside from what has been promised, to examine what has been performed, no positive and constructive accomplishment of the past five years compares with the support which America has contributed to the financial stability of the world. It clearly marks a new epoch.

This holds a distinctly higher rank than a mere barter and sale. It reaches above the ordinary business transaction into a broader realm. America has disbanded her huge armies and reduced her powerful fleet, but in attempting to deal justly through the sharing of our financial resources we have done more for peace than we could have done with all our military power. Peace, we know, rests to a great extent upon justice, but it is very difficult for the public mind to divorce justice from economic opportunity. The problem for which we have been attempting a solution is in the first instance to place the people of the earth back into avenues of profitable employment. It was necessary to restore hope, to renew courage. A great contribution to this end has been made with American money. The work is not all done yet. No doubt it will develop that this has not been accomplished without some mistakes, but the important fact remains that when the world needed to be revived we did respond. As nations see their way to a safer economic existence, they will see their way to a more peaceful existence. Possessed of the means to meet personal and public obligations, people are reestablishing their self-respect. The financial strength of America has contributed to the spiritual restoration of the world. It has risen into the domain of true business.

The working out of these problems of regulation, government economy, the elimination of waste in the use of human effort and of materials, conservation and the proper investment of our savings both at home and abroad, is all a part of the mighty task which was imposed upon mankind of subduing the earth. America must either perform her full share in the accomplishment of this great world destiny or fail. For almost three centuries we were intent upon our domestic development. We sought the help of the people and the wealth of other lands by which to increase our numerical strength and augment our national fortune. We have grown exceedingly great in population and in riches. This power and this prosperity we can continue for ourselves if we will but proceed with moderation. If our people will but use those resources which have been entrusted to them, whether of command over large numbers of men or of command over large investments of capital, not selfishly but generously, not to exploit others but to serve others, there will be no doubt of an increasing production and distribution of wealth.

All of these efforts represent the processes of reducing our domestic and foreign relations to a system of law. They consist of a determination of clear and definite rules of action. It is a civilizing and humanizing method adopted by means of conference, discussion, deliberation, and determination. If it is to have any continuing success, or any permanent value, it will be because it has not been brought about by one will compelling another by force, but has resulted from men reasoning together. It has sought to remove compulsion from the business life of the country and from our relationship with other nations. It has sought to bestow a greater freedom upon our own people and upon the people of the world. We have worshipped the ideals of force long enough. We have turned to worship at the true shrine of understanding and reason. . . .

This is the land of George Washington. We can do no less than work toward the realization of his hope. It ought to be our ambition to see the institutions which he founded grow in the blessings which they bestow upon our own citizens and increase in the good which their influence casts upon all the world. He did not hesitate to meet peril or encounter danger or make sacrifices. There is no cause which can be supported by any other methods. We cannot listen to the counsels of perfection; we cannot pursue a timorous policy; we cannot avoid the obligations of a common humanity. We must meet our perils; we must encounter our dangers; we must make our sacrifices; or history will recount that the works of Washington have failed. I do not believe the future is to be dismayed by that record. The truth and faith and justice of the ancient days have not departed from us.

REVIEW QUESTIONS

1. Why did the United States provide financial credits and loans to the European nations after World War I?
2. How might a working-class American respond to Coolidge's speech?

25 &. THE GREAT DEPRESSION, 1929–1939

During the 1932 election campaign, Democrat Franklin D. Roosevelt promised the American people a "new deal" and "bold, persistent experimentation" to help pull the nation out of the Great Depression. His charismatic personality and infectious energy struck a resonant chord. Roosevelt bested Herbert Hoover in a landslide, and he brought with him large Democratic majorities in both houses of Congress. On March 4, 1933, millions of Americans huddled around their radios to hear Roosevelt deliver his inaugural address. He promised them immediate action—and he delivered. No sooner did the former New York governor move into the White House than he began making an unprecedented series of executive decisions and signing new legislation that served to transform the very nature of the federal government.

During the "First Hundred Days" of his presidency, Roosevelt and the Democratic Congress repealed the Eighteenth Amendment, ending the thirteen-year experiment with prohibition of alcoholic beverages, intervened to shore up the banking industry, drafted new regulations for the stock market, and created an array of new federal agencies and programs designed to reopen factories, raise farm prices, put people back to work, conserve natural resources, and relieve the distress created by chronic unemployment.

The flurry of governmental activity and Roosevelt's uplifting rhetoric helped restore hope to many among the desperate and destitute, but the Depression persisted. The honeymoon of expectation that Roosevelt enjoyed immediately after his election gave way to strident criticism from both ends of the political spectrum. Conservatives accused him of assaulting the freedoms undergirding capitalism. In 1934 disgruntled conservative Democrats formed the American Liberty League to organize opposition to Roosevelt's "socialistic" programs. Roosevelt denounced the Liberty League as a group of "economic royalists" indifferent to the misery of the masses. "I welcome their hatred," he declared.

Other critics lambasted Roosevelt for not doing enough to help the poor and unemployed. The desperate economic conditions gave new life to the Socialist and Communist parties, both of which had fielded candidates in the 1932 presidential election. Many prominent writers, artists, and academics gravitated to the radical Left, and several labor unions began to witness the effects of communist agitators.

The volatile social tensions of the 1930s also helped spawn a diverse array of "neo-populist" demagogues. The most prominent of these independent operators was Democratic Senator Huey P. Long of Louisiana. In late 1934 he launched his "Share Our Wealth" program as an alternative to the New Deal. Using rabble-rousing techniques that he had refined as governor, Long called for a 100 percent tax on all personal income over $1 million and all fortunes over $5 million. He promised to use the revenue from these new taxes to provide every American with a home, a car, retirement benefits, and free educational opportunities. By 1935 Long boasted almost 8 million followers around the country and was preparing to launch a challenge to Roosevelt's reelection. In September, however, he was gunned down in Louisiana by the relative of a disgruntled political opponent.

Another landslide victory in 1936 emboldened Roosevelt to broaden the scope of his New Deal initiatives. He launched new programs for the unemployed, created the first minimum wage, reorganized the executive branch, and began urban redevelopment programs that included public housing for the homeless. Still, millions of Americans continued to live in squalor, especially in the rural South, where tenants and sharecroppers rarely benefited from the new government programs. By 1938, amid a new recession, the momentum of the New Deal began to wane. Roosevelt had expended most of his creativity and political capital. In the November congressional elections, the Republicans made deep inroads into the Democratic majorities in both houses. Foreign crises began to distract the attention of the administration and the nation, and Roosevelt began to focus on international diplomacy and military preparedness.

Even more so than her husband, Eleanor Roosevelt understood the human impact of the Depression, and she used her platform as First Lady to minister to the needs of the destitute and to reach out to disadvantaged minorities. She broke precedent to hold her own weekly press conferences, traveled throughout the country to meet with people of all walks of life, gave numerous lectures and radio addresses, and expressed her candid opinions in a daily syndicated newspaper column titled "My Day." In the process of such ceaseless agitation, Eleanor Roosevelt became a beloved symbol of the New Deal's concern for common folk and their daily distress.

FROM Two Views of the Great Depression (1932)

For those already living at barely a subsistence level, the onset of the Great Depression had an impact different from its effect on those enjoying affluence. The following accounts convey the difficulties of surviving the economic downturn. The first interview is with a retired black worker named Clifford Burke, living in Chicago. The second is the recollection of Jane Yoder, whose immigrant father was a blacksmith in a small Illinois mining town. The Yoders had seven children. In 1929 the mines closed down, and her father was forced to move from town to town in search of work. Take note of their references to New Deal programs, such as the Works Progress Administration, intended to relieve the distress of prolonged unemployment by providing government jobs.

From *Hard Times: An Oral History of the Great Depression*, pp. 82–83, 85–87. Copyright 1970, 1986 by Studs Terkel. Reprinted by permission of The New Press. www.thenewpress.com

A Black Man's Perspective

The Negro was born in depression. It didn't mean too much to him, The Great American Depression, as you call it. There was no such thing. The best he could be is a janitor or a porter or a shoeshine boy. It only became official when it hit the white man. If you can tell me the difference between the depression today and the Depression of 1932 for a black man, I'd like to know it. Now, it's worse, because of the prices. Know the rents they're payin' out here? I hate to tell ya. . . .

We had one big advantage. Our wives, they could go to the store and get a bag of beans or a sack of flour and a piece of fat meat, and they could cook this. And we could eat it. Steak? A steak would kick in my stomach like a mule in a tin stable. Now you take the white fella, he couldn't do this. His wife would tell him: Look, if you can't do any better than this, I'm gonna leave you. I seen it happen. He couldn't stand bringing home beans instead of steak and capon. And he couldn't stand the idea of going on relief like a Negro.

You take a fella had a job paying him $60, and here I am making $25. If I go home taking beans to my wife, we'll eat it. It isn't exactly what we want, but we'll eat it. The white man that's making big money, he's taking beans home, his wife'll say: Get out. (Laughs.)

Why did these big wheels kill themselves? They weren't able to live up to the standards they were accustomed to, and they got ashamed in front of their women. You see, you can tell anybody a lie, and he'll agree with you. But you start layin' down the facts of real life, he won't accept it. The American white man has been superior so long, he can't figure out why he should come down.

I remember a friend of mine, he didn't know he was a Negro. I mean he acted like he never knew it. He got tied downtown with some stock. He blew about twenty thousand. He came home and drank a bottle of poison. A bottle of iodine or something like that. It was a rarity to hear a Negro killing himself over a financial situation. He might have killed himself over some woman. Or getting in a fight. But when it came to the financial end of it, there were so few who had anything. (Laughs).

I made out during that . . . *Great* Depression. (Laughs.) Worked as a teamster for a lumber yard. Forty cents an hour. Monday we'd have a little work. They'd say come back Friday. There wasn't no need to look for another job. The few people working, most all of them were white.

So I had another little hustle. I used to play pool pretty good. And I'd ride from poolroom to poolroom on this bicycle. I used to beat these guys, gamble what we had. I'd leave home with a dollar. First couple of games I could beat this guy, I'd put that money in my pocket. I'd take the rest of what I beat him out of and hustle the day on that. Sometimes I'd come home with a dollar and a half extra. That was a whole lot of money. Everybody was out trying to beat the other guy, so he could make it. It was pathetic.

I never applied to the PWA (Public Works Administration) or WPA (Works Progress Administration), 'cause as long as I could hustle, there was no point in beating the other fellow out of a job, cuttin' some other guy out.

A Woman's Account

We were struggling, just desperate to be warm. No blankets, no coats. At this time I was in fourth grade. Katie[1] went to Chicago and bought an Indian blanket coat. . . .

Before that I had one coat. It must have been a terrible lightweight coat or what, but I can remember being cold, just shivering. And came home, and nothing to do but go to bed, then you put the coat on the bed and you got warm.

The cold that I've known. I never had boots. I think when I got married, I had my first set of boots. In rainy weather, you just ran for it, you ran between the raindrops or whatever. This was luxuriating to have boots. You simply wore your old shoes if it was raining. Save the others. You always polished them and put shoe trees in them. You didn't have unlimited shoe trees, either. When the shoes were worn out, they're used around the house. And of the high heels, you cut the heels down and they're more comfortable. . . .

---

[1]An older sister.

If we had a cold or we threw up, nobody ever took your temperature. We had no thermometer. But if you threw up and were hot, my mother felt your head. She somehow felt that by bringing you oranges and bananas and these things you never had—there's nothing wrong with you, this is what she'd always say in Croatian; you'll be all right. Then she gave you all these good things. Oh, gee, you almost looked forward to the day you could throw up. I could remember dreaming about oranges and bananas, dreaming about them. . . .

I can think of the WPA . . . my father got immediately employed in this WPA. This was a godsend. This was the greatest thing. It meant food, you know. Survival, just survival.

How stark it was for me to come into nurses' training and have the girls . . . give their impressions of the WPA. How it struck me. Before I could ever say that my father was employed in the WPA, discussions in the bull sessions in our rooms immediately was: these lazy people, the shovel leaners. I'd just sit there and listen to them. I'd look around and realize: sure, Susan Stewart was talking this way, but her father was a doctor, and her mother was a nurse. Well, how nice. They had respectable employment. In my family, there was no respectable employment. I thought, you don't know what it's like.

How can I defend them? I was never a person who could control this. It just had to come out or I think I'd just blow up. So I would say, "I wonder how much we know until we go through it. Just like the patients we take care of. None of them are in the hospital by choice." I would relate it in abstractions. I think it saved me from just blowing up.

I would come back after that and I'd just say: Gee, these are just two separate, separate worlds.

REVIEW QUESTIONS

1. What did Burke mean when he asserted that the "Negro was born in depression"?

2. Why did Burke feel so many whites committed suicide as a result of the economic collapse? What stereotypes did he hold about whites?
3. Describe some of the hardships that Yoder endured as a child. What did she consider

to be luxuries that many people now take for granted?
4. What seemed to cause the differences in opinion regarding government relief programs?

HERBERT HOOVER

Government's Role in Fighting the Great Depression (1932)

Herbert Hoover did his best to revive economic growth amid the Great Depression, but he balked at the idea that the federal government should help individuals ravaged by hunger and homelessness. In this 1931 radio speech on Abraham Lincoln's birthday, he explained his reasoning. His refusal to offer humanitarian assistance helped cost him reelection in 1932.

From, "Radio Address on Lincoln's Birthday," in *The State Papers and Other Public Writings of Herbert Hoover*, ed. William Starr Myers (Garden City, NY: Doubleday, 1934), 1:503–05.

By the magic of the radio, I am able to address several hundred public gatherings called this evening throughout our country in celebration of the birth of Abraham Lincoln. It is appropriate that I should speak from this room in the White House where Lincoln strived and accomplished his great service to our country.

*   *   *

In Lincoln's day the dominant problem in our form of government turned upon the issue of states rights. Though less pregnant with disaster, the dominant problem today in our form of government turns in large degree upon the issue of the relationship of federal, state, and local government responsibilities. We are faced with unceasing agitation that the federal government shall assume new financial burdens, that it shall undertake increased burdens in regulation of abuses and in the prosecution of crime.

It is true that since Lincoln's time many forces have swept across state borders and have become more potent than the state or local community can deal with alone either financially or by jurisdiction. Our concept of federal, state, and local responsibilities is possible of no unchangeable definitions and it must shift with the moving forces in the nation, but the time has come when we must have more national consideration and decision of the part which each shall assume in these responsibilities.

The federal government has assumed many new responsibilities since Lincoln's time, and will probably assume more in the future when the states and local communities cannot alone cure abuse or bear the entire cost of national programs, but there is an essential principle that should be maintained in these matters. I am convinced that where federal action is essential then in most cases it should limit its responsibilities to supplement the States and local communities, and that it should not assume the major role or the entire responsibility, in replacement of the States or local government. To do otherwise threatens the whole foundations of local government, which is the very basis of self-government.

The moment responsibilities of any community, particularly in economic and social questions, are shifted from any part of the nation to Washington, then that community has subjected itself to a remote bureaucracy with its minimum of understanding and of sympathy. It has lost a large part of its voice and its control of its own destiny. Under federal control the varied conditions of life in our country are forced into standard molds, with all their limitations upon life, either of the individual or the community. Where people divest themselves of local government responsibilities they at once lay the foundation for the destruction of their liberties.

And buried in this problem lies something even deeper. The whole of our governmental machinery was devised for the purpose that through ordered liberty we give incentive and equality of opportunity to every individual to rise to that highest achievement of which he is capable. At once when government is centralized there arises a limitation upon the liberty of the individual and a restriction of individual opportunity.

The true growth of the nation is the growth of character in its citizens. The spread of government destroys initiative and thus destroys character. Character is made in the community as well as in the individual by assuming responsibilities, not by escape from them. Carried to its logical extreme, all this shouldering of individual and community responsibility upon the government can lead but to the superstate where every man becomes the servant of the State and real liberty is lost. Such was not the government that Lincoln sought to build. There is an entirely different avenue by which we may both resist this drift to centralized government and at the same time meet a multitude of problems. That is to strengthen in the Nation a sense and an organization of self-help and cooperation to solve as many problems as possible outside of government. We are today passing through a critical test in such a problem arising from the economic depression.

Due to lack of caution in business and to the impact of forces from an outside world, one-half of which is involved in social and political revolution, the march of our prosperity has been retarded. We are projected into temporary unemployment, losses, and hardships. In a nation rich in resources, many people were faced with hunger and cold through no fault of their own. Our national resources are not only material supplies and material wealth but a spiritual and moral wealth in kindliness, in compassion, in a sense of obligation of neighbor to neighbor and a realization of responsibility by industry, by business, and the community for its social security and its social welfare.

The evidence of our ability to solve great problems outside of government action and the degree of moral strength with which we emerge from this period will be determined by whether the individuals and the local communities continue to meet their responsibilities.

Throughout this depression I have insisted upon organization of these forces through industry, through local government and through charity, that they should meet this crisis by their own initiative, by the assumption of their own responsibilities. The federal government has sought to do its part by example in the expansion of employment, by affording credit to drought sufferers for rehabilitation, and by cooperation with the community, and thus to avoid the opiates of government charity and the stifling of our national spirit of mutual self-help.

We can take courage and pride in the effective work of thousands of voluntary organizations for provision of employment, for relief of distress, that have sprung up over the entire Nation. Industry and business have recognized a social obligation to their employees as never before. The State and local governments are being helpful. The people are themselves succeeding in this task. Never before in a great depression has there been so systematic a protection against distress. Never before has there been so little social disorder. Never before has there been such an outpouring of the spirit of self-sacrifice and of service.

The ever-growing complexity of modern life, with its train of evermore perplexing and difficult problems, is a challenge to our individual characters and to our devotion to our ideals. The resourcefulness of America when challenged has never failed. Success is not gained by leaning upon government to solve all the problems before us. That way leads to enervation of will and destruction of character.

Victory over this depression and over our other difficulties will be won by the resolution of our people to fight their own battles in their own communities, by stimulating their ingenuity to solve their own problems, by taking new courage to be masters of their own destiny in the struggle of life. This is not the easy way, but it is the American way. And it was Lincoln's way.

The ultimate goal of the American social ideal is equality of opportunity and individual initiative. These are not born of bureaucracy. This ideal is the expression of the spirit of our people. This ideal obtained at the birth of the Republic. It was the ideal of Lincoln. it is the ideal upon which the nation has risen to unparalleled greatness.

We are going through a period when character and courage are on trial, and where the very faith that is within us is under test. Our people are meeting this test. And they are doing more than the mediate task of the day. They are maintaining the ideals of our American system. By their devotion to these ideals we shall come out of these times stronger in character, in courage, and in faith.

*   *   *

REVIEW QUESTIONS

1. What distinctions did Hoover draw between the roles of the federal, state, and local governments in dealing with the Great Depression?
2. Why was Hoover so insistent that the federal government stay out of providing assistance to individuals suffering from joblessness, homelessness, and hunger?

FRANKLIN D. ROOSEVELT

FROM First Inaugural Address (1933)

As Roosevelt took office the nation faced a banking crisis as well as a deepening depression. He had yet to formulate the specific programs that would make up the New Deal, but he knew that the nation expected quick action and bold leadership. In his inaugural address he sought to provide both.

New York Times, March 5, 1933.

This is a day of national consecration, and I am certain that my fellow Americans expect that on my induction into the Presidency I will address them with a candor and a decision which the present situation of our Nation impels.

This is pre-eminently the time to speak the truth, the whole truth, frankly and boldly. Nor need we shrink from honestly facing conditions in our country today. This great nation will endure as it has endured, will revive and will prosper.

So first of all let me assert my firm belief that the only thing we have to fear is fear itself—nameless, unreasoning, unjustified terror which paralyzes needed efforts to convert retreat into advance.

In every dark hour of our national life a leadership of frankness and vigor has met with that understanding and support of the people themselves which is essential to victory. I am convinced that you will again give the support to leadership in these critical days.

In such a spirit on my part and on yours we face our common difficulties. They concern, thank God, only material things. Values have shrunken to fantastic levels; taxes have risen; our ability to pay has fallen; government of all kinds is faced by serious curtailment of income; the means of exchange are frozen in the currents of trade; the withered leaves of industrial enterprise lie on every side; farmers find no markets for their produce; the savings of many years in thousands of families are gone.

More important, a host of unemployed citizens face the grim problem of existence, and an equally great number toil with little return. Only a foolish optimist can deny the dark realities of the moment.

Yet our distress comes from no failure of substance. We are stricken by no plague of locusts. Compared with the perils which our forefathers conquered because they believed and were not afraid, we have still much to be thankful for. Nature still offers her bounty and human efforts have multiplied it. Plenty is at our doorsteps, but a generous use of it languishes in the very sight of the supply. Primarily this is because the rulers of the exchange of mankind's goods have failed, through their own stubbornness and their own incompetence, have admitted their failure, and abdicated. Practices of the unscrupulous money changers stand indicted in the court of public opinion, rejected by the hearts and minds of men. . . .

Our greatest primary task is to put people to work. This is no unsolvable problem if we face it wisely and courageously.

It can be accomplished in part by direct recruiting by the Government itself, treating the task as we would treat the emergency of a war, but at the same time, through this employment, accomplishing greatly needed projects to stimulate and reorganize the use of our natural resources.

Hand in hand with this we must frankly recognize the overbalance of population in our industrial centers and, by engaging on a national scale in a redistribution, endeavor to provide a better use of the land for those best fitted for the land.

The task can be helped by definite efforts to raise the values of agricultural products and with this the power to purchase the output of our cities.

It can be helped by preventing realistically the tragedy of the growing loss through foreclosure of our small homes and our farms.

It can be helped by insistence that the Federal, State, and local governments act forthwith on the demand that their cost be drastically reduced. It can be helped by the unifying of relief activities which to-day are often scattered, uneconomical, and unequal. It can be helped by national planning for and supervision of all forms of transportation and of communications and other utilities which have a definitely public character.

There are many ways in which it can be helped, but it can never be helped merely by talking about it. We must act and act quickly.

Finally, in our progress toward a resumption of work we require two safeguards against a return of the evils of the old order; there must be a strict supervision of all banking and credits and investments; there must be an end to speculation with other people's money, and there must be provision for an adequate but sound currency.

There are the lines of attack. I shall presently urge upon a new Congress in special session detailed measures for their fulfillment, and I shall seek the immediate assistance of the several States.

Through this program of action we address ourselves to putting our own national house in order and making income balance outgo. . . .

In the field of world policy I would dedicate this Nation to the policy of the good neighbor—the neighbor who resolutely respects himself and, because he does so, respects the rights of others—the neighbor who respects his obligations and respects the sanctity of his agreements in and with a world of neighbors.

If I read the temper of our people correctly, we now realize as we have never realized before our interdependence on each other; that we can not merely take but we must give as well; that if we are to go forward, we must move as a trained and loyal army willing to sacrifice for the good of a common discipline, because without such discipline no progress is made, no leadership becomes effective.

We are, I know, ready and willing to submit our lives and property to such discipline, because it makes possible a leadership which aims at a larger good. This I propose to offer, pledging that the larger purposes will bind upon us all as a sacred obligation with a unity of duty hitherto evoked only in time of armed strife.

With this pledge taken, I assume unhesitatingly the leadership of this great army of our people dedicated to a disciplined attack upon our common problems.

Action in this image and to this end is feasible under the form of government which we have inherited from our ancestors. Our Constitution is so simple and practical that it is possible always to meet extraordinary needs by changes in emphasis and arrangement without loss of essential form. That is why our constitutional system has proved itself the most superbly enduring political mechanism the modern world has produced. It has met every stress of vast expansion of territory, of foreign wars, of bitter internal strife, of world relations.

It is to be hoped that the normal balance of executive and legislative authority may be wholly adequate to meet the unprecedented task before us. But it may be that an unprecedented demand and need for undelayed action may call for temporary departure from that normal balance of public procedure.

I am prepared under my constitutional duty to recommend the measures that a stricken nation in the midst of a stricken world may require. These measures, or such other measures as the Congress may build out of its experience and wisdom, I shall

seek, within my constitutional authority, to bring to speedy adoption.

But in the event that the congress shall fail to take one of these two courses, and in the event that the national emergency is still critical, I shall not evade the clear course of duty that will then confront me. I shall ask the congress for the one remaining instrument to meet the crisis—broad Executive power to wage a war against the emergency, as great as the power that would be given to me if we were in fact invaded by a foreign foe.

For the trust reposed in me I will return the courage and the devotion that befit the time. I can do no less.

We face the arduous days that lie before us in the warm courage of national unity; with the clear consciousness of seeking old and precious moral values; with the clean satisfaction that comes from the stern performance of duty by young and old alike. . . .

In this dedication of a nation we humbly ask the blessing of God. May He protect each and every one of us! May He guide me in the days to come!

REVIEW QUESTIONS

1. What measures did Roosevelt pledge to put before the Congress?
2. How was Roosevelt prepared to govern if Congress blocked his initiatives?
3. Give examples of Roosevelt's efforts to bolster morale and instill hope among the public.

Letters to the Roosevelts during the Depression

As the human consequences of the prolonged Depression unfolded, people grew desperate. Many of them looked to Franklin and Eleanor Roosevelt for help. Indeed, the Roosevelts received over 15 million letters from struggling Americans. Many Americans who felt compelled to write the Roosevelts were supportive of the New Deal.

Minnie Hardin, a hardworking Indiana woman struggling to make ends meet during the Great Depression, sent a blistering letter to Eleanor Roosevelt criticizing the New Deal for helping many people who were not willing to help themselves. Three letters are excerpted here.

From Roosevelt Papers, Series 190, Miscellaneous, 1937, Franklin D. Roosevelt Library. Reprinted in *Down and Out in the Great Depression: Letters from the Forgotten Man* by Robert S. McElvaine. Copyright © 1983 by the University of North Carolina Press. Foreword © 2008. Used by permission of the publisher. www.uncpress.unc.edu.

Goff, Kansas
May 10, 1935
Mrs. Franklin D. Roosevelt:

My Dear Friend:

For the first time of my lifetime I am asking a favor and this one I am needing very badly and I am coming to you for help.

Among your friends do you know of one who is discarding a spring coat for a new one. If so could you beg the old one for me. I wear a size 40 to 42 I have not had a spring coat for six years and last Sunday when getting ready to go to church I see my winter coat had several very thin places in the back that is very noticeable My clothes are very plain so I could wear only something plain. we were hit very hard by the drought and every penny we can save goes for feed to put in crop.

Hoping for a favorable reply.

Your friend Mrs. J. T.

Mr. and Mrs. Roosevelt
Wash. D.C.
February 1936

Dear Mr. President,

I am a boy of 12 years. I want to tell you about my family. My father hasn't worked for 5 months. He went plenty times to relief, he filled out application. They won't give us anything. I don't know why. Please you do something. We haven't paid 4 months rent, Everyday the landlord rings the bell, we don't open the door for him. We are afraid that will be put out, been put out before, and don't want to happen again. We haven't paid the gas bill, and the electric bill, haven't paid grocery bill for 3 months. My bother goes to Lane Tech. High School. He's eigh-

teen years old, hasn't gone to school for 2 weeks because he got no carfare. I have a sister she's twenty years, she can't find work. My father he staying home. All the time he's crying because he can't find work. I told him why are you crying daddy, and daddy said why shouldn't I cry when there is nothing in the house. I feel sorry for him. That night I couldn't sleep. The next morning I wrote this letter to you. In my room. We're American citizens and were born in Chicago, Ill. and I don't know why they don't help us Please answer right away because we need it. Will starve. Thank you.

God bless you.

[Anonymous]
Chicago, Ill.

Mrs. Roosevelt:

I suppose from your point of view the work relief, old age pensions, slum clearance and all the rest seems like a perfect remedy for all the ills of this country, but I would like for you to see the results, as the other half see them.

We have always had a shiftless, never-do-well class of people whose one and only aim in life is to live without work. I have been rubbing elbows with this class for nearly sixty years and have tried to help some of the most promising and have seen others try to help them, but it can't be done. We cannot help those who will not try to help themselves and if they do try, a square deal is all they need, and by the way that is all this country needs or ever has needed: a square deal for all and then, let each paddle their own canoe, or sink.

There has never been any necessity for anyone who is able to work, being on relief in this locality, but there have been many eating the bread of charity and they have lived better than ever before. I have had taxpayers tell me that their children came from school and asked why they couldn't have nice lunches like the children on relief. The women and children around here have had to work at the fields to help save the crops and several women fainted while at work and at the same time we couldn't go up or down the road without stumbling over some of the reliefers, moping around carrying dirt from one side of the road to the other and back again, or else asleep. I live alone on a farm and have not raised any crops for the last two years as there was no help to be had. I am feeding the stock and have been cutting the wood to keep my home fires burning. There are several reliefers around here now who have been kicked off relief but they refuse to work unless they can get relief hours and wages, but they are so worthless no one can afford to hire them.

As for the clearance of the real slums, it can't be done as long as their inhabitants are allowed to reproduce their kind. I would like for you to see what a family of that class can do to a decent house in a short time. Such a family moved into an almost new, neat, four-room house near here last winter. They even cut down some of the shade trees for fuel, after they had burned everything they could pry loose. There were two big idle boys in the family and they could get all the fuel they wanted, just for the cutting, but the shade trees were closer and it was taking a great amount of fuel, for they had broken out several windows and they had but very little bedding. There were two women there all the time and three part of the time and there was enough good clothing tramped in the mud around the yard to have made all the bedclothes they needed. It was clothing that had been given them and they had worn it until it was too filthy to wear any longer without washing, so they threw it out and begged more. I will not try to describe their filth for you would not believe me. They paid no rent while there and left between two suns owing everyone from whom they could get a nickels worth of anything. They are just a fair sample of the class of people on whom so much of our hard earned tax money is being squandered and on whom so much sympathy is being wasted.

As for the old people on beggars' allowances: the have provided homes for all the old people who never liked to work, where they will be neither cold nor hungry: much better homes than most of them have ever tried to provide for themselves. They have lived many years through the most prosperous times of our country and had an opportunity to prepare for old age, but they spent their lives in idleness or worse and now they expect those who have worked like slaves, to provide a living for them and all their worthless descendants. Some of them are asking for from thirty to sixty dollars a month when I have known them to live on a dollar a week rather than go to work. There is many a little child doing without butter on its bread, so that some old sot can have his booze and tobacco: some old sot who spent his working years loafing around pool rooms and saloons, boasting that the world owed him a living.

Even the child welfare has become a racket. The parents of large families are getting divorces, so that the mothers and children can qualify for aid. The children have to join the ranks of the "unemployed" as they grow up, for no child that has been raised on charity in this community has ever amounted to anything.

You people who have plenty of this world's goods and whose money comes easy, have no idea of the heart-breaking toil and self-denial which is the lot of the working people who are trying to make an honest living, and then to have to shoulder all these unjust burdens seems like the last straw. During the worst of the depression many of the farmers had to deny their families butter, eggs, meat, etc. and sell it to pay their taxes and then had to stand by and see the dead-beats carry it home to their families by the arm load, and they knew their tax money was helping pay for it. One woman saw a man carry out eight pounds of butter at one time. The crookedness, selfishness, greed and graft of the crooked politicians is making one gigantic racket out of the new deal, and it is making this a nation of dead-beats and beggars and if it continues the people who will work will soon be nothing but slaves for the pampered poverty rats and I am afraid these human parasites are going to become a menace to the country unless they are disfranchised. No one should have the right to vote theirself [*sic*] a living at the expense of the taxpayers. They learned their strength at the last election and also learned that they can get just about what they want by "voting right." They have had a taste of their coveted life of idleness, and at the rate they are increasing, they will soon control the country. The twentieth child arrived in the home of one chronic reliefer [*sic*] near here some time ago.

Is it any wonder the taxpayers are discouraged by all this penalizing of thrift and industry to reward shiftlessness, or that the whole country is on the brink of chaos?

Minnie A. Hardin
Columbus, Ind.

REVIEW QUESTIONS

1. In the first letter what was the source of the writer's economic difficulties?
2. How did the economic circumstance of the second writer differ from that of the first?
3. Why was Hardin so opposed to government efforts to help the poor and disadvantaged?
4. To what extent are Hardin's views still relevant today?
5. What did the letters imply about attitudes toward the office of the presidency? Toward the Roosevelts?

HUEY LONG

Share Our Wealth (1935)

Huey Long cemented his control as governor of Louisiana by using state power and state funds to improve social services; to build roads, bridges, and schools; and to reform tax codes. In 1932 he was elected to the U.S. Senate. Initially he supported Roosevelt's New Deal measures, but by 1935 he had broken with the president and launched his own "Share Our Wealth" movement as an alternative to the New Deal. He developed a large grassroots following across the country before being assassinated in 1935.

From *Congressional Record*, 74th Cong., 1st Sess., May 7, 1935, pp. 7049–50.

. . . Here is what we stand for in a nutshell:

1. We propose that every family in America shall at least own a homestead equal in value to not less than one-third the average family wealth. The average family wealth of America, at normal values, is approximately $16,000. So our first proposition means that every family shall have a home and the comforts of a home up to a value of not less than $5,000.

2. We propose that no family shall own more than 300 times the average family wealth, which means that no family shall possess more than a wealth of $5,000,000. And we think that is too much. The two propositions together mean that no family shall own less than one-third of the average family wealth, nor shall any family own more than 300 times the average family wealth. That is to say that none should be so poor as to have less than

one-third of the average, and none should be so rich as to have more than 300 times the average.

3. We next propose that every family shall have an income equal to at least one-third of the average family income in America. If all were allowed to work, according to our statistics, there would be an average family income of from $5,000 to $10,000 per year. So, therefore, in addition to the home which every family would own and the comforts of life which every family would enjoy, every family would make not less than $2,000 to $3,000 per year upon which to live and educate their children.

4. We propose that no family shall have an income of more than 300 times the average family income. Less the income taxes, this would mean an annual income of $1,000,000 would be the maximum allowed any one family in 1 year. The third and fourth propositions simply mean that no family should earn less than one-third the average, and no family should earn more than 300 times the average; none to make too much, none to make too little. Everyone to have the things required for life; every man a king.

5. We propose a pension to the old people. Under our proposal taxes would not be levied upon the sons and daughters, nor the working people to support their aged fathers and mothers. But on the contrary, such support as would be given for old-age pensions would be borne solely by the surplus money which the Government would rake off the big fortunes and big inheritances.

6. We propose to care for the veterans of our wars, including the immediate cash payment of the soldiers' bonus, and last, but not least, we propose that every child in America have a right to education and training, not only through grammar and high school, but also through colleges and universities. And this education and training would be of such extent as will equip each child to battle on fair terms in the work which it is compelled to perform

throughout life. We would not have it that a child could go to college or university provided his parents had the money on which to send him, but it would be the right of every child under our plan to the costs, including living expenses of college and university training, which could be done by our country at a cost considerably less than is required for the military training which has been given our youth in the past. . . .

Let no one tell you that it is difficult to redistribute the wealth of this land; it matters not how rich or great one may be, when he dies his wealth must be redistributed anyway. The law of God shows how it has been throughout time. Nothing is more sensible or better understood than the redistribution of property. The laws of God command it. It is required of all nations that live. . . .

So let us be about our work. It is simple. Why lie ye here idle? There is enough for all. Let there be peace in the land. Let our children be happy. . . .

How wonderful, how great, how fruitful to all this great land of ours can be. We only have to eliminate useless greed, provide that none shall be too big and none too small. Beautiful America can rise to the opportunity before it. It means to us all:

Every man a king.

REVIEW QUESTIONS

1. What did the "Share Our Wealth" program seek to accomplish with regard to personal incomes?
2. Where did Long propose to find the revenue to fund his proposed programs? How realistic was this notion?
3. How accurate were those who charged that Long's program represented an American version of socialism?

DOROTHY THOMPSON

FROM Roosevelt's "Court-Packing" Plan (1937)

President Franklin Roosevelt's 1937 attempt to restructure the Supreme Court, which critics labeled his "court-packing plan," aroused intense opposition in Congress, even among Democrats. Dorothy Thompson, the distinguished journalist and one of the earliest enemies of Nazism, lambasted Roosevelt's efforts to reshape the Supreme Court.

From "Roosevelt's 'Court-Packing' Plan," *The Washington Star*, February 10, 1937. Copyright © 1937 by Dorothy Thompson. Reprinted with the permission of McIntosh & Otis, Inc. [Editorial insertions appear in square brackets—*Ed.*]

If the American people accept this last audacity of the President without letting out a yell to high heaven, they have ceased to be jealous of their liberties and are ripe for ruin. This is the beginning of pure personal government. Do you want it? Do you like it? Look around about the world—there are plenty of examples—and make up your mind.

The Executive [President Roosevelt] is already powerful by reason of his overwhelming victory in November [1936], and will be strengthened even more if the reorganization plan for the administration, presented some weeks ago, is adopted. We have, to all intents and purposes, a one party Congress, dominated by the President. Although nearly 40 percent of the voters repudiated the New Deal at the polls, they have less than 20 percent representation in both houses of Congress. And now the Supreme Court is to have a majority determined by the President and by a Senate which he dominates. When that happens we will have a one-man Government. It will all be constitutional. So, he claims, is Herr [Adolf] Hitler.

Leave the personality and the intentions of the President out of the picture. They are not the crux of this issue. . . . He may have the liberties of the American people deeply at heart. But he will have a successor who may be none of these things. There have been benevolent dictatorships and benevolent tyrannies. They have even, at times in history,

worked for the popular welfare. But that is not the welfare, which up to now, the American people have chosen.

And let us not be confused by the words "liberal" and "conservative" or misled into thinking that the expressed will of the majority is the essence of democracy. By that definition Hitler, Stalin and Mussolini are all great democratic leaders. The essence of democracy is the protection of minorities. Nor has a majority of this generation the right to mortgage a majority of the next. In the Constitution of the United States is incorporated the rights of the people, rights enjoyed by every American citizen in perpetuity, which cannot be voted away by any majority, ever. Majorities are temporary things. The Supreme Court is there to protect the fundamental law even against the momentary "will of the people." That is its function. And it is precisely because nine men can walk out and say: "You can't do that!" that our liberties are protected against the mob urge that occasionally the Court has been traditionally divorced from momentary majorities. . . .

This is no proposal to change the Constitution. This is no proposal to limit the powers of the Supreme Court. This is a proposal to capture the Supreme Court. . . .

Don't talk of liberalism! The liberal does not believe that the end justifies the means. Long experience has taught him that the means usually determine the end. No human being can believe in the sincerity of this proposal. It is clever, in a world sick of cleverness and longing for plain talk and simple honesty. Must we begin to examine every message from the President to see whether there is a trick in it somewhere?

Are the opposition in Washington phonographs or are they men? If they are men we shall see another little "willful group." They are a handful, but they can do one thing: They can see that this measure is not rushed through without debate, they can see to it that the country has time to think about this, to talk about it, to debate it on every forum platform, to act upon it, individually and in groups, regardless of party.

REVIEW QUESTIONS

1. Do you agree with Thompson that Roosevelt's attempt to restructure the Supreme Court resembled fascism? Explain.
2. Do you agree that the "essence of democracy is the protection of minorities"? Why or why not?

ROY WILKINS

An African American Assessment of the New Deal (1940)

The New Deal and the vocal support for civil rights provided by Franklin and Eleanor Roosevelt gave hope to African Americans. In 1936, Mary McLeod Bethune, a Florida-based educator and activist, became the highest ranking African American woman in government when President Roosevelt named her director of Negro Affairs in the National Youth Administration. Bethune claimed that the 1930s was "the first time in their history" that African Americans viewed the federal government with the "expectancy of sympathetic understanding and interpretation." Yet others were more ambivalent about the New Deal's record on civil rights. In 1940, Roy Wilkins (1901–1981), a black journalist serving as a staff member of the National Association for the Advancement of Colored People (NAACP) assessed the New Deal's record on civil rights.

"The Roosevelt Record," *The Crisis*, November 1940, 343. The publisher wishes to thank the Crisis Publishing Co., Inc., the publisher of the magazine of the National Association for the Advancement of Colored People, for the use of this material first published in the November 1940 issue of *Crisis Magazine*. [Editorial insertions appear in square brackets—*Ed.*]

On the subject of the Negro, the Roosevelt record is spotty, as might be expected in an administration where so much power is in the hands of the southern wing of the Democratic Party. And yet Mr. [Franklin] Roosevelt, hobbled as he has been by the Dixie die-hards, has managed to include Negro citizens in practically every phase of the administration program. In this respect, no matter how far behind the ideal he may be, he is far ahead of any other Democratic president, and of recent Republican ones.

The best proof that Mr. Roosevelt has not catered always to the South and has insisted on carrying the Negro along with his program is to be found in the smearing, race-hating propaganda used against him in the 1936 campaign by southern white groups. Both he and Mrs. Roosevelt were targets of filthy mud-slinging simply because they did not see eye-to-eye with the South on the Negro.

This does not mean that the Roosevelt administration has done all that it could have done for the race. Its policies in many instances have done Negroes great injustice and have helped to build more secure walls of segregation.

On the anti-lynching bill, Mr. Roosevelt has said not a mumbling word. His failure to endorse this legislation . . . is a black mark against him. It does no good to say that the White House could not pass down some word on this bill. The White House spoke on many bills. Mr. Roosevelt might have pressed the anti-lynching bill to a vote, especially during January and February 1938, when there was tremendous public opinion supporting the bill. His failure to act, or even speak, on the anti-lynching bill was the more glaring because, while mobs in America were visiting inhumanities upon Negroes, Mr. Roosevelt periodically was rebuking some foreign government [Nazi Germany] for inhumanity, and enunciating high sentiments of liberty, tolerance, justice, etc.

To declare that the Roosevelt administration has tried to include the Negro in nearly every phase of its program for the people of the nation is not to ignore the instances where government policies have harmed the race.

At Boulder dam, for example, the administration continued the shameful policy begun by Hoover of forbidding Negroes to live in Boulder City, the government-built town [for construction workers]. And in its own pet project, the TVA [Tennessee Valley Authority], the administration forbade Negroes to live in Norris [Tennessee], another government-built town at Norris dam.

Full credit must go to the administration for its program of low-cost housing, so sorely needed by low-income families. No one pretends that the American housing program is more than a begin-

ning, but Negroes have shared in it in the most equitable manner. However, there were, outside the slum-clearance program, some damaging practices. The FHA [Federal Housing Authority], which insures mortgages for home buyers, has enforced a regulation that puts the power and approval of the government on ghetto life. No Negro family that sought a home outside the so-called "Negro" neighborhood could get a FHA-insured loan.

The vast programs for youth, the CCC [Civilian Conservation Corps] and the NYA [National Youth Administration], have included our young people, but in the CCC a justifiable complaint has been that Negro instructors, advisers, and reserve army officers were not appointed in any but the tiniest proportion.

There is little need to mention relief and the WPA. Mr. Roosevelt's critics concede what his administration has done in these two branches of his program by concentrating their attack upon the relief that the New Deal has given Negroes. In relief the government set the tone. That tone was so much higher than the city, the county, and state standards for Negroes in certain areas that, even though differentials existed, the net result was more than it would have been without government supervision. Collective bargaining and the Wages and Hours Act have aided Negro workers in private industry.

The farm program has not been ideally administered, but colored people have shared in the benefits. More than 50,000 families have been assisted by the Farm Security Administration.

Mr. Roosevelt had the courage to appoint a Negro to a federal judgeship, the first in the history of the country. His nominee was confirmed by a Democratic Senate without a murmur. Complaint has been made that in naming about a score of colored administrative assistants and advisers, Mr. Roosevelt has kept Negroes out of any real posts in the government. If it be true that Mr. Roosevelt has created Negro appendages to various bureaus, it cannot be denied that colored people know more about their government and have penetrated nearer to policy-making desks than ever before.

Heavily on the debit side is Mr. Roosevelt's approval of the War Department's notorious Jim

Crow [system of racial segregation] in the armed services.

[The] most important contribution of the Roosevelt administration to the age-old color line problem in America has been its doctrine that Negroes are a part of the country and must be considered in any program for the country as a whole. The inevitable discriminations notwithstanding, this thought has been driven home in thousands of communities by a thousand specific acts. For the first time in their lives, government has taken on meaning and substance for the Negro masses.

REVIEW QUESTIONS

1. In Wilkins's view, what was the primary factor limiting Roosevelt's efforts to treat African Americans equally?
2. Based on this editorial, what is your assessment of Roosevelt's record on civil rights?

PEARL S. BUCK

American Women (1938)

Pearl Sydenstricker Buck (1892–1973) was a celebrated American writer, novelist, and humanitarian. Born in West Virginia, the daughter of Presbyterian missionaries, she spent most of her life before 1934 in Zhenjiang, China, although she attended college and graduate school in the United States. In 1930, she published her first novel, East Wind, West Wind. *Her next novel,* The Good Earth, *focused on the lives of Chinese peasants; it won a Pulitzer Prize in 1932. Six years later, Buck became the first American woman to receive a Nobel Prize in Literature. In 1930, she wrote an essay assessing the status of American women as viewed through the lens of her experiences in China.*

"American Women," originally published in *Harper's Magazine* (August 1938). Reprinted by permission of Inkwell Management on behalf of the Estate of Pearl S. Buck.

I am an American woman, but I had no opportunity until a few years ago to know women in America. Living as I did in China, it is true that I saw a few American women; but that is not the same thing. One was still not able to draw many conclusions from them about American women. I gathered, however, that they felt that girls in China had a hard time of it, because there every family liked sons better than daughters, and, in the average family, did not give them the same education or treatment. In America, however, they said people welcomed sons and daughters equally and treated them the same. This, after years in a country [that] defines a woman's limitations very clearly, seemed nothing short of heaven—if true.

Therefore when I came to America to live I was interested particularly in her women. And during these immediate past years I have come to know a good many of them—women in business, artists, housewives in city and country, women young and old. I have taken pains to know them.

More than that, I have made my own place as a woman in America. And I find that what I anticipated before I came here is quite wrong. It seems to me that women are very badly treated in America. A few of them know it, more of them dimly suspect it, and most of them, though they know they ought to be glad they live in a Christian country where women are given an education, do not feel as happy in their lonely hearts as they wish they did.

The reason for this unhappiness is a secret sense of failure, and this sense of failure comes from a feeling of inferiority, and the feeling of inferiority comes from a realization that actually women are not much respected in America.

Tradition is very strong in this backward country of ours. We Americans are a backward nation in everything except in the making and using of machines. And we are nowhere more backward than we are in our attitude toward our women. We still, morally, shut the door of her home on a woman. We say to her, "Your home ought to be enough for you if you are a nice woman. Your husband ought to be enough—and your children."

If she says, "But they aren't enough—what shall I do?" we say, "Go and have a good time, that's a nice girl. Get yourself a new hat or something, or go to the matinee or join a bridge club. Don't worry your pretty head about what is not your business."

So, though I am impressed with the fact that American women do not, as a group, seem happy, privileged as they are, I am not surprised. I know that happiness comes to an individual only as a result of personal fulfillment through complete functioning of all the energies and capabilities with which one is born. I do not for a moment mean that all women must go out and find jobs and "do something" outside the home. That would be as silly and

general a mistake as our present general clinging to tradition. I simply mean let us be realistic. Let us face the fact that as a nation we are in a medieval state of mind about the place of women in society.

We are so clever with machines, we Americans. But we have done a silly thing with our women. We have put modern high-powered engines into old antiquated vehicles. It is no wonder the thing is not working.

And there are only two courses to follow if we do want it to work. We must go back to the old, simple, one-horsepower engine or else we must change the body to suit the engine—one or the other. If the first, then tradition must be held to from the moment a woman is born, not, as it now is, clamped upon her when, after a free and extraordinarily equal childhood and girlhood with boys, she attempts to enter into a free and equal adult life with men and finds it denied her, to discover then that her education has had nothing to do with her life.

Or else we must be willing to let her go on as she began. This means that American men must cease being "sweet boys" and grow up emotionally as well as physically and face women as adult men. But they, poor things, have not been fitted for that either! Besides, of course, they are afraid of what women might do.

REVIEW QUESTIONS

1. In what ways were American women "badly treated," according to Buck?
2. How does Buck define happiness?
3. To what extent do American girls and women today suffer under the same cult of domesticity limiting their horizons and stunting their potential?

26 ✑ THE SECOND WORLD WAR, 1939–1945

During the 1920s, most Americans ignored foreign relations. Their focus was on the prosperity and frivolity of the Roaring Twenties. The refusal by Congress to join the League of Nations in 1919 signaled a return to the isolationist sentiment that had governed the nation's foreign policy during the nineteenth century. Woodrow Wilson's liberal internationalism was deemed bankrupt by his Republican opponents. "We seek no part in directing the destiny of the world," President Warren G. Harding announced in 1924. Yet in reality the United States could no longer isolate itself from world affairs. The nation's economy and its interests were now global in nature. American investments abroad increased sevenfold during the 1920s, and the rapidly industrializing American economy grew dependent on raw materials imported from abroad.

The history of American foreign relations between 1920 and the mid-1930s thus seems paradoxical in hindsight: at the same time that the United States was becoming more dependent on international trade, its statesmen were disavowing the use of force in international affairs. They instead placed their faith in democratic principles and international treaties to preserve the peace and protect American economic interests abroad.

The capstone of this reliance on treaties to preserve world peace was the Kellogg-Briand Pact of 1928 (also known as the Pact of Paris). The French foreign minister, Aristide Briand, proposed that the United States and France sign a treaty disavowing war as a method of settling disputes between the two countries. The American secretary of state, Frank Kellogg, embraced the concept but insisted that it be a multilateral pact. The two diplomats then convinced Great Britain, Japan, Italy, Belgium, Poland, Germany, Czechoslovakia, and six other countries to join them in signing the treaty. The U.S. Senate ratified it in 1929. But the authors of the pact were naive; they failed to recognize that it was not treaties or idealistic rhetoric that sustained world peace but individual national interests mediated by the balance of power—a mechanism that would require the *timely threat or use of force to ensure its survival. One critic dismissed the treaty as a hollow cluster of pious phrases representing nothing more than "an international kiss."*

The inability of the Kellogg-Briand Pact to maintain global peace was vividly revealed in the world's response to the Japanese invasion of Manchuria in 1931. In direct violation of the Kellogg-Briand Pact, the Japanese army took control of northeastern China and set up their own puppet state of Manchukuo. President Hoover and Secretary of State Henry L. Stimson condemned the Japanese actions and refused to recognize the new regime in Manchukuo. The Japanese paid no attention and consolidated their control over Chinese territory. The unwillingness of Europe and the United States to use economic or military force against Japan mirrored their timid response to aggression by Nazi Germany and Fascist Italy during the 1930s. The Western democracies—France, Great Britain, and the United States—proved unable or unwilling to act collectively against Japanese expansionism in East Asia, German militancy in Europe, and Italian aggression in North Africa.

In 1937 the Japanese launched a massive invasion of China. Japan's naked aggression outraged public opinion in the West, called into question the passive stance of the United States, and heightened the sense of international urgency. Secretary of State Cordell Hull denounced the Japanese invasion, but his strong words fell on deaf ears. The Japanese were convinced that Western democracies were not willing to use force to stop their conquest of China. The United States endorsed the League of Nations's condemnation of Japanese aggression but opposed any economic sanctions against Japan. By 1938 Japan had assumed effective control over China.

The debate between isolationism and interventionism suddenly shifted focus on December 7, 1941, when the Japanese unleashed a surprise air raid on U.S. air and naval bases in Hawaii. The next day President Roosevelt asked Congress for a declaration of war against Japan. Soon thereafter Germany declared war on the United States. The world war that Americans had struggled to keep at bay had arrived at last.

World War II was the most significant event of the twentieth century. The conflict eventually engulfed five continents, leaving few people untouched and over 50 million dead, most of them civilians. The Japanese attack on Pearl Harbor unified Americans as nothing had done before. Men and women rushed to join the armed forces. Eventually over 16.4 million people would serve in the military during the war, including 350,000 women who performed various noncombat roles. Almost 300,000 Americans would lose their lives in the conflict. This was total war on a nightmarish scale. Whole cities were destroyed, nations dismembered, and societies transformed. Devilish new instruments of destruction were invented—plastic explosives, proximity fuses, rockets, jet airplanes, and atomic weapons—and systematic genocide emerged as an explicit war aim of the Germans and Japanese.

The war also led to an unprecedented expansion of the federal government. The number of civilian government employees more than tripled during the war, from 1.1 million to 3.8 million. And nationwide mobilization created an alliance between the defense industry and the federal government that became known as the military-industrial complex.

While the war raged in Asia and in Europe, its massive requirements served to transform social and economic life at home, changing the way Americans worked and lived. Total war required record levels of federal spending that provided a powerful catalyst for industry and manufacturing. This created 17 million new jobs which, along with military service, led to full employment of the nation's workforce. The war economy thus pulled the nation out of its prolonged depression and set in motion a massive internal migration. Some 6 million people left farms to take up work in the cities. California, speckled with defense plants, was an especially powerful magnet, adding some two million residents during the war. Several million whites and blacks left the rural South, lured by jobs in defense plants in the North and West.

Women were aggressively recruited for defense-related jobs. Between 1940 and 1945, 6.3 million women entered the workforce, and for the first time in history working women who were married outnumbered those who were single. By 1945 women constituted 37 percent of the workforce. Substantial numbers of African Americans participated in the wartime migration into military service and defense industries. Nearly 1 million blacks served in the armed forces, but mostly in segregated units usually led by white officers. Millions more found their way into the civilian workforce. In the process, they encountered even more obstacles than did women. Prejudice against blacks in the workplace remained rampant; they continued to be the last hired and first fired.

While millions of people were migrating across the country in search of new and better jobs during the war, one group of Americans was being forcibly moved and quarantined. In the aftermath of the attack on Pearl Harbor, anti-Japanese hysteria and racial prejudice ran high, especially on the West Coast. Exaggerated fears of possible Japanese attacks on the mainland and sabotage efforts led President Roosevelt to approve an army order in 1942 requiring that some 110,000 Japanese Americans, including 40,000 children, be "relocated" from their homes and "interned" in barbed-wire enclosed prison camps in seven southern and western states.

By the spring of 1945 the war in Europe was essentially over, but fighting in the Pacific persisted. The desperate Japanese launched kamikaze (suicide) air assaults on British and American ships. Such fanatical defensive measures gravely concerned Allied strategists as they planned the invasion of Japan for late 1945. They estimated that 35 percent of the allied assault force, some 250,000 men, would be killed or wounded. Some analysts predicted that the figure would be twice that high. This sobering prospect combined with the death of President Roosevelt in April to dull the celebrations of the German surrender on May 8.

Two months later, the new president, Harry S. Truman, learned of an alternative way to end the war with Japan. In July a team of American scientists detonated an atomic bomb in the New Mexico desert. A few days later, while meeting with Winston Churchill and Josef Stalin in Germany, Truman issued what has become known as the Potsdam Declaration: if the Japanese did not offer unconditional surrender, they would face "prompt and utter destruction." When Japan rejected the ultimatum, Truman ordered an atomic bomb dropped on the island nation. On August 6 a B-29 bomber named the Enola Gay released a five-ton uranium bomb over the port city of Hiroshima, subjecting the residents to what one called "a hell of unspeakable torments."

More than 80,000 people were killed immediately by the bomb blast. Thousands more died months and years later as a result of radiation poisoning. Four square miles of the city were flattened. Three days later, on August 9, another bomb was dropped on Nagasaki, with similar results. On August 14 Japan surrendered.

On September 2, 1945, the most devastating conflict in world history was officially over, but it left in its wake power vacuums in Europe and Asia that a rejuvenated Soviet Union and a newly "internationalist" United States sought to fill to protect their military, economic, and political interests. Instead of peace resulting from the end of World War II, a new and protracted "cold war" between the Soviet Union and the United States came to dominate world affairs in the postwar era.

CHARLES A. LINDBERGH

FROM Address to America First Rally (1941)

Charles Lindbergh was the young aviator who electrified the world in 1927 when he flew alone nonstop from New York to Paris in thirty-three hours. After his historic flight, he became an international celebrity. During the late 1930s he emerged as a leading spokesman for isolationism. The largest of the isolationist groups was the America First organization. When war did erupt, however, Lindbergh participated, secretly flying some fifty combat missions in Asia, shooting down one Japanese fighter plane.

From "The Text of Colonel Lindbergh's Address to the America First Committee Here," *New York Times*, April 24, 1941.

. . . I know I will be severely criticized by the interventionists in America when I say we should not enter a war unless we have a reasonable chance of winning. . . . But I do not believe that our American ideals, and our way of life, will gain through an unsuccessful war. And I know that the United States is not prepared to wage war in Europe successfully at this time. . . .

I have said before, and I will say again, that I believe it will be a tragedy to the entire world if the British Empire collapses. That is one of the main reasons why I opposed this war before it was declared, and why I have constantly advocated a negotiated peace. I did not feel that England and France had a reasonable chance of winning. France has now been defeated; and, despite the propaganda and confusion of recent months, it is now obvious that England is losing the war. I believe this is realized even by the British government. But they have one last desperate plan remaining. They hope that they may be able to persuade us to send another American Expeditionary Force to Europe, and to share with England militarily, as well as financially, the fiasco of this war. . . .

*   *   *

. . . There is a policy open to this nation that will lead to success—a policy that leaves us free to follow our way of life, and to develop our own civilization. It is not a new and untried idea. It was advocated by Washington.[1] It was incorporated in the Monroe Doctrine. Under its guidance the United States became the greatest nation in the world.

It is based upon the belief that the security of the nation lies in the strength and character of its own people. It recommends the maintenance of armed forces sufficient to defend this hemisphere from attack by any combination of foreign powers. It demands faith in an independent American destiny. This is the policy of the America First Committee today. It is a policy not of isolation, but of independence; not of defeat, but of courage. It is a policy that led this nation to success during the most trying years of our history, and it is a policy that will lead us to success again. . . .

War is not inevitable for this country. Such a claim is defeatism in the true sense. No one can make us fight abroad unless we are willing ourselves to do so. No one will attempt to fight us here if we are ourselves as a great nation should be armed. Over a hundred million people in this nation are opposed to entering the war. If the principles of democracy mean anything at all, that is reason enough for us to stay out. If we are forced into a war against the wishes of an overwhelming major-

---

[1] George Washington (1732–1799).

ity of our people, we will have proved democracy such a failure at home that there will be little use of fighting for it abroad.

The time has come when those of us who believe in an independent American destiny must band together and organize for strength. We have been led toward war by a minority of our people. This minority has power. It has influence. It has a loud voice. But it does not represent the American people. During the last several years I have traveled over this country from one end to the other. I have talked to many hundreds of men and women, and I have letters from tens of thousands more, who feel the same way as you and I.

Most of these people have no influence or power. Most of them have no means of expressing their convictions, except by their vote which has always been against this war. They are the citizens who have had to work too hard at their daily jobs to organize political meetings. Hitherto, they have relied upon their vote to express their feelings; but now they find that it is hardly remembered except in the oratory of a political campaign. These people—the majority of hardworking American citizens, are with us. They are the true strength of our country. And they are beginning to realize, as you and I, that there are times when we must sacrifice our normal interests in life in order to insure the safety and the welfare of our nation. . . .

REVIEW QUESTIONS

1. Contrast Lindbergh's arguments against helping the Allies with Roosevelt's proposals.
2. Assess the viability of Lindbergh's defensive military strategy.
3. Assess Lindbergh's distinction between isolation and independence.
4. To whom was Lindbergh referring when he said that a "minority" had led the United States toward war?

FRANKLIN D. ROOSEVELT

War Message to Congress (1941)

The morning after the Japanese attack on Pearl Harbor, President Franklin Roosevelt appeared before Congress to request an immediate declaration of war against Japan. On the same day, Congress—with only one dissenting vote cast by Montana representative Jeannette Rankin, a dedicated pacifist—declared war.

From *Congressional Record,* 77th Cong., 1st Sess., December 8, 1941, p. 9519.

Yesterday, December 7, 1941—a date which will live in infamy—the United States of America was suddenly and deliberately attacked by naval and air forces of the empire of Japan.

The United States was at peace with that nation and, at the solicitation of Japan, was still in conver-sation with its government and its emperor looking toward the maintenance of peace in the Pacific.

Indeed, one hour after Japanese air squadrons had commenced bombing in the American Island of Oahu the Japanese Ambassador to the United States and his colleague delivered to our Secretary of State a formal reply to a recent American message. And, while this reply stated that it seemed useless to continue the existing diplomatic negotiations, it contained no threat or hint of war or of armed attack.

It will be recorded that the distance of Hawaii from Japan makes it obvious that the attack was deliberately planned many days or even weeks ago. During the intervening time the Japanese Government has deliberately sought to deceive the United States by false statements and expressions of hope for continued peace.

The attack yesterday on the Hawaiian Islands has caused severe damage to American naval and military forces. I regret to tell you that very many American lives have been lost. In addition American ships have been reported torpedoed on the high seas between San Francisco and Honolulu.

Yesterday the Japanese Government also launched an attack against Malaya. Last night Japanese forces attacked Guam. Last night Japanese forces attacked the Philippine Islands. Last night the Japanese attacked Wake Island. And this morning the Japanese attacked Midway Island.

Japan has therefore undertaken a surprise offensive extending throughout the Pacific area. The facts of yesterday and today speak for themselves. The people of the United States have already formed their opinions and well understand the implications to the very life and safety of our nation.

As Commander in Chief of the Army and Navy I have directed that all measures be taken for our defense. Always will our whole nation remember the character of the onslaught against us.

No matter how long it may take us to overcome this premeditated invasion, the American people in their righteous might, will win through to absolute victory.

I believe that I interpret the will of the Congress and of the people when I assert that we will not only defend ourselves to the uttermost but will make it very certain that this form of treachery shall never again endanger us.

Hostilities exist. There is no blinking at the fact that our people, our territory and our interests are in grave danger.

With confidence in our armed forces, with the unbounding determination of our people, we will gain the inevitable triumph. So help us God.

I ask that the Congress declare that since the unprovoked and dastardly attack by Japan on Sunday, Dec. 7, 1941, a state of war has existed between the United States and the Japanese Empire.

REVIEW QUESTIONS

1. Why did Roosevelt consider it so important to highlight the "dastardly" nature of Japanese attacks?
2. Why did Roosevelt emphasize that Japan had also attacked areas other than Hawaii?

FRANKLIN D. ROOSEVELT AND WINSTON CHURCHILL

The Atlantic Charter (1941)

In August 1941, several months before the attack on Pearl Harbor, President Roosevelt met with British prime minister Winston Churchill aboard a warship off Newfoundland to discuss American efforts to help Britain stave off German attacks. In the process the two Western leaders articulated the basic principles and high ideals on which their alliance was based. The Atlantic Charter echoed many of the themes of Woodrow Wilson's Fourteen Points. It condemned aggression, affirmed the right of self-determination, and endorsed the principles of collective security and arms reduction. As such it provided the foundation on which the United States, Great Britain, and later, albeit ambivalently, the Soviet Union, established their military strategy and political objectives.

From U.S. Department of State, *Peace and War: United States Foreign Policy, 1931–1941* (Washington, DC, 1943), pp. 718–19.

The President of the United States of America and the Prime Minister, Mr. Churchill, representing His Majesty's Government in the United Kingdom, being met together, deem it right to make known certain common principles in the national policies of their respective countries on which they base their hopes for a better future for the world.

FIRST, their countries seek no aggrandizement, territorial or other;

SECOND, they desire to see no territorial changes that do not accord with the freely expressed wishes of the peoples concerned;

THIRD, they respect the right of all peoples to choose the form of government under which they will live; and they wish to see sovereign rights and self-government restored to those who have been forcibly deprived of them;

FOURTH, they will endeavor, with due respect for their existing obligations, to further the enjoyment by all States, great or small, victor or vanquished, of access, on equal terms, to the trade and to the raw materials of the world which are needed for their economic prosperity;

FIFTH, they desire to bring about the fullest collaboration between all nations in the economic field with the object of securing, for all, improved labor standards, economic adjustment and social security;

SIXTH, after the final destruction of the Nazi tyranny, they hope to see established a peace which will afford to all nations the means of dwelling in safety within their own boundaries, and which will afford assurance that all the men in all the lands may live out their lives in freedom from fear and want;

SEVENTH, such a peace should enable all men to traverse the high seas and oceans without hindrance;

EIGHTH, they believe that all of the nations of the world, for realistic as well as spiritual reasons, must come to the abandonment of the use of force. Since no future peace can be maintained if land, sea or air armaments continue to be employed by nations which threaten, or may threaten, aggression outside of their frontiers, they believe, pending the establishment of a wider and permanent system of general security, that the disarmament of such nations is essential. They will likewise aid and encourage all other practicable measures which will lighten for peace-loving peoples the crushing burden of armaments.

REVIEW QUESTIONS

1. In affirming "sovereign rights" and "self-government," the Atlantic Charter created what kind of dilemma for European nations that possessed colonies?

2. Why did economic issues play such an important role in the Atlantic Charter?

3. Do you think the eighth point was realistic? Explain.

A. PHILIP RANDOLPH

FROM Call to Negro America to March on Washington (1941)

In May 1941, A. Philip Randolph (1889–1979), the African American head of the Brotherhood of Sleeping Car Porters, threatened a "thundering march" on Washington of 150,000 blacks "to wake up and shock white America as it has never been shocked before." Such a dramatic public event, he decided, was the only way to convince President Roosevelt to ensure that minorities had equal access to jobs in the rapidly expanding defense industries and government agencies. Just before the scheduled march, President Roosevelt issued Executive Order 8802, which created a Fair Employment Practices Committee (FEPC) to eliminate racial discrimination in government hiring. Randolph thereupon canceled the march. But the mere creation of a new federal agency did not ensure justice. Randolph therefore kept the pressure on the administration to provide adequate funding and staffing for the FEPC. Although black employment in federal jobs increased from 60,000 in 1941 to 200,000 in 1945, the FEPC could not directly regulate private employers or labor unions. Moreover, despite these limitations, attempts to make the FEPC a permanent government agency never generated broad-based political support.

From "Call to Negro America to March on Washington for Jobs and Equal Participation in National Defense," *Black Worker* 14, May 1941. Reprinted by permission of the A. Philip Randolph Institute.

We call upon you to fight for jobs in National Defense. We call upon you to struggle for the integration of Negroes in the armed forces. . . .

We call upon you to demonstrate for the abolition of Jim-Crowism in all Government departments and defense employment.

This is an hour of crisis. It is a crisis of democracy. It is a crisis of minority groups. It is a crisis of Negro Americans.

What is this crisis?

To American Negroes, it is the denial of jobs in Government defense projects. It is racial discrimination in Government departments. It is widespread Jim-Crowism in the armed forces of the Nation.

While billions of the taxpayers' money are being spent for war weapons, Negro workers are finally being turned away from the gates of factories, mines and mills—being flatly told, "NOTHING DOING." Some employers refuse to give Negroes jobs when they are without "union cards," and some unions refuse Negro workers union cards when they are "without jobs."

What shall we do?

What a dilemma!

What a runaround!

What a disgrace!

What a blow below the belt!

Though dark, doubtful and discouraging, all is not lost, all is not hopeless. Though battered and bruised, we are not beaten, broken, or bewildered.

Verily, the Negroes' deepest disappointments and direst defeats, their tragic trials and outrageous oppressions in these dreadful days of destruction and disaster to democracy and freedom, and the rights of minority peoples, and the dignity and independence of the human spirit, is the Negroes' greatest opportunity to rise to the highest heights of struggle for freedom and justice in Government, in industry, in labor unions, education, social service, religion, and culture.

With faith and confidence of the Negro people in their own power for self-liberation, Negroes can break down that barriers of discrimination against employment in National Defense. Negroes can kill the deadly serpent of race hatred in the Army, Navy, Air and Marine Corps, and smash through and blast the Government, business and labor-union red tape to win the right to equal opportunity in vocational training and re-training in defense employment.

Most important and vital of all, Negroes, by the mobilization and coordination of their mass power, can cause PRESIDENT ROOSEVELT TO ISSUE AN EXECUTIVE ORDER ABOLISHING DISCRIMINATIONS IN ALL GOVERNMENT DEPARTMENT, ARMY, NAVY, AIR CORPS AND NATIONAL DEFENSE JOBS.

Of course, the task is not easy. In very truth, it is big, tremendous and difficult.

It will cost money.

It will require sacrifice.

It will tax the Negroes' courage, determination and will to struggle. But we can, must and will triumph.

The Negroes' stake in national defense is big. It consists of jobs, thousands of jobs. It may represent millions, yes hundreds of millions of dollars in wages. It consists of new industrial opportunities and hope. This is worth fighting for.

But to win our stakes, it will require an "all-out," bold and total effort and demonstration of colossal proportions.

Negroes can build a mammoth machine of mass action with a terrific and tremendous driving and striking power that can shatter and crush the evil fortress of race prejudice and hate, if they will only resolve to do so and never stop, until victory comes.

Dear fellow Negro Americans, be not dismayed by these terrible times. You possess power, great power. Our problem is to harness and hitch it up for action on the broadest, daring and most gigantic scale.

In this period of power politics, nothing counts but pressure, more pressure, and still more pressure, through the tactic and strategy of broad, organized, aggressive mass action behind the vital and important issues of the Negro. To this end, we propose that ten thousand Negroes MARCH ON WASHINGTON FOR JOBS IN NATIONAL DEFENSE AND EQUAL INTEGRATION IN THE FIGHTING FORCES OF THE UNITED STATES.

An "all-out" thundering march on Washington, ending in a monster and huge demonstration at Lincoln's Monument will shake up white America.

It will shake up official Washington.

It will give encouragement to our white friends to fight all the harder by our side, with us, for our righteous cause.

It will gain respect for the Negro people.

It will create a new sense of self-respect among Negroes.

But what of national unity?

We believe in national unity which recognizes equal opportunity of black and white citizens to jobs in national defense and the armed forces, and in all other institutions and endeavors in America. We condemn all dictatorships, Fascist, Nazi and Communist. We are loyal, patriotic Americans all.

But if American democracy will not defend its defenders; if American democracy will not protect its protectors; if American democracy will not give jobs to its toilers because of race or color; if American democracy will not insure equality of opportunity, freedom and justice to its citizens, black and white, it is a hollow mockery and belies the principles for which it is supposed to stand. . . .

Today we call on President Roosevelt, a great humanitarian and idealist, to . . . free American Negro citizens of the stigma, humiliation and insult of discrimination and Jim-Crowism in Government departments and national defense.

The Federal Government cannot with clear conscience call upon private industry and labor unions to abolish discrimination based on race and color as long as it practices discrimination itself against Negro Americans.

REVIEW QUESTIONS

1. What kind of equality did Randolph advocate? How does his outlook compare with that of Booker T. Washington?
2. Why did Randolph focus on a protest march as his preferred tactic? What other options might have been available?
3. Assess the advantages and disadvantages of Randolph's linking of domestic racial equality and global freedom.

Women in War Industries

Encouraged by government recruiting campaigns, some 6 million women took jobs in defense plants during the first three years of the war. Many of them left conventional domestic jobs—as maids, cooks, waitresses—to join industrial assembly lines. Others had never worked outside the home. It is not surprising that they encountered prejudice among their male co-workers. Yet the overall experience was quite positive for many women, and it created long-lasting changes in outlook and perspective. The two following accounts are representative of the experiences of wartime working women.

Excerpts from oral history interviews with Inez Sauer and Sybil Lewis from *The Homefront*. Copyright © 1984 by Mark Jonathan Harris, Franklin D. Mitchell, and Steven J. Schechter. Used by permission of the University of Southern California, History Department.

Inez Sauer, Chief Clerk, Tool Room

I was thirty-one when the war started and I had never worked in my life before. I had a six-year-old daughter and two boys, twelve and thirteen. We were living in Norwalk, Ohio, in a large home in which we could fit about 200 people playing bridge, and once in a while we filled it.

I remember my husband saying to me, "You've lived through a depression and you weren't even aware it was here." It was true. I knew that people were without work and having a hard time, but it never seemed to affect us or our friends. They were all of the same ilk—all college people and all golfing and bridge-playing companions. I suppose you'd call it a life of ease. We always kept a live-in maid, and we never had to go without anything.

Before the war my life was bridge and golf and clubs and children. . . . When the war broke out, my husband's rubber-matting business in Ohio had to close due to the war restrictions on rubber. We also lost our live-in maid, and I could see there was no way I could possibly live the way I was accustomed to doing. So I took my children home to my parents in Seattle.

The Seattle papers were full of ads for women workers needed to help the war effort. "Do your part, free a man for service." Being a D.A.R.,[1] I really wanted to help the war effort. I could have worked for the Red Cross and rolled bandages, but I wanted to do something that I thought was really vital. Building bombers was, so I answered an ad for Boeing.

My mother was horrified. She said no one in our family had ever worked in a factory. "You don't know what kind of people you're going to be associated with." My father was horrified too, no matter how I tried to impress on him that this was a war effort on my part. He said, "You'll never get along with the people you'll meet there." My husband thought it was utterly ridiculous. I had never worked. I didn't know how to handle money, as he put it. I was nineteen when I was married. My husband was ten years older, and he always made me feel like a child, so he didn't think I would last very long at the job, but he was wrong.

They started me as a clerk in this huge tool room. I had never handled a tool in my life outside of a hammer. Some man came in and asked for a bastard file. I said to him, "If you don't control your language, you won't get any service here." I went to my supervisor and said, "You'll have to correct this man. I won't tolerate that kind of language." He laughed and laughed and said, "Don't you know what a bastard file is? It's the name of a very coarse file." He went over and took one out and showed me.

*　　*　　*

The first year, I worked seven days a week. We didn't have any time off. They did allow us Christmas off, but Thanksgiving we had to work. That

was a hard thing to do. The children didn't understand. My mother and father didn't understand, but I worked. I think that put a little iron in my spine too. I did something that was against my grain, but I did it and I'm glad. . . .

Because I was working late one night I had a chance to see President Roosevelt. They said he was coming on the swing shift, after four o'clock, so I waited to see him. They cleared out all the aisles of the main plant, and he went through in a big, open limousine. He smiled and he had his long cigarette holder, and he was very, very pleasant. "Hello there, how are you? Keep up the war effort. Oh, you women are doing a wonderful job." We were all thrilled to think the President could take time out of the war effort to visit us factory workers. It gave us a lift, and I think we worked harder.

Boeing was a real education for me. It taught me a different way of life. I had never been around uneducated people before, people that worked with their hands. I was prudish and had never been with people that used coarse language. Since I hadn't worked before, I didn't know there was such a thing as the typical male ego. My contact with my first supervisor was one of animosity, in which he stated, "The happiest duty of my life will be when I say goodbye to each of you women as I usher you out the front door." I didn't understand that kind of resentment, but it was prevalent throughout the plant. Many of the men felt that no woman could come in and run a lathe, but they did. I learned that just because you're a woman and have never worked is no reason you can't learn.

The job really broadened me. I had led a very sheltered life. I had had no contact with Negroes except as maids or gardeners. My mother was a Virginian, and we were brought up to think that colored people were not of the same economic or social level. I learned differently at Boeing. I learned that because a girl is a Negro she's not necessarily a maid, and because a man is a Negro doesn't mean that all he can do is dig. In fact, I found that some of the black people I got to know there were very superior—and certainly equal to me—equal to anyone I ever knew.

----

[1]Daughter of the American Revolution.

Before I worked at Boeing I also had had no exposure to unions. After I was there for awhile, I joined the machinists union. We had a contract dispute, and we had a one-day walkout to show Boeing our strength. We went on this march through the financial district in downtown Seattle.

My mother happened to be down there seeing the president of the Seattle First National Bank at the time. Seeing this long stream of Boeing people, he interrupted her and said, "Mrs. Ely, they seem to be having a labor walkout. Let's go out and see what's going on." So my mother and a number of people from the bank walked outside to see what was happening. And we came down the middle of the street— I think there were probably five thousand of us. I saw my mother, I could recognize her—she was tall and stately—and I waved and said, "Hello, mother." That night when I got home, I thought she was never going to honor my name again. She said, "To think my daughter was marching in that labor demonstration. How could you do that to the family?" But I could see that it was a new, new world.

My mother warned me when I took the job that I would never be the same. She said, "You will never want to go back to being a housewife." At that time I didn't think it would change a thing. But she was right, it definitely did.

I had always been in a shell; I'd always been protected. But at Boeing I found a freedom and an independence that I had never known. After the war I could never go back to playing bridge again, being a club woman and listening to a lot of inanities when I knew there were things you could use your mind for. The war changed my life completely. I guess you could say, at thirty-one, I finally grew up.

*   *   *

Sybil Lewis, Riveter

When I first arrived in Los Angeles, I began to look for a job. I decided I didn't want to do maid work anymore, so I got a job as a waitress in a small black restaurant. I was making pretty good money, more than I had in Sapulpa, Oklahoma, but I didn't like the job that much; I didn't have the knack for getting good tips. Then I saw an ad in the newspaper offering to train women for defense work. I went to Lockheed Aircraft and applied. They said they'd call me, but I never got a response, so I went back and applied again. You had to be pretty persistent. Finally they accepted me. They gave me a short training program and taught me how to rivet. Then they put me to work in the plant riveting small airplane parts, mainly gasoline tanks.

The women worked in pairs. I was the riveter and this big, strong white girl from a cotton farm in Arkansas worked as the bucker. The riveter used a gun to shoot rivets through the metal and fasten it together. The bucker used a bucking bar on the other side of the metal to smooth out the rivets. Bucking was harder than shooting rivets; it required more muscle. Riveting required more skill.

I worked for a while as a riveter with this white girl when the boss came around one day and said, "We've decided to make some changes." At this point he assigned her to do the riveting and me to do the bucking. I wanted to know why. He said, "Well, we just interchange once in a while." But I was never given the riveting job back. This was the first encounter I had with segregation in California, and it didn't sit too well with me. It brought back some of my experiences in Sapulpa—you're a Negro, so you do the hard work. I wasn't failing as a riveter—in fact, the other girl learned to rivet from me—but I felt they gave me the job of bucker because I was black. . . .

The war years had a tremendous impact on women. I know for myself it was the first time I had a chance to get out of the kitchen and work in industry and make a few bucks. This was something I had never dreamed would happen. In Sapulpa all that women had to look forward to was keeping house and raising families. The war years offered new possibilities. You came out to California, put on your pants, and took your lunch pail to a man's job. This was the beginning of women's feeling that they could do something more. We were trained to do this kind of work because of the war, but there was no question that this was just an interim period. We were all told that when the war was over, we would not be needed anymore.

REVIEW QUESTIONS

1. Assess whether factory work for women offered more sacrifices or opportunities.
2. What racial or gender stereotypes emerged in these accounts? What did such attitudes suggest about the prospects for social progress in the postwar era?
3. How do you think these women would educate their own children about their vocational futures?

FROM *Korematsu v. United States* (1944)

In the aftermath of the Japanese attack on Pearl Harbor, Lieutenant General John L. DeWitt grew concerned about the prospect of saboteurs being among the West Coast's large population of Japanese Americans. To deal with this threat, which he and others greatly exaggerated, General DeWitt ordered that all Japanese and Japanese Americans on the Pacific Coast be transferred to inland detention camps where they were placed behind barbed-wire fences and under the scrutiny of armed guards. President Roosevelt and Congress supported the detention program. In 1944 the issue gained a hearing before the Supreme Court when Fred Korematsu appealed his conviction for violating the detention order. Justice Hugo Black delivered the majority opinion upholding the detention program on the grounds of military necessity. Three justices dissented. The internment program understandably embittered many Japanese Americans. Some 5,000 decided to renounce their American citizenship and to move to Japan at the end of the war. Not until 1988 did the Congress finally admit the injustice of the internment program and award $20,000 to each of the 62,000 surviving detainees.

From U.S. Supreme Court, *Korematsu v. U.S.* (1944) in *Supreme Court Reporter* (St. Paul, MN: West Publishing, 1946), 65:194–95, 197–98, 201–02, 203–06. [Editorial insertions appear in square brackets—*Ed.*]

MR. JUSTICE BLACK delivered the opinion of the Court:

. . . It should be noted, to begin with, that all legal restrictions which curtail the civil rights of a single racial group are immediately suspect. That is not to say that all such restrictions are unconstitutional. It is to say that courts must subject them to the most rigid scrutiny. Pressing public necessity may sometimes justify the existence of such restrictions; racial antagonism never can. . . .

Exclusion Order No. 34, which the petitioner knowingly and admittedly violated, was one of a number of military orders and proclamations, all of which were substantially based upon Executive Order No. 9066. That order, issued after we were at war with Japan, declared that the successful prosecution of the war requires every possible protection against espionage and against sabotage to national defense material, national defense premises, and national defense utilities. . . .

We uphold the exclusion order as of the time it was made and when the petitioner violated it. . . . In doing so, we are not unmindful of the hardships imposed by it upon a large group of American citizens. But hardships are part of war, and war is an aggregation of hardships. All citizens alike, both in and out of uniform, feel the impact of war in greater or lesser measure. Citizenship has its responsibilities, as well as its privileges, and, in time of war, the burden is always heavier.

Compulsory exclusion of large groups of citizens from their homes, except under circumstances of direst emergency and peril, is inconsistent with our basic governmental institutions. But when, under conditions of modern warfare, our shores are threatened by hostile forces, the power to protect must be commensurate with the threatened danger.

*   *   *

It is said that we are dealing here with the case of imprisonment of a citizen in a concentration camp solely because of his ancestry, without evidence or inquiry concerning his loyalty and good disposition towards the United States. Our task would be simple, our duty clear, were this a case involving the imprisonment of a loyal citizen in a concentration camp because of racial prejudice. Regardless of the true nature of the assembly and relocation centers—and we deem it unjustifiable to call them concentration camps, with all the ugly connotations that term implies—we are dealing specifically with nothing but an exclusion order. To cast this case into outlines of racial prejudice, without reference to the real military dangers which were presented, merely confuses the issue.

Korematsu was not excluded from the Military Area because of hostility to him or his race. He was excluded because we are at war with the Japanese Empire, because the properly constituted military authorities feared an invasion of our West Coast and felt constrained to take proper security measures, because they decided that the military urgency of the situation demanded that all citizens of Japanese ancestry be segregated from the West Coast temporarily, and, finally, because Congress, reposing its confidence in this time of war in our military leaders—as inevitably it must—determined that they should have the power to do just this. There was evidence of disloyalty on the part of some, the

military authorities considered that the need for action was great, and time was short. We cannot—by availing ourselves of the calm perspective of hindsight—now say that, at that time, these actions were unjustified.

*   *   *

MR. JUSTICE ROBERTS, dissenting:

I dissent, because I think the indisputable facts exhibit a clear violation of Constitutional rights.

This is not a case of keeping people off the streets at night . . . nor a case of temporary exclusion of a citizen from an area for his own safety or that of the community, nor a case of offering him an opportunity to go temporarily out of an area where his presence might cause danger to himself or to his fellows.

On the contrary, it is the case of convicting a citizen as a punishment for not submitting to imprisonment in a concentration camp, based on his ancestry, and solely because of his ancestry, without evidence or inquiry concerning his loyalty and good disposition towards the United States. If this be a correct statement of the facts disclosed by this record, and facts of which we take judicial notice, I need hardly labor the conclusion that Constitutional rights have been violated.

*   *   *

MR. JUSTICE MURPHY, dissenting:

This exclusion of "all persons of Japanese ancestry, both alien and non-alien," from the Pacific Coast area on a plea of military necessity in the absence of martial law ought not to be approved. Such exclusion goes over "the very brink of constitutional power," and falls into the ugly abyss of racism.

In dealing with matters relating to the prosecution and progress of a war, we must accord great respect and consideration to the judgments of the military authorities who are on the scene and who have full knowledge of the military facts. The scope of their discretion must, as a matter of necessity and common sense, be wide. And their judgments ought not to be overruled lightly by those whose training and duties ill-equip them to deal intelligently with matters so vital to the physical security of the nation.

At the same time, however, it is essential that there be definite limits to military discretion, especially where martial law has not been declared. Individuals must not be left impoverished of their constitutional rights on a plea of military necessity that has neither substance nor support. Thus, like other claims conflicting with the asserted constitutional rights of the individual, the military claim must subject itself to the judicial process of having its reasonableness determined and its conflicts with other interests reconciled. What are the allowable limits of military discretion, and whether or not they have been overstepped in a particular case, are judicial questions.

The judicial test of whether the Government, on a plea of military necessity, can validly deprive an individual of any of his constitutional rights is whether the deprivation is reasonably related to a public danger that is so "immediate, imminent, and impending" as not to admit of delay and not to permit the intervention of ordinary constitutional processes to alleviate the danger.

*   *   *

[This relocation order] clearly does not meet that test. Being an obvious racial discrimination, the order deprives all those within its scope of the equal protection of the laws as guaranteed by the Fifth Amendment. It further deprives these individuals of their constitutional rights to live and work where they will, to establish a home where they choose and to move about freely. In excommunicating them without benefit of hearings, this order also deprives them of all their constitutional rights to procedural due process. Yet no reasonable relation to an "immediate, imminent, and impending" public danger is evident to support this racial restriction, which is one of the most sweeping and complete deprivations of constitutional rights in the history of this nation in the absence of martial law. . . .

Justification for the exclusion is sought, instead, mainly upon questionable racial and sociological grounds not ordinarily within the realm of expert military judgment, supplemented by certain semi-military conclusions drawn from an unwarranted use of circumstantial evidence. Individuals of Japanese ancestry are condemned because they are said to be "a large, unassimilated, tightly knit racial group, bound to an enemy nation by strong ties of race, culture, custom and religion." They are claimed to be given to "emperor worshipping ceremonies," and to "dual citizenship." Japanese language schools and allegedly pro-Japanese organizations are cited as evidence of possible group disloyalty, together with facts as to certain persons being educated and residing at length in Japan. It is intimated that many of these individuals deliberately resided "adjacent to strategic points," thus enabling them to carry into execution a tremendous program of sabotage on a mass scale should any considerable number of them have been inclined to do so.

The need for protective custody is also asserted. The report refers, without identity, to "numerous incidents of violence," as well as to other admittedly unverified or cumulative incidents. From this, plus certain other events not shown to have been connected with the Japanese Americans, it is concluded that the "situation was fraught with danger to the Japanese population itself," and that the general public "was ready to take matters into its own hands." Finally, it is intimated, though not directly charged or proved, that persons of Japanese ancestry were responsible for three minor isolated shellings and bombings of the Pacific Coast area, as well as for unidentified radio transmissions and night signaling.

The main reasons relied upon by those responsible for the forced evacuation, therefore, do not prove a reasonable relation between the group characteristics of Japanese Americans and the dangers of invasion, sabotage and espionage. The reasons appear, instead, to be largely an accumulation of much of the misinformation, half-truths and insinuations that for years have been directed against Japanese Americans by people with racial and economic prejudices—the same people who have been among the foremost advocates of the evacuation. A military judgment based upon such racial and sociological considerations is not entitled to the great weight ordinarily given the judgments based upon strictly military considerations. Especially is this so when every charge relative to race, religion, culture, geographical location, and legal and economic status has been substantially discredited by independent studies made by experts in these matters. . . .

No one denies, of course, that there were some disloyal persons of Japanese descent on the Pacific Coast who did all in their power to aid their ancestral land. Similar disloyal activities have been engaged in by many persons of German, Italian and even more pioneer stock in our country. But to infer that examples of individual disloyalty prove group disloyalty and justify discriminatory action against the entire group is to deny that, under our system of law, individual guilt is the sole basis for deprivation of rights.

Moreover, this inference, which is at the very heart of the evacuation orders, has been used in support of the abhorrent and despicable treatment of minority groups by the dictatorial tyrannies which this nation is now pledged to destroy. To give constitutional sanction to that inference in this case, however well intentioned may have been the military command on the Pacific Coast, is to adopt one of the cruelest of the rationales used by our enemies to destroy the dignity of the individual and to encourage and open the door to discriminatory actions against other minority groups in the passions of tomorrow.

*   *   *

I dissent, therefore, from this legalization of racism. Racial discrimination in any form and in any degree has no justifiable part whatever in our democratic way of life. It is unattractive in any setting, but it is utterly revolting among a free people who have embraced the principles set forth in the Constitution of the United States. All residents of this nation are kin in some way by blood or culture to a foreign land. Yet they are primarily and necessarily a part of the new and distinct civilization of the United States. They must, accordingly, be treated at all times as the heirs of the American experiment, and as entitled to all the rights and freedoms guaranteed by the Constitution.

*   *   *

MR. JUSTICE JACKSON, dissenting:

Korematsu was born on our soil, of parents born in Japan. The Constitution makes him a citizen of the United States by nativity, and a citizen of California by residence. No claim is made that he is not loyal to this country. There is no suggestion that, apart from the matter involved here, he is not law-abiding and well disposed. Korematsu, however, has been convicted of an act not commonly a crime. It consists merely of being present in the state whereof he is a citizen, near the place where he was born, and where all his life he has lived.

Even more unusual is the series of military orders which made this conduct a crime. They forbid such a one to remain, and they also forbid him to leave. They were so drawn that the only way Korematsu could avoid violation was to give himself up to the military authority. This meant submission to custody, examination, and transportation out of the territory, to be followed by indeterminate confinement in detention camps.

A citizen's presence in the locality, however, was made a crime only if his parents were of Japanese birth. Had Korematsu been one of four—the others being, say, a German alien enemy, an Italian alien enemy, and a citizen of American-born ancestors, convicted of treason but out on parole—only Korematsu's presence would have violated the order. The difference between their innocence and his crime would result, not from anything he did, said, or thought, different than they, but only in that he was born of different racial stock.

Now, if any fundamental assumption underlies our system, it is that guilt is personal and not inheritable. Even if all of one's antecedents had been convicted of treason, the Constitution forbids its penalties to be visited upon him, for it provides that "no attainder of treason shall work corruption of blood, or forfeiture except during the life of the person attainted." But here is an attempt to make an otherwise innocent act a crime merely because this prisoner is the son of parents as to whom he had no choice, and belongs to a race from which there is no way to resign.

REVIEW QUESTIONS

1. Why did Justice Black object to calling relocation centers concentration camps?

2. What did Justice Murphy mean when he stated that "individual guilt is the sole basis for deprivation of rights"? Do you agree?

HARRY S. TRUMAN

The Atomic Bombing of Hiroshima— The Public Explanation (1945)

The following selection is President Truman's public announcement on August 6, 1945, of the dropping of the atomic bomb. His comments were directed as much to the political and military leaders in Japan as they were to the American people.

From U.S. Department of State, Publication No. 2702, *The International Control of Atomic Energy: Growth of a Policy* (Washington, DC, n.d. [1947]), pp. 95–97.

Sixteen hours ago an American airplane dropped one bomb on Hiroshima, an important Japanese Army base. That bomb had more power than 20,000 tons of T.N.T. It had more than two thousand times the blast power of the British "Grand Slam," which is the largest bomb ever yet used in the history of warfare.

The Japanese began the war from the air at Pearl Harbor. They have been repaid many fold. And the end is not yet. With this bomb we have now added a new and revolutionary increase in destruction to supplement the growing power of our armed forces. In their present forms these bombs are now in production and even more powerful forms are in development. It is an atomic bomb. It is a harnessing of the basic power of the universe.

The force from which the sun draws its power has been loosed against those who brought war to the Far East. Before 1939, it was the accepted belief of scientists that it was theoretically possible to release atomic energy. But no one knew any practical method of doing it. By 1942, however, we knew that the Germans were working feverishly to find a way to add atomic energy to the other engines of war with which they hoped to enslave the world. But they failed. . . . The battle of the laboratories held fateful risks for us as well as the battles of the air, land, and sea, and we have now won the battle of the laboratories as we have won the other battles. . . .

With American and British scientists working together we entered the race of discovery against the Germans. The United States had available the large number of scientists of distinction in the many needed areas of knowledge. It had the tremendous industrial and financial resources necessary for the project and they could be devoted to it without undue impairment of other vital war work. In the United States the laboratory work and the production plants, on which a substantial start had already been made, would be out of reach of enemy bombing, while at that time Britain was exposed to constant air attack and was still threatened with the possibility of invasion.

For these reasons Prime Minister Churchill and President Roosevelt agreed that it was wise to carry on the project here. We now have two great plants and many lesser works devoted to the production of atomic power. Employment during peak construction numbered 125,000 and over 65,000 individuals are even now engaged in operating the plants. Many have worked there for two and a half years. Few know what they have been producing. . . .

What has been done is the greatest achievement of organized science in history. It was done under high pressure and without failure. We are now prepared to obliterate more rapidly and completely every productive enterprise the Japanese have above ground in any city. We shall destroy their docks, their factories, and their communications. Let there be no mistakes; we shall completely destroy Japan's power to make war.

It was to spare the Japanese people from utter destruction that the ultimatum of July 26 was issued at Potsdam. Their leaders promptly rejected that ultimatum. If they do not now accept our terms, they may expect a rain of ruin from the air, the like of which has never been seen on this earth. Behind this air attack will follow sea and land forces in such numbers and power as they have not yet seen and with the fighting skill of which they are already well aware. . . .

The fact that we can release atomic energy ushers in a new era in man's understanding of nature's forces. Atomic energy may in the future supplement the power that now comes from coal, oil, and falling water, but at present it cannot be produced on a basis to compete with them commercially. Before that comes, there must be a long period of intensive research. . . .

I shall recommend that the Congress of the United States consider promptly the establishment of an appropriate commission to control the production and use of atomic power within the United States. I shall give further consideration and make further recommendations to the Congress as to how atomic power can become a powerful and forceful influence towards the maintenance of world peace.

REVIEW QUESTIONS

1. According to Truman, why had production of atomic bombs taken place in the United States rather than elsewhere?
2. Why did Truman omit any reference to the thousands of Japanese killed by the atomic bomb?
3. What was Truman's attitude toward sharing nuclear technology with other countries after the war?

KARL T. COMPTON

If the Atomic Bomb Had Not Been Used (1946)

Winston Churchill declared that the atomic bomb was "a miracle of deliverance" that ended the war and thereby saved over a million lives. Not everyone agreed. In fact, wartime documents reveal that some military analysts predicted that an amphibious invasion of Japan would have resulted in approximately 46,000 deaths—slightly more than those suffered during the Normandy invasion. Thus critics then and since have argued that Allied casualties during an invasion of Japan would have been high but acceptable and that the atomic bombs were unnecessary because the Japanese would have soon surrendered anyway. In 1946 physicist Karl T. Compton, who had worked on various scientific projects during World War II, defended the use of the atomic bomb. After reading Compton's article, President Truman wrote him a letter in which he agreed with his account. "The Japanese," he stressed, "were given fair warning and were offered the terms, which they finally accepted, well in advance of the dropping of the bomb. I imagine the bomb caused them to accept the terms."

From "If the Atomic Bomb Had Not Been Used," *Atlantic Monthly* 178 (December 1946), pp. 54–56. Reprinted by permission of Charles A. Compton.

About a week after V-J Day I was one of a small group of scientists and engineers interrogating an intelligent, well-informed Japanese Army officer in Yokohama. We asked him what, in his opinion, would have been the next major move if the war had continued. He replied: "You would probably have tried to invade our homeland with a landing operation on Kyushu about November 1. I think the attack would have been made on such and such beaches."

"Could you have repelled this landing?" we asked, and he answered: "It would have been a very desperate fight, but I do not think we could have stopped you."

"What would have happened then?" we asked.

He replied: "We would have kept on fighting until all Japanese were killed, but we would not have been defeated," by which he meant that they would not have been disgraced by surrender.

It is easy now, after the event, to look back and say that Japan was already a beaten nation, and to ask what therefore was the justification for the use of the atomic bomb to kill so many thousands of helpless Japanese in this inhuman way; furthermore, should we not better have kept it to ourselves as a secret weapon for future use, if necessary? This argument has been advanced often, but it seems to me utterly fallacious.

I had, perhaps, an unusual opportunity to know the pertinent facts from several angles, yet I was without responsibility for any of the decisions.

I can therefore speak without doing so defensively. While my role in the atomic bomb development was a very minor one, I was a member of the group called together by Secretary of War Stimson[1] to assist him in plans for its test, use, and subsequent handling. Then, shortly before Hiroshima, I became attached to General MacArthur[2] in Manila, and lived for two months with his staff. In this way I learned something of the invasion plans and of the sincere conviction of these best-informed officers that a desperate and costly struggle was still ahead. Finally, I spent the first month after V-J Day in Japan, where I could ascertain at first hand both the physical and the psychological state of that country. Some of the Japanese whom I consulted were my scientific and personal friends of long standing.

From this background I believe, with complete conviction, that the use of the atomic bomb saved hundreds of thousands—perhaps several millions—of lives, both American and Japanese; that without its use the war would have continued for many months; that no one of good conscience knowing, as Secretary Stimson and the Chiefs of Staff did, what was probably ahead and what the atomic bomb might accomplish could have made any different decision. Let some of the facts speak for themselves.

---

[1]Henry L. Stimson (1867–1950).
[2]General Douglas MacArthur (1880–1964).

Was the use of the atomic bomb inhuman? All war is inhuman. Here are some comparisons of the atomic bombing with conventional bombing. At Hiroshima the atomic bomb killed about 80,000 people, pulverized about five square miles, and wrecked an additional ten square miles of the city, with decreasing damage out to seven or eight miles from the center. At Nagasaki the fatal casualties were 45,000 and the area wrecked was considerably smaller than at Hiroshima because of the configuration of the city.

Compare this with the results of two B-29 incendiary raids over Tokyo. One of these raids killed about 125,000 people, the other nearly 100,000.

Of the 210 square miles of greater Tokyo, 85 square miles of the densest part was destroyed as completely, for all practical purposes, as were the centers of Hiroshima and Nagasaki; about half the buildings were destroyed in the remaining 125 square miles; the number of people driven homeless out of Tokyo was considerably larger than the population of greater Chicago. These figures are based on information given us in Tokyo and on a detailed study of the air reconnaissance maps. They may be somewhat in error but are certainly of the right order of magnitude.

Was Japan already beaten before the atomic bomb? The answer is certainly "yes" in the sense that the fortunes of war had turned against her. The answer is "no" in the sense that she was still fighting desperately and there was every reason to believe that she would continue to do so; and this is the only answer that has any practical significance.

General MacArthur's staff anticipated about 50,000 American casualties and several times that number of Japanese casualties in the November 1 operation to establish the initial beachheads on Kyushu. After that they expected a far more costly struggle before the Japanese homeland was subdued. There was every reason to think that the Japanese would defend their homeland with even greater fanaticism than when they fought to the death on Iwo Jima and Okinawa. No American soldier who survived the bloody struggles on these islands has much sympathy with the view that

battle with the Japanese was over as soon as it was clear that their ultimate situation was hopeless. No, there was every reason to expect a terrible struggle long after the point at which some people can now look back and say, "Japan was already beaten."

A month after our occupation I heard General MacArthur say that even then, if the Japanese government lost control over its people and the millions of former Japanese soldiers took to guerrilla warfare in the mountains, it could take a million American troops ten years to master the situation.

That this was not an impossibility is shown by the following fact, which I have not seen reported. We recall the long period of nearly three weeks between the Japanese offer to surrender and the actual surrender on September 2. This was needed in order to arrange details of the surrender and occupation and to permit the Japanese government to prepare its people to accept the capitulation. It is not generally realized that there was threat of a revolt against the government, led by an Army group supported by the peasants, to seize control and continue the war. For several days it was touch and go as to whether the people would follow their government in surrender.

The bulk of the Japanese people did not consider themselves beaten; in fact they believed they were winning in spite of the terrible punishment they had taken. They watched the paper balloons take off and float eastward in the wind, confident that these were carrying a terrible retribution to the United States in revenge for our air raids.

We gained a vivid insight into the state of knowledge and morale of the ordinary Japanese soldier from a young private who had served through the war in the Japanese Army. He had lived since babyhood in America, and had graduated in 1940 from Massachusetts Institute of Technology. This lad, thoroughly American in outlook, had gone with his family to visit relatives shortly after his graduation. They were caught in the mobilization and he was drafted into the Army.

This young Japanese told us that all his fellow soldiers believed that Japan was winning the war. To them the losses of Iwo Jima and Okinawa were parts of a grand strategy to lure the American forces closer and closer to the homeland, until they could be pounced upon and utterly annihilated. He himself had come to have some doubts as a result of various inconsistencies in official reports. Also he had seen the Ford assembly line in operation and knew that Japan could not match America in war production. But none of the soldiers had any inkling of the true situation until one night, at ten-thirty, his regiment was called to hear the reading of the surrender proclamation.

Did the atomic bomb bring about the end of the war? That it would do so was the calculated gamble and hope of Mr. Stimson, General Marshall,[3] and their associates. The facts are these. On July 26, 1945, the Potsdam Ultimatum called on Japan to surrender unconditionally. On July 29 Premier Suzuki issued a statement, purportedly at a cabinet press conference, scorning as unworthy of official notice the surrender ultimatum, and emphasizing the increasing rate of Japanese aircraft production. Eight days later, on August 6, the first atomic bomb was dropped on Hiroshima; the second was dropped on August 9 on Nagasaki; on the following day, August 10, Japan declared its intention to surrender, and on August 14 accepted the Potsdam terms.

On the basis of these facts, I cannot believe that, without the atomic bomb, the surrender would have come without a great deal more of costly struggle and bloodshed.

Exactly what role the atomic bomb played will always allow some scope for conjecture. A survey has shown that it did not have much immediate effect on the common people far from the two bombed cities; they knew little or nothing of it. The even more disastrous conventional bombing of Tokyo and other cities had not brought the people into the mood to surrender.

The evidence points to a combination of factors. (1) Some of the more informed and intelligent elements in Japanese official circles realized that they were fighting a losing battle and that complete destruction lay ahead if the war continued. These

elements, however, were not powerful enough to sway the situation against the dominating Army organization, backed by the profiteering industrialists, the peasants, and the ignorant masses. (2) The atomic bomb introduced a dramatic new element into the situation, which strengthened the hands of those who sought peace and provided a face-saving argument for those who had hitherto advocated continued war. (3) When the second atomic bomb was dropped, it became clear that this was not an isolated weapon, but that there were others to follow. With dread prospect of a deluge of these terrible bombs and no possibility of preventing them, the argument for surrender was made convincing. This I believe to be the true picture of the effect of the atomic bomb in bringing the war to a sudden end, with Japan's unconditional surrender.

If the atomic bomb had not been used, evidence like that I have cited points to the practical certainty that there would have been many more months of death and destruction on an enormous scale. Also the early timing of its use was fortunate for a reason which could not have been anticipated. If the invasion plans had proceeded as scheduled, October, 1945, would have seen Okinawa covered with airplanes and its harbors crowded with landing craft poised for the attack. The typhoon which struck Okinawa in that month would have wrecked the invasion plans with a military disaster comparable to Pearl Harbor.

These are some of the facts which led those who know them, and especially those who had to base decisions on them, to feel that there is much delusion and wishful thinking among those after-the-event strategists who now deplore the use of the atomic bomb on the ground that its use was inhuman or that it was unnecessary because Japan was already beaten. And it was not one atomic bomb, or two, which brought surrender; it was the experience of what an atomic bomb will actually do to a community, plus the *dread of many more,* that was effective.

If 500 bombers could wreak such destruction on Tokyo, what will 500 bombers, each carrying an atomic bomb, do to the City of Tomorrow? It is this

---

[3]General George Marshall (1880–1959).

deadly prospect which now lends such force to the two basic policies of our nation on this Subject: (1) We must strive generously and with all our ability to promote the United Nations' effort to assure future peace between nations; but we must not lightly surrender the atomic bomb as a means for our own defense. (2) We should surrender or share it only when there is adopted an international plan to enforce peace in which we can have great confidence.

REVIEW QUESTIONS

1. Do you agree that there was no fundamental difference between firebombing Tokyo and dropping atomic bombs on Hiroshima and Nagasaki? Why or why not?

2. Should the United States have shared the technical information about atomic bombs with other nations or kept it a secret?

27 ❧ THE COLD WAR AND THE FAIR DEAL, 1945–1952

On April 12, 1945, an inexperienced Harry S. Truman became president as a result of Franklin Roosevelt's death. Truman immediately confronted issues of bewildering magnitude and complexity. The protracted world war had altered the balance of power in Europe, dislodged colonial empires, and created social and political turbulence within nations. Of immediate concern was the disintegration of the wartime alliance with the Soviet Union. Having "liberated" Eastern Europe from Nazi control, the Soviets were imposing their political and military will on the region, determined to absorb the area into their own sphere of influence. While the United States insisted that the peoples of Eastern Europe should determine their own postwar status through democratic elections and free trade, the Soviets were even more determined to create a buffer of "friendly states" along their western border so as to prevent another invasion of their homeland (Russia had been invaded three times since the early nineteenth century).

Throughout 1946 and 1947 political leaders subservient to Soviet desires consolidated their control over Eastern Europe, especially Poland. At the same time, the Soviets established a puppet regime in newly created East Germany. Former British prime minister Winston Churchill warned that the Soviets had pulled down an "iron curtain" of repression across the eastern half of Europe.

In the process of pursuing such conflicting objectives in Eastern Europe, both sides helped escalate tensions and intensify an emerging "cold war" (a phrase popularized by the prominent American journalist Walter Lippmann). By 1947 American officials had become convinced that Soviet foreign policy was not pursuing legitimate security concerns; instead, they had come to view Josef Stalin as a paranoid dictator driven by an uncompromising communist ideology that envisioned world domination.

In early 1947 Truman's key foreign policy aides—Secretary of State and former army chief of staff George C. Marshall, Under Secretary of State Dean G.

Acheson, and career foreign service officer George F. Kennan—fashioned a new diplomatic strategy to deal with the burgeoning cold war. Truman was tired of "babying the Russians" and wanted a tougher stance. The lesson that he and others had drawn from the failed statesmanship of the 1930s was that appeasing aggressive dictators was disastrous. His advisers responded with what became known as the "containment policy."

The first application of this containment doctrine focused on the eastern Mediterranean. Since 1946 the Greek government had been locked in a civil war with communist guerrillas. At the same time, its neighbor Turkey was facing unrelenting pressure from the Soviet Union to gain naval access to the Mediterranean. The British had provided financial and military support to the Greeks and Turks, but in early 1947 they informed the United States that they could no longer provide such assistance because of their own economic distress.

Truman acted swiftly. On March 12, 1947, he asked a joint session of Congress to provide $400 million worth of military and economic assistance to Greece and Turkey. He portrayed the situation in stark terms: failure to act would encourage further Soviet expansion around the world. In stating the case for such assistance, the president outlined what became known as the Truman Doctrine. The United States, he said, must be willing to support free peoples everywhere in order to resist the cancer of "totalitarian regimes." Failure to do so would "endanger the peace of the world" and the "welfare of our own nation."

The Truman Doctrine laid the foundation for American foreign policy for the next forty years. It committed the United States to the role of a worldwide policeman. Critics, including George Kennan, warned that the United States could not alone suppress every communist insurgency around the world. The prominent journalist Walter Lippmann derided the new containment doctrine as a "strategic monstrosity" that would entangle the United States in endless international disputes.

Truman's policies could not keep pace with the dynamic changes reshaping the world order. In 1949 the Chinese Communists led by Mao Zedong won a civil war against the "nationalist" forces of Generalissimo Jiang Jieshi (Chiang Kai-shek) and forced the nationalist Chinese off the mainland onto the island of Formosa (Taiwan). Dean Acheson, who became secretary of state in 1949, quickly asserted that "the Communist regime serves not [Chinese] interests but those of Soviet Russia." The victory of Mao's forces prompted Truman's critics to ask "Who lost China?" Republicans believed that the United States should have acted more aggressively to support Jiang's nationalist cause.

Truman faced new problems as well. The global competition between the United States and the Soviet Union forced Americans to confront the deeply embedded racism that still governed social relations in their own country. It was difficult for American diplomats in Africa to convince new nations on that continent that the United States was their friend when so many vestiges of racism still existed in American society. As a result, the cold war served as a stimulus to the civil rights movement. At the same time, the discovery that the Soviet Union had detonated an atomic bomb in 1949, years in advance of American predictions, gave Republicans another weapon in their fight with the administration. The Soviets, they reasoned, must have gained access to secret American documents through their espionage network in the United States. Scattered evidence of successful Soviet espionage in North America gave fuel to the partisan claim that the Truman administration was "soft on Communism" and helped launch the anti-communist crusade led by Republican senator Joseph McCarthy.

The invasion of South Korea in June 1950 by 75,000 Soviet-equipped North Korean troops surprised the world and heightened fears of possible communist infiltration at home. Senator McCarthy stepped up his campaign of accusations and half-truths. Truman first pushed through the United Nations a resolution of condemnation. He then ordered General Douglas MacArthur to send military equipment to the South Koreans and to use American airpower to blunt the North Korean advance. Truman never asked Congress for a declaration of war. Officially, the Korean conflict was a police action supported by the United Nations. Critics labeled it "Mr. Truman's War."

In September General MacArthur assumed the offensive with a brilliant maneuver that outflanked the North Koreans and sent them reeling. Sensing a great victory, MacArthur and Truman convinced the United Nations to allow the allied forces to cross the 38th parallel, "liberate" North Korea from communist control, and unify the divided nation under democratic rule. A policy of containment now gave way to a policy of liberation. The plan was working to perfection by mid-October as the American-dominated U.N. forces pushed across North Korea toward the Yalu River border with China. Concerned about Chinese entry into the conflict, Truman flew to Midway Island to consult with MacArthur. The American general dismissed concerns about the Chinese, arguing that they could not mount significant opposition and that American airpower would neutralize them in any event. Truman remained skeptical and ordered MacArthur to use only South Korean forces in the vanguard of the coalition as it approached the Chinese border.

But MacArthur refused to be bridled by his civilian commander-in-chief. He disobeyed the president and moved American and British troops close to the Yalu River on November 24. Two days later 300,000 Chinese "volunteers" streamed across the border, attacking in waves inspired by blaring bugles. The U.N. forces fell back in the most brutal fighting of the war. Three weeks later they recrossed the 38th parallel. In the midst of the retreat, MacArthur asked permission to bomb bridges on the Yalu River as well as Chinese bases across the border. He also asked for a naval blockade of the Chinese coast and suggested the possible use of Nationalist Chinese forces in Korea.

Truman feared that such drastic measures would provoke World War III with China and possibly the Soviet Union. His assessment of the situation was bleak: the best that could be achieved was a negotiated restoration of the dividing line at the 38th parallel. To MacArthur this smacked of appeasement, and he publicly criticized Truman, saying that "there is no substitute for victory." Truman now had no choice but to relieve the popular but erratic and insubordinate MacArthur. The cashiered general returned to a hero's welcome in the United States, including a ticker-tape parade down New York City's Fifth Avenue. His Republican supporters called for Truman's impeachment and urged MacArthur to run for president. But the congressional testimony of General Omar Bradley, chairman of the Joint Chiefs of Staff, blunted MacArthur's case. Expanding the fighting into China, Bradley asserted, would be "the wrong war, at the wrong place, at the wrong time, and with the wrong enemy."

As the months passed and the war raged on, public opinion soured on Truman and the American commitment in Korea. By the onset of the 1952 election campaign, the battlefront in Korea had stabilized at the 38th parallel and voters simply wanted the conflict ended. Negotiations begun in July 1951 dragged on for two years while intense but sporadic fighting continued. When an armistice agreement was finally concluded by the Eisenhower administration in 1953, the Korean conflict had cost over $20 billion and 33,000 American lives. Over 2 million Koreans had been killed. Communism had been contained, but at a high cost.

MR. X [GEORGE F. KENNAN]

FROM The Sources of Soviet Conduct (1947)

George F. Kennan was a career diplomat with extensive service abroad as well as in Washington. In 1947 he was tapped to head the state department's new policy-planning staff, which was to provide long-range analyses and plans for the conduct of American foreign relations. This article was a distillation of a long cable message that Kennan had prepared a year before while serving in the U.S. embassy in Moscow. Published in the July 1947 issue of the prestigious journal Foreign Affairs *under the pseudonym "Mr. X," it offered an unofficial summary of administration assessments of the Soviet threat. As he himself later admitted, Kennan failed to specify what he meant by containment—economic? political? military? Kennan's vague language also implied a global commitment to contain communism militarily anywhere and everywhere in the world. Policymakers in later years would fail to distinguish between areas vital to American interests and regions of less significance.*

The political personality of Soviet power as we know it today is the product of ideology and circumstances: ideology inherited by the present Soviet leaders from the movement in which they had their political origin, and circumstances of the power which they have exercised for nearly three decades in Russia. . . . The main concern [of the Kremlin] is to make sure that it has filled every nook and cranny available to it in the basin of world power. But if it finds unassailable barriers in its path, it accepts these philosophically and accommodates itself to them. The main thing is that there should always be pressure, increasing constant pressure, toward the desired goal. There is no trace of any feeling in Soviet psychology that the goal must be reached at any given time.

These considerations make Soviet diplomacy at once easier and more difficult to deal with than the diplomacy of individual aggressive leaders like Napoleon and Hitler. On the one hand it is more sensitive to contrary force, more ready to yield on individual sectors of the diplomatic front when that force is felt to be too strong, and thus more rational in the logic and rhetoric of power.

On the other hand it cannot be easily defeated or discouraged by a single victory on the part of its opponents. And the patient persistence by which it is animated means that it can be effectively countered not by sporadic acts which represent the momentary whims of democratic opinion but only by intelligent long-range policies on the part of Russia's adversaries—policies no less steady in their purpose, and no less variegated and resourceful in their application, than those of the Soviet Union itself.

In these circumstances it is clear that the main element of any United States policy toward the Soviet Union must be that of a long-term, patient but firm and vigilant containment of Russian expansionist tendencies. It is important to note, however, that such policy has nothing to do with outward histrionics: with threats or blustering or superfluous gestures of outward "toughness." . . . The Russian leaders are keen judges of human psychology, and as such they are highly conscious that loss of temper and self-control is never a source of strength in political affairs. They are quick to exploit such evidences of weakness. For these reasons, it is the *sine qua non* of successful dealing with Russia that the foreign government in question should remain at all times cool and collected and that its demands on Russian policy should be put forward in such a manner as to leave the way open for a compliance not too detrimental to Russian prestige.

In the light of the above, it will be clearly seen that the Soviet pressure against the free institutions of the Western world is something that can be contained by the adroit and vigilant application of counter-force at a series of constantly shifting geographical and political points, corresponding to the shifts and maneuvers of Soviet policy, but which cannot be charmed or talked out of existence. The Russians look forward to a duel of infinite duration, and they see that already they have scored great successes. . . .

It is clear that the United States cannot expect in the foreseeable future to enjoy political intimacy with the Soviet regime. It must continue to regard the Soviet Union as a rival, not a partner, in the political arena. It must continue to expect that Soviet policies will reflect no abstract love of peace and stability, no real faith in the possibility of a permanent happy coexistence of the Socialist and capitalist worlds, but rather a cautious, persistent pressure toward the disruption and weakening of all rival influence and rival power.

Balanced against this are the facts that Russia, as opposed to the Western world in general, is still by far the weaker party, that Soviet policy is highly flexible, and that Soviet society may well contain deficiencies which will eventually weaken its own total potential. This would of itself warrant the United States entering with reasonable confidence upon a policy of firm containment, designed to confront the Russians with unalterable counter-force at every point where they show signs of encroaching upon the interests of a peaceful and stable world. . . .

It would be an exaggeration to say that American behavior unassisted and alone could exercise a power of life and death over the Communist movement and bring about the early fall of Soviet power in Russia. But the United States has it in its power to increase enormously the strains under which Soviet policy must operate, to force upon the Kremlin a far greater degree of moderation and circumspection than it has had to observe in recent years, and in this way to promote tendencies which must eventually find their outlet in either the break-up or the gradual mellowing of Soviet power. . . .

REVIEW QUESTIONS

1. According to Kennan, what did Soviet leaders value or respect?
2. How did Kennan propose that the United States increase the "strains" within the Soviet system?
3. How do you think Soviet officials would have responded to Kennan's analysis?

WALTER LIPPMANN

A Critique of Containment (1947)

Kennan's "containment doctrine" elicited a spirited critique from Walter Lippmann, a Pulitzer Prize–winning journalist widely recognized as one of the most authoritative commentators on political and diplomatic affairs during the 1940s.

... My objection, then, to the policy of containment is not that it seeks to confront the Soviet power with American power, but that the policy is misconceived, and must result in a misuse of American power. For as I have sought to show, it commits this country to a struggle which has for its objective nothing more substantial than the hope that in ten or fifteen years the Soviet power will, as the result of long frustration, "break up" or "mellow." In this prolonged struggle the role of the United States is, according to Mr. X, to react "at a series of constantly shifting geographical and political points" to the encroachments of the Soviet power.

The policy, therefore, concedes to the Kremlin the strategic initiative as to when, where and under what local circumstances the issue is to be joined. It compels the United States to meet the Soviet pressure at these shifting geographical and political points by using satellite states, puppet governments and agents which have been subsidized and supported, though their effectiveness is meager and their reliability uncertain. By forcing us to expend our energies and our substance upon these dubious and unnatural allies on the perimeter of the Soviet Union, the effect of the policy is to neglect our natural allies in the Atlantic community, and to alienate them.

*   *   *

All the other pressures of the Soviet Union at the "constantly shifting geographical and political points," which Mr. X is so concerned about—in the Middle East and in Asia—are, I contend, secondary and subsidiary to the fact that its armed forces are in the heart of Europe. It is to the Red Army in Europe, therefore, and not to ideologies, elections, forms of government, to socialism, to communism, to free enterprise, that a correctly conceived and soundly planned policy should be directed. ...

We may now consider how we are to relate our role in the United Nations to our policy in the conflict with Russia. Mr. X does not deal with this question. But the State Department, in its attempt to operate under the Truman Doctrine, has shown where that doctrine would take us. It would take us to the destruction of the U.N. ...

The U.N., which should be preserved as the last best hope of mankind that the conflict can be settled and a peace achieved, is being chewed up. The seed corn is being devoured. Why? Because the policy of containment, as Mr. X has exposed it to the world, does not have as its objective a settlement of the conflict with Russia. It is therefore implicit in the policy that the U.N. has no future as a universal society, and that either the U.N. will be cast aside like the League of Nations, or it will be transformed into an anti-Soviet coalition. In either event the U.N. will have been destroyed. ...

REVIEW QUESTIONS

1. What did Lippmann mean by a "misuse of American power"?
2. Why did Lippmann contend that the objectives of Truman's containment doctrine conflicted with those of the United Nations?
3. Which analysis do you find more persuasive, Kennan's or Lippmann's? Why?

FROM The Truman Doctrine (1947)

Although the catalyst for this speech was the crisis in Greece and Turkey, President Truman and his advisers seized the opportunity to explain their broader concept of the postwar world and America's obligations. By pledging to resist communism anywhere and everywhere, Truman established a dangerous precedent.

From *Congressional Record*, 80th Cong., 1st Sess., March 12, 1947, p. 1981.

The gravity of the situation which confronts the world today necessitates my appearance before a joint session of the Congress. The foreign policy and the national security of this country are involved.

One aspect of the present situation, which I wish to present to you at this time for your consideration and decision, concerns Greece and Turkey.

The United States has received from the Greek Government an urgent appeal for financial and economic assistance. Preliminary reports from the American Economic Mission now in Greece and reports from the American Ambassador in Greece corroborate the statement of the Greek Government that assistance is imperative if Greece is to survive as a free nation.

I do not believe that the American people and the Congress wish to turn a deaf ear to the appeal of the Greek Government. The very existence of the Greek state is today threatened by the terrorist activities of several thousand armed men, led by Communists, who defy the Government's authority at a number of points, particularly along the northern boundaries. . . . Meanwhile, the Greek Government is unable to cope with the situation. The Greek Army is small and poorly equipped. It needs supplies and equipment if it is to restore the authority to the Government throughout Greek territory.

Greece must have assistance if it is to become a self-supporting and self-respecting democracy. The United States must supply this assistance. We have already extended to Greece certain types of relief and economic aid but these are inadequate. There is no other country to which democratic Greece can turn. No other nation is willing and able to provide the necessary support for a democratic Greek Government.

The British Government, which has been helping Greece, can give no further financial or economic aid after March 31. Great Britain finds itself under the necessity of reducing or liquidating its commitments in several parts of the world, including Greece.

We have considered how the United Nations might assist in this crisis. But the situation is an urgent one requiring immediate action, and the United Nations and its related organizations are not in a position to extend help of the kind that is required. . . .

Greece's neighbor, Turkey, also deserves our attention. The future of Turkey as an independent and economically sound state is clearly no less important to the freedom loving peoples of the world than the future of Greece. The circumstances in which Turkey finds itself today are considerably different from those of Greece. Turkey has been spared the disasters that have beset Greece. And during the war, the United States and Great Britain furnished Turkey with material aid. Nevertheless, Turkey now needs our support.

Since the war Turkey has sought additional financial assistance from Great Britain and the United States for the purpose of effecting the modernization necessary for the maintenance of its national integrity. That integrity is essential to the preservation of order in the Middle East.

The British Government has informed us that, owing to its own difficulties, it can no longer extend financial or economic aid to Turkey. As in the case of Greece, if Turkey is to have the assistance it needs, the United States must supply it. We are the only country able to provide that help.

I am fully aware of the broad implications involved if the United States extends assistance to Greece and Turkey, and I shall discuss these implications with you at this time.

One of the primary objectives of the foreign policy of the United States is the creation of conditions in which we and other nations will be able to work out a way of life free from coercion. This was a fundamental issue in the war with Germany and Japan. Our victory was won over countries which sought to impose their will, and their way of life, upon other nations.

To ensure the peaceful development of nations, free from coercion, the United States has taken a leading part in establishing the United Nations. The United Nations is designed to make possible lasting freedom and independence for all its members. We shall not realize our objectives, however, unless we are willing to help free peoples to maintain their free institutions and their national integrity against aggressive movements that seek to impose on them totalitarian regimes. This is no more than a frank recognition that totalitarian regimes imposed on free peoples, by direct or indirect aggression, undermine the foundations of international peace and hence the security of the United States.

The peoples of a number of countries of the world have recently had totalitarian regimes forced upon them against their will. The Government of the United States has made frequent protests against coercion and intimidation, in violation of the Yalta Agreement, in Poland, Rumania and Bulgaria. I must also state that in a number of other countries there have been similar developments.

At the present moment in world history nearly every nation must choose between alternative ways of life. The choice is too often not a free one.

One way of life is based upon the will of the majority, and is distinguished by free institutions, representative government, free elections, guarantees of individual liberty, freedom of speech and religion, and freedom from political oppression.

The second way of life is based upon the will of the minority forcibly imposed upon the majority. It relies upon terror and oppression, a controlled press and radio, fixed elections, and the suppression of personal freedoms.

I believe that it must be the policy of the United States to support free peoples who are resisting attempted subjugation by armed minorities or by outside pressures. I believe that we must assist free peoples to work out their own destinies in their own way.

I believe that our help should be primarily through economic and financial aid which is essential to economic stability and orderly political processes. The world is not static, and the status quo is not sacred. But we cannot allow changes in the status quo in violation of the charter of the United Nations by such methods as coercion, or by such subterfuges as political infiltration. In helping free and independent nations to maintain their freedom, the United States will be giving effect to the principles of the charter of the United Nations.

It is necessary only to glance at a map to realize that the survival and integrity of the Greek nation are of grave importance in a much wider situation. If Greece should fall under the control of an armed minority, the effect upon its neighbor, Turkey, would be immediate and serious. Confusion and disorder might well spread throughout the entire Middle East.

Moreover, the disappearance of Greece as an independent state would have a profound effect upon those countries in Europe whose peoples are struggling against great difficulties to maintain their freedoms and their independence while they repair the damages of war.

It would be an unspeakable tragedy if these countries, which have struggled so long against overwhelming odds, should lose that victory for which they sacrificed so much. Collapse of free institutions and loss of independence would be disastrous not only for them but for the world. Discouragement and possibly failure would quickly be the lot of neighboring peoples striving to maintain their freedom and independence.

Should we fail to aid Greece and Turkey in this fateful hour, the effect will be far reaching to the west as well as to the east. We must take immediate and resolute action.

I therefore ask the Congress to provide authority for assistance to Greece and Turkey in the amount of $400,000,000 for the period ending June 30, 1948.

In addition to funds, I ask the Congress to authorize the detail of American civilian and military personnel to Greece and Turkey, at the request of those countries, to assist in the tasks of reconstruction, and for the purpose of supervising the use of such financial and material assistance as may be furnished. I recommend that authority also be provided for the instruction and training of selected Greek and Turkish personnel.

Finally, I ask that the Congress provide authority which will permit the speediest and most effective use, in terms of needed commodities, supplies, and equipment, of such funds as may be authorized. . . .

The seeds of totalitarian regimes are nurtured by misery and want. They spread and grow in the evil soil of poverty and strife. They reach their full growth when the hope of a people for a better life has died. We must keep that hope alive. The free peoples of the world look to us for support in maintaining their freedoms.

If we falter in our leadership, we may endanger the peace of the world—and we shall surely endanger the welfare of this nation.

Great responsibilities have been placed upon us by the swift movement of events. I am confident that the Congress will face these responsibilities squarely.

REVIEW QUESTIONS

1. How was American national security affected by events in Greece and Turkey?
2. Truman outlined two alternative ways of life. What were they and which one corresponded to the United States? The Soviet Union?
3. Did Truman's speech imply American military as well as economic involvement in the affairs of other nations?

FROM The Marshall Plan (1947)

Secretary of State George C. Marshall knew that the political stability of western Europe depended on its economic health. In this address to the all-male Harvard University graduating class of 1947, he outlined the rationale for a massive infusion of American aid into the postwar recovery in Europe. He did not yet know the details of administering such a program, but he was confident of its necessity.

From *Congressional Record*, 80th Cong., 1st Sess., December 19, 1947, pp. 11, 749–51.

I need not tell you gentlemen that the world situation is very serious. That must be apparent to all intelligent people. I think one difficulty is that the problem is one of such enormous complexity that the very mass of facts presented to the public by press and radio make it exceedingly difficult for the man in the street to reach a clear appraisal of the situation. Furthermore, the people of this country are distant from the troubled areas of the earth and it is hard for them to comprehend the plight and consequent reactions of the longsuffering peoples, and the effect of those reactions on their governments in connection with our efforts to promote peace in the world.

In considering the requirements for the rehabilitation of Europe, the physical loss of life, the visible destruction of cities, factories, mines, and railroads was correctly estimated, but it has become obvious during recent months that this visible destruction was probably less serious than the dislocation of the entire fabric of European economy.

For the past 10 years conditions have been highly abnormal. The feverish preparation for war and the more feverish maintenance of the war effort engulfed all aspects of national economies. Machinery has fallen into disrepair or is entirely obsolete. . . . Raw materials and fuel are in short supply. Machinery is lacking or worn out. The farmer or the peasant cannot find the goods for sale which he desires to purchase. So the sale of his farm produce for money which he cannot use seems to him an unprofitable transaction. He, therefore, has withdrawn many fields from crop cultivation and is using them for grazing. He feeds more grain to stock and finds for himself and his family an ample supply of food, however short he may be on clothing and the other ordinary gadgets of civilization.

Meanwhile people in the cities are short of food and fuel. So the governments are forced to use their foreign money and credits to procure these necessities abroad. This process exhausts funds which are urgently needed for reconstruction. Thus a very serious situation is rapidly developing which bodes no good for the world. The modern system of the division of labor upon which the exchange of products is based is in danger of breaking down.

The truth of the matter is that Europe's requirements for the next 3 or 4 years of foreign food and other essential products—principally from America—are so much greater than her present ability to pay that she must have substantial additional help, or face economic, social, and political deterioration of a very grave character.

The remedy lies in breaking the vicious circle and restoring the confidence of the European people in the economic future of their own countries and of Europe as a whole. The manufacturer and the farmer throughout wide areas must be able and willing to exchange their products for currencies the continuing value of which is not open to question.

Aside from the demoralizing effect on the world at large and the possibilities of disturbances arising as a result of the desperation of the people concerned, the consequences to the economy of the United States should be apparent to all. It is logical that the United States should do whatever it is able to do to assist in the return of normal economic health in the world, without which there can be no political stability and no assured peace.

Our policy is directed not against any country or doctrine but against hunger, poverty, desperation, and chaos. Its purpose should be the revival of a working economy in the world so as to permit the emergence of political and social conditions in which free institutions can exist. Such assistance, I am convinced, must not be on a piecemeal basis as various crises develop. Any assistance that this Government may render in the future should provide a cure rather than a mere palliative.

Any government that is willing to assist in the task of recovery will find full cooperation, I am sure, on the part of the United States Government. Any government which maneuvers to block the recovery of other countries cannot expect help from us. Furthermore, governments, political parties, or groups which seek to perpetuate human misery in order to profit therefrom politically or otherwise will encounter the opposition of the United States.

It is already evident that, before the United States Government can proceed much further in its efforts to alleviate the situation and help start the European world on its way to recovery, there must be some agreement among the countries of Europe as to the requirements of the situation and the part those countries themselves will take in order to give proper effect to whatever action might be undertaken by this Government.

It would be neither fitting nor efficacious for this Government to undertake to draw up unilaterally a program designed to place Europe on its feet economically. This is the business of the Europeans. The initiative, I think, must come from Europe. The role of this country should consist of friendly aid in the drafting of a European program and of later support of such a program so far as it may be practical for us to do so. The program should be a joint one, agreed to by a number, if not all European nations.

An essential part of any successful action on the part of the United States is an understanding on the part of the people of America of the character of the problem and the remedies to be applied. Political passion and prejudice should have no part. With foresight, and a willingness on the part of our people to face up to the vast responsibility which history has clearly placed upon our country, the difficulties I have outlined can and will be overcome.

REVIEW QUESTIONS

1. What was the most acute economic problem facing Europe after the end of World War II?
2. How do you think the Soviet Union would have responded to Marshall's speech?

HARRY S. TRUMAN

FROM Statement on the Korean War (1950)

President Truman saw the North Korean invasion of South Korea as analogous with what German dictator Adolf Hitler had done in the 1930s—intimidating Western democracies through bold aggressions. This time, he pledged, there would be no appeasement. Yet Truman also did not want the Korean conflict to escalate into another world war. This brought him into conflict with General Douglas MacArthur, who wanted to expand the fighting to mainland China. In April 1951 Truman made the difficult decision to remove MacArthur from his command.

From *Department of State Bulletin* 24 (April 16, 1951): 603–05.

. . . The Communists in the Kremlin are engaged in a monstrous conspiracy to stamp out freedom all over the world. If they were to succeed, the United States would be numbered among their principal victims. It must be clear to everyone that the United States cannot—and will not—sit idly by and await foreign conquest. The only question is: When is the best time to meet the threat and how?

In the simplest terms, what we are doing in Korea is this:

We are trying to prevent a third world war.

I think most people in this country recognized that fact last June. And they warmly supported the decision of the Government to help the Republic of Korea against the Communist aggressors. Now, many persons, even some who applauded our decision to defend Korea, have forgotten the basic reason for our action. . . .

The aggression against Korea is the boldest and most dangerous move the Communists have yet made.

The attack on Korea was part of a greater plan for conquering all of Asia. . . . They want to control all of Asia from the Kremlin. This plan of conquest is in flat contradiction to what we believe. We believe that Korea belongs to the Koreans. We believe that India belongs to the Indians. We believe that all

the nations of Asia should be free to work out their affairs in their own way. This is the basis of peace in the Far East and it is the basis of peace everywhere else.

The whole Communist imperialism is back of the attack on peace in the Far East. It was the Soviet Union that trained and equipped the North Koreans for aggression. The Chinese Communists massed forty-four well-trained and well-equipped divisions on the Korean frontier. These were the troops they threw into battle when the North Korean Communists were beaten.

The question we have to face is whether the Communist plan of conquest can be stopped without general war. Our Government and other countries associated with us in the United Nations believe that the best chance of stopping it without general war is to meet the attack in Korea and defeat it there.

That is what we have been doing. It is a difficult and bitter task. But so far it has been successful. So far, we have prevented World War III. So far, by fighting a limited war in Korea, we have prevented aggression from succeeding and bringing on a general war. And the ability of the whole free world to resist Communist aggression has been greatly improved. . . .

But you may ask: Why can't we take steps to punish the aggressor? Why don't we bomb Manchuria and China itself? Why don't we assist nationalist Chinese troops to land on the mainland of China?

If we were to do these things we would be running a very grave risk of starting a general war. If that were to happen, we would have brought about the exact situation we are trying to prevent. . . .

I believe that we must try to limit the war to Korea for these vital reasons: to make sure that the precious lives of our fighting men are not wasted; to see that the security of our country and the free world is not needlessly jeopardized; and to prevent a third world war.

A number of events have made it evident that General MacArthur did not agree with that policy. I have therefore considered it essential to relieve General MacArthur so that there would be no doubt or confusion as to the real purpose and aim of our policy.

It was with the deepest personal regret that I found myself compelled to take this action. General MacArthur is one of our greatest military commanders. But the cause of world peace is more important than any individual.

The change in commands in the Far East means no change whatever in the policy of the United States. We will carry on the fight in Korea with vigor and determination in an effort to bring the war to a speedy and successful conclusion.

The new commander, Lt. Gen. Matthew Ridgway, has already demonstrated that he has the great qualities of military leadership needed for this task. We are ready, at any time, to negotiate for a restoration of peace in the area. But we will not engage in appeasement. We are only interested in real peace. Real peace can be achieved through a settlement based on the following factors:

One: the fighting must stop.

Two: concrete steps must be taken to insure that the fighting will not break out again.

Three: there must be an end to the aggression.

A settlement founded upon these elements would open the way for the unification of Korea and the withdrawal of all foreign forces.

In the meantime, I want to be clear about our military objective. We are fighting to resist an outrageous aggression in Korea. We are trying to keep the Korean conflict from spreading to other areas. But at the same time we must conduct our military activities so as to insure the security of our forces. This is essential if they are to continue the fight until the enemy abandons its ruthless attempt to destroy the Republic of Korea.

That is our military objective—to repel attack and to restore peace. In the hard fighting in Korea, we are proving that collective action among nations is not only a high principle but a workable means of resisting aggression. Defeat of aggression in Korea may be the turning point in the world's search for a practical way of achieving peace and security. . . .

We do not want to widen the conflict. We will use every effort to prevent that disaster. And in so doing we know that we are following the great principles of peace, freedom, and justice.

REVIEW QUESTIONS

1. How did Truman link American security concerns with the situation in Korea?
2. Truman asserted that the United States should not appease aggressors, but at the same time he insisted that the fighting in Korea should remain limited. Was this possible?
3. Did the Korean War establish any important precedents for future American actions? If so, what were they?

JOSEPH MCCARTHY

Democrats and Communists (1950)

As suggested by the following speech delivered to a Republican women's club in Wheeling, West Virginia, Senator Joseph McCarthy from Wisconsin became a master at making outlandish charges about domestic subversion—and getting away with it. He declared that the United States was losing the Cold War because the Truman administration was infested with scores of known communists; moreover, he claimed to have the names of 205 of them. Those who questioned his methods found themselves the subject of vicious attacks and smear campaigns. In July 1950 a Senate subcommittee chaired by Maryland Democrat Millard Tydings dismissed McCarthy's charges as "a fraud and a hoax." McCarthy thereupon turned on Tydings and helped undermine his reelection campaign. McCarthy never identified an actual Communist in the Truman administration.

From *Congressional Record*, 81st Cong., 2nd Sess., February 12, 1950, pp. 1954–57.

Today we are engaged in a final all-out battle between communistic atheism and Christianity. The modern champions of communism have selected this as the time, and ladies and gentlemen, the chips are down—they are truly down. . . .

Five years after a world war has been won, men's hearts should anticipate a long peace, and men's minds should be free from the heavy weight that comes with war. But this is not such a period—for this is not a period of peace. This is a time of the "cold war." This is a time when all the world is split into two vast, increasingly hostile camps—a time of a great armaments race. . . .

At war's end we were physically the strongest nation on earth—and at least potentially the most powerful intellectually and morally. Ours could have been the honor of being a beacon in the desert of destruction, a shining living proof that civilization was not yet ready to destroy itself. Unfortunately, we have failed miserably and tragically to arise to the opportunity.

The reason why we find ourselves in a position of impotency is not because our only powerful potential enemy has sent men to invade our shores, but rather because of the traitorous actions of those who have

been treated so well by this Nation. It has not been the less fortunate or members of minority groups who have been selling this Nation out, but rather those who have had all the benefits that the wealthiest nation on earth has had to offer—the finest homes, the finest college education, and the finest jobs in Government we can give.

This is glaringly true in the State Department. There the bright young men who are born with silver spoons in their mouths are the ones who have been the worst. . . . In my opinion the State Department, which is one of the most important government departments, is thoroughly infested with Communists.

I have in my hand 205 cases of individuals who would appear to be either card carrying members or certainly loyal to the Communist party, but who nevertheless are still helping to shape our foreign policy.

One thing to remember in discussing the Communists in our Government is that we are dealing with spies who get 30 pieces of silver to steal the blueprints of a new weapon. We are dealing with a far more sinister type of activity because it permits the enemy to guide and shape our policy.

REVIEW QUESTIONS

1. According to McCarthy, what forces were arrayed against each other in 1950?
2. In what respects did McCarthy's remarks have a populist theme?

3. Why do you think McCarthy stressed the economic motivations of supposed communists working in the State Department? Did this contradict any of his earlier assertions?

WILLIAM O. DOUGLAS

FROM The Black Silence of Fear (1952)

By 1952 a few prominent leaders began to criticize the excesses and dangers of the anti-communist movement led by Wisconsin Senator Joseph McCarthy. Among the most articulate was Supreme Court Justice William O. Douglas (1898–1980). Born in Minnesota and raised in California and Washington state, Douglas graduated from Columbia University School of Law in 1925. He became a distinguished professor at the Yale University Law School before being appointed to the Supreme Court in 1939. Throughout his long career on the bench, he steadfastly defended civil liberties.

From "The Black Silence of Fear," *New York Times Magazine*, January 13, 1952, pp. 7, 37–38. Reprinted by permission of the Estate of William O. Douglas. [Editorial insertions appear in square brackets—*Ed.*]

There is an ominous trend in this nation. We are developing tolerance only for the orthodox point of view on world affairs, intolerance for new or different approaches. . . .

. . . We have over the years swung from tolerance to intolerance and back again. There have been years of intolerance when the views of minorities have been suppressed. But there probably has not been a period of greater intolerance than we witness today. To understand this, I think one has to leave the country, go into the back regions of the world, lose himself there, and become absorbed in the problems of the peoples of different civilizations. When he returns to America after a few months he probably will be shocked. He will be shocked not at the intentions or purposes or ideals of the American people. He will be shocked at the arrogance and

intolerance of great segments of the American press, at the arrogance and intolerance of many leaders in public office, at the arrogance and intolerance reflected in many of our attitudes toward Asia. He will find that thought is being standardized, that the permissible area for calm discussion is being narrowed, that the range of ideas is being limited, that many minds are closed. . . .

This is alarming to one who loves his country. It means that the philosophy of strength through free speech is being forsaken for the philosophy of fear through repression.

That choice [to limit free speech] in Russia is conscious. Under Lenin the ministers and officials were encouraged to debate, to advance new ideas and criticisms. Once the debate was over, however, no dissension or disagreement was permitted. But even that small degree of tolerance for free discussion that Lenin permitted disappeared under Stalin. Stalin maintains a tight system of control, permitting no free speech, no real clash in ideas, even in the inner circle. We are, of course, not emulating either Lenin or Stalin. But we are drifting in the direction of repression, drifting dangerously fast. . . .

The drift goes back, I think, to the fact that we carried over to days of peace the military approach to world affairs. . . .

. . . Today in Asia we are identified not with ideas of freedom, but with guns. Today at home we are thinking less and less in terms of defeating communism with ideas, more and more in terms of defeating communism with military might.

The concentration on military means has helped to breed fear. It has bred fear and insecurity partly because of the horror of atomic war. But the real reason strikes deeper. In spite of our enormous expenditures, we see that Soviet imperialism continues to expand and that the expansion proceeds without the Soviets firing a shot. The free world continues to contract without a battle for its survival having been fought. It becomes apparent, as country after country falls to Soviet imperialistic ambitions, that military policy alone is a weak one, that military policy alone will end in political bankruptcy and futility. Thus fear mounts.

Fear has many manifestations. The Communist threat inside the country has been magnified and exalted far beyond its realities. Irresponsible talk by irresponsible people has fanned the flames of fear. Accusations have been loosely made. Character assassinations have become common. Suspicion has taken the place of goodwill. Once we could debate with impunity along a wide range of inquiry. Once we could safely explore to the edges of a problem, challenge orthodoxy without qualms, and run the gamut of ideas in search of solutions to perplexing problems. Once we had confidence in each other. Now there is suspicion. Innocent acts become tell-tale marks of disloyalty. The coincidence that an idea parallels Soviet Russia's policy for a moment of time settles an aura of suspicion around a person.

Suspicion grows until only the orthodox idea is the safe one. Suspicion grows until only the person who loudly proclaims that orthodox view, or who, once having been a Communist, has been converted, is trustworthy. Competition for embracing the new orthodoxy increases. Those who are unorthodox are suspect. Everyone who does not follow the military policymakers is suspect. Everyone who voices opposition to the trend away from diplomacy and away from political tactics takes a chance. Some who are opposed are indeed "subversive." Therefore, the thundering edict commands that all who are opposed are "subversive." Fear is fanned to a fury. Good and honest men are pilloried. Character is assassinated. Fear runs rampant. . . .

Fear has driven more and more men and women in all walks of life either to silence or to the folds of the orthodox. Fear has mounted: fear of losing one's job, fear of being investigated, fear of being pilloried. This fear has stereotyped our thinking, narrowed the range of free public discussion, and driven many thoughtful people to despair. This fear has even entered universities, great citadels of our spiritual strength, and corrupted them. We have the spectacle of university officials lending themselves to one of the worst witch-hunts we have seen since early days.

This fear has affected the youngsters. . . . Youth, like the opposition party in a parliamentary system, has served a powerful role. It has cast doubts on our policies, challenged our inarticulate major premises, put the light on our prejudices, and exposed our inconsistencies. Youth has made each generation indulge in self-examination.

But a great change has taken place. Youth is still rebellious; but it is largely holding its tongue. There is the fear of being labeled a "subversive" if one departs from the orthodox party line. That charge, if leveled against a young man or young woman, may have profound effects. It may ruin a youngster's business or professional career. No one wants a Communist in his organization nor anyone who is suspect. . . .

This pattern of orthodoxy that is shaping our thinking has dangerous implications. No one man, no one group can have the answer to the many perplexing problems that today confront the management of world affairs. The scene is a troubled and complicated one. The problems require the pooling of many ideas, the exposure of different points of view, the hammering out in public discussions of the pros and cons of this policy or of that. . . .

The great danger of this period is not inflation, nor the national debt, nor atomic warfare. The great, the critical danger is that we will so limit or narrow the range of permissible discussion and permissible thought that we will become victims of the orthodox school. If we do, we will lose flexibility. We will lose the capacity for expert management. We will then become wedded to a few techniques, to a few devices. They will define our policy and at the same time limit our ability to alter or modify it. Once we narrow the range of thought and discussion, we will surrender a great deal of our power. We will become like the man on the toboggan who can ride it but who can neither steer it nor stop it.

The mind of man must always be free. The strong society is one that sanctions and encourages freedom of thought and expression. . . . Our real power is our spiritual strength, and that spiritual strength stems from our civil liberties. If we are true to our traditions, if we are tolerant of a whole market place of ideas, we will always be strong. Our weakness grows when we become intolerant of opposing ideas, depart from our standards of civil liberties, and borrow the policeman's philosophy from the enemy we detest.

REVIEW QUESTIONS

1. Douglas claims that intolerance is bred by fear. What had generated such fear among Americans after World War II?
2. Why is he concerned about the forces of conformity and "orthodoxy" becoming so pervasive?
3. In what ways does he see the United States coming to resemble Soviet society?

28 ✌ COLD WAR AMERICA, 1950–1959

The dominant theme of American life after 1945 was unprecedented prosperity coupled with persistent—if little noticed—poverty. Between 1945 and 1960 the economy soared, propelled by a boom in residential construction and by the high levels of defense spending spurred by the Cold War. People weary of the sacrifices and rationing required by World War II eagerly purchased new consumer goods, such as electric refrigerators, dishwashers, washing machines, television sets, high-fidelity phonographs, and transistor radios.

The postwar consumer culture was centered in the new suburban communities that sprouted like mushrooms across the landscape. By 1960 some 60 million people, one third of the total population, lived in suburbs outside the cities that nurtured them. The prescribed role for middle-class women in this new suburban culture was focused on traditional domesticity. Women who worked in defense plants during the war were encouraged to return to the domestic circle and devote their attention to husbands and children. Even though the number of working women increased during the 1950s, the stereotypic image of the middle-class housewife remained that of a doting spouse who cooked the meals and transported the kids in her station wagon.

Religious life also prospered in the postwar era. With the nation locked into an ideological battle with communism (which prohibited or suppressed religious expression), spiritual belief took on new political significance. In 1954 Congress added the phrase "under God" to the Pledge of Allegiance, and the next year it required that the phrase "In God We Trust" be placed on all currency. Attendance at churches and synagogues soared, movies with biblical themes were box office hits, and religious books were often bestsellers. Yet not all observers were comforted by a religious revival animated by a "feel good" theology. The preeminent theologian Reinhold Niebuhr criticized the superficiality associated with much of the era's religious enthusiasm.

Dwight D. Eisenhower was elected in 1952 in large part because voters believed the military hero could end the stalemated war in Korea and lead the United States through the confrontations of the Cold War. Americans yearned for peace and stability, and "Ike" promised to provide both. To satisfy the right wing of the Republican Party, Eisenhower tapped John Foster Dulles as his secretary of state. A dogmatic, humorless Calvinist descended from missionaries and diplomats, Dulles resolved to wage holy war against "atheistic communism." Impatient with the containment program of Truman and the Democrats, he advocated a more aggressive policy designed to "liberate" the "captive peoples" of Eastern Europe and China from communist tyranny. Moreover, Dulles believed that the Soviets responded only to force, and this sometimes required engaging in "brinkmanship," a willingness to take crises to the edge of war to stem communist aggression.

Dulles's crusading rhetoric pleased Republican conservatives, but Eisenhower preferred a less confrontational approach. As a former commanding general he knew when and where to fight. For example, when the Hungarians and Poles revolted against Soviet rule in 1956, the United States did not intervene to help "liberate" them. Eisenhower realized that there was no feasible way to do so. He, more than Dulles, understood the limits of American power.

Eisenhower also understood the financial limits of a worldwide crusade against communism. The former general was determined to reduce military spending so as to maintain a balanced budget and a thriving economy. He and Dulles thus fastened on what came to be called a policy of "massive retaliation." Instead of relying on expensive conventional military forces to provide national security and preserve international order, they decided to use the threat of massive nuclear retaliation to keep the Soviets in line and at the same time reduce defense spending. This would give the United States what Dulles called "a bigger bang for the buck."

The threatened use of nuclear weapons, however, made little sense in dealing with trouble spots in Southeast Asia. In Indochina, for example, the United States had provided France with $1.2 billion in military aid between 1950 and 1954 in its war against Ho Chi Minh and his communist Viet Minh followers. Eisenhower adopted a rationale that later American presidents would repeat: if the communists gained control of Indochina, then the neighboring countries would soon fall like dominoes. In 1954 the French sought to draw the elusive Viet Minh into the open for a single climactic battle at Dien Bien Phu. But the idea backfired, and the French found themselves surrounded and cut off. The French government issued a desperate plea for American air strikes, but Eisenhower refused. He did not want to involve the United States in another Asian war on the heels of the armistice in Korea.

The beleaguered French army at Dien Bien Phu surrendered in May 1954. At the Geneva Peace Conference the parties agreed to divide Indochina at the

17th parallel, creating the temporary states of North and South Vietnam. An election scheduled for 1956 would decide under what form of government the infant nation would be unified (though the United States subsequently refused to support the election because it feared that Ho Chi Minh would win by a large margin). Just as the United States had filled the breach created by the departure of the British from Greece, the American government now agreed to replace the French in Vietnam, offering its support to the new South Vietnamese leader, Ngo Dinh Diem.

Perhaps the greatest challenge associated with the Cold War was that its ideological emphasis made every trouble spot in the world fertile ground for Soviet-American competition. To deal with unrest in the Middle East, for example, President Eisenhower requested from Congress in 1957 a resolution empowering him to use military force in the Middle East against any manifestation of "international communism." This came to be known as the Eisenhower Doctrine, which transferred the authority to wage war from Congress to the executive branch (a shift that had begun during the Korean War but had never received explicit recognition or approval). In the summer of 1957 Eisenhower invoked his new authority, dispatching 15,000 marines to Lebanon.

In the domestic arena the most important development during the 1950s involved civil rights and race relations. The social changes wrought by World War II gave added impetus to the efforts to end racial segregation. The massive migration of blacks from the South to other regions of the country created new political dynamics that bolstered the efforts of the National Association for the Advancement of Colored People (NAACP) and other organizations to tear down racial barriers. Led by attorney Thurgood Marshall, the NAACP in 1950 mounted a legal challenge against the "separate but equal" doctrine that the Supreme Court had sanctioned in the case of Plessy v. Ferguson *(1896).*

Their opportunity arose when Oliver Brown, a resident of Topeka, Kansas, filed suit against the local school board. He objected to the requirement that his daughter be bused across town to attend an all-black school. Initially, a federal appeals court rejected Brown's suit because the segregated schools in Topeka satisfied the "equality test." But after two years of testimony and arguments, the Supreme Court overturned the lower court in its famous decision, Brown v. Board of Education of Topeka, Kansas *(1954). The Court's landmark ruling set in motion a series of events that would give rise to a national civil rights movement dedicated to desegregation and true racial equality.*

Busy Wife's Achievements (1956)

After the end of the Second World War, the United States experienced a period of unprecedented economic growth lasting well into the 1960s. Prosperity also brought dramatic changes to the role of women. With the end of the war, millions of men returned to the civilian workforce, displacing many women who had been urged to fill the vacancies created by men leaving for service in the armed forces. In addition, the postwar era witnessed the "baby boom," as married couples sought to make up for the time lost during the war in forming families. At the same time, the suburban revolution fostered a revival of conventional notions of feminine domesticity that reinforced traditional stereotypes about gender roles at home, in the workplace, and in social life. During the postwar era, Life *magazine was among the most popular publications in the United States. In 1956 the magazine's editors published an article describing the "typical" middle-class American housewife.*

Marjorie Sutton is home manager, mother, hostess and useful civic worker

At the kitchen counter which doubles as her office, Marjorie Sutton of Los Angeles for a brief moment straddles her two equally busy roles as a happy, successful housewife and as a useful civic worker.

At 32, Mrs. Sutton is admittedly lucky. She is pretty and popular. Her husband earns an average of $25,000. She has a spacious home, a gardener and a full-time maid. Thus freed of much of a housewife's drudgery, she has a unique opportunity to work for her community—and she does. She is a sponsor of the Campfire Girls, serves on P.T.A. committees, helps raise funds for Centinela Hospital and Goodwill Industries, sings in the choir at Hollywood's First Presbyterian, and inevitably is drawn into many of her husband's civic interests.

But Marge Sutton thinks of herself primarily as a housewife and, having stepped from high school into marriage, has made a career of running her home briskly and well. She does much of the cooking, makes clothes for her four children (ages 6–14) and for herself and, as a hostess, she entertains an endless stream of guests—1,500 a year, she estimates.

Marjorie Hayworth and George Sutton were married when he was 17 and she 16 and both were in high school. George rejected a football scholarship to go to work at his father's Ford agency (he took it over in 1948) and Marge left school to set up housekeeping.

With great understatement, George says, "Marge likes to keep busy." In her daily round she attends club or charity meetings, drives the children to school, does the weekly grocery shopping (average bill: $100), makes ceramics and is planning to study French. A conscientious mother, she spends a lot of time with her children, helping with homework and on costumes for parties, listening to their stories and problems. Her husband comes home for lunch almost every day and Marge makes it a point, whatever her schedule, to be there too. She shares his enthusiasm for driving their Model T. "She'd be a racer if I'd let her," says George.

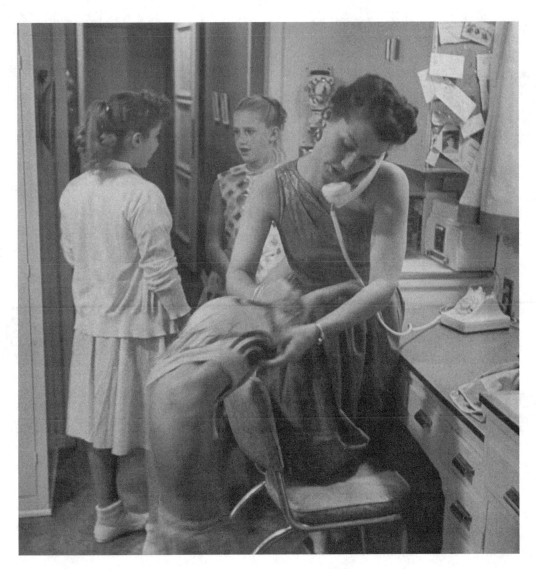

TELEPHONE ON SHOULDER, *Marge Sutton discusses P.T.A. while skinning shirt from son Gart. Lolly (right) and a guest are in background.*

DRIVING THE MODEL T, *vintage 1921, Marge steers with Gart beside her, Christie in back seat, husband George, Marshall and Lolly on running boards.*

FEEDING "FRIENDLY INDIANS," *a father and son group, Marge serves punch. George, who is helping serve, is known in [the] group as "Big Thunderbird."*

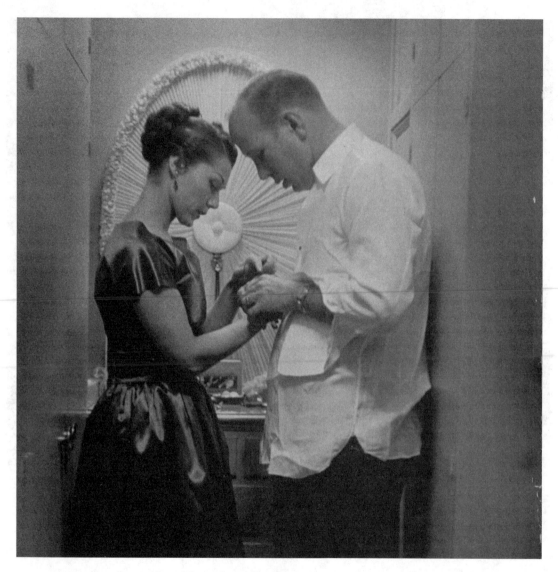

HELPFUL HUSBAND *George Sutton fastens bracelet for Marge as they get set to go out. She made [her] dress herself.*

HOSTESS BY CANDLELIGHT, *Marge ladles nonalcoholic eggnog (the Suttons do not drink) for two of the 50 guests whom she and George invited in for a pre-Christmas session of carol-singing after Sunday evening church service.*

TRIMMING THE TREE, *a 16-foot fir which the family cut in the San Bernardino Mountains, Marge leans over the banister in the front hallway while Marshall, 8, Lolly, 10, and Gart, 6, watch wide-eyed.*

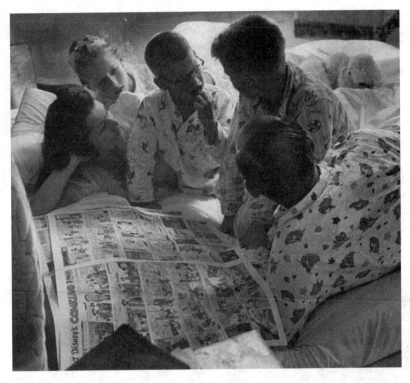

SUNDAY RITUAL *has George Sutton read Lolly, Gart and Marshall funnies at 7 a.m. before church.*

CHURCH CHORE *finds Marge, as the decorations chairman, trimming Hollywood Presbyterian altar.*

LESSON SESSION *brings Marge to Lolly's room to drill her on spelling a hard word,* "*necessity.*"

KEEPING IN SHAPE, *Marge bounces high off the trampoline under the eye of Instructor Joe Smith during her twice-weekly session at the Centinela Valley YMCA in Inglewood. Her interest in the trampoline started during a "slim and trim" class which she took at the "Y" to help preserve her size 12 figure.*

Many evenings the Suttons entertain two to 200 guests—church groups, their children's clubs, business friends. This leaves little time for reading or solitude but they try to arrange a few evenings alone. "We're a big family," says George, "and it's nice to have a quiet meeting of the board of directors now and then."

REVIEW QUESTIONS

1. If you were a college student in the 1950s, what message about prevailing social values and gender roles would you derive from reading this article?
2. In what way does the article reflect the prevailing ideological Cold War confrontation with communism and the Soviet Union?

BETTY FRIEDAN

FROM *The Feminine Mystique* (1963)

Born in 1921, Betty Friedan graduated with honors from Smith College in Massachusetts and pursued a doctoral degree in psychology at the University of California at Berkeley before dropping out to marry. She raised three children during the 1950s and performed the role of the dutiful housewife and mother. In 1957, however, she experienced a revelation of sorts when she mailed an alumni questionnaire to her Smith College classmates. The replies stunned her. Most of her classmates reported that while their lives were superficially successful, they suffered from an aching "sense of dissatisfaction." This prompted Friedan to spend five years researching a book dealing with what she called the "problem with no name." Published in 1963, The Feminine Mystique dissected the prevailing "mystique" of the blissful suburban housewife and helped launch the feminist movement.

The suburban housewife—she was the dream image of the young American women and the envy, it was said, of women all over the world. The American housewife—freed by science and labor-saving appliances from the drudgery, the dangers of childbirth and the illnesses of her grandmother. She was healthy, beautiful, educated, concerned only about her husband, her children, her home. She had found true feminine fulfillment. As a housewife and mother, she was respected as a full and equal partner to man in his world. She was free to choose automobiles, clothes, appliances, supermarkets; she had everything that women ever dreamed of.

In the fifteen years after World War II, this mystique of feminine fulfillment became the cherished and self-perpetuating core of contemporary American culture. Millions of women lived their lives in the image of those pretty pictures of the American suburban housewife, kissing their husbands good-bye in front of the picture window, depositing their station-wagonsful of children at school, and smiling as they ran the new electric waxer over the spotless kitchen floor. . . .

Their only dream was to be perfect wives and mothers; their highest ambition to have five children and a beautiful house, their only fight to get and keep husbands. They had no thought for the unfeminine problems outside the home; they wanted the men to make the major decisions. They gloried in their role as women, and wrote proudly on the census blank: "Occupation: housewife."

For over fifteen years, the words written for women, and the words women used when they talked to each other, while their husbands sat on the other side of the room and talked shop or politics or septic tanks, were about problems with their children, or how to keep their husbands happy, or improve their children's school, or cook chicken or make slipcovers. . . .

But on an April morning in 1959, I heard a mother of four, having coffee with four other mothers in a suburban development fifteen miles from New York, say in a tone of quiet desperation, "the problem." And the others knew, without words, that she was not talking about a problem with her husband, or her children, or her home. Suddenly they all realized they shared the same problem, the problem that has no name. . . .

The problem lay buried, unspoken, for many years in the minds of American women. It was a strange stirring, a sense of dissatisfaction, a yearning that women suffered in the middle of the twentieth century in the United States. Each suburban wife struggled with it alone. As she made the beds, shopped for groceries, matched slipcover material, ate peanut butter sandwiches with her children, chauffeured Cub Scouts and Brownies, lay beside her husband at night—she was afraid to ask even of herself the silent question—"Is this all?"

For over fifteen years there was no word of this yearning in the millions of words written about women, for women, in all the columns, books and articles by experts telling women their role was to seek fulfillment as wives and mothers. Over and over women heard in voices of tradition and of Freudian sophistication that they could desire no greater destiny than to glory in their own femininity. Experts told them how to catch a man and keep him, how to breastfeed children and handle their toilet training, how to cope with sibling rivalry and adolescent rebellion; how to buy a dishwasher, bake bread, cook gourmet snails, and build a swimming pool with their own hands; how to dress, look, and act more feminine and make marriage more exciting; how to keep their husbands from dying young and their sons from growing into delinquents. They were taught to pity the neurotic, unfeminine, unhappy women who wanted to be poets or physicists or presidents. They learned that truly feminine women do not want careers, higher education, political rights—the independence and the opportunities that the old-fashioned feminists fought for. Some women, in their forties and fifties, still remembered painfully giving up those dreams, but most of the younger women no longer even thought about them. A thousand expert voices applauded their femininity, their adjustment, their new maturity. All they had to do was devote their lives from earliest girlhood to finding a husband and bearing children. . . .

The feminine mystique says that the highest value and the only commitment for women is the fulfillment of their own femininity. It says that the great mistake of Western culture, through most of its history, has been the under-valuation of this femininity. It says this femininity is so mysterious and intuitive and close to the creation and origin of life that man-made science may never be able to understand it. But however special and different, it is in no way inferior to the nature of man; it may even in certain respects be superior. The mistake, says the mystique, the root of women's troubles in the past is that women envied men, women tried to be like men, instead of accepting their own nature, which can find fulfillment only in sexual passivity, male domination, and nurturing maternal love.

*   *   *

. . . The logic of the feminine mystique redefined the very nature of woman's problem. When woman was seen as a human being of limitless human potential, equal to man, anything that kept her from realizing her full potential was a problem to be solved: barriers to higher education and political participation, discrimination or prejudice in law or morality. But now that woman is seen only in terms of her sexual role, the barriers to the realization of her full potential, the prejudices which deny her full participation in the world, are no longer problems. The only problems now are those that might disturb her adjustment as a housewife. So career is a problem, education is a problem, political interest, even the very admission of women's intelligence and individuality is a problem. And finally there is the problem that has no name, a vague undefined wish for "something more" than washing dishes, ironing, punishing and praising the children. . . .

If an able American woman does not use her human energy and ability in some meaningful pursuit (which necessarily means competition, for there is competition in every serious pursuit of our society), she will fritter away her energy in neurotic symptoms, or unproductive exercise, or destructive "love."

It is time to stop giving lip service to the idea that there are no battles left to be fought for women in America, that women's rights have already been won. It is ridiculous to tell girls to keep quiet when they enter a new field, or an old one, so the men will not notice they are there. In almost every professional field, in business and in the arts and sciences, women are still treated as second-class citizens. It would be a great service to tell girls who plan to work in society to expect this subtle, uncomfortable discrimination—tell them not to be quiet, and hope it will go away, but fight it. A girl should not expect special privileges because of her sex, but neither should she "adjust" to prejudice and discrimination.

She must learn to compete then, not as a woman, but as a human being. Not until a great many women move out of the fringes into the mainstream will society itself provide the arrangements for their new life plan. . . .

REVIEW QUESTIONS

1. What did Friedan mean by the "problem with no name"?
2. What was the "feminine mystique" and what did it suggest about the historical causes of female unhappiness?
3. Describe how this excerpt might have helped inspire a new generation of feminist activists.

REINHOLD NIEBUHR

FROM Varieties of Religious Revival (1955)

Reinhold Niebuhr (1892–1971) was the foremost Christian theologian of the twentieth century. A graduate of Yale Divinity School, he pastored a church in Detroit during the 1930s before joining the faculty of Union Theological Seminary in New York City. In the midst of the surge of popular interest in Christianity during the Cold War, he raised penetrating questions about the depth of spiritual commitment evident in the movement.

From *The New Republic* 132, June 6, 1955, pp. 13–16. Reprinted by permission of The New Republic, Copyright © 1955, The New Republic, Inc.

No one can question the fact that we are experiencing a marked increase of interest in religion if not a revival of religious faith. The interpretations of the causes and possible consequences of this phenomenon may differ. It may be viewed with contradictory emotions of satisfaction or alarm by those who rather too simply regard religion as *per se* either good or bad. But about the evidences of this revival there can be no doubt.

Both church statistics and public-opinion polls, as well as the sale of religious literature, can be regarded as telling evidence. Church membership in the three faiths of Catholicism, Judaism and Protestantism has reached the surprising percentage of 60 percent of the population. It is also significant that 15 percent more of the population actually claim to be members of congregations than the church statistics actually establish. . . .

The popularity of television and radio religious broadcasts need not be numbered among the significant indices. . . . The sale of religious books, running into millions of copies for the "best sellers," may be a more important index, though this index immediately confronts us with the problem of gauging the inner significance of the current revival. For the most popular books on religion will be regarded by both the religious and the irreligious as evidence of the spread of a very dubious religion. Beginning with the best seller from the pen of the late Rabbi Joshua Liebman in 1946, and culminating in the phenomenal sale of the books by Norman Vincent Peale, this religious literature must be regarded as evidence of a rather frantic effort of the naturally optimistic American soul to preserve its optimism in the age of anxiety.

The themes of "peace of mind" and "positive thinking" either express a religion of self-assurance or they are pious guides to personal success. They can not be taken seriously by responsible religious or secular people because they do not come to terms with the basic collective problems of our atomic age, and because the peace which they seek to inculcate is rather too simple and neat. It is not like the "peace of God which passeth understanding." That peace passes understanding precisely because it is at peace with pain in it. The pain is caused by love and responsibility. In short, many of the indices of religiosity point to types of religion which are only remotely related to the main themes of the historic faiths. Interest in them can not, therefore, be attributed to a revival of these faiths.

The popularity of evangelists such as Billy Graham in Europe, as well as in America, is a quite different index of religious interest, but probably the interest is not as significant as usually assumed. Billy Graham expounds a fundamentalist version of the Christian faith. His faith is certainly superior to the success cults. It expresses some of the central themes of the Christian faith. He demands that men be confronted with God in Christ; and hopes that this confrontation will lead to conversion. Billy Graham carries on the traditions of our old frontier evangelistic piety, probably on a higher level than Billy Sunday achieved a generation back. Such evangelism may discipline certain disordered individual lives. But the secular critics of religion do not have to take seriously a version of the Christian faith which suggests that the dilemma of our age is due to a "wickedness" which conversion can cure.

Billy Graham sincerely carries on the individualistic and perfectionist illusions of the evangelistic Christianity of the old "Bible Belt." The moral dilemmas of the atomic age are certainly among the causes of the decay of secular religious alternatives to the historic faiths. But this kind of simple religious moralism was ironically refuted on a recent weekend when Billy Graham preached to the President [Dwight D. Eisenhower] in the morning and appeared on a television program in the afternoon. On television he suggested that conversion to Christianity could solve the problem of the hydrogen bomb. He preached to a President whose loyalty board had eliminated a very high-minded scientist from our atomic energy program because *inter alia* he was not sufficiently "enthusiastic" about the production of the hydrogen bomb.

One wonders what the President thought about this curious juxtaposition of events. But at any rate, it is obvious that contemporary moral dilemmas refute both the secular and the religious moralists who think that we could solve our problems if either "evil" men would become "good" or "ignorant" men "intelligent." There is always validity in the religious challenge, which converts drunkards and adulterers from their evil ways, and which convicts all of us who regard ourselves as "normal" of really being quite self-centered. But any religious or secular interpretation of life which would solve our collective moral and political dilemmas simply either by conversion or enlightenment has obviously not measured the depth of the problem.

Reference to President Eisenhower's devotion to Billy Graham suggests another index of the religious revival which may well leave both the religious and the secularists somewhat apprehensive. I refer to the development of the idea that the religious faith is a part of the "American way of life." Foreign observers are baffled by this phenomenon in a nation which they regard as, in many respects, the most "secular" of all cultures and which certainly is, in the sense that it is more technocratic than any European culture, and reveals fewer evidences of religious influence upon its traditions. But we Americans have somehow combined good plumbing with religious faith in the "American way of life."

The Refutation of Secular Religions

But an analysis of the dubious and even dangerous manifestations of modern religiosity has not brought us closer to the real religious issue of our day, nor explained the real revival of interest in, if not adherence to, the historic Christian and Jewish faiths. One index of that genuine revival is the increased interest in religious courses in our colleges and universities and the increased sympathy for religious faith among "intellectuals." The fact is that the religious faith which was regarded as completely outmoded in the days when those of us who are not old were in college, has become a live option, not only for the "simple and the credulous" but for the sophisticated. How can we explain that startling change?

Perhaps one inclusive answer can be given: the secular alternatives to the historic faiths have been refuted by history. These secular alternatives were also "religions" in the sense that they answered the question about the meaning of human existence. They answered the question in terms of simple rational intelligibility rather than in terms of that paradoxical combination of mystery and meaning which characterizes the Biblical faiths. These Biblical faiths believe in a God who can not be quite comprehended, in the "mystery" of creation, and in the mystery of redemption and revelation. In the Christian faith, the crux of the revelation of the divine mystery is asserted to ban historical drama in which the relation between the divine justice and mercy is revealed in such a way that those who confront the divine through this revelation are at once convicted of their sin and forgiven so that they can walk in the "newness of life."

. . . Will Herberg is probably right in asserting that the chief cause of the growth of the religious communities is the desire of "belonging" which men feel, particularly in the anonymity of our urban centers.

. . . The revival of religious faith today, despite the traditional and modern corruptions of religious faith proves that the enigmas of history, of man's freedom and responsibility and of his guilt, can not be solved as easily as modern culture assumed. The human being develops grace and wisdom by discerning the meaning of existence in a realm of mystery, and meaning by a commitment of faith. He is conscious of a responsible freedom which is not easily explained in any system of coherence elaborated by either the philosophies or the sciences; and he knows himself to be guilty, ultimately considered, and therefore in need of forgiveness. This mystery and meaning of freedom, sin, and grace are the perennial sources of the religious life. They have expressed themselves anew against the prejudices of a secular age.

It must, however, be recognized that the only religious faith which can be the source of charity and wisdom is one which knows the religious life itself to be as ambiguous as all human life is. The worship of God is claimed too simply as the ally of our cause against the foe.

This recognition of the ambiguity in the religious life itself must include an appreciation of the contributions which secular protests against religion have made and are making to the purification of religion; and of the necessity of all forms of rational discipline for the guidance of man in the moral and social complexities of our common life. This appreciation does not, however, invalidate the witness of a genuine religion against secular aberrations which deny the dignity of man and subordinate him to a social or political process, or which make the worship of reason the basis of a new fanatic unreasonableness, as grievous as the old religious fanaticism.

REVIEW QUESTIONS

1. Which indicators of religious revival were most reliable to Niebuhr?
2. What were some of the fundamental issues that religious life had to address?
3. Why does Niebuhr describe religious life as ambiguous?

JOHN FOSTER DULLES

Massive Retaliation (1954)

John Foster Dulles (1888–1959) was a prominent Wall Street lawyer before becoming secretary of state in 1953. He sharply criticized former president Truman's containment policy for being too complacent. Dulles viewed the conflict with the Soviet Union as a stark contrast between good and evil. He was convinced that the Soviets were intent on dominating the world and that the United States was the epitome of democratic idealism. He wanted the United States not simply to contain the spread of communism but to defeat it. In practice, however, he sought to meet the Soviet threat without bankrupting the nation's economy or overtaxing its military resources. This led him to the concept of "massive retaliation," which he articulated in this 1954 address.

From *Department of State Bulletin* 30 (January 25, 1954): 107–10.

The Soviet Communists are planning for what they call "an entire historical era," and we should do the same. They seek, through many types of maneuvers, gradually to divide and weaken the free nations by overextending them in efforts which, as Lenin put it, are "beyond their strength, so that they come to practical bankruptcy." Then, said Lenin, "our victory is assured." Then, said Stalin, will be "the moment for the decisive blow."

In the face of this strategy, measures cannot be judged adequate merely because they ward off an immediate danger. It is essential to do this, but it is also essential to do so without exhausting ourselves.

When the Eisenhower administration applied this test, we felt that some transformations were needed. It is not sound military strategy permanently to commit U.S. land forces to Asia to a degree that leaves us no strategic reserves. It is not sound economics, or good foreign policy, to support permanently other countries; for in the long run, that creates as much ill will as good will. Also, it is not sound to become permanently committed to military expenditures so vast they lead to "practical bankruptcy."

Change was imperative to assure the stamina needed for permanent security. But it was equally imperative that change should be accompanied by understanding of our true purposes. Sudden and spectacular change had to be avoided. Otherwise, there might have been a panic among our friends and miscalculated aggression by our enemies. We can, I believe, make a good report in these respects.

We need allies and collective security. Our purpose is to make these relations more effective, less costly. This can be done by placing more reliance on deterrent power and less dependence on local defensive power.

This is accepted practice so far as local communities are concerned. We keep locks on our doors, but we do not have an armed guard in every home. We rely principally on a community security system so well equipped to punish any who break in and steal that, in fact, would-be aggressors are generally deterred. That is the modern way of getting maximum protection at a bearable cost.

What the Eisenhower administration seeks is a similar international security system. We want, for ourselves and the other free nations, a maximum deterrent at a bearable cost. Local defense will always be important. But there is no local defense which alone will contain the mighty land power of the Communist world. Local defenses must be reinforced by the further deterrent of massive retaliatory power. A potential aggressor must know that he cannot always prescribe battle conditions that suit him. Otherwise, for example, a potential aggressor, who is glutted with manpower, might be tempted to attack in confidence that resistance would be confined to manpower. He might be tempted to attack in places where his superiority was decisive.

The way to deter aggression is for the free community to be willing and able to respond vigorously at places and with means of its own choosing.

So long as our basic policy concepts were unclear, our military leaders could not be selective in building our military power. If an enemy could pick his time and place and method of warfare—and if our

policy was to remain the traditional one of meeting aggression by direct and local opposition—then we needed to be ready to fight in the Arctic and in the Tropics; in Asia, the Near East, and in Europe; by sea, by land, and by air; with old weapons and with new weapons. . . .

Before military planning could be changed, the President and his advisers, as represented by the National Security Council, had to make some basic policy decisions. This has been done. The basic decision was to depend primarily upon a great capacity to retaliate, instantly, by means and at places of our choosing. Now the Department of Defense and the Joint Chiefs of Staff can shape our military establishment to fit what is our policy, instead of having to try to be ready to meet the enemy's many choices. That permits of a selection of military means instead of a multiplication of means. As a result, it is now possible to get, and share, more basic security at less cost.

Let us now see how this concept has been applied to foreign policy, taking first the Far East.

In Korea this administration effected a major transformation. The fighting has been stopped on honorable terms. That was possible because the aggressor, already thrown back to and behind his place of beginning, was faced with the possibility that the fighting might, to his own great peril, soon spread beyond the limits and methods which he had selected.

The cruel toll of American youth and the non-productive expenditure of many billions have been stopped. Also our armed forces are no longer largely committed to the Asian mainland. We can begin to create a strategic reserve which greatly improves our defensive posture.

This change gives added authority to the warning of the members of the United Nations which fought in Korea that, if the Communists renewed the aggression, the United Nations response would not necessarily be confined to Korea. . . .

In the ways I outlined we gather strength for the longterm defense of freedom. We do not, of course, claim to have found some magic formula that insures against all forms of Communist successes. It is normal that at some times and at some places there may be setbacks to the cause of freedom. What we do expect to insure is that any setbacks will have only temporary and local significance, because they will leave unimpaired those free world assets which in the long run will prevail.

If we can deter such aggression as would mean general war, and that is our confident resolve, then we can let time and fundamentals work for us. . . .

REVIEW QUESTIONS

1. What is the essential reasoning behind Dulles's policy of deterrence?
2. Assess the strengths and weaknesses of using the threat of atomic weapons as the basis of a "massive retaliation" strategy.

FROM The Eisenhower Doctrine (1957)

During the 1950s most of the newly independent nations in Africa and Asia refused to choose sides between the Soviet Union and the United States, preferring instead to remain neutral ("nonaligned"). In the view of Dulles and other policymakers, however, there could be no neutrality amid such an ideological conflict. Dulles often referred to such nonaligned status as "immoral." Concerns over the vulnerability of nonaligned nations in the Middle East to communist subversion led Eisenhower and Congress to articulate a rationale for American intervention.

From *United States Statutes at Large*, 71:5–6.

Resolved, That the President be and hereby is authorized to cooperate with and assist any nation or group of nations in the general area of the Middle East desiring such assistance in the development of economic strength dedicated to the maintenance of national independence.

SEC. 2. The President is authorized to undertake, in the general area of the Middle East, military assistance programs with any nation or group of nations of that area desiring such assistance. Furthermore, the United States regards as vital to the national interest and world peace the preservation of the independence and integrity of the nations of the Middle East. To this end, if the President determines the necessity thereof, the United States is prepared to use armed force to assist any such nation or group of nations requesting assistance against armed aggression from any country controlled by international communism: *Provided*,

That such employment shall be consonant with the treaty obligations of the United States and with the Constitution of the United States.

SEC. 3. The President is hereby authorized to use during the balance of the fiscal year 1957 for economic and military assistance under this joint resolution not to exceed $200,000,000 from any appropriation now available for carrying out the provisions of the Mutual Security Act of 1954. . . .

SEC. 4. The President should continue to furnish facilities and military assistance, within the provisions of applicable law and established policies, to the United Nations Emergency Force in the Middle East, with a view to maintaining the truce in that region.

SEC. 5. The President shall within the months of January and July of each year report to the Congress his action hereunder.

SEC. 6. This joint resolution shall expire when the President shall determine that the peace and security of the nations in the general area of the Middle East are reasonably assured by international conditions created by action of the United Nations or otherwise except that it may be terminated earlier by a concurrent resolution of the two Houses of Congress.

REVIEW QUESTIONS

1. Did the Eisenhower Doctrine place any limits on American assistance?
2. Did the resolution define "peace and security"?
3. The resolution focused on external threats posed by countries controlled by communism. What did this imply about the way policymakers viewed the spread of communism?

FROM *Brown v. Board of Education of Topeka* (1954)

After trying for almost a half century, the National Association for the Advancement of Colored People (NAACP) finally succeeded in getting the Supreme Court to review the "separate but equal" principle articulated in the Plessy v. Ferguson *case of 1896. In the mid-1950s the vast majority of public schools, especially in the South, were racially separate but far from equal in resources or facilities. In the* Brown *case, however, the Court did not stress this fact; instead it advanced a different line of reasoning that ultimately invalidated racially based school segregation. While the decision did not transform school systems overnight, the unanimous Court provided the foundation for great advances over the next ten years.*

From *Supreme Court Reporter* (St. Paul, MN: West Publishing, 1954), 74:687–92. [Editorial insertions appear in square brackets—*Ed.*]

CHIEF JUSTICE WARREN: These cases come to us from the states of Kansas, South Carolina, Virginia, and Delaware. They are premised on different facts and different local conditions, but a common legal question justifies their consideration together in this consolidated opinion.

In each of the cases, minors of the Negro race, through their legal representatives, seek the aid of the courts in obtaining admission to the public schools of their community on a nonsegregated basis. In each instance, they have been denied admission to schools attended by white children under laws requiring or permitting segregation according to race. This segregation was alleged to deprive the plaintiffs of the equal protection of the laws under the Fourteenth Amendment. In each of the cases other than the Delaware case, a three-judge federal district court denied relief to the plaintiffs on the so-called "separate but equal" doctrine announced by this Court in *Plessy v. Ferguson* (1896).

Under that doctrine, equality of treatment is accorded when the races are provided substantially equal facilities, even though these facilities be separate.... The plaintiffs contend that segregated public schools are not "equal" and cannot be made "equal," and that hence they are deprived of the equal protection of the laws. Because of the obvious importance of the question presented, the Court took jurisdiction. . . .

Reargument was largely devoted to the circumstances surrounding the adoption of the Fourteenth Amendment in 1868. It covered exhaustively consideration of the Amendment in Congress, ratification by the states, then existing practices in racial segregation, and the views of proponents and opponents of the Amendment.

This discussion and our own investigation convince us that, although these sources cast some light, it is not enough to resolve the problem with which we are faced. At best, they are inconclusive. The most avid proponents of the post-[Civil] War Amendments undoubtedly intended them to remove all legal distinctions among "all persons born or naturalized in the United States." Their opponents, just as certainly, were antagonistic to both the letter and the spirit of the Amendments and wished them to have the most limited effect. What others in Congress and the state legislatures had in mind cannot be determined with any degree of certainty.

An additional reason for the inconclusive nature of the Amendment's history, with respect to segregated schools, is the status of public education at that time. In the South, the movement toward free common schools, supported by general taxation, had not yet taken hold. Education of white children was largely in the hands of private groups. Education of Negroes was almost nonexistent, and practically all of the race were illiterate. In fact, any education of Negroes was forbidden by law in some states.

Today, in contrast, many Negroes have achieved outstanding success in the arts and sciences as well as in the business and professional world. It is true that public education had already advanced further in the North, but the effect of the amendment on Northern States was generally ignored in the congressional debates. Even in the North, the conditions of public education did not approximate those existing today. The curriculum was usually rudimentary; ungraded schools were common in rural areas; the school term was but three months a year

in many states; and compulsory school attendance was virtually unknown. As a consequence, it is not surprising that there should be so little in the history of the Fourteenth Amendment relating to its intended effect on public education.

In the first cases in this Court construing the Fourteenth Amendment, decided shortly after its adoption, the Court interpreted it as proscribing all state-imposed discriminations against the Negro race. The doctrine of "separate but equal" did not make its appearance in this Court until 1896 in the case of *Plessy v. Ferguson*, involving not education but transportation. . . .

In approaching this problem, we cannot turn the clock back to 1868 when the Amendment was adopted, or even to 1896 when *Plessy v. Ferguson* was written. We must consider public education in the light of its full development and its present place in American life throughout the Nation. Only in this way can it be determined if segregation in public schools deprives these plaintiffs of the equal protection of the laws.

Today, education is perhaps the most important function of state and local governments. Compulsory school attendance laws and the great expenditures for education both demonstrate our recognition of the importance of education to our democratic society. It is required in the performance of our most basic public responsibilities, even service in the armed forces. It is the very foundation of good citizenship. Today it is a principal instrument in awakening the child to cultural values, in preparing him for later professional training, and in helping him to adjust normally to his environment.

In these days, it is doubtful that any child may reasonably be expected to succeed in life if he is denied the opportunity of an education. Such an opportunity, where the state has undertaken to provide it, is a right which must be made available to all on equal terms.

We come then to the question presented: Does segregation of children in public schools solely on the basis of race, even though the physical facilities and other "tangible" factors may be equal, deprive the children of the minority group of equal educational opportunities? We believe that it does.

In *Sweatt v. Painter*, in finding that a segregated law school for Negroes could not provide them equal educational opportunities, this Court relied in large part on "those qualities which are incapable of objective measurement but which make for greatness in a law school." In *McLaurin v. Oklahoma State Regents*, the Court, in requiring that a Negro admitted to a white graduate school be treated like all other students, again resorted to intangible considerations: ". . . his ability to study, to engage in discussions and exchange views with other students, and, in general, to learn his profession."

Such considerations apply with added force to children in grade and high schools. To separate them from others of similar age and qualifications solely because of their race generates a feeling of inferiority as to their status in the community that may affect their hearts and minds in a way unlikely ever to be undone. The effect of this separation on their educational opportunities was well stated by a finding in the Kansas case by a court which nevertheless felt compelled to rule against the Negro plaintiffs:

"Segregation of white and colored children in public schools has a detrimental effect upon the colored children. The impact is greater when it has the sanction of the law; for the policy of separating the races is usually interpreted as denoting the inferiority of the Negro group. A sense of inferiority affects the motivation of a child to learn. Segregation with the sanction of law, therefore, has a tendency to retard the educational and mental development of Negro children and to deprive them of some of the benefits they would receive in a racially integrated school system."

Whatever may have been the extent of psychological knowledge at the time of *Plessy v. Ferguson*, this finding is amply supported by modern authority. Any language in *Plessy v. Ferguson* contrary to this finding is rejected.

We conclude that in the field of public education the doctrine of "separate but equal" has no place. Separate educational facilities are inherently unequal. Therefore, we hold that the plaintiffs and others similarly situated for whom the actions have been brought are, by reason of the segregation complained of, deprived of the equal protection of the laws guaranteed by the Fourteenth Amendment. . . .

REVIEW QUESTIONS

1. In reaching its decision, did the Court rely on the original intentions of the congressional framers of the Fourteenth Amendment? Why or why not?
2. According to the Court, were racially separate schools permissible as long as they were equal in quality and resources? Why or why not?

FROM Southern Declaration on Integration (1956)

The Brown *decision provoked violent opposition in the South. Hastily formed White Citizens' Councils used economic pressure to coerce political leaders into opposing Court-ordered integration. State legislatures vowed to resist federal efforts to intervene in their schools, and some revived the rhetoric of nullification and secession. In 1956, 96 of the 128 southern senators and representatives in Congress signed a so-called Southern Manifesto castigating the Supreme Court's reasoning in the* Brown *case.*

From "Text of 96 Congressmen's Declaration on Integration." *New York Times*, March 12, 1956. [Editorial insertions appear in square brackets—*Ed.*]

... We regard the decision of the Supreme Court in the school cases as clear abuse of judicial power. It climaxes a trend in the Federal judiciary undertaking to legislate, in derogation of the authority of Congress, and to encroach upon the reserved rights of the states and the people.

The original Constitution does not mention education. Neither does the Fourteenth Amendment nor any other amendment. The debates preceding the submission of the Fourteenth Amendment clearly show that there was no intent that it should affect the systems of education maintained by the states. . . .

When the amendment was adopted in 1868, there were thirty-seven states of the Union. Every one of the twenty-six states that had any substantial racial differences among its people either approved the operation of segregated schools already in existence or subsequently established such schools by action of the same law-making body which considered the Fourteenth Amendment.

As admitted by the Supreme Court in the public school case (*Brown v. Board of Education*), the doctrine of separate but equal schools "apparently originated in *Roberts v. City of Boston* (1849), upholding school segregation against attack as being violative of a state constitutional guarantee of equality." This constitutional doctrine began in the North—not in the South—and it was followed not only in Massachusetts, but in Connecticut, New York, Illinois, Indiana, Michigan, Minnesota, New Jersey, Ohio, Pennsylvania and other northern states until they, exercising their rights as states through the constitutional processes of local self-government, changed their school systems.

In the case of *Plessy v. Ferguson* in 1896 the Supreme Court expressly declared that under the Fourteenth Amendment no person was denied any of his rights if the states provided separate but equal public facilities. This decision has been followed in many other cases. It is notable that the Supreme Court, speaking through Chief Justice [William H.] Taft, a former President of the United States, unanimously declared in 1927 in *Lum v. Rice* that the "separate but equal" principle is ". . . within the discretion of the state in regulating

its public schools and does not conflict with the Fourteenth Amendment."

This interpretation, restated time and again, became a part of the life of the people of many of the states and confirmed their habits, customs, traditions and way of life. It is founded on elemental humanity and common sense, for parents should not be deprived by Government of the right to direct the lives and education of their own children.

Though there has been no constitutional amendment or act of Congress changing this established legal principle almost a century old, the Supreme Court of the United States, with no legal basis for such action, undertook to exercise their naked judicial power and substituted their personal political and social ideas for the established law of the land.

This unwarranted exercise of power by the court, contrary to the Constitution, is creating chaos and confusion in the states principally affected. It is destroying the amicable relations between the white and Negro races that have been created through ninety years of patient effort by the good people of both races. It has planted hatred and suspicion where there has been heretofore friendship and understanding.

Without regard to the consent of the governed, outside agitators are threatening immediate and revolutionary changes in our public school systems. If done, this is certain to destroy the system of public education in some of the states.

With the gravest concern for the explosive and dangerous condition created by this decision and inflamed by outside meddlers:

We reaffirm our reliance on the Constitution as the fundamental law of the land.

We decry the Supreme Court's encroachments on rights reserved to the states and to the people, contrary to established law and to the Constitution.

We commend the motives of those states which have declared the intention to resist forced integration by any lawful means.

We appeal to the states and people who are not directly affected by these decisions to consider the constitutional principles involved against the time when they too, on issues vital to them, may be the victims of judicial encroachment.

Even though we constitute a minority in the present Congress, we have full faith that a majority of the American people believe in the dual system of government which has enabled us to achieve our greatness and will in time demand that the reserved rights of the states and of the people be made secure against judicial usurpation.

We pledge ourselves to use all lawful means to bring about a reversal of this decision which is contrary to the Constitution and to prevent the use of force in its implementation.

In this trying period, as we all seek to right this wrong, we appeal to our people not to be provoked by the agitators and troublemakers invading our states and to scrupulously refrain from disorder and lawless acts.

REVIEW QUESTIONS

1. According to the declaration, why did the Court rule as it did in the *Brown* case?
2. What were the implications of the charge that "outside agitators" were trying to force changes in southern public schools?

DWIGHT D. EISENHOWER

FROM The Situation in Little Rock (1957)

In the late summer of 1957 the school board of Little Rock, Arkansas, tried to implement the initial phase of its desegregation plan mandated by the federal government. Governor Orville Faubus, however, thwarted their efforts. Concerned that he would not be reelected if he allowed the racial integration of schools, he called out the National Guard to prevent the first African American students from attending Central High School. After a three-week stalemate, a federal judge ordered the guardsmen off the school grounds. As the soldiers departed, they were replaced by an enraged white mob. The mayor appealed to President Eisenhower, who dispatched units of the 101st Airborne Division to disperse the mob, restore order, and protect the black students. Eisenhower was a reluctant participant in the Little Rock crisis, and he took pains to explain his actions.

From *Public Papers of the Presidents of the United States: Dwight D. Eisenhower, 1957*, no. 198 (Washington, DC, 1958), pp. 689–94.

My Fellow Citizens. . . . I must speak to you about the serious situation that has arisen in Little Rock. . . . In that city, under the leadership of demagogic extremists, disorderly mobs have deliberately prevented the carrying out of proper orders from a federal court. Local authorities have not eliminated that violent opposition and, under the law, I yesterday issued a proclamation calling upon the mob to disperse.

This morning the mob again gathered in front of the Central High School of Little Rock, obviously for the purpose of again preventing the carrying out of the court's order relating to the admission of Negro children to that school.

Whenever normal agencies prove inadequate to the task and it becomes necessary for the executive branch of the federal government to use its powers and authority to uphold federal courts, the President's responsibility is inescapable.

In accordance with that responsibility, I have today issued an Executive Order directing the use of troops under federal authority to aid in the execution of federal law at Little Rock, Arkansas. This became necessary when my Proclamation of yesterday was not observed, and the obstruction of justice still continues. It is important that the reasons for my action be understood by all our citizens.

As you know, the Supreme Court of the United States has decided that separate public educational facilities for the races are inherently unequal and therefore compulsory school segregation laws are unconstitutional. . . .

During the past several years, many communities in our southern states have instituted public school plans for gradual progress in the enrollment and attendance of school children of all races in order to bring themselves into compliance with the law of the land.

They thus demonstrated to the world that we are a nation in which laws, not men, are supreme. I regret to say that this truth—the cornerstone of our liberties—was not observed in this instance. . . .

Here is the sequence of events in the development of the Little Rock school case. In May of 1955, the Little Rock School Board approved a moderate plan for the gradual desegregation of the public schools in that city. It provided that a start toward integration would be made at the present term in the high school, and that the plan would be in full operation by 1963. . . . Now this Little Rock plan was challenged in the courts by some who believed that the period of time as proposed in the plan was too long.

The United States Court at Little Rock, which has supervisory responsibility under the law for the plan of desegregation in the public schools, dismissed the challenge, thus approving a gradual

rather than an abrupt change from the existing system. The court found that the school board had acted in good faith in planning for a public school system free from racial discrimination.

Since that time, the court has on three separate occasions issued orders directing that the plan be carried out. All persons were instructed to refrain from interfering with the efforts of the school board to comply with the law.

Proper and sensible observance of the law then demanded the respectful obedience which the nation has a right to expect from all its people. This, unfortunately, has not been the case at Little Rock. Certain misguided persons, many of them imported into Little Rock by agitators, have insisted upon defying the law and have sought to bring it into disrepute. The orders of the court have thus been frustrated.

The very basis of our individual rights and freedoms rests upon the certainty that the President and the Executive Branch of Government will support and insure the carrying out of the decisions of the federal courts, even, when necessary, with all the means at the President's command. . . .

Mob rule cannot be allowed to override the decisions of our courts.

Now, let me make it very clear that federal troops are not being used to relieve local and state authorities of their primary duty to preserve the peace and order of the community. . . .

The proper use of the powers of the Executive Branch to enforce the orders of a federal court is limited to extraordinary and compelling circumstances. Manifestly, such an extreme situation has been created in Little Rock. This challenge must be met and with such measures as will preserve to the people as a whole their lawfully protected rights in a climate permitting their free and fair exercise.

The overwhelming majority of our people in every section of the country are united in their respect for observance of the law—even in those cases where they may disagree with that law. . . . A foundation of our American way of life is our national respect for law.

In the South, as elsewhere, citizens are keenly aware of the tremendous disservice that has been done to the people of Arkansas in the eyes of the nation, and that has been done to the nation in the eyes of the world.

At a time when we face grave situations abroad because of the hatred that communism bears toward a system of government based on human rights, it would be difficult to exaggerate the harm that is being done to the prestige and influence, and indeed to the safety, of our nation and the world.

Our enemies are gloating over this incident and using it everywhere to misrepresent our whole nation. We are portrayed as a violator of those standards of conduct which the peoples of the world united to proclaim in the Charter of the United Nations. There they affirmed "faith in fundamental human rights" and "in the dignity and worth of the human person" and they did so "without distinction as to race, sex, language or religion." And so, with deep confidence, I call upon the citizens of the State of Arkansas to assist in bringing to an immediate end all interference with the law and its processes. If resistance to the federal court orders ceases at once, the further presence of federal troops will be unnecessary and the City of Little Rock will return to its normal habits of peace and order and a blot upon the fair name and high honor of our nation in the world will be removed.

Thus will be restored the image of America and of all its parts as one nation, indivisible, with liberty and justice for all.

REVIEW QUESTIONS

1. Under what conditions did Eisenhower believe that intervention by the executive branch was justified?
2. How might the Soviet Union have exploited the controversy in Little Rock?
3. How would a proponent of segregation have rebutted Eisenhower's stance?

DWIGHT D. EISENHOWER

FROM Farewell Address (1961)

After serving two full terms as president, Dwight D. Eisenhower retired from public life in 1961. Before turning the White House over to his Democratic successor, John F. Kennedy, he delivered a farewell address in which he expressed his hopes and fears for the nation and presented his personal disappointments and accomplishments. His speech turned out to be more prophetic than commentators at the time recognized.

From *Public Papers of the Presidents of the United States: Dwight D. Eisenhower, 1960–1*, no. 421 (Washington, DC, 1961), pp. 1035–40.

My Fellow Americans:

Three days from now, after half a century in the service of our country, I shall lay down the responsibilities of office as, in traditional and solemn ceremony, the authority of the Presidency is vested in my successor. . . .

We now stand ten years past the midpoint of a century that has witnessed four major wars among great nations. Three of them involved our own country. Despite these holocausts America is today the strongest, the most influential and most productive nation in the world. Understandably proud of this preeminence we yet realize that America's leadership and prestige depend, not merely upon our unmatched material progress, riches and military strength, but on how we use our power in the interests of world peace and human betterment.

Throughout America's adventure in free government, our basic purposes have been to keep the peace; to foster progress in human achievement, and to enhance liberty, dignity and integrity among people and among nations. To strive for less would be unworthy of a free and religious people. Any failure traceable to arrogance, or our lack of comprehension or readiness to sacrifice would inflict upon us grievous hurt both at home and abroad.

Progress toward these noble goals is persistently threatened by the conflict now engulfing the world. It commands our whole attention, absorbs our very beings. We face a hostile ideology—global in scope, atheistic in character, ruthless in purpose, and insidious in method. Unhappily the danger it poses promises to be of indefinite duration. To meet it successfully, there is called for, not so much the emotional and transitory sacrifices of crisis, but rather those which enable us to carry forward steadily, surely, and without complaint the burdens of a prolonged and complex struggle—with liberty the stake. Only thus shall we remain, despite every provocation, on our charted course toward permanent peace and human betterment. . . .

A vital element in keeping the peace is our military establishment. Our arms must be mighty, ready for instant action, so that no potential aggressor may be tempted to risk his own destruction.

Our military organization today bears little relation to that known by any of my predecessors in peacetime, or indeed by the fighting men of World War II or Korea. Until the latest of our world conflicts, the United States had no armaments industry. American makers of plowshares could, with time and as required, make swords as well. But now we can no longer risk emergency improvisation of national defense; we have been compelled to create a permanent armaments industry of vast proportions. Added to this, three and a half million men and women are directly engaged in the defense establishment. We annually spend on military security more than the net income of all United States corporations.

This conjunction of an immense military establishment and a large arms industry is new in the American experience. The total influence—economic, political, even spiritual—is felt in every city, every state house, every office of the federal government. We recognize the imperative need for this development. Yet we must not fail to comprehend its grave implications. Our toil, resources, and livelihood are all involved; so is the very structure of our society.

In the councils of government, we must guard against the acquisition of unwarranted influence, whether sought or unsought, by the military-industrial complex. The potential for the disastrous rise of misplaced power exists and will persist. We must never let the weight of this combination endanger our liberties or democratic processes. We should take nothing for granted. Only an alert and knowledgeable citizenry can compel the proper meshing of the huge industrial and military machinery of defense with our peaceful methods and goals, so that security and liberty may prosper together.

Akin to, and largely responsible for the sweeping changes in our industrial-military posture, has been the technological revolution during recent decades.

In this revolution, research has become central; it also becomes more formalized, complex, and costly. A steadily increasing share is conducted for, by, or at the direction of, the federal government. . . .

The prospect of domination of the nation's scholars by federal employment, project allocations, and the power of money is ever present—and is gravely to be regarded.

Yet, in holding scientific research and discovery in respect, as we should, we must also be alert to the equal and opposite danger that public policy could itself become the captive of a scientific-technological elite.

It is the task of statesmanship to mold, to balance, and to integrate these and other forces, new and old, within the principles of our democratic system—ever aiming toward the supreme goals of our free society.

Another factor in maintaining balance involves the element of time. As we peer into society's future, we—you and I, and our government—must avoid the impulse to live only for today, plundering, for our own ease and convenience, the precious resources of tomorrow. We cannot mortgage the material assets of our grandchildren without risking the loss also of their political and spiritual heritage. We want democracy to survive for all generations to come, not to become the insolvent phantom of tomorrow. Down the long lane of the history yet to be written America knows that this world of ours, ever growing smaller, must avoid becoming a community of dreadful fear and hate, and be, instead, a proud confederation of mutual trust and respect.

Such a confederation must be one of equals. The weakest must come to the conference table with the same confidence as do we, protected as we are by our moral, economic, and military strength. That table, though scarred by many past frustrations, cannot be abandoned for the certain agony of the battlefield. Disarmament, with mutual honor and confidence, is a continuing imperative. Together we must learn how to compose differences, not with arms, but with intellect and decent purpose.

Because this need is so sharp and apparent I confess that I lay down my official responsibilities in this field with a definite sense of disappointment. As one who has witnessed the horror and the lingering sadness of war—as one who knows that another war could utterly destroy this civilization which has been so slowly and painfully built over thousands of years—I wish I could say tonight that a lasting peace is in sight.

Happily, I can say that war has been avoided. Steady progress toward our ultimate goal has been made. But, so much remains to be done. As a private citizen, I shall never cease to do what little I can to help the world advance along that road. . . .

REVIEW QUESTIONS

1. How did Eisenhower characterize the Soviet Union?
2. Given Eisenhower's description of communism, does his call for disarmament seem contradictory? Why or why not?
3. In light of the international environment during the 1950s, was Eisenhower's ability to keep the nation out of war a major or minor accomplishment? Explain.

29 ❧ A NEW FRONTIER AND A GREAT SOCIETY, 1960–1968

The election of John F. Kennedy as president in 1960 ushered in a decade of ener-getic idealism that bore fruit in the founding of the Peace Corps, the War on Pov-erty, and Great Society programs of federal assistance to the poor. The 1960s also witnessed a dramatic new phase of the civil rights movement. Kennedy was one of the first political leaders to recognize the vast number of Americans not only mired in poverty but also hidden from public awareness. And, even though Ken-nedy himself was reluctant to assault racial injustice in the segregated South because of the political clout of southern Democrats, events eventually forced him and his successor, Lyndon B. Johnson, to make civil rights a primary concern.

During the 1950s Dr. Martin Luther King Jr., an ordained black minister, emerged as the heroic, charismatic leader of the national civil rights movement. He fastened upon a brilliant strategy—nonviolent civil disobedience—to gain the attention and sympathy of a complacent nation. Through boycotts, marches, sit-ins, and other forms of protest, King and the Southern Christian Leadership Conference (SCLC), which he founded, forced authorities to confront the injus-tices of racism. His passionate commitment and uplifting rhetoric helped excite national concern, and his efforts led directly to major new legislation such as the Civil Rights Act of 1964, which prohibited racial discrimination in employment and public facilities, and the Voting Rights Act of 1965, which outlawed literacy tests and other measures used by local registrars to deny blacks access to the bal-lot. In 1964 King was awarded the Nobel Peace Prize for his efforts.

Yet as time passed the civil rights movement began to fragment. The legal and political gains did not translate into immediate economic and social advances. Black neighborhoods continued to be plagued by crime and drug addiction, fatherless households, and intense frustration and alienation. On August 11, 1965, only five days after the passage of the Voting Rights Act, Watts, a black neighborhood in Los Angeles, erupted in a chaos of looting, arson, and violence. During the next three years, 300 more race riots occurred in inner-city communities across the nation. Over 200 people were killed, 7,000 injured, and 40,000 arrested. For many urban blacks outside the South, the mainstream civil rights movement had brought little tangible improvement in their lives. Most African Americans lived not in the rural South but in major cities such as New York, Philadelphia, Detroit, Newark, Chicago, and Los Angeles. Blacks living in urban ghettos faced chronic poverty, unemployment, decaying housing and schools, and police brutality.

Young black activists outside the South grew impatient with Dr. King's leadership and his commitment to integration within the larger white society. Black militants such as Stokely Carmichael and H. Rap Brown rejected the nonviolent civil disobedience promoted by King and the SCLC. For them, "Black Power" became the rallying cry in the mid-1960s.

The concept of Black Power grew out of the tradition of black nationalism— the belief that people with African roots share a distinctive culture and destiny. It fed on the seething discontent with the pace of social change within the black ghettos of urban America. Malcolm X was the most compelling proponent of black nationalism. A convert to the Black Muslim (the Nation of Islam) faith led by Elijah Muhammad, he urged African Americans to take control of their communities "by any means necessary," including violence. Unlike King and the other leaders of SCLC, Malcolm X was not interested in promoting integration. "Our enemy is the white man," he exclaimed. His goal was a separate, self-reliant black community within the United States. Yet during late 1964 Malcolm X began to moderate his stance. He broke with the Black Muslims and began to talk of racial cooperation. His defection cost him his life. On February 21, 1965, Malcolm X was shot and killed by three Black Muslim assassins.

The militance displayed by Malcolm X survived among the younger proponents of Black Power. During the summer of 1966 Stokely Carmichael led the Student Nonviolent Coordinating Committee (SNCC) away from its original commitment to peaceful social change. His successor, H. Rap Brown, told the members of SNCC to grab their guns, burn the cities, and shoot the "honky to death." A group of young black militants in California led by Huey Newton and Bobby Seale shared these strong feelings and organized the Black Panther Party to engage in guerrilla violence against white authorities.

During each summer between 1965 and 1968, urban America was aflame with racial rioting. In 1967, for example, eighty-seven people were killed and over 16,000 arrested. The violence prompted President Johnson in 1967 to appoint a special National Advisory Commission on Civil Disorders headed by Governor Otto Kerner of Illinois to determine the causes of the racial turmoil. The Kerner Commission Report appeared in 1968. It called for a "compassionate, massive and sustained" commitment to racial equality and social justice "backed by the resources of the most powerful and richest nation on this earth." Unfortunately, only a month after the report appeared, Martin Luther King Jr. was assassinated in Memphis. His tragic death sparked another outbreak of racial rioting across the country.

By the end of the 1960s the quest for racial equality had become interwoven with other powerful social currents, including the anti-war protests and the feminist movement. The combined energies of these and other crusades, coupled with the conservative backlash they provoked, threatened to unravel American society by the end of the 1960s.

JOHN F. KENNEDY

Inaugural Address (1961)

John Fitzgerald Kennedy (1917–1963) was the youngest president ever elected, and he self-consciously sought to inspire young adults to get more involved in politics and social reform. Born into a wealthy Catholic Massachusetts family, a graduate of Harvard University and a World War II naval hero, he served in the Senate before gaining the Democratic nomination in 1960. He and his advisers viewed his victory over Republican vice president Richard Nixon as a mandate for change and an activist presidency. His inauguration occurred on a bitterly cold day, but Kennedy's uplifting rhetoric caught the attention and imagination of the huge crowd.

From *Public Papers of the Presidents of the United States: John F. Kennedy, 1961*, no. 1 (Washington, DC, 1962), pp. 1–3.

We observe today not a victory of party but a celebration of freedom—symbolizing an end as well as a beginning—signifying renewal as well as change. For I have sworn before you and Almighty God the same solemn oath our forebears prescribed nearly a century and three-quarters ago.

The world is very different now. For man holds in his mortal hands the power to abolish all forms of human poverty and all forms of human life. And yet the same revolutionary beliefs for which our forebears fought are still at issue around the globe—the belief that the rights of man come not from the generosity of the state but from the hand of God.

We dare not forget today that we are the heirs of that first revolution. Let the word go forth from this time and place, to friend and foe alike, that the torch has been passed to a new generation of Americans—born in this century, tempered by war, disciplined by a hard and bitter peace, proud of our ancient heritage—and unwilling to witness or permit the slow undoing of those human rights to which this nation has always been committed, and to which we are committed today at home and around the world.

Let every nation know, whether it wishes us well or ill, that we shall pay any price, bear any burden, meet any hardship, support any friend, oppose any foe to assure the survival and the success of liberty.

This much we pledge—and more.

To those old allies whose cultural and spiritual origins we share, we pledge the loyalty of faithful friends. United, there is little we cannot do in a host of cooperative ventures. Divided, there is little we can do—for we dare not meet a powerful challenge at odds and split asunder.

To those new states whom we welcome to the ranks of the free, we pledge our word that one form of colonial control shall not have passed away merely to be replaced by a far more iron tyranny. We shall not always expect to find them supporting our view. But we shall always hope to find them strongly supporting their own freedom—and to remember that, in the past, those who foolishly sought power by riding the back of the tiger ended up inside.

To those people in the huts and villages of half the globe struggling to break the bonds of mass misery, we pledge our best efforts to help them help themselves, for whatever period is required—not because the Communists may be doing it, not because we seek their votes, but because it is right. If a free society cannot help the many who are poor, it cannot save the few who are rich.

To our sister republics south of our border, we offer a special pledge—to convert our good words into good deeds—in a new alliance for progress—to assist free men and free governments in casting off the chains of poverty. But this peaceful revolution of hope cannot become the prey of hostile powers. Let all our neighbors know that we shall join with them to oppose aggression or subversion anywhere in the Americas. And let every other power know that this hemisphere intends to remain the master of its own house. . . .

In your hands, my fellow citizens, more than mine, will rest the final success or failure of our course. Since this country was founded, each generation of Americans has been summoned to give testimony to its national loyalty. The graves of young Americans who answered the call to service surround the globe.

Now the trumpet summons us again—not as a call to bear arms, though arms we need—not as a call to battle, though embattled we are—but a call to bear the burden of a long twilight struggle, year in and year out, "rejoicing in hope, patient in tribulation," a struggle against the common enemies of man: tyranny, poverty, disease, and war itself.

Can we forge against these enemies a grand and global alliance, North and South, East and West, that can assure a more fruitful life for all mankind? Will you join in that historic effort?

In the long history of the world, only a few generations have been granted the role of defending freedom in its hour of maximum danger. I do not shrink from this responsibility—I welcome it. I do not believe that any of us would exchange places with any other people or any other generation. The energy, the faith, the devotion which we bring to this endeavor will light our country and all who serve it—and the glow from that fire can truly light the world.

And so, my fellow Americans: ask not what your country can do for you—ask what you can do for your country.

My fellow citizens of the world: ask not what America will do for you, but what together we can do for the freedom of man. Finally, whether you are citizens of America or citizens of the world, ask of us here the same high standards of strength and sacrifice which we ask of you. With a good conscience our only sure reward, with history the final judge of our deeds, let us go forth to lead the land we love, asking His blessing and His help, but knowing that here on earth God's work must truly be our own.

REVIEW QUESTIONS

1. Kennedy asserted that America would "pay any price" to defend liberty. What kind of foreign policy commitments might this have entailed?
2. What did Kennedy identify as the "common enemies of man"? To defeat these enemies, would government power have to be expanded? Why?
3. Explain how the Soviet Union might have responded to this speech.

MICHAEL HARRINGTON

FROM *The Other America* (1962)

Throughout the 1950s public attention was focused on the amazing affluence generated by the American economy. Yet as social analyst Michael Harrington revealed in The Other America *(1962), 40 to 50 million Americans, some 20 percent of the total population, were in fact mired in poverty. This "underclass" was largely hidden from view. They included the elderly and the "unseen" residents of urban slums and rural hovels. President Kennedy read several reviews of Harrington's book and was so stunned by its revelations that he created a task force to design federal programs to address the nation's chronic pockets of poverty. Kennedy was assassinated before the programs could be implemented, but under Lyndon B. Johnson the government initiated a comprehensive—and ultimately ineffective—"war on poverty."*

There is a familiar America. It is celebrated in speeches and advertised on television and in the magazines. It has the highest mass standard of living the world has ever known.

In the 1950s this America worried about itself, yet even its anxieties were products of abundance. The title of a brilliant book was widely misinterpreted, and the familiar America began to call itself "the affluent society." There was introspection about Madison Avenue and tail fins; there was discussion of the emotional suffering taking place in the suburbs. In all this, there was an implicit assumption that the basic grinding economic problems had been solved in the United States. In this theory the nation's problems were no longer a matter of basic human needs, of food, shelter, and clothing. Now they were seen as qualitative, a question of learning to live decently amid luxury.

While this discussion was carried on, there existed another America. In it dwelt somewhere between 40,000,000 and 50,000,000 citizens of this land. They were poor. They still are.

To be sure, the other America is not impoverished in the same sense as those poor nations where millions cling to hunger as a defense against starvation. This country has escaped such extremes. That does not change the fact that tens of millions of Americans are, at this very moment, maimed in body and spirit, existing at levels beneath those necessary for human decency. If these people are not starving, they are hungry, and sometimes fat with hunger, for that is what cheap foods do. They are without adequate housing and education and medical care.

The Government has documented what this means to the bodies of the poor, and the figures will be cited throughout this book. But even more basic, this poverty twists and deforms the spirit. The American poor are pessimistic and defeated, and they are victimized by mental suffering to a degree unknown in Suburbia.

This book is a description of the world in which these people live; it is about the other America. Here are the unskilled workers, the migrant farm workers, the aged, the minorities, and all the others who live in the economic underworld of American life. . . . I would ask the reader to respond critically to every assertion, but not to allow statistical quibbling to obscure the huge, enormous, and intolerable fact of poverty in America. For, when all is said and done, that fact is unmistakable, whatever its exact dimensions, and the truly human reaction can only be outrage. . . .

The millions who are poor in the United States tend to become increasingly invisible. Here is a great mass of people, yet it takes an effort of the intellect and will even to see them. . . .

The other America, the America of poverty, is hidden today in a way that it never was before. Its millions are socially invisible to the rest of us. No wonder that so many misinterpreted Galbraith's[1] title and assumed that "the affluent society" meant

---

[1]Economist John Kenneth Galbraith (1908–2006).

that everyone had a decent standard of life. The misinterpretation was true as far as the actual day-to-day lives of two-thirds of the nation were concerned. Thus, one must begin a description of the other America by understanding why we do not see it.

There are perennial reasons that make the other America an invisible land. Poverty is often off the beaten track. It always has been. The ordinary tourist never left the main highway, and today he rides interstate turnpikes. He does not go into the valleys of Pennsylvania where the towns look like movie sets of Wales in the thirties. He does not see the company houses in rows, the rutted roads (the poor always have bad roads whether they live in the city, in towns, or on farms), and everything is black and dirty. And even if he were to pass through such a place by accident, the tourist would not meet the unemployed men in the bar or the women coming home from a runaway sweatshop. . . .

If the middle class never did like ugliness and poverty, it was at least aware of them. "Across the tracks" was not a very long way to go. There were forays into the slums at Christmas time; there were charitable organizations that brought contact with the poor. Occasionally, almost everyone passed through the Negro ghetto or the blocks of tenements, if only to get downtown to work or to entertainment.

Now the American city has been transformed. The poor still inhabit the miserable housing in the central area, but they are increasingly isolated from contact with, or sight of, anybody else. Middle-class women coming in from Suburbia on a rare trip may catch the merest glimpse of the other America on the way to an evening at the theater, but their children are segregated in suburban schools. The business or professional man may drive along the fringes of slums in a car or bus, but it is not an important experience to him. The failures, the unskilled, the disabled, the aged, and the minorities are right there, across the tracks, where they have always been. But hardly anyone else is.

In short, the very development of the American city has removed poverty from the living, emotional experience of millions upon millions of middle-class Americans. Living out in the suburbs, it is easy to assume that ours is, indeed, an affluent society.

This new segregation of poverty is compounded by a well-meaning ignorance. A good many concerned and sympathetic Americans are aware that there is much discussion of urban renewal. Suddenly, driving through the city, they notice that a familiar slum has been torn down and that there are towering, modern buildings where once there had been tenements or hovels. There is a warm feeling of satisfaction, of pride in the way things are working out: the poor, it is obvious, are being taken care of.

The irony in this . . . is that the truth is nearly the exact opposite to the impression. The total impact of the various housing programs in postwar America has been to squeeze more and more people into existing slums. More often than not, the modern apartment in a towering building rents at $40 a room or more. For, during the past decade and a half, there has been more subsidization of middle- and upper-income housing than there has been for the poor. . . .

And finally, the poor are politically invisible. It is one of the cruelest ironies of social life in advanced countries that the dispossessed at the bottom of society are unable to speak for themselves. The people of the other America do not, by far and large, belong to unions, to fraternal organizations, or to political parties. They are without lobbies of their own; they put forward no legislative program. As a group, they are atomized. They have no face; they have no voice.

Thus, there is not even a cynical political motive for caring about the poor, as in the old days. Because the slums are no longer centers of powerful political organizations, the politicians need not really care about their inhabitants. The slums are no longer visible to the middle class, so much of the idealistic urge to fight for those who need help is gone. Only the social agencies have a really direct involvement with the other America, and they are without any great political power. . . .

That the poor are invisible is one of the most important things about them. They are not simply neglected and forgotten as in the old rhetoric of reform; what is much worse, they are not seen.

REVIEW QUESTIONS

1. According to Harrington, America was commonly described as an "affluent society." What was implied by this phrase, and why did Harrington deny its validity?

2. Why were the poor so invisible to middle-class Americans?

3. Did the poor have political power? Why or why not?

MARTIN LUTHER KING JR.

FROM Letter from a Birmingham Jail (1963)

During the 1960 presidential campaign John F. Kennedy had promised to provide "moral leadership" to improve race relations in the United States. Once in office, however, he moved cautiously, fearful of alienating the powerful coalition of conservative southern Democrats in Congress. The mantle of "moral leadership" was instead taken up by Dr. Martin Luther King Jr., the inspirational black Baptist minister from Atlanta who helped found the Southern Christian Leadership Conference (SCLC) in 1957. In early 1963 King and the SCLC resolved to assault segregation in Birmingham, Alabama. They organized an economic boycott of white businesses and staged a series of protest marches. Birmingham police used dogs and fire hoses to break up the rallies, and they arrested King and many of his lieutenants. While in jail he used smuggled paper and pen to write a powerful response to criticism he had received from local white ministers.

While confined here in the Birmingham City Jail, I came across your recent statement calling our present activities "unwise and untimely."

. . . I am here, along with several members of my staff, because we were invited here. I am here because I have basic organizational ties here. Beyond this, I am in Birmingham because injustice is here. Just as the 8th-century prophets left their little villages and carried their "thus saith the Lord" far beyond the boundaries of their home town, and just as the Apostle Paul left his little village of Tarsus and carried the gospel of Jesus Christ to practically every hamlet and city of the Greco-Roman world, I too am compelled to carry the gospel of freedom beyond my particular home town. . . . Injustice anywhere is a threat to justice everywhere. . . .

You deplore the demonstrations that are presently taking place in Birmingham. But I am sorry that your statement did not express a similar concern for the conditions that brought the demonstrations into being. I am sure that each of you would want to go beyond the superficial social analyst who looks merely at effects, and does not grapple with underlying causes. I would not hesitate to say that it is unfortunate that so-called demonstrations are taking place in Birmingham at this time, but I would say in more emphatic terms that it is even more unfortunate that the white power structure of this city left the Negro community with no other alternative.

In any nonviolent campaign there are four basic steps: 1) collection of the facts to determine whether injustices are alive; 2) negotiation; 3) self-purification; and 4) direct action. We have gone through all of these steps in Birmingham. There can be no gainsaying of the fact that racial injustice engulfs this community. Birmingham is probably the most thoroughly segregated city in the United States. Its ugly record of police brutality is known in every section of this country. Its unjust treatment of Negroes in the courts is a notorious reality. There have been more unsolved bombings of Negro homes and churches in Birmingham than any city in this nation. These are the hard, brutal, and unbelievable facts. . . .

We know through painful experience that freedom is never voluntarily given by the oppressor; it must be demanded by the oppressed. Frankly I have never yet engaged in a direct action movement that was "well timed," according to the timetable of those who have not suffered unduly from the disease of segregation. For years now I have heard the word "Wait!" It rings in the ear of every Negro with a piercing familiarity. This "wait" has almost always meant "never." It has been a tranquilizing Thalidomide, relieving the emotional stress for a moment, only to give birth to an ill-formed infant of frustration. We must come to see with the distinguished jurist of yesterday that "justice too long delayed is justice denied." We have waited for more than 340 years for our constitutional and God-given rights. The nations of Asia and Africa are moving with jetlike speed toward the goal of political independence, and we still creep at horse and buggy pace toward the gaining of a cup of coffee at a lunch counter. . . .

You express a great deal of anxiety over our willingness to break laws. This is certainly a legitimate concern. Since we so diligently urge people to obey the Supreme Court's decision of 1954 outlawing segregation in the public schools, it is rather strange and paradoxical to find us consciously breaking laws. One may well ask, "How can you advocate breaking some laws and obeying others?" The answer is found in the fact that there are two types of laws: There are *just* laws and there are *unjust* laws. I would be the first to advocate obeying just laws. One has not only a legal but a moral responsibility to obey just laws. Conversely, one has a moral responsibility to disobey unjust laws. I would agree with Saint Augustine that "An unjust law is no law at all."

Now what is the difference between the two? How does one determine when a law is just or unjust? A just law is a man-made code that squares with the moral law or the law of God. An unjust law is a code that is out of harmony with the moral law. To put it in the terms of Saint Thomas Aquinas, an unjust law is a human law that is not rooted in eternal and natural law. Any law that uplifts human personality is just. Any law that degrades human personality is unjust.

All segregation statutes are unjust because segregation distorts the soul and damages the personality. It gives the segregator a false sense of superiority and the segregated a false sense of inferiority. . . . So segregation is not only politically, economically, and sociologically unsound, but it is morally wrong and sinful. Paul Tillich has said that sin is separation. Isn't segregation an existential expression of man's tragic separation, an expression of his awful estrangement, his terrible sinfulness? So I can urge men to obey the 1954 decision of the Supreme Court because it is morally right, and I can urge them to disobey segregation ordinances because they are morally wrong. . . .

Let me give another explanation. An unjust law is a code inflicted upon a minority which that minority had no part in enacting or creating because it did not have the unhampered right to vote. Who can say the legislature of Alabama which set up the segregation laws was democratically elected? Throughout the state of Alabama all types of conniving methods are used to prevent Negroes from becoming registered voters and there are some counties without a single Negro registered to vote despite the fact that the Negro constitutes a majority of the population. Can any law set up in such a state be considered democratically structured? . . .

We can never forget that everything Hitler did in Germany was "legal" and . . . it was "illegal" to aid and comfort a Jew in Hitler's Germany. But I am sure that, if I had lived in Germany during that time, I would have aided and comforted my Jewish brothers even though it was illegal. If I lived in a Communist country today where certain principles dear to the Christian faith are suppressed, I believe I would openly advocate disobeying these anti-religious laws. . . .

We will have to repent in this generation not merely for the vitriolic words and actions of the bad people, but for the appalling silence of good people. We must come to see that human progress never rolls in on wheels of inevitability. It comes through the tireless efforts and persistent work of men willing to be co-workers with God, and without this hard work time itself becomes an ally of the forces of social stagnation. . . .

You spoke of our activity in Birmingham as extreme. At first I was rather disappointed that fellow clergymen would see my nonviolent efforts as those of the extremist. I started thinking about the fact that I stand in the middle of two opposing forces in the Negro community. One is a force of complacency made up of Negroes who, as a result of long years of oppression, have been so completely drained of self-respect and a sense of "somebodiness" that they have adjusted to segregation, and of a few Negroes in the middle class who, because of a degree of academic and economic security, and because at points they profit by segregation, have unconsciously become insensitive to the problems of the masses. The other force is one of bitterness and hatred and comes perilously close to advocating violence. It is expressed in the various black nationalist groups that are springing up over the nation, the largest and best known being Elijah Muhammad's Muslim movement. This movement is nourished by the contemporary frustration over the continued existence of racial discrimination. It

is made up of people who have lost faith in America, who have absolutely repudiated Christianity, and who have concluded that the white man is an incurable "devil."

I have tried to stand between these two forces saying that we need not follow the "donothingism" of the complacent or the hatred and despair of the black nationalist. There is the more excellent way of love and nonviolent protest. I'm grateful to God that, through the Negro church, the dimension of nonviolence entered our struggle. If this philosophy had not emerged I am convinced that by now many streets of the South would be flowing with floods of blood. And I am further convinced that if our white brothers dismiss us as "rabble rousers" and "outside agitators"—those of us who are working through the channels of nonviolent direct action—and refuse to support our nonviolent efforts, millions of Negroes, out of frustration and despair, will seek solace and security in black nationalist ideologies, a development that will lead inevitably to a frightening racial nightmare.

Oppressed people cannot remain oppressed forever. The urge for freedom will eventually come. This is what has happened to the American Negro. Something within has reminded him of his birthright of freedom; something without has reminded that he can gain it. . . .

So the question is not whether we will be extremist but what kind of extremist will we be. Will we be extremists for hate or will we be extremists for love? Will we be extremists for the preservation of injustice—or will we be extremists for the cause of justice? . . .

The contemporary Church is so often a weak, ineffectual voice with an uncertain sound. It is so often the arch-supporter of the *status quo*. Far from being disturbed by the presence of the Church, the power structure of the average community is consoled by the Church's silent and often vocal sanction of things as they are.

But the judgment of God is upon the Church as never before. If the Church of today does not recapture the sacrificial spirit of the early Church, it will lose its authentic ring, forfeit the loyalty of millions and be dismissed as an irrelevant social club with no meaning for the 20th century. . . . I am thankful to God that some noble souls from the ranks of organized religion have broken loose from the paralyzing chains of conformity and joined us as active partners in the struggle for freedom . . . they have gone with the faith that right defeated is stronger than evil triumphant. These men have been the leaven in the lump of the race. Their witness has been the spiritual salt that has preserved the true meaning of the Gospel in these troubled times. They have carved a tunnel of hope through the dark mountain of disappointment. . . . But even if the Church does not come to the aid of justice, I have no despair about the future. I have no fear about the outcome of our struggle in Birmingham, even if our motives are presently misunderstood. We will reach the goal of freedom in Birmingham and all over the nation, because the goal of America is freedom. Abused and scorned though we may be, our destiny is tied up with the destiny of America. . . .

One day the South will recognize its real heroes. They will be the James Merediths, courageously and with a majestic sense of purpose, facing jeering and hostile mobs and the agonizing loneliness that characterizes the life of the pioneer. They will be old, oppressed, battered Negro women, symbolized in a seventy-two-year-old woman of Montgomery, Alabama, who rose up with a sense of dignity and with her people decided not to ride the segregated buses, and responded to one who inquired about her tiredness with ungrammatical profundity: "My feets is tired, but my soul is rested." They will be young high school and college students, young ministers of the Gospel and a host of the elders, courageously and nonviolently sitting in at lunch counters and willingly going to jail for conscience's sake. One day the South will know that when these disinherited children of God sat down at lunch counters they were in reality standing up for the best in the American dream and the most sacred values in our Judeo-Christian heritage, and thus carrying our whole nation back to great wells of democracy which were dug deep by the founding fathers in the formulation of the Constitution and the Declaration of Independence. . . .

I hope this letter finds you strong in the faith. I also hope that circumstances will soon make it possible for me to meet each of you, not as an integrationist or a civil rights leader, but as a fellow clergyman and a Christian brother. Let us all hope that the dark clouds of racial prejudice will soon pass away, that the deep fog of misunderstanding will be lifted from our fear-drenched communities, and that in some not too distant tomorrow the radiant stars of love and brotherhood will shine over our great nation with all of their scintillating beauty. . . .

REVIEW QUESTIONS

1. King describes two kinds of laws. What are they, and what criteria does King use in deciding when to obey them?
2. What were the two "opposing forces" in the "Negro community" according to King? What did each side advocate?
3. Do you think whites would have felt threatened by King's strategy of nonviolent civil disobedience? Explain.

ABBEY LINCOLN

FROM Who Will Revere the Black Woman? (1966)

Centuries of racism affected black men and women differently. In a 1966 essay in
Negro Digest, *Abbey Lincoln (born Anna Marie Wooldridge in 1930), a celebrated*
jazz singer, songwriter, actress, and civil rights activist from rural Michigan, high-
lighted the historic abuse of "black womanhood" by both whites and black men. In
doing so, she posed an uncompromising challenge to civil rights activists to address
the distinctive issues facing African American women.

From "Who Will Revere the Black Woman?" Originally published in *Negro Digest* (September 1966), pp. 16–20. Reprinted by permission of the Estate of Abbey Lincoln and the Anna Marie
Wooldridge Revocable Living Trust. [Editorial insertions appear in square brackets—*Ed.*]

Mark Twain said, in effect, that when a country enslaves a people, the first necessary job is to make the world feel that the people to be enslaved are sub-human. The next job is to make his fellow-countrymen believe that man is inferior and then, the unkindest cut of all is to make that man believe himself inferior.

A good job has been done in this country, as far as convincing them [African Americans] of their inferiority is concerned. The general white community has told us in a million different ways and in no uncertain terms that "God" and "nature" made a mistake when it came to fashioning us and ours. . . .

[S]trange as it is, I've heard it echoed by too many Black full-grown males that Black woman-hood is the downfall of the Black man in that she (the Black woman) is "evil," "hard to get along with," "domineering," "suspicious," and "narrow-minded." In short, a black, ugly, evil you-know-what.

As time progresses, I've learned that this description of my mothers, sisters, and partners in crime is used as the basis and excuse for the further shoving, by the Black man, of his own head into the sand of oblivion. Hence, the black mother, housewife, and all-round girl Thursday is called

upon to suffer both physically and emotionally every humiliation a woman can suffer and still function. . . .

Raped and denied the right to cry out in her pain, she has been named the culprit and called "loose," "hot-blooded," "wanton," "sultry," and "amoral." She has been used as the white man's sexual outhouse, and shamefully encouraged by her own ego-less man to persist in this function. Wanting, too, to be carried away by her "Prince Charming," she must, in all honesty, admit that he has been robbed of his crown by the very assaulter and assassin who has raped her. Still, she looks upon her man as God's gift to Black womanhood and is further diminished and humiliated and outraged when the feeling is not mutual. . . .

At best we are made to feel that we are poor imitations and excuses for white women. Evil? Evil, you say. The black woman is hurt, confused, frustrated, angry, resentful, frightened and evil! Who in the hell dares suggest that she should be otherwise? These attitudes only point up her perception of the situation and her healthy rejection of same.

Maybe if our women get evil enough and angry enough, they'll be moved to some action that will bring our men to their senses. There is one unalterable fact that too many of our men cannot seem to face. And that is, we "black, evil, ugly" women are a perfect and accurate reflection of you "black, evil, ugly" men. Play hide and seek as long as you can and will, but your every rejection and abandonment of us is only sorry testament of how thoroughly and carefully you have been blinded and brainwashed. And let it be further understood that when we refer to you we mean, ultimately, us. For you are us, and vice versa.

We are the women who were kidnapped and brought to this continent as slaves. We are the women who were raped, are still being raped, and our bastard children snatched from our breasts and scattered to the winds to be lynched, castrated, de-egoed, robbed, burned, and deceived. . . .

We are the women who dwell in the hell-hole ghettos all over the land. We are the women whose bodies are sacrificed, as living cadavers, to experimental surgery in the white man's hospitals for the sake of white medicine. We are the women who are invisible on the television and movie screens, on the Broadway stage. We are the women who are lusted after, sneered at, leered at, hissed at, yelled at, grabbed at, tracked down by white degenerates in our own pitiable, poverty-stricken and prideless neighborhoods.

We are the women whose hair is compulsively fried, whose skin is bleached, whose nose is "too big," whose mouth is "too big and loud," whose behind is "too big and broad," whose feet are "too big and flat," whose face is "too black and shiny," and whose suffering and patience is [sic] too long and enduring to be believed. . . .

We are the women whose husbands and fathers and brothers and sons have been plagiarized, imitated, denied, and robbed of the fruits of their genius, and who consequently we see as emasculated, jailed, lynched, driven mad, deprived, enraged and made suicidal. We are the women who nobody, seemingly, cares about, who are made to feel inadequate, stupid and backward, and who inevitably have the most colossal inferiority complexes to be found.

And who is spreading the propaganda that "the only free people in the country are the white man and the black woman"? If this be freedom, then Heaven is hell, right is wrong, and cold is hot.

Who will revere the black woman? Who will keep our neighborhoods safe for black innocent womanhood? Black womanhood is outraged and humiliated. Black womanhood cries for dignity and restitution and salvation. Black womanhood wants and needs protection, and keeping, and holding. Who will assuage her indignation? Who will keep her precious and pure? Who will glorify and proclaim her beautiful image? To whom will she cry rape?

REVIEW QUESTIONS

1. According to Lincoln, how had black women been abused and stereotyped by men during the twentieth century?
2. How had such abuse affected black women? How was such abuse to be confronted and stopped?

GEORGE C. WALLACE

FROM The Civil Rights Movement: Fraud, Sham, and Hoax (1964)

George Wallace served as the feisty racist governor of Alabama during the early 1960s. In 1958 he had lost the gubernatorial election to a rabid segregationist, and Wallace crudely vowed that he would "never be out-niggered again." He won the governorship in 1962 and pledged: "Segregation now! Segregation tomorrow! Segregation forever!" In June 1963 Wallace stood defiantly in a doorway at the University of Alabama to prevent the first black student from registering, only to step aside when federal marshals threatened his arrest. Wallace's theatrical defense of segregation and his opposition to civil rights legislation and related Supreme Court rulings, communism, and "left-wing" liberalism made him a hero among white conservatives. In 1964 he challenged Lyndon Johnson for the Democratic presidential nomination. Although unsuccessful, he displayed an ability to exploit the "white backlash" against political and social liberalism. This signaled an emerging conservative revolt that would flower in the 1970s and 1980s.

From the Alabama Department of Archives and History, Montgomery, Alabama.

We come here today in deference to the memory of those stalwart patriots who on July 4, 1776, pledged their lives, their fortunes, and their sacred honor to establish and defend the proposition that governments are created by the people, empowered by the people, derive their just powers from the consent of the people, and must forever remain subservient to the will of the people.

Today, 188 years later, we celebrate that occasion and find inspiration and determination and courage to preserve and protect the great principles of freedom enunciated in the Declaration of Independence.

It is therefore a cruel irony that the President of the United States has only yesterday signed into law the most monstrous piece of legislation[1] ever enacted by the United States Congress.

It is a fraud, a sham, and a hoax.

This bill will live in infamy. To sign it into law at any time is tragic. To do so upon the eve of the celebration of our independence insults the intelligence of the American people.

It dishonors the memory of countless thousands of our dead who offered up their very lives in defense of principles which this bill destroys.

Never before in the history of this nation have so many human and property rights been destroyed by a single enactment of the Congress. It is an act of tyranny. It is the assassin's knife stuck in the back of liberty.

With this assassin's knife and a blackjack in the hand of the Federal force-cult, the left-wing liberals will try to force us back into bondage. Bondage to a tyranny more brutal than that imposed by the British monarchy which claimed power to rule over the lives of our forefathers under sanction of the Divine Right of kings.

[1]Civil Rights Act of 1964.

Today, this tyranny is imposed by the central government which claims the right to rule over our lives under sanction of the omnipotent black-robed despots who sit on the bench of the United States Supreme Court.

This bill is fraudulent in intent, in design, and in execution. It is misnamed. Each and every provision is mistitled. It was rammed through the Congress on the wave of ballyhoo, promotions, and publicity stunts reminiscent of P. T. Barnum.

It was enacted in an atmosphere of pressure, intimidation, and even cowardice, as demonstrated by the refusal of the United States Senate to adopt an amendment to submit the bill to a vote of the people. . . .

It threatens our freedom of speech, of assembly, or association, and makes the exercise of these Freedoms a federal crime under certain conditions.

It affects our political rights, our right to trial by jury, our right to the full use and enjoyment of our private property, the freedom from search and seizure of our private property and possessions, the freedom from harassment by Federal police and, in short, all the rights of individuals inherent in a society of free men.

Ministers, lawyers, teachers, newspapers, and every private citizen must guard his speech and watch his actions to avoid the deliberately imposed booby traps put into this bill. It is designed to make Federal crimes of our customs, beliefs, and traditions.

Therefore, under the fantastic powers of the Federal judiciary to punish for contempt of court and under their fantastic powers to regulate our most intimate aspects of our lives by injunction, every American citizen is in jeopardy and must stand guard against these despots. . . .

I am having nothing to do with enforcing a law that will destroy our free enterprise system. I am having nothing to do with enforcing a law that will destroy neighborhood schools. I am having nothing to do with enforcing a law that will destroy the rights of private property.

I am having nothing to do with enforcing a law that destroys your right—and my right—to choose my neighbors—or to sell my house to whomever I choose. I am having nothing to do with enforcing a law that destroys the labor seniority system.

I am having nothing to do with this so-called civil rights bill.

The liberal left-wingers have passed it. Now let them employ some pinknik social engineers in Washington, D.C., to figure out what to do with it. . . .

It has been said that power corrupts and absolute power corrupts absolutely. There was never greater evidence as to the proof of this statement than in the example of the present Federal Judiciary. . . .

I feel it important that you should know and understand what it is that these people are trying to do. The written opinions of the court are filled with double talk, semantics, jargon, and meaningless phrases. The words they use are not important. The ideas that they represent are the things which count.

It is perfectly obvious from the left-wing liberal press and from the left-wing law journals that what the court is saying behind all the jargon is that they don't like our form of government.

They think they can establish a better one. In order to do so it is necessary that they overthrow our existing form, destroy the democratic institutions created by the people, change the outlook, religion, and philosophy, and bring the whole area of human thought, aspiration, action and organization, under the absolute control of the court. Their decisions reveal this to be the goal of the liberal element on the court which is in a majority at present.

It has reached the point where one may no longer look to judicial decisions to determine what the court may do. However, it is possible to predict with accuracy the nature of the opinions to be rendered.

One may find the answer in the Communist Manifesto. The Communists are dedicated to the overthrow of our form of government. They are dedicated to the destruction of the concept of private property. They are dedicated to the object of destroying religion as the basis of moral and ethical values. . . .

I do not call the members of the United States Supreme Court Communists. But I do say, and I submit for your judgment the fact that every single decision of the court in the past ten years which related in any way to each of these objectives has been decided against freedom and in favor of tyranny. . . .

The Federal court rules that your children shall not be permitted to read the bible in our public school systems. Let me tell you this, though. We still read the bible in Alabama schools and as long as I am governor we will continue to read the bible no matter what the Supreme Court says. . . .

But yet there is hope.

There is yet a spirit of resistance in this country which will not be oppressed. And it is awakening. And I am sure there is an abundance of good sense in this country which cannot be deceived. . . .

Being a southerner is no longer geographic. It's a philosophy and an attitude. One destined to be a national philosophy—embraced by millions of Americans—which shall assume the mantle of leadership and steady a governmental structure in these days of crises.

Certainly I am a candidate for President of the United States. If the left-wingers do not think I am serious—let them consider this.

I am going to take our fight to the people—the court of public opinion—where truth and common sense will eventually prevail. . . . Conservatives of this nation constitute the balance of power in presidential elections.

I am a conservative.

I intend to give the American people a clear choice. I welcome a fight between our philosophy and the liberal left-wing dogma which now threatens to engulf every man, woman, and child in the United States.

I am in this race because I believe the American people have been pushed around long enough and that they, like you and I, are fed up with the continuing trend toward a socialist state which now subjects the individual to the dictates of an all-powerful central government.

I am running for President because I was born free. I want to remain free. I want your children

and mine and our prosperity to be unencumbered by the manipulations of a soulless state.

I intend to fight for a positive, affirmative program to restore constitutional government and to stop the senseless bloodletting now being performed on the body of liberty by those who lead us willingly and dangerously close to a totalitarian central government.

In our nation, man has always been sovereign and the state has been his servant. This philosophy has made the United States the greatest free nation in history.

This freedom was not a gift. It was won by work, by sweat, by tears, by war, by whatever it took to be—and to remain free. Are we today less resolute, less determined and courageous than our fathers and our grandfathers?

Are we to abandon this priceless heritage that has carried us to our present position of achievement and leadership? I say if we are to abandon our heritage, let it be done in the open and full knowledge of what we do.

We are not unmindful and careless of our future. We will not stand aside while our conscientious convictions tell us that a dictatorial Supreme Court has taken away our rights and our liberties.

We will not stand idly by while the Supreme Court continues to invade the prerogatives left rightfully to the states by the constitution.

We must not be misled by left-wing incompetent news media that day after day feed us a diet of fantasy telling us we are bigots, racists and hate-mongers to oppose the destruction of the constitution and our nation.

A left-wing monster has risen up in this nation. It has invaded the government. It has invaded the news media. It has invaded the leadership of many of our churches. It has invaded every phase and aspect of the life of freedom-loving people.

It consists of many and various and powerful interests, but it has combined into one massive drive and is held together by the cohesive power of the emotion, setting forth civil rights as supreme to all.

But, in reality, it is a drive to destroy the rights of private property, to destroy the freedom and liberty of you and me. And, my friends, where there are no property rights, there are no human rights. Red China and Soviet Russia are prime examples.

Politically evil men have combined and arranged themselves against us. The good people of this nation must now associate themselves together, else we will fall one by one, an unpitied sacrifice in a struggle which threatens to engulf the entire nation.

We can win. We can control the election of the president in November. Our object must be our country, our whole country and nothing but our country.

If we will stand together—the people of this state—the people of my state—the people throughout this great region—yes, throughout the United States—then we can be the balance of power. We can determine who will be the next president. . . .

Let it be known that we will no longer tolerate the boot of tyranny. We will no longer hide our heads in the sand. We will reschool our thoughts in the lessons our forefathers knew so well.

We must destroy the power to dictate, to forbid, to require, to demand, to distribute, to edict, and to judge what is best and enforce that will of judgment upon free citizens. We must revitalize a government founded in this nation on faith in God.

I ask that you join with me and that together, we give an active and courageous leadership to the millions of people throughout this nation who look with hope and faith to our fight to preserve our constitutional system of government with its guarantees of liberty and justice for all within the framework of our priceless freedoms.

REVIEW QUESTIONS

1. According to Wallace, what were some of the freedoms endangered by the Civil Rights Act of 1964?
2. Why was Wallace especially critical of the Supreme Court?
3. Did Wallace direct his speech to appeal to the emotions or the intellect of his audience? Explain.

BARRY GOLDWATER

FROM Extremism in the Defense of Liberty Is No Vice (1964)

In July 1964 Barry Goldwater, a Republican senator from Arizona, launched the modern conservative movement with a rousing speech in San Francisco accepting his party's nomination for the presidency. Goldwater had earlier written two books, The Conscience of a Conservative *(1960) and* Why Not Victory? *(1962), both of which sold millions of copies and established him as the nation's most prominent conservative leader. He lost the 1964 election to Lyndon B. Johnson, but his campaign set in motion the surge of political conservatism that reshaped the landscape of national politics. Goldwater was reelected to the Senate in 1968, 1974, and 1980. He died in 1998.*

New York Times, July 17, 1964, p. 10. Reprinted by permission of the Arizona Historical Foundation from the Personal and Political Papers of Senator Barry M. Goldwater. [Editorial insertions appear in square brackets—*Ed.*]

. . . The good Lord raised this mighty Republic to be a home for the brave and to flourish as the land of the free—not to stagnate in the swampland of collectivism, not to cringe before the bullying of communism.

Now my fellow Americans, the tide has been running against freedom. Our people have followed false prophets. We must, and we shall, return to proven ways—not because they are old, but because they are true. We must, and we shall, set the tides running again in the cause of freedom. And this party, with its every action, every word, every breath, and every heartbeat, has but a single resolve, and that is freedom—freedom made orderly for this nation by our constitutional government; freedom under a government limited by the laws of nature and of nature's God; freedom balanced so that order lacking liberty will not become the slavery of the prison cell; balanced so that liberty lacking order will not become the license of the mob and of the jungle.

Now, we Americans understand freedom. We have earned it; we have lived for it, and we have died for it. This nation and its people are freedom's model in a searching world. We can be freedom's missionaries in a doubting world. But, ladies and gentlemen, first we must renew freedom's mission in our own hearts and in our own homes.

During four futile years, the Administration which we shall replace has distorted and lost that vision. It has talked and talked and talked and talked the words of freedom, but it has failed and failed and failed in the works of freedom.

Now failure cements the wall of shame in Berlin; failures blot the sands of shame at the Bay of Pigs [in Cuba]; failures mark the slow death of freedom in Laos; failures infest the jungles of Vietnam, and failures haunt the houses of our once great alliances and undermine the greatest bulwark ever erected by free nations, the NATO community. Failures proclaim lost leadership, obscure purpose, weakening will, and the risk of inciting our sworn enemies to new aggressions and to new excesses.

And because of this Administration we are tonight a world divided. We are a nation becalmed.

We have lost the brisk pace of diversity and the genius of individual creativity. We are plodding along at a pace set by centralized planning, red tape, rules without responsibility and regimentation without recourse.

Rather than useful jobs in our country, our people have been offered bureaucratic "make work"; rather than moral leadership, they have been given bread and circuses. They have been given spectacles, and, yes, they've even been given scandals.

Tonight there is violence in our streets, corruption in our highest offices, aimlessness amongst our youth, anxiety among our elders, and there's a virtual despair among the many who look beyond material success for the inner meaning of their lives. And where examples of morality should be set, the opposite is seen. Small men seeking great wealth or power have too often and too long turned even the highest levels of public service into mere personal opportunity.

Now, certainly simple honesty is not too much to demand of men in government. We find it in most. Republicans demand it from everyone. They demand it from everyone no matter how exalted or protected his position might be. The growing menace in our country tonight, to personal safety, to life, to limb and property, in homes, in churches, on the playgrounds, and places of business, particularly in our great cities, is the mounting concern, or should be, of every thoughtful citizen in the United States.

Security from domestic violence, no less than from foreign aggression, is the most elementary and fundamental purpose of any government, and a government that cannot fulfill this purpose is one that cannot long command the loyalty of its citizens.

History shows us, demonstrates that nothing, nothing prepares the way for tyranny more than the failure of public officials to keep the streets safe from bullies and marauders.

Now we Republicans see all this as more—much more—than the result of mere political differences or mere political mistakes. We see this as the result of a fundamentally and absolutely wrong view of man, his nature, and his destiny. Those who seek to live your lives for you, to take your liberties in return for relieving you of yours; those who elevate the state and downgrade the citizen, must see ultimately a world in which earthly power can be substituted for Divine Will, and this nation was founded upon the rejection of that notion and upon the acceptance of God as the author of freedom.

Now those who seek absolute power, even though they seek it to do what they regard as good, are simply demanding the right to enforce their own version of heaven on earth, and let me remind you they are the very ones who always create the most hellish tyranny. Absolute power does corrupt, and those who seek it must be suspect and must be opposed. Their mistaken course stems from false notions, ladies and gentlemen, of equality. Equality, rightly understood, as our founding fathers understood it, leads to liberty and to the emancipation of creative differences; wrongly understood, as it has been so tragically in our time, it leads first to conformity and then to despotism.

Fellow Republicans, it is the cause of Republicanism to resist concentrations of power, private or public—which enforce such conformity and inflict such despotism. It is the cause of Republicanism to ensure that power remains in the hands of the people—and, so help us God, that is exactly what a Republican President will do with the help of a Republican Congress.

It is further the cause of Republicanism to restore a clear understanding of the tyranny of man over man in the world at large. It is our cause to dispel the foggy thinking which avoids hard decisions in the delusion that a world of conflict will somehow mysteriously resolve itself into a world of harmony, if we just don't rock the boat or irritate the forces of aggression—and this is hogwash. It is, further, the cause of Republicanism to remind ourselves, and the world, that only the strong can remain free; that only the strong can keep the peace.

Now I needn't remind you, or my fellow Americans regardless of party, that Republicans have shouldered this hard responsibility and marched in this cause before. It was Republican leadership under Dwight Eisenhower that kept the peace, and passed along to this administration the mightiest

arsenal for defense the world has ever known. And I needn't remind you that it was the strength and the believable will of the Eisenhower years that kept the peace by using our strength, by using it in the Formosa Straits, and in Lebanon, and by showing it courageously at all times.

It was during those Republican years that the thrust of Communist imperialism was blunted. It was during those years of Republican leadership that this world moved closer, not to war, but closer to peace, than at any other time in the last three decades.

And I needn't remind you, but I will, that it's been during Democratic years that our strength to deter war has been stilled and even gone into a planned decline. It has been during Democratic years that we have weakly stumbled into conflict, timidly refusing to draw our own lines against aggression, deceitfully refusing to tell even our people of our full participation, and tragically, letting our finest men die on battlefields unmarked by purpose, unmarked by pride or the prospect of victory.

Yesterday, it was Korea; tonight it is Vietnam. Make no bones of this. Don't try to sweep this under the rug. We are at war in Vietnam. And yet the President [Lyndon Johnson], who is the Commander in Chief of our forces, refuses to say, refuses to say mind you, whether or not the objective over there is victory, and his Secretary of Defense [Robert McNamara] continues to mislead and misinform the American people, and enough of it has gone by.

And I needn't remind you, but I will, it has been during Democratic years that a billion persons were cast into Communist captivity and their fate cynically sealed.

Today—today in our beloved country we have an Administration which seems eager to deal with Communism in every coin known—from gold to wheat, from consulates to confidences, and even human freedom itself.

Now the Republican cause demands that we brand Communism as the principal disturber of peace in the world today. Indeed, we should brand it as the only significant disturber of the peace. And we must make clear that until its goals of conquest are absolutely renounced, and its relations with all nations tempered, Communism and the governments it now controls are enemies of every man on earth who is or wants to be free.

Now, we here in America can keep the peace only if we remain vigilant, and only if we remain strong. Only if we keep our eyes open and keep our guard up can we prevent war. And I want to make this abundantly clear—I don't intend to let peace or freedom be torn from our grasp because of lack of strength or lack of will—and that I promise you Americans.

I believe that we must look beyond the defense of freedom today to its extension tomorrow. I believe that the Communism which boasts it will bury us will, instead, give way to the forces of freedom. And I can see in the distant and yet recognizable future the outlines of a world worthy of our dedication, our every risk, our every effort, our every sacrifice along the way. Yes, a world that will redeem the suffering of those who will be liberated from tyranny.

I can see, and I suggest that all thoughtful men must contemplate, the flowering of an Atlantic civilization, the whole of Europe reunified and freed, trading openly across its borders, communicating openly across the world.

This is a goal far, far more meaningful than a moon shot. It's a truly inspiring goal for all free men to set for themselves during the latter half of the twentieth century. . . .

I would remind you that extremism in the defense of liberty is no vice!

And let me remind you also that moderation in the pursuit of justice is no virtue!

By the—the beauty of the very system we Republicans are pledged to restore and revitalize, the beauty of this Federal system of ours is in its reconciliation of diversity with unity. We must not see malice in honest differences of opinion, and no matter how great, so long as they are not inconsistent with the pledges we have given to each other in and through our Constitution.

Our Republican cause is not to level out the world or make its people conform in computer regimented sameness. Our Republican cause is to free our people and light the way for liberty throughout the world. Ours is a very human cause for very humane goals. This party, its good people, and its unquenchable devotion to freedom, will not fulfill the purposes of this campaign, which we launch here and now, until our cause has won the day, inspired the world, and shown the way to a tomorrow worthy of all our yesteryears.

I repeat, I accept your nomination with humbleness, with pride, and you and I are going to fight for the goodness of our land.

Thank you.

REVIEW QUESTIONS

1. What was Goldwater's attitude toward the growing conflict in Vietnam?
2. Like most acceptance speeches, Goldwater focuses on the failures of the opposition and tends to speak in general terms. What specific initiatives does he mention or imply?
3. Why did he feel the need to stress that "extremism in the defense of liberty is no vice"?

JOAN BAEZ

I Do Not Believe in War (1964)

In 1964, the prominent folk singer Joan Baez grew so upset with the American bombing of North Vietnam that she refused to pay her federal taxes as a symbolic protest. Her letter to the Internal Revenue Service explaining her motives encapsulates many of the concerns of the growing anti-war movement.

Dear friends:

What I have to say is this:

I do not believe in war.

I do not believe in the weapons of war.

Weapons and war have murdered, burned, distorted, crippled, and caused endless varieties of pain to men, women, and children for too long. Our modern weapons can reduce a man to a piece of dust in a split second, can make a woman's hair fall out or cause her baby to be born a monster. They can kill the part of a turtle's brain that tells him where he is going, so instead of trudging to the ocean he trudges confusedly towards the desert, slowly, blinking his poor eyes, until he finally scorches to death and turns into a shell and some bones.

I'm not going to volunteer the 60% of my year's income tax that goes to armaments. There are two reasons for my action. One is enough to say that no man has the right to take another man's life. Now we plan and build [nuclear] weapons that can take thousands of lives in a second, millions of lives in a day, billions in a week.

No one has the right to do that.

It is madness.

It is wrong.

My other reason is that modern war is impractical and stupid. We spend billions of dollars a year on [nuclear] weapons which scientists, politicians, military men, and even presidents all agree must never be used. That is impractical. The expression "National Security" has no meaning. It refers to our Defense System, which I call our Offense System, and which is a farce. It continues expending, heaping up, one horrible kill machine upon another until, for some reason or another, a button will be pushed and our world, or a good portion of it will be blown to pieces. That is not security. That is stupidity.

People are starving to death in some places of the world. They look to this country with all its wealth and its power. They look at our national budget. They despise us. That is impractical and stupid.

Maybe the line should have been drawn when the bow and arrow were invented, maybe the gun, the cannon, maybe. Because now it is all wrong, all impractical, and all stupid. So all I can do is draw my own line now. I am no longer supporting my portion of the arms race.

Sincerely,

Joan Baez

REVIEW QUESTIONS

1. Why did Baez refuse to pay her federal taxes?
2. Was she opposed to the combat in Vietnam or all wars in general?

MALCOLM X

FROM "The Black Revolution" Speeches (1964)

Born Malcolm Little in 1925, Malcolm X was the son of a Baptist preacher who pro-
moted black separatism and was murdered by unknown assailants in Michigan. At
age six, the fatherless Malcolm was taken to a foster home. He dropped out of school
in the eighth grade and embarked on a crime spree that landed him in a federal
prison at age twenty-one. There he discovered the writings of Elijah Muhammad,
leader of the Black Muslims. Muhammad portrayed whites as servants of the devil;
blacks therefore had to separate themselves from the white community. Mal-
colm became a loyal disciple of Elijah Muhammad. Upon his release from prison, he
became minister of a Black Muslim temple in Harlem, a black neighborhood in New
York City. Clashes with the Black Muslim leadership over which tactics to use in
fighting racism led to his suspension from the organization in late 1963. He then
traveled to Mecca, where he adopted the beliefs of orthodox Muslims and founded
the Organization of Afro-American Unity. In 1964 he delivered the following
address.

From *Two Speeches by Malcolm X*, pp. 7–8, 23–24. Copyright © 1965, 1990 by Betty Shabazz
and Pathfinder Press. Reprinted by permission.

Friends and enemies, tonight I hope that we can have a little fireside chat with as few sparks as possible being tossed around. . . . I hope that this little conversation tonight about the black revolution won't cause many of you to accuse us of igniting it when you find it at your doorstep. . . .

I'm still a Muslim but I'm also a nationalist, meaning that my political philosophy is black nationalism, my economic philosophy is black nationalism, my social philosophy is black nationalism. And when I say that this philosophy is black nationalism, to me this means that the political philosophy of black nationalism is that which is designed to encourage our people, the black people, to gain complete control over the politics and the politicians of our own community.

Our economic philosophy is that we should gain economic control over the economy of our own community, the businesses and the other things which create employment so that we can provide jobs for our own people instead of having to picket and boycott and beg someone else for a job.

And, in short, our social philosophy means that we feel that it is time to get together among our own kind and eliminate the evils that are destroying the moral fiber of our society, like drug addiction, drunkenness, adultery that leads to an abundance of bastard children, welfare problems. We believe that we should lift the level or the standard of our own society to a higher level wherein we will be satisfied and then not inclined toward pushing ourselves into other societies where we are not wanted.

*   *   *

Why is America in a position to bring about a bloodless revolution? Because the Negro in this country holds the balance of power and if the Negro in this country were given what the Constitution says he is supposed to have, the added power of the Negro in this country would sweep all of the racists and the segregationists out of office. It would change the entire political structure of the country. It would wipe out the Southern segregationism that now controls America's foreign policy, as well as America's domestic policy.

And the only way without bloodshed that this can be brought about is that the black man has to be given full use of the ballot in every one of the 50 states. But if the black man doesn't get the ballot, then you are going to be faced with another man who forgets the ballot and starts using the bullet.

Revolutions are fought to get control of land, to remove the absentee landlord and gain control of the land and the institutions that flow from that land. The black man has been in a very low condition because he has had no control whatsoever over any land. He has been a beggar economically, a beggar politically, a beggar socially, a beggar even when it comes to trying to get some education. So that in the past the type of mentality that was developed in this colonial system among our people, today is being overcome. And as the young ones come up they know what they want. And as they listen to your beautiful preaching about democracy and all those other flowery words, they know what they're supposed to have.

So you have a people today who not only know what they want, but also know what they are supposed to have. And they themselves are clearing another generation that is coming up that not only will know what it wants and know what it should have, but also will be ready and willing to do whatever is necessary to see that what they should have materializes immediately. Thank you.

REVIEW QUESTIONS

1. What were the economic and social philosophies of the Black Muslims?
2. According to Malcolm X, what would help prevent racial bloodshed from occurring? Was he optimistic about this? Explain.
3. Compare the views of Malcolm X and Dr. King. What were the essential differences?

STOKELY CARMICHAEL

FROM Black Power (1966)

Born in 1942 in the West Indies and raised in New York City, Stokely Carmichael joined the Student Nonviolent Coordinating Committee (SNCC) while enrolled at Howard University. In the mid-1960s, he emerged as the chairman of the organization and shifted its emphasis from voter registration to self-reliance and violent social change. His successor, H. Rap Brown, was even more militant, once asserting that "Violence is as American as cherry pie." Carmichael eventually changed his name to Kwame Ture and moved to the African nation of Guinea.

From "Black Power," *The New York Review of Books* 7 (September 22, 1966): 5–6, 8. Reprinted with permission from the author's estate.

One of the tragedies of the struggle against racism is that up to now there has been no national organization which could speak to the growing militancy of young black people in the urban ghetto. There has been only a civil rights movement, whose tone of voice was adapted to an audience of liberal whites. It served as a sort of buffer zone between them and angry young blacks. None of its so-called leaders could go into a rioting community and be listened to. In a sense, I blame ourselves—together with the mass media—for what has happened in Watts, Harlem, Chicago, Cleveland, Omaha. Each time the people in those cities saw Martin Luther King get slapped, they became angry; when they saw four little black girls bombed to death, they were angrier; and when nothing happened, they were steaming. We had nothing to offer that they could see, except to go out and be beaten again. We helped to build their frustration.

For too many years, black Americans marched and had their heads broken and got shot. They were saying to the country, "Look, you guys are supposed to be nice guys and we are only going to do what we are supposed to do—why do you beat us up, why don't you give us what we ask, why don't you straighten yourselves out?" After years of this, we are at almost the same point—because we demonstrated from a position of weakness. We cannot be expected any longer to march and have our heads broken in order to say to whites: come on, you're nice guys. For you are not nice guys. We have found you out.

An organization which claims to speak for the needs of a community—as does the Student Nonviolent Coordinating Committee—must speak in the tone of that community, not as somebody else's buffer zone. This is the significance of black power as a slogan. For once, black people are going to use the words they want to use—not just the words whites want to hear. And they will do this no matter how often the press tries to stop the use of the slogan by equating it with racism or separatism.

An organization which claims to be working for the needs of a community—as SNCC does—must work to provide that community with a position of strength from which to make its voice heard. This is the significance of black power beyond the slogan.

Black power can be clearly defined for those who do not attach the fears of white America to their questions about it. We should begin with the basic fact that black Americans have two problems: they are poor and they are black. All other problems arise from this two-sided reality: lack of education, the so-called apathy of black men. Any program to end racism must address itself to that double reality.

Almost from its beginning, SNCC sought to address itself to both conditions with a program aimed at winning political power for impoverished Southern blacks. We had to begin with politics because black Americans are a propertyless people in a country where property is valued above all. We had to work for power, because this country does not function by morality, love, and nonviolence, but by power. Thus we determined to win political power, with the idea of moving on from there into activity that would have economic effects. With power, the masses could *make or participate in making* the decisions which govern their destinies, and thus create basic change in their day-to-day lives. . . .

SNCC today is working in both North and South on programs of voter registration and independent political organizing. In some places, such as Alabama, Los Angeles, New York, Philadelphia, and New Jersey, independent organizing under the black panther symbol is in progress. The creation of a national "black panther party" must come about; it will take time to build, and it is much too early to predict its success. We have no infallible master plan and we make no claim to exclusive knowledge of how to end racism; different groups will work in their own different ways. SNCC cannot spell out the full logistics of self-determination but it can address itself to the problem by helping black communities define their needs, realize their strength, and go into action along a variety of lines which they must choose for themselves. . . .

Ultimately, the economic foundations of this country must be shaken if black people are to control their lives. The colonies of the United States—and this includes the black ghettoes within its borders, north and south must be liberated. For a century, this nation has been like an octopus of exploitation, its tentacles stretching from Mississippi and Harlem to South America, the Middle East, southern Africa, and Vietnam; the form of exploitation varies from area to area but the essential result has been the same—a powerful few have been maintained and enriched at the expense of the poor and voiceless colored masses. This pattern must be broken. As its grip loosens here and there around the world, the hopes of black Americans become more realistic. For racism to die, a totally different America must be born.

This is what the white society does not wish to face; this is why that society prefers to talk about integration. But integration speaks not at all to the problem of poverty, only to the problem of blackness. Integration today means the man who "makes it," leaving his black brothers behind in the ghetto as fast as his new sports car will take him. It has no relevance to the Harlem wino or to the cotton-picker making three dollars a day. . . .

Integration, moreover, speaks to the problem of blackness in a despicable way. As a goal, it has been based on complete acceptance of the fact that *in order to have* a decent house or education, blacks must move into a white neighborhood or send their children to a white school. This reinforces, among both black and white, the idea that "white" is automatically better and "black" is by definition inferior. This is why integration is a subterfuge for the maintenance of white supremacy. It allows the nation to focus on a handful of Southern children who get into white schools, at great price, and to ignore the 94 percent who are left behind in unimproved all-black schools. Such situations will not change until black people have power—to control their own school boards, in this case. Then Negroes become equal in a way that means something, and integration ceases to be a one-way street. Then integration doesn't mean draining skills and energies from the ghetto into white neighborhoods; then it can mean white people moving from Beverly Hills into Watts. . . . Then integration becomes relevant. . . .

Whites will not see that I, for example, as a person oppressed because of my blackness, have common cause with other blacks who are oppressed because of blackness. This is not to say that there are no white people who see things as I do, but that it is black people I must speak to first. It must be the oppressed to whom SNCC addresses itself primarily, not to friends from the oppressing group.

From birth, black people are told a set of lies about themselves. We are told that we are lazy—yet I drive through the Delta area of Mississippi and watch black people picking cotton in the hot sun for fourteen hours. We are told, "If you work hard, you'll succeed"—but if that were true, black people would own this country. We are oppressed because we are black—not because we are ignorant, not because we are lazy, not because we're stupid (and got good rhythm), but because we're black.

*   *   *

The need for psychological equality is the reason why SNCC today believes that blacks must organize in the black community. Only black people can convey the revolutionary idea that black people are able to do things themselves. Only they can help create in the community an aroused and continuing black consciousness that will provide the basis for political strength. In the past, white allies have furthered white supremacy without the whites involved realizing it—or wanting it, I think. Black people must do things for themselves; they must get poverty money they will control and spend themselves, they must conduct tutorial programs themselves so that black children can identify with black people. This is one reason Africa has such importance: The reality of black men ruling their own nations gives blacks elsewhere a sense of possibility, of power, which they do not now have.

This does not mean we don't welcome help, or friends. But we want the right to decide whether anyone is, in fact, our friend. In the past, black Americans have been almost the only people whom everybody and his momma could jump up and call their friends. We have been tokens, symbols, objects—as I was in high school to many young whites, who liked having "a Negro friend." We want to decide who is our friend, and we will not accept someone who comes to us and says: "If you do X, Y, and Z, then I'll help you." We will not be told whom we should choose as allies. We will not be isolated from any group or nation except by our own choice. We cannot have the oppressors telling the oppressed how to rid themselves of the oppressor. . . .

Black people do not want to "take over" this country. They don't want to "get whitey"; they just want to get him off their backs, as the saying goes. . . . The white man is irrelevant to blacks, except as an oppressive force. Blacks want to be in his place, yes, but not in order to terrorize and lynch and starve him. They want to be in his place because that is where a decent life can be had.

But our vision is not merely of a society in which all black men have enough to buy the good things of life. When we urge that black money go into black pockets, we mean the communal pocket. We want to see money go back into the community and used to benefit it. We want to see the cooperative concept applied in business and banking. We want to see black ghetto residents demand that an exploiting landlord or storekeeper sell them, at minimal cost, a building or a shop that they will own and improve cooperatively; they can back their demand with a rent strike, or a boycott, and a community so unified behind them that no one else will move into the building or buy at the store. The society we seek to build among black people, then, is not a capitalist one. It is a society in which the spirit of community and humanistic love prevail. The word love is suspect; black expectations of what it might produce have been betrayed too often. But those were expectations of a response from the white community, which failed us. The love we seek to encourage is within the black community, the only American community where men call each other "brother" when they meet. We can build a community of love only where we have the ability and power to do so: among blacks.

As for white America, perhaps it can stop crying out against "black supremacy," "black nationalism," "racism in reverse," and begin facing reality. The reality is that this nation, from top to bottom, is racist; that racism is not primarily a problem of "human relations" but of an exploitation maintained—either actively or through silence—by the society as a whole. . . .

We have found that they usually cannot condemn themselves, and so we have done it. But the rebuilding of this society, if at all possible, is basically the responsibility of whites—not blacks. We won't fight to save the present society, in Vietnam or anywhere else. We are just going to work, in the way we see fit, and on our goals we define, not for civil rights but for all our human rights.

REVIEW QUESTIONS

1. What did Carmichael mean by "black power"?
2. Why did Carmichael reject the principle of racial integration?
3. What did he mean when he said that blacks should create a society that was not capitalist?

LYNDON B. JOHNSON

FROM Peace without Conquest (1965)

President Lyndon B. Johnson tried repeatedly to convince the public of the strategic importance of South Vietnam and to rally popular support for American military intervention. In this 1965 speech he presented themes and assumptions that would frequently reappear in his later pronouncements.

From U.S. Department of State, *Bulletin* 52 (April 26, 1965): 607. [Editorial insertion appears in square brackets—*Ed.*]

. . . Over this war, and all Asia, is the deepening shadow of Communist China. The rulers in Hanoi [North Vietnam] are urged on by Peking. This is a regime which has destroyed freedom in Tibet, attacked India, and been condemned by the United Nations for aggression in Korea. It is a nation which is helping the forces of violence in almost every continent. The contest in Vietnam is part of a wider pattern of aggressive purpose.

Why are these realities our concern? Why are we in South Vietnam? We are there because we have a promise to keep. Since 1954 every American President has offered support to the people of South Vietnam. We have helped to build, and we have helped to defend. Thus, over many years, we have made a national pledge to help South Vietnam defend its independence. And I intend to keep our promise.

To dishonor that pledge, to abandon this small and brave nation to its enemy, and to the terror that must follow, would be an unforgivable wrong.

We are also there to strengthen world order. Around the globe, from Berlin to Thailand, are people whose well-being rests, in part, on the belief that they can count on us if they are attacked. To leave Vietnam to its fate would shake the confidence of all these people in the value of American commitment, the value of America's word. The result would be increased unrest and instability, and even wider war.

We are also there because there are great stakes in the balance. Let no one think for a moment that retreat from Vietnam would bring an end to conflict. The battle would be renewed in one country and then another. The central lesson of our time is that the appetite of aggression is never satisfied. To withdraw from one battlefield means only to prepare for the next. We must say in Southeast Asia, as we did in Europe, in the words of the Bible: "Hitherto shalt thou come, but no further."

There are those who say that all our effort there will be futile, that China's power is such it is bound to dominate all Southeast Asia. But there is no end to that argument until all the nations of Asia are swallowed up.

There are those who wonder why we have a responsibility there. We have it for the same reason we have a responsibility for the defense of freedom in Europe. World War II was fought in both Europe and Asia, and when it ended we found ourselves with continued responsibility for the defense of freedom.

Our objective is the independence of South Vietnam, and its freedom from attack. We want nothing for ourselves, only that the people of South Vietnam be allowed to guide their own country in their own way.

We will do everything necessary to reach that objective. And we will do only what is absolutely necessary.

In recent months, attacks on South Vietnam were stepped up. Thus it became necessary to increase our response and to make attacks by air. This is not a change of purpose. It is a change in what we believe that purpose requires.

We do this in order to slow down aggression. We do this to increase the confidence of the brave people of South Vietnam who have bravely borne this brutal battle for so many years and with so many casualties.

And we do this to convince the leaders of North Vietnam, and all who seek to share their conquest, of a very simple fact:

We will not be defeated.

We will not grow tired.

We will not withdraw, either openly or under the cloak of a meaningless agreement. . . .

Once this is clear, then it should also be clear that the only path for reasonable men is the path of peaceful settlement.

Such peace demands an independent South Vietnam securely guaranteed and able to shape its own relationships to all others, free from outside interference, tied to no alliance, a military base for no other country.

These are the essentials of any final settlement.

We will never be second in the search for such a peaceful settlement in Vietnam.

There may be many ways to this kind of peace: in discussion or negotiation with the governments concerned; in large groups or in small ones; in the reaffirmation of old agreements or their strengthening with new ones. We have stated this position over and over again fifty times and more, to friend and foe alike. And we remain ready, with this purpose, for unconditional discussions.

And until that bright and necessary day of peace we will try to keep conflict from spreading. We have no desire to see thousands die in battle, Asians or Americans. We have no desire to devastate that which the people of North Vietnam have built with toil and sacrifice. We will use our power with restraint and with all the wisdom we can command. But we will use it. . . .

We will always oppose the effort of one nation to conquer another nation.

We will do this because our own security is at stake.

But there is more to it than that. For our generation has a dream. It is a very old dream. But we have the power and now we have the opportunity to make it come true.

For centuries, nations have struggled among each other. But we dream of a world where disputes are settled by law and reason. And we will try to make it so.

For most of history men have hated and killed one another in battle. But we dream of an end to war. And we will try to make it so.

For all existence most men have lived in poverty, threatened by hunger. But we dream of a world where all are fed and charged with hope. And we will help to make it so.

The ordinary men and women of North Vietnam and South Vietnam—of China and India—of Russia and America—are brave people. They are filled with the same proportions of hate and fear, of love and hope. Most of them want the same things for themselves and their families. Most of them do not want their sons ever to die in battle, or see the homes of others destroyed. . . .

Every night before I turn out the lights to sleep, I ask myself this question: Have I done everything that I can do to unite this country? Have I done everything I can to help unite the world, to try to bring peace and hope to all the peoples of the world? Have I done enough?

Ask yourselves that question in your homes and in this hall tonight. Have we done all we could? Have we done enough? . . .

REVIEW QUESTIONS

1. In what way did Johnson believe that American credibility was at stake in Vietnam? Why was such credibility so important?

2. Did Johnson make reference to domestic political concerns? How might partisan politics have affected his outlook on Vietnam?

3. How would the North Vietnamese have responded to this speech?

INTERPRETING VISUAL SOURCES: THE CIVIL RIGHTS MOVEMENT

The civil rights movement was one of the most important developments in the twentieth century. In 1900 state-mandated segregation was pervasive across the South and racist violence against African Americans was widespread across the nation. Vigilante justice that often ended in the lynching of blacks was all too common.

Yet by the end of World War II, forces converged to spawn an organized crusade for civil rights and social justice. One of those factors was the war itself. Mobilization enabled a million African Americans to serve in the armed forces and broaden their horizons. Even more blacks were able to gain better jobs and working conditions in the defense industries. Waging a war against fascism and its theories of racial superiority led growing numbers of Americans to challenge racism in the United States. Blacks protested all kinds of discrimination, including social segregation. Membership in the National Association for the Advancement of Colored People (NAACP) soared.

After the war ended, the ideological conflict with the Soviet Union led many people to argue that racism was impeding the national effort in the Cold War. In early 1953, when Dwight D. Eisenhower assumed the presidency, he endorsed civil rights in principle, and during his first three years in office, public services in Washington, D.C., were desegregated, as were navy yards and veterans' hospitals. At the same time, challenges to segregated public schools were emerging across the nation.

When the Supreme Court in 1954 issued its pathbreaking decision in Brown v. Board of Education of Topeka, Kansas *outlawing segregated schools, it provided an essential catalyst to the civil rights movement. Equally influential was Rosa Parks's decision to violate the local ordinance in Montgomery, Alabama, requiring blacks to give up their seats to whites on public buses. Her courageous decision set in motion the Montgomery bus boycott. Its success convinced civil rights activists that the time was ripe for a sustained assault on all forms of racial discrimination. By the early 1960s the South was awash in civil disobedience against racism, which in turn was met by "massive resistance." Demonstrators— women, men, and children—braved fire hoses, police dogs, beatings, and humili- ation. Photographers, both black and white, captured on film the often horrific scenes, and the stunning images that appeared in newspapers and magazines helped prick consciences and galvanize national support for the struggle. The Civil Rights Act of 1964 and the Voting Rights Act of 1965 resulted largely from the grassroots movement for civil rights and social justice.*

The Lynching of Rubin Stacy (1935)

The Lynching of Rubin Stacy
Photo 12/Alamy Stock Photo

Race relations in the United States took a decided turn for the worse after 1890. In the South, whites grew concerned about a new generation of African Americans, born in freedom after the Civil War, who were reluctant to abide by traditional notions of white supremacy. By the early twentieth century, state after state had established laws to disenfranchise black voters; impose segregation in public facilities, schools, and transportation; and reinforce the sharecropping and tenantry systems that denied blacks social mobility and economic opportunity. Accompanying such legal and extra-legal efforts to impose racial subordination were increasing acts of violence designed to frighten and intimidate the African American community.

Between 1882 and 1968, some 4,742 blacks were killed by lynch mobs. The victims were often accused of crimes against whites, but it mattered little to the vigilantes whether the charges were true. On occasion blacks were tortured, killed, and mutilated for no reason other than the color of their skin. Lynchings became so commonly accepted that they operated as a form of community recreation and social spectacle. The spectators, many of them children, took grisly delight in the abuses meted out on blacks. "To kill the victim was not enough," one historian has written; "the execution became public theater, a participatory ritual of torture and death, a voyeuristic spectacle prolonged as long as possible (once for seven hours) for the benefit of the crowd."

This photograph shows the lynching of Rubin Stacy on July 19, 1935, in Ft. Lauderdale, Florida. He had been arrested for "assaulting" a white woman named Marion Jones. While six deputies were transporting Stacy to the Dade County jail in Miami, a mob of some 100 whites ran the police car off the road, overpowered the guard, and took control of the handcuffed Stacy. They riddled his body with bullets before hanging him. Later investigations revealed that Stacy, a homeless tenant farmer, had gone to the home of Mrs. Jones and had asked for food. She grew frightened and called police. There was no assault.

Rosa Parks Being Fingerprinted (1955)

The modern civil rights movement began with the refusal of Rosa Parks, a forty-three-year-old seamstress and officer in the local NAACP chapter, to give up her seat to a white man on a bus in Montgomery, Alabama, on December 1, 1955. The bus driver warned Parks that he would have her arrested if she did not move. "You may do that," she replied in a soft voice.

Her arrest led African American community leaders to organize a massive boycott of the city bus system. For months blacks in Montgomery formed carpools, hitchhiked, or simply walked. On February 22, 1956, Parks was indicted with the Reverend Martin Luther King Jr., and 100 other blacks for violating the city's anti-boycott ordinance. But the boycott continued throughout 1956. The boycotters finally won a federal case they had initiated to protest the segregation ordinance, and in November 1956 the Supreme Court let stand a lower court opinion that "the separate but equal doctrine can no longer be safely followed as a correct statement of the law." Alabama's bus-segregation laws were deemed unconstitutional. On December 21, 1956, the first integrated bus rolled through the streets of Montgomery.

CHARLES MOORE

Martin Luther King Jr., Arrested on a Loitering Charge (1958)

MARTIN LUTHER KING JR., ARRESTED ON A LOITERING CHARGE
Charles Moore/Getty Images

As the twenty-six-year-old minister at the Dexter Avenue Baptist Church, the Reverend Martin Luther King Jr. emerged as the courageous leader of the Montgomery bus boycott. After the boycott ended late in 1956, King became the nation's foremost champion of civil rights. On September 3, 1958, he attended a court hearing for his colleague Ralph David Abernathy. As he entered the courtroom, police officers told him to move on; King held his ground and was arrested. The officers marched King to police headquarters and shoved him against the receiving desk. The sergeant tossed the officers the keys to a cell while King's distraught wife, Coretta, looked on. Charles Moore, a newspaper photographer for the Montgomery Advertiser, *was at the courtroom when King was arrested and followed him to the police station. His photographs of the incident were reproduced across the world, and the powerful images helped galvanize public support for the civil rights movement.*

Elizabeth Eckford Badgered by a Mob as She Enters Little Rock High School (1957)

In 1954 the Supreme Court issued its opinion in the landmark case of Brown v. Board of Education of Topeka, Kansas. *The justices unanimously declared that racially segregated public schools were unconstitutional. A year later the Court ordered that the process of integrating the nation's public schools occur "with all deliberate speed." Reaction among segregationists was swift and violent. Virginia senator Harry F. Byrd called on southerners to use "massive resistance" to thwart the court ruling. By the end of 1956, in six southern states, not a single African American child attended school with whites. Arkansas governor Orville Faubus called out the National Guard to prevent nine black students, aged fourteen to sixteen, from entering Central High School in Little Rock.*

On September 4, 1957, Elizabeth Eckford rode a public bus to the high school. When soldiers prevented her entry to the school, she turned around to confront a hysterical white mob. "They moved closer and closer," Eckford recalled. "Somebody started yelling, 'Lynch her. Lynch her.'" A white woman finally led Eckford to the safety of a bus that took her home. Two weeks later a federal court order forced Faubus to remove the troops, and on September 23 the nine courageous black students entered a side door of the high school and began attending classes. The mob outside the school went berserk, forcing school officials to take the students home. The chaotic scene in Little Rock finally convinced President Dwight Eisenhower to dispatch federal troops to protect the black students.

FRED BLACKWELL

Sit-in at F. W. Woolworth's Counter (1963)

SIT-IN AT F. W. WOOLWORTH'S COUNTER
© Fred Blackwell

After the Montgomery bus boycott of 1955–56, Martin Luther King's philosophy of "militant non-violence" inspired others to challenge deeply entrenched patterns of racial segregation in the South. The momentum and energy of the broadening efforts spawned the first genuine mass movement in African American history when four black college freshmen sat down and demanded service at a whites-only Woolworth's lunch counter in Greensboro, North Carolina, on February 1, 1960.

Within a week, the "sit-in" movement had spread to six more cities across the state, and within two months, demonstrations had occurred in fifty-four cities in nine states. In some locations the sit-in students, both black and white, were attacked, but they all followed the directions of student leader John L. Lewis: "Do show yourself friendly on the counter at all times. Do sit straight and always face the counter. Don't strike back, or curse if attacked." But above all, he concluded, "Remember the teachings of Jesus, Gandhi, Thoreau, and Martin Luther King Jr."

On May 28, 1963, a group of Tougaloo College students and professors organized a sit-in at the Woolworth's lunch counter in Jackson, Mississippi. After they sat down and requested service, the waitresses closed the counter. The sit-in continued, however, and soon scores of angry whites, including students from Jackson High School arriving for lunch, began taunting and assaulting them. A group of almost 100 white policemen watched the melee from outside the store; they refused to intervene. For almost three hours, the demonstrators were kicked and beaten, burned with cigarettes, and covered with salt, pepper, sugar, ketchup, and mustard. Finally, the store owner succeeded in begging the police to end the fracas. This photograph shows students Anne Moody (far right) and Joan Trumpauer seated next to Professor John Salter Jr.

BILL HUDSON

William Gadsden Attacked by Police Dogs (1963)

WILLIAM GADSDEN ATTACKED BY POLICE DOGS
Bill Hudson/AP Photo

In the spring of 1963 Martin Luther King and the SCLC launched a series of nonviolent demonstrations in Birmingham, Alabama, the most segregated city in the South. One of King's lieutenants, Fred Shuttlesworth, remembered that "we wanted confrontation, nonviolent confrontation, to see if it would work on a massive scale. Not just for Birmingham—for the nation. We were trying to launch a systematic, wholehearted battle against segregation which would set the pace for the nation." The Birmingham police commissioner, Eugene "Bull" Connor, served as the perfect foil for King's strategy of nonviolent civil disobedience. Connor ordered police to use attack dogs, tear gas, electric cattle prods, and fire hoses on the protesters while millions of outraged Americans watched the confrontations on television.

On May 3, 1963, hundreds of demonstrators, blacks and whites, assembled near the Sixteenth Street Baptist Church. Connor ordered them ousted and arrested. The shocking pictures of police dogs attacking demonstrators galvanized support for the civil rights movement around the nation—and the world. Congressman Peter Rodino was attending a conference in Geneva, Switzerland, when this photograph appeared in European newspapers. One of the conference delegates asked him, "Is this the way you practice democracy?" Rodino said he had no answer.

SECTION REVIEW QUESTIONS

1. Why did parents allow their children to attend lynchings?
2. Women played a central role in the civil rights movement. What impressions does the photograph portray of Rosa Parks?
3. Martin Luther King Jr. promoted the tactic of nonviolent civil disobedience for several reasons. What role did such photographic images play in his strategy?
4. What role do you think you would have played in the turmoil surrounding racial integration had you been a student in the late 1950s or early 1960s?

30 ✑ REBELLION AND REACTION: THE 1960s AND 1970s

During the decade and a half after John Kennedy entered the White House in 1961, the fabric of American society unraveled. A variety of social groups—middle-class white youths, racial and ethnic minorities, feminists, and others—challenged the consensus that had governed American society since the end of World War II. The tragic shootings of public figures—John and Robert Kennedy, Martin Luther King Jr., George Wallace—heightened the sense of chaos. Racial violence and the war in Vietnam fueled social tensions. Intense debates over the volatile issue of abortion further fragmented the nation. To be sure, the end of American involvement in Vietnam in 1973 removed a major source of controversy. But revelations of the Watergate scandal provided another wound to the body politic. The fact that American society survived such prolonged tensions and trauma testifies to the resilience of the Republic.

The civil rights and anti-war movements drew their energies from a youth revolt that began in the 1950s and blossomed in the 1960s and early 1970s. During the late 1950s, the baby boom generation began to enter high school. By the sixties they were enrolled in colleges in record numbers. While the vast majority of these young Americans entered the mainstream of social life, a growing minority grew alienated from the conformity and materialism they saw corrupting middle-class culture. Generational unrest appeared early in the 1950s with the emergence of the Beat poets and alienated teenagers personified by actor James Dean in films such as Rebel Without a Cause *and by Holden Caulfield in J. D. Salinger's bestselling novel* Catcher in the Rye.

By the late 1960s a full-fledged cultural rebellion was under way, and all forms of authority were being questioned. The so-called counterculture celebrated personal freedom at the expense of traditional social mores. Youthful rebels—dubbed hippies—defied parental authority and college officials. In "dropping out" of conventional society, they grew long hair, wore eccentric clothes, gathered in urban or rural communes, used mind-altering drugs, relished "hard" rock music, and engaged in casual sex.

Other young rebels chose to change society rather than abandon it. During the late 1950s small groups of college students began to explore the promise of radical politics, and people began to refer to the emergence of a "New Left." Unlike the Old Left of the 1930s that had relied on Marxist theory and presumed that the contradictions inherent in capitalism would eventually bring about its own collapse, the leaders of the New Left asserted that fundamental social and political changes had to be initiated by well-organized young intellectuals.

The most prominent of the groups representing the New Left was the Students for a Democratic Society (SDS). In 1962 the organization distributed the Port Huron Statement, a manifesto that promoted "participatory democracy"—rather than the traditional political parties as the vehicle for social change—and envisioned universities as the locus of the new movement. SDS was not willing to wait decades for the dialectic of materialism to run its course. They wanted to effect changes immediately. The Port Huron Statement thus decried the apathy on college campuses and urged young people to take collective action against racism, poverty, and the military-industrial complex. Thereafter, members of SDS and other like-minded college students fanned out across the country, seeking to organize poor people into political action groups and to help southern blacks register to vote.

During the mid-1960s the youth revolt spread from the inner cities and rural South to college campuses across the nation. As student activists returned from working as volunteers in the civil rights movement or in anti-poverty programs, they brought with them a militant idealism that initially manifested itself in protests against university regulations and later focused its energies on opposition to the Vietnam War and the draft.

Beginning with the start of the American bombing campaign in 1965 and fueled by the rising numbers of ground forces fighting and dying in Vietnam, organized anti-war protests and teach-ins occurred at hundreds of universities across the country. Such domestic dissent seemed only to harden the commitment of the Johnson and Nixon administrations to the war in Vietnam and produced a social backlash against the protesters. By the end of the 1960s militants were resorting to violence to draw attention to their cause. Dozens of bombings rocked college campuses in 1969 and 1970. One such explosion killed a student at the University of Wisconsin.

President Nixon's announcement of the "incursion" of South Vietnamese and American troops into Cambodia in the spring of 1970 unleashed dozens of anti-war demonstrations on college campuses. At Kent State University in Ohio, students set fire to the ROTC building. The governor dispatched National Guard units to quell the unrest, and the next day a confrontation occurred at the commons in the center of the campus. As demonstrators hurled rocks and epithets at the troops, the Guardsmen panicked and opened fire, killing four students and wounding many others.

After the American withdrawal from Vietnam in 1973, the anti-war movement subsided. But youthful activism persisted and quickly found new causes to promote. The idealism and energy generated by the civil rights movement and anti-war activities helped inspire organized efforts to gain equality and benefits for other groups: women, Native Americans, gays and lesbians, migrant workers, and the elderly. Still other idealists focused their attention on the degradation of the environment and sought to promote an ecological consciousness.

TOM HAYDEN

FROM The Port Huron Statement (1962)

In 1962 sixty members of the Students for a Democratic Society (SDS) gathered at a conference center at Port Huron on the southern shore of Lake Huron, about fifty miles north of Detroit. Led by Tom Hayden, a graduate student at the University of Michigan and editor of the campus newspaper, they drafted a statement of principles and objectives that came to be known as the Port Huron Statement.

From *Democracy Is in the Streets: From Port Huron to the Siege of Chicago*, by J. Miller, pp. 329–45. Reprinted by permission of Tom Hayden.

We are people of this generation, bred in at least modest comfort, housed now in universities, looking uncomfortably to the world we inherit. When we were kids the United States was the wealthiest and strongest country in the world; the only one with the atom bomb, the least scarred by modern war, an initiator of the United Nations that we thought would distribute Western influence throughout the world. Freedom and equality for each individual, government of, by, and for the people—these American values we found good, principles by which we could live as men. Many of us began maturing in complacency.

As we grew, however, our comfort was penetrated by events too troubling to dismiss.

First, the permeating and victimizing fact of human degradation, symbolized by the Southern struggle against racial bigotry, compelled most of us from silence to activism. Second, the enclosing fact of the Cold War, symbolized by the presence of the Bomb, brought awareness that we ourselves, and our friends, and millions of abstract "others" we knew more directly because of our common peril, might die at any time. We might deliberately ignore, or avoid, or fail to feel all other human problems, but not these two, for these were too immediate and crushing in their impact, too challenging in the demand that we as individuals take the responsibility for encounter and resolution.

While these and other problems either directly oppressed us or rankled our consciences and became our own subjective concern, we began to see complicated and disturbing paradoxes in our surrounding America. The declaration "all men are created equal . . ." rang hollow before the facts of Negro life in the South and the big cities of the North. The proclaimed peaceful intentions of the United States contradicted its economic and military investments in the Cold War status quo.

We witnessed, and continue to witness, other paradoxes. With nuclear energy whole cities can easily be powered, yet the dominant nation-states seem more likely to unleash destruction greater than that incurred in all wars of human history. Although our own technology is destroying old and creating new forms of social organization, men still tolerate meaningless work and idleness. While two-thirds of mankind suffers undernourishment, our own upper classes revel amidst superfluous abundance. Although the world population is expected to double in forty years, the nations still tolerate anarchy as a major principle of international conduct and uncontrolled exploitation governs the sapping of the earth's physical resources. Although mankind desperately needs revolutionary leadership, America rests in national stalemate, its goals ambiguous and tradition-bound instead of informed and clear, its democratic system apathetic and manipulated rather than "of, by, and for the people."

Not only did tarnish appear on our image of American virtue, not only did disillusion occur when the hypocrisy of American ideals was discovered, but we began to sense that what we had originally seen as the American Golden Age was actually the decline of an era. The world-wide outbreak of revolution against colonialism and imperialism, the entrenchment of totalitarian states, the menace of war, overpopulation, international disorder, supertechnology—these trends were testing the tenacity of our own commitment to democracy and freedom and our abilities to visualize their application to a world in upheaval.

Our work is guided by the sense that we may be the last generation in the experiment with living. But we are a minority—the vast majority of our people regard the temporary equilibriums of our society and world as eternally functional parts. In this is perhaps the outstanding paradox: we ourselves are imbued with urgency, yet the message of our society is that there is no viable alternative to the present. Beneath the reassuring tones of the politicians, beneath the common opinion that America will "muddle through," beneath the stagnation of those who have closed their minds to the future, is the pervading feeling that there simply are no alternatives, that our times have witnessed the exhaustion not only of Utopias, but of any new departures as well.

Feeling the press of complexity upon the emptiness of life, people are fearful of the thought that at any moment things might be thrust out of control. They fear change itself, since change might smash whatever invisible framework seems to hold back chaos for them now.

For most Americans, all crusades are suspect, threatening. The fact that each individual sees apathy in his fellows perpetuates the common reluctance to organize for change. The dominant institutions are complex enough to blunt the minds of their potential critics, and entrenched enough to swiftly dissipate or entirely repel the energies of protest and reform, thus limiting

human expectancies. Then, too, we are a materially improved society, and by our own improvements we seem to have weakened the case for further change.

Some would have us believe that Americans feel contentment amidst prosperity—but might it not better be called a glaze above deeply felt anxieties about their role in the new world? And if these anxieties produce a developed indifference to human affairs, do they not as well produce a yearning to believe there *is* an alternative to the present, that something *can* be done to change circumstances in the school, the work-places, the bureaucracies, the government?

It is to this latter yearning, at once the spark and engine of change, that we direct our present appeal. The search for truly democratic alternatives to the present, and a commitment to social experimentation with them, is a worthy and fulfilling human enterprise, one which moves us and, we hope, others today.

On such a basis do we offer this document of our convictions and analysis: as an effort in understanding and changing the conditions of humanity in the late twentieth century, an effort rooted in the ancient, still unfulfilled conception of man attaining determining influence over his circumstances of life.

*   *   *

Values

Making values explicit—an initial task in establishing alternatives—is an activity that has been devalued and corrupted. The conventional moral terms of the age, the politician moralities—"free world," "peoples democracies"—reflect realities poorly, if at all, and seem to function more as ruling myths than as descriptive principles. But neither has our experience in the universities brought us moral enlightenment. Our professors and administrators sacrifice controversy to public relations; their curriculums change more slowly than the living events of the world, their skills and silence are purchased by investors in the arms race: passion is called unscholastic. The questions we might want raised—what is really important? can we live in a different and better way? if we wanted to change society, how would we do it?—are not thought to be questions of a "fruitful, empirical nature," and thus are brushed aside.

*   *   *

. . . It has been said that our liberal—and socialist—predecessors were plagued by vision without program, while our own generation is plagued by program without vision. All around us there is astute grasp of method, technique—the committee, the ad hoc group, the lobbyist, the hard and soft sell, the make, the projected image—but, if pressed critically, such expertise is incompetent to explain its implicit ideals. It is highly fashionable to identify oneself by old categories, or by naming a respected political figure, or by explaining "how we would vote" on various issues.

Theoretic chaos has replaced the idealistic thinking of old—and, unable to reconstitute theoretic order, men have condemned idealism itself. Doubt has replaced hopefulness and men act out a defeatism that is labeled realistic. The decline of utopia and hope is in fact one of the defining features of social life today. The reasons are various: the dreams of the older left were perverted by Stalinism and never re-created; the congressional stalemate makes men narrow their view of the possible; the specialization of human activity leaves little room for sweeping thought; the horrors of the twentieth century, symbolized in the gas ovens and concentration camps and atom bombs, have blasted hopefulness. To be idealistic is to be considered apocalyptic, deluded. To have no serious aspirations, on the contrary, is to be "tough-minded."

In suggesting social goals and values, therefore, we are aware of entering a sphere of some disrepute. Perhaps matured by the past, we have no sure formulas, no closed theories—but that does not mean values are beyond discussion and tentative determination. A first task of any social movement is to convince people that the search for orienting theories and the creation of human values is complex but worthwhile. We are aware that to avoid platitudes we must analyze the concrete conditions of social order. But to direct such an analysis we must use the guideposts of basic principles. Our own social values involve conceptions of human beings, human relationships, and social systems.

We regard *men* as infinitely precious and possessed of unfulfilled capacities for reason, freedom, and love. In affirming these principles we are aware of countering perhaps the dominant conceptions of man in the twentieth century: that he is a thing to be manipulated, and that he is inherently incapable of directing his own affairs. We oppose the depersonalization that reduces human beings to the status of things—if anything, the brutalities of the twentieth century teach that means and ends are intimately related, that vague appeals to "posterity" cannot justify the mutilations of the present. We oppose, too, the doctrine of human incompetence because it rests essentially on the modern fact that men have been competently manipulated into incompetence—we see little reason why men cannot meet with increasing skill the complexities and responsibilities of their situation, if society is organized not for minority, but for majority, participation in decision-making.

Men have unrealized potential for self-cultivation, self-direction, self-understanding, and creativity. It is this potential that we regard as crucial and to which we appeal, not to the human potentiality for violence, unreason, and submission to authority. The goal of man and society should be human independence: a concern not with image or popularity but with finding a meaning in life that is personal and authentic; a quality of mind not compulsively driven by a sense of powerlessness, nor one which unthinkingly adopts status values, nor one which represses all threats to its habits, but one which has full, spontaneous access to present and past experiences, one which easily unites the fragmented parts of personal history, one which openly faces problems which are troubling and unresolved; one with an intuitive awareness of possibilities, an active sense of curiosity, an ability and willingness to learn.

This kind of independence does not mean egotistic individualism—the object is not to have one's way so much as it is to have a way that is one's own. Nor do we deify man—we merely have faith in his potential.

Human relationships should involve fraternity and honesty. Human interdependence is contemporary fact; human brotherhood must be willed, however, as a condition of future survival and as the most appropriate form of social relations. Personal links between man and man are needed, especially, to go beyond the partial and fragmentary bonds of function that bind men only as worker to worker, employer to employees, teacher to student, American to Russian.

Loneliness, estrangement, isolation describe the vast distance between man and man today. These dominant tendencies cannot be overcome by better personnel management, nor by improved gadgets, but only when a love of man overcomes the idolatrous worship of things by man. As the individualism we affirm is not egoism, the selflessness we affirm is not self-elimination. On the contrary, we believe in generosity of a kind that imprints one's unique individual qualities in the relation to other men, and to all human activity. Further, to dislike isolation is not to favor the abolition of privacy; the latter differs from isolation in that it occurs or is abolished according to individual will.

We would replace power rooted in possession, privilege, or circumstance by power and uniqueness rooted in love, reflectiveness, reason, and creativity. As a *social system* we seek the establishment of a democracy of individual participation, governed by two central aims: that the individual share in those social decisions determining the quality and direction of his life; that society be organized to encourage independence in men and provide the media for their common participation.

In a participatory democracy, the political life would be based in several root principles: that decision-making of basic social consequence be carried on by public groupings; that politics be seen positively, as the art of collectively creating an acceptable pattern of social relations; that politics has the function of bringing people out of isolation and into community, thus being a necessary, though not sufficient, means of finding meaning in personal life; that the political order should serve to clarify problems in a way instrumental to their solution; it should provide outlets for the expression of personal grievance and aspiration; opposing views should be organized so as to illuminate choices and facilitate the attainment of goals; channels should be commonly available to relate men to knowledge and to power so that private problems—from bad recreation facilities to personal alienation—are formulated as general issues.

The economic sphere would have as its basis the principles: that work should involve incentives worthier than money or survival. It should be educative, not stultifying; creative, not mechanical; self-directed, not manipulated; encouraging independence, a respect for others, a sense of dignity, and a willingness to accept social responsibility since it is this experience that has crucial influence on habits, perceptions, and individual ethics; that the economic experience is so personally decisive that the individual must share in its full determination; that the economy itself is of such social importance that its major resources and means of production should be open to democratic participation and subject to democratic social regulation.

Like the political and economic ones, major social institutions—cultural, educational, rehabilitative, and others—should be generally organized with the well-being and dignity of man as the essential measure of success.

In social change or interchange, we find violence to be abhorrent because, it requires generally the transformation of the target, be it a human being or a community of people, into a depersonalized object of hate. It is imperative that the means of violence be abolished and the institutions—local, national, international—that encourage nonviolence as a condition of conflict be developed. These are our central values, in skeletal form. It remains vital to understand their denial or attainment in the context of the modern world.

*   *   *

Tragically, the university could serve as a significant source of social criticism and initiator of new modes and molders of attitudes. But the actual intellectual effect of the college experience is hardly distinguishable from that of any other communications channel—say, a television set—passing on the stock truths of the day. Students leave college somewhat more "tolerant" than when they arrived, but basically unchallenged in their values and political orientations. With administrators ordering the institution, and faculty the curriculum, the student learns by his isolation to accept elite rule within the University, which prepares him to accept later forms of minority control. The real function of the educational system—as opposed to its more rhetorical function of "searching for truth"—is to impart the key information and styles that will help the student get by, modestly but comfortably, in the big society beyond. . . .

The very isolation of the individual—from power and community and ability to aspire—means the rise of a democracy without publics. With the great mass of people structurally remote and psychologically hesitant with respect to democratic institutions, those institutions themselves attenuate and become, in the fashion of the vicious circle, progressively less accessible to those few who aspire to serious participation in social affairs. The vital democratic connection between community and leadership, between the mass and the several elites, has been so wrenched and perverted that disastrous policies go unchallenged time and again. . . .

REVIEW QUESTIONS

1. According to Hayden, what two phenomena disrupted the complacency of his generation?
2. What factors did Hayden cite as impeding the formulation of new values and a larger social vision?
3. How did Hayden define the concept of participatory democracy?

SUSAN BROWNMILLER

FROM Abortion Is a Woman's Right (1999)

A woman's legal access to abortion was one of the first issues addressed by the women's liberation movement between 1969 and 1973, when the Supreme Court issued its monumental ruling in Roe v. Wade, *declaring that women had a "constitutional right" to end a pregnancy. State laws imposing excessive restrictions on abortions were overturned. Susan Brownmiller, a Brooklyn-born feminist, journalist, author, and activist, was at the forefront of the efforts leading to* Roe v. Wade. *In her memoir, titled* In Our Time, *she recalled the context of the pro-choice crusade and her own experience with an illegal abortion.*

Nineteen sixty-nine was a precisely defined moment, the year when women of childbearing age transformed a quiet back-burner issue promoted by a handful of stray radicals and moderate reformers into a popular struggle for reproductive freedom. The women had been dubbed the Pill Generation, and indeed, earlier in the decade many had heeded the persuasive call of the sexual revolution, only to be disenchanted. Exploring their sexual freedom with an uncertain knowledge of birth control and haphazard employment of its techniques, they had discovered the hard way that unwanted pregnancy was still a woman's problem.

Unlike the isolated women of their parents' generation who sought individual solutions [to pregnancy] in furtive silence, they would bring a direct personal voice to the abortion debate. They would reveal their own stories, first to one another and then to the public. They would borrow the confrontational tactics of the radical-left movements from which they had come. They would break the law, and they would raise a ruckus to change the law, devising original strategies to fight for abortion through the courts.

Before the new militance erupted, abortion was a criminal act in every state unless a commit-tee of hospital physicians concurred that the pregnancy endangered the woman's life. Three states had extended the largesse to women whose health was threatened—broadly interpreted, health could mean mental health, if two psychiatrists so attested—but no more than ten thousand "therapeutic" abortions were performed in a year. To the general public, abortion was the stuff of lurid tabloid headlines that underscored its peril: A young woman's body found in a motel room; she'd bled to death from a botched operation. A practitioner and a hapless patient entrapped in a midnight raid on what the police dubbed "an abortion mill." There were shining exceptions like the legendary Robert Spencer of Ashland, Pennsylvania, who ran a spotless clinic and charged no more than one hundred dollars, but venality [corruption] ran high in an unlawful business in which practitioners were raided and jailed and patients were pressured to be informers. Money was not the only commodity exchanged on the underground circuit; some abortionists extorted sexual payment for their secret work.

One million women braved the unknown every year, relying on a grapevine of whispers and misinformation to terminate their pregnancies by illegal means. Those lucky enough to secure the address of a good practitioner, and to scrounge up the requisite cash, packed a small bag and headed for San Juan, Havana, London, or Tokyo, or perhaps across town. The less fortunate risked septic infection and a punctured uterus from back-alley amateurs willing to poke their insides with a catheter, a knitting needle, or the unfurled end of a wire hanger. Still others damaged their health with lye or Lysol, the last-ditch home treatments. *Life* magazine estimated in 1967 that "five thousand of the desperate" died every year.

The writer Jane O'Reilly's story gives the lie to the too simple myth that "rich" women could always find a connection. In the summer of 1957, she was a Catholic debutante from St. Louis who was looking forward to her senior year at Radcliffe [College] when she discovered she was pregnant. Dr. Spencer was in one of his periodic shutdowns, Cuba sounded unreal and scary, and the trusted family doctor to whom she appealed insisted that she tell her parents. A classmate finally came up with an address in New York and lent her the six hundred dollars. O'Reilly recalls that a man with a mustache placed her on a kitchen table, prodded her with a knitting needle, and gave her some pills.

A month later she fainted in her college dormitory shower. Whatever had been done to her in New York, Jane O'Reilly was still pregnant. Moving out of the dorm, she joked about putting on weight and took her finals shrouded in a raincoat.

The next day she gave birth at a Salvation Army hospital and signed away her baby daughter. For the next thirty-four years on every May 10, her daughter's birthday, O'Reilly plunged into a sobbing depression. In 1991 the pain partially lifted when her daughter found her through an adoption search.

Women of my generation still need to bear witness; we still carry the traumas. For my first abortion in 1960, I took the Cuba option that had scared O'Reilly. Here's what I remember: Banging on a door during the midday siesta in a strange neighborhood in Havana. Wriggling my toes a few hours later, astonished to be alive. Boarding a small plane to Key West and hitchhiking back to New York bleeding all the way. Bleeding? I must have been hemorrhaging. In which state did I leave the motel bed drenched with my blood?

REVIEW QUESTIONS

1. Prior to the *Roe v. Wade* decision in 1973, abortions were banned in all states except in rare cases when authorities ruled the woman's life was at stake. What options did women have for dealing with unwanted pregnancies?
2. How does Brownmiller's own experience with abortion affect the persuasiveness of her essay's argument?

GLORIA STEINEM

Equal Rights for Women—Yes and No (1970)

Like the civil rights movement, the women's rights movement developed a more radical wing as it matured. In the late 1960s, a younger generation of women activists began calling for a more comprehensive "women's liberation movement." Ohio-born Gloria Marie Steinem, a prominent journalist and social and political activist, emerged as one of the movement's most effective leaders. As a columnist for New York *magazine, she published in 1969 a seminal article titled "After Black Power,*

Women's Liberation," which, along with her ardent support of abortion rights, helped cement her stature as a national feminist leader. In 1972 Steinem co-founded *Ms.* magazine, which soon became the leading national publication promoting feminism. Steinem was at the forefront of the nationwide campaign to ratify the *Equal Rights Amendment (ERA)* to the U.S. Constitution. The proposed amendment stated that "equality of rights under the law shall not be denied or abridged by the United States or by any State on account of sex." In early May 1970, a Congressional committee hosted hearings on the ERA, and Steinem appeared before the committee to testify in support of it. Two years later, both houses of the Democratic-controlled Congress passed the ERA and sent it to the state legislatures for ratification. By 1982, however, the ERA had fallen short of gaining the necessary ratification by thirty-eight state legislatures, and the proposed amendment died.

From Congress, Senate, Committee on the Judiciary, *The "Equal Rights" Amendment: Hearings before the Subcommittee on Constitutional Amendments of the Committee on the Judiciary*, 91st Cong., 2d Sess., May 5–7, 1970.

My name is Gloria Steinem. I am a writer and editor, and I am currently a member of the policy council of the Democratic committee. And I work regularly with the lowest-paid workers in the country, the migrant workers, men, women, and children both in California and in my own State of New York. . . .

During 12 years of working for a living, I have experienced much of the legal and social discrimination reserved for women in this country. I have been refused service in public restaurants, ordered out of public gathering places, and turned away from apartment rentals; all for the clearly-stated, sole reason that I am a woman. And all without the legal remedies available to blacks and other minorities. I have been excluded from professional groups, writing assignments on so-called "unfeminine" subjects such as politics, full participation in the Democratic Party, jury duty, and even from such small male privileges as discounts on airline fares. . . .

However, after 2 years of researching the status of American women, I have discovered that in reality, I am very, very lucky. Most women, both wage-earners and housewives, routinely suffer more humiliation and injustice than I do.

*   *   *

. . . We have all been silent for too long. But we won't be silent anymore.

The truth is that all our problems stem from the same sex based myths. We may appear before you as white radicals or the middle-aged middle class or black soul sisters, but we are all sisters in fighting against these outdated myths. Like racial myths, they have been reflected in our laws. Let me list a few.

That woman are biologically inferior to men. In fact, an equally good case can be made for the reverse. Women live longer than men, even when the men are not subject to business pressures. . . .

*   *   *

Another myth, that some are already treated equally in this society. I am sure there has been ample testimony to prove that equal pay for equal work, equal chance for advancement, and equal training or encouragement is obscenely scarce in every field, even those—like food and fashion industries—that are supposedly "feminine."

*   *   *

Women suffer this second class treatment from the moment they are born. They are expected to be, rather than achieve, to function biologically rather than learn. . . .

*   *   *

Another myth, that children must have full-time mothers. American mothers spend more time with their homes and children than those of any other society we know about. In the past, joint families, servants, a prevalent system in which grandparents raised the children, or family field work in the agrarian systems—all these factors contributed more to child care than the labor-saving devices of which we are so proud.

The truth is that most American children seem to be suffering from too much mother, and too little father. Part of the program of Women's Liberation is a return of fathers to their children. If laws permit women equal work and pay opportunities, men will then be relieved of their role as sole breadwinner. Fewer ulcers, fewer hours of meaningless work, equal responsibility for his own children: these are a few of the reasons that Women's Liberation is Men's Liberation too.

*   *   *

Women are not more moral than men. We are only uncorrupted by power. But we do not want to imitate men, to join this country as it is, and I think our very participation will change it. Perhaps women elected leaders—and there will be many of them—will not be so likely to dominate black people or yellow people or men; anybody who looks different from us.

After all, we won't have our masculinity to prove.

REVIEW QUESTIONS

1. What forms of sexual discrimination had Steinem personally experienced?
2. Which "sexual myths" does Steinem highlight?

PHYLLIS SCHLAFLY

FROM What's Wrong with "Equal Rights" for Women? (1972)

During the 1970s social conservatives launched a concerted counterattack against the feminist movement, arguing that traditional gender roles were the foundation of human civilization. To these conservatives, the essential elements of social well-being—the family, religious belief, patriotism, respect for authority—depended on men and women knowing their place and working together to promote social cohesion. One of the most effective leaders of the anti-feminist movement was Phyllis Schlafly, a conservative Roman Catholic Republican activist living outside of St. Louis. An attorney by training and a talented grassroots organizer as well as Congressional candidate, Schlafly in 1972 founded a national organization called STOP ERA (Stop Taking Our Privileges) in an effort to reaffirm the primacy of marriage and motherhood for American women. Feminists, she asserted, were striving to "remake our laws, revise the marriage contract, restructure society, remold our children to conform to liberationist values instead of God's values, and replace the image of woman as virtue and mother with the image of the prostitute, swinger, and lesbian." In 1972 Schlafly explained her anti-feminist stance in her influential national newsletter, the Phyllis Schlafly Report.

From *Phyllis Schlafly Report* 5, No. 7, February 1972. Reprinted by permission of Phyllis Schlafly.

Of all the classes of people who ever lived, the American woman is the most privileged. We have the most rights and rewards, and the fewest duties. Our unique status is the result of a fortunate combination of circumstances.

1. We have the immense good fortune to live in a civilization which respects the family as the basic unit of society. This respect is part and parcel of our laws and our customs. It is based on the fact of life—which no legislation or agitation can erase—that women have babies and men don't.

If you don't like this fundamental difference, you will have to take up your complaint with God because He created us this way. The fact that women, not men, have babies is not the fault of selfish and domineering men, or of the establishment, or of any clique of conspirators who want to oppress women. It's simply the way God made us.

*   *   *

The Greatest Achievement of Women's Rights

This is accomplished by the institution of the family. Our respect for the family as the basic unit of society, which is ingrained in the laws and customs of our Judeo-Christian civilization, is the greatest single achievement in the entire history of women's rights. It assures a woman the most precious and important right of all—the right to keep her own baby and to be supported and protected in the enjoyment of watching her baby grow and develop.

*   *   *

The Financial Benefits of Chivalry

2. The second reason why American women are a privileged group is that we are the beneficiaries of a tradition of special respect for women which dates from the Christian Age of Chivalry. The honor and respect paid to Mary, the Mother of Christ, resulted in all women, in effect, being put on a pedestal.

. . . In America, a man's first significant purchase is a diamond for his bride, and the largest financial investment of his life is a home for her to live in. American husbands work hours of overtime to buy a fur piece or other finery to keep their wives in fashion, and to pay premiums on their life insurance policies to provide for her comfort when she is a widow (benefits in which he can never share).

*   *   *

The Real Liberation of Women

3. The third reason why American women are so well off is that the great American free enterprise system has produced remarkable inventors who have lifted the backbreaking "women's work" from our shoulders.

*   *   *

The real liberation of women from the backbreaking drudgery of centuries is the American free enterprise system which stimulated inventive geniuses to pursue their talents—and we all reap the profits. The great heroes of women's liberation are not the straggly-haired women on television talk shows and picket lines, but Thomas Edison who brought the miracle of electricity to our homes to give light and to run all those labor-saving devices—the equivalent, perhaps, of a half-dozen household servants for every middle-class American woman. Or Elias Howe who gave us the sewing machine which resulted in such an abundance of readymade clothing. Or Clarence Birdseye who invented the process for freezing foods. Or Henry Ford, who mass-produced the automobile so that it is within the price-range of every American, man or woman.

*   *   *

The Fraud of the Equal Rights Amendment

In the last couple of years, a noisy movement has sprung up agitating for "women's rights." Suddenly, everywhere we are afflicted with aggressive females on television talk shows yapping about how mistreated American women are, suggesting that marriage has put us in some kind of "slavery," that housework is menial and degrading, and—perish the thought—that women are discriminated against. New "women's liberation" organizations are popping up, agitating and demonstrating, serving demands on public officials, getting wide press coverage always, and purporting to speak for some 100,000,000 American women.

It's time to set the record straight. The claim that American women are downtrodden and unfairly treated is the fraud of the century. The truth is that American women never had it so good. Why should we lower ourselves to "equal rights" when we already have the status of special privilege?

*   *   *

What "Women's Lib" Really Means

Many women are under the mistaken impression that "women's lib" means more job employment opportunities for women, equal pay for equal work, appointments of women to high positions, admitting more women to medical schools, and other desirable objectives which all women favor. We all support these purposes, as well as any necessary legislation which would bring them about.

But all this is only a sweet syrup which covers the deadly poison masquerading as "women's lib." The women's libbers are radicals who are waging a total assault on the family, on marriage, and on children. Don't take my word for it—read their own literature and prove to yourself what these characters are trying to do.

The most pretentious of the women's liberation magazines is called *Ms.*, and subtitled "The New Magazine For Women," with Gloria Steinem listed as president and secretary.

Reading the Spring 1972 issue of *Ms.* gives a good understanding of women's lib, and the people who promote it. It is anti-family, anti-children, and pro-abortion. It is a series of sharp-tongued, high-pitched whining complaints by unmarried women. They view the home as a prison, and the wife and mother as a slave. To these women's libbers, marriage means dirty dishes and dirty laundry. One article lauds a woman's refusal to carry up the family laundry as "an act of extreme courage." Another tells how satisfying it is to be a lesbian.

*   *   *

Women's Libbers Do *Not* Speak for Us

The "women's lib" movement is *not* an honest effort to secure better jobs for women who want or need to work outside the home. This is just the superficial sweet-talk to win broad support for a radical "movement." Women's lib is a total assault on the role of the American woman as wife and mother, and on the family as the basic unit of society.

Women's libbers are trying to make wives and mothers unhappy with their career, make them feel that they are "second-class citizens" and "abject slaves." Women's libbers are promoting free sex instead of the "slavery" of marriage. They are promoting Federal "day-care centers" for babies instead of homes. They are promoting abortions instead of families.

*   *   *

Tell your Senators NOW that you want them to vote NO on the Equal Rights Amendment. Tell your television and radio stations that you want equal time to present the case FOR marriage and motherhood.

REVIEW QUESTIONS

1. How does Schlafly justify the traditional role of women as being centered on marriage and motherhood?
2. According to Schlafly, what role has "free enterprise" played in reinforcing traditional gender roles?

SHIRLEY CHISHOLM

FROM I'd Rather Be Black than Female (1970)

Born in Brooklyn, New York, in 1924, and educated at Brooklyn College and Columbia University, Shirley Chisholm (1924–2005) in 1968 became the first African American woman elected to Congress. She served seven terms in the House of Representatives and ran for the Democratic presidential nomination in 1972. In announcing her candidacy, she stressed, "I am not the candidate of black America, although I am black and proud. I am not the candidate of the women's movement of this country, although I am a woman and I am equally proud of that. I am the candidate of the people, and my presence before you now symbolizes a new era in American political history." Two years earlier, in 1970, Chisholm reflected on the obstacles and resistance she encountered as an African American woman seeking political office.

From "I'd Rather Be Black than Female," *McCall's* (August 1970), p. 6. [Editorial insertions appear in square brackets—*Ed.*]

Being the first black woman elected to Congress has made me some kind of phenomenon. There are nine other blacks in Congress; there are ten other women. I was the first to overcome both handicaps at once. Of the two handicaps, being black is much less of a drawback than being female.

If I said that being black is a greater handicap than being a woman, probably no one would question me. Why? Because "we all know" there is preju-dice against black people in America. That there is prejudice against women is an idea that still strikes nearly all men—and, I am afraid, most women—as bizarre.

Prejudice against blacks was invisible to most white Americans for many years. When blacks finally started to "mention" it, with sit-ins, boycotts, and freedom rides, Americans were incredulous. "Who, us?" they asked in injured tones. "We're prejudiced?" It was the start of a long, painful reeducation for white America. It will take years for whites—including those who think of themselves as liberals—to discover and eliminate the racist attitudes they all actually have.

How much harder will it be to eliminate the prejudice against women? I am sure it will be a longer struggle. Part of the problem is that women in America are much more brainwashed and content with their roles as second-class citizens than blacks ever were.

Let me explain. I have been active in politics for more than twenty years. For all but the last six, I have done the work—all the tedious details that make the difference between victory and defeat on election day—while men reaped the rewards, which is almost invariably the lot of women in politics.

It is still women—about three million volunteers—who do most of this work in the American political world. The best any of them can hope for is the honor of being district or county vice-chairman, a kind of separate-but-equal position with which a woman is rewarded for years of faithful envelope stuffing and card-party organizing. In such a job, she gets a number of free trips to state and sometimes national meetings and conventions, where her role is supposed to be to vote the way her male chairman votes.

When I tried to break out of that role in 1963 and run for the New York State Assembly seat from Brooklyn's Bedford-Stuyvesant [neighborhood], the resistance was bitter. From the start of that campaign, I faced undisguised hostility because of my sex.

But it was four years later, when I ran for Congress, that the question of my sex became a major issue. Among members of my own party, closed meetings were held to discuss ways of stopping me.

My opponent, the famous civil-rights leader James Farmer, tried to project a black, masculine image; he toured the neighborhood with sound trucks filled with young men wearing Afro haircuts, dashikis [colorful West African shirts], and beards. While the television crews ignored me, they were not aware of a very important statistic, which both I and my campaign manager, Wesley MacD. Holder,

knew. In my district there are 2.5 women for every man registered to vote. And those women are organized—in PTAs, church societies, card clubs, and other social and service groups. I went to them and asked [for] their help. Mr. Farmer still doesn't quite know what hit him.

When a bright young woman graduate starts looking for a job, why is the first question always: "Can you type?" A history of prejudice lies behind that question. Why are women thought of as secretaries, not administrators? Librarians and teachers, but not doctors and lawyers? Because they are thought of as different and inferior. The happy homemaker and the contented darky are both stereotypes produced by prejudice.

Women have not even reached the level of tokenism that blacks are reaching. No women sit on the Supreme Court. Only two have held Cabinet rank, and none do at present. Only two women hold ambassadorial rank. But women predominate in the lower-paying, menial, unrewarding, dead-end jobs, and when they do reach better positions, they are invariably paid less than a man gets for the same job.

If that is not prejudice, what would you call it?

A few years ago, I was talking with a political leader about a promising young woman as a candidate. "Why invest time and effort to build the girl up?" he asked me. "You know she'll only drop out of the game to have a couple of kids just about the time we're ready to run her for mayor."

Plenty of people have said similar things about me. Plenty of others have advised me, every time I tried to take another upward step, that I should go back to teaching, a woman's vocation, and leave politics to the men. I love teaching, and I am ready to go back to it as soon as I am convinced that this country no longer needs a woman's contribution.

When there are no children going to bed hungry in this rich nation, I may be ready to go back to teaching. When there is a good school for every child, I may be ready. When we do not spend our wealth on hardware to murder people, when we no longer tolerate prejudice against minorities, and when the laws against unfair housing and unfair employment practices are enforced instead of evaded, then there may be nothing more for me to do in politics.

But until that happens—and we all know it will not be this year or next—what we need is more women in politics, because we have a very special contribution to make. I hope that the example of my success will convince other women to get into politics—and not just to stuff envelopes, but to run for office.

It is women who can bring empathy, tolerance, insight, patience, and persistence to government—the qualities we naturally have or have had to develop because of our suppression by men. The women of a nation mold its morals, its religion, and its politics by the lives they live. At present, our country needs women's idealism and determination, perhaps more in politics than anywhere else.

REVIEW QUESTIONS

1. According to Chisholm, why is being a woman a greater challenge than being African American in the political arena?
2. What distinctive qualities does she claim women bring to public service?

CÉSAR CHÁVEZ

Address to the Commonwealth Club of California (1984)

Born in 1927 in Yuma, Arizona, the son of Mexican immigrants, César Chávez served in the U.S. Navy during the Second World War and afterward worked as a migrant laborer and community organizer focused on registering Latinos to vote. In 1965, along with Dolores Huerta, he created the United Farm Workers, a union for migrant lettuce workers and grape pickers, many of them undocumented immigrants who could be deported at any time. Chávez led nonviolent protest marches, staged hunger strikes, and managed nationwide boycotts—all intended to bring justice to migrant workers. Some twenty years later, he gave a speech in San Francisco in which he reflected on the movement for social justice he had organized.

César Chávez, Address to the Commonwealth Club of California, November 9, 1984. ™/© 2018 the César Chávez Foundation. www.chavezfoundation.org. [Editorial insertions appear in square brackets—*Ed.*]

Twenty-one years ago last September, on a lonely stretch of railroad track paralleling U.S. Highway 101 near Salinas, 32 Bracero farm workers lost their lives in a tragic accident.

The Braceros had been imported from Mexico to work on California farms. They died when their bus . . . drove in front of a freight train. . . . Most of the bodies lay unidentified for days. No one, including the grower who employed the workers, even knew their names.

Today, thousands of farm workers live under savage conditions—beneath trees and amid garbage and human excrement—near tomato fields in San Diego County, tomato fields which use the most modern farm technology. Vicious rats gnaw on them as they sleep. They walk miles to buy food at inflated prices. And they carry in water from irrigation pumps.

Child labor is still common in many farm areas. As much as 30 percent of Northern California's garlic harvesters are under-aged children. Kids as young as six years old have voted in state-conducted union elections since they qualified as workers.

Some 800,000 under-aged children work with their families harvesting crops across America. Babies born to migrant workers suffer 25 percent higher infant mortality than the rest of the population. Malnutrition among migrant worker children is 10 times higher than the national rate. Farm workers' average life expectancy is still 49 years—compared to 73 years for the average American.

All my life, I have been driven by one dream, one goal, one vision: To overthrow a farm labor system in this nation which treats farm workers as if they were not important human beings. Farm workers are not agricultural implements. They are not beasts of burden—to be used and discarded. That dream was born in my youth. It was nurtured in my early days of organizing. It has flourished. It has been attacked.

I'm not very different from anyone else who has ever tried to accomplish something with his life. My motivation comes from my personal life—from watching what my mother and father went through when I was growing up; from what we experienced as migrant farm workers in California.

That dream, that vision, grew from my own experience with racism, with hope, with the desire to be treated fairly and to see my people treated as human beings and not as chattel [property]. It grew from anger and rage—emotions I felt 40 years ago when people of my color were denied the right to see a movie or eat at a restaurant in many parts of California. It grew from the frustration and humiliation I felt as a boy who couldn't understand how the growers could abuse and exploit farm workers when there were so many of us and so few of them.

Later, in the 1950s, I experienced a different kind of exploitation. In San Jose, in Los Angeles and in other urban communities, we—the Mexican American people—were dominated by a majority that was Anglo [white]. I began to realize what other minority people had discovered: That the only answer—the only hope—was in organizing.

More of us had to become citizens. We had to register to vote. And people like me had to develop the skills it would take to organize, to educate, to help empower the Chicano people. I spent many years—before we founded the union—learning how to work with people.

We experienced some successes in voter registration, in politics, in battling racial discrimination—successes in an era when Black Americans were just beginning to assert their civil rights and when political awareness among Hispanics was almost non-existent. But deep in my heart, I knew I could never be happy unless I tried organizing the farm workers. I didn't know if I would succeed. But I had to try.

All Hispanics—urban and rural, young and old—are connected to the farm workers' experience. We had all lived through the fields—or our parents had. We shared that common humiliation. How could we progress as a people, even if we lived in the cities, while the farm workers—men and women of our color—were condemned to a life without pride? How could we progress as a people while the farm workers—who symbolized our history in this land—were denied self-respect? How could our people believe that their children could become lawyers and doctors and judges and business people while this shame, this injustice was permitted to continue?

Those who attack our union often say, "It's not really a union. It's something else: A social movement. A civil rights movement. It's something dangerous." They're half right.

The United Farm Workers is first and foremost a union. A union like any other. A union that either produces for its members on the bread and butter issues or doesn't survive. But the UFW has always been something more than a union—although it's never been dangerous if you believe in the Bill of Rights. The UFW was the beginning! We attacked that historical source of shame and infamy that our people in this country lived with. We attacked that injustice, not by complaining; not be seeking hand-outs; not by becoming soldiers in the War on Poverty.

We organized!

Farm workers acknowledged we had allowed ourselves to become victims in a democratic society—a society where majority rule and collective bargaining are supposed to be more than academic theories or political rhetoric. And by addressing this historical problem, we created confidence and pride and hope in an entire people's ability to create the future.

*   *   *

The union's survival—its very existence—sent out a signal to all Hispanics: That we were fighting for our dignity, That we were challenging and overcoming injustice, That we were empowering the least educated among us—the poorest among us.

The message was clear: If it [the crusade for social justice] could happen in the fields, it could happen anywhere—in the cities, in the courts, in the city councils, in the state legislatures. I didn't really appreciate it at the time, but the coming of our union signaled the start of great changes among Hispanics that are only now beginning to be seen.

I've traveled to every part of this nation. I have met and spoken with thousands of Hispanics from every walk of life—from every social and economic class.

One thing I hear most often from Hispanics, regardless of age or position—and from many non-Hispanics as well—is that the farm workers gave them hope that they could succeed and the inspiration to work for change.

*   *   *

It doesn't really matter whether we have 100,000 members or 500,000 members. In truth, hundreds of thousands of farm workers in California—and in other states—are better off today because of our work. And Hispanics across California and the nation who don't work in agriculture are better off today because of what the farm workers taught people about organization, about pride and strength, about seizing control over their own lives.

Tens of thousands of the children and grand-children of farm workers—and the children and grandchildren of poor Hispanics—are moving out of the fields and out of the barrios [poor neighborhoods] and into the professions and into business and into politics. And that movement cannot be reversed!

Our union will forever exist as an empowering force among Chicanos in the Southwest. And that means our power and our influence will grow and not diminish.

History and inevitability are on our side. The farm workers and their children—and the Hispanics and their children—are the future in California. And corporate growers are the past!

Those politicians who ally themselves with the corporate growers and against the farm workers and the Hispanics are in for a big surprise.

They want to make their careers in politics. They want to hold power 20 and 30 years from now—in Modesto, in Salinas, in Fresno, in Bakersfield, in the Imperial Valley, and in many of the great cities of California—those communities will be dominated by farm workers and not by growers, by the children and grandchildren of farm workers and not by the children and grandchildren of growers.

These trends are part of the forces of history that cannot be stopped! No person and no organization can resist them for very long. They are inevitable! Once social change begins, it cannot be reversed.

You cannot uneducate the person who has learned to read. You cannot humiliate the person who feels pride. You cannot oppress the people who are not afraid anymore. . . .

Regardless of what the future holds for the union, regardless of what the future holds for farm workers, our accomplishments cannot be undone! "La Causa"—our cause—doesn't have to be experienced twice. The consciousness and pride that were raised by our union are alive and thriving inside millions of young Hispanics who will never work on a farm!

Like the other immigrant groups, the day will come when we win the economic and political rewards . . . in keeping with our numbers in society. The day will come when the politicians do the right thing by our people out of political necessity and not out of charity or idealism.

That day may not come this year.

That day may not come during this decade.

But it will come, someday!

And when that day comes, we shall see the fulfillment of that passage from the Book of Matthew in the New Testament, "That the last shall be the first and the first shall be last."

And on that day, our nation shall fulfill its creed—and that fulfillment shall enrich us all.

REVIEW QUESTIONS

1. What were the grievances that Chávez cited on behalf of migrant farm workers?
2. Chávez claims that the United Farm Workers gave its members more than higher wages; it gave them hope. In what ways does hope drive movements for social change?

TOM GRACE

The Shooting at Kent State (1970)

Tom Grace, one of the students wounded at Kent State, provided the following account of the incident.

From "Coda: Kent State," in *From Camelot to Kent State* by Joan Morrison and Robert K. Morrison, pp. 329–35. Copyright © 1987 by Joan Morrison and Robert K. Morrison. Reprinted by permission.

My first class of the day was at nine-fifty-five and my girlfriend was in the same class. Because of all the tumultuous disorder that had gone on for the preceding days, the professor, being an understanding man, gave people the option of leaving and taking the exam at an other time if the events had interfered with their studying, or going ahead and taking the test. My girlfriend chose to make an exit; history was not her strong point. As far as I was concerned, I had no problem taking the test. So she left and I stayed. . . .

Toward the end of the class, I recall a student standing and saying that there was going to be a rally on the commons as soon as the class was over. I sat there for a few minutes deliberating as to whether I should go or not, and I remembered my earlier assurances to my girlfriend.

Then I thought to myself, this is too momentous; it's too important for me to stay away. Certainly I couldn't see any harm in my going over just to watch. So I went over there really with the intention of more or less surveying the scene, not knowing what I was going to find.

It was only a short five-minute walk to the commons. I found several hundred students, and some of my roommates, Alan Canfora and Jim Riggs, had flags, black flags, I believe. Alan had spray-painted "KENT" on it, and the other one was just a black flag, and they were waving these things about. So I was drawn to them right away.

There was some chanting going on: "One, two, three, four, we don't want your fucking war" and "Pigs off campus."

The crowd had grouped around the victory bell, which had been historically used to signal victories in Kent State football games, and the bell was being sounded to signal students to congregate. There were at the very least another thousand or so observers and onlookers ringing the hills that surround this part of the commons.

At that point, a campus policeman in a National Guard jeep ordered the crowd, through the use of a bullhorn, to disperse and go to their homes. The policeman was riding shotgun, and I believe a National Guardsman was driving the jeep. "All you bystanders and innocent people go to your homes for your own safety," is what we heard. I think he had the best intentions in terms of asking the crowd to disperse, but it did nothing but whip the crowd into a further frenzy. We have to remember here the mind-set of people and everything that had gone on. A very adversarial atmosphere existed, and we felt that this was our campus, that we were doing nothing wrong, and that they had no right to order us to disperse. If anyone ought to leave, it's them, not us. That's how I felt.

I was standing there yelling and screaming along with everyone else, and then someone flung either a rock or a bottle at the jeep, which bounced harmlessly off the tire. I don't think it was necessarily meant to bounce off the tire; fortunately the person was not a very good shot. That, of course, alarmed the occupants of the jeep. I think they realized at that point because of the crescendo the chants had reached, and also the fact that people were pitching objects in their direction—that we weren't going to leave.

So the jeep drove back to the National Guard lines which had formed on the other side of the commons in front of the remains of the burned ROTC building. Then the National Guardsmen leveled their bayonets at us and started to march across the commons in our direction, shooting tear gas as they came.

I was teargassed along with perhaps a thousand other people. Unlike some of the students, who delayed to throw rocks or tear-gas canisters back in the direction of the National Guard, I chose to leave the area as fast as I could. I retreated to a girls' dormitory where there were some first-floor restrooms. The female students had opened up the windows and were passing out moistened paper towels so people could relieve the effects of the tear gas. So I went and I cleansed my eyes to the best of my ability, and that seemed to take care of me at the moment.

In the meantime, one group of National Guardsmen had advanced the same way that I had retreated, but they did not chase the students further. But another troop of the National Guard had gone right past and proceeded downhill onto the practice football field. There was a rather abrupt drop-off and a chain-link fence where some construction had been going on, and on the other three sides the National Guardsmen were ringed by students.

I cautiously moved a little closer and watched. Some students were throwing rocks at the National Guard, and some of the National Guard were picking up the rocks and throwing them back at the students. I didn't see any National Guardsmen hit by rocks. They seemed to be bouncing at their feet.

Then I remember that the National Guard troop seemed to get into a little huddle before leaving the practice football field. They reformed their lines and proceeded back up the hill. It was almost like the parting of the Red Sea. The students just moved to one side or the other to let the National Guardsmen pass, because no one in their right mind would have stood there as bayonets were coming.

A lot of people were screaming, "Get out of here, get off our campus," and in the midst of all this were some students, oddly enough, who were still wandering through the area with their textbooks, as if they were completely unaware of all that was taking place. I felt that I was still keeping a safe distance. I was 150, 165 feet away. I know that because it's since been paced off.

When the National Guardsmen got to the top of the hill, all of a sudden there was just a quick movement, a flurry of activity, and then a crack, or two cracks of rifle fire, and I thought, Oh, my God! I turned and started running as fast as I could. I don't think I got more than a step or two, and all of a sudden I was on the ground. It was just like somebody had come over and given me a body blow and knocked me right down.

The bullet had entered my left heel and had literally knocked me off my feet. I tried to raise myself, and I heard someone yelling, "Stay down, stay down! It's buckshot!" I looked up, and about five or ten feet away from me, behind a tree, was my roommate Alan Canfora. That was the first time I had seen him since we were down on the other side of the commons, chanting antiwar slogans.

So I threw myself back to the ground and lay as prone as possible to shield myself as much as I could, although like most people I was caught right in the open. I couldn't run, because I had already been hit. There was no cover. I just hugged the ground so as to expose as little of my body as possible to the gunfire. It seemed like the bullets were going by within inches of my head. I can remember seeing people behind me, farther down the hill in the parking lot, dropping. I didn't know if they were being hit by bullets or they were just hugging the ground. We know today that it only lasted thirteen seconds, but it seemed like it kept going and going and going. And I remember thinking, When is this going to stop?

So I was lying there, and all of a sudden this real husky, well-built guy ran to me, picked me up like I was a sack of potatoes, and threw me over his shoulder. He carried me through the parking lot in the direction of a girls' dormitory. We went by one body, a huge puddle of blood. Head wounds always bleed very badly, and his was just awful.

The female students were screaming as I was carried into the dormitory and placed on a couch, bleeding all over the place. A nursing student applied a tourniquet to my leg. I never really felt that my life was in danger, but I could look down at my foot and I knew that I had one hell of a bad wound. The bullet blew the shoe right off my foot, and there was a bone sticking through my green sock. It looked like somebody had put my foot through a meatgrinder.

The ambulances came. Some attendants came in, put me on a stretcher, and carried me outside. The blood loss had lessened because of the tourniquet that was on my leg. I remember having my fist up in the air as a sign of defiance. They put me into the top tier in the ambulance rather than the lower one, which was already occupied. I remember my foot hitting the edge of the ambulance as I went in. From that moment on, until the time that I actually went under from the anesthesia at Robinson Memorial Hospital, I was probably in the most intense pain that I've ever experienced in my life.

They had the back doors closed by this time, and the ambulance was speeding away from the campus. I looked down and saw Sandy Scheuer. I had met Sandy about a week or two beforehand for the first and only time. She had been introduced to me by one of the guys who lived downstairs in my apartment complex. They were casual friends, and she struck me as being a very nice person. She had a gaping bullet wound in the neck, and the ambulance attendants were tearing away the top two buttons of her blouse and then doing a heart massage. I remember their saying that it's no use, she's dead. And then they just pulled up the sheet over her head.

The ambulance got to the hospital, and it was a scene that's probably been played out any number of times when you have a big disaster. There were people running around, stretchers being wheeled in, and I was just put out in a hallway because the medical personnel were attending to the more severely wounded. I had the tourniquet on my leg, so I wasn't bleeding all over the place, but the pain kept getting more excruciating. I was screaming by that time, "Get me something for this pain!" Then I was wheeled into an elevator and brought up to one of the other floors. I remember receiving some anesthesia and being told to count backward from ten. I didn't get very far, and then I was out.

The next thing I remember was waking up in a hospital bed. I looked up at the ceiling and then all of a sudden it came to me what had occurred. I didn't know how long I had been out, and I sat up as quickly as I could and looked down to see if my foot was still there. I could see the tips of my toes sticking out of a cast. I just lay back, and I breathed a big sigh of relief....

Today, if I engage in any strenuous exercise, I'll have a noticeable limp for a couple of days afterward. But on the whole, I consider myself to be rather fortunate. I could have lost my foot; I could have been killed. Four people had been shot to death: Sandy Scheuer, Jeff Miller, Allison Krause, and Bill Schroeder. My roommate Alan Canfora was struck by gunfire. He was among the least injured of the thirteen people who were either mortally wounded or recovered.

Eventually federal indictments against enlisted men and noncommissioned officers in the Ohio National Guard were handed down. But, as it turned out, the judge ruled that the Justice Department failed to prove a case of conspiracy to violate our civil rights and dismissed the case before it was ever sent to the jury. That was the end of criminal proceedings against the Ohio National Guard. They got off scot-free.

But I think there are some guardsmen who are sorry for what happened. One guy in particular seemed to be genuinely remorseful. I remember his testimony. He has very poor eyesight, and on May 4 he couldn't get the gas mask on over his glasses, so he had to wear the gas mask without glasses. He was blind as a bat without them, and he admitted he just knew he was shooting in a certain direction. That was a startling admission. There was a guy out there who could hardly see, blasting away with an M-1.

... Every year from May 1971, which was the first anniversary of the killings, there has been a commemorative ceremony at Kent State that has attracted anywhere from one thousand students to eight thousand. So the issue has been kept alive there, and I'd say that the main focus now is to erect a proper and suitable memorial to the people who were killed there. The university has finally agreed to do that. They have commissioned a study as to what the memorial should look like, and what it should say.

I'm more concerned about what it says than what it looks like. Ever since I was young, I've been an avid reader of history, with a particular focus on the American Civil War, and for that reason I have more than the usual interest in the subject. When I go down to the Gettysburg battlefield or Antietam, I can read on those monuments about what took place there, what the casualty figures were, and I can try to envision what took place. Somebody should be able to do that at Kent State as well.

I think the memorial should state: "On May 4, 1970, units of the Ohio National Guard—Company H, 107th Armored Cavalry (Troop G) and Company A, 145th Infantry Regiment—shot and killed four student protesters and wounded nine others during a demonstration against the U.S. invasion of Cambodia." Straight-out, simple facts.

REVIEW QUESTIONS

1. How did this student view the presence of the guardsmen on campus?
2. Did you find Grace's account of the events convincing?
3. What would you suggest as the appropriate inscription on the memorial? Explain.

RICHARD M. NIXON AND JOHN DEAN

The President and John Dean in the Oval Office (1973)

No sooner was the June 1972 break-in at the Democratic Party headquarters in the Watergate office complex in Washington, D.C., reported in the news media than the Nixon White House began concerted efforts to cover up the incident. The president, for example, ordered the CIA to stop an FBI investigation of the Watergate burglary. He also told aides to keep mum in appearances before the grand jury investigating the incident: "I don't give a shit what happens. I want you to stonewall it." When the Supreme Court forced Nixon to hand over secret tape recordings he had made of meetings in the Oval Office, it became evident that Nixon and his White House aides had used illegal methods to undermine the president's political "enemies." The mushrooming scandal eventually led to Nixon's resignation on August 9, 1974, the only resignation of a U.S. president. The publication of transcripts of the secret tape recordings of conversations in the Oval Office revealed Nixon's role in the cover-up. On February 28, 1973, Nixon met with John Dean, the White House legal counsel. Nixon's profanity-laced conversation focused on ways to protect himself during upcoming Senate hearings dealing with the Watergate episode.

From "Transcript of a recording of a meeting between the President and John Dean in the Oval Office, on February 28, 1973, from 9:12 to 10:23 A.M." nixonlibrary.gov. [Editorial insertions are from the original source—*Ed.*]

February 28, 1973 (9:12 to 10:23 A.M.)

DEAN: [Gordon] Liddy and [James] McCord, who sat through the [break-in] trial, will both be on appeal and there is no telling how long that will last. It is one of these things we will just have to watch.

PRESIDENT NIXON: My view though is to say nothing about them on the ground that the matter is still in the courts and on appeal. Second my view is to say nothing about the [Senate] hearings at this point, except that I trust they will be conducted the proper way and I will not comment on the hearings while they are in pro-cess. Of course if they break through—if they get muckraking—it is best not to cultivate that thing here in the White House. If it is done at the White House again they are going to drop the [adjective deleted] thing. Now there, of course, you say but you leave it all to them. We'll see as time goes on. Maybe we will have to change our policy. But the President should not become involved in any part of this case. Do you agree with that?

DEAN: I agree totally, sir. Absolutely. That doesn't mean that quietly we are not going to be working around the office. You can rest assured that we are not going to be sitting quietly.

PRESIDENT NIXON: I don't know what we can do. The people who are most disturbed by this [unintelligible] are the [adjective deleted] Republicans. A lot of these Congressmen, financial contributors, et cetera, are highly moral. The Democrats are just sort of saying, "[Expletive deleted] fun and games!" . . .

DEAN: The one thing I think they are going to go after with a vengeance—and I plan to spend a great deal of time with next week, as a matter of fact a couple of days getting this all in order—is Herb Kalmbach.

PRESIDENT NIXON: Yes.

DEAN: Herb—they have subpoenaed his records, and he has records that run all over hell's acres on things. . . .

PRESIDENT NIXON: What is holding up his records?

DEAN: They already have gotten to the banks that had them, and what I think we will do is that there will be a logical, natural explanation for every single transaction. It is just a lot of minutia we've got to go through but he's coming in next week, and I told him we would sit down and he is preparing everything. . . .

PRESIDENT NIXON: They can't get his records with regard to his private transactions?

DEAN: No, none of the private transactions. Absolutely, that is privileged material. Anything to do with San Clemente [Nixon's California home] and the like. . . .

PRESIDENT NIXON: Did they ask for them?

DEAN: No. No indication.

PRESIDENT NIXON: Kalmbach is a decent fellow. He will make a good witness.

DEAN: I think he will.

PRESIDENT NIXON: He is smart.

DEAN: He has been tough thus far. He can take it. His skin is thick now. Sure it bothered him when all this press was being played up. *LA Times* were running stories on him all the time and the like. Local stations have been making him more of a personality and his partners have been nipping at him, but Herb is tough now. He is ready and he is going to go through. He is hunkered down and he is ready to handle it, so I am not worried bout Herb at all.

PRESIDENT NIXON: Oh well, it will be hard for him. I suppose the big thing is the financing transaction that they will go after him for. How does the money get to the Bank of Mexico, etc.

DEAN: Oh, well, all that can be explained.

PRESIDENT NIXON: It can?

DEAN: Yes, indeed! Yes, sir! They are going to be disappointed with a lot of the answers they get. When they actually get the facts—because the [*New York*] *Times* and the [*Washington*] *Post* had such innuendo—when they get the facts, they are going to be disappointed.

PRESIDENT NIXON: The one point you ought to get to [Republican Senator Howard] Baker. I tried to get it through his thick skull. His skull is not thick, but tell [Attorney General Richard] Kleindienst in talking to Baker—and Herb should emphasize that the way to have a successful hearing and a fair one is to run it like a court: no hearsay, no innuendo! Now you know—

DEAN: That's a hell of a good point. . . .

PRESIDENT NIXON: [Expletive deleted] Of course, I am not dumb and I will never forget when I heard about this [adjective deleted] forced entry and bugging. I thought, what in hell is this? What is the matter with these people? Are they crazy? I thought they were nuts. A prank! But it wasn't! It wasn't very funny. I think that our Democratic friends know that, too. They know what the hell it was. They don't think we'd be involved in such.

DEAN: I think they do too.

PRESIDENT NIXON: Maybe they don't. They don't think I would be involved in such stuff. They think I have people capable of it. And they are correct, in that [White House aide Charles] Colson would do anything. Well, OK—Have a little fun. And now I will not talk to you again until you have something to report to me.

DEAN: All right, sir.

PRESIDENT NIXON: But I think it is very important that you have these talks with our good friend Kleindienst.

DEAN: That will be done.

PRESIDENT NIXON: Tell him we have to get these things worked out. We have to work together on this thing. I would build him up. He is the man who can make the difference. Also point out to him what we have. [Expletive deleted] Colson's got [characterization deleted], but I really, really,—this stuff here—let's forget this. But let's remember this was not done by the White House. This [Watergate break-in] was done by the Committee to Re-Elect, and [former attorney general John] Mitchell was the Chairman, correct?

DEAN: That's correct!

PRESIDENT NIXON: And Kleindienst owes Mitchell everything. Mitchell wanted him for Attorney General. Wanted him for Deputy, and here he is. Now, [expletive deleted]. Baker's got to realize this, and that if he allows this thing to get out of hand he is going to potentially ruin John Mitchell. He won't. Mitchell won't allow himself to be ruined. He will put on his big stone face. But I hope he does and he will. There is no question what they are after. What the committee is after is somebody at the White House. . . .

REVIEW QUESTIONS

1. What appears to be President Nixon's foremost concern about the upcoming Senate hearings related to the Watergate burglary?
2. Is it appropriate for a U.S. president to exert influence on the U.S. attorney general to influence a criminal investigation?

PHILIP CAPUTO

FROM *A Rumor of War* (1977)

The Vietnam War generated several powerful novels and memoirs. Among the most influential was A Rumor of War, *an autobiographical account of Philip Caputo's experience as a Marine lieutenant among the first American combat troops in Vietnam in 1965–1966. Caputo describes how difficult it was for American troops trained for conventional combat to adjust to the realities of a guerrilla war of attrition against a largely unseen enemy, the Viet Cong—nationalist communists fighting in South Vietnam. Like so many soldiers over the centuries, Caputo's experience of the mundane tedium and discomforts (the jungle heat, biting insects, leeches, and jungle rot fungus from constantly wet boots) as well as intense horrors of actual combat was eye-opening as well as disillusioning. Caputo stressed that he and other U.S. troops were not trained for the kind of irregular guerrilla warfare they experienced. Nor were they prepared for the pervasive corruption they witnessed within the South Vietnamese government and army. Caputo also revealed how he and his platoon killed civilians suspected of aiding the Communist Viet Cong. His riveting meditations on what became America's longest and most frustrating war were widely influential.*

On March 8, 1965, as a young infantry officer, I landed at Danang with a battalion of the 9th Marine Expeditionary Brigade, the first U.S. combat unit sent to Indochina.

*   *   *

For Americans who did not come of age in the early sixties, it may be hard to grasp what those years were like—the pride and overpowering self assurance that prevailed. Most of the thirty-five hundred men in our brigade, born during or immediately after World War II, were shaped by that era, the age of [John F.] Kennedy's Camelot. We went overseas full of illusions, for which the intoxicating atmosphere of those years was as much to blame as our youth.

War is always attractive to young men who know nothing about it, but we had also been seduced into uniform by Kennedy's challenge to "ask what you can do for your country" and by the missionary idealism he had awakened in us. America seemed omnipotent then: the country could still claim it had never lost a war, and we believed we were ordained to play cop to the Communists' robber and spread our own political faith around the world. Like the French soldiers of the late eighteenth century, we saw ourselves as the champions of "a cause that was destined to triumph." So, when we marched into the rice paddies on that damp March afternoon, we carried, along with our packs and rifles, the implicit convictions that the Viet Cong would be quickly beaten and that we were doing something altogether noble and good. We kept the packs and rifles; the convictions, we lost.

The discovery that the men we had scorned as peasant guerrillas were, in fact, a lethal, determined enemy and the casualty lists that lengthened each week with nothing to show for the blood being spilled broke our early confidence. By autumn, what had begun as an adventurous expedition had turned into an exhausting, indecisive war of attrition in which we fought for no cause other than our own survival.

*   *   *

The tedium was occasionally relieved by a large-scale search-and-destroy operation, but the exhilaration of riding the lead helicopter into a landing zone was usually followed by more of the same hot walking, with the mud sucking at our boots and the sun thudding against our helmets while an invisible enemy shot at us from distant tree lines. The rare instances when the VC [Viet Cong] chose to fight a set-piece battle provided the only excitement; not ordinary excitement, but the manic ecstasy of contact. Weeks of bottled-up tensions would be released in a few minutes of orgiastic violence, men screaming and shouting obscenities above the explosions of grenades and the rapid, rippling bursts of automatic rifles.

Beyond adding a few more corpses to the weekly body count, none of these encounters achieved anything; none will ever appear in military histories or be studied by cadets at West Point. Still, they changed us and taught us, the men who fought in them; in those obscure skirmishes we learned the old lessons about fear, cowardice, courage, suffering, cruelty, and comradeship. Most of all, we learned about death at an age when it is common to think of oneself as immortal. Everyone loses that illusion eventually, but in civilian life it is lost in installments over the years. We lost it all at once and, in the span of months passed from boyhood through manhood to a premature middle age. The knowledge of death, of implacable limits placed on a man's existence, served us from our youth as irrevocably as a surgeon's scissors had once severed us from the womb. And yet, few of us were past twenty-five. We left Vietnam peculiar creatures, with young shoulders that bore rather old heads.

My own departure took place in early July 1966. Ten months later . . . an honorable discharge released me from the Marines and the chance of dying an early death in Asia. I felt as happy as a condemned man whose sentence has been commuted, but within a year I began growing nostalgic for the war.

Other veterans I knew confessed to the same emotion. In spite of everything, we felt a strange attachment to Vietnam and, even stranger, a longing to return. The war was still being fought, but this desire to go back did not spring from any patriotic ideas about duty, honor, and sacrifice, the myths with which old men send young men off to get killed, or maimed. It arose, rather, from a recognition of how deeply we had been changed, how different we were from everyone who had not shared with us the miseries of the monsoon, the exhausting patrols, the fear of a combat assault on a hot landing zone. We had very little in common with them. Though we were civilians again, the civilian world seemed alien. We did not belong to it as much as we did to that other world, where we had fought and our friends had died.

I was involved in the antiwar movement at the time and struggled, unsuccessfully, to reconcile my opposition to the war with this nostalgia. Later, I realized a reconciliation was impossible; I would never be able to hate the war with anything like the undiluted passion of my friends in the movement. Because I had fought in it, it was not an abstract issue, but a deeply emotional experience, the most significant thing that had happened to me. It held my thoughts, senses, and feelings in an unbreakable embrace. I would hear in thunder the roar of artillery. I could not listen to rain without recalling those drenched nights on the line, nor walk through woods without instinctively searching for a trip wire or an ambush. I could protest as loudly as the most convinced activist, but I could not deny the grip the war had on me, nor the fact that it had been an experience as fascinating as it was repulsive, as exhilarating as it was sad, as tender as it was cruel.

. . . Anyone who fought in Vietnam, if he is honest about himself, will have to admit he enjoyed the compelling attractiveness of combat. It was a peculiar enjoyment because it was mixed with a commensurate pain. Under fire, a man's powers of life heightened in proportion to the proximity of death, so that he felt an elation as extreme as his dread. His senses quickened, he attained an acuity of consciousness at once pleasurable and excruciating. It was something like the elevated state of awareness induced by drugs. And it could be just as addictive, for it made whatever else life offered in the way of delights or torments seem pedestrian.

*   *   *

. . . The battlefields of Vietnam were a crucible in which a generation of American soldiers were fused together by a common confrontation with death and a sharing of hardships, dangers, and fears. The very ugliness of the war, the sordidness of our daily lives, the degradation of having to take part in body counts made us draw still closer to one another. It was as if in comradeship we found an affirmation of life and the means to preserve at least a vestige of our humanity.

REVIEW QUESTIONS

1. How did the experience of war in Vietnam change Caputo's original idealistic perceptions?
2. What explains the ambivalence Caputo felt toward the war after returning to the United States and participating in the anti-war movement?
3. How does the experience of war create special bonds among combatants?

GLADWIN HILL

FROM Environment May Eclipse Vietnam as College Issue (1969)

As the United States withdrew from the war in Vietnam, many idealistic young people turned their energies to the emerging environmental movement. In 1969, the New York Times *reported on this phenomenon, arguing that environmental activism was "sweeping the nation's campuses."*

"We want to stop the war, end pollution—and beat Stanford!" yelled a Berkeley pep leader at last weekend's big football rally.

The mention of pollution brought a roar of approval from a University of California crowd of 5,000 that almost drowned out the reference to the big game.

Rising concern about the "environmental crisis" is sweeping the nation's campuses with an intensity that may be on its way to eclipsing student discontent over the war in Vietnam.

This is indicated by interviews with students and faculty members from many campuses and with leading [environmental] conservation authorities around the country.

There is a strong feeling on the campuses that the war will be liquidated in due course. Meanwhile, it is physically remote. And, in the wake of the big protest marches, many students feel Vietnam offers only limited scope for student action.

But the deterioration of the nation's "quality of life" is a pervasive, here-and-now, long-term problem that students of all political shadings can sink their teeth and energies into. And they are doing it.

A national day of observance of environmental problems, analogous to the mass demonstrations on Vietnam, is being planned for next spring, with Congressional backing.

From Maine to Hawaii, students are seizing on the environmental ills from water pollution to the global population problem, campaigning against them, and pitching in to do something about them.

"A ground swell of concern is starting, on everything from population and food supply to the preservation of natural areas," commented Dr. Edward Clebsch, assistant professor of botany at the University of Tennessee.

"I've been floored by the intensity of their actions and feelings," said Dr. Vincent Arp, a Bureau of Standards physicist close to the University of Colorado at Boulder. "The student group is going like a bomb."

"They can see it, they can feel it, they can smell it. And they think they can change it," said William E. Felling, a program officer of the Ford Foundation, which contributes to many conservation activities. . . .

Efforts Get Results

Already the student environmental front can point to many accomplishments. Student activists had significant roles in the campaigns to "save" San Francisco Bay and the northern California redwoods, and to block new dams on the Colorado River. . . .

On the University of Texas campus at Austin there are at least six environmental groups with interests ranging from water pollution to conservation law. One group, in the College of Engineering, has filed 5 formal complaints against the University itself for pollution in a nearby creek. At the University of Hawaii, there are close to two dozen groups, each organized around a particular cause.

Action Is Keynote

Some groups, like Boston University's Ecology Coalition, have as few as a dozen members. Others have hundreds. But with causes on every hat . . . mass membership and parliamentary formalities mean . . . action, which can be initiated by a handful of people. Then the causes gather their own following.

A few groups cherish the designation of "radical" and its indirect offshoots of the left, movements like the Students for a Democratic Society and California's Peace and Freedom Party.

"Capitalism is predicated on money and growth, and when you're only interested to maximize profits, you maximize pollution. We need a system that takes maximum care of earth," said Cliff Humphrey, the 32-year-old leader of Ecology Action, one of several groups at Berkeley.

But generally the aura of the environmental "new wave" is conservative, with coats and ties as conspicuous as beards and blue jeans. "There's a role for everybody in ecology," said Keith Lampe, a cofounder of the Yippie movement, who puts out an environment-oriented newsletter from Berkeley. "People with widely different styles and politics can talk to each other with no more tension than a Presbyterian talks with a Methodist."

Few 'Anarchists'

"I doubt if you'll find many anarchist ecologists," commented Steve Berwick, a 28-year-old Yale environmentalist. "Ecology is a system, and anarchy goes against that."

A typical group is Boston University's Ecology Action, whose 75 members are led by Bruce Tissney, a 20-year-old junior geology major. Edwardian rather than hippie in appearance, he has a trimmed red beard, wire-rimmed spectacles, and affects such sartorial accoutrements as a blue plaid vest and matching bow-tie, white shirt, and gold watch and chain.

Ecology Action's two-day educational program last week included "friendly" picketing of the state capitol, a pollution film festival, pamphleteering and lectures, and a mock award of a pollution prize to a local power company. The group has been conferring with state water pollution officials about doing spare time "watchdog" work, and is planning to set up dust-catching devices to monitor air pollution.

There have, across the country, been incidents, but mostly minor—such as the arrest last month of 26 University of Texas students who tried to block the felling of some trees for a campus building extension.

Local Orientation

Some of the campus groups are branches of national organizations such as the Sierra Club (which has just installed a campus coordinator at its San Francisco headquarters), the Wildlife Federation, and the newly established Friends of the Earth. But most of them are spontaneous local movements. Many tend to shun the established national organizations as being dedicated to old-line "conservation" rather than the environmental crisis. They also feel the older groups are wary of "direct action" for fear of losing the tax-exempt status that is their financial base. Ad hoc student groups don't have this problem.

"We don't want to be labeled as 'conservationists' or 'antipollution,'" said Wes Fisher, a 26-year-old ecology student at the University of Minnesota. "Pollution and overpopulation are like a web, and pollution is just the symptom."

The students are employing the gamut of communications and political-pressure techniques—

meetings, lectures, rallies, picketing, research, pamphleteering, letter-writing, petitions, legislative testimony, collaboration with public agencies and contacts with politicians. . . .

The environmental "new wave" gathered in California as far back as 1965, when Berkeley students staged a sitdown protest against a freeway and Stanford students became involved in campaigns for San Francisco Bay, the redwoods, and Point Reyes National Seashore.

*   *   *

Overshadowing Vietnam

There are differing indications on the campuses about how soon environment may overshadow Vietnam in student interest, but the trend is evident.

"A lot of people are becoming disenchanted with the antiwar movement," said Boston University's Bruce Tiffney. "People who are frustrated and disillusioned are starting to turn to ecology."

"I think environment is a bigger issue than the war, and I think people are beginning to sense its urgency," said Robert Benner, a 22-year-old geology student in the University of Colorado conservation movement.

"The country is tired of S.D.S. [Students for a Democratic Society] and ready to see someone like us come to the forefront," remarked Alan Tucker, a member of Ecology Activists at San Francisco State.

"Environmental problems will obviously replace other major issues of today," said Terry Cornelius, president of the University of Washington's committee on the environmental crises. "This is not just a social movement for Biafra or Vietnam, but for everybody and our closed system, Earth."

"Environment will replace Vietnam as a major issue with the students as the Vietnam phase-out proceeds," commented A. Bruce Etherington, chairman of the University of Hawaii's architecture department. "And it will not be just a political lever to be used by radicals."

Many of the "over-30" environmentalists see the student movement as the catalyst if not the main driving force, that will get environmental improvement rolling and overcome the older generation's tacit resignation to the status quo.

"These kids are really remarkable in their understanding and maturity," said 52-year-old Dr. Barry Commoner, the prominent Washington University ecologist who has been addressing many student groups.

Campuses are seen as representing a greatly broadened base for the "conservation constituency" needed to jog bureaucrats and support the politicians through whom environmental reforms generally must clear.

Conservation lawyers look to campuses for the scientific expertise vital in pressing environmental battles in the courts, and for the energy necessary to raise funds for the usually expensive legal proceedings.

Indications are that coming months will see the student conservation tide swelling and manifesting itself in an arresting variety of ways.

Already students are looking forward to the first "D-Day" of the movement, next April 22—when a nationwide environmental "teach-in" [Earth Day], being coordinated from the office of Senator Gaylord Nelson, Wisconsin Democrat, is planned, to involve both college campuses and communities.

Given the present rising pitch of interest, some supporters think, it could be a bigger and more meaningful event than the antiwar demonstrations.

REVIEW QUESTIONS

1. Why was environmentalism deemed to be of greater interest to college students than opposition to the Vietnam War?

2. In what sense was the burgeoning environmental movement a conservative phenomenon?

3. Why were college students viewed as the vanguard necessary to lead the environmental movement?

31 ∾ CONSERVATIVE REVIVAL, 1977–1990

During 1979 President Jimmy Carter and his Democratic administration grew impotent. The stagnant economy remained sluggish, double-digit inflation continued unabated, and failed efforts to free the American hostages in Iran prompted critics to denounce the administration as indecisive and incapable of bold action. Complicating matters was the chronic bickering among the president's key advisers. Carter's inability to mobilize the nation behind his ill-fated energy program revealed mortal flaws in his reading of the public mood and his understanding of legislative politics.

While the Carter administration was foundering, Republican conservatives were forging a plan to win the White House in 1980. Those plans centered on the popularity and charisma of Ronald Reagan, the Hollywood actor turned California governor and political commentator. He was not a deep thinker, but he was a superb analyst of the public mood, an unabashed patriot, and a committed advocate of conservative principles. Reagan was also charming, cheerful, and funny, a likable politician renowned for his relentless anecdotes and deflecting one-liners. Where the moralistic Carter denounced the evils of free enterprise capitalism and tried to scold Americans into reviving long-forgotten virtues of frugality, a sunny Reagan promised a "revolution of ideas" designed to unleash the capitalist spirit, restore national pride, and regain international respect. As a true believer and an able compromiser, Reagan combined the fervor of a revolutionary with the pragmatism of a diplomat. One commentator recognized that he was unique in "possessing the mind of both an ideologue and a politician."

Reagan credited Calvin Coolidge and his treasury secretary, Andrew Mellon, with demonstrating that by reducing taxes and government regulations, the elixir of free-market capitalism would revive the economy. Like his Republican predecessors of the 1920s, he wanted to unleash entrepreneurial energy as never before. By cutting taxes and domestic spending, he claimed, a surging economy would produce more government revenues that would help reduce the budget deficit. As it turned out, the Reagan administrations failed to cut government spending—indeed, the federal budget deficit increased dramatically during his presidency. But inflation and unemployment subsided, and public confidence returned.

At the same time that Reagan was promoting his domestic agenda he was pursuing an aggressive foreign policy. He sent American marines into war-torn Lebanon, launched a bombing raid on terrorist Libya, provided massive aid to the anti-communist Contra rebels in Nicaragua, authorized a marine invasion of Cuban-controlled Grenada, and authorized the largest peacetime defense budget in American history.

In 1983 Reagan escalated the nuclear arms race by authorizing the Defense Department to develop a Strategic Defense Initiative (SDI). It involved a complex anti-missile defense system using super-secret laser and high-energy particle weapons to destroy enemy missiles in outer space. To Reagan its great appeal was the ability to destroy weapons rather than people, thereby freeing defense strategy from the concept of mutually assured destruction that had long governed Soviet and American attitudes toward nuclear war. Journalists quickly dubbed the program "Star Wars" in reference to the popular science-fiction film. Despite skepticism among the media and many scientists that such a "foolproof" celestial defense system could be built, SDI forced the Soviets to launch an expensive research and development program of their own to keep pace.

Reagan easily won reelection in 1984, and his personal popularity helped ensure the election of his vice president, George H. W. Bush, in 1988. Just how revolutionary the Reagan era was remains a subject of intense partisan debate. What cannot be denied, however, is that during the 1980s Ronald Reagan became the most dominant—and beloved—political leader since Franklin Roosevelt. His actions and his beliefs set the tone for the decade and continue to affect American political and economic life.

Yet Reagan's policies did not actually constitute a revolution. Although he had declared in his 1981 inaugural address his intention to "curb the size and influence of the federal establishment," the New Deal welfare state remained intact when Reagan left office. Neither the Social Security system nor Medicare was dismantled or overhauled, and the federal agencies that Reagan threatened to abolish, such as the Department of Education, not only remained intact in 1989 but had increased budgets.

Reagan's administration did bring inflation under control and in the process helped stimulate the longest sustained period of peacetime prosperity in history. Such economic successes, coupled with the nuclear disarmament treaty as well as Reagan's efforts to light the fuse of freedom in Eastern Europe and set in motion forces that would soon cause the collapse of Soviet Communism, put the Democratic Party on the defensive, and forced conventional New Deal "liberalism" into *a panicked retreat. The fact that Reagan's tax policies widened the gap between the rich and poor and created huge budget deficits for future presidents to confront did not seem to faze many voters. Most observers, even Democrats, acknowledged that Reagan's greatest success was in renewing America's soaring sense of possibilities. As columnist George Will recognized, what the United States needed most in 1981, when Reagan was sworn in, was to recover "the sense that it has a competence commensurate with its nobilities and responsibilities."*

Jimmy Carter

A Crisis of Confidence (1979)

In the third year of his presidency, Jimmy Carter had grown frustrated that his efforts to fight inflation, ignite economic growth, and develop an effective energy policy in the face of the high gasoline and oil prices resulting from the actions of the OPEC nations. In July 1979, he abruptly canceled a televised speech and instead holed up at Camp David, the presidential retreat in Maryland, where he hosted for two weeks leaders from all walks of life: business, labor, religion, and politics. On July 15, 1979, he returned to Washington, D.C., and delivered a speech remarkable for its candor. Sounding more like a preacher than a politician, Carter told the American people that the nation was suffering from a "crisis of confidence" and the worship of false values that had paralyzed the national will. Restoring American morale and self-confidence was "the important task" facing the nation. Unfortunately for Carter and his administration, his speech failed in that effort. Republican Ronald Reagan seized upon Carter's speech as the theme of his presidential campaign in 1980. Reagan saw no "crisis of confidence" in the American people; instead, he saw a "crisis of confidence" in Jimmy Carter's leadership.

From *Public Papers of the Presidents of the United States: Jimmy Carter, 1979* Book 2, June 23 to December 31, 1979 (Washington, DC: U.S. Government Printing Office, 1980), pp. 1236–41. [Editorial insertions appear in square brackets—*Ed.*]

Good evening. This is a special night for me. Exactly three years ago, on July 15, 1976, I accepted the nomination of my party to run for president of the United States. I promised you a president who is not isolated from the people, who feels your pain, and who shares your dreams and who draws his strength and his wisdom from you.

During the past three years I've spoken to you on many occasions about national concerns, the energy crisis, reorganizing the government, our nation's economy, and issues of war and especially peace. . . .

Ten days ago I had planned to speak to you again about a very important subject—energy. For the fifth time I would have described the urgency of the problem and laid out a series of legislative recommendations to the Congress. But as I was preparing to speak, I began to ask myself the same question that I now know has been troubling many of you. Why have we not been able to get together as a nation to resolve our serious energy problem?

It's clear that the true problems of our nation are much deeper—deeper than gasoline lines or energy shortages, deeper even than inflation or recession. And I realize more than ever that as president I need your help. . . .

*   *   *

It has been an extraordinary ten days [that have] confirmed my belief in the decency and the strength and the wisdom of the American people, but it also bore out some of my long-standing concerns about our nation's underlying problems.

*   *   *

[A]fter listening to the American people, I have been reminded again that all the legislation in the world can't fix what's wrong with America. So, I want to speak to you first tonight about a subject even more serious than energy or inflation. I want to talk to you right now about a fundamental threat to American democracy.

I do not mean our political and civil liberties. They will endure. And I do not refer to the outward strength of America, a nation that is at peace tonight everywhere in the world, with unmatched economic power and military might.

The threat is nearly invisible in ordinary ways. It is a crisis of confidence. It is a crisis that strikes at the very heart and soul and spirit of our national will. We can see this crisis in the growing doubt about the meaning of our own lives and in the loss of a unity of purpose for our nation.

The erosion of our confidence in the future is threatening to destroy the social and the political fabric of America. . . . Our people are losing that faith, not only in government itself but in the ability as citizens to serve as the ultimate rulers and shapers of our democracy. As a people we know our past and we are proud of it. Our progress has been part of the living history of America, even the world. We always believed that we were part of a great movement of humanity itself called democracy, involved in the search for freedom, and that belief has always strengthened us in our purpose. But just as we are losing our confidence in the future, we are also beginning to close the door on our past.

In a nation that was proud of hard work, strong families, close-knit communities, and our faith in God, too many of us now tend to worship self-indulgence and consumption. Human identity is no longer defined by what one does, but by what one owns.

But we've discovered that owning things and consuming things does not satisfy our longing for meaning. We've learned that piling up material goods cannot fill the emptiness of lives which have no confidence or purpose.

The symptoms of this crisis of the American spirit are all around us. For the first time in the history of our country, a majority of our people believe that the next five years will be worse than the past five years. Two-thirds of our people do not even vote. The productivity of American workers is actually dropping, and the willingness of Americans to save for the future has fallen below that of all other people in the Western world.

As you know, there is a growing disrespect for government and for churches and for schools, the news media, and other institutions. This is not a message of happiness or reassurance, but it is the truth and it is a warning.

*   *   *

Looking for a way out of this crisis, our people have turned to the Federal government and found it isolated from the mainstream of our nation's life. Washington, D.C., has become an island. The gap between our citizens and our government has never been so wide. The people are looking for honest answers, not easy answers; clear leadership, not false claims and evasiveness and politics as usual.

What you see too often in Washington and elsewhere around the country is a system of government that seems incapable of action. You see a Congress twisted and pulled in every direction by hundreds of well-financed and powerful special interests. You see every extreme position defended to the last vote, almost to the last breath by one unyielding group or another.

You often see a balanced and a fair approach that demands sacrifice, a little sacrifice from everyone, abandoned like an orphan without support and without friends. Often you see paralysis and stagnation and drift. You don't like it, and neither do I. What can we do?

First of all, we must face the truth, and then we can change our course. We simply must have faith in each other, faith in our ability to govern ourselves, and faith in the future of this nation. Restoring that faith and that confidence to America is now the most important task we face. It is a true challenge of this generation of Americans.

*   *   *

We know the strength of America. We are strong. We can regain our unity. We can regain our confidence. We are the heirs of generations who survived threats much more powerful and awesome than those that challenge us now. Our fathers and mothers were strong men and women who shaped a new society during the Great Depression, who fought world wars, and who carved out a new charter of peace for the world.

We ourselves are the same Americans who just ten years ago put a man on the Moon. We are the generation that dedicated our society to the pursuit of human rights and equality. And we are the generation that will win the war on the energy problem and in that process rebuild the unity and confidence of America.

We are at a turning point in our history. There are two paths to choose. One is a path I've warned about tonight, the path that leads to fragmentation and self-interest. Down that road lies a mistaken idea of freedom, the right to grasp for ourselves some advantage over others. That path would be one of constant conflict between narrow interests ending in chaos and immobility. It is a certain route to failure.

All the traditions of our past, all the lessons of our heritage, all the promises of our future point to another path, the path of common purpose and the restoration of American values. That path leads to true freedom for our nation and ourselves. We can take the first steps down that path as we begin to solve our energy problem.

Energy [policy] will be the immediate test of our ability to unite this nation, and it can also be the standard around which we rally. On the battlefield of energy we can win for our nation a new confidence, and we can seize control again of our common destiny.

In little more than two decades we've gone from a position of energy independence to one in which almost half the oil we use comes from foreign countries, at prices that are going through the roof. Our excessive dependence on OPEC has already taken a tremendous toll on our economy and our people. This is the direct cause of the long lines which have made millions of you spend aggravating hours waiting for gasoline. It's a cause of the increased inflation and unemployment that we now face. This intolerable dependence on foreign oil threatens our economic independence and the very

security of our nation. The energy crisis is real. It is worldwide. It is a clear and present danger to our nation. These are facts and we simply must face them.

What I have to say to you now about energy is simple and vitally important. Point one: I am tonight setting a clear goal for the energy policy of the United States. Beginning this moment, this nation will never use more foreign oil than we did in 1977—never. From now on, every new addition to our demand for energy will be met from our own production and our own conservation. The generation-long growth in our dependence on foreign oil will be stopped dead in its tracks right now and then reversed as we move through the 1980s. . . .

Point two: To ensure that we meet these targets, I will use my presidential authority to set import quotas. I'm announcing tonight that for 1979 and 1980, I will forbid the entry into this country of one drop of foreign oil more than these goals allow. . . .

Point three: To give us energy security, I am asking for the most massive peacetime commitment of funds and resources in our nation's history to develop America's own alternative sources of fuel—from coal, from oil shale, from plant products for gasohol, from unconventional gas, from the sun. . . .

*   *   *

Point four: I'm asking Congress to mandate, to require as a matter of law, that our nation's utility companies cut their massive use of oil by 50 percent within the next decade and switch to other fuels, especially coal, our most abundant energy source.

Point five: To make absolutely certain that nothing stands in the way of achieving these goals, I will urge Congress to create an energy mobilization board which, like the War Production Board in World War II, will have the responsibility and authority to cut through the red tape, the delays, and the endless roadblocks to completing key energy projects.

We will protect our environment. But when this nation critically needs a refinery or a pipeline, we will build it.

Point six: I'm proposing a bold conservation program to involve every state, county, and city and every average American in our energy battle. This effort will permit you to build conservation into your homes and your lives at a cost you can afford.

*   *   *

Our nation must be fair to the poorest among us, so we will increase aid to needy Americans to cope with rising energy prices. We often think of conservation only in terms of sacrifice. In fact, it is the most painless and immediate way of rebuilding our nation's strength. Every gallon of oil each one of us saves is a new form of production. It gives us more freedom, more confidence, that much more control over our own lives.

So, the solution of our energy crisis can also help us to conquer the crisis of the spirit in our country. It can rekindle our sense of unity, our confidence in the future, and give our nation and all of us individually a new sense of purpose.

*   *   *

I do not promise you that this struggle for freedom will be easy. I do not promise a quick way out of our nation's problems, when the truth is that the only way out is an all-out effort. What I do promise you is that I will lead our fight, and I will enforce fairness in our struggle, and I will ensure honesty. And above all, I will act. We can manage the short-term shortages more effectively and we will, but there are no short-term solutions to our long-range problems. There is simply no way to avoid sacrifice.

*   *   *

Little by little we can and we must rebuild our confidence. We can spend until we empty our treasuries, and we may summon all the wonders of science. But we can succeed only if we tap our greatest resources—America's people, America's values, and America's confidence.

REVIEW QUESTIONS

1. Describe what Carter meant by a crisis of confidence paralyzing the American people.
2. How did he propose to deal with that "crisis of confidence" and get America moving again?

RONALD REAGAN

FROM Acceptance Address, Republican National Convention (1980)

Ronald Reagan won the 1980 Republican presidential nomination because he promised to make America great again. The nation's problems, he claimed, were primarily the result of Jimmy Carter's failed Democratic administration. A former Hollywood actor and California governor, Reagan exuded optimism and leadership at a time when many Americans felt the nation was floundering.

From Republican National Convention Speech, July 17, 1980. Reprinted by permission of the Reagan Foundation.

*   *   *

More than anything else, I want my candidacy to unify our country; to renew the American spirit and sense of purpose. I want to carry our message to every American, regardless of party affiliation, who is a member of this community of shared values.

Never before in our history have Americans been called upon to face three grave threats to our very existence, any one of which could destroy us. We face a disintegrating economy, a weakened defense and an energy policy based on the sharing of scarcity.

The major issue of this campaign is the direct political, personal and moral responsibility of Democratic Party leadership—in the White House and in Congress—for this unprecedented calamity which has befallen us. They tell us they have done the most that humanly could be done. They say that the United States has had its day in the sun; that our nation has passed its zenith. They expect you to tell your children that the American people no longer have the will to cope with their problems; that the future will be one of sacrifice and few opportunities.

My fellow citizens, I utterly reject that view. The American people, the most generous on earth, who created the highest standard of living, are not going to accept the notion that we can only make a better world for others by moving backwards ourselves. Those who believe we can have no business leading the nation.

I will not stand by and watch this great country destroy itself under mediocre leadership that drifts from one crisis to the next, eroding our national will and purpose. We have come together here because the American people deserve better from those to whom they entrust our nation's highest offices, and we stand united in our resolve to do something about it.

We need rebirth of the American tradition of leadership at every level of government and in private life as well. The United States of America is unique in world history because it has a genius for leaders—many leaders—on many levels.

But, back in 1976, Mr. Carter said, "Trust me." And a lot of people did. Now, many of those people are out of work. Many have seen their savings eaten away by inflation. Many others on fixed incomes, especially the elderly, have watched helplessly as the cruel tax of inflation wasted away their purchasing power. And, today, a great many who trusted Mr. Carter wonder if we can survive the Carter policies of national defense.

"Trust me" government asks that we concentrate our hopes and dreams on one man; that we trust him to do what's best for us. My view of government places trust not in one person or one party, but in those values that transcend persons and parties. The trust is where it belongs—in the people. The responsibility to live up to that trust is where it belongs, in their elected leaders. That kind of relationship, between the people and their elected leaders, is a special kind of compact.

Three hundred and sixty years ago, in 1620, a group of families dared to cross a mighty ocean to build a future for themselves in a new world. When they arrived at Plymouth, Massachusetts, they formed what they called a "compact"; an agreement among themselves to build a community and abide by its laws. The single act—the voluntary binding together of free people to live under the law—set the pattern for what was to come.

A century and a half later, the descendants of those people pledged their lives, their fortunes and their sacred honor to found this nation. Some forfeited their fortunes and their lives; none sacrificed honor.

Four score and seven years later, Abraham Lincoln called upon the people of all America to renew their dedication and their commitment to a government of, for and by the people.

Isn't it once again time to renew our compact of freedom; to pledge to each other all that is best in our lives; all that gives meaning to them—for the sake of this, our beloved and blessed land?

Together, let us make this a new beginning. Let us make a commitment to care for the needy; to teach our children the values and the virtues handed down to us by our families; to have the courage to defend those values and the willingness to sacrifice for them.

Let us pledge to restore, in our time, the American spirit of voluntary service, of cooperation, of private and community initiative; a spirit that flows like a deep and mighty river through the history of our nation.

As your nominee, I pledge to restore to the federal government the capacity to do the people's work without dominating their lives. I pledge to you a government that will not only work well, but wisely; its ability to act tempered by prudence and its willingness to do good balanced by the knowledge that government is never more dangerous than when our desire to have it help us blinds us to its great power to harm us.

The first Republican president once said, "While the people retain their virtue and their vigilance, no administration by any extreme of wickedness or folly can seriously injure the government in the short space of four years."

If Mr. Lincoln could see what's happened in these last three-and-a-half years, he might hedge a little on that statement. But, with the virtues that our legacy as a free people and with the vigilance that sustains liberty, we still have time to use our renewed compact to overcome the injuries that have been done to America these past three-and-a-half years.

First, we must overcome something the present administration has cooked up: a new and altogether indigestible economic stew, one part inflation, one part high unemployment, one part recession, one part runaway taxes, one party deficit spending and seasoned by an energy crisis. It's an economic stew that has turned the national stomach.

Ours are not problems of abstract economic theory. Those are problems of flesh and blood; problems that cause pain and destroy the moral fiber of real people who should not suffer the further indignity of being told by the government that it is all somehow their fault. We do not have inflation because—as Mr. Carter says—we have lived too well.

The head of a government which has utterly refused to live within its means and which has, in the last few days, told us that this year's deficit will be $60 billion, dares to point the finger of blame at business and labor, both of which have been engaged in a losing struggle just trying to stay even.

High taxes, we are told, are somehow good for us, as if, when government spends our money it isn't inflationary, but when we spend it, it is.

Those who preside over the worst energy shortage in our history tell us to use less, so that we will run out of oil, gasoline, and natural gas a little more slowly. Conservation is desirable, of course, for we must not waste energy. But conservation is not the sole answer to our energy needs. America must get to work producing more energy. The Republican program for solving economic problems is based on growth and productivity.

*   *   *

Our problems are both acute and chronic, yet all we hear from those in positions of leadership are the same tired proposals for more government tinkering, more meddling and more control—all of which led us to this state in the first place.

Can anyone look at the record of this administration and say, "Well done?" Can anyone compare the state of our economy when the Carter Administration took office with where we are today and say, "Keep up the good work?" Can anyone look at our reduced standing in the world today and say, "Let's have four more years of this?"

I believe the American people are going to answer these questions the first week of November and their answer will be, "No—we've had enough." And, then it will be up to us—beginning next January 20th—to offer an administration and congressional leadership of competence and more than a little courage.

We must have the clarity of vision to see the difference between what is essential and what is merely desirable, and then the courage to bring our government back under control and make it acceptable to the people.

It is essential that we maintain both the forward momentum of economic growth and the strength of the safety net beneath those in society who need help. We also believe it is essential that the integrity of all aspects of Social Security are preserved.

Beyond these essentials, I believe it is clear our federal government is overgrown and overweight.

Indeed, it is time for our government to go on a diet. Therefore, my first act as chief executive will be to impose an immediate and thorough freeze on federal hiring. Then, we are going to enlist the very best minds from business, labor and whatever quarter to conduct a detailed review of every department, bureau and agency that lives by federal appropriations. . . .

*   *   *

I will not accept the excuse that the federal government has grown so big and powerful that it is beyond the control of any president, any administration or Congress. We are going to put an end to the notion that the American taxpayer exists to fund the federal government. The federal government exists to serve the American people. On January 20th, we are going to re-establish that truth. . . .

The Carter Administration lives in the world of make-believe. Every day, drawing up a response to that day's problems, troubles, regardless of what happened yesterday and what will happen tomorrow.

The rest of us, however, live in the real world. It is here that disasters are overtaking our nation without any real response from Washington. This is make-believe, self-deceit and—above all—transparent hypocrisy.

*   *   *

Tonight, let us dedicate ourselves to renewing the American compact. I ask you not simply to "Trust me," but to trust your values—our values—and to hold me responsible for living up to them. I ask you to trust that American spirit which knows no ethnic, religious, social, political, regional, or economic boundaries; the spirit that burned with zeal in the hearts of millions of immigrants from every corner of the Earth who came here in search of freedom.

Some say that spirit no longer exists. But I have seen it—I have felt it—all across the land; in the big cities, the small towns and in rural America. The American spirit is still there, ready to

blaze into life if you and I are willing to do what has to be done; the practical, down-to-earth things that will stimulate our economy, increase productivity and put America back to work. The time is now to resolve that the basis of a firm and principled foreign policy is one that takes the world as it is and seeks to change it by leadership and example; not by harangue, harassment or wishful thinking.

The time is now to say that while we shall seek new friendships and expand and improve others, we shall not do so by breaking our word or casting aside old friends and allies.

And, the time is now to redeem promises once made to the American people by another candidate, in another time and another place. He said, "For three long years I have been going up and down this country preaching that government—federal, state, and local—costs too much. I shall not stop that preaching. As an immediate program of action, we must abolish useless offices. We must eliminate unnecessary functions of government . . . we must consolidate subdivisions of government and, like the private citizen, give up luxuries which we can no longer afford." . . . So said Franklin Delano Roosevelt in his acceptance speech to the Democratic National Convention in July 1932.

The time is now, my fellow Americans, to recapture our destiny, to take it into our own hands. But, to do this will take many of us, working together. I ask you tonight to volunteer your help in this cause so we can carry our message throughout the land. . . .

God bless America.

REVIEW QUESTIONS

1. How did Reagan propose to address what he called an "overgrown and overweight" federal government?
2. What did Reagan mean by his commitment to "recapture our destiny"?

RONALD REAGAN

The "Evil Empire" (1983)

Ronald Reagan skillfully courted the Religious Right during his presidency. In a speech to the Annual Convention of the National Association of Evangelicals in Orlando, Florida, he outlined his crusade against atheistic communism.

From *Public Papers of the Presidents of the United States: Ronald Reagan, 1983* (Washington, DC, 1984), 1:359–64.

. . . There are a great many God-fearing, dedicated, noble men and women in public life, present company included. And, yes, we need your help to keep us ever mindful of the ideas and the principles that brought us into the public arena in the first place. The basis of those ideals and principles is a commitment to freedom and personal liberty that, itself, is grounded in the much deeper realization that freedom prospers only where the blessings of God are avidly sought and humbly accepted.

The American experiment in democracy rests on this insight. Its discovery was the great triumph of our Founding Fathers voiced by William Penn when he said: "If we will not be governed by God, we must be governed by tyrants." Explaining the inalienable rights of men, Jefferson said, "The God who gave us life, gave us liberty at the same time." And it was George Washington who said that "of all the dispositions and habits which lead to political prosperity, religion and morality are indispensable supports."

And finally, that shrewdest of all observers of American democracy, Alexis de Tocqueville, put it eloquently after he had gone on a search for the secret of America's greatness and genius—and he said: "Not until I went into the churches of America and heard her pulpits aflame with righteousness did I understand the greatness and the genius of America. . . . America is good. And if America ever ceases to be good, America will cease to be great."

Well, I'm pleased to be here today with you who are keeping America great by keeping her good.

Only through your work and prayers and those of millions of others can we hope to survive this perilous century and keep alive this experiment in liberty, this last, best hope of man.

I want you to know that this administration is motivated by a political philosophy that sees the greatness of America in you her people, and in your families, churches, neighborhoods, communities—the institutions that foster and nourish values like concern for others and respect for the rule of law under God. Now, I don't have to tell you that this puts us in opposition to, or at least out of step with, a prevailing attitude of many who have turned to a modern-day secularism, discarding the tried and time-tested values upon which our very civilization is based. No matter how well intentioned, their value system is radically different from that of most Americans. And while they proclaim that they're freeing us from superstitions of the past, they've taken upon themselves the job of superintending us by government rule and regulation. Sometime their voices are louder than ours, but they are not yet a majority. . . .

Freedom prospers when religion is vibrant and the rule of law under God is acknowledged. When our Founding Fathers passed the first amendment, they sought to protect churches from government interference. They never intended to construct a wall of hostility between government and the concept of religious belief itself.

The evidence of this permeates our history and our government. The Declaration of Independence mentions the Supreme Being no less than four times. "In God We Trust" is engraved on our coinage. The Supreme Court opens its proceedings with a religious invocation. And the Members of Congress open their sessions with a prayer. I just happen to believe the schoolchildren of the United States are entitled to the same privileges as Supreme Court Justices and Congressmen.

Last year, I sent the Congress a constitutional amendment to restore prayer to public schools. Already this session, there's growing bipartisan support for the amendment, and I am calling on the Congress to act speedily to pass it and to let our children pray.

Perhaps some of you read recently about the Lubbock school case, where a judge actually ruled that it was unconstitutional for a school district to give equal treatment to religious and nonreligious student groups, even when the group meetings were being held during the students' own time. The first amendment never intended to require government to discriminate against religious speech. . . .

More than a decade ago, a Supreme Court decision literally wiped off the books of 50 states statutes protecting the rights of unborn children. Abortion on demand now takes the lives of up to one and a half million unborn children a year. Human life legislation ending this tragedy will some day pass the Congress, and you and I must never rest until it does. Unless and until it can be proven that the unborn child is not a living entity, then its right to life, liberty, and the pursuit of happiness must be protected. . . .

America's goodness and greatness
One recent survey by a Washington-based research council concluded that Americans were far more religious than the people of other nations; 96 percent of those surveyed expressed a belief in God and a huge majority believed the Ten Commandments had real meaning in their lives. And another study has found that an overwhelming majority of Americans disapprove of adultery, teenage sex, pornography, abortion, and hard drugs. And this same study showed a deep reverence for the importance of family ties and religious belief.

I think the items that we've discussed here today must be a key part of the Nation's political agenda. For the first time the Congress is openly and seriously debating issues—and that's enormous progress right there. I repeat: American is in the midst of a spiritual awakening and a moral renewal. And with your Biblical keynote, I say today, "Yes, let justice roll on like a river, righteousness like a never-failing stream."

Now, obviously, much of this new political and social consensus I've talked about is based on a positive view of American history, one that takes pride in our country's accomplishments and record. But we must never forget that no government schemes are going to perfect man. We know that living in this world means dealing with what philosophers would call the phenomenology of evil or, as theologians would put it, the doctrine of sin.

There is sin and evil in the world, and we're enjoined by Scripture and the Lord Jesus to oppose it with all our might. Our nation, too, has a legacy of evil with which it must deal. The glory of this land has been its capacity of transcending the moral evils of our past. For example, the long struggle of minority citizens for equal rights, once a source of disunity and civil war, is now a point of pride for all Americans. We must never go back.

There is no room for racism, anti-Semitism, or other forms of ethnic and racial hatred in this country.

I know that you've been horrified, as have I, by the resurgence of some hate groups preaching bigotry and prejudice. Use the mighty voice of your pulpits and the powerful standing of your churches to denounce and isolate these hate groups in our midst. The commandment given us is clear and simple; "Thou shalt love thy neighbor as thyself."

But whatever sad episodes exist in our past, any objective observer must hold a positive view of American history, a history that has been the story of hopes fulfilled and dreams made into reality. Especially in this century, America has kept alight the torch of freedom, but not just for ourselves but for millions of others around the world.

And this brings me to me final point today. During my first press conference as President, in answer to a direct question, I pointed out that, as good Marxist-Leninists, the Soviet leaders have openly and publicly declared that the only morality they recognize is that which will further their course, which is world revolution. I think I should point out I was only quoting Lenin, their guiding spirit, who said in 1920 that they repudiated all morality that proceeds from supernatural ideas— that's their name for religion—or ideas that are outside class conception. Morality is entirely subordinate to the interests of class war. And everything is moral that is necessary for the annihilation of the old, exploiting social order and for uniting the proletariat.

Well, I think the refusal of many influential people to accept this elementary fact of Soviet doctrine illustrates an historical reluctance to see totalitarian powers for what they are. We saw this phenomenon in the 1930's. We see it too often today.

This doesn't mean we should isolate ourselves and refuse to seek an understanding with them. I intend to do everything I can to persuade them of our peaceful intent, to remind them that it was the West that refused to use its nuclear monopoly in the forties and fifties for territorial gain and which now proposes a 50-percent cut in strategic ballistic missiles and the elimination of an entire class of land-based, intermediate range nuclear missiles.

At the same time, however, they must be made to understand we will never compromise our principles and standards. We will never give away our freedom. We will never abandon our belief in God. And we will never stop searching for a genuine peace. . . .

Yes, let us pray for the salvation of all of those who live in that totalitarian darkness—pray they will discover the joy of knowing God. But until they do, let us be aware that while they preach the supremacy of the state, declare its omnipotence over individual man, and predict its eventual domination of all peoples on the Earth, they are the focus of evil in the modern world. . . .

While America's military strength is important, let me add here that I've always maintained that the struggle now going on for the world will never be decided by bombs or rockets, by armies or military might. The real crisis we face today is a spiritual one; at root, it is a test of moral will and faith.

Whittaker Chambers, the man whose own religious conversion made him a witness to one of the terrible traumas of our time, the Hiss-Chambers case, wrote that the crisis of the Western World exists to the degree in which the West is indifferent to God, the degree to which it collaborates in communism's attempt to make man stand alone without God. And then he said, for Marxism-Leninism is actually the second oldest faith, first proclaimed in the Garden of Eden with the words of temptation, "Ye shall be as gods." The Western World can answer this challenge, he wrote, "but only provided that its faith in God and the freedom He enjoins is as great as communism's faith in Man." I believe we shall rise to the challenge. I believe that communism is another sad, bizarre chapter in human history whose last pages even now are being written. I believe this because the source of our strength in the quest for human freedom is not material, but spiritual. And because it knows no limitation, it must terrify and ultimately triumph over those who would enslave their fellow man. For in the words of Isaiah: "He giveth power to the faint; and to them that have no might He increased strength. . . . But they that wait upon the Lord shall renew their strength; they shall mount up with wings as eagles; they shall run, and not be weary. . . ."

Yes, change your world. One of our Founding Fathers, Thomas Paine, said, "We have it within our power to begin the world over again." We can do it, doing together what no one church could do by itself.

God bless you, and thank you very much.

REVIEW QUESTIONS

1. Do you agree with Reagan's interpretation of the separation between church and state in American history?
2. How do you feel about the incorporation of prayer in public schools?
3. Do you accept Reagan's characterization of the Soviet Union as the source of evil in world affairs?

JESSE JACKSON

FROM **Democratic Nominating Convention Speech (1984)**

In 1984 Jesse Jackson, a prominent African American civil rights activist and Baptist preacher who had been a senior aide to Martin Luther King Jr. during the 1960s, ran for the Democratic presidential nomination, seeking to create a "Rainbow Coalition" of supporters that would cut across all racial and ethnic groups and embolden people of color to run for national office. An inspiring as well as provocative speaker, he surprised analysts by finishing third in the balloting behind Gary Hart and the eventual presidential nominee, former vice president Walter Mondale. Jackson gained more primary votes than any previous African American candidate in American history. His strong showing gained him a visible and influential role at the Democratic National Convention in San Francisco in July. In his fifty-minute prime-time speech to the convention, Jackson displayed the rhetorical skills of a revivalist minister, stressing party unity and racial harmony. The riveting speech with its gospel cadences attracted a huge national television audience and drew repeated ovations, leading Florida Governor Bob Graham to declare: "If you are a human being and weren't affected by what you just heard, you may be beyond redemption."

Reprinted by permission of the Rainbow PUSH Coalition.

Tonight we come together bound by our faith in a mighty God, with genuine respect and love for our country, and inheriting the legacy of a great party, the Democratic Party, which is the best hope for redirecting our nation on a more humane, just and peaceful course.

This is not a perfect party. We are not a perfect people. Yet, we are called to a perfect mission: our mission to feed the hungry; to clothe the naked; to house the homeless; to teach the illiterate; to provide jobs for the jobless; and to choose the human race over the nuclear race.

*   *   *

. . . Leadership must heed the call of conscience, redemption, expansion, healing and unity, for they are the key to achieving our mission. Time is neutral and does not change things. With courage and initiative, leaders can change things.

No generation can choose the age or circumstance in which it is born, but through leadership it can choose to make the age in which it is born, an age of enlightenment, an age of jobs and peace and justice.

Only leadership—that intangible combination of gifts, the discipline, information, circumstance, courage, timing, will and divine inspiration—can lead us out of the crisis in which we find ourselves. The leadership can mitigate the misery of our nation. Leadership can part the waters and lead our nation in the direction of the Promised Land. Leadership can life the boats stuck at the bottom.

*   *   *

This campaign has taught me much; that leaders must be tough enough to fight, tender enough to cry, human enough to make mistakes, humble enough to admit them, strong enough to absorb the pain and resilient enough to bounce back and keep on moving.

For leaders, the pain is often intense. But you must smile through your tears and keep moving with the faith that there is a brighter side somewhere.

*   *   *

America is not like a blanket—one piece of unbroken cloth, the same color, the same texture, the same size. America is more like a quilt— many patches, many pieces, many colors, many sizes, all woven and held together by a common thread. The white, the Hispanic, the black, the Arab, the Jew, the woman, the native American, the small farmer, the businessperson, the environmentalist, the peace activist, the young, the old, the lesbian, the gay and the disabled make up the American quilt.

Even in our fractured state, all of us count and all of us fit somewhere. We have proven that we can survive without each other. But we have not proven that we can win and progress without each other. We must come together.

*   *   *

We must be unusually committed and caring as we expand our family to include new members. All of us must be tolerant and understanding as the fears and anxieties of the rejected and of the party leadership express themselves in so many different ways. Too often what we call hate—as if it were some deeply rooted in philosophy or strategy—it is simply ignorance, anxiety, paranoia, fear and insecurity.

To be strong leaders, we must be long-suffering as we seek to right the wrongs of our Party and our Nation. We must expand our Party, heal our Party and unify our Party. That is our mission in 1984.

*   *   *

President Reagan says the nation is in recovery. Those 90,000 corporations that made a profit last year but paid no Federal taxes are recovering. The 37,000 military contractors who have benefited from Reagan's more than doubling of his military budget in peacetime, surely they are recovering.

The big corporations and rich individuals who received the bulk of a three-year, multibillion tax cut from Mr. Reagan are recovering. But no such recovery is under way for the least of these. Rising tides don't lift all boats, particularly those stuck at the bottom.

For the boats stuck at the bottom there's a misery index. This Administration has made life more miserable for the poor. Its attitude has been contemptuous. Its policies and programs have been cruel and unfair to working people. They must be held accountable in November for increasing infant mortality among the poor. In Detroit—in Detroit, one of the great cities in the western world, babies are dying at the same rate as Honduras, the most underdeveloped Nation in our hemisphere. This Administration must be held accountable for policies that have contributed to the growing poverty in America. There are now 34 million people in poverty, 15 percent of our Nation. Twenty-three million are White, 11 million Black, Hispanic, Asian and others. By the end of this year, there will be 41 million people in poverty. We cannot stand idly by. We must fight for change now.

*   *   *

. . . Our time has come. Our time has come. Suffering breeds character. Character breeds faith, and in the end faith will not disappoint. Our time has come. Our faith, hope and dreams have prevailed. Our time has come. Weeping has endured for nights, but that joy cometh in the morning.

Our time has come. No grave can hold our body down. Our time has come. No lie can live forever. Our time has come. We must leave the racial battle ground and come to the economic common ground and moral higher ground. America, our time has come.

We come from disgrace to amazing grace. Our time has come. Give me your tired, give me your poor, your huddled masses who yearn to breathe free and come November, there will be a change because our time has come.

Thank you and God bless you.

REVIEW QUESTIONS

1. How does Jackson define the mission of the Democratic Party?
2. Describe Jackson's metaphor of America society being like a quilt. Is it effective?

RUSH LIMBAUGH

FROM *The Way Things Ought to Be* (1992)

Born in Cape Girardeau, Missouri, in 1951, Rush Limbaugh became the most popular and influential conservative talk-show host during the 1980s. His rise to fame and fortune was not easy, however. A college dropout, he was fired from radio stations in Missouri and Pennsylvania for being too controversial. "My whole family thought I was destined for failure," he recalled. Yet his persistence paid off. By the mid-1980s, his radio show in Sacramento, California, led the ratings. His success convinced the ABC Radio Network to launch the nationwide Rush Limbaugh Show *in 1988. It soon became America's highest rated show, in part because Limbaugh was so outspoken and confrontational. "It's my job, it's my life, it's my career, it's my passion," Limbaugh once said about his politically charged career as a radio host, commentator, and writer. "I'm doing what I love. I think I'm doing what I was born to do." In 1993 he was inducted into the Radio Hall of Fame. In this selection from his 1992 book,* The Way Things Ought to Be, *he takes on multiculturalism.*

Multiculturalism

A few years ago, radical students at Stanford University protested against a required course in the great texts of Western civilization. They organized a march, led by the Reverend Jesse Jackson, with a chant, "Hey, hey, ho, ho, Western culture's gotta go." And Stanford capitulated and abolished the Western civilization requirement. it was replaced with watered-down courses in which books were supposed to be examined from the perspective of "race, class, and gender," and read-ings from St. Augustine and John Locke were interspersed with such works as the autobiography of Guatemalan Marxist guerilla fighter Rigoberta Menchu and a documentary on Navajo Indians entitled "Our Cosmos, Our Sheep, Our Bodies, Ourselves."

Multiculturalism is billed as a way to make Americans more sensitive to the diverse cultural backgrounds of people in this country. It's time we blew the whistle on that. What is being taught under the guise of multiculturalism is worse than historical revisionism; it's more than a distortion of facts; it's an elimination of facts. In some schools, kids are being taught that the ideas of the Constitution were really borrowed from the Iroquois Indians, and that Africans discovered America by crossing the Atlantic on rafts hundreds of years before Columbus and made all sorts of other scientific discoveries and inventions that were later stolen from them. They are told that the ancient Greeks and Romans stole all of their ideas from the Egyptians and that the Egyptians were black Africans.

In fact, most historians and anthropologists will tell you that while there was a lot of cultural exchange in the ancient world and the Greeks and Romans absorbed some of the Egyptian ideas, it was only one of many influences. And the ancient Egyptians were dark-skinned but not black, even though many scholars have been so intimidated that they will only say this off the record. My purpose here is not to be critical of Africans or African culture, but simply to point out that not one syllable of any of our founding documents can be traced to the roots of tribal Africa—and that neither I nor anyone else is going to improve racial relations by pretending otherwise.

There is a fallacious premise out there that black kids have low self-esteem because they don't have any roots. They don't have anything to relate to in their past except slavery and degradation, and to elevate their self-esteem we must teach them about the great cultures of their ancestors. I think the multiculturalists are perpetrating a tremendous and harmful fraud when they take young black kids in public schools and teach them things that are irrelevant or even counterproductive to their future as Americans. They teach that street slang is just as good as grammatical English, that whites are cold and logical but blacks are warm and intuitive, and that Africans have a different approach to numbers that doesn't emphasize precision.

Well, if you want to get a job with IBM you've got to have the skills that will help you get that job. And that involves a lot of things. Not just the skills, such as logical thinking and mathematics, but language, appearance, showing up on time. And if the

kids have been taught that learning these things means compromising themselves and conforming to white values, how on earth can they be expected to succeed? If you want to prosper in America, if you want access to opportunity in America, you must be able to assimilate: to become part of the American culture. Just as in any other country of the world—if an American moved there, he would have to adapt to its culture if he wanted to succeed. The so-called minorities in this country are not being done any favors when the multiculturalist crowd forces their attitudinal segregation from mainstream society. The politics of cultural pride are actually the politics of alienation, in a different uniform. . . .

What is this American culture toward which we should all aspire? American culture is defined primarily by the idea of self-reliance. That's how this country was built: people of every background fending for themselves and for their families. And it's something we are losing. If you tell someone to get a job, you are using dirty words now; you are being insensitive. Now you are told to define yourself by your place within a tribe or a group.

People have accused me of racism or insensitivity when I challenge the multiculturalist view on history and education. But far from being a racist, far from being a bigot, I have a great deal of compassion and love for people of all backgrounds, and I also love my country. I want this to be a great country, and a great country needs as many great individuals as there can be.

These young black kids in public schools in America are Americans. Not Africans, not Jamaicans, but Americans. And we have to treat them as such. It is in our nation's best interest, and in their best interest too, for them to grow up as good Americans, to know American culture, to learn to prosper in America. And I have that hope. I want everyone to be taught the things that are necessary for them to prosper as Americans, not black something or brown something or red something, but as Americans.

Of course there are people in the multiculturalist movement who have the best of intentions, who think the movement is dedicated to helping members of minority cultures become more well rounded. And I don't want to castigate all advocates of multiculturalism. In fact, if people want to teach ancient African history, or Third World cultures, or women's studies, that's fine—as long as it doesn't become the primary perspective and doesn't supplant the things that all American kids need to know—and as long as it is not coupled with the fraudulent message that the minorities' best opportunity of succeeding in this society is to jealously cling to their past.

REVIEW QUESTIONS

1. How does Limbaugh define "multiculturalism"? What examples does he use to explain the term?
2. According to Limbaugh, every resident should seek to assimilate into "American culture." To him, what is the defining attribute of American culture? Do you agree?

NEIL HICKEY

FROM Is Fox News Fair? (1998)

The polarization of American politics was abetted by major cable news media choosing sides on the liberal/conservative divide. In 1996, Fox News emerged to challenge CNN from the right, while MSNBC did the same from the left. By the end of the century, both upstart news channels had established their brands in the increasingly contentious world of news broadcasting. In 1998, Neil Hickey, an editor of the Columbia Journalism Review, *published an analysis of the upstart Fox News Channel, owned by the global media titan Rupert Murdoch.*

From "Is Fox News Fair?," *Columbia Journalism Review*, March/April 1998, pp. 30–32, 35. Reprinted by permission of Neil Hickey. [Editorial insertions appear in square brackets—*Ed.*]

"I don't think there's ever been anything like it," Brit Hume declares with undisguised enthusiasm. He's talking about the Fox News Channel (FNC), Rupert Murdoch's fledgling, all-news cable network, a competitor to CNN and MSNBC launched on October 6, 1996, with an estimated sticker price of $475 million and now available in 25 million U.S. homes. As the network's managing editor and chief Washington correspondent, Hume is FNC's highest profile figure—twenty-three years a reporter for ABC News, eight years as its chief White House correspondent, an Emmy winner in 1991 for his Gulf War coverage. In a promotional announcement aired often on FNC, Hume tells viewers: "The intention here is to do a broadcast people can trust."

"Trust." "Fairness and balance." "We report, you decide." Those terms punctuate FNC's broadcast day like a drumbeat, along with viewer mail flashed on the screen: "We are thrilled with the unbiased and fair coverage." "Thank you for finally providing a TV home for me." "Until Fox News Channel, I was about 2 give up on news." "It's nice to have a newsperson say, 'You can draw your own conclusions.'" "TV news magazines have fluff. Fox has facts." "Fox News Channel has boldly earned the right to declare they are fair and balanced." "Finally, objective journalism . . . . You're long overdue."

"Thank you for putting together a team that tells the whole story."

For Murdoch, playing the FNC chip is a huge gamble. CNN, in its eighteenth year, is a pillar on the international news scene, and a cash cow for its owner, Time Warner—the world's biggest media conglomerate. MSNBC is the privileged offspring of behemoth parents, GE and Microsoft. Those two cable networks were duking it out vigorously for a share of the relatively small all-news audience— with CNN comfortably the world champ—when FNC entered the ring as a brash challenger. It's looking at losses for the two years 1997 and 1998 of $150 million, and won't be operationally solvent (say its proprietors) until sometime in 2000, with years to go beyond that before News Corp. recoups its investment.

Nonetheless, it's a briar patch that Murdoch, 68, was eager to leap into. He needed news as the final piece of his three-legged stool to be truly a major player in American television, like ABC, CBS, and NBC. Although hugely successful in entertainment (The X-Files, The Simpsons) and sports (National Football League games) via his Fox broadcasting network, the Australian-born magnate never was a presence in national TV news in the U.S.... Now, the recently-forged Fox News division, under Murdoch's chosen instrument for progress, Roger Ailes, 56, is busily trying to change all that by building a national TV news organization and a chain of news-conscious local stations that can play on the same ball field with the big kids.

Having thus committed to a cable news network, the question for Murdoch became: What kind of network? What would be its taste and texture? How would it differ from the entrenched dynamic duo, CNN and MSNBC? The answer emerged from Murdoch's conviction that most TV journalists are far more liberal than the population as a whole.

There is some evidence that he is correct. In a 1996 Freedom Forum/Roper Center survey of 139 Washington-based newspeople, 61 percent of the sample professed to being either "liberal" or "liberal to moderate," and a paltry 9 percent "conservative" or "moderate to conservative." In 1992, Bill Clinton got 89 percent of their votes, George Bush 7 percent.

In a famous Wall Street Journal op-ed piece in February 1996, CBS newsman Bernard Goldberg hurled a hand grenade at his colleagues, saying: "The old argument that the networks and other 'media elites' have a liberal bias is so blatantly true that it's hardly worth discussing anymore." Even Walter Cronkite declared last year that most journalists "are probably tilted toward the liberal side."

Enter Murdoch, stage right. In February 1996, he installed as chairman and C.E.O. of the Fox News division the tough, profane political consultant and TV producer, Ailes, who'd advised a string of Republican office-seekers: Nixon, Reagan, Bush, New York Senator Alfonse D'Amato, and New York Mayor Rudolph Giuliani. Ailes had been a central figure in Joe McGinniss's celebrated book about the 1968 Nixon campaign, The Selling of the President, which depicted Ailes as a ranting, blustery partisan whose showbiz talents cut to the core of Nixon's image problems. (Famous Ailes quote from the book "...a lot of people think Nixon is dull...a bore, a pain in the ass.... He's a funny looking guy. He looks like somebody hung him in a closet overnight and he jumps out in the morning with his suit all bunched up and starts running around saying, 'I want to be President.'")

...The questions persist: Can a news network with executives and onscreen talent so conspicuously and so heavily right of center fulfill a promise of delivering "fair and balanced" news, information, and opinion? Does the oft-repeated slogan, "We report. You decide," accurately describe how the network delivers news? In FNC's round-the-clock format—unlike those of its competitors at CNN and MSNBC—hard news, except for breaking stories, is mostly confined to a few minutes on the hour and half-hour, plus an hour-long newscast at 7 P.M. Most of the rest is chat shows, interviews—discussions of trends, technology, health, entertainment, education, pets, as well as some old newsreels from the Fox Movietone archives.

A close monitoring of the channel over several weeks indicates that the news segments tend to be straightforward, with little hint of political subtext except for stories the news editors feel the "mainstream" press has either down-played or ignored.

Nobody, least of all FNC, downplayed the allegations surrounding President Clinton's relationship with Monica Lewinsky.

Quick off the mark on January 21, the day the story broke, FNC had the first photo of Lewinsky on the air at 9 A.M., and, that same day, the first interview with Gennifer Flowers. It began devoting all of its daytime schedule to the crisis, except for brief segments on other news, along with weekend specials attracting hundreds of viewer phone calls. The network even inaugurated a whole new early-evening series, *Special Report with Brit Hume*, to keep daily tabs on the evolving story "for the duration of the development." Staffers from bureaus around the country were rushed in to reinforce the Washington team. "I've been proudest of our restraint," says FNC vice president John Moody.

Another Clinton story—unrelated to the alleged sex scandal—got the full FNC treatment because, according to Brit Hume, nobody else was doing it. On January 7, the FNC dinner hour news program introduced a report saying: "Hillary Clinton and the White House broke the rules. But the taxpayer may end up paying the bill." The story described a $286,000 sanction imposed by a federal judge against the administration for a "coverup" (in the judge's words) of efforts to keep the proceedings of Hillary Clinton's 1993 health care task force a secret. The White House had been shifty in responding to a legal request for the records, the FNC story suggested; interviewees were adamant that taxpayers ought not get stuck with paying the fine.

If Fox's collective news hole—small for an all-news cable channel—offers largely untilted coverage, its discussion programs regularly and unabashedly convey a right-of-center sensibility, sometimes subtle, at other times overt. In a promo for the *Hannity & Colmes* show, Sean Hannity declared his view that "a liberal is somebody who thinks he has a right to my hard-earned money." A talk show guest, Tim Graham of the Washington-based Media Research Center, declared it "outrageous" that the indictments of two Clinton cabinet members received only "eight or nine seconds of network airtime," and that "so many Clinton scandals don't get sufficiently covered." The host, Eric Burns, wondered if that was because "the media are so liberally biased." Graham answered that if one compares Clinton's coverage to Ronald Reagan's, it's "hard to conclude that there isn't a liberal bias here." He added: "Clearly you can say there's a liberal bias when you've got CNN's president staying in the Lincoln bedroom [in the White House] and nobody seems to care at CNN."

But nobody can object to a "fair and balanced" news service, nor one that simply "reports" and lets you "decide." Those terms have become a marketing device and a fig leaf for Fox staffers who are otherwise perfectly candid (as they were in interviews for this article) about their right-of-center convictions. But the same yardstick must apply to them as they demand from their competitors: keeping the hard news pristinely free of ideology.

Is the output of Fox News Channel, in its totality, truly "fair" and "balanced"? The answer is a qualified no. It's no more fair and balanced than the *National Review* or *The Nation*, which flaunt no such claims. In its patchwork quilt of talk shows, FNC is, inevitably, the product of its creators, interlocutors [on-air staff], and guests. That makes it unmistakably a bully pulpit for conservative sentiment in America—and, consequently, robustly controversial, which, for better or worse, expands the boundaries of our national discourse. It's one more stone in what's becoming an avalanche of news and opinion hurtling at the public. But the antidote to controversial speech, as is regularly pointed out in journalistic circles, is more controversial speech—not less.

Review Questions

1. In your opinion, is the Fox News Channel "fair and balanced"?
2. Do partisan cable news channels benefit or degrade American civic discourse?

32 ❧ TWENTY-FIRST-CENTURY AMERICA, 1993–PRESENT

The United States during the last decade of the twentieth century ricocheted between extremes in search of a stable center. In politics, as an editorial in Business Week *stressed in 1996, "voters want their leaders to govern from the center." In 1992 Bill Clinton defeated George H. W. Bush by portraying himself as a new type of Democrat, a centrist and a Washington outsider committed to reducing the size and cost of government. Once in office, however, he fell under the sway of old-style liberals who convinced him to focus on apportioning government jobs to minorities, promoting gay rights within the military, and allowing his wife, Hillary, to design a government-run healthcare reform package that smacked of New Dealism.*

The results were catastrophic for the Democrats. Republicans scored a major victory in the 1994 elections. For the first time in forty years, they seized control of both houses of Congress and announced that their "Contract with America" involved nothing less than the dismantling of the welfare state. "It's the Russian revolution in reverse," said Republican strategist Bill Kristol. Newt Gingrich, the outspoken new Speaker of the House, declared that "We are at the end of an era." Tom DeLay, Gingrich's lieutenant in the House, brazenly stressed that "we are ideologues."

Yet the radical Republicans soon found themselves the victims of their own hubris. Middle-of-the-road Americans balked at the idea of shutting down the federal government, and the ever-resilient Bill Clinton surprised his opponents by moving decisively toward the political center. He hired a new stable of advisers and began stressing that the "era of Big Government is over." He used his State of the Union address in 1995 to co-opt the Republicans on key issues such as welfare reform and balancing the budget. Clinton now insisted that the Democratic Party had allowed itself to be seduced by "identity politics"—self-interested groups preoccupied with race, ethnicity, gender, and sexual orientation. He promised to abandon such factionalism by moving the party to the center of American values. He began talking about the need to curb teen pregnancy and underage smoking as well as improve the quality of TV programs.

By 1996 the editor of U.S. News and World Report *could remark that Clinton had stopped the Republican "revolution and successfully placed himself in the political center, uniting his own party and widening his appeal to independents." His victory over Bob Dole in the 1996 presidential election confirmed his successful makeover. One of Clinton's top aides declared after the election that "We're going to see government from the center."*

The same conservative forces steering Bill Clinton toward the center were also affecting racial attitudes during the 1990s. People in both political parties began to question the affirmative action policies that had given preferential treatment to women and minorities. When the Supreme Court ruled in Adarand Constructors v. Pena *(1995) that the government required a "compelling interest" to justify affirmative action mandates, efforts spread across the country to set aside race- and gender-based preferences. In 1996 the state of California eliminated affirmative action programs in employment, contracting, and university admissions. Democratic Senator Joseph Lieberman of Connecticut expressed the widespread view that racial and gender preferences were "patently unfair."*

A new generation of conservative African American intellectuals agreed. Thomas Sowell, Shelby Steele, Glen Loury, and Ward Connerly, among others, stressed that affirmative action and social welfare programs had backfired. Instead of liberating and uplifting blacks, they had made them dependent on government assistance and undercut individual initiative. Connerly, a member of the board of regents of the University of California, asked, "Are we going to continue to believe that blacks by definition are disadvantaged? As a black man, I say no."

Another widespread concern during the 1990s was the erosion of civic virtue and public involvement. Between 1960 and 1990, a quarter of the electorate lost interest in voting. In 1994 only 39 percent of the registered voters cast ballots. Apathy at the polls was indicative of a larger trend toward declining participation in community affairs. A dramatic rise in people registering as "independents" rather than Democrats or Republicans, a sharp decline in membership in voluntary associations, and a growing cynicism toward politicians, the political process, and others prompted social scientists to analyze the reasons for a diminishing sense of civic engagement. The Harvard University political scientist Robert Putnam declared in 1995 that the "social fabric is becoming visibly thinner, our connections among each other are becoming visibly thinner. We don't trust one another as much, and we don't know one another as much. And, of course, this is behind the deterioration of the political dialogue, the deterioration of public debate."

Putnam blamed television, VCRs, and computers for distracting people from their social responsibilities; others cited the sharp increase in working wives and the self-absorbed hedonism of the baby boom generation and their children—Generation X. Whatever the case, Americans headed toward the twenty-first century with an uncertain confidence that the center would hold.

But the center did not hold. The presidential election of 2000 was one of the most controversial in history. After the votes were tallied on election night, victory hinged on the state of Florida, where the results were so close that a recount was ordered. For days the outcome remained uncertain as each party accused the other of vote fraud. The Supreme Court finally decided the matter, and it awarded the state's electoral votes and therefore the presidency to Republican George W. Bush. He was the first president since John Quincy Adams to follow his father in the White House. He was also the fifth president to have been elected with fewer popular votes than his opponent, former vice president Al Gore.

Bush not only arrived in the White House amid the controversy of a disputed election, but he also inherited a sputtering economy and a falling stock market. By the spring of 2000, the high-tech companies that had led the soaring stock market during the 1990s had begun to stall. Stock values collapsed, stealing over $2 trillion from household wealth. Consumer confidence and capital investment plummeted with the stock market. By March 2001 the economy was in recession for the first time in over a decade. "These are times of shattered illusions," said economist Robert Samuelson. "The mythology of the 'New Economy' is receding before the reality of declining jobs and profits."

With the collapse of the Soviet Union and the end of the cold war, world politics grew even more unstable during the 1990s. The basic premise of American foreign policy was "unipolar"—to maintain the nation's leadership role in global affairs. Yet the very preponderance of American military power and economic influence created instability. A simmering mistrust of America's geopolitical dominance festered throughout the world at the same time that traditional diplomatic relations were being fractured by growing competition among the world's major civilizations. Where ideologies such as capitalism and communism had earlier been the cause of conflict and tension in foreign relations, issues of religion, ethnicity, and clashing cultural values now divided peoples. "Most important," wrote Harvard University scholar Samuel Huntington, "the efforts of the West to promote its values of democracy and liberalism as universal values, to maintain its military predominance, and to advance its economic interests engender countering responses from other civilizations."

As the twenty-first century unfolded, nations were no longer the sole actors on the stage of world politics. Instead, nebulous multinational groups inspired by religious fanaticism and anti-American rage began to use sophisticated methods of terrorism to gain notoriety and to attack the allies of Israel. The very rootlessness of such zealots—they were alienated from their native societies and able to move around at will in order to infiltrate other countries and cultures—proved to be an ironic strength. Well-financed and well-armed terrorists flourished in the cracks of foundering nations such as Sudan, Somalia, Pakistan, Yemen, and Afghanistan. Throughout the 1990s, the United States fought a losing, secret war against organized terrorism. The ineffectiveness of intelligence agencies in tracking the movements and intentions of militant extremists became tragically evident in 2001.

At 8:45 on the morning of September 11, 2001, a hijacked commercial airliner slammed into the north tower of the World Trade Center in New York City. As people on the streets and in front of television screens watched the famous skyscraper burning, a second jet, traveling at 500 miles per hour, hit the south tower. The fuel-laden planes tore gaping holes in the buildings and turned them into infernos. But worse was to come. The twin towers, both 110 stories tall and filled with thousands of employees, collapsed from the intense heat. Surrounding buildings also collapsed. The southern end of Manhattan—"Ground Zero"—became a hellish scene of twisted steel, suffocating smoke, and wailing sirens.

While the catastrophic drama in New York was unfolding, a third hijacked plane crashed into the Pentagon in Washington, D.C. The fourth airliner, thought to be headed for the White House, missed its mark when passengers, who had heard reports, via cell phones, of the earlier hijackings, assaulted the terrorists to prevent the plane from being used as a weapon. During the struggle in the cockpit, the plane went out of control and plummeted into the Pennsylvania countryside, killing all on board.

Within hours of the hijackings, officials identified the nineteen terrorists as members of al Qaeda ("the base"), a well-financed worldwide network of Islamic extremists led by a wealthy Saudi renegade, Osama bin Laden. For several years, bin Laden had been using remote bases in war-torn Afghanistan as his personal refuge and terrorist training centers. Afghanistan's ruling Taliban regime collaborated with bin Laden's terrorist agenda.

The September 11 terrorist assault on America changed the course of a new presidency, a nation, and the world. The economy, already in decline, went into a free fall. President Bush, who had never professed to know much about international relations or world affairs and had shown only disdain for Clinton's "multilateralism" policy, was suddenly thrust onto center stage as commander-in-chief of a wounded nation.

The Bush administration immediately forged an international coalition to fight terrorism worldwide. On October 7, after the Taliban defiantly refused to turn over bin Laden, the United States and its allies launched a military campaign—Operation Enduring Freedom—to locate and punish terrorists or "those harboring terrorists." On December 9, only two months after the American-led military campaign in Afghanistan had begun, the Taliban regime collapsed entirely.

In the fall of 2002 President Bush unveiled a new national security doctrine that marked a distinct shift from previous administrations. Containment and deterrence had been the guiding strategic concepts of the cold war years. In the war against terrorism, however, such cold-war policies were bankrupt. Fanatics willing to become suicide bombers would not be deterred. President Bush declared that the growing menace posed by "shadowy networks" of terror-

ist groups and unstable rogue nations with weapons of mass destruction required a new doctrine of preemptive military action. "If we wait for threats to fully materialize," he explained, "we will have waited too long. In the world we have entered, the only path to safety is the path of action. And this nation will act."

In 2003 the Bush Doctrine was put into action when the United States and its allies invaded Iraq on the false belief that dictator Saddam Hussein had developed an arsenal of biological and chemical "weapons of mass destruction." The Bush Doctrine made sense to many Americans traumatized by the threat of global terrorism. But to many outside the United States it reinforced fears of American arrogance, interventionism, and unilateralism. As the French foreign minister explained, "We cannot accept either a politically unipolar world, nor a culturally uniform world, nor the unilateralism of a single hyperpower." The ultimate test of the Bush Doctrine would be whether the United States could convert its overwhelming global power into an international consensus for dealing with terrorism and the proliferation of weapons of mass destruction.

George W. Bush was narrowly reelected in 2004. His second presidential term was beset by political problems, a sputtering economy, and growing public dissatisfaction with his performance and the continuing war in Iraq. Even his support among Republicans crumbled, and many social conservatives felt betrayed by his handling of their concerns. The editors of the Economist, *an influential conservative newsmagazine, declared that Bush had become "the least popular re-elected president since Richard Nixon became embroiled in the Watergate fiasco." Soaring gasoline prices and the federal budget deficit fueled public frustration with the Bush administration. The president's efforts to reform the tax code, Social Security, and immigration laws languished during his second term, and the turmoil and violence in Iraq showed no signs of abating. Senator Chuck Hagel, a Nebraska Republican, declared in 2005 that "we're losing in Iraq."*

Soon Bush's troubles mounted when in 2007 home values and housing sales began a precipitous decline. During 2008, the loss of trillions of dollars in home-equity value set off a seismic shock across the economy. Record numbers of mortgage borrowers defaulted on their payments. Foreclosures soared, adding to the glut of homes for sale and further reducing home prices. Banks lost billions, first on shaky subprime mortgages, then on most other categories of debt: credit cards, car loans, student loans, and an array of commercial mortgage-backed securities. The sudden contraction of consumer credit, corporate spending, and consumer purchases pushed the economy into a deepening recession in 2008. By late fall of 2008, the United States was facing its greatest financial crisis since the Great Depression of the 1930s. What had begun as a decline in home prices had become a global economic meltdown—fed by the paralyzing fright of insecurity. "The Age of Prosperity is over," announced the prominent Republican economist Arthur Laffer in 2008.

The economic crisis had potent political effects. As two preeminent econo-mists noted, "In the eight years since George W. Bush took office, nearly every component of the U.S. economy has deteriorated." Even a prominent Republican strategist, Kevin Phillips, deemed Bush "perhaps the least competent president in modern history." Bush's vulnerability excited Democrats about the possibility of regaining the White House in the 2008 election. The early front-runner for the Democratic nomination was New York senator Hillary Rodham Clinton, the highly visible spouse of ex-President Bill Clinton. Like her husband, she displayed an impressive command of policy issues and mobilized a well-funded campaign team. And as the first woman with a serious chance of gaining the presidency, she garnered widespread support among voters eager for female leadership. In the end, however, an overconfident Clinton was upset in the Democratic primaries and caucuses by little-known first-term senator Barack Obama of Illinois, an inspiring speaker who attracted huge crowds by promising a "politics of hope" and bolstering their desire for "change."

Obama was the first African American presidential nominee of either party, the gifted biracial son of a white mother from Kansas and a black Kenyan father who left the household and returned to Africa when Barack was a toddler. The forty-seven-year-old Harvard Law School graduate and former professor, com-munity organizer, and state legislator presented himself as a conciliator who could inspire and unite a diverse people and forge bipartisan collaborations. Obama exuded poise, confidence, and energy. By contrast, his Republican opponent, seventy-two-year-old Arizona senator John McCain, was the oldest presidential candidate in history.

On November 4, 2008, Barack Obama made history by becoming the nation's first person of color elected president. "Change has come to America," he announced in his victory speech. His triumph was decisive and sweeping. The inspirational Obama won the popular vote by seven points: 53 percent to 46 percent. His margin in the electoral vote was even more impressive: 365 to 173.

The new Obama administration inherited two unpopular wars, in Iraq and Afghanistan, and the worst economic crisis in eighty years. President Obama sys-tematically began reducing U.S. troop levels in the Middle East while pursuing legislative initiatives designed to end the Great Recession. He ordered the Trea-sury Department to "bail out" huge financial institutions threatened with bank-ruptcy. Then, in early 2009, after a prolonged debate, Congress passed, and Obama signed, an $832 billion economic stimulus bill called the American Recovery and Reinvestment Act. The bill included cash distributions to the states for construction projects to renew the nation's infrastructure (roads, bridges, levees, government buildings, and the electricity grid), money for renewable energy systems, and $212 billion in tax reductions for individuals and businesses, as well as additional funds for food stamps and unemployment benefits. It was *the largest government infusion of cash into the economy in history. In the end, however, it was not large enough to generate a robust economic recovery.*

The economic crisis merited Obama's full attention, but he chose as his top legislative priority a controversial federal health insurance program. The president's goal in creating the Patient Protection and Affordable Care Act (ACA), which Republican critics labeled "Obamacare," was to make medical insurance and health care accessible for everyone, regardless of income. The $940 billion health-care law, proposed in 2009 and debated bitterly for a year, was signed into law by President Obama on March 23, 2010. In its scope and goals, the ACA was a landmark in the history of health and social welfare—as well as in the expansion of the federal government's power—and conservative Republicans vowed to repeal the act as soon as possible.

President Obama had more success in dealing with foreign affairs than in reviving the American economy. His foremost concern was the overextension of U.S. power abroad. What journalists came to call the Obama Doctrine was very much like the Nixon Doctrine (1970), stressing that the United States could not afford to continue to be the world's principal policeman. Yet it would not be easy to reduce the nation's military commitments abroad, for the fate of America's economy and security was entangled more than ever with the fate of an unstable and increasingly violent world.

On February 27, 2009, Obama announced that all 142,000 U.S. troops would be withdrawn from Iraq by the end of 2011, as had been agreed to by the Iraqi government and the Bush administration in 2008. True to his word, the last U.S. combat troops left Iraq in December 2011. Their exit marked the end of a bitterly divisive war that had raged for nearly nine years, killed over 110,000 Iraqis, and left the war-torn nation shattered and unstable. The U.S. intervention in Iraq had cost over 4,500 American lives (with 30,000 wounded, many grievously so), and $2 trillion.

Perhaps the greatest embarrassment was that the government that the U.S. left behind in Iraq was inept and not even friendly to American interests. America's long and chaotic war in Iraq (Obama called it "disastrous") was an unnecessary intervention, an expensive mistake, and a prolonged distraction for the government, the military, and the nation. As it turned out, there were no weapons of mass destruction, as the Bush administration had claimed. Nor was there a direct link between the al Qaeda terrorists and Saddam Hussein. Al Qaeda, in fact, did not arrive in Iraq until after the American invasion. "The first Iraq war, in which I led a tank platoon, was necessary" said John Nagel, a retired army officer. "This one was not."

At the same time that President Obama was reducing U.S. military involvement in Iraq, he dispatched 21,000 additional troops to Afghanistan in what was called a "surge." While doing so, however, he narrowed the focus of the U.S. mission to suppressing terrorists rather than "nation building"—the idea of transforming strife-torn Afghanistan into a stable capitalist democracy.

The military surge worked as hoped. By the summer of 2011, President Obama announced that the "tide of war was receding" and that the United States had largely achieved its goals in Afghanistan, setting in motion a substantial withdrawal of forces beginning in 2011 and lasting until 2014. Echoing his declarations about Iraq, Obama stressed that the Afghans must determine the future stability of Afghanistan. "We will not try to make Afghanistan a perfect place," he said. "We will not police its streets or patrol its mountains indefinitely. That is the responsibility of the Afghan government." As the troops came home, Americans quickly lost interest in what Obama had earlier called the "good war" in Afghanistan. In April 2014, despite threats by the Taliban to kill voters, Afghans turned out in huge numbers to choose a new president to lead them into the post-American era. But it was an expensive outcome for America's longest war. In the thirteen years since the United States invaded Afghanistan in 2001, America had spent over a trillion dollars there and had suffered 2,300 military deaths.

By the end of Obama's first year in office, American political culture was suffering from a crisis of mutual resentment, so polarized between squabbling Democrats and Republicans that it resembled two separate nations. Each had its own political party, its own cable news station and rabidly partisan commentators, its own newspapers, its own think tanks, and its own billionaire activists.

And both "nations"—blue and red, liberal and conservative—had their own factions committed to a politics of rage. No sooner was Obama sworn in than anti-government conservatives mobilized against him and the "tax-and-spend" liberalism he represented in their eyes. In 2009, anti-Obama conservatives formed a national Tea Party movement, with groups spread across the fifty states. The Tea Party is not so much a cohesive political organization as it is a mood, an attitude, and an ideology, a diverse collection of self-described "disaffected," "angry," and "very conservative" activists, mostly white, male, married, middle-class Republicans over forty-five, boiling mad at the massive government bailouts of huge banks and corporations that had come in the wake of the 2008 economic meltdown. Tea Party members demanded a radically smaller federal government (although most of them supported Social Security and Medicare, the two most expensive federal social programs).

In the 2010 Congressional elections, Democratic House and Senate candidates (as well as moderate Republicans), including many long-serving leaders, were defeated in droves when conservative Republicans, many of them aligned with the Tea Party, gained sixty-three seats to recapture control of the House of Representatives, and won a near majority in the Senate as well. Thereafter, Obama and the Republican-dominated House engaged in a harsh sparring match. With each side refusing to negotiate or compromise, the bickering between both parties prevented meaningful action on the languishing economy, chronic joblessness, and the runaway federal budget deficit.

In 2012, Mitt Romney, a former corporate executive and governor of Massachusetts, won the Republican presidential nomination, but Obama won reelection by gaining the overwhelming support of the nation's fastest growing groups—Latinos, Asian Americans, and African Americans.

During his second term, Barack Obama discovered how hard it was to lead the world's economic and military superpower in the post-Cold War era. He struggled to stabilize a cluster of unstable nations—Iraq, Afghanistan, Libya, Ukraine, and Syria—that craved U.S. resources but resented American meddling.

Unexpected events during the summer of 2014 gave Barack Obama the opportunity to take decisive action. In June, the volatile Middle East took a sudden turn for the worse when Sunni jihadists who had been fighting in Syria invaded northern Iraq and announced the creation of their own nation (caliphate), called the Islamic State (ISIS). ISIS quickly emerged as the largest, best-financed, most heavily armed, and most brutal of the jihadist terrorist groups. If George W. Bush had plunged U.S. power too deeply into Iraq, Obama seemed to have withdrawn U.S. power too quickly. One overreached, the other undershot.

On the domestic front, the bitter polarization of the two major parties continued as compromise *and* moderation *became dirty words. In the 2014 congressional elections, Republicans gained control of the Senate for the first time since 2006. They also strengthened their hold on the House, added governorships, and tightened their control of state legislatures. Republicans campaigned on a single theme: the "failure" of President Obama and the "disaster" of Obamacare. The new Congress included mostly Republicans on the far right, Democrats on the far left, and hardly anyone in the middle. "That alignment," said Gerald Seib of the* Wall Street Journal, *created a Congress "that does less, and does it less well, than any time in memory."*

Obama seemed disheartened by the "gap between the magnitude of our challenges and the smallness of our politics" and blamed Republicans for stalemating his second term. But the president was not blameless. As Ian Bremmer, an international consultant, said, "George W. Bush was a leader who didn't like to think. Barack Obama is a thinker who doesn't like to lead."

Yet during the summer of 2015, in the sunset of his presidency, Obama regained his energy. He also benefited from two surprising U.S. Supreme Court rulings. For years, Republicans had waged all-out war on the Affordable Care Act (Obamacare). Unable to halt the implementation of the new program in Congress, critics turned to the courts to challenge the health-care law. In a surprising 6-3 decision in King v. Burwell, *the Supreme Court saved the controversial law.*

Just a day later, the Supreme Court issued another bombshell ruling when it announced a 5-4 decision in Obergefell v. Hodges, *which banned states from preventing same-sex marriages. The landmark decision infuriated the Religious Right. Rick Scarborough, a Baptist minister in Texas, vowed that he and others would "denounce this practice in our [religious] services, we will not teach it in our schools, we will refuse to officiate at this type of wedding, and we will not accept any encroachments on our First Amendment rights."*

Yet the Supreme Court's affirmation of same-sex marriage reflected the profound change in public attitudes toward lesbian and gay (LGBTQ) rights during the early twenty-first century. In 2008, presidential candidate Barack Obama had felt the need to disavow support for marriage equality. By 2012, he had reversed himself by embracing the right of same-sex marriage. His change of mind reflected a resurgent social transformation in American life.

The momentum of the Court decisions in June 2015 bolstered Obama's efforts in foreign policy. In his 2009 inaugural address, he had vowed to international enemies that "we will extend a hand if you are willing to unclench your fist." That effort finally paid off in 2015, not only with the normalizing of relations with Cuba but also when the United States and five other world powers announced a draft treaty with Iran intended to thwart its efforts to develop a nuclear weapon. In exchange for ending the international trade embargo against Iran, the agreement called for the Iranians to dismantle much of their nuclear program and allow for international inspectors to confirm their actions. Obama warned Congressional critics that voting against such a treaty would mean "a greater chance of war in the Middle East."

The ferocious polarization of American society and politics was on full display during the 2016 presidential campaign. The contest featured a seething sense of anger at the federal government among voters furious at cultural liberalism, bureaucratic incompetence, and the self-serving focus of party leaders. "Both parties have failed us," observed a lifelong conservative.

Many working-class whites felt left behind by the economic recovery. Some had seen their factory jobs go "offshore" through globalization. Others had seen their wages stagnate, their prospects diminished, their hopes crushed. They blamed their troubles on an economic system that favored the wealthy, government-subsidized minorities, low-wage immigrant labor, and the political elite. Their shared anxieties and resentments had coalesced into a grassroots "lily-white" nationalist backlash against the multiculturalism promoted during Obama's presidency.

Seventeen Republicans aspirants competed for the Republican presidential nomination—governors, senators, corporate executives—but one was unique: New Yorker Donald Trump, a billionaire real estate developer and reality television star who had never held elected office but, unlike the other candidates, had national name recognition. As he claimed, "There's nobody like me. Nobody."

Trump positioned himself as an "outsider" eager to "drain the swamp" of corruption created by political "insiders" in Washington, D.C. He skillfully exploited the emotions of people who felt left behind by the economic recovery and resentful of what they perceived to be unregulated immigration. He campaigned against "career politicians" and Washington bureaucrats. "Throw them out!" became a favorite audience response at boisterous rallies at which he gave voice to the grievances of his *supporters, transforming their distress into rage directed at Hillary Clinton, the Democratic candidate.*

Trump vowed to "Make America Great Again." He promised to end Obamacare, cut taxes, abandon the "unfair" NAFTA (North American Free Trade Agreement) and TPP (Trans-Pacific Partnership) trade deals, approve the use of torture on captured terrorists and their families, reverse the Obama administration's environmental protections, and increase funding for the military. Most of all, he repeatedly lashed out at "illegal immigrants," promising to build a towering, "beautiful" wall along the entire border with Mexico—and make the Mexican government pay for it!

Trump focused on the fears and prejudices of his supporters ("Trumpsters"), especially working-class whites in the South and the crucial Midwest "Rust Belt" states—Ohio, Michigan, Pennsylvania, West Virginia, and Wisconsin. "I love the poorly educated," he proudly affirmed. "The hell with political correctness." As a Trump supporter in New Hampshire explained, "He tells us what we all think but are afraid to say." The "country's spiraling downwards, people are not getting pay raises, and we're not the superpower we think we are."

To the surprise of pundits and the chagrin of party leaders, Trump won the Republican nomination in July 2016.

The 2016 contest between Donald Trump and Hillary Clinton was more memorable for its drama and insults than its issues or proposals. Trump dismissed "crooked Hillary" as a "nasty woman," calling her the "most corrupt person ever to seek the presidency." He lampooned her as a creature of the Washington and Wall Street elite who masqueraded as a friend of the people while raking in millions of ill-gotten dollars. If elected president, he promised, he would "put her in jail," leading his supporters to wear T-shirts that read, "Lock Her Up."

For her part, Clinton dismissed Trump as unfit for the highest office in the land, labeling him as dangerous, unpredictable, and lacking the temperament demanded of the U.S. president. She hurt her cause when, in a fit of frustration, she claimed that "you could put half of Trump's supporters into what I call the 'basket of deplorables.'"

Clinton's narrow loss to Trump on November 8 surprised virtually everyone. Trump won 309 electoral votes to her 228. True, Clinton won 3 million more votes than Trump out of the 136 million cast, but she lost by 78,000 votes the crucial swing states of Michigan, Ohio, Pennsylvania, and Wisconsin. Her failure to attract white working-class and lower middle-class males in the Rust Belt states was her downfall, along with the fact that not enough Democratic-leaning minority voters went to the polls.

In his inaugural address, Trump assured the nation that his swearing-in ceremony would be "remembered as the day the people became the rulers of this nation again." He told his ecstatic supporters that "you will never be ignored again," for he intended to uproot the political "establishment." An unapologetic and aggressive hyper-nationalism would be the theme of his administration: "From this day forward, it is going to be only America first—America first."

To generate momentum for his new presidency, Donald Trump signed thirty-two executive orders removing protections for consumers, the environment, food safety, Internet privacy, transgender Americans, and victims of sexual abuse.

Eventually, however, Trump could not govern simply by issuing executive orders; he had to negotiate the passage of legislation. Throughout the presidential campaign, Trump had lambasted Obamacare, promising to replace it "on day one" with a much better health-care program "at a tiny fraction of the cost, and it is going to be so easy." To that end, he and House speaker Paul Ryan unveiled in early 2017 the American Health Care Act (AHCA). It would have removed many of the pillars of Obamacare, including phasing out Medicaid subsidies that had enabled millions of people to gain coverage for the first time.

Yet surveys showed that only 17 percent of voters liked the new bill. For that reason and others, Trump and Ryan could not get the Republican majority in the House to support "Trumpcare." The Republican leadership withdrew the AHCA without a formal vote. Trump, the self-described wizard at "deal-making," had been unable to strike a deal with members of his own party. He admitted to being surprised "that health care could be so complicated."

A similar fate befell Trump's other showcase campaign promise: building a "huge" wall along the Mexican border and forcing Mexico to pay for it. In late April 2017, the president acknowledged that he could not convince Congress that the wall was worth the more than $20 billion it was estimated to cost.

In foreign affairs, Donald Trump's early actions were equally minimal, in part because he had so little preparation for global leadership. Other than hosting several foreign dignitaries, talking tough toward rogue nations North Korea and Iran, and launching a volley of cruise missiles at a Syrian air base in retaliation for a chemical attack by the Syrian government on civilians, the president's view of America's role in the world remained confusing to many people.

President Trump finally achieved a major legislative victory with the passage of a comprehensive tax cut in December 2017. The Republican-controlled Congress passed the Tax Cuts and Job Act without a single Democratic vote. It also repealed the individual mandate at the center of Obamacare. Analysts predicted that this would lead to 13 million fewer people covered by health insurance, mostly young adults likely to opt out. With fewer healthy adults in the ACA pool, those still enrolled would pay higher insurance costs, which would lead still more people to drop their coverage.

Still, Trump's administration struggled to gain momentum. The passage of tax reform initially stimulated the stock market, but in March 2018, Trump suddenly announced punitive tariffs on imported steel and aluminum, infuriating America's most reliable trading partners, and causing a steep decline in the stock market. The firing of FBI Director James Comey and the appointment of Robert S. Mueller III to organize a criminal investigation into the possible Russian involvement in the 2016 elections became significant problems that demanded a great deal of the time and attention of the Trump administration.

This much seemed certain as 2018 unfolded: Donald Trump would continue to fascinate and irritate the nation and the world and enjoy a high level of support among those who voted for him with his efforts to stop the flow of "illegal immigrants" into the country, to negotiate deals with rogue nations like North Korea, and to withdraw the U.S. from some of its major treaty commitments such as the Iran nuclear deal, while beset by the ongoing Russia investigation by special counsel Robert Mueller, burdened by constant turnover and factional drama among his aides, and dogged by aggrieved women claiming he had abused or engaged in affairs with them. The president—a man celebrated for his resilience—seemed determined to fend off all challenges by staying on the offensive. What the future would hold remained predictably unpredictable.

MARY FISHER

The Whisper of AIDS (1992)

During the 1980s, a frightening new disease called AIDS (acquired immunodefi-ciency syndrome) swept across the world. Public health officials reported that gay men and intravenous drug users were especially at risk for developing AIDS. People contracted the human immunodeficiency virus (HIV), which causes AIDS, through contact with the blood or body fluids of an infected person. Those infected with the virus showed signs of extreme fatigue, developed a strange combination of infections, and soon died. The Reagan administration and the Republican party showed little interest in AIDS because it was viewed as a "gay disease." Patrick Buchanan, who served as Reagan's director of communications, said that gay men had "declared war on nature, and now nature is extracting an awful retribution." Buchanan and others convinced President Reagan not to engage the HIV/AIDS issue. As a result, by 2000, AIDS had claimed almost 300,000 American lives, and it had become the leading cause of death among men ages twenty-five to forty-four. At the Republican party presidential convention in 1992, Mary Fisher, a former assistant to President Gerald Ford, delivered a riveting speech about AIDS, which she had contracted from her husband, an intravenous drug user. Her thirteen-minute speech, seen by 27 million viewers, "brought AIDS home to America," according to the New York Times.

"The Whisper of Aids," a speech delivered at the Republican National Convention, August 19, 1992. Reprinted by permission of Mary Fisher.

Less than three months ago, at platform hearings in Salt Lake City, I asked the Republican Party to lift the shroud of silence which has been draped over the issue of HIV/AIDS. I have come tonight to bring our silence to an end.

I bear a message of challenge, not self-congratulation. I want your attention, not your applause. I would never have asked to be HIV-positive. But I believe that in all things there is a good purpose, and so I stand before you and before the nation, gladly.

The reality of AIDS is brutally clear. Two hundred thousand Americans are dead or dying; a million more are infected. Worldwide, forty million, or sixty million or a hundred million infections will be counted in the coming few years. But despite science and research, White House meetings and con-gressional hearings, despite good intentions and bold initiatives, campaign slogans and hopeful promises—despite it all, it's the epidemic which is winning tonight.

In the context of an election year, I ask you here, in this great hall, or listening in the quiet of your home, to recognize that the AIDS virus is not an apolitical creature. It does not care whether you are Democrat or Republican. It does not ask whether you are black or white, male or female, gay or straight, young or old.

Tonight, I represent an AIDS community whose members have been reluctantly drafted from every segment of American society. Though I am white and a mother, I am one with a black infant strug-gling with tubes in a Philadelphia hospital. Though I am female and contracted this disease in marriage, and enjoy the warm support of my family, I am one with the lonely gay man sheltering a flickering candle from the cold wind of his family's rejection.

This is not a distant threat; it is a present danger. The rate of infection is increasing fastest among women and children. Largely unknown a decade ago, AIDS is the third leading killer of young-adult Americans today—but it won't be third for long. Because, unlike other diseases, this one travels. Adolescents don't give each other cancer or heart disease because they believe they are in love. But HIV is different. And we have helped it along. We have killed each other—with our ignorance, our prejudice, and our silence.

We may take refuge in our stereotypes but we cannot hide there long. Because HIV asks only one thing of those it attacks: Are you human? And this is the right question: Are you human? Because people with HIV have not entered some alien state of being. They are human. They have not earned cruelty and they do not deserve meanness. They don't benefit from being isolated or treated as outcasts. Each of them is exactly what God made: a person. Not evil, deserving of our judgment; not victims, longing for our pity. People. Ready for support and worthy of compassion.

My call to you, my Party, is to take a public stand no less compassionate than that of the President [George H. W.] and Mrs. [Barbara] Bush. They have embraced me and my family in memorable ways. In the place of judgment, they have shown affection. In difficult moments, they have raised our spirits. In the darkest hours, I have seen them reaching not only to me, but also to my parents, armed with that stunning grief and special grace that comes only to parents who have themselves leaned too long over the bedside of a dying child.

With the President's leadership, much good has been done; much of the good has gone unheralded; as the President has insisted, "Much remains to be done."

But we do the President's cause no good if we praise the American family but ignore a virus that destroys it. We must be consistent if we are to be believed. We cannot love justice and ignore prejudice, love our children and fear to teach them.

Whatever our role, as parent or policy maker, we must act as eloquently as we speak—else we have no integrity.

My call to the nation is a plea for awareness. If you believe you are safe, you are in danger. Because I was not hemophiliac, I was not at risk. Because I was not gay, I was not at risk. Because I did not inject drugs, I was not at risk.

My father has devoted much of his lifetime to guarding against another holocaust. He is part of the generation who heard Pastor Niemoeller come out of the Nazi death camps to say, "They came after the Jews and I was not a Jew, so I did not protest. They came after the Trade Unionists, and I was not a Trade Unionist, so I did not protest. They came after the Roman Catholics, and I was not a Roman Catholic, so I did not protest. Then they came after me, and there was no one left to protest."

The lesson history teaches is this: If you believe you are safe, you are at risk. If you do not see this killer stalking your children, look again. There is no family or community, no race or religion, no place left in America that is safe. Until we genuinely embrace this message, we are a nation at risk.

Tonight, HIV marches resolutely towards AIDS in more than a million American homes, littering its pathway with the bodies of the young. Young men. Young women. Young parents. Young children. One of the families is mine. If it is true that HIV inevitably turns to AIDS, then my children will inevitably turn to orphans. . . .

I want my children to know that their mother was not a victim. She was a messenger. I do not want them to think, as I once did, that courage is the absence of fear; I want them to know that courage is the strength to act wisely when most we are afraid. I want them to have the courage to step forward when called by their nation, or their Party, and give leadership—no matter what the personal cost. I ask no more of you than I ask of myself, or of my children.

To the millions of you who are grieving, who are frightened, who have suffered the ravages of AIDS firsthand: Have courage and you will find comfort.

To the millions who are strong, I issue this plea: Set aside prejudice and politics to make room for compassion and sound policy. . . .

To all within sound of my voice, I appeal: Learn with me the lessons of history and of grace, so my children will not be afraid to say the word AIDS when I am gone. Then their children, and yours, may not need to whisper it at all.

God bless the children, and bless us all—good night.

REVIEW QUESTIONS

1. Fisher told America that, "We may take refuge in our stereotypes but we cannot hide there long." What were the stereotypes about AIDS that she mentioned?
2. Fisher insisted that she was less a victim than a messenger. What was her essential message to the nation?

BILL GATES

FROM *The Road Ahead* (1996)

Beginning in the 1970s, the computer revolution and the later development of the Internet transformed communication. The idea of a programmable machine that would rapidly perform mental tasks had been around since the eighteenth century, but it took the Second World War to gather the intellectual and financial resources needed to create such a "computer."

In 1946, a team of engineers at the University of Pennsylvania developed ENIAC (electronic numerical integrator and computer), the first all-purpose, all-electronic digital computer. It required 18,000 vacuum tubes to operate. The following year, researchers at Bell Telephone Laboratories invented the transistor, which replaced the bulky vacuum tubes and enabled much smaller, yet more powerful, computers—as well as new devices such as hearing aids and transistor radios.

The next major breakthrough was the invention in 1971 of the microprocessor—virtually a tiny computer on a silicon chip. The microprocessor chip revolutionized computing by allowing storage of far more data in much smaller machines.

The microchip made possible the personal computer. In 1975, engineer Ed Roberts developed the Altair 8800, the prototype of the personal computer. Its potential excited Bill Gates, a Harvard University sophomore, who improved the software of the Altair 8800, dropped out of college, and formed a company called Microsoft.

During the 1980s, IBM (International Business Machines), using a microprocessor made by the Intel Corporation and an operating system provided by Microsoft, helped transform the personal computer into a mass consumer product. In 1963, a half-million computer chips were sold worldwide; by 1970, the number was 300 million.

Computer chips transformed a variety of electronic products—televisions, calculators, wristwatches, clocks, ovens, phones, laptops, and automobiles—while facilitating efforts to land astronauts on the moon and launch satellites into space. The development of the Internet, electronic mail (e-mail), and cell-phone technology during the 1980s and 1990s allowed for instantaneous communication, thereby accelerating the globalization of the economy and dramatically increasing productivity in the workplace.

In 1995, Bill Gates first published a book titled The Road Ahead *in which he envisioned the impact of the computer revolution he was helping to guide.*

Personal computers have already changed our work habits, but it is the evolving Internet that will really change our lives. As information machines are connected on the Internet, people, entertainment, and information services suddenly become accessible. As the Internet's popularity and capability increase, you'll be able to stay in touch with anyone, anywhere, who wants to stay in touch with you and to browse through any of thousands of sources of information, day or night. A little further along, you'll be able to answer your apartment intercom from your office or answer any mail from your home. Your misplaced or stolen camera will send you a message telling you exactly where it is, even if it's in a different city. Information that once was difficult to retrieve will be easier and easier to find:

Is my bus running on time?

Are there any accidents right now on the route I usually take to the office?

Does anyone want to trade his or her Thursday theater tickets for my Wednesday tickets?

What is my child's school-attendance record?

What's a good recipe for halibut?

Which store, anywhere, can deliver by tomorrow morning for the lowest price a wristwatch that can take my pulse?

What would somebody pay for my old Mustang convertible?

How is the hole in a needle manufactured?

Are my shirts ready yet at the laundry?

What's the cheapest way to subscribe to the *Wall Street Journal*?

What are the symptoms of a heart attack?

Was there any interesting testimony at the county courthouse today?

Do fish see in color?

What does the Champs-Élysées look like right now?

Where was I at 9:02 P.M. last Thursday?

Let's say you're thinking about trying a new restaurant and want to see its menu, the wine list, and the specials of the day. Maybe you're wondering what your favorite food reviewer said about it. You may also want to know what sanitation score the health department gave the place. If you're leery of the restaurant's neighborhood, you might want to see a safety rating based on police reports. Still interested in going? You'll want reservations, a map, and directions based on current traffic conditions. You'll take the directions in printed form or have them read to you—and updated—as you drive.

All of this information will be readily accessible and completely personalized for you. You'll be able to explore whatever parts of it interest you in whatever ways and for however long you want. You'll watch a [television] program when it's convenient for you instead of when a broadcaster chooses to air it. You'll shop, order food, contact friends, or publish information for other people to use when and as you want to. Your nightly newscast will start at a time you determine and last exactly as long as you want it to, and it will cover subjects selected by you or by a service that knows your interests. You'll be able to ask for reports from Tokyo or Boston or Seattle, request more detail on a news item, or inquire whether your favorite columnist has commented on an event. If you prefer, your news will be delivered to you on paper.

Early forms of some of these services are showing up on the Internet already, but they only hint at what's to come. A massive shift in the way people communicate and relate to information is under way.

Change of this magnitude makes people nervous. Every day, all over the world, people are asking about the implications of the network, often with apprehension. What will happen to our jobs? Will we withdraw from the physical world and live vicariously through our computers? Will the gulf between the haves and have-nots widen irreparably? Will a computer be able to help the disenfranchised in East St. Louis or the starving in Ethiopia? Without a doubt, major challenges will accompany the network and the changes it will bring about. . . .

Information technology is not a panacea. This disappoints people who demand to know how PCs and the Internet will solve all human problems. I wonder whether in Gutenberg's age people asked: "What good is this press? Is it going to feed people? Will it help overcome illness? Will it make the world more just?" Eventually it facilitated all of these things, of course, but in 1450 it was probably hard to tell that it would.

One thing is clear: We don't have the option of turning away from the future. No one gets to vote on whether technology is going to change our lives. No one can stop productive change in the long run because the marketplace inexorably embraces it. Gov-

ernments can try to slow the rate of change within their own borders by restricting the use of certain technologies, but these policies risk leaving a country isolated from the world economy, preventing its companies from being competitive and its consumers from getting the latest products and the best prices.

I believe that because progress will come no matter what, we need to make the best of it—not try to forestall it.

REVIEW QUESTIONS

1. How accurate were Gates's predictions about the impact of computers on everyday life?
2. What issues created by the computer revolution did Gates not foresee?

Contract with America (1994)

On September 27, 1994, over three hundred Republican candidates for Congress, led by Representatives Newt Gingrich of Georgia and Dick Armey of Texas, pledged themselves to a "Contract with America." The document represented their shared platform for the upcoming election. The contract struck a responsive chord with the voters, who gave the Republicans a stunning victory at the polls. For the first time in forty years, Republicans gained control of both houses of Congress (230 to 205 in the House and 53 to 47 in the Senate). After being elected the Speaker of the House, Gingrich began transforming the elements of the Contract with America into legislation.

From *Contract with America: The Bold Plan by Representative Newt Gingrich, Representative Dick Armey, and the House Republicans to Change the Nation*, Ed Gillespie and Bob Schellhas, eds. (New York: Times Books, 1994), pp. 7–11. Copyright © 1994 by the Republican National Committee. Reprinted by permission of the Republican National Committee.

As Republican Members of the House of Representatives and as citizens seeking to join that body we propose not just to change its policies, but even more important, to restore the bonds of trust between the people and their elected representatives.

That is why in this era of official evasion and posturing, we offer instead a detailed agenda for national renewal, a written commitment with no fine print.

This year's election offers the chance, after four decades of one-party control, to bring to the House a new majority that will transform the way Congress works. That historic change would be the end of government that is too big, too intrusive, and too easy with the public's money. It can be the beginning of a Congress that respects the values and shares the faith of the American family.

Like Lincoln, our first Republican president, we intend to act "with firmness in the right, as God gives us to see the right." To restore accountability to Congress. To end its cycle of scandal and disgrace. To make us all proud again of the way free people govern themselves.

On the first day of the 104th Congress, the new Republican majority will immediately pass the following major reforms, aimed at restoring the faith and trust of the American people in their government:

FIRST, require all laws that apply to the rest of the country also apply equally to the Congress;

SECOND, select a major, independent auditing firm to conduct a comprehensive audit of Congress for waste, fraud or abuse;

THIRD, cut the number of House committees, and cut committee staff by one third;

FOURTH, limit the terms of all committee chairs;

FIFTH, ban the casting of proxy votes in committee;

SIXTH, require committee meetings to be open to the public;

SEVENTH, require a three-fifths majority vote to pass a tax increase;

EIGHTH, guarantee an honest accounting of our Federal Budget by implementing zero base-line budgeting.

Thereafter, within the first 100 days of the 104th Congress, we shall bring to the House Floor the following bills, each to be given full and open debate, each to be given a clear and fair vote and each to be immediately available this day for public inspection and scrutiny.

1. THE FISCAL RESPONSIBILITY ACT
A balanced budget/tax limitation amendment and a legislative line-item veto to restore fiscal responsibility to an out-of-control Congress, requiring them to live under the same budget constraints as families and businesses.

2. THE TAKING BACK OUR STREETS ACT
An anti-crime package including stronger truth-in-sentencing, "good faith" exclusionary rule exemptions, effective death penalty provisions, and cuts in social spending from this summer's "Crime" bill to fund prison construction and additional law enforcement to keep people secure in their neighborhoods and kids safe in their schools.

3. THE PERSONAL RESPONSIBILITY ACT
Discourage illegitimacy and teen pregnancy by prohibiting welfare to minor mothers and ending increased AFDC (Aid to Families with Dependent Children) for additional children while on welfare, cut spending for welfare programs, and enact a tough two-years-and-out provision with work requirements to promote individual responsibility.

4. THE FAMILY REINFORCEMENT ACT
Child support enforcement, tax incentives for adoption, strengthening rights of parents in their children's education, stronger child pornography laws, and an elderly dependent care tax credit to reinforce the central role of families in American society.

5. THE AMERICAN DREAM RESTORATION ACT
A $500 per child tax credit, begin repeal of the marriage tax penalty, and creation of American Dream Savings Accounts to provide middle class tax relief.

6. THE NATIONAL SECURITY RESTORATION ACT
No U.S. troops under U.N. command and restoration of the essential parts of our national security funding to strengthen our national defense and maintain our credibility around the world.

7. THE SENIOR CITIZENS FAIRNESS ACT
Raise the Social Security earnings limit which currently forces seniors out of the work force, repeal the 1993 tax hikes on Social Security benefits and provide tax incentives for private long-term care insurance to let Older Americans keep more of what they have earned over the years.

8. THE JOB CREATION AND WAGE ENHANCEMENT ACT
Small business incentives, capital gains cut and indexation, neutral cost recovery, risk assessment/cost-benefit analysis, strengthening the Regulatory

Flexibility Act and unfunded mandate reform to create jobs and raise worker wages.

9. THE COMMON SENSE LEGAL REFORM ACT
"Loser pays" laws, reasonable limits on punitive damages and reform of product liability laws to stem the endless tide of litigation.

10. THE CITIZEN LEGISLATURE ACT
A first-ever vote on term limits to replace career politicians with citizen legislators.

REVIEW QUESTIONS

1. Summarize how Republicans wanted to change the operations of the House of Representatives.
2. Which groups did the contract favor? Which did it slight?
3. Did the contract's proposed changes constitute reforms or a revolution? Explain.

PATRICK J. BUCHANAN

FROM To Reunite a Nation (2000)

Patrick J. Buchanan ran for the Republican presidential nomination three times, in 1992, 1996, and 2000. In each instance, he centered his conservative campaigns on growing public support for the restriction of immigration to the United States. Born in 1938 and raised in a Catholic family in Washington, D.C., he attended Georgetown University and the Columbia University School of Law before making his name as a feisty conservative political activist and journalist. He served as President Richard Nixon's speechwriter and later served as a popular political commentator on cable news programs. In 2000, he gave a speech at the Richard M. Nixon Library that highlighted his concerns about "illegal immigration."

From "To Reunite a Nation," speech delivered at the Richard M. Nixon Library, January 18, 2000. Reprinted by permission of Patrick J. Buchanan and Creators Syndicate, Inc. [Editorial insertions appear in square brackets—*Ed.*]

Like all of you, I am awed by the achievements of many recent immigrants. Their contributions to Silicon Valley are extraordinary. The over-representation of Asian-born kids in advanced high school math and science classes is awesome, and, to the extent that it is achieved by a superior work ethic, these kids are setting an example for all of us. The contributions that immigrants make in small businesses and hard work in tough jobs that don't pay well merits our admiration and deepest respect. And, many new immigrants show a visible love of this country and an appreciation of freedom that makes you proud to be an American.

Northern Virginia, where I live, has experienced a huge and sudden surge in immigration. It has become a better place, in some ways, but nearly unrecognizable in others, and no doubt worse in some realms, a complicated picture over all. But it is clear to anyone living in a state like California or Virginia that the great immigration wave, set in motion by the Immigration Act of 1965, has put an indelible mark upon America.

We are no longer a biracial society; we are now a multi-racial society. We no longer struggle simply to end the divisions and close the gaps between black and white Americans; we now grapple, often awkwardly, with an unprecedented ethnic diversity. We also see the troubling signs of a national turning away from the idea that we are one people, and the emergence of a radically different idea, that we are separate ethnic nations within a nation. . . .

Concerns of this sort are even older than the Republic itself. In 1751, Ben Franklin asked: "Why should Pennsylvania, founded by the English, become a Colony of Aliens, who will shortly be so numerous as to Germanize us instead of our Anglifying them?" Franklin would never find out if his fears were justified. German immigration was halted by the Seven Years' War; then slowed down by the Great Lull in immigration that followed the American Revolution. A century and half later, during what is called the Great Wave, the same worries were in the air.

In 1915 Theodore Roosevelt told the Knights of Columbus: "There is no room in this country for hyphenated Americanism. . . . The one absolutely certain way of bringing this nation to ruin, of preventing all possibility of its continuing to be a nation at all, would be to permit it to become a tangle of squabbling nationalities." Congress soon responded by enacting an immigration law [1924] that brought about a virtual forty-year pause to digest, assimilate, and Americanize the diverse immigrant wave that had rolled in between 1890 and 1920.

Today, once again, it is impossible not to notice the conflicts generated by a new "hyphenated Americanism." In Los Angeles, two years ago, there was an anguishing afternoon in the Coliseum where the U.S. soccer team was playing Mexico. The Mexican-American crowd showered the U.S. team with water bombs, beer bottles and trash. The "Star Spangled Banner" was hooted and jeered. A small contingent of fans of the American team had garbage hurled at them. The American players later said that they were better received in Mexico City than in their own country.

Last summer, El Cenizo, a small town in south Texas, adopted Spanish as its official language. All town documents are now to be written, and all town business conducted, in Spanish. Any official who cooperates with U.S. immigration authorities was warned he or she would be fired. To this day, Governor [George W.] Bush is reluctant to speak out on this de facto secession of a tiny Texas town to Mexico.

Voting in referendums that play a growing part in the politics of California is now breaking down sharply on ethnic lines. Hispanic voters opposed Proposition 187 to cut off welfare to illegal aliens, and they rallied against it under Mexican flags. They voted heavily in favor of quotas and ethnic preferences in the 1996 California Civil Rights Initiative, and, again, to keep bilingual education in 1998. These votes suggest that in the California of the future, when Mexican-American voting power catches up with the Mexican-American population, any bid to end racial quotas by referendum will fail. A majority of the state's most populous immigrant group now appears to favor . . . separate language programs, rather than to be assimilated into the American mainstream. . . .

I don't want to overstate the negatives. But in too many cases the American Melting Pot has been reduced to a simmer. At present rates, mass immigration reinforces ethnic subcultures, reduces the incentives of newcomers to learn English; and extends the life of linguistic ghettos that might otherwise be melded into the great American mainstream. If we want to assimilate new immigrants—and we have no choice if we are to remain one nation—we must slow down the pace of immigration.

Whatever its shortcomings, the United States has done far better at alleviating poverty than most countries. But an America that begins to think of itself as made up of disparate peoples will find social progress far more difficult. It is far easier to look the other way when the person who needs help does not speak the same language, or share a common culture or common history.

Americans who feel it natural and right that their taxes support the generation that fought World War II—will they feel the same way about those from Fukien Province or Zanzibar? If America continues on its present course, it could rapidly become a country with no common language, no common culture, no common memory and no common identity. And that country will find itself very short of the social cohesion that makes compassion possible.

REVIEW QUESTIONS

1. Assess the effectiveness of Buchanan's arguments. Does he make an effective case for restricting immigration? Does he at times make sweeping statements unsupported by evidence?

2. In what ways are Buchanan's concerns about immigration relevant today?

GEORGE W. BUSH

FROM Address to Congress and the Nation (2001)

The terrorist assaults on the United States in September 2001 shocked the world and led President George W. Bush to launch a global war on terror "to answer these attacks and rid the world of evil," as if he were launching a religious crusade, warning other nations that "either you are with us or you are with the terrorists."

From Address before a Joint Session of the Congress on the United States Response to the Terrorist Attacks of September 11 [September 20, 2001], in *Public Papers of the Presidents of the United States: George W. Bush*, 2001, book II, ed. (Washington, DC: U.S. Government Printing Office, 2001), pp. 1140–44.

. . . My fellow citizens, for the last nine days, the entire world has seen for itself the state of union, and it is strong. Tonight, we are a country awakened to danger and called to defend freedom. Our grief has turned to anger and anger to resolution. Whether we bring our enemies to justice or bring justice to our enemies, justice will be done.

*   *   *

On September the 11th, enemies of freedom committed an act of war against our country. Americans have known wars, but for the past 136 years they have been wars on foreign soil, except for one Sunday in 1941. Americans have known the casualties of war, but not at the center of a great city on a peaceful morning.

Americans have known surprise attacks, but never before on thousands of civilians. All of this was brought upon us in a single day, and night fell on a different world, a world where freedom itself is under attack.

Americans have many questions tonight. Americans are asking, "Who attacked our country?" The evidence we have gathered all points to a collection of loosely affiliated terrorist organizations known as al Qaeda. They are some of the murderers indicted for bombing American embassies in Tanzania and Kenya and responsible for bombing the USS *Cole*.

Al Qaeda is to terror what the Mafia is to crime. But its goal is not making money, its goal is remaking the world and imposing its radical beliefs on people everywhere. The terrorists practice a fringe form of Islamic extremism that has been rejected by Muslim scholars and the vast majority of Muslim clerics; a fringe movement that perverts the peaceful teachings of Islam. The terrorists' directive commands them to kill Christians and Jews, to kill all Americans and make no distinctions among military and civilians, including women and children.

This group and its leader, a person named Osama bin Laden, are linked to many other organizations in different countries, including the Egyptian Islamic Jihad, the Islamic Movement of Uzbekistan. There are thousands of these terrorists in more than 60 countries. They are recruited from their own nations and neighborhoods and brought to camps in places like Afghanistan where they are trained in the tactics of terror. They are sent back to their homes or sent to hide in countries around the world to plot evil and destruction.

The leadership of al Qaeda has great influence in Afghanistan and supports the Taliban regime in controlling most of that country. In Afghanistan we see al Qaeda's vision for the world. Afghanistan's people have been brutalized, many are starving and many have fled.

Women are not allowed to attend school. You can be jailed for owning a television. Religion can be practiced only as their leaders dictate. A man can be jailed in Afghanistan if his beard is not long enough.

The United States respects the people of Afghanistan—after all, we are currently its largest source of humanitarian aid—but we condemn the Taliban regime. It is not only repressing its own people, it is threatening people everywhere by sponsoring and sheltering and supplying terrorists.

By aiding and abetting murder, the Taliban regime is committing murder. And tonight the United States of America makes the following demands on the Taliban:

Deliver to United States authorities all of the leaders of al Qaeda who hide in your land.

Release all foreign nationals, including American citizens you have unjustly imprisoned. Protect foreign journalists, diplomats and aid workers in your country. Close immediately and permanently every terrorist training camp in Afghani-

stan. And hand over every terrorist and every person and their support structure to appropriate authorities.

Give the United States full access to terrorist training camps, so we can make sure they are no longer operating.

These demands are not open to negotiation or discussion. The Taliban must act and act immediately. They will hand over the terrorists or they will share in their fate.

I also want to speak tonight directly to Muslims throughout the world. We respect your faith. It's practiced freely by many millions of Americans and by millions more in countries that America counts as friends. Its teachings are good and peaceful, and those who commit evil in the name of Allah blaspheme the name of Allah.

The terrorists are traitors to their own faith, trying, in effect, to hijack Islam itself. The enemy of America is not our many Muslim friends. It is not our many Arab friends. Our enemy is a radical network of terrorists and every government that supports them.

Our war on terror begins with al Qaeda, but it does not end there. It will not end until every terrorist group of global reach has been found, stopped and defeated.

Americans are asking "Why do they hate us?" They hate what they see right here in this chamber: a democratically elected government. Their leaders are self-appointed. They hate our freedoms: our freedom of religion, our freedom of speech, our freedom to vote and assemble and disagree with each other.

They want to overthrow existing governments in many Muslim countries such as Egypt, Saudi Arabia and Jordan. They want to drive Israel out of the Middle East. They want to drive Christians and Jews out of vast regions of Asia and Africa.

These terrorists kill not merely to end lives, but to disrupt and end a way of life. With every atrocity, they hope that America grows fearful, retreating from the world and forsaking our friends. They stand against us because we stand in their way.

We're not deceived by their pretenses to piety. We have seen their kind before. They're the heirs of all the murderous ideologies of the 20th century. By sacrificing human life to serve their radical visions, by abandoning every value except the will to power, they follow in the path of fascism, Nazism and totalitarianism. And they will follow that path all the way to where it ends in history's unmarked grave of discarded lies.

Americans are asking, "How will we fight and win this war?" We will direct every resource at our command—every means of diplomacy, every tool of intelligence, every instrument of law enforcement, every financial influence, and every necessary weapon of war—to the destruction and to the defeat of the global terror network.

Now, this war will not be like the war against Iraq a decade ago, with a decisive liberation of territory and a swift conclusion. It will not look like the air war above Kosovo two years ago, where no ground troops were used and not a single American was lost in combat.

Our response involves far more than instant retaliation and isolated strikes. Americans should not expect one battle, but a lengthy campaign unlike any other we have ever seen. It may include dramatic strikes visible on TV and covert operations secret even in success. We will starve terrorists of funding, turn them one against another, drive them from place to place until there is no refuge or no rest. And we will pursue nations that provide aid or safe haven to terrorism. Every nation in every region now has a decision to make: Either you are with us or you are with the terrorists.

From this day forward, any nation that continues to harbor or support terrorism will be regarded by the United States as a hostile regime. Our nation has been put on notice, we're not immune from attack. We will take defensive measures against terrorism to protect Americans.

Today, dozens of federal departments and agencies, as well as state and local governments, have responsibilities affecting homeland security. These efforts must be coordinated at the highest level. So tonight, I announce the creation of a Cabinet-level position reporting directly to me, the Office of Homeland Security. . . .

These measures are essential. The only way to defeat terrorism as a threat to our way of life is to stop it, eliminate it and destroy it where it grows. Many will be involved in this effort, from FBI agents, to intelligence operatives, to the reservists we have called to active duty. All deserve our thanks, and all have our prayers.

And tonight a few miles from the damaged Pentagon, I have a message for our military: Be ready. I have called the armed forces to alert, and there is a reason. The hour is coming when America will act, and you will make us proud.

This is not, however, just America's fight. And what is at stake is not just America's freedom. This is the world's fight. This is civilization's fight. This is the fight of all who believe in progress and pluralism, tolerance and freedom.

We ask every nation to join us. We will ask and we will need the help of police forces, intelligence services and banking systems around the world. The United States is grateful that many nations and many international organizations have already responded with sympathy and with support—nations from Latin America to Asia to Africa to Europe to the Islamic world.

Perhaps the NATO charter reflects best the attitude of the world: An attack on one is an attack on all. The civilized world is rallying to America's side.

They understand that if this terror goes unpunished, their own cities, their own citizens may be next. Terror unanswered can not only bring down buildings, it can threaten the stability of legitimate governments. And you know what? We're not going to allow it. . . .

After all that has just passed, all the lives taken and all the possibilities and hopes that died with them, it is natural to wonder if America's future is one of fear. Some speak of an age of terror. I know there are struggles ahead and dangers to face. But this country will define our times, not be defined by them.

As long as the United States of America is determined and strong, this will not be an age of terror. This will be an age of liberty here and across the world. Great harm has been done to us. We have suffered great loss. And in our grief and anger we have found our mission and our moment.

Freedom and fear are at war. The advance of human freedom, the great achievement of our time and the great hope of every time, now depends on us. Our nation, this generation, will lift the dark threat of violence from our people and our future. We will rally the world to this cause by our efforts, by our courage. We will not tire, we will not falter and we will not fail. . . .

I will not forget the wound to our country and those who inflicted it. I will not yield, I will not rest, I will not relent in waging this struggle for freedom and security for the American people. The course of this conflict is not known, yet its outcome is certain. Freedom and fear, justice and cruelty, have always been at war, and we know that God is not neutral between them.

Fellow citizens, we'll meet violence with patient justice, assured of the rightness of our cause and confident of the victories to come.

In all that lies before us, may God grant us wisdom and may he watch over the United States of America. Thank you.

REVIEW QUESTIONS

1. According to Bush, what were the goals of al Qaeda?
2. The president told the other nations of the world: "Either you are with us or you are with the terrorists." Was this a valid assertion?

BARACK OBAMA

FROM **A New Beginning (2009)**

Barack Obama, an attorney and former U.S. Senator from Illinois, became the forty-fourth president of the United States on January 19, 2009. His surprising victory resulted largely from the energy and charisma he displayed during the campaign. Amid the continuing Great Recession, voters embraced Obama's echoing theme of the "politics of hope and change" (from the largely ineffective policies of the Bush administration). Obama denounced the prevailing Republican "economic philosophy that says we should give more and more to those with the most and hope that prosperity trickles down to everyone else." He described the 2008 financial meltdown as the "final verdict on this failed philosophy." Voters entrusted him to deal with thorny issues such as economic recovery, reform of the financial industry, national health-care legislation, and energy policy. President-elect Obama acknowledged the daunting challenges facing the nation and his new administration. The United States was embroiled in two wars, in Iraq and Afghanistan. The economy was in shambles, unemployment was soaring, and the national debt was hemorrhaging. In his inaugural address, President Obama highlighted the departures he would make from the policies of the George W. Bush administration. He also stressed the "new beginning" symbolized by his inauguration as the first African American president, describing himself as a "man whose father less than sixty years ago might not have been served at a local restaurant."

Speech delivered January 20, 2007. whitehouse.gov.

My fellow citizens: I stand here today humbled by the task before us, grateful for the trust you've bestowed, mindful of the sacrifices borne by our ancestors.

I thank President Bush for his service to our nation as well as the generosity and cooperation he has shown throughout this transition.

*   *   *

That we are in the midst of crisis is now well understood. Our nation is at war against a far-reaching network of violence and hatred. Our economy is badly weakened, a consequence of greed and irresponsibility on the part of some, but also our collective failure to make hard choices and prepare the nation for a new age. Homes have been lost, jobs shed, businesses shuttered. Our health care is too costly, our schools fail too many—and each day brings further evidence that the ways we use energy strengthen our adversaries and threaten our planet.

These are the indicators of crisis, subject to data and statistics. Less measurable, but no less profound, is a sapping of confidence across our land; a nagging fear that America's decline is inevitable, that the next generation must lower its sights.

Today I say to you that the challenges we face are real. They are serious and they are many. They will not be met easily or in a short span of time. But know this America: They will be met.

On this day we gather because we have chosen hope over fear, unity of purpose over conflict and discord. On this day we come to proclaim an end to the petty grievances and false promises, the recriminations and worn-out dogmas that for far too long have strangled our politics. We remain a young nation. But in the words of Scripture, the time has come to set aside childish things. The time has come to reaffirm our enduring spirit; to choose our better history; to carry forward that precious gift, that noble idea passed on from generation to generation: the God-given promise that all are equal, all are free, and all deserve a chance to pursue their full measure of happiness.

*   *   *

For everywhere we look, there is work to be done. The state of our economy calls for action, bold and swift. And we will act, not only to create new jobs, but to lay a new foundation for growth. We will build the roads and bridges, the electric grids and digital lines that feed our commerce and bind us together. We'll restore science to its rightful place, and wield technology's wonders to raise health care's quality and lower its cost. We will harness the sun and the winds and the soil to fuel our cars and run our factories. And we will transform our schools and colleges and universities to meet the demands of a new age. All this we can do. All this we will do.

Now, there are some who question the scale of our ambitions, who suggest that our system cannot tolerate too many big plans. Their memories are short, for they have forgotten what this country has already done, what free men and women can achieve when imagination is joined to common purpose, and necessity to courage. What the cynics fail to understand is that the ground has shifted beneath them, that the stale political arguments that have consumed us for so long no longer apply.

The question we ask today is not whether our government is too big or too small, but whether it works—whether it helps families find jobs at a decent wage, care they can afford, a retirement that is dignified. Where the answer is yes, we intend to move forward. Where the answer is no, programs will end. And those of us who manage the public's dollars will be held to account, to spend wisely, reform bad habits, and do our business in the light of day, because only then can we restore the vital trust between a people and their government.

Nor is the question before us whether the market is a force for good or ill. Its power to generate wealth and expand freedom is unmatched. But this crisis has reminded us that without a watchful eye, the market can spin out of control. The nation cannot prosper long when it favors only the prosperous. The success of our economy has always depended not just on the size of our gross domestic product, but on the reach of our prosperity, on the ability to extend opportunity to every willing heart—not out of charity, but because it is the surest route to our common good.

*   *   *

So let us mark this day with remembrance of who we are and how far we have traveled. In the year of America's birth, in the coldest of months, a small band of patriots huddled by dying campfires on the shores of an icy river. The capital was abandoned. The enemy was advancing. The snow was stained with blood. At the moment when the outcome of our revolution was most in doubt, the father of our nation ordered these words to be read to the people:

"Let it be told to the future world . . . that in the depth of winter, when nothing but hope and virtue could survive . . . that the city and the country, alarmed at one common danger, came forth to meet [it]."

America: In the face of our common dangers, in this winter of our hardship, let us remember these timeless words. With hope and virtue, let us brave once more the icy currents, and endure what storms may come. Let it be said by our children's children that when we were tested we refused to let this journey end, that we did not turn back nor did we falter, and with eyes fixed on the horizon and God's grace upon us, we carried forth that great gift of freedom and delivered it safely to future generations.

Thank you. God bless you. And God bless the United States of America.

REVIEW QUESTIONS

1. What specific initiatives did Obama promise in his inaugural address?
2. How did Obama respond to those who questioned the scope of his proposals?

FROM *Obergefell v. Hodges* (2015)

During the early twenty-first century, thirty-seven states passed laws allowing for same-sex marriages. In response, thirteen other states enacted laws limiting marriage to the union of a man and a woman. In 2015, the Supreme Court heard the case of James Obergefell. When his partner, John Arthur, became terminally ill, they decided to marry in Maryland, where same-sex marriage was legal. When Arthur died, however, the couple's home state of Ohio, which banned same-sex marriage, refused to list Obergefell as Arthur's surviving spouse on the death certificate. Obergefell's attorneys argued that gay and lesbian Americans should have equal access to the constitutional right of marriage. The right to marry, they added, accords couples a fundamental human dignity. Attorneys for Ohio countered that allowing same-sex marriages would infringe upon the states' right to decide the issue and that gay unions would undermine the longstanding institution of marriage. On June 26, 2015, the Supreme Court voted 5-4 in favor of Obergefell, explaining that state bans on same-sex marriages violated the due process and equal protection clauses of the Fourteenth Amendment. Writing for the majority, Justice Anthony Kennedy declared that marriage is a fundamental right "inherent in the liberty of the person" and is therefore protected by the due process clause, which prohibits the states from depriving any person of "life, liberty, or property without due process of law." He added that the close connection between liberty and equality meant that the marriage right is also guaranteed by the equal protection clause, which forbids the states from "deny[ing] to any person . . . the equal protection of the laws." Kennedy then argued at length that "the reasons marriage is fundamental," including its connection with individual liberty, "apply with equal force to same-sex couples."

From *Obergefell v. Hodges*, No. 14-556, slip op. at 23 (U.S. June 26, 2015).

JAMES OBERGEFELL, et al., PETITIONERS

v.

RICHARD HODGES, DIRECTOR, OHIO DEPARTMENT OF HEALTH, et al.;

Justice [Anthony] Kennedy delivered the opinion of the Court. The Constitution promises liberty to all within its reach, a liberty that includes certain specific rights that allow persons, within a lawful realm, to define and express their identity. The petitioners in these cases seek to find that liberty by marrying someone of the same sex and having their marriages deemed lawful on the same terms and conditions as marriages between persons of the opposite sex.

*   *   *

Before addressing the principles and precedents that govern these cases, it is appropriate to note the history of the subject now before the Court.

From their beginning to their most recent page, the annals of human history reveal the transcendent importance of marriage. The lifelong union of a man and a woman always has promised nobility and dignity to all persons, without regard to their station in life. Marriage is sacred to those who live by their religions and offers unique fulfillment to those who find meaning in the secular realm. Its dynamic allows two people to find a life that could not be found alone, for a marriage becomes greater

than just the two persons. Rising from the most basic human needs, marriage is essential to our most profound hopes and aspirations.

*   *   *

That history is the beginning of these cases. The respondents say it should be the end as well. To them, it would demean a timeless institution if the concept and lawful status of marriage were extended to two persons of the same sex. Marriage, in their view, is by its nature a gender-differentiated union of man and woman. This view long has been held and continues to be held in good faith by reasonable and sincere people here and throughout the world.

The petitioners acknowledge this history but contend that these cases cannot end there. Were their intent to demean the revered idea and reality of marriage, the petitioners' claims would be of a different order. But that is neither their purpose nor their submission. To the contrary, it is the enduring importance of marriage that underlies the petitioners' contentions. This, they say, is their whole point. Far from seeking to devalue marriage, the petitioners seek it for themselves because of their respect and need for its privileges and responsibilities. And their immutable nature dictates that same-sex marriage is their only real path to this profound commitment.

*   *   *

Until the mid-20th century, same-sex intimacy long had been condemned as immoral by the state itself in most Western nations, a belief often embodied in the criminal law. For this reason, among others, many persons did not deem homosexuals to have dignity in their own distinct identity. A truthful declaration by same-sex couples of what was in their hearts had to remain unspoken. Even when a greater awareness of the humanity and integrity of homosexual persons came in the period after World War II, the argument that gays and lesbians had a just claim to dignity was in conflict with both law and widespread social conventions. Same-sex intimacy remained a crime in many States. Gays and lesbians were prohibited from most government employment, barred from military service, excluded under immigration laws, targeted by police, and burdened in their rights to associate. . . .

For much of the 20th century, moreover, homosexuality was treated as an illness. When the American Psychiatric Association published the first Diagnostic and Statistical Manual of Mental Disorders in 1952, homosexuality was classified as a mental disorder, a position adhered to until 1973. . . .

In the late 20th century, following substantial cultural and political developments, same-sex couples began to lead more open and public lives and to establish families. This development was followed by a quite extensive discussion of the issue in both governmental and private sectors and by a shift in public attitudes toward greater tolerance. As a result, questions about the rights of gays and lesbians soon reached the courts, where the issue could be discussed in the formal discourse of the law. . . .

*   *   *

Under the Due Process Clause of the Fourteenth Amendment, no State shall "deprive any person of life, liberty, or property, without due process of law." The fundamental liberties protected by this Clause include most of the rights enumerated in the Bill of Rights. . . . In addition these liberties extend to certain personal choices central to individual dignity and autonomy, including intimate choices that define personal identity and beliefs.

*   *   *

This analysis compels the conclusion that same-sex couples may exercise the right to marry. The four principles and traditions to be discussed demonstrate that the reasons marriage is fundamental under the Constitution apply with equal force to same-sex couples.

A first premise of the Court's relevant precedents is that the right to personal choice regarding marriage is inherent in the concept of individual autonomy. This abiding connection between marriage and liberty is why *Loving* invalidated interracial marriage bans under the Due Process Clause. . . .

Choices about marriage shape an individual's destiny. As the Supreme Judicial Court of Massachusetts has explained, because "it fulfils yearnings for security, safe haven, and connection that express our common humanity, civil marriage is an esteemed institution, and the decision whether and whom to marry is among life's momentous acts of self-definition."

. . . A second principle in this Court's jurisprudence is that the right to marry is fundamental because it supports a two-person union unlike any other in its importance to the committed individuals. . . .

A third basis for protecting the right to marry is that it safeguards children and families and thus draws meaning from related rights of childrearing, procreation, and education. . . .

As all parties agree, many same-sex couples provide loving and nurturing homes to their children, whether biological or adopted. And hundreds of thousands of children are presently being raised by such couples. . . .

Excluding same-sex couples from marriage thus conflicts with a central premise of the right to marry. Without the recognition, stability, and predictability marriage offers, their children suffer the stigma of knowing their families are somehow lesser. They also suffer the significant material costs of being raised by unmarried parents, relegated through no fault of their own to a more difficult and uncertain family life. The marriage laws at issue here thus harm and humiliate the children of same-sex couples. . . .

Fourth and finally, this Court's cases and the Nation's traditions make clear that marriage is a keystone of our social order.

For that reason, just as a couple vows to support each other, so does society pledge to support the couple, offering symbolic recognition and material benefits to protect and nourish the union. Indeed, while the States are in general free to vary the benefits they confer on all married couples, they have throughout our history made marriage the basis for an expanding list of governmental rights, benefits, and responsibilities. . . . The States have contributed to the fundamental character of the marriage right by placing that institution at the center of so many facets of the legal and social order.

There is no difference between same- and opposite-sex couples with respect to this principle. Yet by virtue of their exclusion from that institution, same-sex couples are denied the constellation of benefits that the States have linked to marriage. This harm results in more than just material burdens. Same-sex couples are consigned to an instability many opposite-sex couples would deem intolerable in their own lives. As the State itself makes marriage all the more precious by the significance it attaches to it, exclusion from that status has the effect of teaching that gays and lesbians are unequal in important respects. It demeans gays and lesbians for the State to lock them out of a central institution of the Nation's society. Same-sex couples, too, may aspire to the transcendent purposes of marriage and seek fulfillment in its highest meaning.

The limitation of marriage to opposite-sex couples may long have seemed natural and just, but its inconsistency with the central meaning of the fundamental right to marry is now manifest. With that knowledge must come the recognition that laws excluding same-sex couples from the marriage right impose stigma and injury of the kind prohibited by our basic charter.

*   *   *

The right of same-sex couples to marry that is part of the liberty promised by the Fourteenth Amendment is derived, too, from that Amendment's guarantee of the equal protection of the laws. The Due Process Clause and the Equal Protection Clause are connected in a profound way, though they set forth independent principles.

*   *   *

These considerations lead to the conclusion that the right to marry is a fundamental right inherent in the liberty of the person, and under the Due Process and Equal Protection Clauses of the Fourteenth Amendment couples of the same-sex may not be deprived of that right and that liberty. The Court now holds that same-sex couples may exercise the fundamental right to marry. No longer may this liberty be denied to them.

*   *   *

Chief Justice John Roberts, with whom Justice Antonin Scalia and Justice Clarence Thomas join, dissenting.

Petitioners make strong arguments rooted in social policy and considerations of fairness. They contend that same-sex couples should be allowed to affirm their love and commitment through marriage, just like opposite-sex couples. That position has undeniable appeal; over the past six years, voters and legislators in eleven States and the District of Columbia have revised their laws to allow marriage between two people of the same sex.

But this Court is not a legislature. Whether same-sex marriage is a good idea should be of no concern to us. Under the Constitution, judges have power to say what the law is, not what it should be. The people who ratified the Constitution authorized courts to exercise "neither force nor will but merely judgment." *The Federalist* No. 78, p. 465 (C. Rossiter ed. 1961) (A. Hamilton) [capitalization altered].

Although the policy arguments for extending marriage to same-sex couples may be compelling, the legal arguments for requiring such an extension are not. The fundamental right to marry does not include a right to make a State change its definition of marriage. And a State's decision to maintain the meaning of marriage that has persisted in every culture throughout human history can hardly be called irrational. In short, our Constitution does not enact any one theory of marriage. The people of a State are free to expand marriage to include same-sex couples, or to retain the historic definition.

Today, however, the Court takes the extraordinary step of ordering every State to license and recognize same-sex marriage. Many people will rejoice at this decision, and I begrudge none their celebration. But for those who believe in a government of laws, not of men, the majority's approach is deeply disheartening. Supporters of same-sex marriage have achieved considerable success persuading their fellow citizens—through the democratic process—to adopt their view. That ends today. Five lawyers have closed the debate and enacted their own vision of marriage as a matter of constitutional law. Stealing this issue from the people will for many cast a cloud over same-sex marriage, making a dramatic social change that much more difficult to accept.

The majority's decision is an act of will, not legal judgment. The right it announces has no basis in the Constitution or this Court's precedent. The majority expressly disclaims judicial "caution" and omits even a pretense of humility, openly relying on its desire to remake society according to its own "new insight" into the "nature of injustice." *Ante*, at 11, 23. As a result, the Court invalidates the marriage laws of more than half the States and orders the transformation of a social institution that has formed the basis of human society for millennia, for the Kalahari Bushmen and the Han Chinese, the Carthaginians and the Aztecs. Just who do we think we are?

It can be tempting for judges to confuse our own preferences with the requirements of the law. But as this Court has been reminded throughout our history, the Constitution "is made for people of fundamentally differing views." *Lochner v. New York*, 198 U.S. 45, 76 (1905) (Holmes, J., dissenting). Accordingly, "courts are not concerned with the wisdom or policy of legislation." *Id.*, at 69 (Harlan, J., dissenting).

The majority today neglects that restrained conception of the judicial role. It seizes for itself a question the Constitution leaves to the people, at a time when the people are engaged in a vibrant debate on that question. And it answers that question based not on neutral principles of constitutional law, but on its own "understanding of what freedom is and must become." *Ante*, at 19. I have no choice but to dissent.

Understand well what this dissent is about: It is not about whether, in my judgment, the institution of marriage should be changed to include same-sex couples. It is instead about whether, in our democratic republic, that decision should rest with the people acting through their elected representatives, or with five lawyers who happen to hold commissions authorizing them to resolve legal disputes according to law. The Constitution leaves no doubt about the answer.

REVIEW QUESTIONS

1. How persuasive are Justice Kennedy's arguments for same-sex marriages? Is his use of the Fourteenth Amendment justified?
2. Examine the claim of the dissenting justices that the majority opinion favoring same-sex marriage was "an act of will, not legal judgment." Do you agree or disagree?

DONALD TRUMP

FROM Address to a Joint Session of Congress (2017)

The 2016 presidential campaign was unique in political history. Brash New Yorker Donald Trump, a billionaire real estate developer and reality television star who had never held elected office, won the Republican nomination. As he bragged, "There's nobody like me. Nobody."

The tempestuous presidential campaign pitted Trump against former Secretary of State Hillary Clinton, and it quickly grew bitter, with each accusing the other of being unqualified for the nation's highest office. Trump positioned himself as an "outsider" eager to "drain the swamp" of corruption created by "political insiders" in Washington, D.C. In pledging to "Make America Great Again," he skillfully exploited the emotions of people left behind by the economic recovery and resentful of unregulated immigration, "unfair" multi-nation trade agreements, and unending U.S. military involvement in the Middle East.

Americans had never seen a candidate as unconventional, unpredictable, and inexplicable as Donald John Trump, yet his shoot-from-hip combativeness appealed to many voters fed up with conventional politics. They embraced his pledge "to drain the swamp" of political corruption and cronyism in Washington, D.C., and they gave him just enough votes to defeat Hillary Clinton and win the presidency. Just weeks after his presidential inauguration, Trump addressed Congress in a televised speech.

Donald Trump, "Remarks by President Trump in a Joint Address to Congress." Speech issued on February 28, 2017. www.whitehouse.gov. [Editorial insertions appear in square brackets—*Ed.*]

I am here tonight to deliver a message of unity and strength, and it is a message deeply delivered from my heart. A new chapter of American Greatness is now beginning. A new national pride is sweeping across our nation. And a new surge of optimism is placing impossible dreams firmly within our grasp.

What we are witnessing today is the Renewal of the American Spirit. Our allies will find that America is once again ready to lead. All the nations of the world—friend or foe—will find that America is strong, America is proud, and America is free.

In nine years, the United States will celebrate the 250th anniversary of our founding—250 years since the day we declared our Independence. It will be one of the great milestones in the history of the world. But what will America look like as we reach our 250th year? What kind of country will we leave for our children?

I will not allow the mistakes of recent decades past to define the course of our future. For too long, we've watched our middle class shrink as we've exported our jobs and wealth to foreign countries.

We've financed and built one global project after another, but ignored the fates of our children in the inner cities of Chicago, Baltimore, Detroit—

and so many other places throughout our land. We've defended the borders of other nations, while leaving our own borders wide open, for anyone to cross—and for drugs to pour in at a now unprecedented rate. And we've spent trillions of dollars overseas, while our infrastructure at home has so badly crumbled.

Then, in 2016, the earth shifted beneath our feet. The rebellion [the Trump presidential campaign] started as a quiet protest, spoken by families of all colors and creeds—families who just wanted a fair shot for their children, and a fair hearing for their concerns. But then the quiet voices became a loud chorus—as thousands of citizens now spoke out together, from cities small and large, all across our country.

Finally, the chorus became an earthquake—and the people turned out by the tens of millions, and they were all united by one very simple, but crucial demand, that America must put its own citizens first . . . because only then, can we truly MAKE AMERICA GREAT AGAIN.

Dying industries will come roaring back to life. Heroic veterans will get the care they so desperately need. Our military will be given the resources its brave warriors so richly deserve. Crumbling infrastructure will be replaced with new roads, bridges, tunnels, airports and railways gleaming across our beautiful land. Our terrible drug epidemic will slow down and ultimately, stop. And our neglected inner cities will see a rebirth of hope, safety, and opportunity.

Above all else, we will keep our promises to the American people. It's been a little over a month since my inauguration, and I want to take this moment to update the nation on the progress I've made in keeping those promises. . . .

We have begun to drain the swamp of government corruption by imposing a five-year ban on lobbying by executive branch officials—and a lifetime ban on becoming lobbyists for a foreign government.

We have undertaken a historic effort to massively reduce job-crushing regulations, creating a deregulation task force inside of every government agency; imposing a new rule which mandates that for every one new regulation, two old regulations must be eliminated; and stopping a regulation that threatens the future and livelihoods of our great coal miners.

We have cleared the way for the construction of the Keystone and Dakota Access Pipelines—thereby creating tens of thousands of jobs—and I've issued a new directive that new American pipelines be made with American steel. We have withdrawn the United States from the job-killing Trans-Pacific Partnership. . . .

At the same time, my Administration has answered the pleas of the American people for immigration enforcement and border security. By finally enforcing our immigration laws, we will raise wages, help the unemployed, save billions of dollars, and make our communities safer for everyone. We want all Americans to succeed—but that can't happen in an environment of lawless chaos. We must restore integrity and the rule of law to our borders.

For that reason, we will soon begin the construction of a great wall along our southern border. It will be started ahead of schedule and, when finished, it will be a very effective weapon against drugs and crime. As we speak, we are removing gang members, drug dealers and criminals that threaten our communities and prey on our citizens. Bad ones are going out as I speak tonight and as I promised. . . .

We are also taking strong measures to protect our Nation from Radical Islamic Terrorism. . . . We cannot allow a beachhead of terrorism to form inside America—we cannot allow our Nation to become a sanctuary for extremists. That is why my Administration has been working on improved vetting procedures, and we will shortly take new steps to keep our Nation safe—and to keep out those who would do us harm.

As promised, I directed the Department of Defense to develop a plan to demolish and destroy ISIS—a network of lawless savages that have slaughtered Muslims and Christians, and men, women, and children of all faiths and beliefs. We will work with our allies, including our friends and allies in the Muslim world, to extinguish this vile enemy from our planet.

I have also imposed new sanctions on entities and individuals who support Iran's ballistic missile program, and reaffirmed our unbreakable alliance with the State of Israel.

Finally, I have kept my promise to appoint a Justice to the United States Supreme Court—from my list of twenty judges—who will defend our Constitution. I am honored to have Maureen Scalia with us in the gallery tonight. Her late, great husband, Antonin Scalia, will forever be a symbol of American justice. To fill his seat, we have chosen Judge Neil Gorsuch, a man of incredible skill, and deep devotion to the law. He was confirmed unanimously to the Court of Appeals, and I am asking the Senate to swiftly approve his nomination.

Tonight, as I outline the next steps we must take as a country, we must honestly acknowledge the circumstances we inherited. Ninety-four million Americans are out of the labor force. Over 43 million people are now living in poverty, and over 43 million Americans are on food stamps. More than one in five people in their prime working years are not working. We have the worst financial recovery in 65 years.

In the last eight years, the past Administration has put on more new debt than nearly all other Presidents combined. We've lost more than one-fourth of our manufacturing jobs since NAFTA was approved, and we've lost 60,000 factories since China joined the World Trade Organization in 2001. Our trade deficit in goods with the world last year was nearly $800 billion. And overseas, we have inherited a series of tragic foreign policy disasters.

Solving these, and so many other pressing problems, will require us to work past the differences of party. It will require us to tap into the American spirit that has overcome every challenge throughout our long and storied history.

But to accomplish our goals at home and abroad, we must restart the engine of the American economy—making it easier for companies to do business in the United States, and much, much harder for companies to leave our country.

Right now, American companies are taxed at one of the highest rates anywhere in the world. My economic team is developing historic tax reform that will reduce the tax rate on our companies so they can compete and thrive anywhere and with anyone . . . . At the same time, we will provide massive tax relief for the middle class.

We must create a level playing field for American companies and workers . . . . Currently, when we ship products out of America, many other countries make us pay very high tariffs and taxes—but when foreign companies ship their products into America, we charge them . . . almost nothing. . . .

I believe strongly in free trade but it also has to be FAIR TRADE . . . . The first Republican President, Abraham Lincoln, warned that the "abandonment of the protective [tariff] policy by the American Government . . . will produce want and ruin among our people."

Lincoln was right—and it is time we heeded his . . . words. I am not going to let America and its great companies and workers be taken advantage of us [sic] any longer. I am going to bring back millions of jobs. Protecting our workers also means reforming our system of legal immigration. The current, outdated system depresses wages for our poorest workers, and puts great pressure on taxpayers. . . .

Another Republican President, Dwight D. Eisenhower, initiated the last truly great national infrastructure program—the building of the interstate highway system. The time has come for a new program of national rebuilding.

America has spent approximately $6 trillion in the Middle East—all the while our infrastructure at home is crumbling. With this $6 trillion we could have rebuilt our country—twice. And maybe even three times if we had people who had the ability to negotiate.

To launch our national rebuilding, I will be asking Congress to approve legislation that produces a $1 trillion investment in the infrastructure of the United States—financed through both public and private capital—creating millions of new jobs. This effort will be guided by two core principles: Buy American, and Hire American.

Tonight, I am also calling on this Congress to repeal and replace Obamacare with reforms that expand choice, increase access, lower costs, and at the same time, provide better healthcare.

Mandating every American to buy government-approved health insurance was never the right solution for our country. The way to make health insurance available to everyone is to lower the cost of health insurance, and that is what we are going to do. . . .

Everything that is broken in our country can be fixed. Every problem can be solved. And every hurting family can find healing, and hope.

Our citizens deserve this, and so much more—so why not join forces to finally get it done? On this and so many other things, Democrats and Republicans should get together and unite for the good of our country, and for the good of the American people.

My administration wants to work with members of both parties to make childcare accessible and affordable, to help ensure new parents have paid family leave, to invest in women's health, and to promote clean air and clear water, and to rebuild our military and our infrastructure.

True love for our people requires us to find common ground, to advance the common good, and to cooperate on behalf of every American child who deserves a brighter future. . . .

Finally, to keep America safe we must provide the men and women of the United States military with the tools they need to prevent war and—if they must—to fight and to win.

I am sending Congress a budget that rebuilds the military . . . and calls for one of the largest increases in national defense spending in American history. My budget will also increase funding for our veterans.

Our veterans have delivered for this Nation—and now we must deliver for them. The challenges we face as a Nation are great. But our people are even greater. And none are greater or braver than those who fight for America in uniform. . . .

Our foreign policy calls for a direct, robust and meaningful engagement with the world. It is American leadership based on vital security interests that we share with our allies across the globe. We strongly support NATO, an alliance forged through the bonds of two world wars that dethroned fascism, and a Cold War [that] defeated communism.

But our partners must meet their financial obligations. And now, based on our very strong and frank discussions, they are beginning to do just that . . . . We expect our partners, whether in NATO, the Middle East, or in the Pacific—to take a direct and meaningful role in both strategic and military operations, and pay their fair share of the cost. . . .

On our 100th anniversary, in 1876, citizens from across our Nation came to Philadelphia to celebrate America's centennial. At that celebration, the country's builders and artists and inventors showed off their creations.

Alexander Graham Bell displayed his telephone for the first time.

Remington unveiled the first typewriter. An early attempt was made at electric light.

Thomas Edison showed an automatic telegraph and an electric pen.

Imagine the wonders our country could know in America's 250th year.

Think of the marvels we can achieve if we simply set free the dreams of our people . . . .

This is our vision. This is our mission. But we can only get there together. We are one people, with one destiny. We all bleed the same blood. We all salute the same great American flag. And we are all made by the same God. . . .

The time for small thinking is over. The time for trivial fights is behind us. We just need the courage to share the dreams that fill our hearts. The bravery to express the hopes that stir our souls. And the confidence to turn those hopes and dreams to action. . . .

REVIEW QUESTIONS

1. What major themes did Trump emphasize in the speech?
2. Trump insisted that, "Everything that is broken in our country can be fixed. Every problem can be solved. And every hurting family can find healing, and hope." Do you agree?
3. What impresses you about this speech? What concerns you?